# America's Economic Heritage

# America's Economic Heritage

## From a Colonial to a Capitalist Economy, 1634-1900

Meyer Weinberg

GREENWOOD PRESS
Westport, Connecticut • London, England

**Library of Congress Cataloging in Publication Data**

Weinberg, Meyer, 1920-
  America's economic heritage.

  Includes bibliographies and indexes.
  Contents: v. 1. From a colonial to a capitalist
economy, 1634-1900 — v. 2. A mature economy, post 1900.
  1. United States—Economic conditions—Sources.
I. Title.
HC103.W38 1983      016.330973      83-10877
ISBN 0-313-23751-4 (lib. bdg. : set)
ISBN 0-313-24135-X (lib. bdg. : v. 1)
ISBN 0-313-24136-8 (lib. bdg. : v. 2)

Library of Congress Catalog Card Number: 83-10877
ISBN: 0-313-24135-X

First published in 1983

Greenwood Press
A division of Congressional Information Service, Inc.
88 Post Road West
Westport, Connecticut 06881

Printed in the United States of America

10 9 8 7 6 5 4 3 2 1

---

**Copyright Acknowledgments**

Grateful acknowledgment is given for permission to use the following:

A quotation from *American Scientist,* Vol. 48, No. 1, journal of Sigma Xi, The Scientific Research Society, C.E.H. Bawn, "Some Impressions of Soviet Science." Reprinted by permission.

Extracts from the book entitled *Building an American Industry . . . An Autobiography* by Jacob Dolson Cox, Jr. published in 1951 © the Cleveland Twist Drill Company. Reprinted by permission.

Reprinted with permission from "The Case for More Basic Research," in *Chemical and Engineering News XXXVII* (January 19, 1959) by Walter J. Murphy. Copyright 1959 American Chemical Society.

From *Farm Boy to Financier* by Frank A. Vanderlip, copyright 1935 by Hawthorn Properties. Permission to reprint given by Frank A. Vanderlip, Jr.

From *Father of Radio: The Autobiography of Lee de Forest.* Copyright © 1950 by Lee de Forest. Used by permission of Follett Publishing Company.

From *Fifty Billion Dollars, My Years with the RFC, 1932-45* by Jesse Jones and Edward Angly. Reprinted with permission of Macmillan Publishing Co., Inc. Copyright 1951 by The Chronicle Company, renewed 1979 by Houston Endowment Inc.

# CONTENTS

# FOREWORD

## HAROLD D. WOODMAN

The economic history of the United States is an astonishing success story. It's a story that began inauspiciously in 1607 when a handful of English settlers founded Jamestown on the coast of present-day Virginia—and somehow managed to survive. Or at least the settlement survived, for most of the first settlers and many of those who followed succumbed to the rigors of weather, inadequate food, and disease or the attacks of unfriendly Indians. In the decades that followed, other settlements along the North American coast survived the initial difficult years and, like the Virginia colony, became thriving communities. Most of the residents were English, but some Dutch, French, and others chose to settle in the English colonies and a growing number of enslaved black Africans became unwilling residents.

Virginians found that their tobacco had a ready market in Europe; merchants from Boston, New York, Philadelphia, and other cities in the northern colonies, protected by the English navy and by legislation excluding foreigners from trade with the English colonies, provided the ships to carry the tobacco to markets abroad. Grains and other foodstuffs, ships stores, and other commodities also entered the trade to Europe and the West Indies. Earnings from these exports helped to pay for the import of manufactured goods from England and elsewhere. By 1776, when the thirteen colonies declared their independence from England, their population had reached about two and a half million. Most of the people were farmers, but commerce and trade supported a growing urban population of merchants, artisans, sailors, dockworkers, and others.

By the standards of the day, the new nation was wealthy. Although exact figures are unavailable, historians agree that the wealth of the United States at the time of the Revolution about equalled that of every western European nation save England. In the decades that followed, Americans pushed westward, carving out new states from the lands ceded by England following the Revolution and from lands bought from the French and taken from the Spanish, the Mexicans, and the Indians. As the nation extended its geographic boundaries, it diversified its economy. By the middle of the nineteenth century, the United States had become a major producer of industrial commodities. Agriculture still remained the primary economic sector, providing work for the majority of the population, a market and the raw materials for much of the industrial output, and the nation's leading exports.

By the end of the nineteenth century the United States had become the world's leading industrial nation. Twentieth-century Americans could and did boast that they lived in the richest nation on earth. The nation's businesses provided a bewildering array of goods to stores and mail order houses that distributed them to a growing population. And an increasing volume of American industrial and agricultural exports entered world markets.

When economic historians speak of this economic success story they usually use terms such as economic growth and economic development, gross national product (GNP) or national income, and per capita product or income. (National product and national income are measures of different things, but when translated into dollar values they become equivalent terms: everything produced earns income for someone—workers, stockholders, bankers, corporations, etc.) Although economists developed these terms and measures for the twentieth century, economic historians have attempted to gather the necessary data to use them to describe the past. It is important, therefore, to understand their meaning.

Economic growth refers to the increase in the output of the economy. Because output is in the form of a variety of goods and services that cannot be compared and totaled—bushels of corn, tons of steel, patients treated by doctors, etc.—it must be converted into comparable numbers. Economists use dollars to make the conversion. Each good and service is assigned a dollar value, its market value at the time it was produced. The sum of the values of the economy's output of all goods and services is the gross national product. (Items are counted only once in calculating GNP. For example, the value of automobiles includes the value of the steel used in producing them. The value of the steel that is included in the value of automobiles is excluded from the total steel output so as to avoid double-counting.) When economists compare the GNP for two or more time periods they can determine the amount and the rate of economic growth. The same procedure can be used to compare the economic growth of one area or region with another and one nation with another—the latter comparison, of course, requiring that the value of goods in the two nations be converted to a single currency.

Although valuable for some purposes, this measurement is pretty crude and apt to be misleading. If, for example, the years between the two periods being compared were marked by inflation, the GNP for the second period would be higher than that of the first even if output did not increase. The same amount of goods and services would now have a higher value simply because of price increases. To avoid this problem, economists deflate the second figure by the inflation rate. For example, if prices increase by 10 percent, this 10 percent is subtracted from the GNP in the second period. The result would be a new figure which more accurately measures the real output of goods and services.

Still, the figures remain too crude for certain kinds of measurements. The missing ingredient is population. Suppose, for example, that the GNP (adequately adjusted for inflation or deflation) doubled between period A and period B, but during the same time the population also doubled. Growth would have taken place, but insofar as the people were concerned, little change had occurred. Twice the amount of goods and services now had to be distributed to twice the number of people. To deal with this problem, economists use per capita figures when making comparisons. By dividing the population into the GNP they get a per capita GNP. Comparing per capita GNPs gives a more precise comparison if the relative wealth and the well-being of the population over time is the comparison sought. (Per capita GNP figures clearly reveal what is called the "population problem." A nation may experience an increase in its GNP, but if the growth rate of the population exceeds that of the GNP, the result will be increasing poverty.)

When significant per capita economic growth occurs, economists usually refer to the change as economic *development* rather than simply *growth* because the figures reveal that for some reason or set of reasons, production has become more efficient, that is, the output per person has increased. This increase may result from the discovery and exploitation of new or better resources as, for example, occurs with the movement onto more fertile land allowing farmers using the same techniques to increase their output or with the discovery of oil which increases the value of the output from a parcel of land. Unless additional new or better resources are constantly being discovered and exploited, this source of economic development is apt to be a one-time occurrence without lasting results.

Innovation is another source of economic development. Its most obvious form is technological innovation   new machines that increase the productivity of a worker. Important also, however, is organizational innovation—new methods to organize the production and distribution of goods. Such innovations, when they are widespread and recurring, usually bring structural changes in economic organization, changes in the nature of work, and social changes, as, for example, occurred when production of clothing moved out of the home and into the factory.

Thus, new discoveries and innovations might have very different long-term effects. If the change involves only a small part of the economy, its effects will be slight. But if a discovery or innovation stimulates others which in turn stimulate still others, the effects will be profound. The building of the railroad, for example, created a market for iron, steel, coal, lumber, and tools, thereby stimulating the growth of manufacturing and mining and an increase in employment. The railroad also opened new areas to commercial production which created markets for equipment and consumer goods. Innovations that have this ripple effect (economists term the connections "linkages") will usually bring long-term economic development. The long-run changes may prove to be beneficial, but often their immediate effect will be extremely disruptive, producing structural unemployment and bankruptcies in some areas as the economy adjusts to the changes.

When economic historians gather the necessary figures they can provide concrete data to describe America's economic success story. At the same time, however, there is much that these figures do not reveal. Per capita income figures provide no information about the *distribution* of income, and therefore high per capita income figures may hide the existence of poverty among sections of the population. Nor do the figures provide information about the costs of economic development in the form of such things as polluted air and water, repetitious, meaningless work, overcrowded cities, and added health hazards to workers and consumers—to name but a few. And finally, although the figures show *what* happened, they can at best only suggest *why* it happened.

Economic historians must be able to show the record of economic change, but they must also seek to explain why that change occurred. At first glance, the task seems easy enough. Machines replace hand labor which increases output or the railroad replaces wagons which lowers transportation costs or the assembly line replaces stationary work stations which speeds assembly time. But such explanations usually prove inadequate because they are incomplete. Usually many innovations take place simultaneously, and therefore the historian faces the task of explaining the relative importance of each. Furthermore, innovations are usually interrelated and interdependent. The trucking industry, highway construction, and the businesses providing fuel, repairs, and other services cannot be viewed in isolation from one another or apart from the extent of the demand for over-the-road transportation facilities.

But explaining cause and effect and mutual interaction, difficult as it often is, is only part of the historian's task. To an American living in the late twentieth century, it may appear obvious that if a new machine is developed which cuts labor costs and increases output that new machine will be purchased and used by a manufacturer. Let us examine some of the assumptions implicit in our finding it obvious that the new machine will be used.

One set of assumptions concerns the costs involved. We assume that the new machine will produce savings that exceed the cost of the machine. The machine's cost will include more than its purchase price; maintenance and training costs must also be counted. If the new machine requires that workers using it have extensive training or if maintenance and repair of the new machine requires the expansion of maintenance facilities including training maintenance workers and purchasing maintenance supplies and equipment, the real cost of the new machine increases, perhaps far beyond its purchase price. If the new machine replaces an old one, then the cost of the new must include the loss involved in scrapping the old. Other possible new costs might include costs of reorganizing the shop to accommodate the new machine, of providing new power sources that might be needed, of changing other equipment and procedures so that the new machine fits into the flow of production. The list could easily be extended, but the point should be clear: when we assume that the new machine will be introduced we assume that the costs of introduction will not exceed the benefits. But we make another cost assumption as well. We assume that a manufacturer can afford to introduce the new machine. Even if the long-term benefits exceed the costs, the manufacturer may lack the funds or the credit needed to buy the machine.

Another set of assumptions concerns the market. We assume the existence of competition which impels a manufacturer to introduce a cost cutting machine in order to get an edge on his competition. If producers have arranged a cartel or some other form of agreement dividing the market and thereby avoiding competition or if the producer has a monopoly, especially one with government support, the inducement to introduce the new machine will be diminished. Another assumption about the market is that there will be a demand for the increased output from the new machine. If the demand for the commodity being produced is saturated, increased production might merely create a surplus that drives prices down and destroys the advantages of the new machine. And finally, we assume the existence of an adequate supply of machines, replacement parts, power, and raw materials.

These assumptions about costs and the market may appear to be purely economic in nature, but they are only partly so because they really rest upon other assumptions that are political, social, and psychological. Or, to put the matter in a different way, they are based upon assumptions concerning human behavior. Ultimately understanding this behavior becomes the most difficult task faced by the economic historian seeking to explain economic development—or the lack of development.

People raised in the twentieth-century United States take certain behavior patterns for granted. Because we share so many perceptions, expectations, and attitudes we behave in fairly predictable ways. We know what is expected of us as workers, employers, landlords, tenants, students, teachers, consumers, and voters—and we act accordingly. We respond to certain kinds of market signals by buying, selling, investing, and saving in response to price, advertising, fad and fashion, interest rates, retirement goals, and the like. Of course our actions are not completely predictable and different people will respond in different ways to various market signals. But most of the variation occurs within a rather narrow range, making the behavior socially acceptable and reasonably predictable. Those whose actions transcend the boundaries of acceptable behavior are deemed odd or dangerous and are punished by ridicule, ostracism, or by the force of the law, depending upon the nature of their deviant behavior.

In brief, most Americans have what some have called a "modern" (in contrast to a "traditional") outlook or what others have termed a "bourgeois ideology." Our behavior is fairly predictable because we share this ideology, that is, because we interpret the world in which we live in similar ways. Because so much of this behavior is automatic we consider it natural rather than learned. But in fact, of course, it is learned from our parents, our peers, our teachers and from what we read and see about us as we grow up—in short, from what the sociologists call the "socialization process." Consider how much of our early training and schooling is concerned with teaching characteristics such as promptness, reliability, individualism, and self reliance, and how early we learn the difference between mine and thine, a difference that gradually becomes enshrined as the idea of private property and the rights and privileges associated with it. We learn to be consumers by having our wants stimulated by enticing advertising and store displays and by seeing the possessions of the people in the books used to teach us to read.

People born and raised in other societies or in other times learn to behave in different ways because they are socialized in different cultures with different ideologies. Behavior which seems natural to us may look odd, deviant, even illegal to such people.

When the socialization process is described in this way the world appears static. There seems to be little room for substantial change. If everyone is brought up to learn to live within the society in which he or she is born, how does change occur? We may expect that in any given society at any given time certain individuals will not behave according to the social norms. But in some instances such people are scorned or ignored or even destroyed, while in other places they gain support and begin the process of change. How can the difference be explained?

More specifically, why did England in the eighteenth century and the United States in the nineteenth century become modernized, industrialized, and thoroughly bourgeois while Spain and China did not? We can point to inventions such as the steam engine, to improved transportation facilities such as canals and railroads, to improvements in the organization of production such as the factory system, and to the development of necessary credit facilities such as banks. These and other changes promoted rapid economic development in England and the United States. Their absence in other countries hindered development.

But the historian must confront the problem of explaining why these development producing institutions arose in England and the United States and not in Spain and China. The complexity of the problem becomes evident when we notice that latecomers to the development process could benefit from the example of others that came earlier, as indeed they often do. But not always. If Japan and Germany entered the development process, many of their neighbors did not. Today, many of the leaders of undeveloped or less developed nations are eager to move their countries onto the path of economic development (or, at least, they say they are) but find the task very difficult.

Obviously there is no easy answer to this problem. If there were, it would not be a problem because people in less developed nations would simply adopt the methods used in the successful nations and thereby achieve the economic development and the wealth they seek. Instead, some seem to cling to older, traditional ways of doing things while others seem to discard growth inhibiting traditions with relative ease. The problem is not one of individual psychology or even national character, although both of these are involved; nor are traditional ways merely the product of habit or inertia. They are grounded in political, social, and economic relations in which certain groups or classes reap benefits in the form of wealth, power, and status. Therefore, discarding traditional ways means discarding the traditional social organization and altering class relations. This makes the change truly revolutionary and it is often marked by violent and bloody upheavals. The change, in short, is political as well as economic, and its success or failure depends upon the relative strengths of those opposing and those favoring change.

Economic historians cannot provide nations seeking economic development with a simple, easily followed success formula. Such a formula might have to include the suggestion that the traditional ruling class commit suicide, a bit of advice that is unlikely to be followed. But this need not concern us. Historians are not policy makers, although we would like to believe that our investigations may prove valuable to those who make or influence policy.

By investigating the history of a country that achieved rapid economic development, historians can gain insight into the process that might be of value to policy makers, but will certainly help to advance our understanding of the past. A meaningful study requires that historians look beyond the bare bones of economics and investigate the cultural and social traditions of the people. Only then is it possible to understand why the same or similar kinds of economic pressures, problems, and opportunities often elicit quite different responses among different peoples.

Meyer Weinberg's massive documentary history provides some of the raw material needed for such an investigation. Through the documents the reader may see how Americans perceived the world in which they lived and learn something about how and why these perceptions changed over time. To appreciate these changing perceptions the reader must view the documents from the perspective of the time in which they were written. How did the authors of the documents view their world? What interpretation did they give to events and why did they respond as they did to the opportunities and problems they faced? Modern readers, of course, have the benefit of hindsight; they know the future which the authors of the documents could not know. This provides insights into the direction thoughts and perceptions were moving, but it can also be misleading because it may suggest a reading which those who lived then could neither understand nor accept.

Although we know that the beginnings of the United States date from the early seventeenth century, we often forget the significance of this fact. Jamestown was named for King James I, the colony for the virgin queen Elizabeth I, who died in 1603. The early settlers therefore had grown up in late Elizabethan England; they were products of the English Renaissance. England was already undergoing massive social and economic changes associated with developing commerce, some industrialization, and the modernization of agriculture - -all of which affected the outlook of portions of the population. Nevertheless, culture and politics remained medieval. The resulting tensions culminated in civil war in the mid-seventeenth century and in a bloodless "Glorious Revolution" in 1688-1689, which propelled England into the modern age. Those who embarked for the colonies during these years brought with them the experiences and the ideas associated with these events. Those who had arrived earlier closely followed changes in England, and these changes in the mother country therefore affected colonial ideology and institutions.

It is essential that the documents in Part I be read with this context in mind. It is also important to remember that the authors of the documents were responding to particular problems and opportunities they faced in the New World where traditional ways and the institutions that supported them had never been fully established and where change therefore faced less opposition and came easier.

The first document, an extract from John Winthrop's *Journal*, will illustrate my point. Note the explicit acceptance of the social hierarchy in Winthrop's description of the election of a committee to decide on the division of lands. He complains that the electors passed over the "chief men" and selected a majority of the "inferior sort." It is significant that this important decision was to be made by an elected committee which could include the inferior sort. This process could not have occurred in the England Winthrop and his fellow colonists had recently left because the distribution of land in England would require the expropriation of the landowners. Moreover, in England, the inferior sort had little voice in any major decisions, even those that might profoundly affect their lives and well-being.

Winthrop claims he was not personally offended by not being selected—which was probably not true—but, he says, other "chief men" were upset. The minister, John Cotton, seems to have convinced the people that it was God's will that the chief men not be bypassed, because Winthrop reports that after Cotton spoke to the people they agreed to a new election. Clearly the "inferior sort" were pressing for an increased voice in decisions, although their deference to older traditions led them to back down when pressed to do so. Winthrop explains the source of their concern: they feared "that the richer men would give the poorer sort no great proportions of land." Land was the major source of wealth and the basis for political power in England, and therefore it is not surprising that the inferior sort would seek to increase their landholdings and would fear that the elite might not support their efforts. Winthrop, whose views concerning social structure and the importance of the popular will seem very undemocratic, argues for a land distribution system that seems to be very democratic. He says that he and the other magistrates deemed it unwise to allow people to own more land than they could profitably use. Instead, vacant land should be held for distribution to later immigrants.

Placing the documents in the proper context so that they can be fully understood both for what they reveal about the outlook of their authors as well as about trends in economic and social change is difficult for those who are not experts in the periods and problems involved. But Weinberg provides invaluable aids for readers without that expertise. After each document he gives the source from which the document was extracted. In most cases the sources are published, and therefore interested readers may find the full document and others relating to it in any good library. In addition, the bibliography provides at least one article or book, but usually several, for each of the 785 documents. These are scholarly books and articles by modern experts; they will lead readers into the issues being considered in the document, provide the necessary historical background, and in many cases, introduce some of the controversies among historians concerning the significance of the events and issues discussed.

I suspect that few readers will start at the beginning and read through this massive collection. Most will seek out certain problems or issues to pursue over time. Weinberg has organized his collection to facilitate this approach. He has divided each chronological part into sections containing documents relating to a particular sector of the economy or particular problems or social relations. This allows readers to skip from part to part in order to

follow a specific matter over a long time span. For example, readers
interested in the problem of the relationship between government and the
economy may easily follow this matter through the documents printed in
the appropriate sections of each of the four time periods in to which the collection is divided. Many documents fit in more than one category and therefore some documents relevant to a particular problem may be found in
other sections. Thus, documents concerning the conflict over the Second
Bank of the United States are relevant both to government-business relations and to finance. Weinberg has chosen to place them in the section on
finance. Readers will have no difficulties finding the documents they seek if
they consult the detailed table of contents and the comprehensive index.

The documents concerning government-business relations, supple-
mented, when necessary, with items from the bibliography, will provide
readers with valuable insights into the sources of that peculiar and often
contradictory attitude Americans have towards government in a private
enterprise economy. One conclusion will become immediately obvious.
Despite all the talk about laissez-faire and despite all the complaints about
government interference, government has played a significant part in the
economy throughout our history. Where Western Europeans often dis-
trusted and feared government, Americans usually looked to government to
solve problems. An interesting and revealing manifestation of this difference is the contrasting meaning given to the word "liberal." In the
United States, a liberal advocates increased government involvement in
economic affairs, but in Western Europe a liberal is one who opposes
government intervention in the economy. Liberalism arose in Europe in
opposition to the remnants of mercantilism with its government-sanctioned
special privileges and monopolies; the liberal slogan was "laissez-faire."

Americans also opposed government-sanctioned special privileges (see,
for example, documents 238, 239, and 241) but the opposition was not to
government interference as such, but rather to monopoly which imposed
unfair exactions on the common people. The bank, not the government,
was the menace; indeed, the government in the capable hands of Andrew
Jackson could solve the problem. Later, reformers looked to the government to control big business, insure full employment, and in general keep
the economy functioning. These views did not (and do not) prevent
Americans from complaining about government interference. But the complaints, although often expressed in general terms condemning big government, are usually directed towards particular government actions that seem
troublesome, expensive, or unneeded by particular groups.

I have presented only a few brief examples to illustrate how this collection, along with its splendid organizational and bibliographic aids, will be
of value to general readers and students interested in American economic
history. Teachers can send their students to particular documents or to
particular themes in the documents to illustrate concepts covered in texts

and lectures and to give students the experience of reading and evaluating contemporary documents. The collection provides endless subjects for term papers along with the bibliographic guides to help students get started.

But the collection can also help the advanced student researcher and even the professional historian. Of course, no collection of documents, even one as extensive as this, can replace archival research for the serious historian. The documents Weinberg has chosen to reprint reflect his views about what is significant, and, although his views are well informed, others may not share them. Nevertheless, the historian embarking upon an investigation of an aspect of one of the many problems in American economic history and students of comparative economic development will find this collection with its bibliography and ample index a useful starting point for their investigations.

Meyer Weinberg is to be commended for his enormous effort in preparing this collection.

# PREFACE

This work is a first-hand view of American economic history. The view is achieved by reproducing the texts of 785 significant primary historical sources. Virtually every source in the collection has met the following tests: (1) it is an eyewitness account; (2) it is recounted by an especially qualified contemporary observer, usually the actor himself; (3) it is representative of countless like events; (4) in the case of an invention, it is a statement by the inventor or by an early user of the invention; (5) in the case of government policy, it is a statement by a responsible official involved in that area of policy; and (6) it illuminates an important aspect of American economic history.

Broadly, the work is divided into two volumes. The first volume consists of three parts: I—Colonial history to 1815 (137 pages); II—1815 to 1860 (196 pages); and III—1860 to 1900 (230 pages) and IV—Post 1900 (451 pages). Each source is introduced with a summary statement giving something of the historical setting of the source. Individuals mentioned in the source as well as the author of it are identified. Within each section, sources are arranged around nine different themes: Land, Agriculture, Commerce, Labor, Manufacturing, Foreign Trade, Government, Money and Banking, and Industrial Research. The applicability of these themes varies, of course, from period to period. Sub-themes are treated as parts of the major themes. Through explicit cross-references as well as entries in a detailed index, the reader's attention is called to related material appearing in more than one period.

The economic historian is heir to a superb series of sources simply because of the relative lack of division of labor in early American life. During the years 1789-1825, a man who was president or vice-president or secretary of state might also have been an operator of a nailery, or a tobacco planter, or a wholesale merchant, or a slave-owner—and if his name was Thomas Jefferson, he was all these. The sources are drawn from a wide variety of places. With respect to selected letters by George Washington, Benjamin Franklin, Thomas Jefferson, Alexander Hamilton, and James Madison, I have utilized microfilms of the originals in the Division of Manuscripts, Library of Congress. If, after inspection, I found the early or earliest printed version of the letter to be accurate, credit was given to the printed work. If, however, I found a significant discrepancy between the original and the printed version, a footnote reference is made to the manuscript collection only.

I have tried to present to the reader a broad sampling of various types of printed primary sources. For the colonial period, for example, extracts are reproduced from proceedings of parliamentary committees and from royal instructions to colonial governors. Letters are a rich source of knowledge about economic processes and events. Diaries and autobiographies reveal much. After 1865, transcripts of congressional and other federal inquiries start to become valuable, though these come into their own only after 1900. Engineering and technical journals contain extensive contemporary materials.

Researchers in American economic history have become familiar with certain standard primary sources. Neither students nor general readers, however, consult these sources. I have reproduced extracts from a number both for their own value and as a guide for the interested reader. These include: the McLane Report on manufactures (1833); the Pujo investigation of high finance (1913); the Armstrong investigation of life insurance (1906); the Collom report on regulation of railroads (1885); the Ku Klux Klan hearings (1871-1872); the Industrial Commission hearings (1899-1901); the Industrial Relations Study (1914); the Public Lands Report (1880); the earliest dependable study of foreign investment in the United States (1853); and many more. I have also used the relevant correspondence and writings of several leading statesmen; these include John Quincy Adams (*Memoirs* and *Writings*), Sam Houston, Stephen F. Austin, John Calhoun, William Seward, Rufus King, and Henry Clay in addition to those mentioned earlier. Nowadays, when a certain degree of economic ignorance has become part of the qualification for high governmental office, the contemporary reader may be startled at the detailed knowledge of economic affairs demonstrated by these and other politicians of earlier years.

The class coloring of historical documentation has long been known. Written documents are the product of literate persons, yet economic history is made by illiterate persons as well. I have been pleased to find authoritative narratives by slaves, shoemakers, dirt farmers, railroad brakemen, and sheep shearers. More numerous are accounts by organizers of small and large corporations, cotton and tobacco planters, factory managers, and importers.

I have tried to emphasize connections between economic and general history. This is done placing the document in a broader setting so as to establish clearly its connection with larger trends and developments. Sometimes this has required a comment on the political context of the document or pointing out an interconnection between the industry at issue and other ones. Thus, the volumes contain materials relating to the history of corporate law, the politics of slavery, the economics of literature, and the diplomacy of territorial expansion. I have treated technology as a fundamental dimension of economic history.

The bibliography, arranged by source number, lists from one to five secondary works for each of the 785 sources. In addition to book-length studies, a special effort was made to locate articles in leading research journals covering the fields of interest in this work.

The "old" economic history, which held forth until a generation ago, had little room for individuals. More an extension of the narrative style characteristic of political and social history, it stressed large-scale institutional change. Long-term trends in basic divisions of the subject occupied most of the space and some well-known leaders were cited occasionally to illustrate a generalization. The "new" economic history, heavily dependent on econometrics, was severely analytical and mined the past for its relevance to economic theory. It outstripped its predecessor in attending to long-term changes and often supplied theoretical explanations of the dynamic of these developments. But whatever its accomplishments, it was even less hospitable to the individual than the old economic history.

The present work presents the broad sweep of American economic history as delineated by individuals located along various axes of historical development. An account does not automatically become authoritative simply because its author was an eye-witness to an event, yet the historian's proverbial dependence on such accounts, properly sifted, remains well-taken. What, then, are the advantages of a first-hand view of American, or for that matter, any economic history?

First, an awareness of authenticity is heightened. An immediacy is created that few narratives can match. The reader shares with the first-hand source a common experience of an emotion that makes the subject matter far more than a past fact. Second, historical events can all the more readily be viewed in their human dimension. The result is not so much to reduce economic history to individual action as to place economic history in a human context. The play of motives, personal interest, prejudices, and personal insight sheds light on the historical character of the subject matter at hand. Third, first hand accounts often are insightful. To be sure, while the inventor may well be the best authority on his or her creation, this does not always hold true. Nevertheless, it is especially enlightening to read the analysis of Eli Whitney of the cotton gin or of the Rust brothers of their mechanical cotton picker. Jefferson's directions to Lewis and Clark on the eve of their pioneering journey throw a unique light on the commerical situation of the United States at the outset of the nineteenth century. Simon Ramo's analysis of the contemporary corporate merger movement gains something special from his own background in high corporate affairs. Fourth, clashes of policies and interpretations are graphically present in the first-hand accounts. The present work is not designed as a debate handbook, nor has there been an effort to edit into the work a homogeneous viewpoint. A very wide variety of interpretations can be found herein. The first concern has been whether a given account presents a uniquely valuable view of its subject matter. Inevitably, different viewpoints are expressed.

During the past generation of the ascendancy of the new, econometric history, research in the primary sources of American economic history has suffered a set-back. Accordingly, another purpose of this work is to direct the attention of students and researchers to promising sources that may be unknown to them.

I wish to thank the Manuscript Division of the Library of Congress for its cooperation. The libraries of the University of Chicago and the University of Massachusetts, Amherst, opened their holdings to me without complaint or grimace. Betty Craker, my secretary, typed a long and complex manuscript with care and intelligence. During the summer of 1982, Josephine Ryan helped prepare the final manuscript for typing and assisted with permissions. An anonymous publisher's reader made many excellent suggestions, most of which were incorporated within the final draft. Aiding in the making of the index were Dan Weinberg, Ben Weinberg, Sue Simmons, David Spencer, Steve Gilson, and Maureen McAnnery. To all these persons I express my gratitude and relief.

# PART I
# A COLONIAL ECONOMY— TO 1815

# A.

## ACQUIRING NEW LAND

### 1. HOW THE BOSTON LANDS WERE DISTRIBUTED (1634)

While the earliest Puritan leaders were men who appreciated the value of land, their land distribution policy was guided by considerations of community purpose. The new Puritan commonwealth needed settlers, room for expansion, and specialized occupations. Land policy must serve these ends. John Winthrop, the author of the following extract, was the first governor of Massachusetts Bay Colony, organized in 1629.

This day...the inhabitants of Boston met to choose seven men who should divide the town lands among them. They chose by papers, and in their choice left out Mr. Winthrop, Coddington, and other of the chief men; only they chose one of the elders and a deacon, and the rest of the inferior sort, and Mr. Winthrop had the greater number before one of them by a voice or two. This they did, as fearing that the richer men would give the poorer sort no great proportions of land, but would rather leave a great part at liberty for new comers and for common, which Mr. Winthrop had oft persuaded them unto, as best for the town, etc. Mr. Cotton and divers others were offended at this choice, because they declined the magistrates; and Mr. Winthrop refused to be one upon such an election as was carried by a voice or two, telling them, that though, for his part, he did not apprehend any personal injury, nor did doubt of their good affection towards him, yet he was much grieved that Boston should be the first who should shake off their magistrates, especially Mr. Coddington, who had been always so forward for their enlargement; adding further reason of declining this choice, to blot out so bad a precedent. Whereupon, at the motion of Mr. Cotton, who showed them, that it was the Lord's order among the Israelites to have all such business committed to the elders, and that it had been nearer the rule to have chosen some of each sort, etc., they all agreed to go to a new election, which was referred to the next lecture day.

The reason why some were not willing that the people should have more land in the bay than they might be likely to use in some other more necessary employments, and partly that there might be place to receive such as should come after; seeing it would be very prejudicial to the commonwealth, if men should be forced to go far off for land, while others had much, and could make no use of it, more than to please their eye with it.

John Winthrop, Winthrop's Journal, ed. J. K. Hosmer, I, (New York:  Scribner's 1908), pp. 143-144.

## 2.   INSTRUCTIONS TO A LAND AGENT (1767)

The Royal Proclamation of 1763 suspended further migration west of the Alleghenies.  This provision, along with others, all but excluded colonists from the profitable Indian trade and stopped the transfer of Indian lands to speculators.  The Crown, however, was unable to police the Proclamation, and the settlers--among them, George Washington--were unable to resist the temptations involved.  William Crawford, to whom Washington writes here, was a surveyor and one of Washington's comrades-in-arms.  He had just moved to Pennsylvania where he became a judge and a land agent for Washington.

I would recommend, it to you to keep this whole matter a secret, or trust it only with those, in whom you can confide, and who can assist you in bringing it to bear by their discoveries of land. And this advice proceeds from several very good reasons, and in the first place, because I might be censured for the opinion I have given in respect to the King's proclamation, and then, if the scheme I am now proposing to you was known, it might give the alarm to others, and, by putting them upon a plan of the same nature, (before we could lay a proper foundation for success ourselves,) set the different interests a clashing, and, probably, in the end, overturn the whole.  All which may be avoided by a silent management, and the [operation] snugly carried on by you under the guise of hunting other game, which you may, I presume, effectually do, at the same time you are in pursuit of land, which when fully discovered, advise me of it, and if there appears but a bare possibility of succeeding any time hence, I will have the lands immediately surveyed, to keep others off, and leave the rest to time and my own assiduity to accomplish.

The other matter, just now hinted at and which I proposed in my last to join you, in attempting to secure some of the most valuable

lands in the King's part, which I think may be accomplished after a
while, notwithstanding the proclamation, that restrains it at present, and prohibits the settling of them at all; for I can never
look upon that proclamation in any other light (but this I say between ourselves), than as a temporary expedient to quiet the minds
of the Indians, and must fall, of course, in a few years, especially
when those Indians are consenting to our occuping the lands.  Any
person, therefore, who neglects the present opportunity of hunting
out good lands, and in some measure marking and distinguishing them
for his own (in order to keep others from settling them), will
never regain it.  Therefore if you will be at the trouble of seeking
out the lands, I will take upon me the part of securing them, so
all the cost and charges of surveying, and patenting &c, after which
you shall have such a reasonable proportion of the whole, as we may
fix upon at our first meeting; as I shall find it absolutely necessary, and convenient for the better furthering of the design, to
let some few of my friends be concerned in the scheme, and who must
partake of the advantages.


    Letter, George Washington to William Crawford, September 21,
1767, Worthington C. Ford (ed.), Writings of George Washington,
II, (New York:  G. P. Putnam's Sons, 1889), pp. 223, 220, 222.


3.    CONFISCATION OF LOYALIST ESTATES WAS A JUST POLICY (1770's)


    During the Revolution, "loyalists"--i.e., American
colonists who supported the King's cause--suffered confiscation of their estates.  Critics of the Revolution
seized on this practice as an unjust one.  Franklin is
here answering such a British critic, Francis Maseres,
a legal light in England who had served as Attorney-
General of Quebec from 1766 to 1769.


    All the estates in England and south of Scotland, and most of
those possessed by the descendants of the English in Ireland, are
held from ancient confiscations made of the estates of Caledonians
and Britons, the original possessors in your island, or the native
Irish, in the last century only.  It is but a few months since,
that your Parliament has, in a few instances, given up confiscations
incurred by a rebellion suppressed forty years ago.  The war against
us was begun by a general act of Parliament, declaring all our estates confiscated; and probably one great motive to the loyality of
the royalists was the hope of sharing in these confiscations.  They
have played a deep game, staking their estates against ours; and
they have been unsuccessful.  But it is a surer game, since they had
promises to rely on from your government, of indemnification in case
of loss; and I see your Parliament is about to fulfill those promises.  To this I have no objection, because, though still our

enemies, they are men; they are in necessity; and I think even a
hired assassin has a right to his pay from his employer.  It seems
too more reasonable, that the expense of paying these should fall
upon the government who encouraged the mischief done, rather than
upon us who suffered it; the confiscated estates making amends but
for a very small part of that mischief.  It is not, therefore,
clear, that our retaining them is chargeable with injustice.


Letter, Benjamin Franklin to Francis Maseres, June 26, 1785,
Jared Sparks (ed.), Works of Benjamin Franklin, X, pp. 192-193.


4.  "MAKE HAY WHILE THE SUN SHINES" (1784)


Land speculation was one of the most animating
economic pursuits of early America.  Ownership of
land served as an entry into farming but also as a
means of accumulating capital.  Trade in land was one
of the few ready sources of capital in those days.
Since much of the landed estate of the country was in
the public domain, influence in governmental affairs
was essential for speculators to acquire choice pieces
of land.  Here is an example of this phenomenon.
William Blount was a prominent speculator in western
lands and served in the North Carolina and federal
legislatures; Lachlin McIntosh had just been elected
to the Continental Congress as a delegate from Georgia;
while Stephen Heard, governor of Georgia during the
Revolutionary War, had settled on a farm in his state,
near the town of Washington.  The latter three persons,
as well as a fourth, were serving as land commissioners
for Georgia and they were to make recommendations for
land grants.


Before you reach the Long Island I pursue you will find yourselves much fatigued with travelling, and I am not without my fears
that you will be discouraged from attempting the intended Visit, to
the Bent of Tenesee but I hope a View of the advantages, which present themselves will be sufficient to induce you to persvere--
    The Object of the Tenesee Company in purchasing the Bent and
(I suppose) your's in Accepting the appointment as commissioners
must have been the same, I mean private Emolument and in Order that
we may both obtain our purposes it is Necessary, We should understand each Other and that our Acts should tend to our mutiose advantage, that is that our Intrust should be joint which can only be by
each of you, Accepting an equal Share with the original Petitioners
whose Names are known to you and if this is agreeable to you, please
signify your Approbation to Missers. Dondeldson, Martin & Severe
and it shall bend the company to admit you each as joint Adventurers,
and if you think writings Necessary they will on the part of the

Company enter into such as may be proper.  You have power, to make the company such, compensation as may be deemed Adequate and satisfactory, No Bond nor no Oath has been required nor no Instructions, given you from whence as well as the General disposition of the best informed part of your legislature, I think it ardent they intended and wished you to be liberal and if you accede to my Proposition of our Interest being the same you will have a share of your own liberty--It was the Opinion of Gen$^l$. M$^c$.Intosh that the whole of the bent should be granted the company without any other consideration except that of settling a Number of People on it; for these seven weeks past I have been attending the legislature of this State, now siting at this place that body have passed an act ceeding to the Congress of the United States all the Teretory owned by this State lying West of the Apalachan mountain the leading step to this act was a similar Act passed by the State of Virginia and I suspect Your State will also be under the Necessity of following her Example and should this be the case as I am sure it will had you not at any rate better make a liberal Grant to the Company than leave it for the State to give to Congress--The quantity of Land contained in the Bent is unknown in my Petition, I composed it to contain 300,000. Acres more or less it may contain some more tho Not much so that should you grant the whole of the bent for 300,000 Acres more or less I think it would be most prudent but should you think otherwise, I wish whatever quantity you may think best to grant should be bounded by Natural Boundaries except the Northern line & that may be bounded by the Southern line of this State and let it be expressed to contain as much more or less.  Your Brother Commissioners will Show you a letter I have just recved from my friend in Congress by which you will see it will be very eaesey to people the Bent, Such Another appertunity may never present itself of Making a Spec and there's an old Proverb which says "make Hay while the sun shines," of which I wish you to be mindful

Letter, William Blount to Lachlin McIntosh, John Morrell, William Downes, and Stephen Heard, May 31, 1784, Alice Barnwell Keith (ed.), The John Gray Blount Papers, I, (Raleigh, N.C.: State Department of Archives and History, 1952), pp. 169-170.

### 5.   UNCULTIVATED LAND AND UNEMPLOYED POOR (1785)

Property or sustenance Thomas Jefferson regarded as a natural right.  Visiting Fontainbleau, he was led to the following reflections as he observed the King's hunting grounds and a very poor old woman with whom Jefferson walked along the road.  The splendor of the hunting grounds and the poverty of the woman reminded him of the distortion of natural right in a country where great extremes of poverty existed side-by-side.

The solitude of my walk led me into a train of reflections on
that unequal division of property which occasions the numberless
instances of wretchedness which I had observed in this country & is
to be observed all over Europe.  The property of this country
[France] is absolutely concentrated in a very few hands, having
revenues of from half a million of guineas a year downwards.  These
employ the flower of the country as servants, some of them having
as many as 200 domestics, not labouring.  They employ also a great
number of manufacturers, & tradesmen, & lastly the class of labouring husbandmen.  But after all there comes the most numerous of all
the classes, that is, the poor who cannot find work.  I asked myself
what could be the reason that so many should be permitted to beg who
are willing to work, in a country where there is a very considerable
proportion of uncultivated lands?  These lands are undisturbed only
for the sake of game.  It should seem then that it must be because
of the enormous wealth of the proprietors which places them above
attention to the increase of their revenues by permitting these
lands to be laboured.  I am conscious that an equal division of property is impracticable.  But the consequences of this enormous in-
equality producing so much misery to the bulk of mankind, legislators cannot invent too many devices for subdividing property, only
taking care to let their subdivisions go hand in hand with the natural affections of the human mind.  The descent of property of
every kind therefore to all the children, or to all the brothers &
sisters, or other relations to equal degree is a politic measure,
and a practicable one.  Another means of silently lessening the in-
equality of property is to exempt all from taxation below a certain
point, & to tax the higher portions of property in geometrical progression as they rise.  Whenever there is in any country, uncultivated lands and unemployed poor, it is clear that the laws of property have been so far extended as to violate natural right.  The
earth is given as a common stock for man to labour & live on.  If
for the encouragement of industry we allow it to be appropriated,
we must take care that other employment be provided to those excluded from the appropriation.  If we do not the fundamental right
to labour the earth returns to the unemployed.  It is too soon yet
in our country to say that every man who cannot find employment but
who can find uncultivated land shall be at liberty to cultivate it,
paying a moderate rent.  But it is not too soon to provide by every
possible means that as few as possible shall be without a little
portion of land.  The small land owners are the most precious part
of a state.

Letter, Thomas Jefferson to Rev. James Madison, October 28,
1785, Ford (ed.), Writings of Thomas Jefferson, VII, pp. 35-36.

### 6.  SELL WESTERN LAND IN SMALLER PARCELS (1788)

Spain formally owned both Louisiana to the west of
the United States, and Florida to the south.  Spanish

land policy throughout Latin America favored the large
operator.  But in Florida and Louisiana a very different
policy was followed--one of encouraging Americans to
emigrate by the offer of free land.  This move, in turn,
created a pressure on the American government to revise
its own land system.  Ironically, then, one strong force
acting to make land more easily available was the semi-
feudal Spanish state-interest in America.  Below,
St. Clair, governor of the Northwest Territory, writes
to Jay, Minister for Foreign Affairs in the government of
the Confederation soon to be replaced by a government
under the Federal Constitution.

It is for a considerable time that the Spaniards have been
offering a thousand acres of land gratis to every American who would
remove into the West or Florida, to pay ten dollars for every hun-
dred-weight of tobacco he could raise and deliver at New Orleans,
an exemption from all taxes, and a proportionate price for provisions and other articles the produce of his farm, but they have
lately gone a step farther.  If I am well informed, Colonel Morgan,
who was lately in treaty with the Board of Treasury for a tract of
land on the Mississippi, has obtained of Mr. Gardoqui a grant of a
very large tract upon the Spanish side, opposite to the mouth of
the Ohio, which he engages to settle with Americans.  They are to
have the same privileges with those who remove into Florida.
He is now at Fort Pitt, and it is supposed will carry a good
many people from that country.  Upon Kentucky is, however, his
chief dependence, for in that quarter are many thousands of people
who have been tempted by the accounts published of its amazing fertility to quit their ancient settlements without having secured a
foot of land there, and can not obtain lands but at a price that is
beyond their reach.  There is no doubt many of those will readily
join him, for they have no country, and indeed that attachment to
the natale solum that has been so powerful and active a principle
in other countries is very little felt in America.
I have been casting about for some way to counteract Mr.
Morgan, and I can not think of any so likely to succeed as for
Congress to change the mode of disposing of the Western lands in
large tracts, at least to change it for a part of them, and lay them
open to be taken up by the people who settle upon them.  The country
upon the Mississippi, and between that and the Wabash, would
accommodate the people of Kentucky who have no lands, and I believe
it would tempt them to remove to it rather than the Spanish side,
and it might be disposed of in the manner the proprietors of
Pennsylvania sold the lands they had purchased of the Indians.  It
was thus:  The lands were set at five pounds sterling per hundred
acres; no more than three hundred acres were allowed to be taken
up by one man.  He made a description, in writing of the piece
wanted, bounding it either upon lands already granted, or some
creek or river, or marked trees, that rendered it sufficiently
certain, and carried it to the office of the Surveyor-General
where it we entered into a book kept for the purpose.  The
Surveyor-General issued an order for making the survey returnable

within a certain time to his office, and the applicant took
possession.  The purchase-money ran upon interest from the date
of the order of survey, and was discharged when it was in the
person's power, though to make them more industrious a time was
fixed within which the patents should be taken out, but no advantage was taken of their overpassing that time; on the payment of
principal and interest the patents issued.  I believe there is not
an instance, though it was a very extensive country, at least, the
instances were few, were the patents had not been taken out, and
all the land, good and bad, had been sold.  Although this mode
would not so suddenly extinguish any part of the debt as that now
in use, yet an interest equal to the interest of the debt, so far
as the lands went, would be accruing to the United States, and the
principal would come in at last, and the people, who are of infinite
value, that will otherwise be more than lost, will be secured.  The
present inhabitants of that country, when they see it gathering
strength by the accession of new inhabitants will be more contented
to remain in it.


    Letter, Arthur St. Clair to John Jay, December 13, 1788,
William Henry Smith (ed.), The St. Clair Papers, II, (Cincinnati,
Ohio:  Robert Clarke Co., 1882), pp. 103-105.


        7.  SPECULATION IN AMERICAN LAND IS THE BASIS
              OF EVERY FORTUNE THERE (1795)


        With the outbreak of the French Revolutionary
wars, capital in Europe sought safety overseas.  For
nearly two centuries, American land as a profitable
investment had been proclaimed to Englishmen, especially.
Here is an appeal to continental European investors,
written by Talleyrand.


    Summarizing the purpose of this memoir I believe I have given
an exact idea of speculations which can be made on uncultivated
lands in the United States of America.  I have announced that these
speculations, still little known by most European capitalists, nevertheless were very well known, very extensive and already reduced to
a regular system by all American proprietors and by a small number
of rich Europeans who have participated in their success, but that
this kind of speculation employs far from the quantity of money it
is susceptible of employing and assures very great profits to those
who wish to profit from this circumstance to undertake it.
    I have shown then on what principles these speculations were
founded and I have shown that the population of America, growing
with great rapidity and tending to spread over the lands not yet
occupied, creates a constant demand which cannot be stopped and

which should necessarily assure an advantageous resale to capitalists who have in their hands vast expanses of uncultivated lands.

I have shown that there can be no danger in accumulating a large mass of this kind of property because it can neither deteriorate nor require any expense of preservation to the one who possesses it.

I have shown that no other property was as solid nor as imperishable. Passing then to the means of making the resale and of realizing the profits I have shown how, by the mere effect of time and of the natural population growth, the price of lands cannot fail to rise, I have compared the present price of American lands with the price which they will have when America is settled like Europe, and I have shown the annual increase which this calculation promises to the whole of the lands in the different states of the Union. Then reducing this calculation to the states of New York and Pennsylvania I have shown how much more rapidly these states approach such a density of population as that of France and England because they continually receive the emigration of the northern states where the population is superfluous. The result of these figures has proved that the value of uncultivated land in these two states rises at a rate of about 20% per year which, adding to the capital, acts exactly in the same manner as a savings bank, but at a far higher compound interest and with infinitely greater safety for the lender. Finally I have made known the art of doubling one's capital much more quickly by means of forming settlements which, directing the population toward a particular point, enable you to enjoy in very few years increases which the land, left to itself and the sole effect of time, would receive only more slowly although just as surely.

In support of these developments I have cited generally known facts, examples of which, confirmed by a multitude of other particular facts, go much beyond the calculations and reasoning which I have presented. I have shown how the land had doubled in value in the hands of inactive speculators who awaited the rise brought about by time, and how it was increased more rapidly for those who added to the action of time the activity of their own industry and the advance of certain sums.

All that I have included in this memoir--facts, reasoning, figures--is known to everyone in the United States of America. This theory is here the basis of every fortune. I believe it would be desirable for all the rich men of Europe to have their fortunes repose on as solid bases.

Hans Huth and Wilma J. Pugh (eds.), Talleyrand In America As A Financial Promoter 1794-96, (Washington, D.C.:  Government Printing Office, 1942), pp. 174-175.  (Annual Report of the American Historical Association for the year 1941, Vol. II).

## 8.   HOW TO INCREASE LAND SALES (1810)

In 1810 the United States was like an atom--
mostly empty space.  The public domain was placed
on sale to actual settlers who were scarce at the land
offices, partly because they could not get up the
$422.20 for a purchase and partly because it was
cheaper to squat on the land, without benefit of
title.  Many speculators sought a low land price,
even if all buyers paid the same price.  Albert
Gallatin in this letter to John Eppes refers to a
differential price as between large and small
purchases.  Eppes was chairman of the Committee on
Ways and Means of the U.S. House of Representatives;
Gallatin was Secretary of the Treasury.

Not less than ten land offices are now in full operation,
offering a great choice of good lands, situated in various climates,
and suited to the habits of the citizens of every portion of the
Union.  They are sold at the rate of two dollars and sixty-four
cents, if paid for at the time of purchase, and in tracts of one
hundred and sixty acres.  As much is sold as there is actual demand
for land in similar situations at that price.  The sales are, however, almost exclusively confined to those who are, or intend to
become, actual settlers, and all the money which can be raised by
that description of purchasers is annually paid to the United
States.  In order to increase immediately the amount of sales, a
different capital from that which has heretofore been applied to
that object--the capital of persons who will purchase for the purpose of selling again with a profit--must be brought into action.
But it is evident that no person will purchase lands at the present
price as an object of speculation whilst the United States continue
to sell at the same price in small tracts.  To effect the proposed
object it would be necessary not only to reduce the price, but to
make a difference between that of lands sold in large tracts and
that asked for small tracts, sufficient to encourage purchases on
an extensive scale.  That alteration might produce an additional
revenue, but appears to me extremely injurious in other respects.
The present system of sales has been tried, and answers the expectations of the Legislature.  A gradual increase must, notwithstanding some temporary fluctuations, necessarily take place.  On that
I would rely; nor would I venture to suggest any other change than
that already proposed on a former occasion,--a moderate and general
reduction of prices, discontinuing at the same time all sales on
credit, but continuing to sell at the same rate large or small
tracts of land.

Letter, Albert Gallatin to John Eppes, February 26, 1810,
H. Adams (ed.), Writings of Albert Gallatin, I, pp. 470-471.

9.  THE NEED TO SEPARATE THE INDIAN FROM THE LAND (1814)


    One theory of land rights held that ownership
passed with conquest.  J. Q. Adams theorized that
ownership was determined by the level of economic
use; white farmers would use the land more intensively
and it would be unjust to leave the same land to be
used only for occasional hunting by Indians.  (See
Sources No. 123 and 124).  At this time Adams was one
of four American envoys negotiating an end to the War
of 1812 at Ghent, Belgium; Monroe, to whom he writes
here, was Secretary of State.


    It was impossible for such people [the Indians] ever to be said
to have possessions.  Their only right upon land was a right to use
it as hunting grounds; and when those lands where they hunted became necessary or convenient for the purposes of settlement, the
system adopted by the United States was by amicable arrangement
with them to compensate them for renouncing the right of hunting
upon them, and for removing to remoter regions better suited to
their purposes and mode of life.  This system of the United States
was an improvement upon the former practice of all European nations,
including the British.  The original settlers of New England had
set the first example of this liberality towards the Indian, which
was afterwards followed by the founder of Pennsylvania.  Between
it and taking the lands for nothing, or exterminating the Indians
who had used them, there was no alternative.  To condemn vast
regions of territory to perpetual barrenness and solitude, that
a few hundred savages might find wild beasts to hunt upon it, was
a species of game law that a nation descended from Britons would
never endure.  It was as incompatible with the moral as with the
physical nature of things.  If Britain meant to preclude forever
the people of the United States from settling and cultivating those
territories, she must not think of doing it by a treaty.  She must
formally undertake and accomplish their utter extermination.  If
the government of the United States would ever submit to such a
stipulation, which I hoped they would not, all its force, and all
that of Britain combined with it, would not suffice to carry it
long into execution.  It was opposing a feather to a torrent.  The
population of the United States in 1810 passed seven millions.  At
this hour it undoubtedly passed eight.  As it continued to increase in such proportions, was it in human experience or in human
power to check its progress by a bond of paper, purporting to ex-
clude posterity from the natural means of subsistence which they
would derive from the cultivation of soil?


    Letter, John Quincy Adams to James Monroe, September 5, 1814,
W. C. Ford (ed.), Writings of John Quincy Adams, V, (New York:
McMillan Co., 1913-1917), pp. 115-116.

# B.

## SUBSISTENCE AND MONEY FARMING

### 10.  CORN WAS VERY SCARCE (1643)

In the sacred Puritan commonwealth of Massachusetts
Bay, every event had a primary religious significance.
If corn was scarce, this must be attributed to "the just
hand of the Lord."  Divine purpose was always expressed
through public spirit and was opposed to self-love.
Nevertheless, economic life was not exempt from the
virtues and temptations of organized society.  This extract is from John Winthrop's journal.

Corn was very scarce all over the country, so as by the end of
the 2d month, many families in most towns had none to eat, but were
forced to live of clams, muscles, cataos, dry fish, etc., and sure
this came by the just hand of the Lord, to punish our ingratitude
and covetousness.  For corn being plenty divers years before, it was
so undervalued, as it would not pass for any commodity:  if one
offered a shop keeper corn for any thing, his answer would be, he
know not what to do with it.  So for laborers and artificers; but
now they would have done any work, or parted with any commodity, for
corn.  And the husbandman, he now made his advantage, for he would
part with no corn, for the most part, but for ready money or for
cattle, at such a price as should be 12d. in the bushel more to him
than ready money.  And indeed it was a very sad thing to see how
little of a public spirit appeared in the country, but of self-love
too much.  Yet there were some here and there, who were men of
another spirit, and were willing to abridge themselves, that others
might be supplied.  The immediate causes of this scarcity were the
cold and wet summer, especially in the time of the first harvest;
also, the pigeons came in such flocks, (above 10,000 in one flock,)
that beat down, and eat up a very great quantity of all sorts of

English grain, much corn spent in setting out the ships, ketches, etc.; lastly, there were such abundance of mice in the barns, that devoured much there. The mice also did much spoil in orchards, eating off the bark at the bottom of the fruit trees in the time of the snow, so as never had been known the like spoil in any former winter. So many enemies doth the Lord arm against our daily bread, that we might know we are to eat it in the sweat of our brows.

Winthrop, Winthrop's Journal, II, pp. 91-92.

### 11. A VIRGINIA PLANTER AND HIS LONDON AGENT (1720)

Debts, orders, personal affairs, shipping, tobacco prices and freight rates--all were fit subjects between a planter and his agent. Robert Carter who writes this letter was a wealthy landowner who had served as treasurer and president of the Virginia colonial assembly. At his death he is said to have left 300,000 acres of land, 1,000 slaves and £10,000.

This letter accompanies the "Carter." She is loaded at £10 per ton, which I hope will in some measure retrieve the great, great losses upon he[r] late voyages. Captain Kent is threatened mightily to be remembered when a scarce year comes, but that humor will go near soon to blow over. There is no reason that we who venture our money should be losers by it.

There is in her 60 hogsheads of my crop tobacco coming to you, and 10 more stemmed are designed to you per the "Mercury," which makes your quota 100 hogshead, according to your desire. If you do not give us eleven pence per pound, now freights are so high we shall get nothing.

The goods you sent me came in good order, but the two coats for my two youngest girls were never sent. Pray let me have them the next year. All that were at the opening the goods that came for my children can vouch for the truth of this.

Herein is an invoice for goods to supply my families the next year, wherein I have been as good a husband as possibly I can. You tell me you lay out my money with as much caution as if it were your own. This I must confess is all I can desire, yet give me leave to say some of them seems to be extraordinary dear. The earrings and the tombstone cost abundance more than I expected or intended. I shall be obliged to you to let me be the master of my own money. You talk vainly to me in making Mrs. Heath my pattern. Had I but one daughter, and she the descendant of two successive muckworms, perhaps a parallel might not be improper: my circumstances are other ways. I must cut my coat according to my cloth and bless God I am able to do so well as I do.

I'm heartily sorry for poor Ben Graves's misfortune. He's an honest brickman, and I believe will hardly long want an employ. I

shall be very well pleased to hear he gets a good one.  His brother
Adam made a wrong step when he left the "Carter"; however, methinks
you should be so generous to the memory of that good man, his father,
to find him a suitable berth in some of your ships, and, if my word
will go any length with you, 'tis my desire you take care of him.

Your debts I take the same care of as I do my own; get them,
when I can, without law.  Thos. Cunningham hath paid me upon your
account his debt of 26/3.  Patrick Connolly is in my debt as well as
yours.  He hath two hogsheads on board the "Carter"; to whom he intends them yet I don't know.  I shall give you a line more about some
other of your debts in another letter.

Mr. Heath's debts are so scattered I don't know what will become
of many of them, but we shall write to him a joint letter.  I find
he does not come into my proposal about Mr. Jackson's debt.  To give
him satisfaction in that matter I have sent him the stated account
for our records of that estate, whereby it appears I have paid off
more debts than the estate amounted to, including the value of the
land I sold, and sure Mr. Heath is not such a violent lover of money
to desire I should pay other men's debts out of my own estate.

I should be obliged to you if you took more frequent opportunity
to give me an account of the welfare of my sons.  I have not had one
line concerning them since the "Carter".  I want very much to know
what I am to trust to in relation of their maintenance.  You gave me
your opinion the two eldest would stand me in £40 apiece (?).  If you
run me out any more money upon them, I'm upon thoughts of removing
them to Manchester School, where I am well advised I can maintain
them for a great deal less and their education every whit as good.

I drew on you the other day for £200 payable to Edmund Jenings,
Esq., which requested you to answer at time.  Some more drafts I
shall be forced to make ere long.  Have had great losses of my
negroes in my families this last winter, the recruiting at which
swallows a great deal of money.  If you had sent me an account
current I could have been more exact in my care not to outrun the
constable.

You press me to send you a certificate for the cannister of tea
you sent me two years ago.  It is here inclosed according to your
form, signed by Mr. Pra[tt] and Mrs. John Robinson, whose hands and
persons are well enough known in England.

You make a proposal about selling the "Carter".  I have [no?]
reason to fall into it, I'm sure.  I can hardly believe you are in
earnest:  when that time comes you'll be the greatest sufferer; unless another ship supplies her place, your business will soon droop
here.

The ship "Catherine's" accounts you say are not yet made up.
When they are I shall be glad to get my money back again.  I hope if
the "Carter" makes anything by this voyage I shall be in the way of
getting my debt from Hastewell's estate.  You must expect never to
escape dunning till you have licked me whole in that matter....

Letter, Robert Carter to William Dawkins, July 13, 1720, Louis
B. Wright (ed.), Letters of Robert Carter, 1720-1727, (San Marino,
California:  Huntington Library, 1940), pp. 10-13.

12.  A VIRGINIA PLANTER WRITES HIS GENERAL OVERSEER (1721)


     The general overseer was the prime dependence of
an absentee planter.  There was little he was not responsible for.  Robert Carter writes the following:


     You are first of all to acquaint yourself with the condition
the several plantations are in and to use your utmost diligence and
endeavor to get the crops all planted and to see that the overseers
mind their business and keep their homes.  You are to take an
account as soon as you can of my goods at the several quarters.  I
now give you a copy of my last letter to Natt Hedgeman, by which
you will know what goods went up in the last sloop.  You must take
especial care of my arms at the several quarters, and give me an
account what they are and in what order they are.  Last winter I
sent up a set of [...] arms to Natt Hedgeman--that is, a case of
pistols and holsters, sword and belt, and carabine and belt.  You
must take these arms into your custody and be answerable for them
as he was.  You must be very careful and diligent in r[ea]ping and
getting in the wheat as soon as it is ripe.  You must [take care]
in all respects [to] perform the articles of your agreement.  As
soon as conveniently you can you must get a particular account of
my stocks of cattle and hogs, their age and orts.  You must write
to me by all opportunities, letting me know your wants and in what
circumstances everything is and goes forward.  Mr. Hooper will do
you all the service he can, by writing or other ways.
     Doctor Thomas Turner undertakes the care of my families; you
must be sure to send for him as often as there is occasion.  Be
sure to keep a particular account in writing of everything you
deliver out, as nails, tar, etc.


     Letter, Robert Carter to John Johnson, June 22, 1721, Wright
(ed.), Letters of Robert Carter, pp. 105-106.



13.  AMERICAN SILK CULTIVATION WILL FREE ENGLAND
     FROM FOREIGN DEPENDENCE (1749)


     This is a model mercantilist argument to en-
courage colonial silk cultivation presented in the
British Parliament.  Promised advantages are:  (1)
low-cost raw materials to British industry; (2) increased employment in England; (3) avoidance of poor-
taxes, (4) widened American market for British manufacturers; and (5) retaining specie money in England.

A petition of the merchants, weavers, throwsters, dyers, and
other manufacturers of raw and thrown silks, in behalf of themselves
and many thousand labouring people, depending on the silk trade, was
presented to the House [of Commons], and read; setting forth, that
the petitioners have, within these few years, improved the manufacture of raw silk into thrown, and afterwards into plain and wrought
silks and velvets, so as not only to supply our home consumption, but
to export great quantities, whereby several thousands of persons have
been employed:  and that the supply of fine short raw silk has been
heretofore from Italy and Spain, (except a small precarious portion
thereof from China) the throwing of which gave employment to great
numbers of young and infirm people:  and that the Spaniards are vigorously attempting the increase and improvement of the manufacture
of wrought silks and velvets in that kingdom; for the encouragement
whereof, the exportation of raw silk thence is absolutely prohibited;
and the raw short silk of Italy, which has been always freely exported, except from Piedmont, has this year been also prohibited to
be exported from any of those territories; where great encouragement
is given to promote the manufacture of wrought silks and velvets,
having now a favourable opportunity by great numbers of weavers, late
inhabitants of Genoa, who, during the intestine troubles there,
sheltered themselves in many other towns through the Italian dominions:  and that the price of thrown silk, the only species now
allowed to be exported from Italy, is lately risen from 30 to 40 per
cent. which has already occasioned the putting down a great many
looms, and will soon occasion the putting down many more, to the
great prejudice of the silk manufacture, and the ruin of great numbers of poor families, who, for want of employ, must become burthen-
some to their respective parishes:  and that the petitioners apprehend it to be of the utmost importance to secure to these kingdoms
so valuable a branch of business as the silk manufacture is; which
nothing can more certainly effect, than producing a supply of raw
silk in some of his Majesty's dominions; and which, the petitioners
are informed, from undoubted authority, may be done in the southern
colonies of America, where the soil and climate are as favourable as
in any part of Italy, for the quick growth of mulberry trees, and the
breeding and nurture of silk worms; and from whence five hundred
pounds of weight of raw silk has been imported into London, from
Carolina and Georgia since the late general peace, which, upon trial,
has been found to answer, in the several operations, all the purposes
of the best Italian organzine:  and that the petitioners conceive if
proper encouragement was given to the production of raw silk in his
Majesty's colonies in America, it would be a means, in a few years,
of securing a constant and considerable supply thereof for the manufactures of this kingdom, and be a saving to the nation of some hundred thousand pounds, annually paid to Italy and Spain, for their
thrown and raw silks, besides many other great and national advantages which would accrue by the returns thereof in goods to America:
and therefore praying the House to take the premises into consideration; and to give such relief therein as the nature of the case
shall require.

Stock (ed.), Proceedings And Debates Of The British Parliaments
Respecting North America, V, pp. 373-374.

## 14.  THE SHORTCOMINGS OF LONDON FACTORS (1770)

A catalogue of complaints which could have been
repeated by almost any tobacco planter is in this extract written by George Washington, a planter who had
served as Justice of Fairfax and represented that area
in the House of Burgesses.

This Letter accompanies my Invoices for Potomack and York Rivers
as also Mr. & Miss. Custis's --Agreeable to the several Orders therein containd you will please to dispatch the Goods & by the first Ships
bound to the respective Rivers--Those for Potomack will come I hope
by a more careful hand than the last did as I neither receivd the
Goods nor Letters by Captn. Saunderson till the middle of June nor
coud ever discover in what Ship--by what Captn.--or to what part of
the Country they came (the duplicate by Peterson giving no insight
into any of these matters but left me in full belief that the Ship
was lost as such a length of time had elapsd between the date of
your Letter and the recept of it)--In short I do not know to this
hour how the Goods came to this River as it was by Accident I heard
they were stored at Boyds hold about 60 miles from this place and
was obligd to send for them at my own expence which will often
happen if they are sent into any other River than the one they are
destind to, but why this shoud have been the case in the Instance
before us I am at a loss to guess as there were two Ships Saild
from London to Potomack after Johnstown did; and a little before or
nearly the time of the date of your letter by Saunderson, to wit,
Grig in the service of Molleson and Walker belonging to Debert's,
Lee, & Sayre.
When I opened the Packages a piece of Duffield chargd  4. 13s
was found eaten to a honey comb (by Moth)--Whether this was the
effect of long lying or carelessness of the Woolen Draper I shall
not undertake to determine but certain it is, that I shall not be
able to get a single Garment out of the whole piece--By Merchants
more accustomd to ye importation of Goods than I am, I have been
told that it must have been packd up in the order I receivd it, as
there is no such thing as Moths eating in a close Parcel--If this
really was the case, it is a species of Dealing which does not
reflect much honr. upon the reputation of Messr. Mauduit Wright &
Co.
By Captn. Peterson I have Shipd you 32 hhds. of Mr. Custis's
Tobo. and all mine consisting of 17 more, the Sales of which I hope
and flatter myself will be equal to other Tobacco's made in the
same Neighbourhood; but which give me leave to add, has not been the
case hitherto notwithstanding you seem to think that I cannot be
otherwise than pleased with the last Acct. you rendered.
That 11 1-2d. a lb. is such a price as a Planter (in a tolerable good year) may afford to make Tobacco for, I shall not deny;
but it does not follow as a consequence that I should be satisfied

therewith in behalf of myself & Ward when a Succession of short
Crops have given a Universal start to Tobo. and when I know (if the
veracity of some Gentlemen with whom I conversed at Williamsburg
when I was down there last is to be credited) that other Crops made
in York & James City Counties not six miles from Mr. Custis's Plantation & mind have sold at 12d. & 12 1-2 p. lb; and the common transfer Tobo. a large proportion of which we pay towards the support of
a Minister in York County, when prizd and Shipd to London fetchd 12d
so, and what reason can be assigned then for my being pleasd with
11d & 11 1-2 (averaging about £12 a hhd.) when the commonest Arrono-
ko Tobo. fetchd this in evry Port in Great Britain I know not; as it
is by someone presumable, that the Tobacco which Mr. Valentine now
makes, & Stems a fourth or a third of in order to make it good,
should be of Inferior quality to the general run of purchased
Tobaco., or worse than that which he himself has applied to the payment of the Minister's Salery; to do which, and to answer all other
Publick Claims it is well known that the most indifferent of our
(Inspected) Tobo. is always appropriated—Upon the whole, the repeated disappointments which I meat with has reduced me to a dele-
mma which I am not very well reconcild to—To decline a Correspondence either altogether or in part which has subsisted for so many
years is by no means my Inclination; and to persevere in a Consignment which seems to lend to the prejudice of myself and Ward, not
only in the Sales of our Tobacco, but the purchase of Goods, is
hardly to be expected.

  That my Goods are for the most part exceedingly dear bought and
the directions which are given for the choice of Particular Articles
not always attended to, I have no scruples in declaring—The first
is no otherwise to be proved than by a comparison of the prices &
quality—The second is to be evincd by numberless instances, two of
which I shall give as the most recent and Important—Having occasion
for Window Glass for a House I was building I sent for my quantity
9 by 11; and got it in 8 by 10—this was a considerable disappointment, & no small disadvantage to me, but not equal to the one that
followd upon the Heels of it: I mean the Chariot, which I begd
might be made of well seasond materials, and by a masterly Workman;
instead of which, it was made of wood so exceedingly Green that the
Pannels slipd out of the mouldings before it was two months in use—
Split from one end to the other—and became so open at the joints,
tho every possible care was taken of it, that I expect very little
further Service from it with all the Repairs I can bestow.

  Besides this we frequently have slight goods & sometimes old &
unsaleable articles put of upon us, and at such advanced Prices that
one would be Inclind to think the Tradesmen did not expect to be
paid in part for them; for it is a fact incontestably true that
Linnens & other Articles that have their prices proportiond to their
respective qualities, are to be bought in the Factors Stores here
almost as cheap as we Import them, after the Merchant has laid on a
sufficient advance for his profit—Disagreeable it is to me to mention these things to you, but when it is considered that my own
dealings are confind wholly, & my Wards principally to your House,
it is not to be wondered at that I should be dissatisfied with ill
bought Goods, or a more indifft. price for Tobo. than is given to my
Neighbours.

I am very glad that by meeting with Colo. Stewart you have got quit of the troublesome Doctr. McLean--the Nett sum of £302 I shoud have been very well content to have received, as I lent this money to that Gentleman to be returnd or not, as it suited his convenience; never expecting or desiring a farthing of Interest for the use of it.

You will perceive in looking over the several Invoices that some of the Goods there required, are upon condition that the Act of Parliament Imposing a Duty upon Tea, Paper &c. for the purpose of raising a Revenue in America is totally repeald; & I beg the favour of you to be governd strictly thereby, as it will not be in my power to receive any Articles contrary to our Non-Importation Agreement to which I have Subscribed, & shall Religiously adhere to, if it was, as I coud wish it to be, ten times as strict.

Letter, George Washington to Robert Cary, August, 1770, Commons (ed.). Documentary History of American Industrial Society, I, pp. 301-305.

15.  "ERRORS IN THE RURAL MANAGEMENT OF NEW ENGLAND" (1775)

The anonymous author of American Husbandry, published in 1775, finds faults with New England farming which could not be blamed on topography or climate. In short, besides the proverbial "rocky soil" and "bitter cold" of New England, another obstacle to good farming were the human failings of the farmer.

The cultivated parts of New England are more regularly inclosed than Canada, but the planters do not sufficiently attend to this circumstance; many estates and farms are in this respect in such condition that in Great Britain they would be thought in a state of devastation; yet here it all arises from carelessness. Live hedges are common, yet the plenty of timber in many parts of the province is such that they neglect planting these durable, useful, and excellent fences, for the more easy way of posts and rails, or boards, which last but a few years and are always out of repair. This is a negligence and a want of foresight that is unpardonable: but though the new settlers see the inconvenience of it on the lands of the old ones, and find live hedges in many places substituted, yet do they go on with the practice, as if it was the best in the world. In many plantations, there are only a few inclosures about the houses, and the rest lie like common fields in England, the consequence of which is much useless labour in guarding crops from cattle.
.  .  .  .  .  .  .  .  .  .  .  .  .  .  .  .  .  .  .  .  .  .  .  .  .  .  .  .  .  .  .  .  .  .  .  .  .  .  .  .  .  .  .  .  .
And this mention of cattle leads me to observe that most of the farmers in this country are, in whatever concerns cattle, the most negligent ignorant set of men in the world. Nor do I know any country in which animals are worse treated. Horses are in general,

even valuable ones, worked hard and starved:  they plough, cart, and
ride them to death, at the same time that they give very little heed
to their food; after the hardest day's works, all the nourishment
they are like to have is to be turned into a wood, where the shoots
and weeds form the chief of the pasture; unless it be after the hay
is in, when they get a share of the after-grass.  A New Englander
(and it is the same quite to Pennsylvania) will ride his horse full
speed twenty or thirty miles; tye him to a tree, while he does
business, then re-mount, and gallop back again.  This bad treatment
extends to draft oxen; to their cows, sheep, and swine; only in a
different manner, as may be supposed.   There is scarce any branch of
rural economy which more demands attention and judgment than the
management of cattle; or one which, under a judicious treatment, is
attended with more profit to the farmer in all countries; but the
New England farmers have in all this matter the worst notions imaginable.

I must, in the next place, take notice of their tillage, as being weakly and insufficiently given:  worse ploughing is no where to
be seen, yet the farmers get tolerable crops; this is owing, particularly in the new settlements, to the looseness and fertility of
old woodlands, which, with very bad tillage, will yield excellent
crops:  a circumstance the rest of the province is too apt to be
guided by, for seeing the effects, they are apt to suppose the same
treatment will do on land long since broken up, which is far enough
from being the case.  Thus, in most parts of the province, is found
shallow and unlevel furrows, which rather scratch than turn the
land; and of this bad tillage the farmers are very sparing, rarely
giving two ploughings if they think the crop will do with one; the
consequence of which is their products being seldom near so great as
they would be under a different management.   Nor are their implements well made, or even well calculated for the work they are designed to perform; of this among other instances I may take the
plough.  The beam is too long; the supporters ought to be moveable,
as they are in ploughs in England and in Scotland; the plough share
is too narrow, which is a common fault; and the wheels are much too
low; were they higher, the draft would be proportionably lighter.
In other parts of the province, I have indeed seen better ploughs,
but they are in few hands, and, besides, are not quite free from
these defects.

The harrows are also of a weak and poor construction; for I
have more than once seen them with only wooden teeth, which however
it may do for mere sand in tilth, must be very inefficacious on
other soils, but the mischief of using such on one sort of land is
that the slovens are always ready to extend them for cheapness to
the rest.   The carts and waggons are also in some parts of the province very awkward ill made things, in which the principles of
mechanics are not at all considered.

. . . . . . . . . . . . . . . . . . . . . . . . . . . . . . . . . .
New Englanders are also deficient in introducing those new articles of culture, which have become common in different parts of
Great Britain; among others, let us instance carrots, parsnips, potatoes, Jerusalem artichokes, beets, lucerne, sainfoine, and particularly cabbages; these articles are many of them better adapted to
the climate of New England than of Great Britain; yet they are not

attended to half so much:  but the farmers of this country would
find their interest more in the introduction of these articles, than
could ever happen to any people in the mother country, where land is
so scarce that they cannot afford to make trial of anything that
they are not previously certain will answer; whereas in these colonies the case is different; land costs nothing; they have enough of
various soils to try every thing, without the loss of the land bringing them into those difficulties which it must ever do in countries
where a considerable rent, tythe, and poor's taxes are paid.  But
this circumstance, which is such an undoubted advantage, in fact
turns out the contrary; and for this reason, they depend on this
plenty of land as a substitute for all industry and good management;
neglecting the efforts of good husbandry, which in England does more
than the cheapness of the soil does in America.


     Harry J. Carman (ed.), American Husbandry (1775), (New York:
Columbia University Press, 1939), pp. 55-56, 59-60, 62-63.


        16.  "CURSES ON YOU, USURER!" (1780)


     Thomas Hart, a planter and land speculator, Sheriff
of Orange County, North Carolina and uncle of Senator
Thomas Hart Benton (See Source No. 246), writes a blunt
and friendly letter indicating the close social relations
existing in the North Carolina backcountry among members
of the commercial-planting ruling group.


     I have (Once more) Sent a waggon and two Hhd$^s$. tob$^o$. to your
place, and what will you send me in Return, I Suppose a half Bush$^1$.
Salt, or Gall$^n$. of Rum for a 100$^{wt}$ Tob$^o$, Something like this, I make
no doubt,--What a Sett of Atheistical fellows must there be in Newbern that thinks there is Neither God nor Devil to punish them in a
Nother World, for their usury to us in this, I must send down Debow
Once more to preach up the Doctrine of Regeneration or the New Birth
to you, for If over there was a Sett of men on the fact of this
Globe, who stood more in Need of being Regenerated and Born anew, I
wonder trully how many poor Sons of Bitches with tears in their Eyes
have I Seen within these Six weeks past, Comming from your place,
Some with 5 or 6 Bush$^{ls}$. Salt in their waggons, Some [with] 8 or 10
Gall$^s$. of Rum, and others with Cargoes [of less?] Vallue, all declaring themselves Broken [miserably] but None of them without a
Good Store of [curses which] they bestow (with a very Liberal hand)
on the Good folks of Newbern, and how can you bear with all this,
can you expect to thrive Under the Heavy Curses of the Rightious
folks of this Country, had Not you better try to do Something that
may entitle you to Our Blessing Instead of Our Curses, come do (for
Godsake) begin with me, and let us See what you can do.  The Winter
is very hard and Corn very Scarce, I have therefore Sent down a
Cupple of Good Horses, what will you give me for them, two Good

Horses & two Hh$^{ds}$. Tob$^{o}$.  Undoubtedly is worth two Hh$^{ds}$. o good Rum,
and a little sugar besides, or the devil is in it, but you wont purchase anything that you Can't Immediately put on Board, therefore do
Recommend him to Some of your Good Gent$^{m}$. in Newbern who will deal
Cleverly with him.
    I Remember you told me whenever you heard any person [complain-
ing] against Others, for making Money too fast, you looked on him as
an envious man, who was disturb'd Only with his own [mis] fortune,
which forbid him Reaping equal [amounts with] those he envy'd,
there may be a good [deal of truth?] in this Observation, If we will
admitt the [......] in [......]  Same degeneracy with the People of
Newbern, but you must not admit of this, or this Preaching of Debow
will be in Vain to you, for while ever you Can flatter yourselves
that you are virtuous as [Others] there is little hopes of Conviction, and while you Continue to Make Money out of us, we must Content Ourselves with heaping our Curses on you, and much you lose for
that--

    Letter, Thomas Hart to William Blount, January 25, 1780, Keith
(ed.), Blount Papers, I, pp. 8-9.


        17.  "THE MOST DELUSIVE OF ALL SNARES" (1786)


        Long experience led Virginia tobacco planters to
stress independence from London merchants.  Imperial
regulations determined, however, that American tobacco
flow predominantly to London.  So long as the planters
retained title to the tobacco, they controlled somewhat
the price of the product.  To do otherwise, warned
Thomas Jefferson, was to destroy the planter's bargaining
position.  Jefferson was United States Minister to France
and Mrs. Paradise, a wealthy American, was married to
John Paradise, a well-known British linguist.


    I concur with you in opinion that it is for Mr. Paradise's in-
terest to go as soon as possible to America, and also to turn all
his debts into one, which may be to Mr. Gist or any other:  upon
condition that the person giving him this credit shall be satisfied
to receive annually his interest in money, and shall not require
consignments of tobacco.  This is the usual condition of the tobacco
merchants.  No [burthen] can be more oppressive to the mind or fortune, and long experience has proved to us that there never was an
instance of a man's getting out of debt who was once in the hands of
a tobacco merchant & bound to consign his tobacco to him.  It is the
most delusive of all snares.  The merchant feeds the inclination of
his customer to be credited till he gets the burthen of debt so increased that he cannot throw it off at once.  He then begins to give
him less for his tobacco & ends with giving him what he pleases for
it, which is always so little that let the demands of the customer

for necessaries be reduced ever so low in order to get himself out of debt, the merchant lowers his price in the same proportion so as always to keep such a balance against his customer as will oblige him to continue his consignments of tobacco. Tobacco always sells better in Virginia than in the hands of a London merchant. The confidence which you have been pleased to place in me induces me to take the liberty of advising you to submit to any thing rather than to an obligation to ship your tobacco. A mortgage of property, the most usurious interest, or any thing else will be preferable to this. If Mr. Paradise can get no single money lender to pay his debts, perhaps those to whom he owes might be willing to wait, on his placing in the hands of trustees in London whom they should approve, certain parts of his property, the profits of which should suffice to pay them within a reasonable time.

Letter, Thomas Jefferson to Mrs. Lucy Ludwell Paradise, August 27, 1786, The Papers of Thomas Jefferson, Vol. 24, Library of Congress.

## 18.  RELATIVE PROFITABILITY OF AMERICAN OVER BRITISH AGRICULTURE (1792)

Arthur Young, the British authority, had written George Washington for information on the profitability of American agriculture. Washington asked Jefferson to supply him with the requested data.

Mr. Young calculates the employment of £5040. worth of land and £1200. farmer's capital, making an aggregate capital of £6240. in England, which he makes yield 5. p$^r$. cent extra, or 10. p$^r$. cent on y$^e$. whole. I will calculate, in the Virginia way, the employment of the same capital, on a supposition of good management in the manner of the country.

1.   Supposing negro laborers to be hired.
2.   Supposing them to be bought.

1.   Suppose labourers to be hired, one half men @ £18. the other half women @ £14. for labor, subsistence, cloth$^g$. (I always mean sterlg money).

Int. of £4160 for 3310. a$^s$. of land @ 25/y$^e$. acre . . . . £208--0--0
    of £2080 for farmer's capital of stock, tools, &c   104--0--0
    6240
Taxes @ 7$^d$. the acre (I do not know what they are) . . .   96--10--0
Hire of 33. labourers @ £16 . . . . . . . . . . . . .   528--0--0
                   Produce to be sold annually.
Wheat 6600. bushels @ 3/. . . . . . . . . . . . . . £990
Meat & other articles @ £5. for each laborer. .  165    1155--0
Net profit over & above the 5. p$^r$. cent above charged   219--10
Add annual rise in the value of lands . . . . . . . .   165--10
Real profit over & above the 3. p$^r$. cent above charged   385--

which is 6 1/5 per cent extra, or 11 1/3 p.$^r$ cent on the whole capital.
2.  Suppose labourers to be bought, one half men, & one half women @ £60. sterl. on an average.                                    £
Int. of £3125. for 2500. a. of land @ 25/                156--5--0
     of  1562--10. farmer's capital of stock,              78--2--6
                    utensils, &c                    £
     of  1500--     for purchase of 25. laborers 75
         6187--10
                        Subsistence, clothing, &c    150  225--0--0
[I allow nothing for losses by death, but on the contrary shall presently take credit 4. p.$^r$ cent p.$^r$ annum for their increases over & above keep.$^g$ up their own numbers.]
Taxes @ 7.$^d$ the acre. . . . . . . . . . . . . . . .      72--18--4
                    Produce to be sold annually   £   532-- 5--10
Wheat 5000 bush. @ 3/. . . . . . . . . . . .   750
Meat and other articles @ £5. for each labourer 125  875-- 0--0
Net profit over & above the 5. p.$^r$ cent above
    charged  . . . . . . . . . . . . . . . . . . . .    342--15--10
Add 5 p.$^r$ cent annual rise in the value of land . .  156-- 5--0
4. p.$^r$ cent increase of negroes more y$^n$ keep.$^g$ up
    original number . . . . . . . . . . . . . . .       60-- 0
Real profit over & above the 5. p.$^r$ cent above
    charged  . . . . . . . . . . . . . . . . . . . .    559-- 0--10
Which is 9. p.$^r$ cent extra, or 14. p.$^r$ cent on the whole capital.

    In the preceding estimate I have supposed that 200. bushels of wheat may be sold for every labourer employed, which may be thought too high.  I know it is too high for common land, & common management, but I know also that on good land & with good management it has been done thro' a considerable neighborhood and for many years. On the other hand I have overrated the cost of laboring negroes, and I presume the taxes also are overrated.  I have observed that our families of negroes double in about 25. years, which is an increase of the capital, invested in them, of 4. percent over & above keeping up the original number.


    Letter, Thomas Jefferson to George Washington, June 18, 1792, The Papers of Thomas Jefferson, Vol. 75, Library of Congress.



            19.  "PETITION AGAINST EXCISE [ON WHISKEY]" (1792)


        Congress had laid a tax on the manufacture of spiritous liquors distilled from domestic produce.  This struck at the rural distillers of corn and rye whiskey in Western Pennsylvania.  Their petition against the tax contains an accurate portrayal of the problems of pioneer farming in remote areas.  Albert Gallatin, at this time, represented Fayette County in the Pennsylvania legislature.

Our peculiar situation renders this duty still more unequal and oppressive to us.  Distant from a permanent market, and separate from the eastern coast by mountains which render the communication difficult and almost impracticable, we have no means of bringing the produce of our lands to sale either in grain or in meal.  We are therefore distillers through necessity, not choice, that we may comprehend the greatest value in the smallest size and weight.

The inhabitants of the eastern side of the mountains can dispose of their grain without the additional labor or distillation at a higher price than we can, after we have bestowed that labor upon it.  Yet with this additional labor we must also pay a high duty from which they are exempted, because we have no means of selling our surplus produce but in a distilled state.

Another circumstance which renders this duty ruinous to us is our scarcity of cash.  Our commerce is not, as on the eastern coast, carried on so much by absolute sale as by barter, and we believe it to be a fact that there is not among us a quantity of circulating cash sufficient for the payment of this duty alone.

We are not accustomed to complain without reason; we have punctually and cheerfully paid former taxes on our estates and possessions, because they were proportioned to our real wealth.  We believe this to be founded on no such equitable principles, and are persuaded that your Honorable House will find on investigation that its amount, if duly collected, will be four times as large as any taxes which we have hitherto paid on the whole of our lands and other property.

Henry Adams (ed.), The Writings of Albert Gallatin, I, (New York:  Antiquarian Press, Ltd., 1960), pp. 3-4.

20.  "IT THROWS NO CLASS OF PEOPLE OUT OF BUSINESS" (1793)

For the modern reader, perhaps the most striking part of the letter is Whitney's contention that his cotton gin "makes the labor fifty times less, without throwing any class of people out of business."  In an expanding industry, the labor-displacing effect of a labor-saving invention is entirely counteracted by the need for additional labor as a result of growing demand.  That this did not always happen is attested by the fact that Whitney felt moved to make a special comment about it.  As it turned out, the cotton gin, one of history's most productive farm implements, provided the technological base for the emergence of a new agricultural industry of immense importance to the young nation. With the expansion of British demand for cotton, cotton became the largest single earner of foreign exchange.

I went from N. York with the family of the late Major General Greene to Georgia.  I went immediately with the family to their

Plantation about twelve miles from Savannah with an expectation of
spending four or five days and then proceed into Carolina to take
the school as I have mentioned in former letters.  During this time
I heard much said of the extreme difficulty of ginning Cotton, that
is, seperating it from its seeds.  There were a number of very respectable Gentlemen at Mrs. Grenne's who all agreed that if a machine
could be invented which would clean the cotton with expedition, it
would be a great thing both to the Country and to the inventor.  I
involuntarily happened to be thinking on the subject and struck out
a plan of a Machine in my mind, which I communicated to Miller, (who
is agent to the Executors of Genl. Greene and resides in the family,
a man of respectibility and property) he was pleased with the Plan
and said if I would pursue it and try an experiment to see if it
would answer, he would be at the whole expense, I should loose
nothing but my time, and if I succeeded we would share the profits.
Previous to this I found I was like to disappointed in my school,
that is, instead of a hundred, I found I could get only fifty Guineas
a year.  I however held the refusal of the school untill I tried some
experiments.  In about ten Days I made a little model, for which I
was offered, if I would give up all right and title to it, a Hundred
Guineas.  I concluded to relinquish my school and turn my attention
to perfecting the Machine.  I made one before I came away which required the labor of one man to turn it and with which one man will
clean ten times as much cotton as he can in any other way before
known and also cleanse it much better than in the usual mode.  This
machine may be turned by water or with a horse, with the greatest
ease, and one man and a horse will do more than fifty men with the
old machines.  It makes the labor fifty times less, without throwing
any class of people out of business.

I returned to the Northward for the purpose of having a machine
made on a large scale and obtaining a Patent for the invintion.  I
went to Philadelphia soon after I arrived, made myself acquainted
with the steps necessary to obtain a Patent, took several of the
steps and the Secretary of State Mr. Jefferson agreed to send the
Pattent to me as soon it could be made out—so that I apprehended no
difficulty in obtaining the Patent—Since I have been here I have employed several workmen in making machines and as soon as my business
is such that I can leave it a few days, I shall come to Westboro'.
I think it is probable I shall go to Philadelphia again before I come
to Westboro', and when I do come I shall be able to stay but a few
days.  I am certain I can obtain a patent in England.  As soon as I
have got a Patent in America I shall go with the machine which I am
now making, to Georgia, where I shall stay a few weeks to see it at
work.  From thence I expect to go to England, where I shall probably
continue two or three years.  How advantageous this business will
ventually prove to me, I cannot say.  It is generally said by those
who know anything about it, that I shall make a Fortune by it.  I
have no expectation that I shall make an independent fortune by it,
but I think I had better pursue it than any other business into
which I can enter.  Something which cannot be foreseen may frustrate
my expectations and defeat my Plan; but I am now so sure of success
that ten thousand dollars, if I saw the money counted out to me,
would not tempt me to give up my right and relinquish the object.  I
wish you, sir, not to show this letter nor communicate anything of

its contents to any body except My Brothers and Sister, <u>enjoining</u>
it on them to keep the whole a <u>profound</u> <u>secret</u>.


Letter, Eli Whitney to his father, September 11, 1793, M. B.
Hammond (ed.), "Correspondence of Eli Whitney," <u>American Historical</u>
<u>Review</u>, III, (October, 1897), pp. 99-100.


21.   IS YOUR COTTON GIN "BUT A MACHINE OF THEORY"?  (1793)


As indicated in the preceding document, Whitney
applied for a patent for the cotton gin by contacting
Thomas Jefferson, then Secretary of State.  Jefferson,
himself a tinkerer, did not mind twitting the inventor.
Throughout history, inventors have had to battle against
indifference and outright resistance.  Perhaps most galling
was the genial skepticism typified by the last sentence
in Jefferson's letter.  Note, however, Jefferson's concrete
questions with a view towards using the invention on his
own plantation.


SIR,--Your favor of Oct. 15. inclosing a drawing of your cotton
gin, was received on the 6th inst.  The only requisite of the law
now uncomplied with is the forwarding a model, which being received
your patent may be made out & delivered to your order immediately.
As the state of Virginia, of which I am, carries on household
manufactures of cotton to a great extent, as I also do myself, and
one of our great embarrassments is the cleaning the cotton of the
seed, I feel a considerable interest in the success of your invention, for family use.  Permit me therefore to ask information from
you on these points.  Has the machine been thoroughly tried in the
ginning of cotton, or is it as yet but a machine of theory?  What
quantity of cotton has it cleaned on an average of several days, &
worked by hand, & by how many hands?  What will be the cost of one
of them made to be worked by hand?  Favorable answers to these questions would induce me to engage one of them to be forwarded to
Richmond for me.  Wishing to hear from you on the subject I am &c.
P.S.  Is this the machine advertised the last year by Pearce
at the Patterson manufactory?


Letter, Thomas Jefferson to Eli Whitney, November 16, 1793,
<u>The Papers of Thomas Jefferson</u>, Vol. 94, Library of Congress.

22.  HOW TO CLEAR LAND FOR A FARM (1794)

This material was written by Tench Coxe, the
publicist of American economic development who held
the office of Commissioner of the Revenue.

The settler in making this clearing must take care to burn the
brush and wood, in such manner as to preserve the ashes.  Out of the
wood ashes, thus saved, he should make as much pot ash, or pearl ash,
as he can, and he should dispose of this for ready money, strong
clothing, axes, spades, ploughs, or such other things for his farm,
or family, as it would otherwise be necessary for him to procure, by
selling or bartering, grain or cattle, if he had them to spare.  It
is believed, that the pot ash or pearl ash will procure him as much
value as all the expense and labor of the clearing, during the season would be worth in cash.  He will therefore obtain as much money
or goods as will enable him to hire assistance, in the next season,
either to farm, or to clear land, or to make his improvements, so as
to save his own time, or labor intirely, for clearing more land or
to help him in doing it.  He must again make pot ash or pearl ash,
and he must again apply the money or goods, it sells for, to the
clearing of the next season.--In this way it is plain, that he will
derive money enough from the clearing and pot ashes, of every year,
to do much of the same in the year following.  A man who has 40, 50,
or 100 dollars to spare, at the out-set, will get his land cleared,
in this manner very fast indeed.  If he has sugar maple trees on his
land, he may also obtain money, by making sugar in February and
March, and selling or bartering it for cash, or goods to be laid out
in like manner, in hiring hands the next season.  If money is scarce
in a new settlement, and he barters pot ash or maple sugar, for
strong trowsers, shirts, hats or jackets, he will find it easy to
procure laborers for such necessaries.  It is proper to observe, that
if a man burns his wood and brush on every part of his newly cleared
field, it is doubtful whether he does not injure the soil, by burning
the half rotten leaves and light mould, or earth, which have been
made from the rotten leaves of many years.--There is an opinion, that
the ashes left from burning the trees greatly enrich the land, and
that would be certain, if the light mouldy earth and half rotten
leaves were not also consumed by the fire.  The soil of all new
countries appears to have for its upper part, a layer of stratum of
half rotten vegetable materials, which are capable of being burned,
but which it would be a great benefit to plough into the earth.
Potatoes, the best food for new settlements, grow abundantly in that
rotten vegetable soil.  This is very well known.

Tench Coxe, <u>A View of the United States</u>, (Philadelphia:
William Hall, and Wrigley and Berriman, 1794), pp. 452-453.

23.  AFRICAN COTTON WILL LESSEN ENGLAND'S
DEPENDENCE UPON AMERICA (1808)


The African Institution, a kind of would-be
chamber of commerce for the economic development
of Africa, was using a hoary approach to excite
governmental interest in promoting the Institution's
purposes.


The Committee are aware that it may be objected to this attempt
to extend the cultivation of cotton, that the supply of that article is already equal to the demand; and that therefore the measures
pursued by the Committee are impolitic.  But they would observe in
reply to this objection, that cotton is an article the growth of
which in Africa will occasion less of competition with our own
colonies than almost any other article of tropical produce which
could be named; and that it is important to be preparing source
from which a supply of cotton may be drawn, should circumstances
arise to interrupt our commercial relations with America, or with
the other places which now furnish it.  But independently of these
considerations it may be presumed, that in proportion as the natives
of Africa supply us with the raw material, they will be capable of
paying for a larger quantity of the manufactured article....


Second Report of the Committee of the African Institution,
(London, 1808), in Vincent T. Harlow and F. Madden (eds.), British
Colonial Developments, 1774-1834.  Select Documents, (Oxford:
Clarendon Press, 1953), p. 389.

# C.

# A RUDIMENTARY HOME MARKET

24. GETTING FROM PHILADELPHIA TO NEW YORK (1753)

Recall that Philadelphia was one of the largest
cities in the British Empire and that New York was the
second largest in the American colonies.

Burlington Stage-Waggon, revived.  Notice is hereby given to all
persons that are inclinable to transport themselves, goods, wares and
merchandize from the city of Philadelphia, to the city of New York,
or from New York to Philadelphia that they may have the opportunity
of obliging themselves that way twice every week, wind and weather
permitting.  James Wells, and John Weggery with a commodious Stageboat, well fitted for that purpose, will attend at the Crooked
Billet wharff, in Philadelphia, in order to receive goods and passengers on the following days in every week, Viz. on Monday and Tuesday,
likewise on Thursday and Friday; and on Wednesday and Saturday will
set out and proceed with them to Perth-Amboy Ferry, where a house of
good entertainment is kept, and a commodious stageboat waiting for
their reception, Daniel O'Bryant, master, who will, on Friday morning, proceed directly for New York, and give his attendance at the
Whitehall slip, near the Half-moon battery, at the house of Scotch
John, for the purposes aforesaid, and on Saturday proceed from New
York to Perth Amboy ferry house again; and on Monday a stage-waggon
fitted for the purposes aforesaid, kept by John Prigmore, will set
out for Burlington, where the said Wells and Weggery will be ready to
receive passengers, and goods and convey them to Philadelphia, and
on the same day, Viz. Monday, Jonathan Thomas's stage proceeds to
Perth Amboy ferry, where Daniel O'Bryant receives them as aforesaid;
which is judged to be the cheapest, best and quickest way, that merchants, passengers or others, can convey themselves or their effects,

from one city to the other.
. . . . . . . . . . . . . . . . . . . . . . . . . . . . . . . . . . . .
Altho' the owners of the Bordentown stage have been pleased, by way
of hyperbole, to advertise, That their stage can perform the aforesaid passage sooner by 24 hours than any other stages, but have
omitted to inform the publick, that their stage boat from Philadelphia to Bordentown, is frequently three tides upon the water, or the
greatest part thereof, Viz. two tides of flood, and one of ebb; during which time the Burlington stage is capable of landing her passengers at Perth Amboy, and, upon cases of emergency, is capable of performing the whole stage from Philadelphia to New York, in the space
of 24 hours....

The Pennsylvania Journal, July 19, 1753, in William Nelson
(ed.), Documents Relating to the Colonial History of the State of
New Jersey, XIX, (Paterson, N.J.:  Press Printing and Publishing
Co., 1897), pp. 275-277.

### 25.  DIFFICULTIES OF INTERCOLONIAL PAYMENTS (1758)

William Logan, who writes here, lived in Stenton
near Philadelphia, 140 miles from his correspondent
Jared Eliot from New Haven, Connecticut.  Eliot has
been characterized as a "typical pioneer in applied
science", in the fields of agriculture and iron
manufacture, among others.  He was also a Congregational
minister.

I doubt not but thou has long since, and Very often, passed
Censure on me, & as thou Conceived, Justly, for my long Delay in re-
mitting the Cost of the Plow &c. thou Was So kind to procure for me.
In order therefore to clear myself I must inform thee, that it is
Very rare to find an Opportunity of Sending Money in any pacquet by
any Person going directly to, or thro Your Town to the Eastern Governments, Travellers generally Chusing to go by Water from New York
to Avoid Your Sony Roads.  And as such direct Opportunitys are Very
rare, My living 5 miles from the Town, & being much Engaged in Public
Business, Occasions my not hearing of them When they offer.  I Can
Assure thee my keeping thee so long out of they Money has given me
Great Uneasiness, and I have never since the rec't of the Plow had
but one direct Opportunity before this of sending it, and then I Embraced it, which was by a Gentleman about two Years Since going directly to New London thro Connecticut, and I Wrote thee by him and
sent thee the Amount of my Debt, but when that Gentleman got as far
as Rye, He was obliged to return, and brought back both my Letter and
Money.--As I have not this Other Opportunity by Some Young Gentlemen
who have been paying our Country a visit for their Pleasure, I have
Committed to the Care of one of them (his Name is Pease of R.^d

Island) a small bag Containing Eight Dollars, which He has promised
to deliver thee, With this Letter.  I think the Amt. of Y$^e$Plow,
Wheat, &c. which thou Was So kind to send me was about 7 Dollars,
but I thought Best as the Debt Was Due So long to send thee Eight of
them, which I wish safe to thy Hands, & hope it Will be to they
Satisfaction, & With the Reasons I have Given, Will remove any hard
thoughts for my Delay.


Letter, William Logan to Jared Eliot, September 23, 1758,
Jared Eliot, Essays Upon Field Husbandry in New England and Other
Papers, 1748-1762, edited by Harry J. Carman and Rexford S. Tugwell,
(New York:  Columbia University Press, 1934), pp. 226-227.


### 26.  BALTIMORE IS DIVERTING TRADE FROM PHILADELPHIA (1771)


The commercial prosperity of a town—any town—in
pre-Civil War America depended almost wholly on the
availability of cheap water transport.  Commercial competition between cities often took the form of contending
transportation advantages.  Samuel Rhoads who writes here
to Benjamin Franklin was co-founder with Franklin and 5
others of the American Philosophical Society in 1744.  His
title then was Society "mechanician."


The growing trade of Baltimore Town in Maryland, drawn principally from our province west of the Susquehanna, begins to alarm us
with serious apprehensions of such a rival, as may reduce us to the
situation of Burlington and Newcastle on the Delaware; and we can
devise no means of saving ourselves but by a canal from the Susquehanna to the Schuylkill, and amending the navigation of all our
rivers, so far as they lead towards our capital city.  A great number
of thy friends are very anxious for promoting this work, particularly the canal, if it is practicable, through the heart of the country.
And as thou wast kind enough formerly to send me several papers relating to the navigation of Calder River, I request the favor of
adding thereto the last accounts and instructions respecting canals,
the construction of their floodgates, wastegates, &c.  The Assembly
have ordered the Speaker to procure the remainder of the statutes to
complete their set in the State House library, by which, I suppose,
we shall have those relating to canals; but, if they are to be had
singly, please to send one or two, which are the most instructive in
the rates, terms, conditions of carriage, and passing the grounds,
and the cost shall be paid.


Letter, Samuel Rhoads to Benjamin Franklin, May 3, 1771,
Sparks (ed.), Works of Benjamin Franklin, VII, p. 519.

27.  COMMERCIAL STRATEGY OF STATE BOUNDARIES (1784)


    The crucial commercial role of waterways is clarified
in this letter written by Thomas Jefferson, then Delegate
to Congress from Virginia.  Note how a discussion of the
Virginia boundary shifts to Virginia waterways and then to
Ohio, New York, and the Mississippi.  The very great posi-
bilities of a water-network were already clear.


The reasons which call for this boundary [between Virginia and
North Carolina] (which will retain all the waters of the Kanhaway)
are 1.  That within that are our lead mines.  2.  This river rising
in N. Carola. traverses for navigation and commerce to the Western
country: but 3.  It is a channel which can not be opened but at
immense expence and with every facility which an absolute power over
both shores will give.  4.  This river and it's waters forms a band
of good land passing along our whole frontier, and forming on it a
barrier which will be strongly seated.  5.  For 180 miles beyond
these waters is a mountainous barren which can never be inhabited
and will of course form a safe separation between us and any other
state.  6.  This tract of country lies more convenient to receive
it's government from Virginia than from any other state.  7.  It will
preserve to us all the upper parts of Yohogany and Cheat rivers within which much will be to be done to open these which are the true
doors to the Western commerce.  The union of this navigation with
that of the Potowmac is a subject on which I mentioned that I would
take the liberty of writing to you.  I am sure it's value and practicability are both well known to you.  This is the moment however for
seizing it if ever we mean to have it.  All the world is becoming
commercial.  Was it practicable to keep our new empire separated
from them we might indulge ourselves in speculating whether commerce
contributes to the happiness of mankind.  But we cannot separate ourselves from them.  Our citizens have had too full a taste of the comforts furnished by the arts and manufactures to be debarred the use
of them.  We must then in our own defence endeavor to share as large
a portion as we can of this modern source of wealth and power.  That
offered to us from the Western country is under a competition between
the Hudson, the Pawtomac and the Missisipi itself.  Down the last
will pass all heavy commodities.  But the navigation through the gulf
of Mexico is so dangerous, and that up the Missisipi so difficult and
tedious, that it is not probable that European merchandize will return through that channel.  It is most likely that flour, lumber and
other heavy articles will be floated on rafts which will be themselves an article of sale as well as their loading, the navigators
returning by land or in light batteaux.  There will therefore be a
rivalship between the Hudson and Patowmac for the residue of the
commerce of all the country Westward of L. Erie, on the waters of
the lakes, of the Ohio and upper parts of the Missisipi.  To go to N
York, that part of the trade which comes from the lakes or their
waters must first be brought into L. Erie.  So almost must that which
comes from the waters of the lakes.  When it shall have entered L.
Erie, it must coast along it's harbours, the Northern, tho' shortest,

having few harbours, and these unsafe. Having reached Cayahoga, to
proceed on the N. York will be 970 miles from thence and five portages, whereas it is but 430. miles to Alexandria, if it turns into
the Cayahoga and passes through that, Bit Beaver, Ohio, Yohogany (or
Monogalia and Cheat) and Patowmac, and there are but two portages.
For the trade of the Ohio or that which shall come into it from it's
own waters of the Missisipi, it is nearer to Alexandria than to New
York by 730 miles, and is interrupted by one portage only. Nature
then has declared in favour of the Patowmac, and through that
channel offers to pour into our lap the whole commerce of the Western
World. But unfortunately the channel by the Hudson is already open
and known in practice; ours is still to be opened. This is the moment in which the trade of the West will begin to get into motion
and to take it's direction. It behoves us then to open our doors to
it. I have lately pressed this subject on my friends in the General
Assembly, proposing to them to endeavor to have a tax laid which
shall bring into a separate chest from five to ten thousand pounds
a year, to be employed first in opening the upper waters of the
Ohio and Patowmac, where a little money and time will do a great
deal, leaving the great falls for the last part of the work.

    Letter, Thomas Jefferson to George Washington, March 15, 1784,
Julian P. Boyd (ed.), The Papers of Thomas Jefferson, VII, (Princeton, New Jersey:  Princeton University Press, 1953), pp. 25-27.


    28.  THE DISCONTENTS OF PLANTERS AND MERCHANTS (1785)


        The revolution was over but the commercial supremacy
    of England persisted.  James Madison, leader of the Virginia
    House of Delegates from Orange County, writes of this to
    Monroe who represented Virginia in Congress and Lee, the
    President of Congress.


    I observe in a late newspaper that the commercial discontents
of Boston are spreading to New York and Philadelphia. Whether they
will reach Virginia or not I am unable to say. If they should, they
must proceed from a different interest; from that of the planters,
not that of the Merchants. The present system here is as favorable
to the latter as it is ruinous to the former. Our trade was never
more compleatly monopolized by G.B., when it was under the direction of the British Parliament than it is at this moment. But as
our Merchants are almost all connected with that country & that
only, and as we have neither ships nor seamen of our own, nor likely
to have any in the present course of things, no mercantile complaints
are heard. The planters are dissatisfied, and with reason, but they
enter little into the science of commerce, and rarely of themselves
combine in defence of their interests. If any thing could rouse
them to a proper view of their situation one might expect it from
the contrast of the market here with that of other States. Our

staple has of late been as low as a guinea per hundred on Rappahannock, and not above 32 or 33s. on James River. The current
prices in Philadelphia during the same period have been 44s. of
this currency for tobacco of the latter inspections and in like
proportion for that of the former. The prices of imports of every
kind in those two Markets furnish a contrast equally mortifying to
us. I have not had the same information from other States northward of us, but I have little doubt that it would teach us the same
lesson. Our planters cannot suffer a loss of less than 50 per c$^t$.
on the staple of the Country if to the direct loss in the price of
the staple be added their indirect loss in the price of what they
purchase with their staple. It is difficult notwithstanding to
make them sensible of the utility of establishing a Philadelphia or
a Baltimore among ourselves, as one indispensable step towards relief, and the difficulty is not a little increased by the pains
taken by the Merchants to prevent such a reformation, and by the
opposition arising from local views.

. . . . . . . . . . . . . . . . . . . . . . . . . . . . . . . . . . .

     The revolution has robbed us of our trade with the West Indies,
the only one which yielded us a favorable balance, without opening
any other channels to compensate for it. What makes the British
monopoly the more mortifying is the abuse which they make of it.
Not only the private planters who have resumed the practice of
shipping their own Tobacco, but many of the Merchants particularly
the natives of the Country who have no connections in G.B. have
rec$^d$ acc$^t$s of sales this season, which carry the most visible &
shameful frauds in every article. In every point of view indeed
the trade of this Country is in a deplorable Condition. A comparison
of current prices here with those in the Northern States, either at
this time or at any time since the peace [in 1783], will shew that
the loss direct on our produce & indirect on our imports is not less
than 50 per ct. Till very lately the price of our Staple has been
down at 32 & 33s. on James River & 28s. on Rappahannock. During
the same period the former was selling in Philadelphia, & I suppose
in other Northern ports, at 44s. of this Currency, and the latter in
proportion; tho' it cannot be denied that Tobacco in the Northern
ports is intrinsically worth less than it is here; being at the same
distance from its ultimate market, & burdened with the freight from
this to the other States. The price of merchandise here is at least
as much above as that of Tobacco is below the Northern standard.


     Letters, James Madison to James Monroe and Richard Henry Lee,
June 21, 1785 and July 7, 1785, The Papers of James Madison, Vol. 5,
Library of Congress.


### 29.  RETAIL CREDIT IN VIRGINIA (1785)


     Before the revolution, British mercantile credit
was the basis for American consumer credit. After the
revolution, British credit became tight but American

consumers continued to insist on credit from their
retailers.  When he wrote this, Madison was still
the member of the House of Delegates from Orange
County.  He stayed in this office until 1786.

Our internal trade is taking an arrangement from which I hope
good consequences.  Retail Stores are spread[g] all over the country,
many of them carried on by native adventurers, some of them branched
out from the principal Stores at the heads of navigation.  The distribution of the business however into the importing & the retail
departments has not yet taken place.  Should the port bill be established it will I think quickly add this amendment which indeed
must in a little time follow of itself.  It is the more to be
wished for as it is the only radical cure for credit to the consumer
which continues to be given to a degree which if not checked will
turn the diffusive retail of merchandize into a nuisance.  When the
Shop keeper buys his goods of the wholesale merchant, he must buy
at so short a credit, that he can venture to give none at all.

Letter, James Madison to Thomas Jefferson, August 20, 1785,
The Papers of James Madison, Vol. 5, Library of Congress.

## 30.  COMMERCE OF THE ILLINOIS COUNTRY (1790)

Having acquired this area in 1783, seven years
earlier, the American government had not yet succeeded
in regulating the trade of the area in the interest of
American traders.  This problem was solved only after
1803, by virtue of the Louisiana Purchase.  Arthur St.
Clair, then Governor of North West Territory, writes:

The commerce of the Illinois country is of some importance in
itself, but more so when considered as connected with the Spanish
side of the Mississippi.  The villages on that side of the river
having been originally settled by the French, and under the same
government as that part which is now in the possession of the
United States, the connection between them is still very intimate,
and favors a commercial intercourse which, though illicit, might be
carried on by the citizens of America without risk.  It is carried
on at present without risk, but is, unfortunately, almost entirely
in the hands of the British.  Even such the greatest part of the
merchandise for the trade of the Missouri River is brought from
Michilimackinac by that of the Illinois, partly by the Spanish subjects themselves, and partly by British traders.  The manner is
this:  The Spanish subjects either introduce them at once, in consequence of a secret connection with their commandants, or they are
brought down to Cahokia and landed there, and afterwards carried
over to St. Louis, as opportunities can be found.  What is brought

by the British traders, the Spanish subjects purchase and pay for on
the American side, taking all the risk that attends the introducing
them into their own country upon themselves.  The furs in which
these goods are generally paid for (deer skins answering better than
furs at the New Orleans market), are carried to Canada by the same
communication; that is to say, up the Illinois River, up the Chicago,
and from thence by a small portage into Lake Michigan, and along that
lake to Michilimackinac; or from the Chicago up the river Au Plain,
and by a portage into the same lake.

In the spring of the year the waters of the Michigan and the
Chicago rise each to such a height that the intermediate space is
entirely overflowed, and is passable by the vessels in use there,
which are bark canoes, but which carry a very considerable burden,
and are navigated by three or by five persons.

The commerce of that country is of some importance, also, as an
object of revenue; for if the impost on importations were extended
to it, some money would be produced by it; but the principal advantage would be that it would contribute to turn the trade into the
channel of the United States.

Smith (ed.), St. Clair Papers, II, pp. 174-175.


31.   LIGHTHOUSES IN THE UNITED STATES (1790)


The new Congress had enacted a law providing for
Federal contributions toward the building and upkeep of
lighthouses, a concrete indication of the commercial
astuteness of the new government.  Following is the
report of a state-by-state survey written by Alexander
Hamilton, then Secretary of the Treasury.


NEW HAMPSHIRE
In this State is only one light-house, situated on a point of
land on the island of Newcastle, three miles from Portsmouth, with-
out the walls of the fort which commands the entrance of the
Piscataqua river.  It is under the superintendent of a commissary,
who is captain of the fort; and is at present, in good repair.  The
annual expense of maintaining it is estimated at $217 20.
MASSACHUSETTS
In this State are six light-houses, at the following places,
Viz:
    Boston
    Cape Ann
    Plymouth
    Plum Island
    Nantucket
    Portland
The whole expense attending the support of these establishments,
including the officers' salaries, is estimated at $5736 00.  The

officers appointed for their management are, at Boston, Captain
Thomas Knox, with an annual salary of            $400 00
At Cape Ann, Mr. Samuel Houston, with ditto,     $400 00
At Plymouth, the widow of the late General Thomas, with ditto,
                                                   233 50
At Plum Island, Mr. Lowell, with ditto,            220 00
At Nantucket, Mr. Paul Pinkham, with ditto         250 00
        At Portland, the building not being perfectly completed, no
person is yet appointed to superintend it.
        Exclusive of the above, there is an officer styled & commissary,
who has the charge of supplying the whole.  This office is now filled
by Mr. Divens, but what allowance he has for executing it, the
Secretary has not yet ascertained.
        When the building at Portland is completed, the expense of
maintaining it, and the allowance of the commissary superintending
the whole, will probably make the total amount of the light-house
establishment in the State of Massachusetts about 6,--- per annum.
CONNECTICUT
        In this State there is only one light-house, which is situated
at the port of New London; it is built of stone, and has lately
been repaired.  In the month of May last, the General Assembly
ordered some buoys to be fixed in the harbor for the safety of the
navigation, but nothing has been yet done in consequence of the Act.
        The annual expense of this establishment is estimated at $450.
        At new Haven there is a pier in the harbor, which is private
property, and a buoy at the entrance:  two other buoys are judged
necessary for the safety of the navigation.
NEW YORK
        At New York there is a light-house, and was lately a beacon
at Sandy Hook, the annual expense of which (exclusive of an allowance to the wardens of the port) is about $1500.
        The number of the wardens if four, who have (besides other
duties incident to their office) the charge of supplying and superintending this establishment.  They have each an allowance of one
dollar and a half per day when employed in visiting the words, exclusive of their provisions, & The master warden is Mr. Thomas
Randall.  The beacon has been recently blown down, and will require
to be replaced; which can be done at an inconsiderable expense.
NEW JERSEY
        There is no light-house, nor any establishment of that nature
here.
PENNSYLVANIA
        There is a light-house at Cape Henlopen, and several buoys,
beacons, and piers, for the security of the navigation on the bay
and river Delaware.  The annual expense of these establishments,
which have been under the care of a board of wardens of the port of
Philadelphia, is estimated by the present master warden at $4133.
        This office is now filled by Capt. William Allibone.
DELAWARE
        There is no light-house nor other establishment of this nature,
those on the bay and river Delaware answering for the State.


        Letter, Alexander Hamilton to George Washington, June 18, 1790,
J. C. Hamilton (ed.), <u>Works of Alexander Hamilton</u>, IV, pp. 24-26.

32.  THE SLOWNESS OF COMMUNICATION (1791)

The rigors of this 1,700 mile journey on horseback
suggest the economic impracticability of extended land
shipments.  Note, too, the lack of confidentiality in
communications--another obstacle to commerce over a distance.  Washington, who writes, became President in 1789.


No letters from the Northward or Eastward of this, bearing
date between the 15th and 30th of May, have come to my hands -- and
having abundant evidence before I reached Charleston of the slow
movements of the mail through the three southernmost States, I
did, before I left that place on the 9th of that month direct that
all letters which might be for and following me should be returned
to Fredericksburg as the first place I should touch the post line
upon my return.  But these directions not arriving in Richmond in
time (as I conjecture) the letters of that interval, agreeably to
the superscriptions which I am informed were on them, were forwarded from that place to Taylor's Ferry, in expectation of meeting
me there.  But to this circumstance, which was unknown to me -- and
to finding from better information that I set out with, that it
would be more convenient to cross James River higher up than at
Taylor's; is to be ascribed my missing the communications which were
made between the 15th and 30th of May, as mentioned before.  These
dispatches I may be long without, and perhaps never get; for there
are no cross-posts in those parts, and the letters, which will have
to pass through many hands, may find some who are not deficient in
curiosity.
My return to this place [Mount Vernon] is sooner than I expected, owing to the uninterruptedness of my journey by sickness,
from bad weather, or accidents of any kind whatsoever.  Having obtained before I left Philadelphia the most accurate account I could
get there, of the places and roads through, and by which I was to
perform my tour; and the distances between the former; I formed my
line of march accordingly; fixed each day's journey and the day to
halt; from neither of which I have departed in a single instance,
except staying, from a particular circumstance, two days in Columbia,
and none at Charlotte, instead of one at each -- and crossing James
River at Carter's Ferry in place of Taylor's, as was the original
intention.  But the improbability of performing a tour of 1700 miles
(I have already rode more), with the same set of horses without encountering any accident by which a deviation would be rendered
unavoidable, appeared so great that I allowed eight days for casual-
ties, and six to refresh at this place when I should have returned
to it -- None of the former having happened, account for the 14 days
I shall remain here before the meeting with the commissioners.


Letter, George Washington to Alexander Hamilton, June 13,
1791, The Papers of George Washington, Library of Congress.

### 33.  THE NEED FOR CHEAP INLAND WATER TRANSPORT
### IN WESTERN NEW YORK (1791)

The attraction of immigrant laborers and of commercial opportunities waited upon the development of transportation.  New York's farm resources were, near the end
of the 18th century, still utilized mainly along the southeastern half of the state.  It took considerable imagination
to see the possibilities of what later became the Erie Canal.
Elkanah Watson, the writer of this extract, had been a large-
scale farmer and had recently organized the Bank of Albany
(New York).

The further we explored these western waters, the more we were
impressed with the vast importance of assisting nature, in the whole
extent of the contemplated improvements, so that loaded boats, coming from the Hudson River, can reach our utmost borders without
interruption.  Let any man contemplate a good map; and he cannot
fail to be thus impressed.  Let the same man realize the policy and
necessity of the measure by exploring these waters in person; and
the first impression will not fail to be heightened to an enthusiasm
bordering on infatuation.

The improvements I had all along contemplated, either at a remote period or as near at hand, led me to attend, with a circumspect
and inquisitive eye, to the actual state of these waters.  The prospect is truly animating; when we give a loose rein to imagination,
and take a deep plunge into futurity.

For luxuriance of soil, mildness of climate, and easy access to
market, no other part of the world, so distant from the sea as our
western country, presents such irresistible allurements to emigrants,
as well from the eastern hive as from Europe.  We saw, at every step,
the bold and venerable forests settling before the strokes of the
axe, and farms and population increasing on all sides.  Nothing will
tend with so much certainty to accelerate the progress of these
great events, and to open a door to the happiness of unborn millions,
as to render a water communication at once cheap and easy of access.
Exclusive of continuing an intercourse with the greatest chain of
lakes in the known world, it will give a powerful stimulus to a new
creation in the very heart of this State; and this will be greatly
facilitated, by the admission of boats from fifteen to twenty tons
burden.  Hitherto, no boats have been able to navigate these waters,
carrying over eight or ten barrels; and the expense has everbalanced
the benefits.  Again, by traversing from the harbor of Oswego about
sixty miles on the south shore of Lake Ontario, vessels of sixty or
seventy tons burden may receive the whole produce of the Genesee
country, at the outlet of Genesee River, and also at the outlet of
Lake Erie, at Fort George, which can be easily conveyed in vessels
thence to the harbor of Oswego, and thence be taken, in large
bateaux, through the proposed navigation, to the Hudson River, to be
re-shipped either at Albany or at New York, for foreign markets.

On this momentous subject, a single question arises.  Are we
advanced to a sufficient state of maturity, to justify an undertaking of this magnitude?  If we proceed on the European mode of
calculation, waiting in the first instance to find the country,
through which canals are to pass, in a state of maturity and improvement, the answer is at hand;--No!  But, calculating on the more
enlarged American scale, and considering the physical circumstances
of the country in question, should canals precede the settlements,
it will be justified on the principles of sound policy.  In return
it will inevitably follow, that a vast wilderness will, as it were
by magic, rise into instant cultivation.  If executed gratuitously
by the public, the State will in effect be retarded only a few years,
in receiving a tenfold return for all its disbursements.  If, on the
other hand, it should be performed by private individuals, having a
toll in view, their remuneration would probably be small for a few
years; but the increasing benefit which will arise from this species
of property, will keep equal pace with the augmenting settlement of
cultivation of the country.


Elkanah Watson, Men and Times of the Revolution, (New York:
Dana and Company, 1856, 2nd. ed.), edited by Winslow C. Watson,
pp. 358-360.


34.  A LABOR FORCE FOR DIGGING A CANAL (1792)


Companies organized to build canals were the
largest business enterprises of the time.  They were
without question the largest employers of wage-labor.
This in itself is a prime reason why canal companies
needed relatively large capitals, and therefore also
why they were among the earliest users of the corporate
form of business.


For completing the works at the Falls, for removing the ob-
structions by rocks, &c. between Schohara Creek and the Falls, for
clearing the river from the Falls to Fort Schuyler, and removing
the timber out of Wood Creek, to the Oneida Lake, and for accomplishing all this in the next season, your committee are of opinion that
at least,
     40 Carpenters should be engaged in four companies.
     10 Masons in one company.
      5 Miners.
      1 Black Smith.
      2 Lime-Burners.
     200 Able-bodied labourers, to be engaged for the whole season,
--that is, from the month of May to October, both inclusive:  That
the 200 labourers should be divided into eight companies, with an

overseer to each; That the wages of each should be stipulated that
they should furnish themselves with provisions and liquor, to avoid
those bickerings which constantly result from complaints of bad provisions, &c—That each company of carpenters, and miners, masons and
blacksmiths, and each company of labours should be allowed a person
to cook their victuals—that each individual find his own bedding.—
That as the carpenters, &c. may not be able to purchase provisions
in the country, a stock of provisions and liquors would be laid in,
and sold them at prime cost, with the charges of transportation
added:  That the working hours should be stipulated to prevent controversy.

The expence of those workmen &c. may be,—

```
 40 Carpenters for 160 days at 9s. per day .............. 2880
 10 Masons         do    do    9s. --- ---  ...............  720
  5 Miners         do    do    9s. --- ---  ...............  360
  1 Blacksmith     do    do    9s. --- ---  ...............   72
  2 Lime Burners   do    do    9s. --- ---  ...............  144
200 Labourers      do    do    4s. --- ---  ............... 6400
  8 Overseers      do    do    9s. --- ---  ...............  576
```

Additional pay to 4 Master Carpenters and a Master Mason
   160 days at 4s......................................... 160
Clerk of the Checque for 160 days (who is also to deliver
   the provisions and tools, and keep all the accounts)
   at 10s...................................................  80
11 Cooks for 160 days at 1s................................. 352
1 Surveyor with four Assistants (to be employed when
   requisite) at 40s. per day. estimated at................ 170
A person to attend at the Falls during the winter to receive
   the timber &c. and to kept as an assistant during
   the next season, per annum.............................. 150

                                              12,064

Report of a Committee Appointed to Explore the Western Waters
in the State of New York, (Albany, New York:  Barker and Southwick,
1792), in E. B. O'Callaghan (ed.), Documentary History of the
State of New York, III, (Albany, New York:  Weed, Parsons and Co.,
1850), pp. 1100-1101.

### 35.  DIFFICULTIES OF HEAVY CONSTRUCTION (1795)

Tench Coxe, U.S. Commissioner of the Revenue, wrote
to Thomas Blount that no bid had been received from North
Carolina offering to build a lighthouse.  Blount here lists
three types of reasons why there was such a reluctance to
engage in a heavy construction project.  Inadequate transportation and the lack of machinery to burrow through solid
rock made the job seem impossible.

But for the following Reasons, was not surprized that offers to build them had not been rec^d. from Persons residing there first, Every man there can employ his Capital advantageously in Commerce or Agriculture & of course no one has a surplusage to tempt him into more arduous & les profitable Enterprises.--
Secondly, Many of the materials necessary for such Buildings, such as Stone which is not found near either of the places & Bricks which cannot be made there, must be carried from distant places with a degree of Difficulty & at a rate of Expense which theppeople of that Country do not generally well know how to calculate--
Thirdly, Masons, Bricklayers & other Workman that must necessarily be employed in the erection of such Buildings are not sufficiently numerous at any one place in the State to perform the work within the time that could be allowed for finishing it and the Expense & Diffi-culty of procuring them elsewhere & conveying them there are wither not known be men unacquainted with that sort of Business as the peo-ple of that Country generally are, or consider'd too great to be en-countered, & fourthly, The site of the Light House is almost as re-mote from the Seaport Towns of that State as from Philadelphia or New York which are in many respects more convenient to it than either of them as the materials for build must be carried to it by water in vessels capable of going to Sea (Pamlico Sound through which they must pass being at times as boisterous as the ocean) & many of them can be furnished cheaper & better from ether of these places [Philadelphia or New York] than from any part of North Carolina.--Besides, there arises out of the nature of the Sites two objections to your Plans, which to people who know them appear in-superable--The first lies against the foundation of the Light House. You say it must be sunk 13 feet below the bottom of the Water table, or Surface of the Earth, and well informed men of whom I have asked & received Information say, it is impossible to sink it more than 8, or 9 feet--Because, as all Hills found upon the Banks are composed altogether of Sand which has often, within the memory of people now living, shifted, it will be found necessary, there being no Land nay where on the Banks that has a Clay foundation, to place the Building upon one of the low, flat, stiff spots called by the people who in-habit the Banks, Savannas, which lie from 6 to 8 feet lower than the Sand Hills & under which water is generally found within 8 or 9 feet of the surface of the Earth.
The second lies against the foundation of the Beacon House which you say must be sunk 9 1/2 feet below the surface of the Earth.  Now, the Site of this Building being a Rock, or bed of Oyster Shells & not more than one foot, above the surface of the surround-ing water at common Tide, it is conceived that the foundation cannot be sunk at all, but must rest on the surface of the rock & be solid to the height of 4 or 5 feet which is as high as the Tide at any time rises.--People acquainted with the Coast of North Carolina know too that the undertaker of the Light House will find an Inconven-ience & Expense of considerable importance in the necessity of Boating in flat bottomed Boats, his materials for building of every kind at least one mile through the Sound (for the Vessel that carries them from where they are made or purchased can no where get nearer to the Shore) & a considerable distance up a small Creek--

and again in Hauling them from the Creek to the Spot on which the
Building is to Stand the Distance being three miles & the way so
Sandy that Oxen cannot be used because the Sand would split their
feet.


        Letter, Thomas Blount to Tench Coxe, December 18, 1795, Keith
(ed.), Blount Papers, II, pp. 620-621.


                    36.  MARKETING NAILS IN VIRGINIA (1796)


        Jefferson learned an object lesson in the diffi-
        culties of manufacture and distribution of goods which
        competed with those of a foreign make. (See Source
        No. 68).  He writes here to Archibald Stuart, Revolu-
        tionary soldier and statesman and close friend of both
        Jefferson and Madison.  Jefferson designed Stuart's
        house in Staunton, Virginia.


        I troubled you once before on the subject of my nails, and
must trouble you once more, but hope my present plan will protect
you from all further embarrassment with it.  I set out with refusing
to retail, expecting the merchants of my neighborhood and the upper
country would have given a preference to my supplies, because delivered here [Monticello] at the Richmond wholesale prices, and at
hand to be called for in small parcels, so that they need not to
keep large sums invested in that article & lying dead on their hands.
The importing merchants however decline taking them from a principle
of suppressing every effort towards domestic manufacture, & the merchants who purchase here being much under the influence of the importers, take their nails from them with their other goods.  I have
determined therefore to establish deposits of my nails to be retailed
at Milton, Charlottesville, Staunton, Wormester, & Warren, but first
at the three first places, because I presume my present works, which
turn out a ton a month, will fully furnish them, and two additional
fires which will be at work in a short time, will raise it to a ton
and a half a month, and enable me to extend my supplies to Wormester
& Warren.  I shall retail at Richmond wholesale prices, laying on 5
percent at Milton & Charlottesville for commission to the retailers,
and 10. percent at the other places for commission & transportation.
My present retailing prices at Staunton would be

| Sixes | $12_d 1/2^d$ | per lb. | equal to 7/3 1/2 per M |
| Eights | $12^d$ | " | equal to 10/ |
| Tens | $11_d 1/2^d$ | " | equal to 12/5 1/2 |
| Twelves | $11^d$ | " | equal to 14/8 |
| Sixteens | $10_d 1/2^d$ | " | equal to 17/6 |
| Twenties | $10^d$ | " | equal to 20/10 |

It is tolerably certain that the moment my deposit opens there will
be an entire stoppage to the sale of all imported nails, for a body

can <u>retail</u> them in the upper country at the Richmond <u>wholesale</u>
prices, advanced only 5 or 10 percent. and as I mean to employ only
one person in each place to retail, it will be of some advantage to
the merchant who will undertake it, to have the entire monopoly of
the nail business, & so draw to his store every one who wants nails,
besides the commission of 5 percent, which in an article to be sold
for ready money only, and where he does not employ a farthing of his
own capital, I am advised is a sufficient allowance for commission.
I should expect them to send me a copy of their sales once a month,
and to hold the proceeds ready for my draughts at stated periods,
say monthly.   I trouble you to engage some person whom you can recommend for punctuality, to retail for me.   I heard very favorable
accounts of a Mr. Stuart, merchant of Staunton, & should not hesitate
to prefer him if he will undertake it.   If not, pray do me the favor
to find some other.   I have written you the details, not that you
need put this letter into his hands.   As soon as you will name to
me the person you engage I will send him an assortment of nails by
the first waggons which will take them in.


Letter, Thomas Jefferson to Archibald Stuart, January 3, 1796,
Ford (ed.), <u>Writings of Thomas Jefferson</u>, VII, pp. 49-51.


### 37.   BOSTON GAINS FROM TURNPIKES (1800)


An instructive little exercise in understanding
the commercial value of improved transportation:  lay
a map of New England alongside this extract and trace
the lines and counter-lines of commercial interest.  The
"Court" was the state legislature; the letter was written
from Boston by Fisher Ames, a lawyer, Federalist leader,
and a member of the Governor's Council of Massachusetts.
He writes to Christopher Gore, a prominent Boston lawyer
who was in London acting as a commissioner under the
fourth article of Jay's Treaty to settle American spolia-
tion claims against England.


The Court will break up to-day, after passing...turnpike acts,
to bring the produce of Vermont to this market, and which will recover to Boston a large part of the back country, which has for many
years gone to New York.   A turnpike is granted from the line of
Connecticut to the thirty-milestone, on the road west of Dedham and
Medfield, and which joins the Connecticut turnpike from Hartford
ferry to the aforesaid line, adjoining this State at Douglas.   This
will divert the cheese, butter, &c., &c., which has gone to Providence more and more, and restore to the South End rum-and-molasses
shops, the Jonathans who used to have their sweet communion with
them.   These regulations will really tend to raise Boston; and if
your Middlesex Canal should succeed, the success will be hastened.

Do I not write like a patriot? yet I sell neither rum nor molasses.


   Letter, Fisher Ames to Christopher Gore, March 5, 1800, Seth
Ames (ed.), Works of Fisher Ames, I, (Boston:  Little, Brown & Co.,
1854), p. 277.



   38.  SHIPPING FLOUR FROM LOUISVILLE TO NEW ORLEANS (1802)


       New Orleans was by far the most important market
   for western flour.  Because of poor (and expensive) land
   transportation it was simply uneconomical to ship the
   flour directly by land to the much "nearer" east coast.
   The ratio of down-river to up-river shipments on the
   Mississippi was about 9-1, at least before the advent of
   the steamboat.  During the first years of the 19th century,
   New Orleans became a leading port for receipt of produce
   from the western United States.  Michaux, the narrator of
   the following, was a French botanist and traveller.


   The freightage of a boat to convey the flour to Low Louisiana
costs about a hundred dollars.  They contain from two hundred and
fifty to three hundred barrels, and are navigated by five men, of
whom the chief receives a hundred dollars for the voyage, and the
others fifty each.  They take, from Louisville, where nearly the
whole embarkations are made, from thirty to thirty-five days to go
to New Orleans.  They reckon it four hundred and thirty-five miles
from Louisville to the embouchure of the Ohio, and about a thousand
miles thence to New Orleans, which makes it, upon the whole, a passage of fourteen hundred and thirty-five miles; and these boats have
to navigate upon the river a space of eight or nine hundred miles
without meeting with any plantations.  A part of the crew return to
Lexington by land, which is about eleven hundred miles, in forty or
forty-five days.  This journey is extremely unpleasant, and those
who dread the fatigues of it return by sea.  They embark at New
Orleans for New York and Philadelphia, whence they return to
Pittsburgh, and thence go down the Ohio as far as Kentucky.
   An inspector belonging to the port of Louisville inserted in
the Kentucky Gazette of the 6th of August 1802, that 85,570 barrels
of flour, from the 1st of January to the 30th of the June following,
went out of that port to Low Louisiana.  More than two thirds of
this quantity may be considered as coming from Ohio and the settlements situated upon the rivers Monogahela and Alleghany.  The spring
and autumn are principally the seasons in which this exportation is
made.  It is almost null in summer, an epoch at which almost all
the mills are stopped for the want of water.

Francois Andre Michaux, <u>Travels to the West of the Alleghany Mountains</u>, (London:  B. Crosby and Co., 1805), reprinted in Reuben S. Thwaites (ed.), <u>Early Western Travels:  1748–1846</u>, III, (Cleveland, Ohio:  Arthur H. Clark, 1904), pp. 239–240.


## 39.  EARLY COTTON TRADE (1802)


The general direction of cotton was toward England whether it was sent directly to east coast port cities or indirectly via New Orleans.  At many points British finance facilitated movement of the valuable cargo.  Cotton factors, who were middlemen between eastern providers of imported goods and manufactures and southern planters or merchants, earned a commission on cotton sales and on the eastern goods he traded.  Cotton farmers in the southwest, distant from the Mississippi, traded their crop for imported goods brought via land transport from eastern cities and then to Nashville and thereafter to river ports.

There are very few cultivators who take upon themselves to export the produce of their labour, consisting chiefly of cotton; the major part of them sell it to the tradespeople at Nashville, who send it by the river to New Orleans, where it is expedited to New York and Philadelphia, or exported direct to Europe.  These tradesmen, like those of Lexington, do not pay always in cash for the cotton they purchase, but make the cultivators take goods in exchange, which adds considerably to their profit.  A great quantity of it is also sent by land to Kentucky, where each family is supplied with it to manufacture articles for their domestic wants.

Michaux, <u>Travels</u>, pp. 252–253.


## 40.  THE IMPROPRIETY OF UNLIMITED FEDERAL INTERNAL IMPROVEMENTS (1802)


Jefferson, who was President at this time, was a cautious friend of internal improvements when it was a matter of federal financing.  When, however, it was a matter of imagining the constructive aspects of internal improvements, Jefferson's mind knew few limits.  (See Source No. 27).

You know my doubts or rather convictions about the unconstitutionality of the act for building piers in the Delaware, and the

fears that it will lead to a bottomless expense, & to the greatest
abuses.  There is however one intention of which the act is susceptible & which will bring it within the constitution; and we ought
always to presume that the real intention which is alone consistent
with the constitution.  Altho the power to regulate commerce does
not give a power to build piers, wharfs, open ports, clear the
beds of rivers, dig canals, build warehouses, build manufacturing
machines, set up manufactories, cultivate the earth, to all of
which the power would go, if it went to the first, yet a power to
provide and maintain a navy, is a power to provide receptacles for
it and places to cover & preserve it.  In choosing the places where
this money should be laid out, I should be much disposed, as far as
contracts will permit, to confine it to such place or places as the
ships of war may lie at, and be protected from ice; & I should be
for stating this in a message to Congress, in order to prevent the
effect of the present example.  This act has been built on the
exercise of the power of building light houses, as a regulation of
commerce.  But I well remember the opposition, on this very ground,
to the first act for building a light house.  The utility of the
thing has sanctioned the infraction.  But if on that infraction we
build a 2$^d$, on that 2$^d$ a 3$^d$, &c., any one of the powers in the
constitution may be made to comprehend every power of government.


Letter, Thomas Jefferson to Albert Gallatin, October 13, 1802,
The Papers of Thomas Jefferson, Vol. 126, Library of Congress.


41.  THE TRADE AND TRANSPORTATION OF PITTSBURGH (1802)


Here is a perceptive look at one of the youngest
of western cities, written by Michaux.


Pittsburgh is not only the staple of the Philadelphia and
Baltimore trade with the western country, but of the numerous settlements that are formed upon the Monongahela and Alleghany.  The territorial produce of that part of the country finds an easy and advantageous conveyance by the Ohio and Mississippi.  Corn, hams and dried
pork are the principal articles sent to New Orleans, whence they are
re-exported into the Carribbees.  They also export for the consumption of Louisiana, bar-iron, coarse linen, bottles manufactured at
Pittsburgh, whiskey, and salt butter.  A great part of these provisions come from Redstone, a small commercial town, situated upon the
Monongahela, about fifty miles beyond Pittsburgh.  All these advantages joined together have, within these ten years, increased tenfold the population and price of articles in the town, and contribute to its improvements, which daily grow more and more rapid.
The major part of the merchants settled in Pittsburgh, or in
the environs, are the partners, or else the factors, belonging to
the houses at Philadelphia.  Their brokers at New Orleans sell, as
much as they can, for ready money; or rather, take in exchange

cottons, indigo, raw sugar, the produce of Low Louisiana, which they
send off by sea to the houses at Philadelphia and Baltimore, and
thus cover their first advances.  The bargemen return thus by sea
to Philadelphia or Baltimore, whence they go by land to Pittsburgh
and the environs, where the major part of them generally reside.
Although the passage from New Orleans to one of these two ports is
twenty or thirty days, and that they have to take a route by land
of three hundred miles to return to Pittsburgh, they prefer this
way, being not so difficult as the return by land from New Orleans
to Pittsburgh, this last distance being fourteen or fifteen hundred
miles.  However, when the barges are only destined for Limeston, in
Kentucky, or for Cincinnati, in the state of Ohio, the bargemen
return by land, and by that means take a route of four or five
hundred miles.

The navigation of the Ohio and Mississippi is so much improved
of late that they can tell almost to a certainty the distance from
Pittsburgh to New Orleans, which they compute to be two thousand
one hundred miles.  The barges in the spring season usually take
forty or fifty days to make the passage, which two or three persons
in a pirogue make in five and twenty days.

What many, perhaps, are ignorant of in Europe is, that they
build large vessels on the Ohio, and at the town of Pittsburgh.
One of the principal ship yards is upon the Monongahela, about two
hundred fathoms beyond the last houses in the town.  The timber they
make use of is the white oak, or quercus alba; the red oak, or
quercus rubra; the black oak, or quercus tinctoria; a kind of nut
tree, or juglans minima; the Virginia cherrytree, or cerasus
Virginia; and a kind of pine, which they use for masting, as well as
for the sides of the vessels which require a slighter wood.  The
whole of this timber being near at hand, the expense of building is
not so great as in the ports of the Atlantic states.  The cordage
is manufactured at Redstone and Lexington, where there are two extensive rope-walks, which also supply ships with rigging that are
built at Marietta and Louisville.  On my journey to Pittsburgh in
the month of July 1802, there was a three-mast vessel of two hundred
and fifty tons, and a smaller one of ninety, which was on the point
of being finished.  These ships were to go, in the spring following,
to New Orleans, loaded with the produce of the country, after having
made a passage of two thousand two hundred miles before they got into
the ocean.  There is no doubt but they can, by the same rule, build
ships two hundred leagues beyond the mouth of the Missouri, fifty
from that of the river Illinois, and even in the Mississippi, two
hundred beyond the place whence these rivers flow; that is to say,
six hundred and fifty leagues from the sea; as their bed in the
appointed space is as deep as that of the Ohio at Pittsburgh; in
consequence of which it must be a wrong conjecture to suppose that
the immense tract of country watered by these rivers cannot be populous enough to execute such undertakings.  The rapid population of
the three new western states, under less favorable circumstances,
proves this assertion to be true.

Michaux, Travels, pp. 158-161.

42.  THE COMMERCIAL IMPORTANCE OF THE CUMBERLAND ROAD (1807)

Both President Jefferson and Treasury Secretary
Gallatin had a very strong appreciation of the necessity
for improving transportation and thereby extending the
effective market.  The Cumberland Road was for long one
of the rare internal improvements financed by Congress.
Note, too, another very frequent obstacle in the way of
internal improvements--localism.  Philadelphia wished
to remain the commercial hub of the state and thus did
not favor new roads to the West.


I enclose a letter from a member of the Legislature of
Pennsylvania, enclosing a rough copy of the Act for the Cumberland
road.  Although the words "if such an alteration can, in the opinion
of the President, be made consistently with the Act of Congress,"
are either very intelligible nor very proper, yet, as in the conflict
of local interests and the silent but steady opposition of
Philadelphia, this was the best that could be obtained, and the Act
explicitly authorizes the President to lay the road over any ground
in the State which he may deem most advantageous, I think the Act
should be accepted.  The two last sections are only intended to prevent owners of land asking exorbitant prices for timber, stones,
gravel, &c., wanted for the road.  The immense importance of that
road, as part of a great Western travelling road, and principally
as the main communication for the transportation of all the foreign
or Atlantic articles which the Western States consume, and even for
the carriage of Western flour and produce to the Potomack, induce
me strongly to wish that that part particularly which lies between
the Potomack and the Monongahela may be completed in the most substantial manner.  And for that purpose I think that the best application of the money already appropriated will be, commencing at
Cumberland, to make in the most complete manner just so many miles
as the money will pay for.  I do not suppose that will effect more
than five or six miles; but I have no doubt of Congress appropriating
then enough to finish it; and as a national object it is of primary
importance.  The thousand tons will be carried westwardly annually,
and perhaps one hundred thousand barrels of flour brought back.  I
think the annual saving in expenses of transportation will exceed
two hundred dollars.


Letter, Albert Gallatin to Thomas Jefferson, April 13,
1807, H. Adams (ed.), Writings of Albert Gallatin, I, pp. 334-335.

43.  "EXCLUSIVE POSSESSION OF THE INDIAN COMMERCE" (1808)


     Commercial advantage had been a basic reason for
the Lewis-Clark expedition.  But commerce in the Missouri
Valley waited on peace with the Indians and superiority
over the British and Canadian fur companies.  Jefferson
saw in Astor's new American Fur Company the means whereby
the main problems of Missouri commerce might be solved.
Jefferson is writing to Meriwether Lewis, at this time
Governor of the Louisiana Territory.


     A powerful company is at length forming for taking up the
Indian commerce on a large scale.  They will employ a capital the
first year of 300,000 D. and raise it afterwards to a million.  The
English Mackinac company will probably withdraw from the competition.
It will be under the direction of a most excellent man, a Mr. Astor,
merch't of New York, long engaged in the business, & perfectly
master of it.  He has some hope of seeing you at St. Louis in which
case I recommend him to your particular attention.  Nothing but the
exclusive possession of the Indian commerce can secure us their
peace.


     Letter, Thomas Jefferson to Meriwether Lewis, July 17, 1808,
The Papers of Thomas Jefferson, Vol. 179, Library of Congress.



          44.  ECONOMIC ADVANTAGES OF CANALS (1810)


     At the time the following was written, there were
fewer than 100 miles of canals in the United States.
Shortage of capital and engineering problems were principal obstacles to expansion of canals.  The author, William
Duane, was a lawyer and publicist of internal improvements
and a close friend of the prominent Philadelphia merchant,
Stephen Girard.


     Of the peculiar benefits of canals, in preference to roads,
much may be said; I shall not, however, be diffuse on the subject.
Canals are important to the farmer and land-holder, because they
enhance the value of the lands, woods, coals, iron, and other mines,
to the extent of at least forty miles on each side of the country
through which they pass; because they enable the farmer to carry his
produce to market, and to return in his boat loaded with goods or
manure, at an expense twenty times less than by roads, and because
all that is saved is actual profit; they are important to him, besides, in case he should want either to drain his lands or to irrigate them; and they also enable him to employ his horses or oxen
entirely upon his farm, and not on the road.

Canals are important to the miner, because they enable him to convey to market, such heavy or bulky articles as would not bear the cost of land transportation.

Canals are important to merchants on the sea coast and in the interior, by affording a certain and cheap conveyance for goods or articles imported by the former, and for the produce returned by the latter; but they are still more important by opening a trade between all parts of our immense continent, which must at no distant day, rival, if not entirely supercede a large foreign trade.

Canals in winter may answer, as in Holland and Flanders, all the purposes of the best constructed roads—as they are thus used, in those countries, by means of sleighs, as much as they are by means of boats in summer.

Canals, including the towing path, do not occupy more ground than our turnpike roads; a canal forty feet wide and a mile long would occupy but five acres of ground. . . .

The enemies of our freedom, or those who are jealous of our happiness, predict our ruin from the extent of our country, and the contrariety of the habits of our people; they tell you that a strong government is alone capable of ruling so unwieldy an empire; and even Washington, but from other motives, from his solicitude for your safety, says, that "in a country so extensive as ours, a government of as much vigor as is consistent with the perfect security of liberty, is indispensible." If there are grounds for those invidious predictions on one side, and for these honest apprehensions on the other, what can so readily or effectually remove them as canals, or where these cannot be made, good roads? Those works, if executed to the extent, to which they may be carried in ten years, would, by greatly facilitating the means of intercourse and thus combining its population, as it were, reduce this immense country to the size of a single state; local interests and prejudices would cease to exist, and we should thus be united by every tie in one common brotherhood.

William J. Duane, Letters Addressed to the People of Pennsylvania Respecting the Interval Improvements of the Commonwealth by Means of Roads and Canals, (Philadelphia, Pennsylvania: Jane Aitken, 1811), pp. 30-33.

45. FOREIGN TRADE RETARDS INTERNAL IMPROVEMENTS (1810)

Philadelphia, the state's center of wealth and political influence, had a large contingent of merchants engaged in importing and exporting. With the virtual cutting off of foreign trade due to the Napoleonic Wars, there now appeared a real possibility of shifting attention over to internal development. Again William Duane writes.

That our foreign trade, however beneficial it may have been in other respects, has had an injurious influence upon our own internal concerns and improvements, there cannot, perhaps, be a better proof, than that which is furnished by the silence, which has prevailed in this commonwealth, respecting a communication with the lakes, during the last fifteen years in particular.  I have not been able to find a single act of the legislature, passed within the time, having any such important object in view, nor have I found more than two publications of any consequence urging the legislature to the undertaking. Our interests and our feelings have been too much involved in the concerns of foreign nations; a host of foreign merchants, having no objects but their own gain, have withdrawn the regards of many of our own good citizens from the real interests of their country, and have largely contributed to reduce the country to its present condition.  It is now, therefore, when foreign trade, the course of domestic apathy, is nearly annihilated, that we should be employed in acquiring what has been done, and in doing what ought to be done.

Duane, Letters Addressed to the People, pp. 53-54.

# D.

# SUPPLYING A LABOR FORCE

### 46. LABOR IS STRONG ENOUGH TO RESIST WAGE CONTROLS (1641)

Strict controls over wages, with heavy penalities on workers who accepted more than the legal maximum, were part of English law. Already, however, conditions of the American environment started to weaken these controls. The "court"-- i.e., the General Court or legislature--of the colony was forced by 1641 to admit this. Winthrop writes of this.

The court having found by experience, that it would not avail by any law to redress the excessive rates of laborers' and workmen's wages, etc. (for being restrained, they would either remove to other places where they might have more, or else being able to live by planting and other employments of their own, they would not be hired at all,) it was therefore referred to the several towns to set down rates among themselves. This took better effect, so that in a voluntary way, by the counsel and persuasion to the elders, and example of some who led the way, they were brought to more moderation than they could be by compulsion. But it held not long.

Winthrop, Winthrop's Journal, II, p. 24.

47.   BOSTON SHOULD REPLACE ITS SLAVES WITH
INDENTURED SERVANTS (1706)


North or South, early American economic development
proceeded partly on the basis of slave labor.  The shift
from slave labor to free labor or to less unfree labor
was occasioned by prospective savings on labor costs.
Here is an early example of a non-sentimental opposition
to slavery.


By last Years Bill of Mortality for the Town of Boston. . .we
are furnished with a list of 44 Negroes dead last year, which being
computed one with another at 30 1. per Head, amounts to the Sum of
One Thousand three hundred and Twenty Pounds, of which we would make
this Remark; That the Importing of Negroes into this or the Neighboring Provinces is not so beneficial either to the Crown or
Country, as White Servants would be.
    For Negroes do not carry Arms to defend the Country, as Whites
do.
    Negroes are generally Eye-Servants, great Thieves, much addict-
ed to Stealing, Lying and Purloining.
    They do not People our Country as Whites would do whereby we
should be strengthened against an Enemy.
    By Encouraging the importing of White Men Servants, allowing
somewhat to the Importer, most Husbandmen in the Country might be
furnished with Servants for 8, 9, or 10 1. a Head, who are not able
to Launch out 40 or 50 1. for a Negro the now common price.
    A Man then might buy a White Man Servant we suppose for 10 1.
to Serve 4 years, and Boys for the same price to Serve 6, 8 or 10
years:  If a White Servant die, the Loss exceeds but 10 1. but if a
Negro dies, 'tis a very great loss to the Husbandman; Three years
Interest of the price of the Negro, will near upon if not altogether
purchase a White Man Servant.
    If Necessity call for it, that the Husbandman must fit out a
man against the Enemy; if he has a Negro he cannot send him, but if
he has a White Servant, 'twill answer the end, and perhaps save his
Son at home.
    Were Merchants and Masters Encouraged as already said to bring
in Men Servants, there needed not be such Complaint against Superi-
ours Impressing our Children to the War, there would then be Men
enough to be had without Impressing.
    The bringing in of such Servants would much enrich this Pro-
vince, because Husbandmen would not only be able far better to manure
what Lands are already under Improvement, but would also improve a
great deal more that lyes waste under Woods, and enable this Province to set about raising of Naval Stores, which would be greatly
advantagious to the Crown of England, and this Province.
    For the raising of Hemp here, so as to make Sail-cloth and
Cordage to furnish but our own Shipping, would hinder the Importing
it, & save a considerable sum in a year to make Returns for which
we now do, and in time might be capacitated to furnish England not
only with Sail Cloth and Cordage, but likewise with Pitch, Tar, Hemp,

and other Stores which they are now obliged to purchase in Foreign Nations.

Suppose the Government here should allow Forty Shillings per head for five years, to such as should Import every of these years 100 White Men Servants, and each to Serve 4 years, the cost would be but 200 l. a year, and a 1000 ls for the 5 years:  The first 100 Servants being free the 4th year, they serve the 5th for Wages, and the 6th there is 100 that goes out into the Woods, and settles a 100 families to Strengthen and Baracado us from the Indians, and so a 100 Families more every year successively.

And here you see that in one year the Town of Boston has lost 1320 l. by 44 Negroes, which is also a Loss to the Country in general, and for a less Loss, (if it may improperly be so called) for a 1000 l. the Country may have 500 Men in 5 years time for the 44 Negroes dead in one year.

A certain person within these 6 years had two Negroes dead computed both at 60 l. which would have procured him six white Servants at 10 l. per head to have Served 24 years, at 4 years apiece, without running such a great risque, and the Whites would have strengthened the Country; that Negroes do not.

"Twould do well that none of those Servants be liable to be Impressed during their Service of Agreement at their first Landing.

That such Servants being Sold or Transported out of this Province during the time of their Service, the Person that buys them be liable to pay 3 l. into the Treasury.


The Boston News-Letter, June 10, 1706, Lyman H. Weeks and Edwin M. Bacon (eds.), An Historical Digest of the Provincial Press, (Boston, Massachusetts:  The Society for Americans, Inc., 1911), pp. 338-340.


48.   THE LOT OF THE INDENTURED SERVANT (1750)


This standard account of an indentured servant's lot differs from many others in that the author does not paint the colonies, Pennsylvania especially, as a heaven-on-earth.  His picture is a truthful one.  (He did go back whence he came.)  The writer, Gottlieb Mittelberger, who had been a teacher in Wurttemberg, lived in Pennsylvania for four years.  His book was first published in 1756.


This is how the commerce in human beings on board ship takes place.  Every day Englishmen, Dutchmen, and High Germans come from Philadelphia and other places, some of them very far away, sometime twenty or thirty or forty hours' journey, and go on board the newly arrived vessel that has brought people from Europe and offers them for sale.  From among the healthy they pick out those suitable for the purposes for which they require them.  Then they negotiate with them as to the length of the period of which they will go into service in order to pay off their passage, the whole amount of which they generally still owe. When an agreement has been reached, adult persons by written contract bind themselves to serve for three, four, five, or six years, according to their health and age. The very young, between the ages of ten and fifteen, have to serve until they are twenty-one, however.

Many parents in order to pay their fares in this way and get off the ship must barter and sell their children as if they were cattle. Since the fathers and mothers often do not know where or to what masters their children are to be sent, it frequently happens that after leaving the vessel, parents and children do not see each other for years on end, or even for the rest of their lives.

People who arrive without the funds to pay their way and who have children under the age of five, cannot settle their debts by selling them. They must give away these children for nothing to be brought up by strangers; and in return these children must stay in service until they are twenty-one years old. Children between five and ten who owe half-fare, that is thirty florins, must also go into service in return until they are twenty-one years old, and can neither set free their parents nor take their debts upon themselves. On the other hand, the sale of children older than ten can help to settle a part of their parents' passage charges.

A wife must be responsible for her sick husband and a husband for his sick wife, and pay his or her fare respectively, and must thus serve five to six years not only for herself or himself, but also for the spouse, as the case may be. If both should be ill on arrival, then such persons are brought directly from the ship into a hospital, but not until it is clear that no purchaser for them is to be found. As soon as they have recovered, they must serve to pay off their fare, unless they have the means immediately to discharge the debt.

It often happens that whole families--husband, wife, and children--being sold to different purchasers, become separated, especially when they cannot pay any part of the passage money. When either the husband or the wife has died at sea, having come more than halfway, then the surviving spouse must pay not only his or her fare, but must also pay for or serve out the fare of the deceased.

When both parents have died at sea, having come more than halfway, then their children, especially when they are still young and have nothing to pawn or cannot pay, must be responsible for their own fares as well as those of their parents, and must serve until they are twenty-one years old. Once free of service, they receive a suit of clothing as a parting gift, and if it has been so stipulated the men get a horse and the women a cow.

When a servant in this country has the opportunity to get married he has to pay £5 to £6, that is, 30 to 36 florins for every year that he would still have had to serve. But many who must purchase and pay for their brides in this manner come to regret their purchases later. They would just as soon surrender their damnably expensive wares again and lose their money into the bargain.

No one in this country can run away from a master who has treated him harshly and get far. For there are regulations and laws that ensure that runaways are certainly and quickly recaptured. Those who arrest or return a fugitive get a good reward. For every

day that someone who runs away is absent from his master he must as
a punishment do service an extra week, for every week an extra
month, and for every month a half year.   But if the master does not
want to take back the recaptured runaway, he is entitled to sell him
to someone else for the period of as many years as he would still
have had to serve.

Occupations vary, but work is strenuous in this new land; and
many who have just come into this country at an advanced age must
labor hard for their bread until they die.   I will not even speak
of the young people.   Most jobs involve cutting timber, felling oak
trees, and levelling, or as one says there, clearing, great tracts
of forest, roots and all.   Such forest land, having been cleared in
this way, is then laid out in fields and meadows.   From the best
wood that has been felled people construct railings or fences around
the new fields.   Inside these, all meadows, all lawns, gardens, and
orchards, and all arable land are surrounded and enclosed by thickly
cut wood planks set in zigzag fashion one above the other.   And
thus cattle, horses, and sheep are confined to pasture land.

Our Europeans who have been purchased must work hard all the
time.   For new fields are constantly being laid out; and thus they
learn from experience that Oak tree stumps are just as hard in
America as they are in Germany.   In these hot regions there is particularly fulfilled in them that with which the Lord God afflicted
man in the first book of Moses, on account of his sin and disobedi-
ence, namely:   "Thou shalt eat thy bread in the sweat of thy brow."
Thus let him who wants to earn his piece of bread honestly and in a
Christian manner and who can only do this by manual labor in his
native country stay there rather than come to America.

For, in the first place, things are no better in Pennsylvania.
However hard one may have had to work in his native land, conditions
are bound to be equally tough or even tougher in the new country.
Furthermore the emigrant has to undertake the arduous voyage, which
means not only that he must suffer more misery for half a year than
he would have to suffer doing the hardest labor, but also that he
must spend approximately two hundred florins which no one will re-
fund to him.   If he has that much money, he loses it; if he does
not have it, he must work off his debt as a slave or as a miserable
servant.   So let people stay in their own country and earn their
keep honestly for themselves and their families.   Furthermore, I
want to say that those people who may let themselves be talked into
something and seduced into the voyage by the thieves of human beings
are the biggest fools if they really believe that in America or
Pennsylvania roasted pigeons are going to fly into their mouths
without their having to work for them.

Gottlieb Mittelberger, Journey to Pennsylvania, translated
and edited by Oscar Handlin and John Clive, (Cambridge,
Massachusetts:   Harvard University Press, 1960), pp. 17-21.
Originally published in 1756.

49.  BEING SOLD AS AN INDENTURED SERVANT (1773)


To a nineteen-year-old indentured servant Johann
Carl Buttner newly-arrived from Germany, the prospect
of servitude did not appear horrifying.


Shortly after, an announcement could have been read not only
on the street corners of Philadelphia, but also in the American newspapers: "That a boat at present lying in the harbor of Philadelphia
had arrived from Europe carrying a load of male and female persons,
and that whoever might wish to purchase some of them, was invited to
visit the boat." Shortly afterwards, professional men arrived from
the cities and owners of plantations from the country, who bargained
with the ship's captain for our persons. We had to strip naked, so
that the prospective purchasers could see that we had perfectly
developed and healthy bodies.  After the purchaser had made a selection, he asked: "How much is this boy or this girl?" Many strong
and healthy young men, and especially the pregnant women brought as
much as sixty pounds sterling ($300.00).  Some of my companions had
to serve ten, twelve, or even more years without receiving anything
more than their board and clothes.  This amount of money was received
by the captain in payment for our transportation to America and for
our board.  The length of service was according to the price.  After
these aliens had worked for the time required, they received a certificate of freedom.  Then they had to decide whether they would hire
themselves out or start in business on their own account.  These servants were not given wholly over to the discretion of their masters,
but were still to some extent under the protection of the law; and
the only difference between them and free citizens was that for the
specified time, they could not work for themselves.  So it is easily
seen that the conditions under which we had to labor after our arrival in North America were in no way a formal and life-long slavery,
and that we could have gone immediately about our own business, had
we been in the position to pay the ship's captain what we owed him.
Even now [1828], as I am informed, the poor European arrivals in
North America have to work out the cost of their transportation after
they land there; but they are no longer exposed to the whims and
avarice of ship's captains, as previously.  In latter times, the
Baron of Gagern, known as a wise and philanthropic man, did very
much to ameliorate the conditions of immigrants, and in Philadelphia
there exists at this time a humanitarian society for their assistance.
     Soon the persons that composed the load of our ship were all
sold except six boys, among whom was myself.  They, like myself,
were unwilling to consent to a long term of service.  This made the
ship's captain wild with anger and he threatened, if we refused
again to take service in America under his conditions, to carry us
to the Antilles, especially to Barbadoes, where the heat is unbearable and where we would have to work with negroes.  We realized that
we would gain nothing by a trip to the West Indies, where our
miserable fate would become even more intolerable, and that there

was no salvation from the power of the ship's captain; so we resolved to work out the cost of transportation in the climate of
Philadelphia.  The captain asked for me thirty pounds sterling and
I had to bind myself for the term of six years to the master or
overseer that paid this amount of money.  The master who paid this
money for me--<u>about</u> <u>one</u> <u>hundred</u> <u>and</u> <u>fifty</u> <u>dollars</u>--was the owner of
a plantation in the province of New Jersey, and a member of the
religious sect of the Quakers.


Johann Carl Buttner, <u>Narrative of Johann Carl Buttner in the</u>
<u>American Revolution</u>, (New York:  C. F. Heartman, 1915), pp. 26-28.
Translated from the 2nd German edition, published in Camenz in
1828.


### 50.   INDENTURED SERVANTS ESCAPE TOO EASILY ON THE WESTERN FRONTIER (1774)


One peculiarity of the pioneer Virginia frontier
was the presence there of tobacco plantations.  Here,
however, is a report of some difficulties in establishing a plantation in western Virginia.  It is written by
Valentine Crawford, an overseer and agent of Washington.
A fortnight earlier than he writes Washington had joined
the other burgesses in a illegal meeting to protest the
dissolution of the Colonial legislature by the royal
governor.


I received your letter by Mr. Creley of the 27th of May and am
Sorrey for the Sudint Braking up of the Esembly before they hitt on
Som Method to Releve our Distress Situation Butt is is a happey
Scurcumstance for us Lordonmore [Lord Dunmore, governor of the
colony] being So warm in our favour which gives us great Reselution
to stand our ground what few of us is Left though the Contre
[country] is very thin we have Bilt Sevrell Forts out Hear which wase
a very great means of the people Standing there ground I have built
one att My house and have got Som Men to garde it and Mr. Simson has
Built a Fort att the place where they are Building of your Mill by
the Esistence of His Neabours and part of your Carpenters and I have
been there Severell times and have Encuraged him all I can to Stand
his Ground and I have Severell times oferd him all the Carpenters
and all the Sarvants but he would not take aney of the Sarvants and
but four of the best of the Carpenters his Reason for not taking of
the Sarvants as there wase a great dale of Companey att the Fort and
drink Midling plenty it would be out of his power to govern them and
he Said they would Run away from him and as to Carpenters he and
Stephens the Millwright had Engaged Som Carpenters them Selves before
this Erouption broake out with the Indens and are Louth to discharge
them and take in these you Engagd for me to take down the Ohio or
att Least aney More of them than Conveniently work as the Says from

the Noys of the Indens and the Crowds of people that Come to the
Fort he Cant get Nothing don with the Small Numbr of hands he has
but I will goe to Simson to Morrow morning and Consult him farther
on the affair and doe Every thing in My power for your Entrast the
thoughts of selling of the Sarvants Elarmed them verey Much for they
dont want to be Sold but the hole of the Sarvants have had Som Short
Spells of Sickness and Som others Cut them Selfes with an ax and Lay
bye Som time and one of the best of Stephens Men Cut him Selfe with
an adze the worst I Ever Saw aney body Cut in My Life So that he has
Not been able to doe one Strok for Near one Month this hapened in
digin the Canews I have Sent you a Scetch of Stephens article when I
waite on Simson if he does Not take the Carpenters all I Shall Ether
Sett them to building of a house att the big Medows or discharge them
intirely for it Seems all Most Emposable to Ceep Men Close to bisness
at a Fort where there is So meney people and So much Confusion if
they Can doe Eney thing it Must be att the Medow as they will be to
them Selfes and as Stevens Seems to be verey Loth to be discharged
and Says he Left som very good Jobs to Serve you.

Letter, Valentine Crawford to George Washington, June 8, 1774,
Commons (ed.), A Documentary History of American Industrial Society,
I, pp. 344-345.

### 51.  ONE YEAR'S JOBS BY A JACK-OF-ALL-TRADES (1784)

The division of labor in colonial America was
rudimentary, thus giving rise to the jack-of-all-trades.
He was a skilled craftsman, rather than an entrepreneur,
who normally worked on raw materials or finished goods in
need of repair.  Note that the following account stresses
work on metal objects since the special degree of knowledge
required to work such materials would not ordinarily be
found among householders.

I Shod Roberts Horse all round & Grate mare before...Made Swivel
and E hooks for Lucaanna Knowles...Fixt Cousin Hazards Gun.  Cut
Skrew for David Willson...I made afew Names for James Robinsson...
Made pr Bitts for Simeon Hazard.  Stratend agun for Philip Rodman...
Put this m. two Gripes on cart Wheel for Robert Knowles...Yesterday
I made Small Swivel for Robert Hazard to make lines with...An he
helpt me mend two ax for Simeon Hazard...Fixt alock for James
Shearman and also one yeasterday...I mended asmall Pott for Lucaanna
Knowles and made Some Nales...Went to Benj[n] Hazards to carry p[r]Flatts
that I mended for Simeon Hazard and then went to Joh Gardiners to See
two Tea Kittles he had to mend and Brought the cover of one home
with me. and mended it...mended akittle leg for Cousin Hazard and
made 5 E hooks for Robert Hazard...I helpt George work Some in the
Shop on Plowshear and Coalter.  Began Tea Kittle Cover for Job

Gardiner to men and mended the Cover for the Same...Mended Kittle
Bail for Cousin Hazard and Spindly for Linnen Wheel for one Shelding
up by wordens Pond...I helpt George Newlay p$^r$plow Irons...I made kee
for lock...Made Flour Brads for Jeremiah Brown Jun$^r$...Made hasp and
two Stapales for door and Putt them in...Hupt Barrel for George
Hazard (of Richard)...made Stapels and Cupels for Robert Knowles...
Mended Hoe for Robert Knowles and wired p$^r$ of Carriers for George
and knew Steeld p$^r$ Coumpersis for William Hifferlard...A$^n$ made four
oaster Rake teeth for old James Congdon...Made Knife Blade for
Stephen Collins...Began achane for Robert Knowles...Knew laid ahoe
for Jonathan Champlin. made Staples 8 and rings 8 for abiger Bobcock
...Made Some Nales made Ring and Staple for amans Saddle--for Samuel
Sheffield...Began Some Hinges for Joseph Segar...Irond asyth Sned
for David Willcocks...I made ahammer for Joseph Holly...I made aside
Pinn for Gun lock for Joshua Card...I Sold Robert Knowles amouse
trap...Mended an old Saddl for Joseph Holly...Sharpened p$^r$ Plow Irons
for William Knowles...Began asteel Trap for William Card...I began
apair of Plowiron to Newlay for William Knowles...Fixt a Spring for
Stephen Hollys Gun...Workt on the Steel yards. Heardend an Hachet
for Stephen Holly...I made ahorse block. I made agate...Made two
Bolts for Christopher Clarke the Sawer...Made aspindle for Wollen
Wheel for William Congdon, mended ashovel for Gideon Bobcock and
carried it to him...I put ahandle to a bake pann cover for Gideon
Babcock...Mended for William Browning...Made Spur Buckel for George
...

Caroline Hazard (ed.), Nailer Tom's Diary...The Journal of
Thomas B. Hazard, (Boston, Massachusetts:  The Merrymount Press,
1930), pp. 57-74.


52.   JOURNEYMEN CARPENTERS COMPLAIN AGAINST
MASTER CRAFTSMEN (1785)


The craft guild system, built upon a progression
of apprentice-journeyman-master craftsmen, did not thrive
in early America.  The labor force was widely dispersed
and the supply of workers almost always strained.  While
all three groups of actors in the system customarily
belonged to common organizations around social welfare
functions, in time a class interest drove journeymen and
master craftsman apart.  In the following document,
journeymen appeal to "employers," that is, businessmen
who supplied masters with work orders.  This represented
a step away from the traditional model.  In a few places,
craft interest had already led to creation of local unions
of journeymen.


A considerable Number of the principal Journeymen Carpenters
in this City, think it incumbent on them to lay before the impartial

Public, the following Impositions which the Masters have long
practiced.

The Master Carpenters have long made it a practice to employ
Journeymen, (so very ignorant of their business, that even some of
them have been at a loss to know the right end of their tools), upon
very low wages, while they charge the employer 12s. per day, the
wages only paid to good workmen, and from which they have 1s. 6d.
per day; for what reason?  Because their ignorant Journeymen are
taught by us, what the Masters ought to instruct them in.

About 12 of these Master Carpenters having agreed to reduce our
Wages to 9s. per day, but still charging the employer 10s. 6d. and
positively insist on having the above allowance made them, even
should the wages be reduced to 6s. per day, we not submit our case
to every candid Reader, who undoubtedly will justify our conduct in
putting a stop to such iniquitous practices; therefore, in order to
do justice to ourselves and the Public in general, we a select number of workmen, who know our Business, and are determined not to be
imposed upon, will engage to finish any piece of work that Gentlemen
may be pleased to employ us upon...sending orders to Mr. Aaron
Aarson's...The Journeymen Carpenters.

N.B.    The Terms of Hire shall be made perfectly satisfactory,
at the low charge of Nine Shillings per Day, as we should sooner
receive our money from the Employer than from any of those Masters,
whose ungenerous conduct justly merits our contempt.

Independent Journal: or, the General Advertiser, September 21,
1785, Gottesmann (ed.), II, pp. 207-208.

### 53.  A MORAVIAN JOURNEYMAN CANNOT HAVE
"AMERICAN FREEDOM" (1785)

Living and working in a close-knit religious
community, the Moravians of North Carolina held fast
to their Central European traditions.  In America,
however, the shortage of labor and the ease of escape to
alternative employments put a strain on the formal controls
of the apprenticeship-journeyman-master hierarchy.  In
the end, "American freedom" had its way.

It was noted that for some time various persons have begun to
oppose man-made rules, calling for American freedom.  Such remarks
show a great lack of understanding, for in the so-called free lands
as well as in others there must be proper submission to authority,
without which no human society can endure.  For example, a journeyman must act in all things according to the instructions of the
master-workman in the shop.  If anyone claims the above mentioned
"freedom" against the rules of the town, he thereby proves that it
would be better for him to live elsewhere.

A desire to shoot is increasing among us.  If a master deliberately gives his journeyman time off for hunting he is doing him
a real injury, for we have seen that gradually a man grows eager for
hunting and neglects his regular work, and it is difficult to bring
him back to orderly ways.  Masters must not put muskets into the
hands of their boys, nor go hunting with them, because of evil results.

Minutes of Salem Board, Congregation Council, August 4, 1785,
Adelaid L. Fries (ed.), Records of the Moravians in North Carolina,
V, (Raleigh, North Carolina:  The North Carolina Historical
Commission, 1941), p. 2097.

## 54.  THE LABOR ECONOMICS OF A NAILERY (1787)

A detailed and comprehensive analysis of the nail
business is here narrated by William Blount, writing from
Philadelphia.  The Blounts were very unusual merchants in
that they did not restrict themselves to trade.  For another
operation of a nailery, see Jefferson's account, Source Nos.
36 and 68.

On my way I called at Morris's [Robert Morris] Work at Trenton
where it appears to me that Nail Rod enough is or might be Slit to
supply all Christemdom with Nails, I also looked at his Nail factory
and of all Works that I have seen I have seen none more easily done
nor none so proper for the employment of Negroes because they may
always be kept at the same spot and at the same Work and there's no
rainey days & they may be [tasked] and I conceive one Week is quite
long enough for any person black or white to learn to make a good
Nail; to be sure he will not by this Time learn to make many in a
day but he will improve every day untill he does become prfect--
Since I have been here I have been making some Inquiry about this
Nail Making Business and I find Nail Rod will cost of Haselhurst who
has the disposing of that made at Morris's Works £33. per Ton that
is for 2240 lb Pennsylvania Currency--Stewart and Barr yesterday
agreed with a Nailer for three Casks of 10$^d$. [Penny] 3 d$^o$. 20$^d$. & 3
ditto 30$^d$. Nails at the average price of 9$^d$. per lb Penn$^a$.  Money
to be paid down on the delivery of the Nails--These Nails are for
Carolina but for whom I dont Know. they say that a Nailer will make
every day that is one day with another 12lb 10$^d$. 16 lb 20$^d$ and 18
to [of] 30$^d$. Nails--those of a less size they do not know how many
is a days Task but I shall inquire--From other Inquires which I have
made I believe more can be done in such large Nails than is mentioned by them but for the present I wish you would callulate
[calculate] on the above price of Iron and Nails and the average
quantity a a Hand can make of these large Nails per day which 15 1/3
lb and see if it will not be very advantageous Work to employ your

Man Pollypus and my man Will and such other ingenious young Negroes
as we can at it--I think it will give to each Hand at least 6/ ready
Mony per day--you are to observe that four Hands can work at each
forge at least two, the Bellows is very small with two handles one
on each side and the Nailers blow for themselves, each Anvil is very
small not above 25 lb weight. these two articles with the addition
of a small Hammer and a Key to head the Nails are all the Tools
necessary in this Business--I have told you a Week is sufficient to
learn a Negroe to make Nails & and thus it has appeared to me and I
am told by a Number of well informed people from the State of
Massachusetts where they punish small offences against the Public by
exacting from the Offenders Labour, that the Labour those Offenders
generally are employed in is that of making Nails and that they
generally make good nails in a Week and from that to a Month altho'
they might never have had a Hammar in hand before--a Nailer I suppose
might easily be had here if wanted by the year but at what price I
can form no Opinion--I think this Business would be better for my
boys to learn than the Trade of a Copper as you Know I some Time
past mentioned--And if a Nailer was employed some white Apprentices
I should suppose as many as we would take might by got bound to it
for seven years or more as their age might chance to be by the
Court--You will observe the Seting this Business in motion will cost
very little, the Tools I have mentioned, the Iron will cost you but
very little more than it does here 1, 2 or 3 Tons will do to begin
with and if you should determine to go largely into the Business a
Credit say of 3 Months may be obtained on all the Nail Rod we shall
want.--Think of this Business and let me know the Result--You may
count on calling will from Hendricks when you please and two of my
other Boys Sam & Watt or Sam and Will--And if the Business should
prove beneficial and as Nails will be ready Mony [many] other Boys
could be bought about 15 or 16 Years of age at from 40 to £50.

Letter, William Blount to J. G. Blount, August 9, 1787, Keith
(ed.), Blount Papers, I, pp. 331-332.


          55.   DOES A SCARCITY OF HANDS PRESENTLY
                RETARD MANUFACTURES?  (1791)


        One of the greatest obstacles in the way of accept-
ing manufactures was the fear that factories would draw
off labor from agriculture.  In a nation of farmers, this
was a formidable fear.  More important, it was a realistic
fear.  Advocates of manufacture were bound to try to allay
it.  This response was written by Alexander Hamilton.


With regard to scarcity of hands, the fact itself must be
applied with no small qualification to certain parts of the United
States.  There are large districts which may be considered as pretty

fully peopled; and which, notwithstanding a continual drain for distant settlement, are thickly interspersed with flourishing and increasing towns.  If these districts have not already reached the
point at which the complaint of scarcity of hands ceases, they are
not remote from it, and are approaching fast towards it; and having,
perhaps, fewer attractions to agriculture than some other parts of
the Union, they exhibit a proportionably stronger tendency towards
other kinds of industry.  In these districts may be discerned no
inconsiderable maturity for manufacturing establishments.

But there are circumstances, which have been already noticed,
with another view, that materially diminish, every where, the effect
of a scarcity of hands.  These circumstances are, the great use
which can be made of women and children, on which point a very pregnant and instructive fact has been mentioned--the vast extension
given by late improvements to the employment of machines--which,
substituting the agency of fire and water, has prodigiously lessened
the necessity for manual labor; the employment of persons ordinarily
engaged in other occupations, during the seasons or hours of leisure,
which, besides giving occasion to the exertion of a greater quantity
of labor, by the same number of persons, and thereby increasing the
general stock of labor, as has been elsewhere remarked, may also be
taken into the calculation, as a resource for obviating the scarcity
of hands; lastly, the attraction of foreign emigrants.  Whoever in-
spects, with a careful eye, the composition of our towns, will be
made sensible to what an extent this resource may be relied upon.
This exhibits a large proportion of ingenious and valuable workmen,
in different arts and trades, who, by expatriating from Europe, have
improved their own condition, and added to the industry and wealth
of the United States.  It is a natural inference, from the experience
we have already had, that, as soon as the United States shall present
the countenance of a serious prosecution of manufactures; as soon as
foreign artists shall be made sensible that the state of things here
affords a moral certainty of employment and encouragement; competent
numbers of European workmen will transplant themselves, effectually
to insure the success of the design.  How, indeed, can it other wise
happen, considering the various and powerful inducements which the
situation of this country offers--addressing themselves to so many
strong passions and feelings, to so many general and particular
interests.

It may be affirmed, therefore, in respect to hands for carrying
on manufactures, that we shall, in a great measure, trade upon a
foreign stock, reserving our own for the cultivation of our lands and
the manning of our ships, as far as character and circumstances shall
incline.  It is not unworthy of remark, that the objection to the
success of manufactures, deduced from the scarcity of hands, is alike
applicable to trade and navigation, and yet these are perceived to
flourish, without any sensible impediment from that cause.


Report on Manufactures (1791), J. C. Hamilton (ed.), Works of
Alexander Hamilton, III, pp. 219-221.

# E.

---

# CONSTRICTED
# MANUFACTURING
# DEVELOPMENT

---

### 56. MANUFACTURES ARE FOUNDED IN POVERTY (1760)

England being at war with France, and with victory
very much in prospect, interest centered on whether
England should take Canada or Guadaloupe from France.
Franklin advised taking Canada; one reason being that
Canada had much unoccupied land and could thus afford
an expanding population sufficient room so as not to
drive people into manufactures.  The example of England
was compelling to Franklin and his contemporaries.  There,
the landless were supplying much of the labor force of
the industrial revolution.  In colonial America, there
could hardly have been said to be a shortage of labor for
industry as factories were rare.

A people, spread through the whole tract of country, on this
side of the Mississippi, and secured by Canada in our hands, would
probably for some centuries find employment in agriculture, and
thereby free us at home effectually from our fears of American manufactures.  Unprejudiced men well know, that all the penal and prohibitory laws that were ever thought on will not be sufficient to
prevent manufactures in a country, whose inhabitants surpass the
number that can subsist by the husbandry of it.  That this will be
the case in America soon, if our people remain confined within the
mountains, and almost as soon should it be unsafe for them to live
beyond, though the country be ceded to us, no man acquainted with
political and commercial history can doubt.  Manufactures are
founded in poverty.  It is the multitude of poor without land in a
country, and who must work for others at low wages or starve, that
enables undertakers to carry on a manufacture, and afford it cheap

enough to prevent the importation of the same kind from abroad, and to bear the expense of its own exportation.

But no man, who can have a piece of land of his own, sufficient by his labor to subsist his family in plenty, is poor enough to be a manufacturer, and work for a master. Hence, while there is land enough in America for our people, there can never be manufactures to any amount or value.

The Interest of Great Britain Considered With Regard to Her Colonies, (1760) in Jared Sparks (ed.), The Works of Benjamin Franklin, IV, (Boston, Massachusetts:  Charles Tappan, 1844), p. 19.

### 57.   AMERICAN MANUFACTURES IN 1768

This barren picture of American manufactures is comprehensible on the assumption that only factory and mill production was reported.  The letter is written to William Franklin, Benjamin's son who was the royal Governor of New Jersey colony.

Mr. Grenville complained in the House [of Commons] that the governors of New Jersey, New Hampshire, East and West Florida, had none of them obeyed the orders sent them, to give an account of the manufactures carried on in their respective provinces.  Upon hearing this, I went after the House was up, and got a sight of the reports made by the other governors.  They are all much in the same strain, that there are no manufactures of any consequence; in Massachusetts a little coarse woollen only, made in families for their own wear; glass and linen have been tried and failed.  Rhode Island, Connecticut and New York much the same.  Pennsylvania has tried a linen manufactory, but it is dropped, it being imported cheaper; there is a glasshouse in Lancaster county, but it makes only a little coarse ware for the country neighbours.  Maryland is clothed all with English manufactures.  Virginia the same, except that in their families they spin a little cotton of their own growing.  South Carolina and Georgia none.  All speak of the dearness of labor, that makes manufactures impracticable.  Only the governor of North Carolina parades with a large manufacture in his country, that may be useful to Britain, of pine boards; they having fifty sawmills on one river.  These accounts are very satisfactory here....

Letter, Benjamin Franklin to William Franklin, March 13, 1768, Sparks (ed.), The Works of Benjamin Franklin, VII, p. 393.

58.  PROBLEMS OF THE SPERMACETI TRUST (1769)


Spermaceti candles were made from the head matter of
whales.  Four colonial centers of this manufacture were
Newport and Providence, Rhode Island, Boston, Massachusetts,
and New York, New York.  The loose form of pool was designed
to exercise monopoly control over the spermaceti industry.
The pool, however, was highly unstable, as the following
complaint made by Jacob Rodriguez Rivera, a Newport, Rhode
Island merchant, makes clear.  The Brown firm involved was
a shipping and banking firm based in Providence, Rhode
Island.


It is the Dartmouth manufacture, those of Mr. Jenks & Co. and
Mr. [George] Rome that prove distructive to this branch [controlling
the price of head matter], and which we aught by all means to unite
if posible.  This, I imagine, will be no dificult task, if they are
modest in their claims of a proportion.  Their own intrest, in my
opinion, must make them ready to unite, as the effects of last year
must furnish them a specimen of what they have to expect if we are
all let loose [to compete with each other], and, to obtain this, I
think there is no great necessity of a circular letter, for if you
approve of this method, as we all here doe, Mr. Slocum will undertake to treat with the Dartmouth manufacture.  You can sound [out]
and secure the new manufacture at Providence (which I am informed
by Mr. I.[saac] Hart they signifyd to him their readiness to unite
when he was up there).  And I will undertake Mr. Rome, and as soon
as the sentements of the whole can be known, a meeting, when you may
think proper, will be necessary to close the matter.
I have communicated your letter to all the United Company here,
and they are all nearly of my opinion, and should you also be of the
same, please to let us know, and at the same time give us whatever
you may judge nessisary.  Should the Bostonians refuse comming into
our measures, I think it highly nessisary that every member of our
United Company should be desbard [disbarred] by our articles from
purchasing any head matter at Boston.


Letter, Jacob Rodriguez Rivera to Messrs. Nicholas Brown & Co.,
February 7, 1769, Jacob R. Marcus (ed.), American Jewry.  Documents.
Eighteenth Century, (Cincinnati, Ohio:  The Hebrew Union College
Press, 1959), p. 396.


59.  ENGLISH COMMERCE REQUIRES AMERICA (1780)


In this document England is reminded by Joseph Galloway
that the American colonies, now in revolt, are an economic
necessity for British trade.  Galloway, who had been elected

speaker of the Pennsylvania colonial assembly from 1766 to
1775, became an active Tory in the Revolution and suffered
a confiscation of his estates.    In 1778, he fled to England
where he became a British pensioner.


When America shall have a separate and distinct interest of her
own to pursue, her views will be enlarged, her policy will be exerted
to her own benefit, and her interest, instead of being united with,
will become not only different from, but opposite to, that of Great
Britain.    She will readily perceive, that manufactures are the great
foundation of commerce, that commerce is the great means of acquiring
wealth, and that wealth is necessary to her own safety.    With these
interesting prospects before her, it is impossible to conceive that
she will not exert her capacity to promote manufactures and commerce.
She will see it to be clearly her interest, not only to manufacture
for herself, but others.    Laws will be made, granting bounties to
encourage it, and duties will be laid to discourage or prohibit
foreign importations.    By these measures her manufactures will increase, her commerce will be extended, and, feeling the benefits of
them as they rise, her industry will be exerted, until she not only
shall supply her own wants, but those of Great Britain itself, with
all the manufactures made with her own materials.    Nor will this
reasoning appear to be merely conjectural, to those who will consider
the roving and fluctuating nature of Commerce. . . .If she [Great
Britain] should give up her dominion over America, her commerce, in
a little time, must perish; should she retain America, nothing can
deprive her of it. . . .Yet should she [America] again be united
with us in the same common interest and policy, the task will not be
difficult to induce her to pursue, what is most profitable to herself, the cultivation of the earth, and the raising raw materials
of Great Britain, for ages to come.


Joseph Galloway, Cool Thoughts on the Consequences to Great
Britain of American Independence, (London:    J. Sillkie, 1780),
pp. 52-54.



## 60.    A LARGE AMERICAN TANNERY (1784)


This "extensive" tannery was located in Elizabethtown,
New Jersey.    Tanning, based primarily on hand labor in small
shops, was one of the leading manufactures in post-
Revolutionary America.


It was one of the most extensive tanneries then in the United
States.    It would contain 1500 hides, if every vat was filled.    The
average time for completing the tanning of the stock was over twelve
months.    The tannery was entirely upon the old plan, without a single

modern improvement, except that the lime vats and water pools were
let off by plugs at the bottom into the adjoining brook.  The vats
were upon a hill, not on underground conductors, and were both
filled and emptied by a wooden bucket with a long handle, so as to
make a dipper.  The bark was ground by two horses.  There was a curb
of 12 or 15 feet in diameter, made of three inch plank, with a rim
15 inches high round the outside; a stone wheel and also a wooden
wheel, of even height, when placed on edge, say 5 1/2 feet high, and
8 to 10 inches thick.  The stone was cut into "bears mouth," five
inches from center to center of each.  The wooden wheel had round
iron pins inserted.  The bark was ground by these wheels rolling
over it, and one-fourth of a cord of bark was a "flooring."  Two
floorings were a fair day's work.


    Memoirs of Col. William Edwards, (Washington, D.C., 1897),
pp. 17-18.


61.  WESTERN EXPANSION BENEFITS EUROPEAN INDUSTRY (1784)


    The right of Americans to ship farm goods down the
Mississippi and to utilize New Orleans as a point of deposit
were matters of basic American economic interest.  Madison
hoped to round up European support for American trading
rights on the Mississippi by forswearing industrial competition with these same European powers.  Madison sat in the
Virginia House of Delegates from Orange County.  Jefferson
had recently gone to France to assist Benjamin Franklin and
John Adams negotiate a commercial treaty with that country.


The settlement of the Western country which will much depend
on the free use of the Mississippi, will be beneficial to all nations
who either directly or indirectly trade with the U.S.  By a free expansion of our people the establishment of internal manufactures will
not only be long delayed but the consumption of foreign manufactures
long continue increasing; and at the same time all the productions
of the American soil required by Europe in return for her manufactures, will proportionably increase.  The vacant land of the United
States lying on the waters of the Mississippi is perhaps equal in
extent to the land actually settled.  If no check be given to emi-
grations from the latter to the former, they will probably keep pace
at least with the increase of our people, till the population of both
becomes nearly equal.  For twenty or twenty-five years we shall
consequently have as few internal manufactures in proportion to our
numbers as at present and at the end of that period our imported

manufactures will be doubled.  It may be observed too, that as the
market for these manufactures will first increase and the provision
for supplying it will follow the price of supplies will naturally
rise in favor of those who manufacture them.  On the other hand as
the demand for the tobacco indigo rice corn &c produced by America
for exportation will neither precede nor keep pace with their increase the price must naturally sink in favor also of those who
consume them.  Reverse the case by supposing the use of the Mississippi denied to us and the consequence is that many of our supernumerary hands who in the former case would be husbandmen on the
waters of the Mississippi, will on the latter supposition be manufacturers on those of the Atlantic and even those who may not be
discouraged from seating the vacant lands will be obliged by the
want of vent for the produce of the soil and of the means of purchasing foreign manufactures to manufacture in a great measure for
themselves.


    Letter, James Madison to Thomas Jefferson, August 20, 1784,
The Papers of James Madison, Vol. 5, Library of Congress.



        62.  "LET OUR WORK-SHOPS REMAIN IN EUROPE" (1783)


        Like Franklin in 1760, Jefferson saw the availa-
    bility of land as a bar on the progress of manufacture.
    (See Source No. 59).  Jefferson added a positive distaste
    for the social aspects of manufacturing.  A quarter-century
    later, however, Jefferson accepted manufacture.  (See
    Source No. 70).  This was Jefferson's answer to Query XIX
    during one of the rare intervals of this period when he
    held no public office.


    We never had an interior trade of any importance.  Our exterior
commerce has suffered very much from the beginning of the present
contest.  During this time we have manufactured within our families
the most necessary articles of clothing.  Those of cotton will bear
some comparison with the same kinds of manufacture in Europe; but
those of wool, flax, and hemp are very coarse, unsightly, and unpleasant:  and such is our attachment to agriculture, and such our
preference for foreign manufactures, that be it wise or unwise, our
people will certainly return as soon as they can, to the raising
raw materials, and exchanging them for finer manufactures than they
are able to execute themselves.
    The political economists of Europe have established it as a
principle that every state should endeavor to manufacture for itself:
and this principle, like many others, we transfer to America,

without calculating the difference of circumstance which should often
produce a difference of result.   In Europe the lands either are
cultivated, or locked up against the cultivator. . .Manufacture
must therefore be resorted to of necessity not of choice, to support
the surplus of their people.   But we have an immensity of land
courting the industry of the husbandman.   Is it best then that all
our citizens should be employed in its improvement, or that one half
should be called off from that to exercise manufactures and handi-
craft arts for the other?   Those who labor in the earth are the
chosen people of God, if ever he had a chosen people, whose breasts
he has made his peculiar deposit for substantial and genuine virtue.
It is the focus in which he keeps alive that sacred fire, which
otherwise might escape from the face of the earth.   Corruption of
morals in the mass of cultivators is a phaenomenon of which no age
nor nation has furnished an example.   It is the mark set on those,
who not looking up to heaven, to their own soil and industry, as
does the husbandman, for their subsistence, depend for it on casual-
ties and caprice of customers.   Dependance begets subservience and
venality, suffocates the germ of virtue, and prepares fit tools for
the designs of ambition.   This, the natural progress and consequence
of the arts, has sometimes perhaps been retarded by accidental circumstances:  but, generally speaking, the proportion which the aggregate of the other classes of citizens bears in any state to that of
its husbandmen, is the proportion of its unsound to its healthy parts
and is a good enough barometer whereby to measure its degree of
corruption.   While we have land to labor then, let us never wish to
see our citizens occupied at a work-bench, or twirling a distaff.
Carpenters, masons, smiths, are wanting in husbandry:  but, for the
general operations of manufacture, let [our] work-shops remain in
Europe.   It is better to carry provisions and materials to work men
there, than bring them to the provisions and materials, and with them
their manners and principles.   The loss by the transportation of
commodities across the Atlantic will be made up in happiness and
permanence of government.   The mobs of great cities add just so much
to the support of pure government, as sores do to the strength of
the human body.   It is the manners and spirit of a people which preserve a republic in vigor.   A degeneracy in these is a canker which
soon eats to the heart of its laws and constitution.

Thomas Jefferson, <u>Notes on the State of Virginia</u>, (Trenton,
New Jersey:  Wilson and Blackwell, 1803), pp. 223-225.


63.   A FRENCH INVENTION OF INTERCHANGEABLE PARTS (1786)

Jefferson was reporting on the work of H. Blanc
who described his innovation four years later in
<u>Memoire Important sur la fabrication des armes de
guerre, a l'assembl'e Nationale</u>, published in Paris.
No conclusive evidence is known which would prove

that American contemporaries were aware of Blanc's
work in arms manufacture.

At this time Jefferson was American Ambassador to
France and Henry was governor of Virginia.  (In an earlier
letter, dated August 30th, 1785 and addressed to John Jay,
Jefferson used the word "interchangeable" and thus went to
the heart of the matter.)

An improvement is made here [France] in the construction of the
musket, which may be worthy of attention.  It consists in making
every part of them so exactly alike, that every part of any one may
be used for the same part in any other musket made by the same hand.
The government here has examined and approved the method, and is establishing a large manufactory for the purpose.  As yet the inventor
has only completed the lock of the musket on this plan.  He will proceed immediately to have the barrel, stock and their parts executed
in the same way.  I visited the workman.  He presented me the parts
of 50 locks taken to pieces and arranged in compartments.  I put
several together myself, taking the pieces at hazard as they came to
hand, and found them fit interchangeably in the most perfect manner.
The tools by which he effects this have, at the same time, so
abridged the labour that he thinks he shall be able to furnish the
musket two livres cheaper than the King's price.  But it will be two
or three years before he will be able to furnish any quantity.

Letter, Thomas Jefferson to Patrick Henry, January 24, 1786,
The Papers of Thomas Jefferson, Vol. 24, Library of Congress.

### 64.  "MANUFACTURES WILL COME OF THEMSELVES" (1787)

Basic to a deprecatory attitude toward high
tariffs was either a lack of interest in hurrying
industrial development or an oversanguine dependence
on foreign suppliers.  Madison represented both sentiments.  (See Source Nos. 61 and 148).  He had recently
attended the Annapolis Convention to revise the Articles
of Confederation, and in three weeks was to take a seat
in Congress; Pendleton, a Revolutionary leader, was
serving as president of the Virginia supreme court of
appeals.

There is a rage at present for high duties, partly for the purpose of revenue, partly of forcing manufactures, which it is difficult to resist.  It seems to be forgotten in the first case that in
the arithmetic of the customs as Dean Swift observes 2 & 2 do not
make four; and in the second that manufactures will come of themselves when we are ripe for them.  A prevailing argument among others

on the subject is that we ought not to be dependent on foreign
nations for useful articles, as the event of a war may cut off all
external supplies.  This argument certainly loses its force when it
is considered that in case of a war hereafter, we should stand on a
very different ground from what we lately did.  Neutral Nations,
whose rights are becoming every day more & more extensive, would not
now suffer themselves to be shut out from our ports, nor would the
hostile Nation presume to attempt it.  As far as relates to implements of war which are contraband, the argument for our fabrication
of them is certainly good.

Letter, James Madison to Edmund Pendleton, January 9, 1787,
The Papers of James Madison, Vol. 6, Library of Congress.


65.  AMERICAN MANUFACTURES ARE PROGRESSING (1789)

Given a general shortage of farm labor, the rise
of even small-scale manufactures posed a potential threat
of aggravating the shortage.  Thus, farmers regarded
factories and mills as competitors for a fixed labor supply.
Friends of American manufacturers insisted that industrial
progress would not diminish the supply of farm labor, as can
be seen in the following extract from a letter from George
Washington to Marquis de LaFayette.  LaFayette, who had
served the American Revolution, continued to be a friend
of the United States as he intervened often in French councils on behalf of the new nation.  Washington was preparing
to become, two months hence, the first president of the
United States under the Federal Constitution.


Though I would not force the introduction of manufactures, by
extravagant encouragements, and to the prejudice of agriculture, yet,
I conceive, much might be done in that way by women, children, and
others; without taking one really necessary hand from tilling the
earth.  Certain it is, great savings are already made in many articles of apparel, furniture, and consumption.  Equally certain it
is, that no diminution in agriculture has taken place, at the time
when greater and more substantial improvements in manufactures were
making, than were ever before known in America.  In Pennsylvania
they have attended particularly to the fabrication of cotton cloths,
hats, and all articles in leather.  In Massachusetts, they are establishing factories of duck, cordage, glass and several other
extensive and useful branches.  The number of shoes made in one
town, and nails in another is incredible.  In that State and
Connecticut are also factories of superfine and other broad cloths.
I have been writing to our friend General Knox this day, to procure
me for myself.  I hope it will not be a great while, before it will
be unfashionable for a gentleman to appear in any other dress.

Indeed we have already been too long subject to British prejudices.
I use no porter or cheese in my family, but such as is made in
America.  Both those articles may now be purchased of an excellent
quality.

    While you are quarrelling among yourselves in Europe -- while
one king is running mad -- and others acting as if they were
already so, by cutting the throats of the subjects of their neighbors.  I think you need not doubt, my dear Marquis, we shall continue
in tranquillity here -- and that population will be progressive so
long as there shall continue to be so many easy means for obtaining
a subsistence, and so ample a field for the exertion of talents and
industry.


    Letter, George Washington to the Marquis de LaFayette,
January 29, 1789, The Papers of George Washington, Library of
Congress.


66.   THE FELONIOUS EXPORT OF BRITISH TEXTILE MACHINERY (1791)


        The laws of Great Britain forbade the exportation
of textile machinery or even technical knowledge about
industrial processes that were used in British enterprises.  One way to evade these prohibitions was to aid
a British technician to emigrate, with or without the
machine, a move which was a felony under British law.
Here, President Washington wishes the governor of Virginia
well in his efforts to ensure such an outcome in a given
case while refusing, for reasons of state, to do as much
himself.  The governor was Beverly Randolph.


    I have attentively considered the request, which your Excellency
has made by desire of the legislature, that I would again open the
business of establishing a woollen manufactory in Virginia -- and it
is with infinite regret that I must decline any further agency in it,
at least so far as relates to carrying on a correspondence with the
person in Great Britain, who has proposed to establish the manufactory.  I am persuaded, that your Excellency and the Legislature will
see upon reelection, the impropriety of my appearing in this business, while I remain in my present situation; for I am told that it
is a felony to export the machines, which it is probable the artist
contemplates to bring with him, and it certainly would not carry an
aspect very favorable to the dignity of the United States for the
President in a clandestine manner to entice the subjects of another
nation to violate its laws.
    I have communicated the subject of your Excellency's letter to
the Secretary of State and the Attorney-General, who are both of the
same sentiment which I have expressed, and for the reason mentioned.

I am, however, happy that my agency is not <u>absolutely</u> <u>necessary</u>
to the completion of this object; for the project has been announced
to Virginia and the original letter from the artist has been trans-
mitted to your Excellency.  This communicates every thing on the
subject of which I am possessed, and leaves it with the State of
Virginia to do whatever may be thought best in the affair.

Impressed as I am with the utility of such an establishment, I
shall ever be ready to give it every aid that I can with propriety;
and I am certain that your Excellency and the Legislature will impute my conduct on this occasion to its true motive.

Letter, George Washington to Beverly Randolph, January 13,
1791, The Papers of George Washington, Library of Congress.

## 67.  THE IRON INDUSTRY IN 1791

In 1791, Treasury Secretary Alexander Hamilton sent
to Congress his Report on Manufactures, "the charter of
American industrialism."  It surveyed the progress of
industry and urged federal encouragement and assistance.
He defended manufactures as a boon to farming and claimed
industry would constitute a solid market for farm goods.
Here are the sections of the Report that deal with the
iron industry.  How modestly the iron industry had progressed is evident from the sparsity of hard facts in
Hamilton's discussion.

Iron-works have greatly increased in the United States, and
are prosecuted with much more advantage than formerly.  The average
price, before the Revolution, was about sixty-four dollars per ton;
at present, it is about eighty -- a rise which is chiefly to be
attributed to the increase of manufactures of the material.

The still further extension and multiplication of such manufactures will have the double effect of promoting the extraction of
the metal itself, and of converting it to a greater number of profitable purposes.

Those manufactures, too, unite, in a greater degree than almost
any others, the several requisites which have been mentioned as
proper to be consulted in the selection of objects.
. . . . . . . . . . . . . . . . . . . . . . . . . . . . . . . . . . .
Steel is a branch which has already made a considerable progress, and it is ascertained that some new enterprises, on a more
extensive scale, have been lately set on foot.  The facility of
carrying it to an extent which will supply all internal demands, and
furnish a considerable surplus for exportation, cannot be doubted.
. . . . . . . . . . . . . . . . . . . . . . . . . . . . . . . . . . .
The United States already, in a great measure, supply themselves with nails and spikes.  They are able, and ought certainly

to do it, entirely.  The first and most laborious operation, in this
manufacture, is performed by water-mills; and of the persons afterwards employed, a great proportion are boys, whose early habits of
industry are of importance to the community, to the present support
of their families, and to their own future comfort.  It is not less
curious than true, that, in certain parts of the country, the making
of nails is an occasional family manufacture.

. . . . . . . . . . . . . . . . . . . . . . . . . . . . . . . . . . . . . .

The manufacture of these articles, like that of some others,
suffers from the carelessness and dishonesty of a part of those who
carry it on.  An inspection in certain cases might tend to correct
the evil.  It will deserve consideration whether a regulation of this
sort cannot be applied, without inconvenience, to the exportation of
the articles, either to foreign countries, or from one State to
another.

The implements of husbandry are made in several States in great
abundance.  In many places, it is done by the common blacksmiths.
And there is no doubt that an ample supply for the whole country
can, with great ease, be procured among ourselves.

Various kinds of edged tools for the use of mechanics are also
made; and a considerable quantity of hollow wares, though the business of castings has not yet attained the perfection which might be
wished.  It is, however, improving, and as there are respectable
capitals, in good hands, embarked in the prosecution of those
branches of iron manufactories, which are yet in their infancy,
they may all be contemplated as objects not difficult to be acquired.

Report On Manufactures (1791), J. C. Hamilton (ed.), Works of
Alexander Hamilton, III, pp. 260-261.


68.   NAIL-MAKING AS A RURAL BY-INDUSTRY (1795)

Having retired as Secretary of State, Jefferson
now became a nail-maker.  (See Source No. 36).  He
writes here to Jean Nicholas Demeunier who was the
editor of Encyclopedie Methodique to which Jefferson
contributed.


In our private pursuits it is a great advantage that every
honest employment is deemed honorable.  I am myself a nail-maker.
On returning home, after an absence of ten years, I found my farms
so much deranged, that I saw evidently they would be a burden to me
instead of a support till I could regenerate them; and consequently
that it was necessary for me to find some other resource in the
mean time.  I thought for a while of taking up the manufacture of
pot-ash, which requires but small advances of money.  I concluded
at length however to begin a manufacture of nails, which needs little
or no capital, & I now employ a dozen little boys from 10. to 16.

years of age, overlooking all the details of their business myself
and drawing from it a profit on which I can get along till I can
put my farms into a course of yielding profit.  My new trade of
nail-making is to me in this country what an additional title of
nobility or the ensigns of a new order are in Europe.


Letter, Thomas Jefferson to Jean Nicholas Demeunier, April 29,
1795, The Papers of Thomas Jefferson, Vol. 98, Library of Congress.


### 69.  ELI WHITNEY'S GUN MANUFACTORY (1801)


Fifteen years had passed since Jefferson observed
Blanc's efforts in France to manufacture arms by interchangeable parts.  Whitney was far from solving the
problem, as Jefferson reported below, writing to James
Monroe, governor of Virginia.


The bearer hereof is Mr. Whitney of Connecticut a mechanic of
the first order of ingenuity, who invented the cotton gin now so
much used to the South; he is at the head of a considerable gun
manufactory in Connecticut, and furnishes the U.S. with muskets,
undoubtedly the best they receive.  He has invented moulds and
machines for making all the pieces of his locks so exactly equal,
that take 100 locks to pieces and mingle their parts and the hundred
locks may be put together as well by taking the first pieces which
come to hand.  This is of importance in repairing, because out of
10 locks e.g. disabled for the want of different pieces, 9 good
locks may be put together without employing a smith.  Leblanc [i.e.,
Blanc] in France had invented a similar process in 1788 [1785] and
had extended it to the barrel, mounting & stock.  I endeavored to
get the U.S. to bring him over, which he was ready for on moderate
terms.  I failed and I do not know what became of him.  Mr. Whitney
has not yet extended his improvements beyond the lock.


Letter, Thomas Jefferson to James Monroe, November 14, 1801,
The Thomas Jefferson Papers, Vol. 117, Library of Congress.


### 70.  AMERICA MUST NOT BECOME A MERE AMSTERDAM (1809)


A striking statement of Jefferson's new acceptance
of manufactures as a legitimate and necessary part of
the national economy.  (By error, this change in view is
usually traced to an 1816 letter to Benjamin Austin.)

Political antagonism to the New England opponents of
his foreign policy led Jefferson the more quickly to
strike at these same men who controlled the cargo-carrying
trade.  His correspondents were Thomas Leiper who was a
prosperous merchant in Philadelphia who in 1809 built an
experimental horse-drawn railroad in that city; and
Benjamin Stoddert, a Georgetown, Maryland merchant who
had served as the first Secretary of the Navy, 1798-1801.


I have lately inculcated the encouragement of manufactures to
the extent of our own consumption at least, in all articles of which
we raise the raw material.  On this the federal [ist party] papers
and meetings have sounded the alarm of Chinese policy, destruction
of commerce, &c.; that is to say, the iron which we make must not be
wrought here into ploughs, axes, hoes, &c., in order that the ship
owner may have the profit of carrying it to Europe and bringing it
back in a manufactured form, as if after manufacturing our own raw
materials for our own use, there would not be a surplus produce
sufficient to employ a due proportion of navigation in carrying it
to market and exchanging it for those articles of which we have not
the raw material.  Yet this absurd hue and cry has contributed much
to federalize New England, their doctrine goes to the sacrificing
agriculture and manufactures to commerce; to the calling all our
people from the interior country to the seashore to turn merchants,
and to convert this great agricultural country into a city of
Amsterdam.  But I trust the good sense of our country will see that
its greatest prosperity depends on a due balance between agriculture, manufactures and commerce, and not in this protuberant navigation which has kept us in hot water from the commencement of our
government, and is now engaging us in war.
. . . . . . . . . . . . . . . . . . . . . . . . . . . . . . . . . .
The converting this great agricultural country into a city of
Amsterdam, a mere head-quarters for carrying on the commerce of all
nations with one another is too absurd.


Letters, Thomas Jefferson to Thomas Leiper and to Benjamin
Stoddert, January 21, 1809 and February 18, 1809, The Papers of
Thomas Jefferson, Vols. 185 and 186, Library of Congress.


## 71.  AMERICAN COTTON MANUFACTURE (1810)

Especially under stresses arising out of the War
of 1812 crisis, the American cotton industry grew
rapidly from 1810 to 1815.  The age of large-scale cotton
factories, however, had not yet arrived.  Tench Coxe writes.

This raw material, being the <u>only</u> <u>redundant</u> <u>one</u> adopted to the
manufacture of clothes for apparel and furniture, produced in the
United States, and being the most susceptible of labor-saving operations, the cotton branch will probably, nay certainly, become, <u>very</u>
<u>soon</u> the most considerable of our manufactures. . . .<u>Capitalists</u> <u>can</u>
<u>most</u> <u>easily</u> <u>extend</u> <u>themselves</u> <u>into</u> <u>the</u> <u>cotton</u> <u>manufacture</u>, <u>because</u>
<u>the</u> <u>raw</u> <u>material</u> <u>is</u> <u>abundant</u> <u>and</u> <u>capable</u> <u>of</u> <u>being</u> <u>conveniently</u> <u>and</u>
<u>promptly</u> <u>increased</u>. The United States have some palpable and great
advantages over their foreign rivals in the cotton branch. Those of
Europe depend upon foreign agriculture for the raw material, for the
indigo dye, and in a considerable degree for their bread stuff.
Those in the East Indies will not be allowed or be able to use labor-
saving machinery. Improvements in the loom, and in other things are
opposed by force in Europe. The expences, costs and charges of
transporting cotton, from the farms and plantations, even near the
coasts of the United States, to the manufactories of Manchester,
Glasgow, and Rouen, and the same charges upon manufactured goods
from Manchester, Glasgow and Rouen, to the houses of the planters and
farmers in America are equal to fifty per cent upon the European
costs of the finer, and seventy per cent on the coarse, heavy, and
bulky goods of those great manufacturing towns. Every person capable
of working in the manufactories of woollen, linen, hempen and silken
cloths, can become, in less than a week, a useful cotton manufacturer. The cotton branch, in the United States is the great resort
of all the unemployed cloth manufacturers, and there is here no em-
pediment to a person changing his trade or employment, or place of
business.

Tench Coxe, <u>A Statement of the Arts and Manufactures of the</u>
<u>United States of America for the Year 1810</u>, (Philadelphia,
Pennsylvania:  A. Cornman, 1814), pp. xxviii-xxix.


72.  MACHINES FOR HOUSEHOLD MANUFACTURE (1812)


Even before the outbreak of the War of 1812 household manufactures were expanding. Wartime shortages and
patriotic pressures combined to multiply the effort. Added
to the founding of several moderately-sized factories, all
this activity gave rise to an excessively optimistic expectation of post-war industrial capacities. In this extract
Jefferson writes to Thaddeus Kosciuszko who was a specialist
in military fortifications who had served with the American
revolutionary forces; presently he was organizing a war of
Polish independence against Russia.


Our manufacturers are now very nearly on a footing with those
of England. She has not a single improvement which we do not
possess, and many of them better adapted by ourselves to our ordinary

use.  We have reduced the large and expensive machinery for most
things to the compass of a private family; and every family of any
size is now getting machines on a small scale for their household
purposes.  Quoting myself as an example, and I am much behind many
others in this business, my household manufactures are just getting
into operation on the scale of a carding machine costing $60 only,
which may be worked by a girl of twelve years old, a spinning
machine, which may be made for $10, carrying 6 spindles for wool, to
be worked by a girl also, another which can be made for $25, carry-
ing 12 spindles for cotton, and a loom, with a flying shuttle,
weaving its twenty yards a day.  I need 2,000 yards of linen, cotton,
and woollen yearly, to clothe my family, which this machinery, costing $150 only, and worked by two women and two girls, will more than
furnish.  For fine goods there are numerous establishments at work
in the large cities, and many more daily growing up; and of Merinos
we have some thousands, and these multiplying fast.  We consider a
sheep for every person as sufficient for their woollen clothing, and
this state and all to the North have fully that, and those to the
South, and West will soon be up to it.  In other articles we are
equally advanced, so that nothing is more certain than that, come
peace when it will, we shall never again go to England for a shilling
where we have gone for a dollar's worth.  Instead of applying to her
manufacturers there, they must starve or come here to be employed.


Letter, Thomas Jefferson to General Thaddeus Kosciuszko,
June 28, 1812, The Papers of Thomas Jefferson, Vol. 196, Library
of Congress.


### 73.  "HINTS TO MANUFACTURERS" (1814)


In 1812, war broke out between the United States
and England, a chapter in the broader Napoleonic Wars
then raging in Europe.  When the flow of British goods
and credit stopped, American producers suddenly confronted
a competitor-free domestic market.
One of the fastest friends of American manufactures,
Hezekiah Niles, warned industrialists not to mistake the
war-boom as a permanent protection against better-quality
foreign goods.  One may doubt that this appeal had any
effect.
Niles, editor, publisher, printer, delivery man, and
janitor for Niles' Weekly Register, was a close friend of
Jefferson, Madison, and other leaders.


GENTLEMEN.--All of who have read the WEEKLY REGISTER are well
assured that the editor is your friend.  He is attached to your
interest, because he believes your prosperity is the interest of
his country; and he earnestly desires you may so conduct your several

businesses, that, when peace comes, your establishments may resist
the shock that <u>must</u> accompany the event, and triumph over domestic
prejudice and foreign influence.  I wish to see the great interests
of the United States thus classed--the agricultural, the manufacturing, and the commercial; as, in the advancement of your business
over the commercial,--while it shall enrich the nation at large--I
perceive the only certain means of rooting up a <u>British</u> feeling that
has disgraced us.  But to do this you must establish a character.
Your profits at present are exceedingly great--your works are more
productive than the mines of <u>Mexico</u>.  There is no objection to
this--if an article that you can afford to make for <u>one</u> dollar, will
bring <u>two</u> dollars in the market, I see no reason why you should not
have it--this is the nature and spirit of trade.  <u>But recollect that
these times will not last forever</u>--and lay up a foundation that shall
sustain you at a general peace.  I have feared that your eagerness
to make money was a little like the conduct of the farmer, who,
having a goose that laid a golden egg each day, would have grasped
the whole at once by killing the goose, by which he lost all.  From
personal observation and general remark, it appears that the character of many of your goods is depreciating, though others have and
deserve the highest praise.  The old <u>wholesome</u> recommendation, "it
is not quite so <u>nice</u> as the imported, but a great deal <u>better</u>," has
lost much of its former force.  If it be lost, your establishments
are ruined.  <u>I am satisfied</u>, that several of the most important
manufactories can produce a greater given quantity of goods for less
money in the United States than they can do in <u>England</u>, and that
many others may be carried on as cheaply.  Be content then with a
present business "better than coining"--get as much as you can for
your goods, but let them be of the <u>best quality</u>.--Then you may
<u>command</u> a preference over foreign manufactures; and if, with <u>this</u>
advantage, and the cost of freight, charges and duties on goods
imported, you cannot meet your great rival--you <u>ought</u> to quit the
business.  If you <u>deserve</u> the encouragement, the double duties may
be continued some time after peace (come when it will) for your
protection--but they will not be exacted of the people merely for
<u>your</u> profit; nor is it right they should be.  You must merit pro-
tection by reasonable demands for good commodities--if you act
otherwise, the law will not be re-enacted.
     These remarks appear (to me) of great importance; I hope that
those whom it may concerns will give them the due consideration.


<u>Niles' Weekly Register</u>, June 4, 1814, p. 217.

# F.

# IMPERIAL REGULATION

74. ROYAL INSTRUCTION TO ENFORCE THE WOOL ACT OF 1699

From the broad sweep and unconditional prohibition
in this law, one could easily judge the power of the wool
lobby in Parliament.

Whereas by an act passed in the 10th year of his late Majesty
King William the Third to Prevent the Exportation of Wool out of
the Kingdoms of Ireland and England into Foreign Parts and for the
Encouragement of Woolen Manufactures in the Kingdom of England, it
is amongst other things enacted that from and after the first day
of December, 1699, no wool, woolfells, shortlings, mortlings, wool
flocks, worsted, bay or woolen yarn, cloth, serge, bays, kerseys,
says, frizes, druggets, cloth serges, shalloons, or any other
drapery, stuffs, or woolen manufactures whatsoever made or mixed
with wool or wool flocks being of the product or manufacture of any
of the English plantations in America shall be laden or laid on
board in any ship or vessel in any place or ports within any of the
said English plantations upon any pretense whatsoever; as also that
no such wool or other of the said commodities being of the product
or manufacture of any of the said English plantations shall be
loaden [sic] on any horse, cart, or other carriage to the intent
and purpose to be exported, transported, carried, or conveyed out of
the said English plantations to any other of our plantations or to
any other place whatsoever upon the same and like pains, penalties,
and forfeitures, to and upon all the offender and offenders therin,
within all and every of our said English plantations respectively
as are provided and prescribed by the said act for the said offenses
committed within our kingdom of Ireland; you are to take effectual

care that the true intent and meaning therof as far forth as it
relates to you be duly put in execution.


Labaree (ed.), Royal Instructions to British Colonial Governors,
II, pp. 784-785.


75.  DISCOURAGE THE COLONIAL IRON MANUFACTURE (1717)


The British iron industry--as in the cases of hats and
textiles--opposed colonial manufacture but favored colonial
mining of iron ore.  In the former case, competition was
stilled; in the second, a cheap source of raw materials was
opened.  Three weeks before the following petition was submitted to the House of Commons another petition was submitted by British iron-finishing interests asking for parliamentary encouragement to the colonial iron industry.


A petition of iron-masters, ironmongers, cutlers, freeholders,
nailers, smiths, and artificers in the iron manufacture, living in
and about the town of Birmingham, in the county of Warwick, was
presented to the House, and read; setting forth, that, should there
be encouragement given to the making and manufacturing of iron in
any plantations belonging to his Majesty's dominions, it will certainly tend to the ruin of the iron-trade of this kingdom, which
employs great numbers of people:  the greatest consumption of our
iron manufacture is now sent abroad to the plantations; which, if
they have encouragement, will have no occasion for our assistance;
and the iron-works of this nation must be totally ruined, for want
of employment for the poor:  and praying such relief as the House
shall seem meet.


Leo F. Stock (ed.), Proceedings And Debates Of the British
Parliaments Respecting North America, III, (Washington, D.C.:
Carnegie Institution of Washington, 1930), p. 398.


76.  THE UNFAIR LOW COST OF PRODUCING HATS IN AMERICA (1731)


British hat-makers testify before a House of Commons
committee against colonial hat-makers.  The following year
Parliament acceded to the demands and passed the Hat Act.

Abraham Jaques, a hat-maker, said, that he was at Boston, in
New England, about a year and half since, and worked there with
a master hat-maker, who commonly finished forty beaver hats in a
week; and that four or five apprentices were employed in the trade,
besides journeymen; and that three of the apprentices came from
Jersey, and were bound only for two, three, or four, years; and
that there was 16 hat-makers in the place, and that most of them
kept four or five apprentices; and that the wages of making a hat
there is but I s. 3 d. English money, but, if made in England, 4 s.
6 d. or 5 s.
. . . . . . . . . . . . . . . . . . . . . . . . . . . . . . . . . .

Wm. Glover, hat-maker, said, that he keeps a publick-house,
where journeymen often resort to him, in order to get work in the
hat-making trade, he being one, that helps journeymen to work in
that business; and said, that they can scarce get work for a great
many of them, to get bread, to maintain their families; and apprehended, that the occasion of it was, from the want of such large
exportations, as formerly were, for hats, and not be reason of the
increase of the number of hat-makers.
. . . . . . . . . . . . . . . . . . . . . . . . . . . . . . . . . .

Ordered, that leave be given to bring in a bill, to prevent
the exportation of hats out of any of the colonies or plantations
in America, and to restrain the number of apprentices, taken by the
hat-makers in the said plantations, and for the better encouraging
the making of hats in Great Britain; and that Mr. Alderman Barnard
and Captain Vernon do prepare, and bring in, the same.
. . . . . . . . . . . . . . . . . . . . . . . . . . . . . . . . . .

Richard Turner, hat-maker, said, that he has often sold great
quantities of hats for exportation to the said plantations in
America; and that they were altogether formerly supplied with the
same from England; but that they are now chiefly from New York, and
New England; and has been informed, that ten thousand beavers hats
are yearly made there.


Stock (ed.), Proceedings And Debates Of The British Parliaments
Respecting North America, IV, pp. 146-147-145.


77.   THE PERNICIOUS LAND BANK OF MASSACHUSETTS (1740)


The land bank projected by John Colman in 1720
(see Source No. 100) was set up in 1740. Here is the
attack upon it as mounted in a petition to the House of
Commons.


A petition of the several merchants of London, and others,
whose names are thereunto subscribed, in behalf of themselves, and
great numbers of merchants, traders, and other inhabitants, in the
province of the Massachusetts Bay, in America, was presented to the

House [of Commons] and read; setting forth, that while his Majesty
and this House have exerted their authority and utmost care, not
only to prevent the increase of paper money in America, but even to
sink and discharge what has already issued under the publick authority, by virtue of acts of assemble there, John Coleman Esquire, and
a very great number of private persons, in the Massachusetts Bay,
his associates, have, without any authority, assumed a power to
erect themselves into a company or society there, by the name of the
land bank, and have chosen and appointed directors, treasurers, and
officers, to carry on the same under large yearly salaries, avowedly
for the purpose of issuing paper bills or notes, to a very large
amount, to be redeemable twenty years hence, or at some other remote distance of time; and have actually issued out their notes, and,
by their numbers and influence, endeavour to force a currency for
the same; and this, notwithstanding that the most considerable inhabitants in the Massachusetts Bay in due time opposed such scheme,
and petitioned the general assembly there to discountenance and
suppress that pernicious project; and notwithstanding that his
Majesty's governor, with the advice of the council there, by publick
proclamations, did discourage the same; so that, by means of the
said land bank, the quantity of paper money there is greatly increased, and many frauds, losses, and prejudices, are likely to ensue
to the petitioners have humbly petitioned his Majesty in Council, for
relief against the said Coleman's scheme, and the Lords of the
committee of his Majesty's most honourable Privy-Council, and the
Lords Commissioners for Trade and Plantations, to whom the petition
has been referred, have concurred in opinion, that that scheme was
of dangerous tendency, and fit to be suppressed as speedily and
effectually as possible, and have given all the orders that were
possible for them to give, that the governors should continue in
the meantime to discourage the said scheme.

   Stock (ed.), Proceedings And Debates Of The British Parliaments
Respecting North America, V, p. 97.


        78.   FREE ENTRY OF COLONIAL IRON WILL DEPRIVE
              BRITISH TANNERS OF BARK (1749)


      A crude input-output analysis!


      A petition of the tanners of leather in and about the town of
Sheffield, in the county of York, whose names are thereunto subscribed, was presented to the House [of Commons], and read; setting
forth, that many furnaces and forges for the making of iron from the
ore in pig, and from thence into bar, for supplying and accommodating the iron manufacture carried on in and about the said town, are
erected and employed; and that, for constantly providing the said

iron works with charcoal, many spring woods are preserved and continued with the neighbourhood thereof; and, for the convenience of
a supply of bark of oak (without which tanned leather cannot be
made) from the falls of such woods, the petitioners have settled
themselves in and about the said town; and have of late years
greatly improved and enlarged the said business and trade, to the
advantage of the kingdom, and the increase of his Majesty's revenue,
and alledging, that should the bill, now depending in the House,
for taking off the duty on pig and bar iron imported from his
Majesty's colonies in America into this kingdom, pass into a law,
the petitioners are apprehensive that it would give such encouragement to the making of bar iron in those colonies (plentifully and
cheaply supplied with wood and materials for that purpose) and to the
importing of it into this kingdom, that English iron could not be
afforded upon equal terms with the American iron; and that, if so,
the said forges, now in full use and employment, the petitioners
conceive; would in great measure be neglected and discontinued;
many spring woods, now preserved for the supply of such forges and
furnances with charcoal, would be cleared or holted, and the petitioners would thereby be deprived of a supply of oak bark sufficient
for the continuance of their trades, to the overthrow of that useful and valuable business, and to the ruin of the petitioners; and
that, should the said bill be confined to the taking off of the
duty on pig iron only, and a duty yet remain upon bar iron imported
from the said colonies, the petitioners cannot be apprehensive of
any such consequences as are to be feared from the present intent
of the bill; because the petitioners conceive, that though the number of furnaces for melting down iron ore should be lessened, a proportionable number of forges would be erected for making pig iron
into bar, as would still require all the charcoal the said county
could supply:  and therefore praying, that so much of the said bill,
as relates to the free importation of American iron in bar, may not
pass into a law; or that the petitioners may have such provision for
preservation of their trade, as the nature of their case requires,
and the House shall think meet.


    Stock (ed.), Proceedings And Debates Of The British Parliaments
Respecting North America, V, p. 391.


79.  "ON THE VERY CONSIDERABLE ILLEGAL TRADE
IN THIS PROVINCE" (1753)


    The expanse of the Atlantic Ocean debilitated the
trade laws of England.  So widespread was smuggling that
one could forgive a merchant for forgetting which was his
major gain--his formal profit or the increment from illicit trade.  Governor Glen presents a succinct catalogue of
trade law violations.

Governors are to do their utmost to enforce the observance
of the Laws, but I am affraid all they can do is very little; in
England indeed if the Laws of Trade are not punctually observ'd,
it must generally be owing to the negligence or connivance of
Officers, there being Cruizing Vessels to intercept the Smugglers
at Sea, Riding Officers to intercept the Goods on shore, Searchers,
Tide Waiters, Land Waiters, Officers to Watch in the Night, others
to tend in the day, and Officers kept on board all Vessels; But here
we have few or no Officers, and these I believe never attend either
the loading or unloading and Ship, and it is not possible they
should attend all, there are for example at present fifty nine Sail
of Vessels in this harbour, some loading others unloading at a dozen
of different Wharffs all along the Bay, a Street of half a mile in
length, how can this great Mass of business be transacted by a
Collector, a Naval Officer, & two Searchers w are all the Officers
that are in Charles Town We have two more Ports of Entry George
Town Winiyaw about 60 or 70 miles to the Northward, and Beaufort
Port Royal about as much to the Southward at each of which there is
a Collector only, all our Coast besides, extending about 150 Miles,
is entirely open, and full of Rivers, Creeks and Inlets, where
Vessels may unload at pleasure without great Risque of beong disturbed, in like manner they may load ennumerated Goods, or such as
are prohibited to be exported, and carry them to Foreign Ports,
besides as our Produce is bulky most Planters keep large decked
boats, to bring it to Market, from the distant Rivers and Plantations to one of the three Ports of Entry, these Boats are kept as
Coasters, but they are capable of performing foreign Voyages, and
are under no regulation of entering or Clearing at any Office.
    Some years ago I was assured that there was very little illegal
Trade carried on here, but I presume they have meant comparatively
with regard to some other Provinces, for I am now convinced and know
for certain that there is a very considerable illegal Trade in this
Province, injurious to the Fair Trader, highly hurtful to the King's
Revenue, and destructive to the Manufactures of Britain, & I see it
is a growing evil, but I can think of no Expedient so likely to prevent it, as a greater number of diligent Officers from England that
know their duty, and if Governors were full empowered, to dismiss
such as misbehave, connive at frauds, or are grossly negligent and
remiss, at least to suspend them, and appoint others, till directions
were sent, or from the Treasury, Your Lordships Board, or from the
Commissioners of the Customs, I am persuaded it would have an excellent effect, but I believe the Governor will not care to have
Contests with a Comptroller about the power of appointing Officers,
for they claim that Right, nor can it be very agreeable to him,
After he has seen occasion to make some alteration to have all that
he has done overthrown, by a letter from the Surveyor General from
the remote parts of Virginia; It is several years since I informed
Your Lordships, how necessary another Searcher and two Waiters were
for this Port, but I cannot think the business can be done with less
than four Waiters and if there were a Searcher and one Waiter at
George Town, and the same at Beaufort Port Royal; they wou'd soon

save three times their Sallaries to the Revenue, and in a great
measure put a stop to illicit Trade.

Letter, James Glen, Royal Governor of South Carolina, to
Board of Trade, March, 1753, Labaree (ed.), Royal Instructions to
British Colonial Governors, II, pp. 886-888.


80.   "ANY SMALL BODY OF BRITISH TRADESMEN" (1768)


The mercantilist theory designated "the nation" as
the beneficiary of economic policy.  During the day-to-
day operations of Parliament, however, it was this or
that group of Englishmen which clearly benefitted from
various trade laws.  Franklin was thus denouncing mercantilism as it operated in practice.


They [i.e., Americans] reflected how lightly the interest of
all America had been estimated here, when the interests of a few of
the inhabitants of Great Britain happened to have the smallest competition with it.  That the whole American people was forbidden the
advantage of a direct importation of wine, oil, and fruit, from
Portugal, but must take them loaded with all the expense of a voyage
one thousand leagues round about, being to be landed first in
England, to be re-shipped for America; expenses amounting, in war
time at least, to thirty pounds per cent more than otherwise they
would have been charged with; and all this, merely that a few
Portugal merchants in London may gain a commission on those goods
passing through their hands, (Portugal merchants, by the by, that
can complain loudly of the smallest hardships laid on their trade by
foreigners, and yet, even in the last year, could oppose with all
their influence the giving ease to their fellow subjects laboring
under so heavy an oppression!)  That, on a slight complaint of a
few Virginia merchants, nine colonies had been restrained from making
paper money, become absolutely necessary to their internal commerce-
from the constant remittance of their gold and silver to Britain.
But not only the interest of a particular body of merchants,
but the interest of any small body of British tradesmen or artificers, has been found, they say, to outweigh that of all the King's
subjects in the colonies.  There cannot be a stronger natural right
than that of al man's making the best profit he can of the natural
produce of his lands, provided he does not thereby hurt the state in
general.  Iron is to be found everywhere in America, and the beaver
furs are the natural produce of that country.  Hats, and nails, and
nails, and steel are wanted there as well as here.  It is of no importance to the common welfare of the empire, whether a subject of
the King's obtains his living by making hats on this or on that side
of the water.  Yet the hatters of England have prevailed to obtain

an act in their own favor, restraining that manufacture in America;
in order to oblige the Americans to send their beaver to England to
be manufactured, and purchase back the hats, loaded with the charges
of a double transportation.  In the same manner have a few nail-
makers, and a still smaller body of steel-makers (perhaps there are
not half a dozen of these in England), prevailed totally to forbid
by an act of Parliament the erecting of slitting-mills, or steel-
furnaces, in America; that the Americans may be obliged to take all
their nails for their buildings, and steel for their tools, from
these artificers, under the same disadvantages.

Causes Of The American Discontents Before 1768 (1768), Sparks
(ed.), Works of Benjamin Franklin, IV, pp. 250-251.


    81.  VIOLATING A NON-IMPORTATION AGREEMENT (1769)

        If American merchants paid royal trade regula-
    tions little heed, they certainly took their own
    more seriously.


The Conduct of Simeon Cooley, in his daring Infractions of the
Non-importation Agreement; his insolent and futile Defense of those
inglorious Measures; with his avowed Resolution obstinately to persevere in counteracting the legal Efforts of a brave and free People
in support of their inestimable Rights "alarmed and insenced" the
Inhabitants of this City [New York], who dreading the destructive
Consequence that might have ensued from so dangerous an Example,
determined, at a General Meeting held on Friday Evening last, to
call the said Cooley to Account; and prevail on him, If Possible,
to desist from his vile Practices, and endeavour to bring him to
such Concessions as should to them appear best calculated to attone
for his repeated and unprecendented offences.  Two Gentlemen were
appointed to inform him of the Sentiments of the Inhabitants, who
required his immediate Attendance at their Place of Meeting, and to
assure him that no injury should be offered to his Person; (to prevent which, every imaginable Precaution was taken) but Cooley,
(influenced perhaps by some illdisposed and Stupid Adviser) refused
to attend the Place appointed, and alledged in Excuse for his Non-
attendance, "that he did not think it consistent with his personal
Safety to meet them There", at the same Time he expressed a Willing-
ness to make the Concessions required, from his Parlour Window.
When the Inhabitants received this disagreeable Intelligence, they
immediately proceeded towards his House; but Cooley, apprized of
their coming, thought proper to decamp, accompanied by a Military
Gentlman, (who covered his Retreat) sought for a Sanctuary within
the Fort Walls, which could afford him but an indifferent Protection
against the keen Reproaches of a guilty Conscience, the only

Punishment he had to dread.  Whilst the Inhabitants were assembled
in the Fields, M--r P--r ordered a File of Soldiers to guard his
(Cooley's) House, who were accordingly drawn up before his Door,
with Their Musquets loaded, &c.  Whether the Author of this un-
warrantable Step, designed a compliment to the Magistracy and Inhabitants of this City, or to recommend himself to his Superiors by
his officious and blundering Zeal, is unknown:  but 'tis more than
probable, that his prescipitate Conduct was dissapproved of by the
latter,...

On Saturday Morning, Cooley consented to meet the Inhabitants;
and Four in the Afternoon being the Time appointed, and the Merchants's Coffee-House the Place, they assembled in Expectation of
this Important Event; but the Majority thinking it a very unsuitable
Place for the Purpose, required his appearance in the Fields, where
he attended, and publickly acknowledged his Crimes; implored the
Pardon of his Fellow Citizens; engaged to store an equivalent to
the Goods he had sold, together with all that he had in Possession
that were imported contrary to Agreement; and so to conduct for the
future as not to render himself obnoxious to the Contempt and just
Resentment of an injured People.

. . . . . . . . . . . . . . . . . . . . . . . . . . . . . . . . . . . . . . . . .

SIMEON CO[O]LEY, Silversmith and Jeweller Begs leave to inform
the Public, that he intends to leave this City this Month, with his
Family; humbly intreats all that stand indebted to him to settle
their accounts directly; all those that have any Demands upon him
are desired to call, and they shall be paid.

New York Gazette and the Weekly Mercury, July 24, 1769,
September 4, 1769, Rita S. Gottesman (ed.), The Arts and Crafts
in New York, 1726-1776, (New York:  New York Historical Society,
1938), pp. 37-39.


82.   OWNERSHIP OF TONNAGE ENGAGED IN COLONIAL
TRADE, BY COLONY (1775)


The tobacco colonies (Maryland and Virginia) depended
the most on British-owned tonnage; this reflected their
great specialization in tobacco cultivation, and underscored their commercial dependence on England.  The New
England colonies owned the largest part of their tonnage,
thus reflecting their direct competition with English-
owned bottoms.  This, too, was symbolic of the relationship between Old and New England.

|  | Proportion belonging to British merchants resident in Europe | Proportion belonging to British merchants occasionally residing in colonies | Proportion belonging to native colonial inhabitants |
|---|---|---|---|
| New England- - - | 1-8th. | 1-8th. | 6-8ths. |
| New York- - - | 2-8ths. | 3-8ths. | 3-8ths. |
| Pennsylvania- - - | 2-8ths. | 3-8ths. | 3-8ths. |
| Maryland and Virginia - | 6-8ths. | 1-8th. | 1-8th. |
| North Carolina- - - | 5-8ths. | 2-8ths. | 1-8th. |
| South Carolina and Georgia - | 5-8ths. | 2-8ths. | 1-8th. |

U.S. Congress, 28th, 1st session, Document No. 15, Serial
No. 440, Jonathan Elliot, The Funding System of the United States
and of Great Britain, (Washington, D.C.:  Blair and Rives, 1845),
p. 14.


83.  ENGLISH MANUFACTURERS FEAR LOSS OF
AMERICAN BUSINESS (1774)


Nearly four months after the Boston Tea Party, Parliament was under some pressure from British manufacturers not
to bring on a retaliatory boycott from the American colonies.  Cushing was a Boston merchant then serving on that
city's Committee of Correspondence.


By the enclosed extract of a letter from Wakefield in Yorkshire
to a friend of mine, you will see that the manufacturers begin to
take the alarm.  Another general non-importation agreement is apprehended by them, which would complete their ruin.  But great pains
are taken to quiet them with the idea, that Boston must immediately
submit, and acknowledge the claims of Parliament, for that none of
the other colonies will adhere to them.  A number of the principal
manufacturers from different parts of the kingdom are now in town,
[i.e., in London] to oppose the new duty on foreign linens, which
they fear may provoke the Germans to lay discouragements on British
manufactures.  They have desired me to meet and dine with them on
Wednesday next, where I shall have an opportunity of learning their
sentiments more fully, and communicating my own.


Letter, Benjamin Franklin to Thomas Cushing, April 2, 1774,
Sparks (ed.), Works Of Benjamin Franklin, VII, p. 119.

# G.

---

# THE WORLD MARKET

---

84.  THE MORALITY OF AMERICAN DEBT DELINQUENCY (ca. 1783)


English creditors clamored for payment once the
revolutionary war ended in 1783, but remittances were
slow.  As a result, American merchants were refused
credit.  Franklin wished to argue away the moral charge
involved.  This he did by portraying American economic
weaknesses as a product of English economic aggression
beginning in 1774.


The first step [in 1774] was shutting up the port of Boston
by an act of Parliament; the next, to prohibit by another the New
England fishery.  An army and a fleet were sent to enforce these
acts.  Here was a stop put at once to all the mercantile operations
of one of the greatest trading cities of America; the fishing vessels all laid up, and the usual remittances, by way of Spain,
Portugal, and the Straits, rendered impossible.  Yet the cry was now
begun against us, These New England people do not pay their debts!
The ships of the fleet employed themselves in cruising separately all along the coast.  The marine gentry are seldom so well
contented with their pay, as not to like a little plunder.  They
stopped and seized, under slight pretences, the American vessels
they met with, belonging to whatever colony.  This checked the
commerce of them all.  Ships, loaded with cargoes destined either
directly or indirectly to make remittance in England, were not
spared.  If the differences between the two countries had been then
accommodated, these unauthorized plunderers would have been called
to account, and many of their exploits must have been found piracy.
But what cured all this, set their minds at ease, made short work,

and gave full scope to their piratical disposition, was another
act of Parliament, forbidding any inquisition into those past facts,
declaring them all lawful, and all American property to be forfeited, whether on sea or land, and authorizing the King's British
subjects to take, seize, sink, burn, or destroy, whatever they could
find of it.  The property suddenly, and by surprise taken from our
merchants by the operation of this act, is incomputable.  And yet
the cry did not diminish, These Americans don't pay their debts!

Had the several states of America, on the publication of this
act seized all British property in their power, whether consisting
of lands in their country, ships in their harbours, or debts in the
hands of their merchants, by way of retaliation, it is probable a
great part of the world would have deemed such conduct justifiable.
They, it seems, thought otherwise, and it was done only in one or
two States. and that under peculiar circumstances of provocation.
And not having thus abolished all demands, the cry subsists, that
the Americans should pay their debts!

General Gage, being with his army (before the declaration of
open war) in peaceable possession of Boston, shut its gates, and
placed guards all around to prevent its communication with the
country.  The inhabitants were on the point of starving.  The general, though they were evidently at his mercy, fearing that, while
they had any arms in their hands, frantic desperation might possibly
do him some mischief, proposed to them a capitulation, in which he
stipulated, that if they would deliver up their arms, they might
leave the town with their family and goods.  In faith of this agreement, they delivered their arms.  But when they began to pack up for
their departure, they were informed, that by the word goods, the
general understood only household goods, that is, their beds, chairs,
and tables, not merchant goods; those he was informed they were indebted for to the merchants of England, and he must secure them for
the creditors.  They were accordingly all seized, to an immense
value, what had been paid for not excepted.  It is to be supposed,
though we have never heard of it, that this very honorable general,
when he returned home, made a just distribution of those goods, or
their value, among the said creditors.  But the cry nevertheless
continued, These Boston people do not pay their debts!

The army, having thus ruined Boston, proceeded to different
parts of the continent.  They got possession of all the capital
trading towns.  The troops gorged themselves with plunder.  They
stopped all the trade of Philadelphia for near a year, of Rhode
Island longer, of New York near eight years, of Charleston in South
Carolina and Savannah in Georgia, I forget how long.  This continued
interruption of their commerce ruined many merchants.  The army also
burnt to the ground the fine towns of Falmouth and Charlestown near
Boston, New London, Fairfield, Norwalk, Esopus, Norfolk, the chief
trading town in Virginia, besides innumerable tenements and private
farm-houses.  This wanton destruction of property operated doubly
to the disabling of our merchants, who were importers from Britain,
in making their payments, by the immoderate loss they sustained
themselves, and also the loss suffered by their country debtors,
who had bought of them the British goods, and who were now rendered
unable to pay.  The debts to Britain of course remained undischarged,
and the clamor continued, These knavish Americans will not pay us!

If I have shown clearly that the present inability of many American merchants to discharge their debts, contracted before the war, is not so much their fault, as the fault of the crediting nation, who, by making an unjust war on them, obstructing their commerce, plundering and devastating their country, were the cause of that inability, I have answered the purpose of writing this paper.

The Retort Courteous, Sparks (ed.), The Writings of Benjamin Franklin, II, pp. 500-503, 508.

85.    TARDY TRADE REMITTANCES TO ENGLAND (1788)

Five years after the resumption of foreign trade following the American Revolution gold and silver money left the country as American merchants attempted to settle balances owed English suppliers.  American paper money and commercial paper circulated at a discount.  Beekman, a partner in a well-known New York City mercantile house, contended that in the light of such difficulties English creditors should at least forgive American debtors the interest charges on pre-war debts, some of which were more than a dozen years old.

I have this Day received a Line from Mr. Cowper, wishing me to signify to him in Reply my Agreement to settle the Account with him on the Score of Interest, as some have done, which I accordingly complied with (through his Urgency) provided you, Gentlemen, could insist on my paying the same.  But from our long and large Commercial Dealings with your House as well as that of our Family; our mutual Satisfaction during that Period; together with the Causes of the Interruption and Delay with respect to the Settlement of the Account subsisting between us, I flatter myself you will feel yourselves induced to give up the matter of Interest, since the Peace (that during the Troubles having been given up on all Sides) as indeed some with whom I have closed Accounts on your Side the Water, have freely and of their own Accord done, without any, the least sollicitation on my Part.

But I am persuaded when I lay before you, Gentlemen the following weighty Considerations they will have no small Influence on your Generosity to act in the same Manner in this Instance.  When you reflect on my former Punctuality; and the true Causes of the Change, owing to the late unhappy War, which has so totally deranged Matters as to put it out of one's Power to do as we would wish.  The Prohibition of Congress at the Commencement of the Contest with respect to our discharging British Debts, when I could easily have done it. The almost Impossibility to collect in old Debts.  The unusual Scarcity of Cash, both Paper Currency and particularly Specie.  The

great Sums I have deposited in our Public Funds, which I know not
when I shall be able to receive.  The great Losses I have sustained
of my Property during the War, and particularly by the Depreciation
of our Currency (a Quantity of which now lays useless by me) together
with my being wholly unengaged in Business during that Period, having
a large Family to maintain, and kept out of my Possessions in this
City and Vicinity for so many Years.  The extreme Difficulty in obtaining Monies even for my new Debts since the Peace, especially
Gold and Silver, for which we must pay an Advance from 7 to 8 per
cent.  The high Price of Bills of Exchange which sweep away the small
Profits on the Merchandize imported.  The Precariousness of Trade at
present, often crediting those whom we may think secure, when perhaps we either totally lose the Debt, or have to take up with a
trifling Proportion of the same--which last Consideration, alas! has
been too much the Case I fear, between many British and American
Merchants, the latter of whom, so far from being able to pay even
the Principle (much less the Interest) have to compound with their
Creditors at an insignificant Rate!

    This, however, I am happy in being able to add, never was and
hope never shall be my Lot, having a good landed Estate wholly un-
incumbered, though such Property at present sells far beneath its
real Value, owing to the great Scarcity of Money; which I am sure
you would not wish me too hastily to sacrifice, when I assure you
that I am determined no one shall be a Loser by me, being able and
willing to discharge my just Debts as fast as Money can be come at--
and desirous at the same time of paying proper Attention to my other
Correspondents, which surely you cannot but applaud.

    In short, you might be sensible, Gentlemen not only of the
Difficulties, but the great Disadvantage the Merchants here labour
under in making Remittances abroad, by reason of the absolute Dearth
of Specie, it having been almost drained out of our Country; and the
Payments made us (whether for old or new Debts) being in our Paper
Currency, we have to allow the exorbitant advance just mentioned in
Exchange, as well as 6 1/2 per cent above par for Specie Bills, which
together, I must say, is allowing Interest sufficient.  And if we
purchase Bills for our Paper Currency we must pay at the Rate of
12 1/2 per cent above par; though Mr. Cowper would never receive
any Payment from me of that kind, having refused me once an Offer
of L100 Sterling, which I could not exchange.


    Letter, James Beekman to Thomas Pierce and Son, Bristol,
England, June 30, 1788, Philip L. White (ed.), The Beekman Mercantile Papers, III, (New York:  New York Historical Society,
1956), pp. 1176-1177.

86.   THE GLASGOW MERCHANTS DUN THE VIRGINIANS (1785)


Two years after the end of the revolutionary war,
British merchants were still pressing unsuccessfully for
payment of pre-revolutionary mercantile debts.  Note the
interest of American merchants in preventing special treatment of British creditors.  Madison was a member of the
Virginia House of Delegates and Jefferson was about to
succeed Franklin as United States Minister to France.


Some proceedings of the Glasgow merchants were submitted to the
H. of D. [Virginia House of Delegates] in which they signified their
readiness to receive their debts in four annual payments, with immediate security and summary recoveries at the successive periods, and
were silent as to the point of interest.  Shortly after were presented memorials from the Merchants of this town [Richmond] &
Petersburg representing the advantage which a compliance with the
Glasgow overtures would give the foreign over the domestic creditors.
Very little attention seemed to be paid by the House to the
overtures....


Letter, James Madison to Thomas Jefferson, January 9, 1785,
The Papers of James Madison, Vol. V, Library of Congress.




87.   "AMERICAN MERCHANTS ARE LAUGHED AT AND ASPERSED" (1785)


Two years after the Revolution, both in Bristol
and London American merchants were regarded as unworthy
credit risks.  A business trip to these cities was so dis-
heartening that even a representative of the house of Blount
considered it advisable after a time not to confess he was
seeking credit.


I arrived here [Bristol] yesterday & to-day applied to Mr.
Cruger who received me with marks of the greatest respect & assured
me upon his honour that from our general Character & his Knowledge
of our Candour, ability & probity, there are no men in America whose
order he would execute on Credit with more Chearfulness; but that he
has been so cruelly used by the Gentlemen of America whose orders he
has already complied with, that he is no longer able to obtain a
Credit with the manufacturers.  He has not failed nor will not tho'
he has furnished Goods to America to amo$^t$. of upwards of £200,000
& received no remittance—-thus you see what a foundation he stands
on—-But most other American Merchants have failed or must inevitably
fail in a short time—-you would be amazed to hear of the villainy of

the Merchants in America--even the great Robert Morris has made
no remittance--I must now inform you that I cannot obtain a Credit,
& believe me it is without vanity I say, our House has as good a
reputation as any American House can have--The manufacturers will
not give Credit to any man concerned in the American business
. . . . . . . . . . . . . . . . . . . . . . . . . . . . . . .
    I arrived [in London] on the 11th Ins$^t$. & found American Credit
at so low an ebb that the best established Houses that have been concerned in that Business could not Ship Goods to America but at the
advanced price of from 15 to 20 P C$^t$. because they have not, nor
cannot gain the Confidence of the Manufacturers, whose suspicions
are justly roused to the highest pitch by the amazing number of
Bankruptcies that happen almost daily in that line--The villainous
Conduct of some Americans (I may say most of them) who came over
immediately after the conclusion of the war & got largely into
business here, has conspired with the general want of punctuality
in the Merchants of our Country, to fix on the whole Nation a stigma
of Dishonesty which Time itself will scarcely be able to obliter-
ate--.


    Letters, Thomas Blount to J. G. and T. Blount, September 5
and 26, 1785, Keith (ed.), Blount Papers, I, pp. 214, 219.



88.  PRINCIPAL RESTRICTIONS ON UNITED STATES
FOREIGN TRADE (1793)


    England was at war with revolutionary France and
America was caught in the middle as it tried to sell to
both sides.  As the combatants proceeded, alliances on the
Continent were developed with the result that American
trade there was also hampered as each side tried to deny
the other access to American goods.  Meanwhile, Congress
requested Secretary of State Thomas Jefferson to report
on both the privileges and restrictions then lying on
American trade with foreign countries.  Here is Jefferson's
summary of the restrictions.


To sum up these restrictions, so far as they are important:
FIRST.  In Europe--
Our bread stuff is at most times under prohibitory duties in
England, and considerably dutied on re-exportation from Spain to
her colonies.
Our tobaccoes are heavily dutied in England, Sweden and France,
and prohibited in Spain and Portugal.
Our rice is heavily dutied in England and Sweden, and prohibited
in Portugal.
Our fish and salted provisions are prohibited in England, and
under prohibitory duties in France.

Our whale oils are prohibited in England and Portugal.

And our vessels are denied naturalization in England, and of late in France.

SECOND.  In the West Indies--

All intercourse is prohibited with the possessions of Spain and Portugal.

Our salted provisions and fish are prohibited in England.

Our salted pork and bread stuff (except maize) are received under temporary laws only, in the dominions of France, and our salted fish pays there a weighty duty.

THIRD.  In the article of navigation--

Our own carriage of our own tobacco is heavily dutied in Sweden, and lately in France.

We can carry no article, not of our own production, to the British ports in Europe.  Nor even our own produce to her American possessions.


Report to Congress, December 16, 1793, Ford (ed.), Writings of Thomas Jefferson, VI, pp. 478-479.


## 89.  THE GROWTH OF COMPETITION IN WORLD AGRICULTURAL MARKETS (1794)


America shipped raw materials and farm products to the outside world, including England, in exchange for manufactured goods.  Farm exports, especially, were crucial.  In 1791, for example, out of nearly $20 million in exports, farm products accounted for nearly one-half, southern staples such as tobacco, rice, and indigo, about a third, forest products, over a tenth, and fisheries products, over a twentieth.  The principal source of food for the countries of western Europe turned out to be themselves, rather than overseas countries such as the United States. Nevertheless, the conspectus of world agricultural competition to the United States, as delineated by John Bordley -- lawyer, large-scale farmer, and organizer of the Philadelphia Society for Promoting Agriculture -- is instructive.


What if to the bread wanted by some countries, which is at present supplied by Poland, America and Barbary, one or two great additional sources of it should be opened?  How would the husbandry and the income of our country be affected by it?  Would there not be then felt a want of manufacturers, consumers of bread who make none, yet who would preserve the value of the produce of our husbandry by such consumption, and furnish other necessaries and comforts from their various occupations?  There is reason to believe that yet a little while, and the productions of the countries on

the Nieper and the Danube will rush through the Straits of Constantinople into the Mediterranean, and thence into all Europe.    The
wheat of the Ukrain, hitherto shut up by the Turk, sells at 1 lbs.
to 2 lbs. sterling a bushel.    The countries so shut up also abound
in cattle, hemp, tobacco, &c. which are to be conveyed through these
straits to a market new and important to those countries; which articles will greatly interfere with and cheapen the produce of our
country.    The Banat is said to be by far the cheapest country in
Europe, in all necessary productions, meat, bread, wine, fruits,
&c.    The culture of Rice was introduced there by the late Emperor
with great and increasing success.    Prices in the vicinity of
Tybiscus river are in sterling, as follow:*  wheat at 17d. an English
bushel; rye, 12d. barley, 7d. 1/4; hay in towns, 10 lbs. a ton;
in the country, 3 lbs. a lean ox 40 lbs. to 50 lbs. a cow 30 lbs.
to 45 lbs. (cattle are dearer than grain, because they are readily
driven to market:  they are driven by thousands annually, from the
Ukrain, through Poland into Silesia and Germany) mutton, 1d. a 1b.
beef, from 1d. to 1d. 1/2; pork, 1d. 1/2, to 2d. wine, 45 gallons
new, in a good vintage, 7 lbs. to 42 lbs. according to quality;
rent, 2 lbs. 6 to 4 lbs. the English acre; and all this cheapness
we presume is owing to the want of a passage through the straits
of Constantinople, to foreign markets--the very markets hitherto
supplied by Poland, America and Barbary.    The Turk is to be forced
by the Czarina and the Emperor to suffer a passage through those
straits:  it already has been of late nearly accomplished.
    You say the above events are problematical, or at a great
distance of time:  but there is one of a different nature and very
influential in the argument which is more certain and nearer at
hand.    With the improvements in government, which the philosophical
spirit of modern times is producing, the condition of mankind will
be bettered, and in no circumstance will it be more perceptible than
in their greater skill in all the arts, as well in agriculture as
others.    Then will France by fully equal, to supply her own demands
for wheat, and Spain and Portugal will be so in no long time.
    ANOTHER new source may be in India.    Sugar has not become a
common article from that quarter till lately.    When in 1792, it
sold there 15 lbs. or 18 lbs. near four Spanish dollars a hundred,
it was sold 50 lbs. to 60 lbs. in London.    A sudden and till then
unknown demand for sugars by Europe and America occasioned an
increased price in India:  and the demand having continued and
increased, has stimulated the Indostans to increase the culture of
sugar canes with great spirit, for supplying Europe and America
with sugar.    The Calcutta gazettes are full of the designs of
planting and cultivating the sugar cane:  and now we are assured by
some of our countrymen, who have been lately in India, that the
wheat of that country is very fine, and is sold at 11d. sterling
for an English bushel.    If then their sugar makes a freight and a
profit when carried to Europe, so may their wheat, provided it
should bear so long a voyage.    It would sell at above 500 per cent.
when their sugars would scarcely obtain 300.    But will the bulk and
price of wheat admit of a freight and profit sufficient for the
adventurer?  Mr. Law, in his sketches of arrangements in Bengal,
for the year 1789, says it would clear 50 per cent.  "I saw, he

says, much extended cultivation and increasing population through Bengal: but there is some apprehension of a want of consumption; grain selling in some places 800 lbs. and upwards for 12d. sterling, (equal to 7d. 1/5 a bushel of 60 lbs.) Wheat might certainly be exported from Bengal with great success.--It would be shipped for 7 lbs. 3 sterling, the English quarter which is under 11d. a bushel. At 58 lbs. a quarter in London, it would yield 50 per cent. profit on cost and charges on freight," &c.

ALTHOUGH wheat from India should not always bear the voyage, yet the flour of it, which is very fine, might. Flour carried from the Delaware to the Ganges, proved perfectly good when returned from thence to Philadelphia in a late voyage. But if neither their wheat nor their flour could be carried to Europe in good condition, yet their rice, the common bread of the country, could. It usually is very cheap; and whilst their labour is but 2d. a day, all the fruits of that labour will continue to be cheap.

WHETHER the great sources of the countries on the Nieper and the Danube shall soon be opened or shall not, there is at present such an apparent probability of it as may induce us farmers to con- sider in time how we are to avert the threatened ill effects of a change that must be as sudden as important. The farmer of flashy ostentation may especially think of retrenching wasteful habits: and whilst legislators may wish that labour be apportioned between hus- bandry and manufactories, and gently promote it, they will be cau- tious how they favour the one at the expence of the other.

In the Ukrain and Poland, and on the Danube, labour is cheap, whilst with us it is the highest in the world. When we shall have driven the Indians from their country, what will be the condition of the people of the hither states, respecting labour which already is so much drained from them by the ultra-montane country? This will not immediately affect all the states; but it soon may, and who can say how soon it will not.


John B. Bordley, "Intimations of Manufactures," Sketches On Rotations of Crops and Other Rural Matters, (Philadelphia, Pennsylvania:  Charles Cist, 1796), pp. 72-76.


### 90.    OUR MERCANTILE INTEREST REQUIRES A DIPLOMATIC CONNECTION (1798)


The new American nation must manage to stay out of war; and, following Washington's advice of a year earlier, European military alliances should be avoided. But, argued Adams, American participation in world commerce demanded an American diplomacy.

Expressing the mercantile interest of the new nation, Adams advocated diplomatic relations with states not allied with either combatant. Thus, he assessed the probable gains

from trade as more valuable than the issue of even-
tual American involvement in the war.  At this time,
J. Q. Adams was American Minister Plenipotentiary in
Prussia and his father was President.


They have told us that we have nothing to do with the affairs
and quarrels of Europe, and that a diplomatic intercourse with its
governments would tend to involve us unnecessarily in its wars, and
they have alarmed us with calculations of the expense to which every
additional minister in Europe would subject the people of the United
States.

The experience of the last six years has abundantly shown how
impossible it is to keep us disconnected with the affairs of Europe,
while we have such essential mercantile connections with the great
maritime states; and the numerous injuries we have suffered alternately from both parties amply prove how essential it is to our
interests to have other friends than either.  In every naval war it
must be the interest of Britain and of France to draw or to force
us into it as parties, while it must always be our unequivocal interest to remain neutral.  In the present war I am confident we have
suffered more for want of a free intercourse, communication and concert, with the neutral states in Europe, than would discharge five
times the expense of maintaining ministers with them, and if we
should finally be forced out of the system which the government has
had so much at heart and compelled to engage in hostilities for our
own defence, it may be in some measure attributed to the neglect of
a good understanding with the nations which have had an interest
similar to ours, that is a neutral interest. . . .


Letter, John Quincy Adams to John Adams, January 31, 1798,
Worthington C. Ford (ed.), Writings of John Quincy Adams, II,
(New York:  Macmillan, 1913), p. 251.


## 91.  SELLING GERMAN LINEN TO AMERICA (1800)


Nearly 20 years after independence was achieved,
the United States was still searching for foreign trade
outlets but the poor reputation of its merchants stood
in the way of success.  To be sure, the Napoleonic Wars
still disrupted regular commerce.  J. Q. Adams, who was
on a diplomatic mission to Berlin, characteristically
used his time searching for concrete solutions.


Mr. Jopfer [the burgomaster], I find, as well as all the other
great linen merchants in the mountain-towns, has made the experiment of opening a trade directly with America; and, like all the
rest, he is not satisfied with the success of his speculation.  The

brothers. . . settled in Philadelphia, procured linens to be sent
them to a very large amount, for which they have not yet made their
payments.  The returns they have made were chiefly in sugar, in
coffee, and in bills payable in England, upon all which great loss
has been sustained by the great failures last winter at Hamburg, and
by the very low course of exchange upon London.  Mr. Jopfer asked me
if I could recommend any mercantile houses to him, in New York,
Philadelphia, or Baltimore, as perfectly sure houses, to whom he
could safely consign linens; and the same question has been asked me
by other merchants in these towns. . . .I will thank you to send
me one or two names of merchants in each of those towns, who do
business upon consignments, and who enjoy the most firmly-established
credit.  But let them be genuine, solid merchants, whose credit is
founded upon their character for honesty, and not as is too common
in our country, upon the extravagant extent of their enterprizes.


    Letter, John Quincy Adams, August 17, 1800, in Port Folio,
(Philadelphia), April 25, 1801, p. 1.  The letter is unsigned and
was written in Waldenburg.


### 92.  THE ST. LOUIS-NEW ORLEANS TRADE (1803)


    In 1816, it cost as much to ship a ton of goods 30
miles on land as it did to transport the same bulk over
the 3,000 miles of the Atlantic Ocean.  Consequently, only
goods that were of high value for their bulk could bear the
cost of land transport.  Whisky was chief among these.
Human cargo in the form of slaves was another.  Before the
steamboat, river freight was carried on rafts, flatboats,
keelboats, barges, among others.  Some of the larger river
boats that carried produce down the Mississippi were sold
upon reaching New Orleans.  The arduous upstream trip on
the Mississippi was overcome only by the steamboat.  Paul
Alliot wrote this work while imprisoned in New Orleans.
He dedicated it to President Thomas Jefferson.


    The fur trade is very considerable and very lucrative.  Although
it is reckoned as five hundred leagues from St. Louis to New Orleans,
yet with the river high, it only takes twenty days to reach the
latter place.  Consequently, the merchants take advantage of that
season to send for their flour, lead, pelts, tobacco, and salt provisions, and, in fine, for all the various things which they exchange
for their hardware, cloth, haberdashery, hats, spices, firearms,
rouge, and powder.  They generally take three months in taking
their merchandise up the river to St. Louis.
    Finally, after having gone fifteen leagues farther, the traveler
reaches the mouth of the Missouri River which is the boundary of the
empire of Louisiana.  There is found the post of Petit Cote, which

is guarded by an officer and fifty soldiers.  There is also there a
small city whose population is two or three hundred inhabitants.
They trade in pelts with the various savage nations who inhabit the
bluffs of that river and who raise the same products as do the
inhabitants of St. Louis.

Those good and courageous people, far distant from all faction,
as well as from perfidy and tyranny, occupy themselves, in the bosom
of peace which they have at last found in a country which was formerly the abode of those men whom nature forms without need and
without criminal passions, in rearing their children, in teaching
them at an early age to love one another, to work, and finally, to
enjoy as a consequence that terrestrial happiness which good
spouses find in their homes.


Paul Alliot, "Historical and Political Reflections on
Louisiana," manuscript in Library of Congress, translated and
reprinted in James Alexander Robertson (ed.), Louisiana under the
Rule of Spain, France, and the United States, 1785-1807, I,
(Cleveland, Ohio:  The Arthur H. Clark Co., 1911), pp. 139, 141.


93.  "THE WHOLE WORLD...OUR JOINT MONOPOLY" (1806)


American trade thrived during major parts of the
Anglo-French Wars as shipments to and from England and
France grew rapidly.  Between 1792 -- a year before the
wars began -- and 1806, American exports grew from $20.8
million to $101.5 million.  British ships stopped American
vessels on the high seas, boarded them, and took off seamen
alleged to be of British nationality.  These episodes, plus
British efforts to prevent U.S. trade with France, strained
Anglo-American relations.  President Jefferson tried to
take the long view in this letter to James Monroe who was in
London as an American negotiator of a commercial treaty with
England.  (The treaty failed of ratification by the Senate
since it was criticized for being too lenient to the
British.)


No two countries upon earth have so many points of common interest & friendship; & their rulers must be great bunglers indeed
if with such dispositions, they break them asunder.  The only ri-
vality that can arise is on the ocean.  England may by petty lar-
ceny, thwartings, check us on that element a little, but nothing she
can do will retard us there one year's growth.  We shall be supported
there by other nations & thrown into their scale to make a part of
the great counterpoise to her navy.  It on the other hand she is
just to us, conciliatory, and encourages the sentiment of family
feelings & conduct, it cannot fail to befriend the security of both.
We have the seamen & materials for 50. ships of the line, & half

that number of frigates and were France to give us the money, &
England the dispositions to equip them, they would give to England
serious proofs of the stock from which they are sprung, & the
school in which they have been taught, and added to the efforts of
the immensity of sea-coast lately united under one power would leave
the state of the ocean no longer problematical.  Were, on the other
hand, England to give the money, & France the dispositions to place
us on the sea in all our force, the whole world, out of the continent of Europe, might be our joint monopoly.  We wish for neither
of these scenes.  We ask for peace & justice from all nations & we
will remain uprightly neutral in fact, tho' leaning in belief to the
opinion that an English ascendancy on the ocean is safer for us than
that of France.  We begin to broach the idea that we consider the
whole gulph Stream as of our waters, in which hostilities & cruising
are to be frowned on for the present and prohibited so soon as either consent or force will permit us.  We shall never permit another
privateer to cruise within it, and shall forbid our harbors to national cruisers.  This is essential for our tranquility & commerce.


Letter, Thomas Jefferson,to James Monroe, May 4, 1806, The
Papers of Thomas Jefferson, Vol. 158, Library of Congress.


94.  ENGLAND WILL USE SOUTH AMERICA (1808)


Spain had long tried to monopolize the economic
advantages that arose from selling to its American
colonies, requiring, for example, that other countries
first ship the goods to Spain itself.  During the Anglo-
French wars of the 1790s, American ships traded directly
with the colonies both legally and otherwise.  When, in
1808, Napoleon's armies conquered Spain, both American
and British exporters saw their commercial opportunities
improve in Spain's colonies.  The conquest of Spain
encouraged nascent nationalist groups in Latin America
to think seriously of independence.  Pinkney, U.S. minister to England, here writes to Secretary of State Madison
about some of these matters.


I have heard it suggested (as a Course of Reasoning not unusual
here [in London] among Merchants & others) that South America, whether dependent or independent must be thrown commercially into the
arms of G.B., that, encouraged to Exertion & roused to activity by
a new order of Things, she will hereafter rival us in all the great
agricultural productions of our Country--that under a System friendly
to the Development of their Resources, our Southern Neighbours will
even surpass us as Cultivators--that G.B. will thus become wholly
independent of the U.S. for articles which she has heretofore been
obliged to take from them, &, in a great Degree too, for the

consumption of her Manufactures--that in other views our Importance
will be greatly diminished, if not absolutely annihilated, by this
new Competition--that this Result, almost inevitable in any View,
is more especially to be counted upon if G.B. compelled by the
Policy of our Govt or following the Impulse of the Jealousy which
is imperted to her, shd foster by her Capital & her Trade to the
full Extent of her Capacity, the prosperity of the South, in contradiction to that of the North--that the charge in Spain is
otherwise likely to enable G.B. to hold towards the U.S. a higher
Tone that formerly.
    It is forgotten [by the British] . . . that [Spanish America]
. . . may & must contribute to nourish our growth, while it can
scarcely rival us in anything!--It is forgotten that, if it continues to lean up the Parent State [Spain], it is not likely under
the Pressure of Colonial Restrictions to flourish to our Prejudice
or never to flourish at all, but may serve to strengthen & enrich
us; and that, if it becomes independent, after our Example, it will
be far more natural that we shd benefit & reflect Luster and Power
upon each other than that G.B. shd find in the South the means of
humbling the other Branches of the great Family of the West.


Letter, William Pinkney to James Madison, September 7, 1808,
Maryland Historical Magazine, (December, 1960), pp. 368-369.


95.  AMERICAN TRADE WITH ASIA STRENGTHENS
ENGLAND'S SILVER POSITION (1808)


    Before the Revolution, American colonists had been
forbidden to trade directly with China and India.  While
the peace treaty of 1783 opened up the area to American
traders, by 1809 shipments to the East made up only two
percent of American exports.  The traders would often go
from America to Europe, sell goods in exchange for metallic money which they then sold in China and India.  Silver
was traditionally valued in those countries for purposes
of hoarding.  Baring, who wrote the following account,
was a partner in the Anglo-American merchant-banking house
of Baring Brothers and had important American connections.


    If the complaints of the West India planter of the neutral
trade of America are founded in error, those of the other great
commercial bodies are supported by still less plausible ground.
The Continent of Europe, it seems, will not take the manufactures
of India from Leadenhall-street, and the Americans are accused of
introducing them into different parts of the world from their own
country.  Considering the [East India] Company in the mixed character of sovereigns and merchants, their first object must be, that
the consumption should not be checked; and I should rather have

expected that the efforts of America to circulate the manufactures
of India in countries to which we have no access, would have been
prompted and encouraged.  If we have always thought it good policy
to permit the intercourse of neutrals with our Indian possessions,
the Americans are, in every respect, to be preferred to those of
the North of Europe.  Their political institutions prevent their
forming any settlements in India, and habits and language will always lead them to ours.  They have no manufactures of their own to
interfere with us, but always go to market with money.  Their intercourse, therefore, in every point of view, must be politically in-
offensive, and commercially beneficial.  If a war with America should
destroy the whole of her trade to India and China, we should probably feel severely the want of silver.  To Bengal the Americans may
be computed to send about half a million sterling annually in Spanish
dollars, and about the same sum to China, which is certainly more
than is sent from Great Britain.  It is immaterial who brings the
silver into the market, of which it facilitates the general circulation.  At Canton, I understand it is indispensable necessary,
as the merchants are obliged to pay the duties in silver; but if
brought there by the Americans, the Company is equally enabled to
circulate the manufactures of the country.  It appears, from a
return made to the House of Commons, that the value of British
manufactures exported to China has been gradually but rapidly increasing.  In 1782 it amounted to £105,041, in 1792 to £559,651,
and in 1805 to £1,102,620.  I am not able to ascertain what quantity
of silver has been sent during the same period, but I have no doubt
that it has diminished since the regular supply of the market by
the Americans; and that our factory has not only been able, by this
circumstance, to increase the sale of our manufactures, but also to
provide, in a greater degree than formerly, for their purchases,
by drafts on the Company at home, and on the different presidencies
in India.

    Alexander Baring, An Inquiry into the Causes and Consequences
of the Orders in Council (London, 1808), in Harlow and Madden (eds.),
British Colonial Developments, pp. 285-286.


            96.   THE AMERICAN TRADE IN RUSSIA (1810)


        The difficulties of selling in the Russian market
resembled somewhat the problem of selling colonial
tobacco to England:  (1) great distance of seller from
the market; (2) small, cohesive group of buyers; (3) no
control over the price of goods traded in return for
American goods.  Following is a letter from John Quincy
Adams, then American Minister to Russia, to William Gray,
a millionaire merchant from Boston who had just been
elected lieutenant-governor of Massachusetts.

Almost all the profitable mercantile business of St. Petersburg
is commission business.  The merchants therefore are all commission
merchants.  The first object of their ambition is to obtain consignments, and their great address consists in making the most of them.
The American business has heretofore been monopolized by a few
houses, and in some instances, unless all the information that I
have obtained here on this matter is erroneous, has fallen into bad
hands.  The practices by which some houses are said to have enriched
themselves upon the plunder (for it deserves no better name) of their
correspondents in America, are numerous and have not always escaped
detection.  Until within these two years the amount of American business was comparatively small, and few of the Americans who came
here knew how their affairs were really transacted.  As the houses
who engrossed all the consignments were much connected with one
another, you will easily perceive how they could sink the price
currents of cargoes to be sold, and raise the market of those to be
purchased, more according to the level of their own interests than
to those of their consigning friends.  The principal houses purchase
on their own accounts, when the prices are at the lowest ebb, immense
provisions of all the articles of export.  The instant an American
vessel is reported to have arrived at Cronstadt, down go the prices
of whatever she brings, and up start those of the Russian exports.
Then the consignee furnishes his friend with a cargo from his own
stores at the increased price, or gives higher than the current price
in market for part of the supply, in order to charge the remainder
at the same price from his own warehouses.  These are among the
fairest and most honest artifices of the trade.  But I have been
told of simulated sales which some consignees make to themselves;
of pretended payments of hush money at the custom house, charged
sometimes to the amount of many thousand rubles under the name of
extra charges, but never paid in reality, only pocketed by the consignee; of twenty thousand rubles offered to a supercargo for the
favor of transacting his owner's business; of purchases made with
the funds of a correspondent and for him by his order, but refused
to be delivered six months after, because in the interval a great
advance had taken place in the price of the articles purchased; of
ostensible accounts of purchase, sale and charges, totally different
from the real transactions of the expense of the consignee, and a
list of and-so-forths all in the same style.  If your business here
in future should bear any comparison in amount with what it has been
the present year, I feel perfectly assured that you would find it
highly for your interest to have an agent of your own to superintend the transactions of all your business, and that it would require
a person not only of incorruptible integrity, but active, intelligent and conversant with the ways and means of the merchants at
this place.

Letter, John Quincy Adams to William Gray, October 8/20, 1810,
W. C. Ford (ed.), Writings of John Quincy Adams, III, pp. 519-521.

# H.

---

# BARTER TRADE

---

97.  THE BARTER VALUE OF THE LABOR EMBODIED
IN A PAIR OF SHOES (1747)


It would be instructive to:  (1) equate some or all of
these measures with other craft work, and (2) derive a common basis--
if such there was--to all the measures.


I think I ought to have according to Rule for Making a pair
of Shoes w$^{th}$ other mens Lether
2/3 of a Bushel of corn  or
12 lb. of Hide  or
a calfskin  or
12 lb. of Beaf  or
8 lb. of Pork  or
1 1/2 Hundred of English Hay brot home
or a Days work  or
1/3 of a cord of wood  or
4$^s$-6$^d$ in Money


Charles L. Hanson (ed.), <u>A Journal for the Years 1739-1803 By</u>
<u>Samuel Lane of Strathan, New Hampshire</u>, (Concord, New Hampshire:
New Hampshire Historical Society, 1937), p. 2.

## 98.  BARTER IN THE PROVINCE OF MAINE (1794)

The following description of barter by Talleyrand
may well contain the sole report of the barter medium
of prostitution.

In very long stretches of completely settled coasts there is
no specie and no one who does not desire to have some, and yet nothing is done to attract any.  There all transactions are in the form
of barter.  Six thousand feet of boards are exchanged for a cow, a
gallon of rum for 6 days of labor, etc.  Even prostitution is bought
more or less publicly and is paid for with pins; that is the small
coin of the country.  But there is no fidelity on any side in these
plainly cunning bargains.  Society is still formless and already
fraud has appeared.  An inhabitant becomes the merchant of a section;
rum, molasses, some coarse cloth, some household utensils and work
tools are the attractions which he offers to a whole bay, which
comes to him from ten miles around.  Then there is begun between the
sellers and buyers a struggle of finesse.  In the intention of the
merchant, selling is only a means of getting the customer in debt,
he offers credit rather than granting it and does not dispute the
conditions so long as they do not dispute the price.  One hundred
per cent profit and often more does not frighten the purchaser, who
manages secretly the resource of not paying.  Thousands of feet of
boards, strings of wampum are stipulated as due on the book of the
merchant, but when due nothing appears; a vessel has entered the
bay, has offered rum for prepared woods and has received preference
over the creditor.

Letter, Talleyrand in September 24, 1794, Hans Huth and Wilma
J. Pugh (eds.), <u>Talleyrand in America As A Financial Promoter, 1794-
96</u>, (Washington, D.C.: Government Printing Office, 1942), p. 82.
(<u>Annual Report</u> of the American Historical Association for the Year
1941, Vol. II).

## 99.  NAILER TOM'S BARTER TRANSACTIONS (1782-1815)

Barter trade was a normal mode of exchange all
over the country.  It was not unusual for one man to
combine barter with cash transactions.  In Nailer Tom's
case, he even had a bank account all the while he was
bartering.

[1782] made p$^r$ Bridle Bitts for Jeremiah Wilson. Scott p$^r$ Shoes
on my mare.  Carried Some Board Nail to Jeffery Watson and gott one

Bushel of Corn and to Andrew Nicholas^is and gott a bridle. & in the
Evaning Carried the widdow Browning Darkmouth to Joseph Congdons on
Cousin Hazards old mare and gott one Bushel of oats of him...[1786]
yeasterday gott of Christopher Robinson two Bushels and two quorts
of Indian Corn for a Note I had against him for Eight Shillings and
three Pence.[1791]Ebinezar Smith helpt me in the Shop.  William
Congdon and wife coum here.  I paid Smith above menfhond a half
bushel of Corn for his days work...[1792]young Mary Jacob Washed
here. and my wife let hur have apeck of Corn toard the same...[1793]
Carried James Helme his Nails that I owed him for the Glass that I
had of him...[1794]A^n went to Boston Neck to carry Robert Hazard
(of R.) 240 Nails that I owed him for two bushels of apples that I
had soum time past...[1797]I paid Ebenezer Smith in Potatoes for
helping me kill my Hogg...[1799]Rec^d of James Carpinter half a
pound of Candles whitch is in full of all accounts...[1800]A^n went
to Little Rest to Geet my Hatt bound and brusht and am to make a
knife blade to pay for it...[1800]John Holway brought home a pece
of Cloth he has been weaveing for me and I paid him in an otter
Trap for the saim so we are Eavan...[1804]Helpt my son Plant Beens
on an acre of Ground I hired of George Hasard--for 15 bushel of
Potatoes and had four and half bushels of him for Seed and I am to
pay him next fall 5 bushels and 20 quorts.  So that the Ground and
Seed coum to 20 bushels and 20 quorts of Potatoes next fall...[1806]
carried a bushel of White beens to send to Samuel Carr Jun^r in Newport to pay for 1 lb. Soughfhong Tea and 3/ worth Sugar I took up
their when I was in Newport last week...[1807]John Oatelys wife
brought home twelve scanes of Lining yearn to pay for work I did
for hur so we are Eavan...[1808]morning I went to Rodman Carpinters.
gott 11 Eeels that Benj T. Peckham left their for me. he owed me 24
toard an Eeel pot I lett him have last year...[1809]Hierd Rouse
Hazard for three Dollars p^r month. to be paid in Money as fast as he
earn it. and four bushels of Corn to be paid Next winter--the time
agreed on is three Month...


Caroline Hazard (ed.), Nailer Tom's Diary, p. 321 and passim.

# I.

## FINANCIAL STRINGENCIES

### 100.  WE MUST HAVE A PAPER MEDIUM (1720)

Because of the persistent failure of New England to
develop adequate exports, the region was heavily indebted
to English merchants.  As a result, gold and silver money
streamed to England, in the process depriving New England
trade of a circulating medium of exchange.  John Colman,
a Boston merchant, suggested there be set up a land bank;
that is, land owners would put up their land on mortgage
and receive up to two-thirds the value in the form of
paper bills.  These bills would circulate as money.  (See
Source No. 77).

But the grant Argument with some men against a _Paper_ _Medium_ is
this:  They say, Paper hath no intrinsick value in it, and ridicule
it, saying, what value is there in a piece of Paper?  But I think
that a very weak argument, and indeed unfair, to compare Bank Bills,
or Province Bills to blank Paper:  What intrinsick value is there
in Silver, or Gold, more than in Iron, Brass, or Tinn, but only the
common acceptance of it by men in Trade, as a _Medium_ _of_ _Exchange_.
Is not every thing in this World, just as men esteem and value it:
If a man give me his Bond, it is as good in my Opinion, as Silver;
and the only reason why it is so, is, because it will pay my Debt,
or command wherewith to Pay it:  Surely then if a Bank Note will
answer for that end, and will purchase for me Food, Physick, and
Cloathing, and all necessaries of Life, it answers all the ends,
which Silver & Gold can answer for:  & then why is there not as much
intrinsick value in one, as in the other:  We find by daily experience, that our Bills will answer all the aforesaid ends:  and therefore I say it is, and ought to be esteemed as good as Silver; Nay,

it is better to us than Silver, because it can't be Ship't off, but
will remain with us:   Another Objection afainst a Private Bank is,
that the Bankers will Emit so much of this Paper Medium, that we
shall be filled with it, and the plenty of it will make it of no
value.   This Objection I think is already obviated, for if it be
under the inspection of the Government, as I have already proposed:
They will appoint Visiters, to whom the Books must always lie open,
so that it will not be in the Power of the Bankers to Emit any thing
more than what the Government approve of.   No doubt but they will
(as the Province Bills sink) find it necessary to allow the Bank
from time to time, to make as many Bank Bills as they sink of
the Province Bills.

   John Colman, The Distressed State Of The Town of Boston Once
More Considered...With a Schaeme For A Bank, (Boston, Massachusetts:
Benjamin Gray, 1720), pp. 87-88, in Andrew M. Davis (ed.), Colonial
Currency Reprints, 1682-1751, II, (Boston, Massachusetts:   The
Prince Society, 1911).


101.   MERCHANTS' NOTES AS CURRENCY (1733)


        In 1733 Massachusetts was deluged by depreciated
    paper currency issued in Rhode Island.   In an attempt to
    displace this currency, a group of Boston merchants issued
    Merchants' Notes--paper money backed by gold with a promise
    of redemption signed by ten merchants.   A proponent of the
    plan discusses two objections.


    1.   That it is an Affair that should have been manag'd by the
Government.   To this I answer.
    That it must be granted, That if the Government could have
done it, it had been best and as acceptable to the Gentlemen of this
Company, as any others whatsoever; but as has been observed before,
the Government have been upon it now for six Years, and nothing
done; and in that time the Bills have fallen more than 20 per Cent
and there was not any prospect of their doing it yet, for a considerable time at least; and long before the Government could have done
it the Rhode Island Bills would have obtained a Currency, and thereby have depreciated our Bills still a great deal more, so that Men
of Interest in the Publick Bills, were driven into it, either to
suffer Rhode-Island to pour One Hundred Thousand Pounds after
another upon us, and thereby not only get from us our Substance
for what cost them nothing but Pen Ink and Paper, but also lose from
six to ten per Cent. per Annum in all the Money they had in Hand or
due to them, or else they must themselves endeavour to withstand
those Rhode-Island Bills, which they judg'd impractable without
providing People with a better and more establish'd Currency:   And

Experience proves they were right in their Judgment, for with these
Notes of Hand they are but just able to keep unwary People from
being impos'd upon by the artifices used to put off these late
Rhode-Island Bills, much less could they, if there had been no good
Bills to have supply'd their Place:  Hungry Persons will be tempted
to eat Trash, if they can't get wholesome Food.
   2.  It is by some objected, That perhaps these Bills or Merchants Notes will be multiplied upon us?  What Security have we
against it?  To this I would say,
   If they are well and punctually paid, the Country can't be
much injured, for the more Bills there are, the more Silver and Gold
must be bro't into the Country and paid to the Possessors, and if
they are not well paid the Signers of the Bills must go to Jail, and
if they should put forth Bills there, few People will be tempted to
take them, but there is all the certainty that there can be in humane Affairs, that they will be well paid; none who know the Circumstances of the Company can scruple their Ability to pay ten times
the Sum, and it will be the Interest & Safety as well as Duty
of the Ten Signers to compel them to it, which they have power also
to do, or otherwise the Signers must pay all themselves, which if
there should be necessity, they doubtless can do:  But besides, it
may be further observed, that as the Signers are Men of some considerable Substance, it will be their Interest, as well as other
Men of Estates, not to increase Bills in such a manner as to depreciate them.  But beyond all this, the precise Sum of 1. 110,000 is
to be Emitted, and no more, by the fundamental & unalterable Articles of the Scheme, and all the Instruments and Securities are
built upon it; nor can there be one Shilling more emitted without
contradicting them, and breach of the most solemn Agreement and
Covenant under Hand & Seal, between the Signers of the Notes, and
each individual Undertakers.


   "Extract of a Letter to a Gentleman in a Neighboring Govern-
ment, Concerning the New Notes of Hand," New England Weekly Journal,
Monday, January 14, 1734, Davis (ed.), Colonial Currency Reprints,
III, (Oxford:  Clarendon Press, 1953), pp. 9-10.



### 102.  COUNTERFEITING DONE PROMPTLY (1777)


     During the Revolution, while New York was under
British occupation, a counterfeiter was permitted to
sell his skilled services.  Presumably, the British
allowed the practice in order to derange the revolu-
tionists' currency.


   Counterfeits.-Persons, going into the other colonies, may be
supplied with any number of counterfeited congress-notes, for the
price of the paper per ream.  They are so nearly and exactly

executed, that there is no risque in getting them off, it being
almost impossible to discover, that they are not genuine. This has
been proved by bills to a very large amount, which have already been
successfully circulated. Enquire for Q.E.D. at the Coffee-House,
from 11P.M. to 4A.M. during the present month.


New York Gazette and Weekly Mercury, April 14, 1777, Rita
S. Gottesman (ed.), The Arts and Crafts in New York, 1777-1799,
(New York, New York:  New York Historical Society, 1954), p. 46.


### 103.  HOW TO FIGHT A WAR WITHOUT MONEY (1779)


Americans had learned by necessity to do without
much specie money in peacetime; paper currency was a
commercial institution even before the Revolution.
Now, during the Revolution, the same held true.  Franklin's
concluding paragraph is a classic of paper finance.
Samuel Cooper was a Boston clergyman and a very active
supporter of the Revolutionary cause.


The depreciation of our money must, as you observe, greatly
affect salary men, widows, and orphans.  Methinks this evil deserves the attention of the several legislatures and ought if
possible to be remedied by some equitable law, particularly adapted
to their circumstances.  I took all the pains I could in Congress
to prevent the depreciation by proposing first that the Bills should
bear Interest; this was rejected, and they were struck as you see
them.  Secondly, after the first Emission, I proposed that we should
stop, strike no more, but borrow on interest those we had issued.
This was not then approved of, and more Bills were issued.  When
from the too great quantity they began to depreciate, we agreed to
borrow on Interest; and I proposed that in order to fix the value
of the Principal, the Interest should be promised in hard Dollars.
This was objected to as impracticable; but I still continue of
Opinion, that by sending out Cargoes to purchase it, we might have
brought in money sufficient for that Purpose, as we brought in powder, &c. &c; and that tho' this operation might have been attended
with some disadvantage, the loss would have been a less Mischief
than that attending the Discredit of the Bills, which threatens to
take out of our Hands the great Instrument of our Defence.  The
Congress did at last come into the proposal of paying the Interest
in real Money.  But when the whole Mass of the Currency was under
way in Depreciation, the Momentum of its Desecent was too great to
be stopped by a Power that might at first have been sufficient to
prevent the beginning of the Motion.  The only remedy now seems to
be a Diminution of the quantity by a vigorous Taxation, of great
nominal sums, which the People are more able to pay, in Proportion

to the quantity and diminished value; and the only Consolation under
the evil is that the Public Debt is proportionably diminished;
with the Depreciation;-and by a kind imperceptible Tax, every one
having paid a Part of it in the fall of Value that took Place between his receiving and paying such Sums as passed thro' his Hands.
For it should always be remembered that the original Intention was
to sink the Bills by Taxes, which as effectually extenguish the
Debt as an actual Redemption.  This Effect of Paper Currency is not
understood on this [i.e., the French] Side of the Water.  And indeed the whole is a Mystery even to the Politicians; how We have
been able to continue a War four years without Money; and how we
could pay with Paper that had no previously fixed fund appropriated
specifically to redeem it-This Currency as we manage it is a
wonderful Machine.  It performs its Office when we issue it; it pays
and clothes troops, and provides victuals and Ammunition; and when
we are obliged to issue a quantity excessive, it pays itself off
by Depreciation.

     Letter, Benjamin Franklin to Samuel Cooper, April 22, 1779,
The Papers of Benjamin Franklin, Library of Congress.


          104.  "A NATIONAL DEBT...WILL BE...A
                NATIONAL BLESSING" (1781)


     In the last period of the Revolutionary War,
Hamilton sketched his conception of the banking and
fiscal policies of an independent United States.  He
argued that the new nation needed the loyalty of monied
men; and a certain new spirit of economic change.  The
public debt could bring both of these about.  Hamilton
is writing to Robert Morris who several weeks earlier had
been selected as superintendent of finance by the Continental Congress; Hamilton had just resigned as aide-de-camp
to General Washington.


     Speaking within moderate bounds our population will be doubled
in thirty years-there will be a confluence of emigrants from all
parts of the world-our commerce will have a proportionable progress-
and of course our wealth and capacity for revenue.  It will be a
matter of choice, if we are not out of debt in twenty years, without at all encumbering the people.
     A national debt if it is not excessive will be to us a national
blessing-it will be a powerful cement of our nation.  It will also
create a necessity for keeping up taxation to a degree which without being oppressive, will be a spur to industry-remote as we are
from Europe and shall be from danger.  It were other wise to be
feared our popular maxims would incline us to too great parsimony

and indulgence.  We labor less now than any civilized nation of
Europe; and a habit of labor in the people, is as essential to the
health and vigor of their minds and bodies, as it is conducive to
the welfare of the State.  We ought not to suffer our self-love
to deceive us in a comparison, upon these points.


    Letter, Alexander Hamilton to Robert Morris, April 30, 1781,
The Papers of Alexander Hamilton, Vol. III, pp. 373-374, Library
of Congress.


### 105.  HEDGING AGAINST INFLATION (1783)


    The end of the Revolutionary War left the
country with a highly depreciated currency and the
possibility of runaway inflation.  The flight to
goods was a panicked reaction to this possibility.
On the other hand, note the sobering tone of the
Blount letter in reply to Williamson.  Williamson
kept funds on deposit with the Blounts for investment purposes.  He also served as confidential agent
for the Blounts, especially in deals concerning
land speculation.


    Accounts concerning the depretiation of Paper are alarming.  I
hope that you will not keep a Shilling of mine in your Hand an Hour
longer than is absolutely necessary.  I do not wish nor expect that
you should attempt to repay this Paper in hard mony.  Only vest it
in Tobacco Pork or any other article not perishable which may be
bought up immediately nearest to the proper hard mony value, and
there keep them.  Unless an opportunity offers of sending them to
Philad$^a$ or some hard mony market.  I believe I can command as much
Cash as will serve me till my Return to the State which I am resolved
shall not be longer distant than April next.  If it should be convenient to lodge 200 Dlrs in Philad$^a$ or Balimor [Baltimore] it may
possibly be needed but at any Rate I can do without it, having saleable Lands in Pennsylvania. one Tract of which I have already sold.
At present the only thing I am anxious about is that the Paper
mony be immediately converted into some permanent property or
Produce.
. . . . . . . . . . . . . . . . . . . . . . . . . . . . . . . . .
    I observe you are allarmed about the Paper Currency which we
cannot say is without cause but have a much more favourable opinion
of it then most People have [ . ]  Goods as well as our produce
[sic] have rose in price very much since that came out which will
in the long run be the making the money of value.  For foreigners
as well as the citizens of other States will shun a Country where
the only circulating Money is Paper And the report of produce being

so high they will no [t] bring people to purchase Cargoes.  if they
did they must purchase to a disadvantage for very few if any make
any difference in the Mony except in a private [sic] manner    We
have sent our Brother Jacob to the N$^{o}$. Counties with your money
with an expectation he can lay it out in Staves & which at a price
that we dan afford to pay you the Specie, should he fail in that
we can lay it out in Naval Stores at a price which we think will
answer if the preference which Spain gives us is of any advantage


    Letters, Hugh Williamson to J. G. Blount, and J. G. and T.
Blount to Hugh Williamson, December 5 and 20, 1783, Keith (ed.),
Blount Papers, I, pp. 137-138, 142.



    106.  EACH BANK SHARE SHOULD HAVE ONE VOTE (1786)


        In 1782, Pennsylvania chartered the Bank of North
    America which soon came under attack for its allegedly
    tight-credit policies.  In 1785, the state legislature
    repealed the bank's charter.  The next year, the legisla-
    ture debated a motion to restore the charter.  (In 1787,
    a new charter was enacted.)  [See Source No. 714.]
        Morris was a highly successful merchant, banker and
    land speculator who had recently served as Superintendent
    of France for the Continental Congress.  As a chief stock-
    holder in the Bank of America, Morris has accepted the
    opportunity in 1785 to become a State Senator in order to
    protect the bank's interest.


    It has been observed in this debate, that the directors of the
bank being chosen by the stockholders,--and these voting according
to property,--the directors are elected by six or seven men, largely
concerned in stock:  and this manner of voting is strongly objected
to.  I ask what should give the right of voting in such an institution, but property?  Shall those who hold a small number of shares,
have equal votes with those who hold a great number?  You may as
well pass an Agrarian law, and divide the property.  Who would invest their money in such an institution, if that regulation were to
take place?  Voting according to property is the only proper mode of
election, although a deviation has taken place.  Shall a man with a
fortieth part of the interest in bank stock which another holds, have
an equal voice with him in the election of those who are to manage
that interest?  Surely not.  It has been said that the directors
exercise a tyranny over the stockholders.  I wish it had been shewn
how:  Their continuance in office is given as a reason:  and it is
urged that they may remain in office as long as they live, which
would be a species of tyranny.  Then continuance in office is a
proof that they enjoy the confidence of the stockholders--not that

they tyrannize over them.  However, a change in the direction was
intended:  and a number of the stockholders went to the late election, with intent to vote-in some new hands.  But the attack on the
bank seeming to render its duration doubtful, they re-elected the
same gentlemen, in order that if the business were to be closed,
it might be done by those, who, having so long conducted it, were
best acquainted with it.

Debates and Proceedings. . .on the Memorials Praying a Repeal or
Suspension of the Law Annulling the Charter of the Bank, Mathew
Carey (ed.), (Philadelphia, Pennsylvania:  Carey and Co., Seddon
and Pritchard, 1804), p. 117.

### 107.   MONEY TROUBLES IN NORTH AMERICA (1789)

The lack of a uniform currency was not necessarily
relieved by barter, for barter depended on an exact coin-
cidence of wants between two holders of surpluses.  The
extract is written by Reverend Marshall, a preacher who
served as leader of Wachovia, the Moravian settlement
in North Carolina.

Hard money, as it is called here, does not circulate any longer,
except a little among ourselves and from occasional travelers.  Even
well-to-do farmers cannot raise it.  The value of the coins varies
greatly.  Gold has generally been clipped; the bank in Philadelphia
has heavy scales and deducts some from it; and much is counterfeited.
Spanish dollars are the safest, but hardly any can be procured any
more.  The French seven-helmet dollars lose 2d between here and
Pennsylvania.  Clipped coins are most common, are under weight, and
circulate only in this state.  Other places will receive it only by
weight as old silver, by which one loses eight or ten per cent.  If
it is sent to Pennsylvania one must find a safe way, and it is still
in danger, and the carriage charge is heavy.
Paper money is of uncertain value, and still not easy to get.
As soon as one tries to force payment he must be content with it,
although at present it is worth only 13 sh. or 13/6d, to 8 shillings hard money.  If one has it, it will not circulate outside
North Carolina, and one can only buy the wares in our poor harbors
to use it in trade.  That does not help for remittance.
The harvests last year and this have been good, but the products of the land cannot be sold in our seaports and are constantly
falling in price.  If the farmer hauls something to market he receives for it either paper money or sugar, rum, coffee, molasses,
salt, iron, with some things his family needs, and may barter these
things in his neighborhood or let them go on credit.  I have been

offered horses, cattle, wheat, corn-meal, tobacco, and the other
things mentioned, which I cannot take because they cannot be used
in our small community, and because everybody is bartering the local
store suffers.

Salem Board Minutes, To the Unity's Vorsteher Collegium,
November, 1789, letter from F. W. Marshall (ed.), Records of the
Moravians, V, p. 2272.

108.   HOW TO REMEDY THE SHORTAGE OF CAPITAL
IN THE UNITED STATES (1794-95)

A shortage of capital, i.e., more profitable
opportunities than could be utilized by the available
capital, characterized 18th century America.  Still,
there remained the technical problem of sending the
gains overseas in the form of interest and profit.
The specie shortage made this difficult.  And the
labor shortage further limited profits from foreign
investments.

It is not by exportations that America can introduce at home
the capital it lacks; its misfortune still is having too little to
export, too much to import, and the rate of exchange attests this
debtor position.  You have equally our opinion on the great landed
properties which America offers ceaselessly to Europe and which
Europe considers without eagerness.  It remains to find some other
marketable asset in a form more suited to European tastes which will
direct toward America the funds of the old world.  The debt of the
United States is too small to offer a sufficient channel.  It is
time to think of another.  In the political state of Europe there
is surely some capital which seeks to escape, but your great uncultivated forests repulse it more than they attract it; it is necessary to have something more manageable, more disposable to the
European to awaken his interest and solicit his confidence.
. . . . . . . . . . . . . . . . . . . . . . . . . . . . . . . . . .
Capital from Europe will not be attracted without imagining
a kind of disposable stock to serve as a temporary storehouse of
funds destined for America and to offer an intermediate use for
them before they spread out in acquisition and improvement of the
lands of the country.

Huth and Pugh (ed.), Talleyrand In America, pp. 85-86.

109.  STIMULATING BANK COMPETITION FOR FEDERAL DEPOSITS (1802)

A request for a federal charter gave President
Jefferson an opportunity to expound the political and
fiscal advantages of bank competition.

The application of the Bank of Baltimore is of great importance.  The consideration is very weighty that it is held by citizens while the stock of the bank is held in so great a proportion
by foreigners.  Were the bank of the U.S. to swallow up the others
and monopolize the whole banking business of the U.S.*, which the
demands we furnish them with tend shortly to [favor] , we might,
on a misunderstanding with a foreign power, be immensely embarrassed
by any disaffection in that bank.  It is certainly for the public
good to keep all the banks competitors for our favors, by a judicious
distribution of them, and thus to engage the individuals who belong
to them in the support of the reformed order of things [i.e., to
Republicanism as opposed to Federalism], or at least in an ac-
quiescence under it.  I suppose that on the condition of participating in the deposits, the banks would be willing to make such
communications of their operations and the state of their affairs
as might satisfy the Sec. of the Treasury of their stability.  It
is recommended to Mr. Gallatin to leave such an opening in his
answer to this letter, as to leave us free to do hereafter what
shall be advisable on a broad view of all the banks in the different
parts of the Union.

Letter, Thomas Jefferson to Albert Gallatin, October 7, 1802,
Ford (ed.), Writings of Thomas Jefferson, VIII, p. 172; checked
against the original manuscript, The Thomas Jefferson Papers, Vol.
126, Library of Congress.
*This is Ford's reading; the original is not clear.

110.  "MAKE ALL THE BANKS REPUBLICAN" (1803)

Wherever possible political advantage and financial
advantage were joined.  The practice was not peculiar to
any single political party.

As to the patronage of the Republican Bank at Providence, I am
decidedly in favor of making all the banks Republican, by sharing
deposits among them in proportion to the dispositions they show;
if the law now forbids it, we should not permit another session of
Congress to pass without amending it.  It is material to the safety

of Republicanism to detach the mercantile interest from its enemies
and incorporate them into the body of its friends.  A merchant is
naturally a Republican, and can be otherwise only from a vitiated
state of things.


Letter, Thomas Jefferson to Albert Gallatin, July 12, 1803,
Ford (ed.), Writings of Thomas Jefferson, VIII, p. 252.


### 111.  HOW THE BANK OF THE UNITED STATES BENEFITS THE FEDERAL GOVERNMENT (1803)


A succinct statement by the Secretary of
the Treasury.


The great advantages we derive from banks, and especially from
the Bank of the United States, are:
1st.  A safe place of deposit for the public moneys.
2nd.  The instantaneous transmission of such moneys from any
one part of the continent to another, the bank giving us immediately
credit at New York, if we want it, for any sum we may have at
Savannah, or at any other of their offices, and vice versa.
3rd.  The great facility which an increased circulation and
discounts give to the collection of the revenue.
For these reasons I am extremely anxious to see a bank at New
Orleans; considering the distance of that place, our own security
and even that of the collector will be eminently promoted, and the
transmission of moneys arising both from the impost and sales of
lands in the Mississippi Territory would without it be a very difficult and sometimes dangerous operation.


Letter, Albert Gallatin to Thomas Jefferson, December 13,
1803, H. Adams (ed.), Writings of Albert Gallatin, I, p. 171.

# J.

# GOVERNMENT AS ORGANIZER

### 112.  A NEW FRAME OF GOVERNMENT WILL REMEDY
### MANY COMMERCIAL EVILS (1786)

Dissatisfaction with the over-decentralized
government of the Articles of Confederation was widespread among the commercial classes of the country,
North and South.

The articles, created by 13 former colonies,
stressed their superior power over the central government.  As a politico-military alliance, it was effective.
After the Revolutionary War, however, merchants and
others attacked the inability of the central government
to enact and administer measures that would protect an
emerging national economic interest.  Madison was discussing the approaching convention of colonies at
Annapolis, Maryland, to discuss amendment of the Articles.
This meeting led to the Constitutional Convention the
following year.  Madison was now a member of the House of
Delegates in Virginia while Jefferson was United States
Minister to France.

Another unhappy effect of a continuance of the present anarchy
of our commerce will be a continuance of the unfavorable balance on
it, which by draining us of our metals furnishes pretexts for the
pernicious substitution of paper money, for indulgences to debtors,
for postponements of taxes.  In fact most of our political evils
may be traced up to our commercial ones, as most of our moral may
to our political.  The lessons which the mercantile interest of
Europe have received from late experience [i.e., Americans default-
ing on their overseas debts] will probably check their propensity

to credit us beyond our resources, and so far the evil of an unfavorable balance will correct itself.  But the Merchants of G.B. if
no others will continue to credit us at least as far as our remittances can be strained, and that is far enough to perpetuate our
difficulties unless the luxurious propensity of our own people can
be otherwise checked.  This view of our situation presents the proposed Convention as a remedial experiment which ought to command
every assent; but if it be a just view it is one which assuredly
will not be taken by all even of those whose intentions are good.


Letter, James Madison to Thomas Jefferson, March 18, 1786,
The Papers of James Madison, Vol. VI, Library of Congress.


### 113.  COMMERCIAL CONSIDERATIONS ON NEUTRALITY (1790)


Thomas Jefferson, as Secretary of State, had been
asked by President Washington to estimate the possible
effects on the United States of British seizure of
Louisiana and the Floridas.  Commercial considerations
played a large part in Jefferson's thoughts on the
matter.


Heads of consideration on the conduct we are to observe in the
war between Spain and Gt. Britain, and particularly should the
latter attempt the conquest of Louisiana and the Floridas.
The dangers of us should Gt. Britain possess herself of these
countries:
She will possess a territory equal to half ours beyond the
Mississippi.
She will seduce that half of ours which is on this side the
Mississippi, by the language, laws, religion, manners, government,
commerce, capital; by the possession of New Orleans, which draws
to it the dependence of all the waters of the Mississippi; by the
markets she can offer them in the Gulph of Mexico and elsewhere.
She will take from the remaining part of our states the markets
they now have for their produce, by furnishing those markets cheaper
with the same articles, tobacco, rice, indigo, bread, lumber, naval
stores, furs.
She will encircle us completely, by these possessions on our
land-board, and her fleets on the sea-board.
Instead of two neighbors balancing each other, we shall have
one, with more than the strength of both.
Would the prevention of this be worth a War?
Consider our abilities to take part in a war, our operations
would be by land only:  how many men should we need employ?  their
cost?  our resources of taxation and credit equal to this.
Weigh the evil of this new accumulation of debt against the
loss of markets, and eternal expense and danger from so overgrown
a neighbor.

But this is on a supposition that France as well as Spain shall be engaged in the war: for with Spain alone, the war would be unsuccessful, and our situation rendered worse.

No need to take a part in the war yet, we may choose our own time. Dealy gives us many chances to avoid it altogether. In such a choice of objects Gt. Britain may not single out Louisiana and the Floridas. She may fail in her attempt on them. France and Spain may recover them.

If all these chances fail we should have to retake them. The benefit between retaking and preventing overbalanced by the benefits of delay. Delay enables us to be better prepared; to obtain from the allies a price for our assistance.

Suppose these are ultimate views, what is to be done at this time?

1st. As to Spain? If she be as sensible as we are that she can not save Louisiana and the Floridas might she not prefer their independence to their subjection to Gt. Britain?

Does not the proposition of the Gt. de Estaing furnish us an opening to communicate our ideas on this subject to the Court of France, and through them to that of Madrid? and our readiness to join them in guaranteeing the independence of those countries?

This might save us from a war, if Gt. Britain respects our weight in a war. And if she does not, the object would place the war on popular ground with us.

2nd. As to England. Say to Beckwith:

That as to a treaty of commerce we would prefer amicable to adverse arrangements, though the latter would be infallible, and in our own power.

That our ideas are, that such a treaty should be founded in perfect reciprocity, and would therefore be its own price.

That as to an alliance we can say nothing till its object be shown, and that it will not be inconsistent with existing engagements.

That in the event of a war between Gt. Britain and Spain, we are disposed to be strictly neutral.

That however we should view with extreme uneasiness any attempts of either power to seize the possessions of the other on our frontier as we consider our own safety interested in a due balance between our neighbors. It might be advantageous to express this latter sentiment; because, if there be any difference of opinion in their Councils, whether to bend their force against North or South America, or the Islands (and certainly there is room for difference): and if these opinions be nearly balanced, that balance might be determined by the prospect of having an enemy more or less according to the object they would select.


Thomas Jefferson, July 12, 1790, "Considerations on Louisiana," in Roberton (ed.), Louisiana, I, pp. 265-267.

114.  CONGRESS IS NOT FILLED WITH STOCK-JOBBERS
AND PAPER-DEALERS (1792)

While on a visit to Mount Vernon, President
Washington heard from some of his neighbors that "all
the capital employed in paper speculation...has furnished effectual means of corrupting...a portion of the
legislature." He communicated this statement to Hamilton
and solicited the latter's comment.

As far as I know, there is not a member of the Legislature who
can properly be called a Stock-Jobber or a paper-Dealer.  There are
several of them who were proprietors of public debt in various ways;
some for money lent and property furnished for the use of the public
during the war, others for sums received in payment of debts -- and
it is supposable enough that some of them had been purchasers of
the public Debt, with intention to hold it as a valuable and convenient property; -- considering an honorable provision for it as a
matter of course.

It is a strange perversion of ideas, and as novel as it is
extraordinary, that men should be deemed corrupt and criminal for
becoming proprietors in the funds of their Country.  Yet I believe
the number of members of Congress is very small who have ever been
considerable proprietors in the funds.  And as to improper speculations on measures depending before Congress, I believe never was
any body of men freer from them.

There are, indeed, several members of Congress who have become
proprietors in the Bank of the United States, and a few of them to
a pretty large amount, say 50 or 60 shares, but all operations of
this kind were necessarily subsequent to the determination upon
the measure.  The subscriptions were of course subsequent and purchases still more so.  Can there be any thing really blamable in
this?  Can it be culpable to invest property in an institution which
has been established for the most important national purposes?  Can
that property be supposed to corrupt the holder?  It would indeed
tend to render him friendly to the preservation of the bank; but
in this, there would be no collision between duty and interest and
it would give him no improper bias on other questions.

To uphold public credit and to be friendly to the Bank must
be presupposed to be corrupt things before the being a proprietor in
the funds or of bank stock, can be supposed to have a corrupting
influence.  The being a proprietor, in either case, is a very
different thing from being, in a proper sense of the term a stock-
jobber.

Letter, Alexander Hamilton to George Washington, August 18,
1792, The Papers of Alexander Hamilton, Vol. 17, pp. 2300-2301,
Library of Congress.

## 115.  "PAPER-MEN" IN CONGRESS  (1793)

On February 28, 1793, Representative Giles moved
several resolutions of censure against Secretary Hamilton;
they were all defeated.  Here is Jefferson's explanation
of the outcome--a simple case of economic self-interest
by Congressmen.


Those who knew the composition of the house 1.  of bank directors  2.  holders of bank stock  3.  stock-jobbers.  4.  blind
devotees, 5.  ignorant persons who did not comprehend them.  6.  lazy
& good-humored persons, who comprehended & acknowledged them, yet
were too lazy to examine, or unwilling to pronounce censure.  The
persons who knew these characters foresaw that the 3. first descriptions making 1/3 of the house, the 3. latter would make 1/2 of the
residue, and of course that they would be rejected by a majority of
2. to 1.  But they thought that even this rejection would do good,
by shewing the public the desperate & abandoned dispositions with
which their affairs were entrusted.  The resolns were proposed, and
nothing spared to present them in the fulness of demonstration.
There were not more than 3. or 4. who voted otherwise than had been
expected.
It is known that [William Vans] Murray of Maryld deals in
paper.
Mar. 23. 1793.  The following list of paper-men is communicated
to me by Mr. Beckley.
[Nathanie] Gilman. S. [tock] H. [older] in U.S. Bank.
[Elbridge] Gerry. S.H.
[Theodore] Sedgewick.
[Fisher] Ames. S.H.
[Benjamin] Goodhue. S.H.
[Benjamin] Bourne of R.I. suspected only.
[Jonathan] Trumbul. S.H.
[Jeremiah] Wadsworth. S.H.
[James] Hillhouse. S.H.
[Amasa] Learned. S.H.
[John] Laurence S.H. & Director
[James] Gordon.
[Elias] Boudinot. S.H.
[Jonathan] Dayton S.H.
[Thomas] Fitsimmons S.H. & Director.
[Daniel] Heister S.H.
[Samuel] Sterret
[William Vans] Murray S.H.
[Hugh] Williamson S.H.
[William L.] Smith S.H. & Director for himself and his proxies his
             vote is near 1/5 of the whole
[George] Cabot. S.H. & Director
[Roger] Sherman. S.H.
[Oliver] Elsworth. qu.
[Rufus] King S.H. & Director.

| [Philemon] Dickinson | Stockholders | H.REPR | SENATE |
|---|---|---|---|
| [Robert] Morris S.H. | Other paper | 16 | 5 |
| [Samuel] Johnson | | 3 | 2 |
| [Ralph] Izard S.H. | | 19 – | 7 – |
| | Suspected | 2 – | 4 – |

Entries in The Anas, March 2 and March 23, 1793, Ford (ed.),
Writings of Thomas Jefferson, I, pp. 222-223.


116.  "IMPROVING OUR CONSTITUTION" FOR COPPER (1800)


Jefferson comments sardonically on the propensity
of economic privilege to stretch the meaning of the
Constitution.  His correspondent Robert Livingston was
chancellor of New York and a frequent holder of posts
in the foreign service.


We are here [i.e., Philadelphia] engaged in improving our
constitution by construction, so as to make it what the majority
thinks it should have been.  The Senate received yesterday a bill
from the Representatives incorporating a company for Roosevelt's
copper mines in Jersey.  This is under the sweeping clause of the
constitution, & supported by the following pedigree of necessities.
Congress are authorized to defend the country : ships are necessary
for that defence : copper is necessary for ships : mines are necessary to produce copper : companies are necessary to work mines : and
"this is the house that Jack built."

Letter, Thomas Jefferson to Robert R. Livingston, April 30,
1800, The Papers of Thomas Jefferson, Vol. 107, Library of Congress.


117.  FISCAL POLICY AND PUBLIC PARSIMONY (1804)


When Jefferson became President the federal
government was paying out annually one-third of its
total revenue in the form of interest on the national
debt.  Also, the federal government was the single
largest spender and customer in the country.  Public
funds had to be spent with a view towards a minimum impact
on the economy.  Here, Gallatin explains the relation of
federal specie payments overseas to the domestic banking
situation.

In every arrangement not connected with this Dept. which may
be adopted, I have but one observation, which is to request that the
Treasury may not be pressed this year beyond our former calculations.
...I allow three hundred thousand dollars to the Secretary of the
Navy for the equipment of the four additional frigates:  he wants
four hundred thousand dollars; but that is too much, as he pays them
only four months' pay and about three months' provisions.  Those together make a considerable sum beyond the estimate of last year,
and, although the revenue exceeds our calculations, the exportation
and debentures this winter and spring are very large.  But it is not
only on account of the Treasury that I wish an abstinence of expenses:  it is on account of the prodigious drain of specie, principally dollars, which has taken place and continues.  There are not
at present one hundred thousand dollars in dollars in Philadelphia,
New York, and Boston put together.  More than three millions of
dollars have been exported within six months from the vaults of the
Bank of the United States alone, and our second instalment to
Great Britain will in July take nearly nine hundred thousand dollars
more.  The principal cause of the drain is that no specie has been
last year or is now imported either from the British or Spanish
American colonies.  Under those circumstances, it is highly desirable to leave as large deposits with the bank as the public service
will permit.  If we press them hard, they must curtail their discounts suddenly to an extent equally injurious to commerce and our
revenue.

Letter, Albert Gallatin to Thomas Jefferson, May 3, 1804,
H. Adams (ed.), Writings of Albert Gallatin, I, p. 191.

118.  GOALS OF THE EXPEDITION (1803)

New means of extending America's commercial reach
were the prime, though not the only, goal set for the
Lewis-Clark expedition.  Meriwether Lewis to whom
Jefferson writes was his private secretary.

The object of your mission is to explore the Missouri river, &
such principal stream of it, as, by it's course & communication with
the waters of the Pacific Ocean, may offer the most direct & practicable water communication across this continent, for the purposes
of commerce.
The interesting points of the portage between the heads of the
Missouri & the water offering the best communication with the Pacific
Ocean should also be fixed by observation, & the course of that
water to the ocean, in the same manner as that of the Missouri.
The commerce which may be carried on with the people inhabiting
the line you will pursue, renders a knolege of these people

important. you will therefore endeavor to make yourself acquainted,
as far as a diligent pursuit of your journey shall admit,
> with the names of the nations & their numbers;
> the extent & limits of their possessions;
> their relations with other tribes or nations;
> their language, traditions, monuments;
> their ordinary occupations in agriculture, fishing,
> hunting, war, arts, & the implements for these;
> their food, clothing, & domestic accomodations;
> the diseases prevalent among them, & the remedies
> they use;
> moral & physical circumstances which distinguish
> them from the tribes we know;
> peculiarities in their laws, customs, & dispositions;
> and articles of commerce they may need or furnish,
> & to what extent.

. . . . . . . . . . . . . . . . . . . . . . . . . . . . . . . . . . . .
In all your intercourse with the natives treat them in the
most friendly & conciliatory manner which their conduct will admit;
allay all jealousies as to the object of your journey, satisfy them
of it's innocence, make them acquainted with the position, extent,
character, peaceable & commercial dispositions of the U.S. of our
wish to be neighborly, friendly & useful to them, & of our dispositions to a commercial intercourse with them; confer with them on
the points most convenient as mutual emporiums, & the articles of
most desirable interchange for them & us. if a few of their influential chiefs, within practicable distance, wish to visit us, arrange
such a visit with them, and furnish them with authority to call on
our officers, on their entering the U.S. to have them conveyed to
this place at public expence.

. . . . . . . . . . . . . . . . . . . . . . . . . . . . . . . . . . . .
Should you reach the Pacific ocean [one full line scratched
out, indecipherable.--Ed.] inform your self of the circumstances
which may decide whether the furs of those parts may not be collected
as advantageously at the head of the Missouri (convenient as is
supposed to the waters of the Colorado & Oregon or Columbia) as at
Nootka sound or any point of that coast; & that trade be consequently
conducted through the Missouri & U.S. more beneficially than by the
circumnavigation now practised.


Instructions from Thomas Jefferson to Meriwether Lewis, June
23, 1803, Reuben C. Thwaites (ed.), Original Journals of the Lewis
and Clark Expedition, 1804-1806, VII, (New York:  Dodd, Mead & Co.,
1905), pp. 248-249, 250, 251.

119.  ACCOMPLISHMENTS OF THE EXPEDITION (1806)

Lewis writes to Jefferson.


     In obedience to your orders we have penetrated the Continent
of North America to the Pacific Ocean and suficiently explored the
interior of the country to affirm that we have discovered the most
practicable communication which does exist across the continent by
means of the navigable branches of the Missouri and Columbia Rivers;
this is by way of the Missouri to the foot of the rapids five miles
below the great falls of that river a distance of 2575 Miles,
thence by land passing the Rocky Mountains to the Kooskooske 340
and from thence by way of the Kooskooske, the S.E. branch of the
Columbia and the latter river to the Ocean of 640 Miles making a
total of 3555 Miles. the Missouri possesses sufficient debth of
water as far as is specifyed for boats of 15 tons burthen, but those
of smaller capacity are to be prefered, the navigation may be deemed
safe and good. of 340 Miles land carriage 200 Miles is along a good
road and 140 over tremendious mountains which for 60 Miles are
covered with eternal snows. notwithstanding the Rocky Mountains thus
present a most formidable barrier to this tract across the continent
a passage is practicable from the last of June to the last of
September, and expence of transportation over land may be reduced
to a mere trifle by means of horses which can be procured in immence
numbers and for the most trivial considerations from the natives
inhabiting the rocky Mountains and Plains of Columbia West of those
Mountains.
. . . . . . . . . . . . . . . . . . . . . . . . . . . . . . . . . . . . . . . . .
     We vew this passage across the continent as affording immence
advantagees to the fir trade but fear that advantages wich it offers
as a communication for the productions of the East Indias to the
United States and thence to.Europe will never be found equal on an
extensive scale to that by the way of the Cape of good hope. still
we beleive that many articles not bulky brittle nor of a perishable
nature may be conveyed to the U'.States by this rout with more
facility and less expence that by that at present practiced.  That
portion of the Continent watered by the Missouri and all it's branches from the Cheyenne upwards is richer in beaver and Otter than any
country on earth particularly that proportion of it's subsiduary
streams lying within the Rocky mountains; the furs of all this
immence tract of country including such as may be collected on the
upper portion of the St. Peters, the Assinniboin & Red rivers may
be conveyed to the mouth of the Columbia by the 1$^{st}$ of August in
each year and from thence be shiped to and arrive at Canton earlier
than the furs which are annually shiped from Montreal arrive in
England.  The N West Company of Canada were they permited by the
U.S. might also convey their furs collected in the Athebaske on the
Saskashawan and South and West of lake Winnipicque by that rout within the same period. in the infancy of this trade across the Continent or during the period that the trading establishments shall be
confined to the branches of the Missouri the men employed in this

trade will be compelled to convey the furs collected on that
quarter as low on the Columbia as tide water in which case they
could not return to the falls of the Missouri untill about the 1$^{st}$.
of October which would be so late in the season that there would be
considerable danger of the river being obstructed by ice before
they could reach S$^{t}$. Louis and the comodities of the East Indias
thus detained untill the following spring. but this dificulty will
vanish when establishments are made on the Columbia and a sufficient
number of men employed at them to convey the East India commodities
to the upper establishment on the Kooskooske and there exchanging
them with the men of the Missouri for their furs in the begining
of July. by these means the furs not only of the Missouri but those
of the Columbia may be shiped to Canton by the season before mentioned and the commit[i]es of the East Indias arrive at S$^{t}$· Louis
by the last of September in each Year. altho' the Columbia dose not
as much as the Missouri abound in beaver and Otter yet it is by no
means despicable in this respect and would furnish a profitable fur
trade, in addition to the otter and beaver considerable quantities
of the finest bear of three species affording a great variety of
colours, the Tyger catt, several species of fox, the Martin and Sea
Otter might be procured beside the rackoon and some other animals
of an inferior class of furs.  If the government will only aid even
on a limited scale the enterprize of her Citizens I am convinced
that we shall soon derive the benifits of a most lucrative trade
from this source. and in the course of 10 or 12 Years a tour
across the Continent by this rout will be undertaken with as little
concern as a voyage across the Atlantic is at present.

    The British N. West company of Canaday have for several years
past carried on a partial trade with the Mandans Minnetares and
Avahaways on the Missouri from their establishments on the Assinniboin
near the entrance of Mouse R. at present I have every reason to
believe that they intend forming an establishment very shortly on
the Missouri near those nations with a view to ingroce the fir trade
of that River.  the known enterprize and resou[r]ces of this Company
latterly stre[n]gthened by an union with its powerful rival the
X.Y. Company have rendered them formidable in that distant part of
the continent to all other traders, and if we are to regard the
trade of the Missouri as an object of importance to the U. States
the strides of this company towards that river cannot be too vigel-
ently watched nor too firmly and spedily opposed by our givernment.


    Letter, Meriwether Lewis to Thomas Jefferson, September 23,
1806, Thwaites (ed.), <u>Original Journals of the Lewis and Clark
Expedition</u>, VII, pp. 334, 335-336.

120.  THE COMMERCIAL DISADVANTAGE OF DISUNION (1813)

Among the New England Federalists, during the War
of 1812, strong pro-British sentiments led to an embryonic
secession movement.  In an incisive paragraph, President
Madison noted the consequent economic disadvantage for New
England.  Later, Madison's basic argument was repeated by
Ruffin in support of southern secession.  (See Source No.
298).

I have never allowed myself to believe that the Union was in
danger, or that a dissolution of it could be desired, unless by a
few individuals, if such there be, in desperate situations or of
unbridled passions.  In addition to the thousand affinities belonging
to every part of the Nation, every part has an interest as deep as
it is obvious, in maintaining the bond which keeps the whole together; and the Eastern part certainly not less than any other.
Looking to the immediate & commercial effect of a dissolution, it
is clear that the Eastern part would be the greatest loser, by such
an event; and not likely therefore deliberately to rush into it;
especially when it takes into view, the groundlessness of the suspicions which alone suggest so dreadful an alternative, and the
turn which would probably grow out of it, to the relations with
Europe.  The great road of profitable intercourse for New England,
even with old England, lies through the Wheat, the Cotton & the
Tobacco fields of her Southern & Western confederates.  On what
basis [could] N. E. & O. E. form commercial stipulations.  On all
the great articles, they would be in direct rivalship.  The real
source of our Revolution was the commercial jealousy of G. B. towards
that part [i.e., New England] of her then Colonies.  If [there be
links] of common interest between the two Countries, they w .
connect the S. & not the N. States, with that part of Europe.

Letter, James Madison to Col. David Humphreys, March 22, 1813,
The Papers of James Madison, Vol. 51, Library of Congress.
The bracketed phrase is G. Hunt's interpretation of an almost-
illegible part of the original letter.

121.   GIRARD AND ASTOR BUY GOVERNMENT BONDS
AT A DISCOUNT (1813)

The wealthy mercantile Federalist aristocracy of
New England opposed the War of 1812 against England.
A great stream of specie flowed from all over the country
to New England coffers during the war, but these wealthy
merchants refused to buy U.S. government bonds.  So poor

was the market for these securities, that these had
to be offered at a 12 per cent discount before even
non-New Englanders like Astor and Girard bought them.
Girard was a wealthy Philadelphia merchant and banker;
Astor was one of the wealthiest financial merchants,
situated in New York City; and Parish was a Scotch-
born financier from Hamburg who dealt widely in trans-
atlantic investments.

     Sir:  In consequence of the notice given by the Treasury
Department, under the date of the 18th of March, 1813, that proposals will be received by you for the whole, or part of the residue
of the loan of sixteen millions of dollars, we herewith beg leave
to offer to take as much stock of the United States, bearing
interest at six per cent. per annum, payable quarter-yearly, (the
stock not to be redeemable before the 31st of December, 1825, at
the rate of eighty-eight dollars for a certificate of one hundred
dollars, as aforesaid,) as will amount to the sum of eight millions
of dollars, or to the residue of the said loan, provided you will
agree to allow us the option of accepting the same terms that may
be granted to persons lending money to the United States, by virtue
of any law authorizing another loan for the service of the year
1813, that Congress may pass before the last day of the present
year.
     It must be further understood and agreed to, that one quarter
per cent, will be allowed us on the amount to which the present
proposal will be accepted.
     Sir:  I will take for myself, and my friends in New York, two
million and fifty-six thousand dollars' worth of the loan authorized
by Congress in February last, receiving six per cent. stock at the
rate of eighty-eight dollars, money for one hundred dollars of six
per cent stock, payable in New York, by instalments, as proposed
by you, or as may be otherwise agreed on.  I understand that, in
case Government should make another loan during the year, I am to
be placed on as good footing as the lenders of money, or contractors
for that loan, will be.  I also understand that I am to receive the
quarter per cent. which is to be paid to persons procuring subscriptions to the present loan.
     GENTLEMEN:  Your proposal for lending seven million fifty-five
thousand eight hundred dollars to the United States, in part of the
sixteen millions loan, is accepted.  You will be pleased to deliver,
before the 15th day of this month, to the cashier of Stephen Girard's
bank, or such other, where, according to your proposals, the payments
are intended to be made, the names of persons embraced by your proposal, together with the sum respectively payable by each.  Each
will be entitled to receive in payment, at his option, either six
per cent. stock at the rate of eighty-eight per cent., or six per
cent. stock at par, and a thirteen years' annuity of one and a
half per cent. of the money loaned; which option must be made at
the time of paying the first instalment.  The payments shall be made
in eight equal instalments on the 15th days of April, May, June,
July, August, September, October, and November.  But every person,

at the time of paying any of the instalments, may pay all or any
number of the subsequent instalments.  Certificates of funding
stock will, on the applications of any subscriber for more than one
hundred thousand dollars, be issued, on payment of any one instalment; for the amount of the next preceding instalment.  In every
other respect, the terms of the public notice of the 20th of
February last will be considered as part of this agreement.


     Letters, Stephen Girard and David Parish to Albert Gallatin,
April 5, 1813; John Jacob Astor to Albert Gallatin, April 5, 1813;
and Albert Gallatin to Girard and Astor, April 7, 1813; Elliot,
Funding System, (New York:  A. M. Kelly, 1968), pp. 565-566.

# PART II
# A COMMERCIAL
# ECONOMY, 1815-1860

# A.

## LAND AS REAL ESTATE

122.  LAND VALUES ON THE WABASH WILL RISE SHARPLY (1817)

Clay's expectations were not over-enthusiastic--if
his land was already paid for.  Clay was Speaker of the
U.S. House of Representatives.  He writes to Thornton who
was Superintendent of the U.S. Patent Office.

I have to say, that, during the summer, I purchased, on the
Wabash, about 2000 Acres of land from the Govt. at its fixed price
of two dollars per acre--The district of Country in which I brought
it is rapidly peopling & settling.  Considering the progress of
population and improvement, and judging from the rise of lands in
the States of Kentucky & Ohio, I do believe that, in a few years,
this land will be worth 15 or 20 dollars per acre.  This agumenta-
tion, which of course, is matter of opinion, founded however upon
the experience of those States and upon observation elsewhere &
reflection, is mainly to be attributed to the growth of our popula-
tion, and <u>the</u> <u>cultivation</u> <u>of</u> <u>the</u> <u>neighbouring</u> <u>lands</u>.  I had the
advantage of information, it is true, in my selection which every
one would not possess himself of, without much more time & research
than I employed.

Letter, Henry Clay to William Thornton, December 6, 1817,
Hopkins and Hargreaves (eds.), <u>Papers of Henry Clay</u>, II, (Lexington,
Kentucky.  University of Kentucky Press, 1961), p. 407.

123.  A PLOW YIELDS NO BETTER TITLE THAN A SPADE (1817)


Madison was attempting to counter the popular argument that Americans had a superior right to the Indian
hunting grounds inasmuch as Americans could make "more
use" of them through agriculture.  (See Source No. 9).


It seemed...that an <u>unqualified</u> right of a civilized people
to land used by people in the hunter-state, on the principle that
the earth was intended for those who would make it most conducive
to the sustenance & increase of the human race, might imply a right
in a people cultivating it with the Spade, to say to one using the
plow, either adopt our mode, or let us substitute it ourselves.
It might also be not easy to repel the claims of those without land
in other Countries, if not in our own, to vacant lands within the
U.S. likely to remain for a <u>long</u> period unproductive of human food.


Letter, James Madison to James Monroe, December 27, 1817,
<u>The Papers of James Madison</u>, Vol. 65, Library of Congress.


124.   CONQUEST CREATES SUPERIOR PROPERTY
RIGHT IN LAND (1823)


Virtually since 1607, American colonization had
proceeded on the assumption that appropriation of
Indian land by force of conquest was justifiable.  In
<u>M'intosh</u>, the Supreme Court gave judicial approval to
this doctrine.  The Court did not examine the contention
that Indian societies had their own formalized conception
of property rights.


We will not enter into the controversy, whether agriculturists,
merchants, and manufacturers, have a right, on abstract principles,
to expel hunters from the territory they possess, or to contract
their limits.  Conquest gives a title which the courts of the
conqueror cannot deny, whatever the private and speculative opinions
of individuals may be, respecting the original justice of the claim
which has been successfully asserted.  The British government, which
was then our government, and whose rights have passed to the United
States, asserted a title to all the lands occupied by Indians within
the chartered limits of the British colonies.  It asserted also a
limited sovereignty over them, and the exclusive right of extin-
guishing the title which occupancy gave to them.  These claims have
been maintained and established as far west as the river Mississippi, by the sword.  The title to a vast portion of the lands we now

hold, originates in them.  It is not for the courts of this country
to question the validity of this title, or to sustain one which is
incompatible with it.

. . . . . . . . . . . . . . . . . . . . . . . . . . . . . . . . .

      But the tribes of Indians inhabiting this country were fierce
savages, whose occupation was war, and whose subsistence was drawn
chiefly from the forest.  To leave them in possession of their
country was to leave the country a wilderness; to govern them as a
distinct people was impossible, because they were as brave and as
high spirited as they were fierce, and were ready to repel by arms
every attempt on their independence.

. . . . . . . . . . . . . . . . . . . . . . . . . . . . . . . . .

      Frequent and bloody wars, in which the whites were not always
the aggressors, unavoidably ensued.  European policy, numbers and
skill, prevailed.  As the white population advanced, that of the
Indians necessarily receded.  The country in the immediate neighborhood of agriculturists became unfit for them.  The game fled into
thicker and more unbroken forests, and the Indians followed.

. . . . . . . . . . . . . . . . . . . . . . . . . . . . . . . . .

      However extravagant the pretension to converting the discovery
of an inhabited country into conquest may appear, if the principle
has been asserted in the first instance, and afterwards sustained;
if a country has been acquired and held under it; if the property of
the great mass of the community originates in it, it becomes the
law of the land, and cannot be questioned.  So, too, with respect
to the concomitant principle, that the Indian inhabitants are to be
            merely as occupants, to be protected, indeed, while in
peace, in possession of their lands, but to be deemed incapable of
transferring the absolute title to others.


      Johnson and Graham's Lessee v. William M'Intosh (8 Wheaton
543), Cotton (ed.), Constitutional Decisions of John Marshall, II,
pp. 19, 20-21, 22.



## 125.  LANDLESS IN THE WEST (1827)


      It is perhaps reason enough to doubt the truth of the
report to say that Hezekiah Niles believed it to be untrue.
But contemporary sources do leave the indistinct impression
that there were landless in the west.  How many is known
only imperfectly.


"The number of persons in the new states and territories, who
were without land two years ago, was investigated by the marshals,
in obedience to a resolution passed in the senate of the United
States, on the motion of colonel Benton.  They were ascertained to
be as follows:--In Ohio, 57,286; Illinois, 9,220; Indiana, 13,485;
Missouri, 10,118; Alabama, 39,368; Mississippi, 5,505; Louisiana,

8,464; Florida, 1,906; Michigan, 985; Arkansas, no return:--in all, upwards of 140,000 heads of families."

We do not know the object of the preceding statement.  Is it, that land may be given to those who have it not?  If so, there are a few of us in the old states that would like to come in for a share!  But we think that, with land at 125 cents per acre, with selections of lots, few "heads of families," capable of holding and rightfully using land, need want it.  With most others, the gift made would soon only swell the monopolies of heartless speculators. "Heads of families!"--What is meant by the words here used?  "Families" in the U.States will average about six persons--in the west, including free laborers, say only five.  It is pretended that 39,308 persons in Alabama, representing 200,000 white people, are without land?  The whole state hardly contains so many heads of families. As we have seen only the preceding summary notice of the document referred to, we shall not impute a want of honesty to the statement, though we are sorry to say that "high pressure" things, presenting gross falsehood in the language of truth, has more than once been sufferd to obtain the quasi sanction of congress in the shape of a report, &c.  It is not true that there were 39,368 "heads of families" in Alabama, 10,118 in Missouri, &c without land, two years ago.


Niles' Weekly Register, December 26, 1829, p. 274.



126.  THE THIRST OF CONGRESSMEN FOR LAND (1838)


Congress was considering a bill to permit actual settlers first chance at federal land once it was placed on the market.  Settlers who were squatting on federal land without title would be assured of one by payment of a nominal sum.  In 1841, such a law was enacted.  Adams' acerbic observations about land-hungry congressmen were very close to the truth.  By now he was a member of the U.S. House of Representatives.


The Pre-emption bill was taken up.  It was debated the whole day with much pertinacity, and Governor Lincoln, the only member of the Committee on the Public Lands representing an interest to pre-serve them as the property of the people, obtained, with the assis-tance of Briggs, two or three palliative amendments, which I believe not worth contending for.  The thirst of a tiger for blood is the fittest emblem of the rapacity with which the members of all the new States fly at the public lands.  The constituents upon whom they depend are all settlers, or tame and careless spectators of the pillage.  They are themselves enormous speculators and land-jobbers. It were a vain attempt to resist them here.
. . . . . . . . . . . . . . . . . . . . . . . . . . . . . . . . . . .

After the recess the Pre-emption bill was again taken up, and passed.  Governor Lincoln and Briggs succeeded in carrying amendments confining the operation of the bill to the benefit of actual bona fide settlers.  They were vehemently opposed by Crary and Casey and the Western members, whose tactics are to abuse without mercy the speculators in debate, and to oppose every possible expedient to guard against them.

Entry for June 14, 1838, C. F. Adams (ed.), Memoirs of John Quincy Adams, X, p. 19.


127.  DANIEL WEBSTER ON THE ECONOMIC
SIGNIFICANCE OF LAND (1838)


The conversion of the public domain into private property and wealth gave rise to countless business transactions and consequently the need for more credit and currency.  The bank-note "inflation" of the 1830's may have been as much a real-estate phenomenon as a currency operation.  Could as great a territory have become private property without repercussions on the means of exchange?  Webster, U.S. Senator from Massachusetts, gave this speech on the floor of the Senate on March 12, 1838.


More than all, the country is new, sir; almost the entire amount of our capital active; and the whole amount of property, in the aggregate, rapidly increasing.  In the last three years thirty-seven millions of acres of land have been separated from the wilderness, purchased, paid for, and become subject to private individual ownership, to transfer and sale, and all other dispositions to which other real estate is subject.  It has thus become property, to be bought and sold for money; whereas while in the hands of government, it called for no expenditure, formed the basis of no transactions, and created no demand for currancy.  Within that short period our people have bought from government a territory as large as the whole of England and Wales, and, taken together, far more fertile by nature.  This seems incredible, yet the return show it.  Suppose all this to have been bought at the minimum price of a dollar and a quarter per acre; and suppose the value to be increased in the common ratio in which we know the value of land is increased, by such purchase, and by the preliminary steps and beginnings of cultivation; an immense augmentation, it will readily be perceived, is made, even in so short a time, of the aggregate of property, in nominal price, and, to a great extent, in real value also.

Niles' Weekly Register, April 7, 1838, p. 92.

128.   REAL ESTATE VALUES IN SAN FRANCISCO
AND MONTEREY (1842-1847)


East or West, settlement pushed land values upward.
The prospect of outright American ownership of California
furthered the upward tendency of land values.  The writer
of this extract, Thomas Larkin, arrived in California in
1832 and soon became one of the wealthiest merchants in
that Mexican province.  During the following 16 years he
was, at one time or another, U.S. Consul in Monterey,
Confidential Agent of the United States, U.S. Navy Agent
for the Territory of California, and U.S. Naval Storekeeper.
He was a prime organizer of the pro-U.S. movement in
California which culminated in the admission of California
as a state in 1850.  In 1847, Buchanan was U.S. Secretary
of State.


As a proof of the nature of real estate in this country which
rise is mostly to be attributed to our taking possession, I would
state that building lots one hundred to one hundred and twenty feet
square in choice situations in this town and the town of San Francisco that cost under one hundred dollars (100$) each two years ago
are now worth two thousand dollars (2,000$).  I have three lots in
the two places that cost five years back fifty dollars (50$) the
alcalde's fees that I can now sell for eight thousand dollars and
they have no improvement of any kind.  Property on the outskirts
of the two towns have increased at less rates.  In towns south of
Monterey there is no advance in real estate, arising from the fact
that but a few Americans reside in them and the uncertainty that
prevails as to whether our line will be so far south as $32^{0}$.


Letter, Thomas O. Larkin to James Buchanan, November 10, 1847,
in George P. Hammond (ed.), The Larkin Papers, VII, (Berkeley,
California:  University of California Press, 1951-1960), pp. 58-59.


129.   ABSENTEE OWNERSHIP IS THE CURSE OF
THE RICE COUNTRY (1847)


In the greatest of the slave states--South Carolina--
absentee ownership was the privilege of the proprietors of
the giant plantations.  Spending a good part of the year
(and of their fortune) in Charlestown society, they could
hardly be classed as active entrepreneurs.  Note that only
the brave ever criticized this practice.  To these owners,
the plantations were real estate investments.  They did not
become sentimental over land.

Absenteeism is the curse and will be, unless diminishe'd, the ruin of the low country, in-as-much as its tendency is to disorganization.   It diminishes the value of Estates, abridges the revenue of the planter, and the comfort of the negroe, except in the case of smart progressing fellows, because they (and there are a number of this kind) manage to convert to their own use and profit a portion of their time and labor which should properly go to swell the income of the owner and so far contribute to the comfortable supply of the whole plantation.

It breaks in upon (has broken in several instances) that tie between master, master's, master's family and slave of which you know the force, and which depends so much upon mutual intimate acquaintance, and occasional, nameless, kindnesses shown.

. . . . . . . . . . . . . . . . . . . . . . . . . . . . . . . . . .

I refer'd (the first time any one has had the temerity to refer to it publicly) to absenteeism and traced its influence on pauperism: and in enumerating as well as I could from memory the Rice plantation and settlements, the proprietors (and in case of Estates, the Executors) of 46 only are bona fide residents.   The proprietors of 50 are, at this moment, absent, and are habitually absent, without the limits of the district from the latter part of May till the beginning of November.   The proprietors of 12 are absentees the year round, having permanent residence of family elsewhere, and coming up occasionally in winter to look after their individual interest.   As you may well suppose the mass of the wealth is owned by the 62 absentees.   The 46 however are creeping up, as they make more of their property and it is among them that you will find the best discipline.

. . . . . . . . . . . . . . . . . . . . . . . . . . . . . . . . . .

Letter, R.F.W. Allston to John C. Calhoun, July 28, 1847, Boucher and Brooks (ed.), Correspondence Addressed to John C. Calhoun, pp. 388-389.

### 130.   LOW LAND PRICE FACILITATES RECKLESS USE OF COTTON ACREAGE (1854)

Olmsted painted a picture which, climate and commodity aside, applied to his native New York just as well.   There, the relatively low price of land dissuaded farmers from making capital improvements on the land.   In the cotton South, this tendency was aggravated by the additional capital required for investment in slaves.   Olmsted was a landscape architect and farmer who made this tour to supply information for a series of articles in the New York Times.

The present facility of acquiring land in the cotton States, the capital needed for its purchase not exceeding, for fresh soil, on an average, three dollars an acre, and the large outlay of capital needed to obtain labor, necessarily induces that mode of agriculture which has desolated so large a portion of the seaboard Slave States.  Twenty slave laborers cost over twenty thousand dollars. They will cultivate four hundred acres of land, which costs less than tenth of that sum.  Knowing that he can buy as much as he wants, at an equally low rate, why, when the production of his land decreases, should the slave owner drain it, or manure it, or, "rest" it, or vary his crops, to prevent further exhaustion?  It will cost twenty dollars' worth of labor to manure an acre.  Why make this expenditure when he can obtain other land at five dollars an acre (fenced and ready for the plough), which, without manure, will return just as much cotton for the same amount of labor (in cultivation merely) as this with it?  Why, when on fresh soil he can get three hundred dollars' worth of cotton a year for each slave employed in cultivating it, should he apply that labor to some other crop on his old land which would return him not more than a hundred dollars for each slave employed?  Why, in these circumstances, should he arrange to remain half his life on the same spot?  and if he is not expecting to remain, why should he expend his costly labor on houses and roads and bridges and fruit trees, or on schools and churches, or on railroads and wharves?  Fifteen years hence his land will no longer be worth cultivating for cotton, and it will then afford no business to a railroad or a steamboat, and in the meantime the difference between wagoning and railing or boating his cotton to the merchant would do but little toward defraying the cost of a railroad or establishing a steamboat route.

Frederick L. Olmsted, A Journey in the Back Country in the Winter of 1853–4, II, (New York:  G. P. Putnam's Sons, 1907), pp. 146–147.

# B.

# EXPANSION OF AGRICULTURE

131.  FARMING NEAR HARRISBURG, PENNSYLVANIA (1821)

Two differences between agriculture south and north
lay in labor requirements and cultivation techniques.  In
southern cotton growing, large masses of unfree workers
were utilized; and cultivation techniques were extensive
rather than intensive.  The prominent politician and practical farmer John C. Calhoun here describes a case of
contrast.

At this time Calhoun was serving as Secretary of War.
The extract is from a letter of September 27, 1821 to John
Ewing Calhoun, a son of the writer's first cousin.

I spent a day with a friend of mine, a farmer, near Harrisburg,
and examined with care every part of his farm.  His land is not so
good naturally as that in Calhoun's settlement, yet he makes much
more to the hand than what we do.  He rents most of his farm for
half of the product.  The part that he cultivates is of considerable
extent, yet he hires steadily, but one negro fellow at 5$ per month.
He informs me that he raises independently of what he gets from his
tenants, in average years, about 800 bushels of corn, 500 of wheat
and nearly the same quantity of oats and rye, besides grass.  He
hires, in harvest, additional labour; but this source of expenditure
he thinks does not exceed $20; and himself and his son in law, who
lives with him aids his labourer particularly in harvest and planting, but the whole of the ploughing, harrowing, and the attending
to his horses, cattle and hogs is done by the single labourer.  I
know my friend to be a man of the strictest veracity, and the statement may be fully relied on.  To us it must appear all most incredible; but when we come to examine his mode of cultivation our

surprise will cease.  Take for instance the Indian corn.  He prepares the ground thoroughly for it before it is planted, but after
that, instead of ploughing, as we do 4, 5, or 6 times, he gives it
but one harrowing and one ploughing.  I saw his field so cultivated.
The corn had been injured by the drought, but still I think it would
give 30 bushels an acre.  I think there are three causes why they
can raise corn with so little labour.  The ground being deeply
ploughed, and the surface thoroughly turned down, much of the weeds'
and grass' seeds do not sprout the next summer; the clover cultivation expels both the grass and weeds to a great extent; and the corn
is planted so close, about 3 feet apart both ways, as to overshadow
and prevent the growth of grass and weeds.  The two first causes may
be introduced with us, and the last by making our ground rich and
obtaining our seed corn from the north might also be, I should
suppose.


    J. Franklin Jameson (ed.), Correspondence of John C. Calhoun,
(Washington, D.C.:  Government Printing Office, 1900), pp. 196-197.
(Annual Report of the American Historical Association for the Year
1899, Vol. II.)



            132.  CREATE A HOME MARKET FOR BREAD STUFFS (1824)


        A short statement of a view that came to dominate
    after the 1820's is made here by Andrew Jackson, at this
    time a U.S. Senator from Tennessee.


    I will ask what is the real situation of the agriculturalist?
Where has the American farmer a market for his surplus products?
Expect for cotton he has neither a foreign nor a home market.  Does
not this clearly prove, when there is no market either at home or
abroad, that there is too much labor employed in agriculture? and
that the channels of labor should be multiplied?  Common sense
points out at once the remedy.  Draw from agriculture the super-
abundant labor, employ its mechanism and manufactures, thereby
creating a home market for your breadstuffs, and distributing labor
to a most profitable account, and benefits to the country will result.  Take from agriculture in the United States six hundred thousand men, women, and children, and you at once give a home market
for more bread stuffs than all Europe now furnishes us.  In short,
sir, we have been too long subject to the policy of the British
merchants.  It is time we should become a little more Americanized,
and instead of feeding the paupers and laborers of Europe, feed our
own, or else in a short time, by continuing our present policy, we
shall all be paupers ourselves.

Letter, Andrew Jackson to Dr. L. H. Coleman, April 26, 1824,
John S. Bassett (ed.), Correspondence of Andrew Jackson, III,
(Washington, D.C.:  Carnegie Institution of Washington, 1928), p.
250.


### 133.  MANUFACTURERS BID UP WAGES BEYOND ABILITY OF FARMERS TO PAY (1832)


Farmers who used hired help did not worry overly
about creating a domestic market for manufacturers.
Despite the assurances of George Washington (source
No. 66A) to the contrary, manufactures were expanding
by recruiting labor from the countryside.  Immigration
was of very minor importance as a source of factory
labor during this period.  These statements were made
by Henry Stark on New Hampshire and by Caleb Page on
Dunbarton.


[NEW HAMPSHIRE]  I would allude to the circumstance that the
price of labor has increased to such an extent that the most rigid
economist cannot till the land by means of hired laborers, and obtain enough produce from it to defray the expenses of cultivation.
For, sir, it is a fact of common notoriety, that the manufacturers
of cotton and woollens are enabled to conduct their business by
paying wages to workmen which no other business in the country will
justify.  The effect of this high price of labor is to induce men
and women to abandon their laudable occupations at home, to the detriment of their farms and households, and of that which is still
more valuable, their morals.  And the effect of this system is so
extensive, that it is with the utmost difficulty the service of men
can be obtained to cultivate the soil.  The price which the manufacturer affords being so much greater than the farmer can possibly
pay, that young men consider themselves destitute of enterprise if
they are content to drive the ox or follow the plough.  Thus, it is
obvious, that this state of things tends directly to degrade the
many, who are agriculturists, and elevate the few, who are manufacturers.  Now, sir, if this discrepancy exists in our present
tariff laws, some course should be taken by the Government, by which
the agriculturist shall be relieved; by which an inducement shall
be given to him that tills the soil, to bestow upon it labor and
capital, which is indispensable to unfold the resources of the
country:  and, sir, till such an experiment shall have its proper
effect, the condition of the agriculturist must inevitably grow
worse.
     What, then, is to be done?  It is obvious that such a course
of legislature enactment should be pursued as will effect a reduction in the profits of manufacturing establishments, by which you

will compel the owners of these corporations to curtail their expenses, and reduce the price of labor at least 33 per cent. By this
measure of the Government will be brought into existence that state
of harmony among the conflicting interests of the country which the
durability of the Union requires.

. . . . . . . . . . . . . . . . . . . . . . . . . . . . . . . . . . .

[DUNBARTON]  This is an agricultural rather than a manufacturing town.  The condition of the people is generally comfortable; and
the only way their interest is effected by the manufacturing establishments, is the difficulty they find in procuring laborers, in
consequence of the exorbitant prices paid by the manufactures in the
large establishments, in order to procure all the laborers in the
country worth hiring.  In this way the manufacturers have contributed more than any other circumstances, to depress the agricultural
interest; we must pay the manufacturers the full price for the goods
we purchase of them, when we can hardly procure laborers to cultivate our farms from which we derive the means of livelihood.  They,
on the contrary, are bolstered up by the tariff, and can give what
wages they please, and command the best help in the country.  As far
as I can learn, the manufacturing interest has tended to depress that
of agriculturalist.  Those living in their neighborhood find, it is
true, a ready market for all they produce; while those farther back
in the country find difficulty in producing any thing for the market, on account of the expense of labor and difficulty of procuring
labor at times even at an exorbitant price.  In other words, it is
considered more respectable to be the well paid drudge of a factory,
than be engaged in the service of the plain living and hard-laboring,
honest yeomantry of the country.

U.S. Congress, 22nd, 1st session, House Doc. No. 308, Documents
Relative To The Manufactures In The United States, I, (Washington,
D.C.:  Duff Green, 1833), pp. 684-685, 742-743.


134.  THE DEFICIENCY IN AMERICAN FARM CAPITAL (1839)


After Western grains started to flood Eastern markets,
farmers on the coast were forced to specialize in non-grain
crops or to increase productivity of their grain acreage,
or to migrate as pioneers or factory workers.  Farmers
who were able to shift over to dairying or horticulture
found they needed much larger capital investments than had
sufficed earlier.  Such farmers, concentrated near urban
markets, paid heed to Buel's preachments.  Jesse Buel, who
writes, was a printer, publisher, editor, judge, and worst
of all -- an agricultural reformer.

The deficiency in farming capital, or rather the stinginess with which capital is employed in improving and maintaining the condition of our lands, is another cause of declension in the profits and character of our Agriculture. The farmer is too prone to invest his surplus means in some new business, or in adding to his acres, instead of applying them to increase the profits of his labor and the products of his farm. He either works more land than he can work well and profitably, or he diverts to other objects the means which would yield a better return if applied to the improvement of the farm. He is apt to consider twenty or thirty dollars an enormous and wasteful outlay upon an acre of land, or upon a choice animal; and yet the interest of this outlay will be ten times paid by the increase of crop or the increase of the animal; and in most cases the principal also will be returned to him in the course of two or three years. Many of the most thriving farmers in southern New York, New Jersey, and Pennsylvania make a quadrennial expenditure of twenty dollars or more to manure an acre; and it has become a maxim with them that the more the outlay for manure, the greater the net profit of their lands. But it is not the outlay for manure alone that demands a liberal expenditure of capital. Good seed, good farm stock, and good implements are all essential to the economy of labor, and to neat and profitable farming.

Harry J. Carman (ed.), Jesse Buel. Agricultural Reformer. Selections From His Writings, (New York: Columbia University Press, 1947), p. 245.


135.  A SLAVE DESCRIBES SUGAR CULTIVATION (1840)


Although a slave, Northup was hired out by his master to work for wages on a Louisiana cane sugar plantation.


The ground is prepared in beds, the same as it is prepared for the reception of the cotton seed, except it is ploughed deeper. Drills are made in the same manner. Planting commences in January, and continues until April. It is necessary to plant a sugar field only once in three years. Three crops are taken before the seed or plant is exhausted.

Three gangs are employed in the operation. One draws the cane from the rick, or stack, cutting the top and flags from the stalk, leaving only that part which is sound and healthy. Each joint of the cane has an eye, like the eye of a potato, which sends forth a sprout when buried in the soil. Another gang lays the cane in the drill, placing two stalks side by side in such manner that joints will occur once in four or six inches. The third gang follows with hoes, drawing earth upon the stalks, and covering them to the depth of three inches.

In four weeks, at the farthest, the sprouts appear above the
ground, and from this time forward grow with great rapidity.  A
sugar field is hoed three times, the same as cotton, save that a
greater quantity of earth is drawn to the roots.  By the first of
August hoeing is usually over.  About the middle of September, whatever is required for seed is cut and stacked in ricks, as they are
termed.  In October it is ready for the mill or sugar-house, and
then the general cutting begins.  The blade of a cane-knife is fifteen inches long, three inches wide in the middle, and tapering
towards the point and handle.  The blade is thin, and in order to be
at all serviceable must be kept very sharp.  Every third hand takes
the lead of two others, one of whom is on each side of him.  The
lead hand, in the first place, with a blow of his knife shears the
flags from the stalk.  He next cuts off the top down as far as it
is green.  He must be careful to sever all the green from the ripe
part, inasmuch as the juice of the former sours the molasses, and
renders it unsalable.  Then he severs the stalk at the root, and
lays it directly behind him.  His right and left hand companions
lay their stalks, when cut in the same manner, upon his.  To every
three hands there is a cart, which follows, and the stalks are
thrown into it by the younger slaves, when it is drawn to the sugar-
house and ground.

If the planter apprehends a frost, the cane is winrowed.  Win-
rowing is the cutting the stalks at the early period and throwing
them lengthwise in the water furrow in such a manner that the tops
will cover the butts of the stalks.  They will remain in this condition three weeks or a month without souring, and secure from
frost.  When the proper time arrives, they are taken up, trimmed
and carted to the sugarhouse.

In the month of January the slaves enter the field again to
prepare for another crop.  The ground is now strewn with the tops,
and flags cut from the past year's cane.  On a dry day fire is set
to this combustible refuse, which sweeps over the field, leaving
it bare and clean, and ready for the hoes.  The earth is loosened
about the roots of the old stubble, and in process of time another
crop springs up from the last year's seed.  It is the same the year
following; but the third year the seed has exhausted its strength,
and the field must be ploughed and planted again.  The second year
the cane is sweeter and yields more than the first, and the third
year more than the second.

During the three seasons I labored on Hawkins' plantation, I
was employed a considerable portion of the time in the sugar-house.
He is celebrated as the producer of the finest variety of white
sugar.  The following is a general description of his sugar-house
and the process of manufacture:

The mill is an immense brick building, standing on the shore
of the bayou.  Running out from the building is an open shed, at
least a hundred feet in length and forty or fifty feet in width.
The boiler in which the steam is generated is situated outside the
main building; the machinery and engine rest on a brick pier, fifteen feet above the floor, within the body of the building.  The
machinery turns two great iron rollers, between two and three feet
in length.  They are elevated above the brick pier, and roll in

towards each other.  An endless carrier, made of chain and wood,
like leather belts used in small mills, extends from the iron
rollers out of the main building and through the entire length of
the open shed.  The carts in which the cane is brought from the
field as fast as it is cut, are unloaded at the sides of the shed.
All along the endless carrier are ranged slave children, whose business it is to place the cane upon it, when it is conveyed through
the shed into the main building, where it falls between the rollers,
is crushed, and drops upon another carrier that conveys it out of
the main building in an opposite direction, depositing it in the
top of a chimney upon a fire beneath, which consumes it.  It is
necessary to burn it in this manner, because otherwise it would soon
fill the building, and more especially because it would soon sour
and engender disease.  The juice of the cane falls into a conductor
underneath the iron rollers, and is carried into a reservoir.  Pipes
convey it from thence into five filterers, holding several hogsheads
each.  These filterers are filled with bone-black, a substance resembling pulverized charcoal.  It is made of bones calcinated in
close vessels, and is used for the purpose of decolorizing, by fil-
tration, the cane juice before boiling.  Through these five filterers it passes in succession, and then runs into a large reservoir
underneath the ground floor, from whence it is carried up, by means
of a steam pump, into a claridier made of sheet iron, where it is
heated by steam until it boils.  From the first clarifier it is
carried in pipes to a second and a third, and thence into close
iron pans, through which tubes pass, filled with steam.  While in a
boiling state it flows through three pans in succession, and is then
carried in other pipes down to the coolers on the ground floor.
Coolers are wooden boxes with sieve bottoms made of the finest wire.
As soon as the syrup passes into the coolers, and is met by the air,
it grains, and the molasses at once escapes through the sieves into
a sistern below.  It is then white or loaf sugar of the finest
kind--clear, clean, and as white as snow.  When cool, it is taken
out, packed in hogsheads, and is ready for market.  The molasses is
then carried from the cistern into the upper story again and by
another process converted into brown sugar.

David Wilson (ed.), Narrative of Solomon Northup, pp. 208-213.


136.  A SLAVE DESCRIBES COTTON CULTURE (1842)

By Solomon Northup, author of the description of
rice, preceding.


The ground is prepared by throwing up beds or ridges, with the
plough--back-furrowing, it is called.  Oxen and mules, the latter
almost exclusively, are used in ploughing.  The women as frequently

as the men perform this labor, feeding, currying, and taking care
of their teams, and in all respects doing the field and stable
work, precisely as do the ploughboys of the North.

The beds, or ridges, are six feet wide, that is, from water
furrow to water furrow.  A plough drawn by one mule is then run
along the top of the ridge or center of the bed, making the drill,
into which a girl usually drops the seed, which she carries in a
bag hung round her neck.  Behind her comes a mule and harrow, covering up the seed, so that two mules, three slaves, a plough and
harrow, are employed in planting a row of cotton.  This is done in
the months of March and April.  Corn is planted in February.  When
there are no cold rains, the cotton usually makes its appearance in
a week.  In the course of eight or ten days afterwards the first
hoeing is commenced.  This is performed in part, also, by the aid
of the plough and mule.  The plough passes as near as possible to
the cotton on both sides, throwing the furrow from it.  Slaves
follow with their hoes, cutting up the grass and cotton, leaving
hills two feet and half apart.  This is called scraping cotton.  In
two weeks more commences the second hoeing.  This time the furrow
is thrown towards the cotton.  Only one stalk, the largest, is now
left standing in each hill.  In another fortnight it is hoed the
third time, throwing the furrow towards the cotton in the same
manner as before, and killing all the grass between the rows.  About
the first of July, when it is a foot high or thereabouts, it is hoed
the fourth and last time.  Now the whole space between the rows is
ploughed, leaving a deep water furrow in the center.  During all
these hoeings the overseer or driver follows the slaves on horseback with a whip, such as has been described.  The fastest hoer takes
the lead row.  He is usually about a rod in advance of his companions.  If one of them passes him, he is whipped.  If one falls behind or is a moment idle, he is whipped.  In fact, the lash is flying from morning until night, the whole day long.  The hoeing season thus continues from April until July, a field having no sooner
been finished once, than it is commenced again.

In the latter part of August begins the cotton picking season.
At this time each slave is presented with a sack.  A strap is
fastened to it, which goes over the neck, holding the mouth of the
sack breast high, while the bottom reaches nearly to the ground.
Each one is also presented with a large basket that will hold about
two barrels.  This is to put the cotton in when the sack is filled.
The baskets are carried to the field and placed at the beginning
of the rows.

. . . . . . . . . . . . . . . . . . . . . . . . . . . . . . . . . .

The cotton grows from five to seven feet, each stalk having a
great many branches, shooting out in all directions, and lapping
each other above the water furrow.

There are few sights more pleasant to the eye, than a wide
cotton field when it is in the bloom.  It presents an appearance
of purity, like an immaculate expanse of light, new-fallen snow.

David Wilson (ed.), Twelve Years A Slave.  Narrative of
Solomon Northup, (Auburn, New York:  Derby and Miller, 1853),
pp. 163–165, 166.

### 137.  NEW YORK CREDIT ENCOURAGES WASTE
### IN MISSISSIPPI (1842)

Perhaps Buckingham was too recent a visitor to
the United States to know it, but he was describing
a very typical process of American economic development rather than something peculiar to Mississippi.
Buckingham was a lecturer from England who had earlier
written a book about the United States.

Of the merchants and traders in Mississippi especially, it had
been the general custom for them to make a visit to New York in the
autumn, and, after visiting the fashionable watering-places, to lay
in a large stock of goods on credit in New York, for sale in Mississippi.  And the eagerness of the New York importer to force his
sales, for the sake of appearing to do an extensive business, and
thus bolstering up his own credit, is scarcely less than that of the
Mississippi buyer to invest largely without payment, and go back with
an immense supply.  This supply was readily sold, either on credit,
or for local banknotes, which were freely advanced, on almost any
security, to persons wishing to speculate.  The proceeds were then
invested by the Mississippi trader in lands, negroes, and houses.
He forthwith became an extensive planter; and in this capacity he
could raise money on his lands and slaves by mortgage, and get advances from New York merchants on his crops of cotton before they
were grown.  In this manner many an adventurer from the State of
Mississippi, not worth 100 dollars, would obtain credit for 50,000;
become nominally possessed of plantations worth 100,000; and setting
up carriages, building villas, and surrounding himself with all kinds
of luxuries, would live at the rate of a man worth 1,000,000.  The
ladies of such a family would of course have their share of expenditure in ornament and fashion; and it is thought that more gold
watches and jewelry of every description had been sold and worn in
the State of Mississippi, within the last three years, than in any
of the oldest States of the Union.

J. S. Buckingham, The Slave States of America, I, (London:
Fisher, Son & Co., 1842), pp. 554-555.

### 138.  THE NEED FOR ORGANIZED CATTLE AND
### WHEAT MARKETS (1844)

Without organized market-places, the commercialization
of agriculture proceeded by fits and starts.  Such market-
places would make a business of the selling of farm commodities.  Until this happened, agriculture could not be said

to be responding to the market so much as to tradition
and guessing.  The writer, Henry Colman, was former
agricultural commissioner of Massachusetts, president
of New York State Agricultural Society, honorary member
of the Royal Agricultural Society of England and former
editor of the New England Farmer.


    With the exception of three or four of our large towns,--as
Boston, New York, and Philadelphia,--we have no established cattle
market in the country; and markets such as Brighton near Boston,
and the Bull's Head near New York, are almost exclusively for the
sale of fat cattle, sheep, and swine.  Our farmers sell, as they
can, to agents or purchasers traveling through the country, and buy
as they can, and where, by chance, after taking in many cases, long
and expensive journeys, they may find the stock which they need.  In
frequent cases, stock, both cattle and swine, are driven through
the country and sold to those who wish to purchase, as accident may
direct.  A wool fair or market, is not, within my knowledge, held
in the country; nor a corn or grain market.  Howard Street, in
Baltimore, affords the only place in the United States resembling
an exclusive market for the sale of grain or flour; and this is
only attended by individual purchasers, and is not a meeting of
farmers, grain dealers, and millers, coming together on particular
days in the week, and at a particular hour in the day, to exhibit
samples, to collect and impart information respecting the grain
prospects of the year, to discuss prices, and to afford to all
parties the advantages of comparison and competition.  In the purchase of wool, agents scour the country, and in general the farmers
are quite at their mercy.  In respect to grain, the farmer carries
his wheat, or other grain, to the miller or the trader, and must
make the best bargain that he can.  In such case, in the first
place, there is no competition; and no possibility of calculating
the quantities on hand for sale; and no mode of fixing any general
or equal price; and, indeed, no certainty to the farmer of finding
any market at all.  These evils might be remedied, and a change
effected, to the great advantage of buyers and sellers, by the adoption of the system of weekly or periodical markets, which prevails
throughout England and Scotland.  Here are wool fairs, for the sale
of wool, of which samples are exhibited; and corn and grain markets,
where wheat, barley, oats, rye, beans, and peas, samples of which
are exhibited, are sold; and markets for the sale of fat cattle,
and markets for the sale of lean cattle, and markets for the sale
of horses, and markets for the sale of sheep and lambs, and markets
for the sale of cheese and butter; these markets sometimes uniting
several objects, or otherwise limited to some single object.
. . . . . . . . . . . . . . . . . . . . . . . . . . . . . . . . . . .
The convenience of these markets, scattered all over the country,
is very great.  They would be useful with us, and I think cannot
be too soon established, especially in our grain-growing districts,
such, for example, as Western New York.  The farmers in this part
of the country would certainly derive great advantages from regular
and quick sales, and from the extended competition to which such
established markets would certainly lead.  Once a week, however, in

the same district, would be too often, as they would be likely to
take the farmers too much from home; and at the breaking up of the
winter, when the state of the roads renders travelling difficult,
or during the busiest season of summer, it might be advisable to
suspend them.  In any event, the hour of opening and of closing
them should be fixed and absolute.  Mutual agreement might determine
this; and the custom, once established, would be as imperative as
any laws on the subject.  If it should be asked how these markets
might be established, I think the agricultural societies in the
different counties could easily arrange the matter; and that it
would be a very useful object of their attention.  I would advise,
further, that a grain market, and a cattle market, should be always
a cash market; and that all giving or taking credit in such cases
should be considered disgraceful both to buyer and seller, and
entirely out of the question.  If bread should not be paid for in
cash, what should be?  I am afraid my advice may be deemed a work
of supererogation, but it is well intended; and whoever contributes
in any way to limit (I am sensible the abolition is hopeless) that
system of private credit and long accounts which prevails to so
great an extent all over the country, does a public benefaction.

Henry Colman, Euiopean Agriculture and Rural Economy, I,
(Boston, Massachusetts:  Arthur D. Phelps, 1846), pp. 298-299, 327.

### 139.  LOOSE RULES OF TENANCY IN THE
UNITED STATES (1844)

Contemporaneously with the New England practice
as described here, tenancy was developing in Illinois
and Iowa; it was au old practice already in New York.
In nearly all these cases, rent was on an area, not a
share, basis.

The leasing of farms, in the United States, is quite rare,
and but in few cases is it arranged by any established rule.  In
New England, in such cases, matters are conducted most loosely.
Farms are frequently "taken to the halves," which is understood to
imply that the farmer returns half of all the produce grown to the
owner; but the landlord is almost entirely in the power of the
farmer; and, after the farmer has, as is but too common, applied to
his own use about half the produce, he divides with the owner the
half which remains.  If the owner furnishes implements, the farmer
returns them as good as he received them; and, if he furnishes stock,
ao on a brecdiug oi a daiiy farm, the tenant pays the legal interest
upon the cost, makes good the stock received when he quits the farm,
which is generally settled by valuers or appraisers, and divides
with his landlord one half the increase.  Our practices, in this

matter, are various and unsettled; and, as long as the hiring of
farms continues with us to be so infrequent,--and is likely to continue so while land remains as easy to be purchased as it now is,--
no exact method will be introduced.

Henry Colman, European Agriculture and Rural Economy, I,
p. 173.


### 140.   TENANTRY GIVES AGRICULTURE A COMMERCIAL CHARACTER (1844)

Colman argued that the necessity for paying a
precise rent would force tenant farmers to keep
detailed financial records.  In England, where the
tenancy relationship was traditional and widespread,
and where formalized rules laid definite obligations
upon the tenant, Colman's argument seemed to hold.  In
America, however, a share-tenant or share-cropper had
little or no such weight of specific obligation hanging
over him, and could thus be as un-"mercantile" as ever.


I shall, perhaps, excite some surprise in stating my belief
that the manner in which farms are held here [i.e., in England], on
hire for a year, or on lease for a term of years, rather than being
owned by the occupants, is itself a powerful instrument or incentive
to agricultural improvement.  In the United States, where farms are
owned by the occupant, the farmer seldom keeps any account, and it
matters not much to him what is the result of the year's management.
The effect of this is to render a man negligent and indifferent to
success or loss.  But when, at the end of every six months, the rent
must be paid, it is not a matter of indifference whether his farming
turns out well or ill; for not only the labor employed is to be paid
for, but the rent of the farm must be punctually discharged.  This
consequently compels him to make every exertion by which he may be
assisted to meet his obligations.  He finds no room for idleness or
neglect; and the continuance of his possession depends upon his good
management and the punctual payment of the rent.  This prompts to
watchfulness, skill, experiment, and improvement; and especially it
gives to farming a commercial or mercantile character, and obliges
the farmer to keep accounts, and so to learn the exact pecuniary result of his operations--a matter in which the farmers of the United
States, as far as my observation goes, who are the owners of the
farms which they occupy, are almost universally deficient.  The
strict responsibility to which the farmers are here held by their
landlords, is undoubtedly a material element in their success.


Henry Colman, European Agriculture and Rural Economy, I, pp.
168-169.

141.   AMERICAN AND BRITISH FARM IMPLEMENTS (1846)

Comparative evaluations of American and British
technology are exceedingly rare.  When given by a qualified observer such as Colman, the evaluation is especially
valuable.

In Paris at the Conservatory of Arts and Trades, at Brussels,
at Utrecht, I found extensive collections of agricultural implements and models of agricultural tools and machinery.  These embraced
many of the most improved implements to be found in England or the
United States.  It may excite a smile of surprise with an Englishman,
that I speak of the United States in this connection.  But I have
seen nothing on the Continent or in Great Britain equal to the collections of agricultural implements which are to be found, for example, in Boston, United States.  The English implements are usually
clumsy, heavy, and inordinately expensive.... They at least answer
the purposes of the ingenious mechanics, who understand very well
when they have got their pail under a cow with a full udder, and
how in the most agreeable manner to abstract the gold from the
pockets of enthusiastic agricultural amateurs.

Henry Colman, European Agriculture and Rural Economy, II,
p. 569.

142.   CHEAP LAND WORKS AGAINST CAPITAL EXPENDITURES
ON FARMS (1849)

The availability of land on tolerable financial
terms made America a special case.  But the same circumstance also encouraged the farmer to neglect long-term
improvements.  The following concerns western New York.
The author, James F. W. Johnston, was reader in chemistry
and mineralogy at the University of Durham, England.  He
had helped train several leading American chemists.

An objection to drainage is made in this country which, though
sometimes urged with us, is by no means of such force in England as
it is in America.  The cost of this improvement, even at the cheapest rate--say four pounds or twenty dollars an acre--is equal to a
large proportion of the present price of the best land in this rich
district of western New York.  From fifty to sixty dollars an acre
is the highest price which farms bring here; and if twenty-five
dollars an acre were expended upon any of it, the price in the
market would not rise in proportion.  Or if forty-dollar land should

actually be improved one-fourth by thorough-drainage, it would
still, it is said, not be more valuable than that which now sells
at fifty dollars; so that the improver would be a loser to the
extent of fifteen dollars an acre.

   This argument will appear to have greater force when it is
understood that there is as yet in New England and New York scarcely
any such thing as local attachment--the love of a place, because it
is a man's own--because he has hewed it out of the wilderness, and
made it what it is; or because his father did so, and he and his
family have been born and brought up, and spent their happy youthful
days upon it.  Speaking generally, every farm from Eastport in
Maine, to Buffalo on Lake Erie, is for sale.  The owner has already
fixed a price in his mind for which he would be willing, and even
hopes to sell, believing that, with the same money, he could do
better for himself and his family by going still farther west.
Thus, to lay out money in improvements is actually to bury what he
does not hope to be able to get out of his land again, when the
opportunity for selling presents itself.


   James F. W. Johnston, Notes on North America.  Agricultural,
Economical, and Social, I, (Boston, Massachusetts:  Charles C.
Little and James Brown, 1851), pp. 162-163.


### 143.  THE LACK OF CAPITAL LEADS TO AN EXHAUSTING SYSTEM OF FARMING (1849)


   The neglect of long-term improvements undoubtedly
was a drawback to American agriculture.  The same circumstance, however, was connected with the easy transformation
of tenant into landowner.  Reference below in this extract
by James Johnston is to the Genesee Valley lands of the
Wadsworth family.


   I may here remark, indeed, as my general impression in regard
to the farming of the whole of north-eastern America it was my fortune to visit--that too little capital is employed in cultivating
the land.  The land itself, and the labour of their families, is
nearly all the capital which most of the farmers possess.  And if
any of them save a hundred dollars, they generally prefer to lend
it on mortgage at high interest, or to embark it in some other pursuit which they think will pay better than farming, than to lay it
out in bettering their farms, or in establishing a more generous
husbandry.

   Of the rich grazing land, an acre and a half fattens off a
beast which in the lean state will cost £5.  Those who hold this
land, therefore, require a capital of £3 or £4 an acre to stock
it.

With a capital of £1 an acre only, an exhausting system of
culture can scarcely fail to be followed--especially as the custom
is to remain only from four to eight years, and during this time
to save as much as enables the tenant to buy a farm somewhere for
himself.

James F. W. Johnston, Notes on North America, I, p. 207.


144.   INTERIOR COTTON PLANTATIONS (1854)


Most cotton planters owned plantations in the interior.
It was they and not the operators of very large plantations
who were typical.  On the other hand, middling and small
planters were dominated by the ambition to rise in the scale
of ownership.


The majority of the interior plantations which came under my
observation belong to resident planters, and are from four hundred
to one thousand acres in extent, the average being perhaps six
hundred acres.  The number of negroes on each varies from ten to
forty, more frequently being between twenty and thirty.  Where there
are fewer than ten negroes, the owners are frequently seen holding
a plow among them; where there are over twenty, a white overseer is
usually employed, the owner perhaps directing, but seldom personally
superintending, the field labor.

The characteristics of this latter class of cotton-planters
vary much.  I shall, I think, be generally rightly understood if I
say that the majority of them possess more dignity of bearing and
manner, that they give a stranger an impression of greater "respectability" than the middle class of farmers at the North and in
England, while they have less general information and less active
and inquiring minds.  The class of farmers in New England and New
York, with whom I compare them, have rarely received any education
beyond that of the public schools, which, in the last generation,
afforded a very meagre modicum of instruction.  The planters of
whom I speak, I judge to have usually spent a short time at
boarding-schools of the country--but in their acquisition of knowledge subsequently to their school-days by newspapers and books,
and by conversation, has been very small.

It is frequently the case, however, that the planter has
started as a poor, and entirely self-dependent young man, the basis
of whose present fortune consisted of his savings from the wages
earned by him as overseer--these are commonly as illiterate as the
very poorest of our Northern agricultural laborers.  Yet again
there are those who, beginning in the same way, have acquired,
while so employed, not only a capital with which to purchase land
and slaves, but a valuable stock of experience and practical information, and somewhat of gentlemanly bearing from intercourse with

their employers.  In respect to the enjoyment of material comforts,
and the exercise of taste in the arrangement of their houses and
grounds, the condition of these planters, while it is superior to
that of the Texans, is far below that of Northern farmers of one
quarter their wealth.


        Frederick L. Olmsted, A Journey in the Back Country in the
Winter of 1853-4, I, pp. 176-178.



        145.  ABSENTEE OWNERSHIP OF COTTON PLANTATIONS (1854)


        A significant analysis of the trend toward increasing
centralization of ownership in cotton cultivation and a
knowing analysis of the economic basis of the hospitable
Southern planters' way of life, written by Frederick Olmsted.


        What proportion of the larger cotton plantations are resided
upon by their owners, I am unable to estimate with confidence.  Of
those having cabin accommodations for fifty slaves each, which came
under my observation from the road, while I was travelling through
the cotton districts bordering the Mississippi River, I think more
than half were unprovided with a habitation which I could suppose
to be the ordinary residence of a man of moderate wealth.  In the
more fertile and less healthy districts I should judge that the
majority of slaves are left by their owners to the nearly unlimited
government of hireling overseers the greater part of the time.  Some
of these plantations are owned by capitalists, who reside permanently
and constantly in the North or in Europe.  Many are owned by wealthy
Virginians and Carolinians who reside on what are called the "show
plantations" of those States; plantations having all the character,
though never the name, of mere country seats, the exhausted soil of
which will scarcely produce sufficient to feed and clothe the resident slaves, whose increase is constantly removed to colonize these
richer fields of the West.
        Still a large number are merely occasionally sojourning places
of their owners, who naturally enough prefer to live as soon as they
can afford to do so, where the conveniences and luxuries belonging
to a highly civilized state of society are more easily obtained than
they can ever be in a country of large plantations.  It is rare
that a plantation would have a dozen intelligent families residing
within a day's ride of it.  Any society that a planter enjoys on his
estate must, therefore, consist in a great degree of permanent
guests.  Hence the name for hospitality of wealthy planters.  A
large plantation is necessarily a retreat from general society, and
is used by its owner, I am inclined to think, in the majority of
cases, in winter, as Berkshire villas and farms are in summer by
rich people of New York and Boston.  I feel assured that this is the

case with the plantations upon the Mississippi, and the bayous of
Louisiana, upon the Arkansas, the Yazoo, and the Red rivers, and
in the lowlands of Carolina and Georgia.  I have never been on a
plantation numbering fifty-field hands, the owner of which was
accustomed to reside steadily through the year upon it.  Still I am
aware there are many such, and possibly it is a minority of them
who are regularly absent with their families from their plantations
during any considerable part of the year.

The summer visitors from the South to our Northern watering-
places are, I judge, chiefly of the migratory, wealthy class.  Such
persons, it is evident are much less influenced in their character
and habits, by association with slaves, than any other at the South.
Their household arrangements, and the customs of their house servants must, of course, assimilate to those of cultivated families
in other parts of the world.  The Irish gentleman and the Irish
peasant are not more unlike, in their habits and manners, than some
of these large planters and the great multitude of slave owners.

The number of the very wealthy is, of course, small, yet as
the chief part of the wealth of these consists in slaves, no inconsiderable proportion of all the slaves belong to men who deputize
their government in a great measure to overseers.  It may be computed, (not, however, with confidence), from the census of 1850,
that about one half the slaves of Louisiana and one third those of
Mississippi and Arkansas, belong to estates of not less than fifty
slaves each, and of these, I believe, nine tenths live on plantations which their owners reside upon, if at all, but transiently.

The number of plantations of this class, and the proportion
of those employed upon them to the whole body of negroes in the
country, is, as I have said, rapidly increasing.  At the present
prices of cotton the large grower has such advantages over the
small, that the owner of a plantation of fifty slaves, favorably
situated, unless he lives very recklessly, will increase in wealth
so rapidly and possess such a credit that he may soon establish or
purchase other plantations, so that at his death his children may
be provided for without reducing the effective force of negroes on
any division of his landed estate.  The excessive credit given to
such planters by negro dealers and tradesmen renders this the more
practicable.  The higher the price of cotton the higher is that of
negroes, and the higher the price of negroes the less is it in the
power of men of small capital to buy them.  Large plantations, of
course, pay a much larger percentage on the capital invested in them
than smaller ones; indeed the only plausible economical defence of
slavery is simply an explanation of the advantages of associated
labor; advantages which are possessed equally by large manufacturing
establishments in which free laborers are brought together and employed in the most effective manner, and which I can see no sufficient reason for supposing could not be made available for agriculture did not the good results flowing from small holdings, on the
whole, counterbalance them.  If the present high price of cotton
and the present scarcity of labor at the South continues, the cultivation of cotton on small plantations will by and by become unusual.

for the same reason that hand-loom weaving has become unusual in
the farm houses of Massachusetts.


    Frederick L. Olmsted, A Journey in the Back Country, I, pp.
128–131.


## 146.  IOWA GRAIN TRADE DERANGED BY PEACE
## AND A RAILROAD (1856)


    The north Iowa grain trade prospered in isolation
from organized markets--which gave local merchants some
power over price--and in response to international emer-
gencies--such as a war in a grain-exporting country.  But
transportation and marketing improvements were surely out-
dating localized trade in farm products.


Sebastopol was invested.  Breadstuffs advanced in Europe.
Russia's ports were blockaded.  Her grain was locked up.  The first
of my fifty-cent wheat brought two dollars and twenty-five cents a
bushel in New York.  I made more than one hundred thousand dollars
between the 1st of August and the 1st of December.  Most of the
money was made the first sixty days, when wheat was low.  I began
buying at fifty cents, and in October was paying a dollar and forty
cents a bushel.  At the latter price only ordinary profits were made.
Everything seemed to favor me that fall.  One propellor, loaded entirely with my wheat and flour, exploded on the lake, and sunk, the
cargo being a total loss, and I made four thousand dollars by it.
It was insured in New York City, and I saved the freight from
Davenport to New York.
    From the 1st of December of that year (1854) until some time
in March, 1856, during the Crimean War, I did a fairly good business.
    Then came a dreadful blow.  First, the news of the taking of
Sebastopol; then, in a short time, the death of Nicholas, Czar of
Russia.  At the news of his death, everyone knew the war was at an
end, and prices of produce fell instantly all over the United
States--wheat from fifty to sixty cents a bushel; flour, three
dollars a barrel, and everything else in proportion; and the decline
continued day after day.  I went to bed, on the night the news
arrived, two hundred thousand dollars poorer than I had arisen the
same morning.
    I had on the market, and unsold, six thousand barrels of flour,
and, in Davenport, one hundred and fifty thousand bushels of wheat,
and all my winter's packing, not a dollar's worth of which had
been sold.
    That drop in prices was an overwhelming catastrophe.  It broke
up nearly every dealer on the Mississippi River, and was really
what finally broke Burrows & Prettyman.  We worked along a number

of years, badly crippled.  This revulsion in the market brought
on stagnation and hard times, and there was not much opportunity
for a man to retrieve his fortunes.

I had made a good deal of money, but had laid it out in building, and in some outside speculations, which entailed heavy losses.

The opening of the Chicago & Rock Island Railroad rather be-
wildered me.  It revolutionized the mode of doing business.  Heretofore, a few men at each business point had done the bulk of the
business required, and a great deal of money and good credit were
necessary.  We always had been compelled to hold our accummulation
from November to April, and not many had either the nerve or the
means to do it.

When the railroad got into operation, produce men were as thick
as potato-bugs.  If a man could raise two hundred and fifty dollars,
he could begin business.  That amount would buy a car-load of wheat.
In the morning he would engage a car, have it put where he could
load it, and have the farmer put his wheat, barley, or oats, as the
case might be, in the car.  By three o'clock in the afternoon the
car would be loaded and shipped.

In the pork season it was the same way.  As I have said before,
the hogs in those days were brought in ready dressed.  A produce
dealer would place a scale on the sidewalk in some convenient place,
weigh his hogs as he bought them, pile them up on the sidewalk, and,
in the afternoon, load them up and ship them.  Dealers were at no
expense of rent or labor.


Fifty Years In Iowa:  Being the Personal Reminiscences of
J.M.D. Burrows, (Davenport, Iowa:  Glass and Co., 1888), pp. 128-
131.

# C.

## AN INDUSTRIALIZING NATION

147.  PUBLIC PREJUDICE AGAINST PATENTS (1816)

The previous year--1815--the U.S. government issued 166 patents.  The rate sped up during 1820-1830 to 535 per year.  But economic historians have not yet studied the value of these patents.  Colonel William Edwards who writes here was a well known inventor in the tanning industry.

For my various improvements I had taken out patents, but such was the public prejudice against patents that I never hazarded a law-suit.  Neither Mr. Fulton for the use of steam, or Mr. Whitney, for the cotton gin, had ever obtained a verdict.  Any one who chose to do so used my improvements.  In after years, I called on such as I conveniently could, and asked them to pay me something, even if little.  I estimate my collections altogether at about $2,500 for forty years of mental effort and expensive experiment.  My patents certainly reduced the cost of tanning from twelve cents per pound to four cents, the saving aggregating millions of dollars in leather sold in New York alone.

Memoirs of Col. William Edwards, pp. 69-70.

148.   A RELUCTANT ENCOURAGEMENT OF DOMESTIC
MANUFACTURE (1817)


In 1817, The American Society for the Encouragement
of Domestic Manufactures elected ex-President Madison a
member.  Thirty-one years earlier, Madison had stated
that manufactures would develop of themselves.  (See
Source No. 64).


Altho' I approve the policy of leaving to the sagacity of individuals, and to the impulse of private interest, the application
of industry & capital, I am equally persuaded, that in this as in
other cases, there are exceptions to the general rule, which do not
impair the principle of it.  Among these exceptions, is the policy
of encouraging domestic manufactures, within certain limits, and in
reference to certain articles.
    Without entering into a detailed view of the subject, it may
be remarked, that every prudent Nation will wish to be independent
of other Nations, for the necessary articles of food, of raiment,
and of defence; and particular considerations applicable to the U.
S. seem to strengthen the motives to this independence.
    Besides the articles falling under this above description,
there may be others for manufacturing which, natural advantages
exist, which require temporary interpositions for bringing them
into regular and successful activity.
    Where the fund of industry is acquired by emigrations from
abroad, and not withdrawn or withheld, from other domestic employments, the case speaks for itself.
    I will only add, that among the articles of consumption and
use the preference in many cases, is decided merely, by fashion or
by habits.  As far as an equality, and still more where a real
superiority is found in the articles manufactured at home, all must
be sensible that it is politic and patriotic to encourage a preference of them, as affording a more certain source of supply for
every class, and a more certain market for the surplus products of
ye agricultural class.


Letter, James Madison to D. Lynch, Jr., June 27, 1817, The
Papers of James Madison, Vol. 64, Library of Congress.




149.   THOSE WITHOUT SKILL IN MANUFACTURE LOSE
THEIR INVESTMENT (1817)


Incorporation in manufacturing had to overcome
the artisan tradition of personal, skilled attention
to the job.  Absentee-ownership of a manufacturing

enterprise seemed to doom that enterprise to losses
arising out of a lack of personal superintendence.
While manufacturing techniques remained crude, the
corporate form in itself meant little.  (See, also,
Source No. 162).  Rufus King, old Federalist leader,
was a U.S. Senator from New York; he writes to his son
Edward who was a bank president.

Lessons in money making I do not think myself very competent
to render; but as regards many ways in which money is lost, I have
not been an inattentive looker on, and can therefore speak from
experience.  Men who have skill and will personally employ it in
superintending and directing manufactures may draw profit from them;
but those who are without such skill and who are to employ, depend
on and pay for agents, who are to superintend manufactures, will be
disappointed if they expect profit.  This has been proved over and
over again in this country, as well as in every other.  I am therefore decisive in my advice to you to take no share in any manufacturing establishment; you would not only not make profit, but
probably as I have done lose your capital.

Letter, Rufus King to Edward King, December 20, 1817, C. R.
King (ed.), The Life and Correspondence of Rufus King, VI,
(New York:  G. P. Putnam's Sons, 1900), p. 86.

## 150.  HOUSING CONSTRUCTION IN A PIONEER CITY (1819)

The customary picture of housing in a pioneer area
is one of a succession of log cabins, each one built by
and for individual pioneers.  In Vandalia, capital of a
state admitted into the union only a year before (1818),
housing was a commodity on the market.  So were the raw
materials, as well as the household utensils.  This co-
existence of a raw pioneer frontier and a commercialized
economy characterized the American colonizing experience.

As it would be three or four months before severe weather
would set in I contracted with an old squatter to build me a cabin
sixteen by fourteen feet in dimensions.  This was the first dwelling
house which was built in Vandalia, the capital of Illinois.  Previous to the building of this cabin Frantz and I were sheltered by
a framework of poles covered with brush.
About this time a number of squatters and their families
arrived at Vandalia with the intention of taking up claims and
improving the same, and as the State House was to be built it was
supposed that mechanics would flock to the new city.

About this time I engaged an expert chopper to fell suitable
timber for me to build more log houses and also as could be sawed
into lumber for frame houses, I had no difficulty in finding men
who desired employment and there was an abundance of the very best
of timber.  However as there were no pine trees in that vicinity,
I in company with an expert woodsman by the name of Ravis went into
the woods and selected the finest walnut trees from which to saw
boards.  We selected about forty and blazed them, which mark was
sufficient to secure them as my property until they were cut down.
We also marked in the same manner such other trees as I deemed necessary for my future operations.  At this time I found that we should
need a place wherein to store provisions for our subsistence and I
concluded to build an addition to my cabin to be used as a storehouse.  This I did and then went to St. Louis to lay in a supply of
such articles as were indispensible to our comfort.  My first stock
of goods consisted of one hundred pounds of tobacco, fifty pounds
of coffee, fifty pounds of sugar, ten pounds of tea, one piece of
brown sheating, one piece of bleached shirting, one piece of drilling, one piece of flannel, one piece of stainett, a small stock of
boots and shoes, and some tinware.  At the same time I purchased
the necessary utensils for use in my own house.  I also purchased
one pine table, six chairs and one small looking-glass.  On my return home from St. Louis, I stopped at a sawmill and purchased lumber for flooring in my cabin and storeroom.  When all was finished
I moved my furniture into the dwelling department and the goods into
the storeroom.  Frantz was as busy as a bee and soon had everything
in nice order.  This commenced our life of semi-civilization.  Emigrants were arriving daily and building themselves primitive habita-
tions.  About this time Esquire Baugh's family arrived and soon
thereafter opened a boarding house in a double cabin Mr. Baugh's
family consisted of himself, his wife and three daughters, fine
looking young ladies.

About this time two young Englishmen named Seemore came to me
and desired to be employed during the winter in sawing lumber for
building purposes with whipsaws.  They represented that they could
saw scantling, sheating, flooring and siding.  We soon agreed in
regard to the prices for the various kinds of work and soon the
young men were busy sawing up the splendid trees which my axemen
had felled.  Thus the work for the winter was in full blast.  The
limbs and tops of the trees were cut up into fire wood and corded
up.  Providence favored up with fine weather for seven months and
at the end of that time I found that we had completed much more work
than I could have possibly expected.

The store which I had opened for the accommodation of the workmen soon proved to be too small.  I was forced to replenish quite
often, and also to increase the quantities of my purchases.  I,
however, limited my purchases to such articles as were strictly
necessary.  A flouring mill was operating in the vicinity which
afforded a supply of breadstuff; game of all kinds consisting of
bear, elk, deer, wild turkeys, wild geese, wild ducks, and fish
were to be found in astonishing quantities.  Beef, pork and flour
were quite cheap, all things considered.

In the spring of 1820 the gentleman who had the contract for the erection of the State House arrived at Vandalia.  He was accompanied by a dozen or more mechanics.  Several state officers came also for the purpose of making the necessary arrangements.

A Mr. McCollum commenced to build a hotel and business was brisk in all departments.  As I needed brick for about a dozen chimneys and for a cellar wall I concluded to burn a small kiln.  I engaged the services of a man who understood the business of brickmaking and as wood was abundant the business was soon commenced.  Ground was broken on the fifth day of May.  About this time contracts were let for the building of three log houses sixteen by eighteen feet each, a small frame house near the store and a frame house for Mr. Ernst's family, eighteen by twenty-four feet square and one story and a half high. To this was to be added a shed twelve by twenty-four feet square to serve as a kitchen.  With these improvements I stopped until I should receive further instructions.

On the fifteenth of May I received a letter from Mr. Ernst, dated Feb. 14, 1820, in which he directed me to build as many houses as possible as he had engaged about one hundred colonists and would charter a vessel to bring them to America.  He also authorized me to draw upon him for such money as I needed.  After the receipt of this letter I concluded that I would build a large frame building before the legislature convened.

I consulted with a Mr. Woods, a master mechanic in regard to the undertaking.  He agreed for a specific price to put up a building which was to be thirty-six feet long and twenty-four feet wide, two stories high.  The price did not suit me but I felt convinced that if accommodations of some sort were not provided for the members of the legislature it would be a death blow to Vandalia.  Events which transpired in a short time proved that I was right.  I finally concluded that the house must be built and so went to work in earnest. The timber which I had was all green and that intended for frame etc. had to be kiln dried.  At a saw mill some twenty miles away, I purchased fifteen hundred feet of dry walnut planks.  This served a good purpose.

Autobiography of Frederick Hollman, (Platteville, Wisconsin: R. I. Dugdale, n.d.), pp. 2-5.


151.    THE GLASS CUTTERS OF BOSTON ARE PROUD
OF THEIR CRAFT (1821)


One may guess that the age of factory production soon left such contests of skill behind.

The glass cutters of Boston have challenged those of New York
at a trial of skill, for a stake of one hundred dollars.


Niles' Weekly Register, December 29, 1821, p. 288.



152.  A COMPARISON OF SCOTTISH AND AMERICAN
COTTON FACTORIES (1822)


Parliament was investigating the laws which forbade
both the exportation from England of certain machinery
and the emigration of certain classes of artisans.  James
Dunlop was one of the few expert witnesses who could speak
with personal authority about the importance of British
machinery and labor for America.  James Dunlop, who writes
here, was a cotton manufacturer in Glasgow and Renfrew, and
represented the master spinners of Renfrewshire at the Parliamentary inquiry.


I returned from America in 1822.  Whilst I was there I had
opportunities of seeing many of the cotton factories in Maryland,
in Pennsylvania, in New Jersey, in Rhode Island, Massachusetts, and
New York, and they were very inferior as compared with our manufactories in Scotland.  I think they are in a similar state to what we
were thirty years ago; there are some exceptions; I was in one of
them that is doing pretty well.  They were rather in a progressive
state.  Excepting a water-wheel that was made in Manchester, I think
all the machinery was made in America, chiefly by Scotchmen.  In the
different factories I went in they were principally worked by men
who had gone from this country.  I think a great many of the artificers in the metals, such as iron and steel turners, and so on, were
British.  Those employed, in fact, to make the iron parts of the
cotton machinery were British; but very few of the spinners there
were people who had left this country; they were chiefly all native
Americans; and appeared to be very active and industrious; but they
have not the skill we have; and I think we have got so much the
start of all the world in machinery, that I think we shall keep it.
Supposing English machinery transported to America, and with
the assistance of English foremen, the population of America would
be soon taught to work in their factories, equal to the men in this
country; but before they would acquire that, we should be ahead of
them a long way again.  I reason, comparing Scotland with England;
we began the business of cotton spinning later, and we were of course
behind; and we have been always behind.  I mean to apply that observation to the population of other foreign countries.  Neverthe
less, the allowing the exportation of English machinery would have
a tendency to advance them rapidly in their manufactures.  And there
is a great disposition on the part of the Americans to procure
English machinery to a large extent, if they could get it.  What

will prevent the Americans coming into competition with us, is the
high price of labour, of coal, and of iron; the iron is chiefly
made from wood; and at a great expense.  I do not think they can
make iron so well as we can, notwithstanding their abundance of charcoal.  The charcoal is a better article than coal for making the
fire, I believe; and as to wages, the artizans there who can work
in wood, receive perhaps from a dollar to a dollar and a half a day;
those who can work in iron, and steel, and brass, have, perhaps,
from nine to twelve dollars a week; twelve is very high, but nine
and ten is very common.  The same class would receive in Glasgow at
this time, from a guinea to 25s. a week, for the best men; the
wages are high just now, the demand for machinery is great.

      The expense of the board of an artizan at any of the factories,
where I was, as compared to the expense in Glasgow, the same comfort
and necessaries afforded to each, is very different, in different
parts of America; in New York, and about the great towns the expense
of living is pretty high; in the country greatly lower, perhaps not
a half; I should suppose, that about a dollar and a half, or from
that to two dollars in the week for board and lodging, would be
sufficient.  I speak of the towns, where it is high; in New Jersey,
going only twenty or thirty miles from town; the expense there in
the country is perhaps a dollar; and those same men will earn from
nine to twelve dollars a week.  In America, the business of mule
spinning is very little known, and I believe they are in a very low
state; I do not know of my own knowledge what wages they have, but
I saw two of my own men there, who were complaining; they said they
hardly made as much as they did in Glasgow; the machinery is bad;
it is chiefly throstler water twist spinning.  I saw some mule
spinning, though not to any great extent; and I saw some cloth woven
from yarn, made in America.  What the comparative expense of manufacturing that was, compared with what the same cloth could have
been sold for in Glasgow, I could not excatly say; but that could
be easily learned from the high duties which the Americans put upon
their imports:  the duty put upon our cotton cloth going into
America, I believe is more than 60 per cent; on some articles they
suppose that a yard of cloth should cost 13 cents, then it pays an
ad valorem duty, something very high; but I cannot speak to the
amount exactly.  Many of the masters of those cotton factories
stated that if they could get English machinery over, they would
order it, but they did not suppose it would be possible to get it.
One of the principal obstacles in the way of the Americans, is their
want of skill, rather than capital, I think; there is a want of
capital too; but it is the want to skill chiefly that keeps them
back.


      Testimony of James Dunlop, George White (ed.), A Digest of the
Minutes of Evidence Taken Before the Committee on Artizans and
Machinery, (London:  Sherwood Jones & Co., 1824), pp. 399-400.

153.   THE PRACTICE OF MECHANICAL ARTS
IN PHILADELPHIA (1824)


One of the founders of the Franklin Institute
relates something about its formation and technical
environment.  The writer is Frederick Fraley who was
president of the American Philosophical Society, and had
been a founding member of the Franklin Institute at
Philadelphia in 1824.


Let us consider for a moment with what we had to deal in its
origin.  There were a few small and isolated workshops in which
mechanical trades were carried on with rude and imperfect tools, and
perfection depended more on the strength and skill of the hand of
the artisan and on the acuteness of his eye, than on any clear men-
tal perception of what he was doing or that the doing of it could
be reduced to anything approaching scientific rules.
I recollect my visits to some of the well-known workshops of
those days, and have seen Patrick Lyon striking vigorous blows on
his anvil, Oliver Evans in his foundry, Jacob Perkins in his fire-
engine manufactory, and the Messrs. Sellers in their then wonder-
working wire works, turning out the marvellous hand and machine
cards.  It was indeed a great privilege to be permitted to visit
those establishments, for they were the pride of their proprietors,
and were not to be entered by all with impunity.
But with the establishment of the Institute came a new phase
of these things.  There had been for some years a sort of mechanics'
club, which zealously guarded additions to its membership, and was
so much attached to ancient mysteries, that it mercilessly black-
bailed all who attempted entrance by the shibboleth of modern ideas.
So it happened that Samuel V. Merrick was excluded from this
venerable, close guild, and he resolved to form an institution on
a more liberal basis and with broader biews, and he joined to himself a few congenial spirits, who went manfully to work and called
a public meeting of Philadelphia citizens, which was largely attended, and which enthusiastically adoped the plans of the founders,
and gave us the great institution in whose Hall you are holding
your present meeting.
. . . . . . . . . . . . . . . . . . . . . . . . . . . . . . . . . . . . .
I cannot close ... without attempting to bring before you, in
contrast, what I saw of machinery and its progress in my youth, and
what I see now.  I shall refer first to the supply of water to the
city of Philadelphia.
Then she was just emerging from the use of wells and handpumps,
and the rude steam engines placed near the Schuylkill River at
Chestnut Street and at the base of the marble building in the Centre
Square at Market and Broad Streets; and the modest basin eighty feet
at its summit, and sixty feet in diameter, were the wonder and boast
of the citizens.  The pipes for the distribution of the water were
wooden logs bored by hand, and it was not until after the establishment of the Institute that iron pipes were cast in this country.

A few had been imported from England, and this fact became a political war-cry, and nearly revolutionized the city government.  About the year 1822 the water-works were established at Fairmount, a transfer of the steam-power having previously been made to that point, a large Boulton & Watt engine having taken the place of the original engines.  The Boulton & Watt engine was a beautiful piece of work, and marked a well-defined phase in mechanical engineering.  For a short time by its side worked a high-pressure engine of great simplicity and with few parts, invented and constructed by Oliver Evans, the great American mechanic, who is probably the inventor of the use of steam under high pressure, and who deserves a high place in the pantheon of inventors.  Recollect that then no other large city in the United States was supplied with water by machinery, and that the representative of city corporations came to study and imitate our example.

Frederick Fraley, "An Essay On Mechanics and the Progress of Mechanical Science--1824 to 1882," Transactions, American Society of Mechanical Engineers, III (1882), pp. 215, 128.

### 154.   INDUSTRY BRINGS GENUINE, NOT BANK-TYPE PROSPERITY TO STEUBENVILLE (1825)

Niles, a sophisticated friend of capitalist industry, was prepared to argue that banks required industrial prosperity for their own prosperity.  He was not yet ready to argue the reverse.

The manufactories of Steubenville, especially the celebrated establishment of Messrs. B. Wells and company, who send to the Atlantic states many thousand dollars' worth of superior superfine cloths every year and a large amount in other woollen goods, more effectually relieve the neighborhood, than it would be relieved of all the [paper] banks in the world were located in the district. It was these creations of value that enabled the banks at that place to maintain their credit during the wreck of such institutions in the western country; and it is proudly mentioned in the "Herald," that it was the "only town between Lancaster in Pennsylvania, and the Mississippi, which could boast of two banks, sustained altogether by private capital and credit."  Besides the great woollen manufactory above alluded to, which is called the "pride of the west," there are, in Steubenville and its immediate neighborhood, as we learn by the "Herald," two steam flour mills--two steam cotton manufactories--one steam paper mill--two breweries--two copperas manufactories--one air foundry, in which are cast all kinds of hollow ware--one steam engine manufactory--one cotton and woollen machinery manufactory--two wool carding machines for country work, one of which is propelled by steam.  These employ a large number

of persons, and the food and materials consumed by them give life
and spirit and "plenty" of money, because it circulates freely, to
the whole district.  Productive industry may be aided by banks--but
banks, without the support of productive industry, will ever "make
to themselves wings and fly away."  They do no more than handle
and turn money--they make none.

Niles' Weekly Register, April 9, 1825, p. 82.


### 155.  WHAT IS NOT A MANUFACTORY?  (1826)

An authoritative indication of a contemporary
definition.

The term "manufactories" is very indefinite; but as commonly
used, does not take in the several establishments of mechanics,
such as tanners, and other workers in leather, hatters and fifty
others, some of whom carry on very extensive businesses, and together employ a yet greater amount of capital and subsist many more
persons, than are employed or subsisted by the "manufactories."

Niles' Weekly Register, August 12, 1826, p. 422.


### 156.  MASS PRODUCTION OF HALL'S RIFLES (1827)

This is the first fully documented, eye-witness
report of an American rifle produced by mass-production
methods, including interchangeable parts.  No such evidence
has yet been brought forward to support the claims to
priority to Eli Whitney or Simeon North.  (See Source No.
171).  The report is that of a board of commissioners
consisting of "practical armorers and intelligent gentlemen."
It was signed by James Carrington, Luther Sage and James
Bell.  Carrington and Sage had both served as inspectors of
contract arms made in New England, representing the Springfield armory; Sage, from 1818 to 1823; Carrington, from
1824 to 1830, except 1825.

In making this examination our attention was directed, in the
first place, for several days, to viewing the operations of the
numerous machines which were exhibited to us by the inventor, John
H. Hall.  Captain Hall has formed and adopted a system in the

manufacture of small arms, entirely novel, and which, no doubt, may
be attended with the most beneficial results to the country,
especially if carried into effect on a large scale.

His machines for this purpose are of several distinct classes,
and are used for cutting iron and steel, and for executing wood
work, all of which are essentially different from each other, and
differ materially from any other machines we have ever seen in
any other establishment.

Their general merits and demerits, when contrasted with the
several machines hitherto in general use for the manufacture of small
arms, will, perhaps, be better understood by pointing out the difference of the results produced by them, than by any very accurate description of the machines themselves.

It is well known, we believe, that arms have never yet been
made so exactly similar to each other by any other process, as to
require no marking of their several parts, and so that those parts
on being changed would suit equally well when applied to every other
arm, (of the same kind) but the machines, we have examined, effect
this with a certainty and precision we should not have believed till
we witnessed their operations.

To determine this point, and test their uniformity beyond all
controversy, we requested Col. Lee, (acting) superintendent of the
United States armory at this place, to send to Hall's armory, five
boxes containing 100 rifles manufactured by him in 1824; and which
had been in the (United States arsenal) since that period. We then
directed two of his workmen to strip off the work from the stocks
of the whole hundred, and also take to pieces the several parts of
the receivers, so called, and scattered them promiscuously over a
long joiners' work bench. One hundred stocks were then brought from
Hall's armory, which had been just finished, and on which no work
or mounting had ever been put. The workmen then commenced putting
the work taken off the stocks brought from the United States arsenal,
on to the 100 new stocks, the work having been repeatedly mixed and
changed by us and the workmen also; all this was done in our presence, and the arms, as fast as they were put together, were handed
to us and minutely examined. We were unable to discover any inaccur-
acy in any of their parts fitting each other, and we are fully persuaded that the parts fitted, after all the changes they must have
undergone by the workmen, as well as those made designedly by us in
the course of two or three days, with as much accuracy and correctness as they did when on the stocks to which they originally belonged.

If the uniformity therefore, in the component parts of small
arms, is an important desideratum, which we presume will not be
doubted by any one the least conversant with the subject, it is, in
our opinion, completely accomplished by the plan which Captain Hall
has carried into effect. By no other process known to us (and we
have seen most, if not all, that are in use in the United States)
could arms be made so exactly alike as to interchange and require
no marks on the different parts; and we very much doubt, whether
the best workmen that may be selected from any armory, with the aid
of the best machines in use, elsewhere, could in a whole life make
a hundred rifles or muskets that would, after being promiscuously

mixed together, fit each other with the exact nicety that is to
be found in those manufactured by Captain Hall.

The quality of the work performed.--We have already remarked
on this point when speaking of the uniformity of the arms we will,
however, further observe, that in point of accuracy, the quality of
the work is greatly superior to any thing we have ever seen or expected to see, in the manufacture of small arms, and cannot, with
any degree of propriety, be compared with work executed by the
usual methods, and it fully demonstrates the practicability of what
has been considered almost or totally impossible, by those engaged
making arms, viz:  of their perfect uniformity.

It appears equally evident to us, that ten thousand arms, in
one parcel, may be made by the new machinery, and all so accurately,
that all their parts will suit equally well when interchanged.

As a brief description of the several machines, embracing the
material peculiarities which distinguish them, is desired, the
following is offered as conveying as correct ideas on the most
material points as we are able to give at this time.  In the first
place they possess the important properties of great stability and
accuracy of construction in all their parts where these properties
are necessary, and in the second place great durability.

The system which Captain Hall has carried into complete effect,
of making all the component parts of his arms alike, renders it impossible for the workmen to deviate from the established models,
without being detected.

It also effectually secures the faithfulness of the inspectors
of those parts, and it will enable them to proceed in the discharge
of their duties with the utmost security in every thing relating to
the forms and dimensions, and relative proportions of the arms and
their component parts.


U.S. Congress, 24th, 1st session, House of Representatives,
Committee on Military Affairs, Report No. 375, February 24, 1836,
Serial No. 292, "Extracts from the report of a board of commissioners, in January, 1827, consisting of practical armorers and intelligent gentlemen, appointed by the United States Ordinance Department,
to examine the machinery invented for fabricating the Hall's rifles,"
pp. 8-10.


### 157.   HOUSEHOLD MANUFACTURE AND THE
### MERCHANT-EMPLOYER (1832)


The merchant-employer was a transitional capitalist.
He owned the raw materials and employed wage labor but
he did not own the tools of the trade and he did not own
a central workplace. S. Williston, the merchant-employer
in this case, had a total capital investment of $15,000,
and his inventory he valued at $10,000:  he purchased

$24,000 worth of raw materials from England and France, and valued his output at $40,000. His markets were New York, West Indies, and even South America!

East Hampton.--Manufacturing of lasting and silk twist buttons is entirely carried on in private families by females, who are paid by groce. Materials are furnished, and contracts made with some hundreds of females residing in several adjouring towns, by one person, who...has been considered the capitalist. They call upon him once a week, and procure moulds, silk, and lasting, &c., and, at the same time, bring the product of their labor of the previous week. A great deal of this labor is performed in vacant times, when they have nothing else to do; which, connected with the circumstance of the operatives being so scattered, renders it difficult to obtain an accurate estimate of this business in the respective towns, and to apportion the time and wages by the day. Six years ago the market was entirely supplied by the foreign article, which has gradually been displaced, until it is now entirely excluded, by the manufacture of this county alone. In the mean time, the prices have fallen more than fifty per cent., while experience and skill have produced an article of double the intrinsic value of that formerly imported. The moulds are made by machinery carried by water power, tended by females.

Documents Relative to the Manufacture in the United States, I, pp. 312-313.


158.  THE FOUR TEXTILE FACTORIES OF LOWELL,
MASSACHUSETTS (1832)


During the preceding decade, Lowell had become a great textile manufacturing center, based on machine industry and corporate organization. The four factories reached far for their raw materials and markets and thus served as a unifying economic force.

COMPANY

| ITEM | Appleton Cotton Manufacturing Company | Lowell Manufacturing Company | Merrimack Cotton Manufacturing Company | Hamilton Cotton Manufacturing Company |
|---|---|---|---|---|
| Foreign materials used in factory: Quantity and Value | | | 163,852 lbs. madder $31,130 <br> 44,534 lbs. indigo 59,898 <br> 114,428 lbs. logwood 2,460 <br> 6,000 lbs. gums 1,650 <br> 10,622 lbs. sumac 420 <br> Berries 1,370 <br> Blanketing 5,100 <br> 4,500 lbs. copper 3,200 <br> 150,000 lbs. sulpher 5,800 | Quercitron bank Pa. 300 <br> Pyro acid 20,000 gals. Mass. 1,720 <br> Various other materials Mass. 5,300 <br><br> Madder ) <br> Indigo ) $5,230 <br> Logwood) |
| Major Markets | | | 1/3 in Mass., rest in N.Y., Pa., and Md. | 1/3 in Mass., rest in N.Y., Phila., and Baltimore |

COMPANY

| ITEM | Appleton Cotton Manufacturing Company | Lowell Manufacturing Company | Merimack Cotton Manufacturing Company | Hamilton Cotton Manufacturing Company |
|---|---|---|---|---|
| Value of land, plant, fixtures | $187,386 | $ 81,741 | $706,009 | $365,119 |
| Value of equipment | 166,169 | 93,464 | 623,837 | 340,285 |
| Value of factory Inventory | 147,978 | 100,000 | 462,037 | 214,682 |
| Domestic materials used in factory: Quantity, source, and value | 441 cords of wood. N.H. $2,646<br>60 tons of coal Pa. 480<br>2,195 gallons oil. Mass. 1,712<br>73,157 lbs. starch. N.H. 4,389<br>1,565,108 lbs. cotton. N.O. & S.C. 172,161.88<br>Other material 13,558 | 4,110,000 lbs. cotton, Ga. $110,000<br>31,800 lbs. starch N.H. 2,208<br>200 tons coal Pa. 1,600<br>Oil & other materials Mass. | 1,471,312 lbs. cotton, N.O. & S.C. $176,248.20<br>44,351 lbs. starch N.H. 2,317.55<br>400 lbs. flour Md. 2,200.00<br>600 cords wood N.H. 2,450.00<br>416 tons coal Pa. 2,900.00<br>5,860 gals. oil Mass. 4,664.61<br>1,300 casks lime Me. 1,820.00<br>260,000 lbs. 5,700.00<br>150,000 potash Vt.&N.H. 7,500<br>1,500 lbs. pearlash Vt.&N.H. 960 | 1,500,000 lbs. cotton. N.O. & S.C. $180,000<br>63,000 lbs. starch Mass. 3,700<br>120 lbs. flour N.H. 720<br>3,050 cords wood Md. $12,200<br>300 tons coal N.H. 2,600<br>3,400 gals. oil Pa. 2,720<br>700 casks lime Mass. 1,050<br>75,000 copperas Me. 1,875<br>45,000 lbs. potash Vt. 2,250<br>Chlorine and other materials Vt. 11,000 |

COMPANY

| ITEM | Appleton Cotton Manufacturing Company | Lowell Manufacturing Company | Merrimack Cotton Manufacturing Company | Hamilton Cotton Manufacturing Company |
|---|---|---|---|---|
| Cotton Cloth produced per yr., value per yard | 4,275,849 yds. @ 10 cents | 1,860,000 yds., @ 13 cents | 6,460,000 yds., = $660,600 | 3,650,000 yds., = $474,500 |
| Males employed over 16 yrs. no. & daily wage | 50 @ $1.16 2/3 | 60 @ 90 cents | 312 @ $1.25 | 154 @ $1.25 |
| Males employed under 16 yrs., no. & daily wage | | | 106 @ 36 cents | |
| Females employed, No. & daily wage | 430 @ $3 per Wk. | 230 @ $3 per Wk. | 1,025 @ 44 cents | 672 @ 52 cents |

Documents Relative to the Manufactures in the United States, I, pp. 340-341. This table has been re-worded and re-arranged by the present editor. Presumably, the Appleton and Lowell firms did not report on foreign materials used because such materials were utilized principally in bleaching and printing operations which were excluded in the returns of the two firms.

159.   THE MECHANIZATION OF TACK-MAKING (1832)


A neglected example of a typical 19th Century
technology.


The making of tacks, by hand, commenced very early in this
town [Abington, Massachusetts], say sixty years since.  The first
attempt was, to cut up old hoops into points, by a very imperfect
kind of shears, and take them up, one by one, and place them in a
common vice, and screw up and unscrew for the purpose of heading
each tack with a hammer.  From this process they were called cut
tacks.  But the mode in making by hand was much improved by moveable
dies, placed in an iron frame, in the shape of an ox bow; the two
ends, in which were placed the dies, being brought together by a
lever pressed by the foot.  In the first process, a man might make
1,000 tacks per day, in the latter 8,000 per day.  This was a great
improvement; and the inventor, (Mr. Ezekiel Reed, then residing in
this town, now of North Bridgewater, and who is a very aged man,
over 80) was entitled to a patent.  He made some attempts to conceal
the operation, but it was so simple and so easily applied, that
others soon got it, and it came into general use.
    With machines, or "tack tools," as they were called, thus im-
proved, from three to four hundred men and boys were employed in
making tacks in this town and vicinity from about the year 1800,
for about 30 years, the business was progressing from a very small
beginning, to employ the number of hands as above.
    In 1815 and '16, a machine was invented by Mr. Jesse Reed,
then of Hanover, in the county of Plymouth, son of the above named
Ezekiel Reed, to make tacks at one operation.  Mr. Melvin Otis,
of Bridgewater, claimed and received a considerable share in the
invention.  Soon afterwards the machines were much improved by the
inventions of Messrs. Thomas Blanchard, of Springfield, and Samuel
Ragers, of East Bridgewater.  These inventors are still living, and
are all natives of Massachusetts.
    For the exclusive patent rights of these inventions, Elihu
Hobart, esq. and the writer of this paid something over twenty
thousand dollars; to which must be added for building of machines
and fixtures to put them into operation by water, ten thousand
dollars more; making thirty thousand dollars expended, in the first
instance, to commence the business of making tacks.  Large sums were
added afterwards.  The price of tacks was reduced over fifty per
cent, immediately, and one man could make more tacks in a day on
one of the patent machines than fifteen could by hand, even in the
last improved mode of moveable dies; by hand 8 or 10,000 per day,
on a machine from 100 to 150,000.  One machine has turned out over
250,000 in a day.
. . . . . . . . . . . . . . . . . . . . . . . . . . . . . . . . .

In no country, perhaps, are the articles of tacks, brads, and
sprigs, made cheaper than in the United States.  The machines for
making tacks, as now improved, work with great facility, and their
invention does honor to the country.  A single machine will turn
out 365 tacks per minute, feed itself, turn the plate, cut and head
them, all complete.  With such machines, aided with American industry, the United States may yet supply the world with tacks; they
will doubtless soon become an article of exportation; several shipments have already been made to advantage; others are now in
contemplation.

Letter, Benjamin Hobart, Abington, Massachusetts to Willard
Phillips, May 30, 1832, Documents Relative to the Manufactures in
the United States, II, pp. 873, 875.

160.   ENGLISH AND SCOTCH ACCENTS IN NEW YORK
MACHINE SHOPS (1850)

Even by mid-century, a native skilled labor
force did not yet exist in sufficient numbers, so
writes James Johnston.

To appreciate the full force of what is said in regard to
American mechanics and American mechanical skill, it is necessary
to be aware of the kind of men with whom their workshops are filled.
I went into some of the machine-shops where the materials for the
new line of steamers were in process of manufacture, and I heard
almost every workman talking with either an English or a Scottish
tongue.  I remarked this to my New York friend who accompanied me.
"Yes," he observed, "but the head-man is an American."  In a
machine-shop the hands are at least as important as the head.  "I
have a clever Englishman in my workshop," said a wholesale hardware
merchant of Philadelphia to me, "and if any English article is
wanted that we have never made, I send for him, and ask him if he
can have it made for me, and he has never failed me yet."
Workshops filled with British workmen are British workshops,
on whichever side of the Atlantic they may be, and engines made in
them are British engines; so that we [Englishmen], in reality, feel
no jealousy at being beaten by ourselves.

Johnston, Notes on North America, II, p. 384.

161.  HOUSEHOLD MANUFACTURING IN MASSACHUSETTS (1832)


Household manufactures were declining rapidly in
Massachusetts.  They retained their hold as by-lines
especially in sailing and whaling villages.


[CHILMARK]  It will readily be seen that we are not a manufacturing town, except in our respective families.  This we do something at.  We make the most of our coarse woollen cloth, all our
woollen stockings, and about 2,000 pair annually for sale; and are
sold in New Bedford and Boston.  Most of our tailoring and shoemaking are done in our houses.
This town contains about 700 inhabitants:  of this population
upwards of fifty seamen are actually employed in whaling voyages,
some in merchant voyages, and some a fishing; consequently, our
male inhabitants are spread in most all parts of the world.
This town is made up of islands, which embrace a territory of
land and water (mostly water) near twenty miles square.  A large
portion of the lands are owned by non-residents, and the inhabitants
are thinly settled, and mostly poor, and their situation is such
that they can obtain but little education.
. . . . . . . . . . . . . . . . . . . . . . . . . . . . . . . . . .
[TISBURY]  It will be proper to remark that we manufacture but
very little, and what we do is mostly for customers living around
us; so it is necessary to make good articles, for they always sell
best.  This town manufactures much of their coarse woollens, and
shoes in their families; and they knit about 1,500 pair per annum
for sale, which are sold in Boston and New Bedford.  The male inhabitants are, many of them, employed in whaling, and other seafaring
voyages.
. . . . . . . . . . . . . . . . . . . . . . . . . . . . . . . . . .
[SAUGUS]  Besides the above named tobacco manufactures, many
cigars are made in families, which probably gives employment to
twenty females, and as many small boys.


Documents Relative to the Manufactures in the United States,
I, pp. 204-205, 208-209, 256-257.


162.  THE SUCCESSFUL MANUFACTURER IS A MONEY LENDER,
EMPLOYER, AND LABORER (1832)


This summary statement was written by Samuel Slater,
the "father" of American factory production.  In 1790 he
had come to this country and helped set up the first textile
factory, based on designs and mechanisms he had observed in
his native England.  Now, forty-two years later, he spoke

authoritatively on some problems of manufactures.
Note his strong artisan's emphasis on the necessity
for personal superintendence.


On the subject of profits, the theoretical economists of this
country have been widely misled from the actual state of things
here, by the scholastic distinctions of European economists. Because
the latter, taking the actual relations of older and richer communities, have distinguished between capitalists, or those who furnish
money and employers, or those who hire money, the former have applied
the same classification to this country, which, being a younger and
a poorer community, has no such distinct and independent relations
or classes. As a general rule, all our able bodied citizens gain
the whole, or a part of their own and the living of their families,
by labor. The richest of them labor for themselves, and employ
others to labor for them. They employ the surplus of profits over
the consumption of themselves and families as a capital for some
business, which themselves follow; or they lend that surplus at an
interest which, with the profits of their personal labor, make up
their income. If a man, therefore, accumulates a surplus of profits
of their personal labor, or income over his expenses, he will employ
that new capital in his business, if by so employing it he can realize a new profit beyond the interest which he can obtain by lending
it to another. If he now employs a thousand dollars, and, with his
personnal labor in the business, makes one hundred dollars a year
more than interest and the expenses of his family, and has another
thousand which may be as well employed, he will put that into the
business also, because it will make his gross income twice as much
as it was before, his family expenses remaining the same, and perhaps require no more of his own labor than his business now requires.
The income, therefore, of nearly all the working classes in this
country, which comprehend its whole population, is compounded of
interest on money, profits on capital employed, and wages of labor.
When, therefore, we inquire as to the rate of profits on capital,
strictly so called--that is to say, the amount of product which
remains after payment of interest, on one hand, and of the wages
of labor on the other--we shall find it much less than superficial
observers and theoretical economists have supposed. There must always be some inducement beyond the legal or common rate of interest,
to tempt a man who has money in stock, or on loan, to transfer that
money to a new employment. He will do so perhaps if morally certain
of a remuneration of one or two per cent. beyond interest. He will
do so, most surely, if, in the triple capacity of money lender,
master, and laborer, he can, by employing his money himself, realize
a gross profit, which, rateably divided between three individuals,
holding the same relation to each other, could not remunerate either
of them, but which, coming to him entire, would be twice or thrice
the common rate of interest on his money.
    It is in this triple capacity of money lender, employer, and
laborer, that our most successful manufacturers have succeeded.
They furnished money for the business and superintended its operation in person. They employed their families in the labors of the
business, and, to the extent of this saving of the wages of

superintendence and labor, realized the gross profits of manufacture.
Instances of ultimate failure among manufacturers of this description are very rare.  Yet would their gross profits fall very far
short of a fair remuneration to each, if those profits should be
divided among three distinct classes of persons, such as our theorists have supposed.  Less successful than the above description of
manufacturers, but more so than another description to be mentioned
hereafter, have been those who, having no money of their own, but
having industry, skill, and prudence, have manufactured on borrowed
capital; and, by personal superintendence and hard labor, have saved
a considerable proportion of the gross profit of manufacture, after
payment of the interest on their loans.  Many of these have succeeded in replacing the money loaned, and saved their mills; but this
saving consists entirely in the saving of them by wages.  Allow
them the common rate of wages which has been paid to others for
similar services, with a very small profit over interest on the
money which they hired, and their mills would not pay the account.
Least successful of all have been those who, themselves engaged in
other pursuits, have invested the nett profits of their own business in manufacturing, and left the latter to the superintendence
of others.  A large proportion of these investments has been wholly
lost throughout the waste, profusion, unskilfulness, and want of
fidelity of agents, superintendents, and other servants, hired at
large salaries, and having no interest in the ultimate prosperity
of the concern.  Many of these adventurers have not only lost the
whole amount of their investments, but have been called upon for
the debts contracted by their agents, in some instances to the
extent of their whole property.  Without, therefore, making any
definite conclusion as to the precise amount of gross profits on
manufacturing business, when conducted by the two first mentioned
classes of adventurers, we may safely affirm, that the aggregate
of those profits, if rateably divided according to the legal rate
of interest, the common rate of profit on capital employed, and
the usual rewards of labor in other callings, among three distinct
and independent classes of individuals holding the relation of money
lenders, employers, and laborers, would afford to neither of those
classes that fair and common remuneration which other branches of
business afford, and that nearly all the prosperous manufacturing
concerns in this State have depended for their prosperity on an
union, in the same persons, of the three capacities which have been
mentioned.


Documents Relative To The Manufactures in the United States,
I, pp. 928-929.

163.  ONLY THE RARE ENGINEER IS ALSO A PRACTICAL
AND THEORETICAL MECHANIC (1838)


Engineering education was most rudimentary in these
days.  William B. Dodd's suggestion, in a letter to the
President Martin Van Buren, of government licensing of
engineers was far ahead of his time.  Dodd could also
have noted that very few practical mechanics were also
theoretical mechanics.  How, then, expect some engineers
to be both?  Dodd wrote beneath his signature the
following:  "Practical and Theoretical Engineer."


Sir:  Having seen a law passed by the Senate and House of
Representatives, and sanctioned by you, respecting the explosion of
steam-boilers, and for the purpose of testing inventions to remedy
the same, I make bold to assert that it is out of the power of man
to make any such discovery except in long practice and experience.
The fault is not in the boilers, but in the men calling themselves
engineers, who are incapable of taking charge of an engine for
these reasons:
1.  Because they know nothing about the nature of steam.
2.  Because they know not how to remedy a defect, if there
is one.
There is not one in every ten that call themselves engineers
that is a practical and theoretical mechanic.  The reason of this
is, because an experienced man will not work for the same wages that
an inexperienced man will.  Your committee may expend millions of
dollars in testing inventions of this kind, and when they leave
off, they will have accomplished no more than the celebrated John
Clark did when he attempted to burn gunpowder in a cylinder without
having it explode.  Engineers are the inventions that your committee
should test; and if found capable of taking charge of an engine, and
holding the lives of thousands of souls in their hands, let such
receive a diploma from Government; and pass a law that such only
shall be employed as engineers who hold such a diploma.  Such a
course would undoubtedly be a great saving of human life, and prevent much imposition.  The engineer who does his duty performs a
hazardous service, and ought to be remunderated accordingly.


Letter, William B. Dodd of Newark, New Jersey, to President
Martin Van Buren, October 1, 1838, U.S. Congress, 25th, 3rd session,
House of Representatives, Document No. 21, Serial No. 345, Steam
Engines...Letter from the Secretary of the Treasury, 1838, p. 398.

164.  BLACKSMITHING AND COUNTRY MACHINE WORK (1838)


A mighty man, and a versatile one, was the
village smith.


Early in October, 1838, I went to Parkesburg, Chester County,
Pennsylvania, as an apprentice, to learn the trades of blacksmithing and country machine work.  These consisted of doing such work
as was required by the farmers and small manufacturers of the neighborhood, such as the shoeing of horses, ironing wagons, carts and
carriages, and all work required of a smith; and in the machine
line, repairs wanted by the farmers on their threshing machines and
other machinery used about the farms, and also both the smith and
machine work for repairs and renewals required by the cotton, woolen,
and other manufacturers, such as grist and saw mills, blast furnaces,
and forge plants.
. . . . . . . . . . . . . . . . . . . . . . . . . . . . . . . . . .
At the shop where I worked there were four smith fires, four
anvils, and for that time a fair supply of small smith tools and
and stocks, taps, and dies for cutting screws.  There were also
two small lathes for turning iron, and a small lathe for doing
pattern work; at times the latter was used for turning and finishing
light brass work, all on wooden shears or beds.  There was also a
very good makeshift of a drill-press bolted up against a ten-inch
wooden post.  All of these tools were of the crudest character, but
capable of doing, in a very elementary way, such machine work as was
required in the neighborhood.  In addition there was a set of rolls
for bending boiler plate, shears and punch, and a kit of small boiler
maker's tools, which put the shop in a position to do boiler making
in a small way.
. . . . . . . . . . . . . . . . . . . . . . . . . . . . . . . . . .
The power to drive these tools was a six-horse-power engine
and boiler; both had, practically speaking, been built in the blacksmith shop by my new master.  It was a rude machine, but worked
quite well, and I don't believe there is today [1912] one mechanic
out of a thousand that could, under the same conditions, build such
an engine.  He would have to make his own drawings and patterns,
make his own forgings, and fit the work all up, without tools,
except makeshifts.  Today as many men work on an engine as there
are parts to it, and each man has a special machine, especially
designed to do his work on.  There are few all-round mechanics today
such as there were sixty years ago; even good, all-round machinists,
valuable as they are today, are getting scarcer daily, and the present shop practice is better calculated to make machines out of men
than to make good all-round mechanics.


The Autobiography of John Fritz, (New York:  Wiley, 1912,
pp. 32-33.

## 165. STATIONARY STEAM ENGINES: DATES
## OF INTRODUCTION (1838)

Steam was used for highly varied purposes. In Louisiana, largest user of steam engines, they could be found in sugar mills; in Pittsburgh, in mills and factories. The great bulk of the steam installations had been made in the preceding fifteen years.

| States | Number | Power [H.P.] | Period when first introduced into use in the State. |
|--------|--------|--------------|------------------------------------------------------|
| Maine - - - - - - - - | 41 | 765 | 1833 |
| New Hampshire - - - - | 6 | 102 | 1833 |
| Massachusetts - - - - | 165 | 2,244 | 1827 |
| Connecticut - - - - - | 47 | 315 | 1830 |
| Rhode Island- - - - - | 58 | 1,430 | 1828 |
| Vermont - - - - - - - | None Returned | None Returned. | |
| New York - - - - - | 87 | 1,425 | |
| New Jersey- - - - - - | 32 | 516 | 1787 to 1834 |
| Pennsylvania- - - - - | 383 | 7,448 | 1791 to 1810 |
| Delaware- - - - - - - | 11 | 88 | 1825 |
| Maryland- - - - - - - | 56 | 683 | 1818 |
| District of Columbia- | 13 | 206 | 1827 |
| Virginia- - - - - - - | 124 | 1,567 | 1821 |
| North Carolina- - - - | 20 | 751 | 1821 |
| South Carolina- - - - | 40 | 675 | 1819 |
| Georgia - - - - - - - | 23 | 799 | 1827 |
| Florida - - - - - - - | 8 | 215 | 1833 |
| Alabama - - - - - - - | 40 | 800 | |
| Louisiana - - - - - - | 274 | 7,796 | 1821 |
| Missouri and- - - - -) Illinois, in part - -) | 56 | 1,120 | 1837 and 1838 |
| Ohio- - - - - - - - - | 83 | 1,786 | 1828 |
| Michigan- - - - - - - | 32 | 368 | 1828 |
| Tennessee - - - - - -) Indiana, and- - - - -) Kentucky - - - - - -) | None Specifically Returned | None Specifically Returned | |
| Wisconsin - - - - - -) Iowa- - - - - - - - -) | None Specifically Returned | None Specifically Returned | |
| United States   Government    - - - - | 17 | 340 | |
| Add standing engines | 1,616 | 31,439 | |
| not returned, but estimated - - - - - | 244 | 4,880 | |
| Total - - | 1,860 | 36,319 | |

U.S. Congress, 25th, 3rd session, House of Representatives, Document No. 21, Serial No. 345, Steam Engines...Letter from the Secretary of the Treasury, 1838, p. 379.

166.    AMERICANS OUTSTRIP ENGLAND IN COMMON
POWER-LOOM WEAVING (1840)


A comparative statement on American and British
technology was written by James Montgomery who was
superintendent of the New York factories in Saco, Maine;
he had earlier been associated with a Scottish textile
mill.


In those departments of the cotton manufacture which relate
to carding and spinning, I consider this country much behind Great
Britain, especially in the carding.  But in those which relate to
weaving by power, the Americans have in every respect equalled,
and in some things surpassed, anything I have yet seen, either in
Glasgow or Manchester.  I refer to common power-loom weaving.  In
fancy weaving, either by power or hand, this country [the United
States], so far as I am informed, has not yet made a beginning.


     James Montgomery, A Practical Detail of the Cotton Manufacture
of the United States of America, (Glasgow:   John Niven, Jr., 1840),
p. 82.


167.    AUTOMATIC TEXTILE MACHINES ARE BUILT TO SUIT AN
INEXPERIENCED LABOR FORCE (1840)


A practical factory manager, with experience on
two continents, is struck by the connection between technology and the character of the labor supply.  Montgomery
writes again.


The great majority of girls employed in the American Factories
are farmers' daughters, who come into the Factory for, perhaps, a
year or two, and frequently for but a few months, until they make a
little money to purchase clothes, &c. and then go home.  In consequence of this continual changing, there are always great numbers
of inexperienced hands in every Factory:  and as the drawing process
requires the utmost care and attention to make correct work as well
as to prevent waste, it is necessary to have the most expert and
experienced hands attending the drawing frames; but this cannot always be obtained in this country as in Great Britain; hence it is
more necessary to have some contrivance connected with the machinery
here, which will, to a certain extent at least, prevent the work
from being injured by inexperience on the part of attendants.  All
the drawing frames, therefore, which I have seen in this country,

are mounted with a self-acting stop-motion, so that when an end
(sliver) breaks, or runs out, that head with which it is connected
instantly stops.
. . . . . . . . . . . . . . . . . . . . . . . . . . . . . . . . . .
      The stop-motion is entirely an American invention, and is
particularly necessary in this country for the reasons already
stated.  But besides the expense of fiting up, it is very liable to
get out of order, and when that is the case, it makes a great deal
of imperfect work, as it usually begets carelessness on the part
of the attendants, who depend almost entirely upon the latch for
stopping the head when the work goes wrong; and when one latch falls,
it frequently brings down others, and breaks or injures the slivers,
besides causing some trouble in putting them all right before the
head can be again started.  Now in Great Britain where there is
always a command of experienced hands, the introduction of this
stop-motion would be attended with no advantage, as, in my opinion,
two active girls by close attention, would do more and better work
on a drawing frame having no self-acting stop-motion, than any I
have yet seen with it, even the most improved.

      Montgomery, A Practical Detail, pp. 57, 59.


                168.   COMPARATIVE COST ADVANTAGES OF AMERICAN
                        TEXTILE MANUFACTURE (1840)


         A catalogue of advantages, written by James Montgomery.


      The amount of goods produced is much greater in America than
in Great Britain; but the hours of labour are somewhat longer in
the former than in the latter country.
      The cost of the buildings, machinery, &c. is a great deal
higher in America than in Britain, as well as the general rate of
wages, particularly in the carding department.
      After comparing the advantages and disadvantages of each, it
appears that the British manufacturer can produce his goods, at
least 19 per cent. cheaper than the American.  This, however, is
more than neutralised, by the cheaper rate at which the latter can
purchase his cotton.
      The circumstance of America being a cotton growing country,
will always give to her manufacturers advantages of which the
British cannot generally avail themselves.  It is very common here
for several manufacturers to join together, and appoint some person
acquainted with the business, to go to the Southern States, and purchase cotton sufficient for a year's consumption.  The person thus
appointed goes to the first markets, and selects such cottons as he
knows will suit those for whom he is purchasing--he buys it at the
cheapest rate, and has it shipped to the nearest port to where it

is to be manufactured. the whole charge for commission will not
amount to one per cent. on the prime cost.
. . . . . . . . . . . . . . . . . . . . . . . . . . . . . . . . . .
        ...the whole expenses attending the purchase and carriage of
cotton, until it is laid down at the Factories, seldom exceed 12 or
13 per cent. on the prime cost, and in many cases are much less.
The Cotton Factories in this country are generally situated near
the sea coast, so that the expense of inland carriage is very trifling, compared with that paid by the majority of Factories in Great
Britain. The carriage from Boston to Lowell is two dollars per ton,
while to many other Factories, the inland carriage is not above one
dollar; at the same time, there are various other Factories, in
different parts of the country, to which the carriage cannot be less
than four dollars.
. . . . . . . . . . . . . . . . . . . . . . . . . . . . . . . . . .
        ...in every description of goods in which the cost of the raw
material exceeds the cost of production, the American manufacturers
have a decided advantage over the British. And they have availed
themselves of this advantage to improve the quality of their goods,
as any person who has had an opportunity of comparing the domestics
manufactured in the two countries, can have no hesitation in giving
the preference to those manufactured in America; and the experience
of every British manufacturer engaged in producing this description
of goods has painfully convinced him, that the superior quality of
the American goods is gradually driving him from every foreign
market.
. . . . . . . . . . . . . . . . . . . . . . . . . . . . . . . . . .
...the manufacturers here can afford to pay higher wages than the
British, because they run their Factories longer hours, and drive
their machinery at a higher speed, from which they produce a much
greater quantity of work; at the same time, they can purchase their
cotton at least one penny a pound cheaper, and their water power
does not cost above one-fourth of the same in Great Britain. But
though wages cannot be reduced much lower than they are at present,
there are other means by which manufacturers might abridge their
expenditure. Their establishments might be erected at much less
expense--a more improved arrangement might be adoped--and the work
conducted with much more economy. All these, however, are matters
which the Americans will very speedily learn; every successive depression of trade will lead them more and more to see the necessity
of managing every department of the business with the least possible
expense; and as soon as they can equal the British in this, they
will be able to compete with them, and that successfully too, in
any market whatever.


        Montgomery, A Practical Detail, pp. 126-127, 129, 130, 138.

169.  HIGH-SPEED MACHINES GIVE A COMPARATIVE ADVANTAGE
TO AMERICAN MANUFACTURING (1840)


Here James Montgomery discusses the fact that high
wages are offset by high per-worker output in America.


Driving machinery at a high speed, however, does not always
meet with the most favorable regard of practical men in Great
Britain; because in that country where power costs so much, whatever
tends to exhaust that power, is a matter of some consideration:
but in this country, where water power is so extensively employed,
it is of much less consequence.  Besides, the expense of labour
being much greater in this country than in Great Britain, the American manufacturers can only compete successfully with the British,
by producing a greater quantity of goods in a given time; hence any
machine that admits of being driven at a higher speed, even though
it should exhaust the power, if it does not injure the work, will
meet with a more favourable reception in this country than in
Great Britain.


Montgomery, A Practical Detail, p. 71.



170.  LOWELL, THE MANCHESTER OF AMERICA (1840)


A succinct characterization is made here by
Montgomery.  (See Source No. 158).


The principal manufacturing town in the United States is that
of Lowell, which may justly be denominated the Manchester of America,
as regards the amount of capital invested for manufacturing purposes, the extent of the business, and the spirited manner in which
it is conducted.  And here, too, the Factory system is perhaps in
more perfect operation than in any other part of the United States.
Here are the largest establishments, the most perfect arrangement,
and the richest corporations.  And it may, without fear of contradiction, be asserted, that the Factories at Lowell produce a greater
quantity of yarn and cloth from each spindle and loom (in a given
time,) than is produced in any other Factories without exception in
the world.


Montgomery, A Practical Detail, p. 162.

171.  HOW TO MANUFACTURE UNIFORM PARTS (1840)


Here is a clear and simple explanation of the essence
of manufacturing interchangeable parts for guns.  It is
written by John Hall who had been employed in federal armor-
ies for a number of years.  (See Source No. 156).


That the plan which I have adopted is applicable to every kind
of arm, a brief explanation of the plan by which it is effected will
satisfy you.  In making a part of an arm like a prescribed model, the
difficulty is exactly the same as that which occurs in making a piece
of iron exactly square.  In such a case, a man would square the second side by the first, the third by the second, and the fourth by
the third; but, on comparing the fourth side with the first, it will
be found that they are not square; the cause is, that in squaring
each side by the preceding side there is a slight but imperceptible
variation, and the comparison of the fourth with the first gives the
sum of the variations of each side from a true square.  And so in
manufacturing a limb of a gun so as to conform to a model, by shifting
the points, as convenience requires, from which the work is gauged
and executed; the slight variations are added to each other in the
progress of the work, so as to prevent uniformity.  The course which
I adopted to avoid this difficulty was, to perform and guage every
operation on a limb from one point, called a bearing, so that the
variation in any operation could only be the single one from that
point.  To illustrate this by the example given above: By my plan,
the tools would be so made, that each side of the square would be
squared from the first side, so that the variation of the fourth side
from the first would be no greater than the second from the first, or
the third from the second.  It is evident that this principle is
applicable in all cases where uniformity is required.
    The plan of manufacturing arms identically is greatly facilitat-
ed by the use of my machinery, which is also of universal application.  That it is so, you will readily understand from the circumstance that the same machinery is made to operate on all the principle limbs of the patent rifle; and on the same principle by which
it can be changed from a limb of one form to another of one arm, it
can be applied to an article of any form whatever.  The machinery
performs the work of the file, though with greater accuracy and
economy, and can be used in almost every case where a file can be.
    The advantages of the machinery in economy and uniformity of
operation may be seen from page 11 of the enclosed document; and it
may be stated generally, with regard to their effects, that one boy,
by the aid of these machines, can perform more work than ten men
with files, in the same time, and with greater accuracy.


Letter, John H. Hall to Joel R. Poinsett, Secretary of War,
February 21, 1840, U.S. Congress, 26th, 1st session, House of
Representatives, Committee on Military Affairs, Report No. 453,
Serial No. 371, p. 6.

172.   MUTUAL MACHINE PIRACY IN IRELAND AND
THE UNITED STATES (1844)


Colman writes a frank, knowing statement about a widespread practice.


The exhibition at Dublin was, in various respects, creditable
to the society.  The collection of grasses and grains, dried specimens of which were exhibited by several nursery-men, were extremely
beautiful, and highly instructive to the farmers.... I saw, likewise, an American straw-cutting machine, very slightly varied from
the original, and which had been patented in Ireland, of which I
could not complain, after many instances of similar plagiarism,
which I had seen, in my own country, exhibited as rare specimens of
Yankee ingenuity.  Of the morality of such tricks, if so they are
to be called, I leave my readers to judge; but in other respects,
from various things which have come under my notice, the account
seems pretty fairly balanced between us.


Colman, European Agriculture and Rural Economy, I, p. 177.


173.   THE MANUFACTURING SOUTH IS NOW WHERE NEW ENGLAND
WAS IN 1822 (1849)


In the following William Gregg writes to James H.
Hammond, a former governor of South Carolina.


The freedom of thought and action of the present day removes
from us the obstacles which many other countries have laboured
against in attempting to revolutionise or improve modes [of] industry.  Added to this we have wonderful advantages over the Eastern
people in commencing the work.  We are not just where they were in
1820 or 22 with this difference that they were dependent on England
for machinery and skilled artisans--with the restrictive laws of
England against them.  We have the advantage of free intercourse
and competition with the Eastern folk, and can procure their machinery as cheap as they can get it.  Machinery mad[e] in providence
can be transported as cheaply to South Carolina as it can be taken
to the interior of any of the Eastern or Northern states.  And to
obtain their most skilful artisans we have only to bid a little
higher for them to avail ourselves of their most talented & best
men.  We can do in 12 years what they have been twenty eight in
doing.  The Augusta Charleston & Graniteville Mills when complete
will contain 1000 looms capable of making 40,000 yards of cloth a
day, this itself is a large commencement & has been done as we may
say in a day.  The State of Georgia has upwards of 2,000,000 of

Charleston Capital employed in her various pursuits.  Show our
people profitable sources of investment and that capital will soon
return.  It would start 2,000 looms.
        Graniteville Stock is above par.  I offered yesterday myself
10 per cent advance for $12,000 worth of it, to a person who had
expressed a wish to sell, the offer was rejected.  I really wished
to make the purchase, & made the offer through a broker so that the
party owning the Stock had no Knowledge of the source from which
the bid came.
        If this State of things continue to exist--there will be no
want of capital to carry out similar enterprises.


        Letter, William Gregg to James H. Hammond, May 30, 1849,
Thomas P. Martin (ed.), "The Advent of William Gregg and the
Graniteville Company," Journal of Southern History, XI (1945), p.
415.


        174.  COAL IN ANGLO-AMERICAN IRON COMPETITION (1849)


        Anthracite or hard coal required little or no
processing before use, and, because it did not crumble,
was transported economically.  Its full heating value
was not utilized, however, until perfection of the hot
blast.  The American iron and steel industry achieved
supremacy, not with anthracite but with bituminous
coal or coke, especially after the Civil War.


        But the advantages arising from .....[Pennsylvania's] rich
deposits of iron ore, have been hitherto more than counterbalanced
by the high prices of fuel in the iron manufacture of Pennsylvania--
this being the principal cause of the inability of American iron
master to compete with the iron manufacturers of Scotland and Wales.
        The fuel of Pennsylvania is almost exclusively anthracite coal,
for the purposes of the iron trade; for though charcoal furnaces
still remain in existence, they are now few and far between.
Pennsylvania resembles any European country in the disappearance of
the natural woods, and the expense of raising timber for fuel, can
no more be borne in Pennsylvania than in any of the countries of
the woods, and the deficiency of the substitute for charcoal in any
of the varieties of coal.
        In the incombustibility of anthracite coal, or in the compara-
tive incompleteness of the combustion which has yet been obtained
in the use of this variety of fuel, is the marked and undoubted disadvantage remaining to be overcome by the iron manufacturers of the
United States.  Iron manufactured from this fuel, is manufactured
at four times the cost of the fuel in the form of coke, in Scotland
and Wales.
. . . . . . . . . . . . . . . . . . . . . . . . . . . . . . . . .

There is...an advantage to Pennsylvania [over Wales] of about $3 in the expenses of the iron ore, but a disadvantage of $7 in the value of the coals; whilst the limestone, though dearer in money, is better in quality in Pennsylvania than in Wales—and this material may be taken as of the same value in both countries—leaving the principal disadvantage of the American iron manufacturer most distinctly apparent in the higher price of the anthracite coals, than of the bituminous coals of Wales.

Some difference there is in favor of Great Britain in the expenses of the labor about the furnace; but labor may be yet largely saved in the iron manufacture of Pennsylvania, where the labor-saving spirit of the country has not yet been in the same operation as in the cotton and other important manufactures of the United States.  But with the difference of $7 in the cost of fuel, which is 30 percent. on a ton of pig iron against it, there can exist no probability of a profitable iron manufacture in the United States.

. . . . . . . . . . . . . . . . . . . . . . . . . . . . . . . . . . . . . . .

Were the full heating powers of anthracite....produced in our iron furnaces, it follows that the principal difficulty would be overcome in Pennsylvania, and that a flourishing iron manufacture would be established by the reversal of the expenses of fuel—which being now adverse by 30 per cent. would become favorable in the same proportion, and this would alone render the United States at once independent of further supplies of iron from any other part of the world.  And with the further saving of furnace room, steam power and labor, it is probable that the increased make of iron would create a further saving, which would render the total difference an average of nine or ten dollars per ton, or one-half of all the expense of making iron at the present time in the United States.

H. Fairbairn, "The Anthracite Iron Manufacture of the United States.  Its Improvement Proposed," Journal of the Franklin Institute, whole volume number XXXXVIII (1849), pp. 394-395, 395-396, 400.

175.   THE SOUTH SHOULD MANUFACTURE COTTON TEXTILES (1849)

General C. T. James was the designer and builder of one-eighth, by his count, of the country's cotton mills. He came from Providence, Rhode Island and later served as a U.S. Senator from that state.  James set out to demonstrate that:  (1) the South had several absolute advantages over New England as a cotton manufacturing region, and (2) New England manufacturing was more than adequately profitable, and none of this needed to be sacrificed if the industry grew up in the South.

Ten of the best plantations would not produce more than
1,800,000 lbs. of cotton.  One mill, of 10,000 spindles, would work
the whole into cloth, No. 15, in the year.  These plantations, including slaves, &c., would be worth at least $738,000.  The mill,
with a working capital of $50,000, would be worth, capital and all,
$250,000.  The cotton, at 6 cents per pound, would be worth
$108,000.  The cloth, 4,500,000 yards, at 7 1/2 cents, (yard wide,)
would be worth $337,500.  Deduct from the amount paid the planter
for cotton, wages of overseers, interest of money, &c., say $28,000,
and you leave him $80,000.  Deduct from the above market value of
cloth, the cost of cotton, steampower, labor, &c., &c., $247,000,
including interest on capital and you leave the manufacturer a clear
ballance of $90,500.  It is evident, then, that a man owning such
a cotton mill, would suffer a very considerable loss, by exchanging
it for cotton plantations, negroes, &c., nominally worth three times
as much.  The value of all productive property is in the ratio of
its productiveness, independent of its actual cost.  Hence, the
mill, with its working capital, at an outlay of $250,000, is about
as valuable to its owner, as cotton lands, fixtures, negroes, &c.,
would be, which cost a million.

. . . . . . . . . . . . . . . . . . . . . . . . . . . . . . . . . . .

In a comparatively short time, hundreds of factories might be
erected at the South, and fully supplied with operatives and managers, and which, even were these to be imported from Europe at the
manufacturer's expense, would be the source of gain to him.  The
expense accuring in transitu, on 1,800,000 lbs. of cotton, delivered
at the northern mill, is about $18,000.  To import 275 operatives
from Europe, would cost $13,750.  These would be sufficient for the
mill.  This item, when compared with the expenses of the transportation of the cotton, would make a saving of $4,250; and as but one
such importation, if even that, would be required, there would
afterward be saved annually, the entire amount of $18,000 to the
planter, by the manufacture of his own cotton.  Again:  interest
on the planter's capital, $43,000, together with 600 hands, and 300
horses and mules, necessary to the production of 1,800,000 lbs. of
cotton, would complete and operate three mills to manufacture the
cotton, returning a gross income of many thousand dollars per annum
more than is realized from its culture.

. . . . . . . . . . . . . . . . . . . . . . . . . . . . . . . . . . .

But the South can do, if so disposed, a great deal more in 40 years
to come, than New England has done in 40 years past.  Nothing is
wanting but enterprise.  Alleged deficiency of capital is no sufficient apology.  New England did not hesitate on that account.  She
saw an opportunity to enrich herself, and improved it.  A lucrative
business will always command capital, and create more.  Planters,
with property of the value of half a million of dollars, would
readily command an available capital of one-half that amount, to
invest in a business known to yield a net profit of 25 per cent, or
more, and which would be certain to return an increase of wealth of
more than 100 per cent to the community, in the short space of two
years; and especially when known, as it is by practical experience,
that it would enhance the value of property at least an hundred
per cent.

. . . . . . . . . . . . . . . . . . . . . . . . . . . . . . . . . . .

Factory labor would be, and is, deemed respectable, and will raise
the poor, destitute, and degraded, to comparative independence,
and moral and social respectability.  In proof of this, where manufactories are established at the South, applications are made for
employment, far beyond the demand, and persons employed soon assume
the industrious habits, and the decency of appearance of the operatives of the North.  Thousands of such, collected in manufacturing
villages, as in New England, might be educated in a degree, at
small expense, instead of growing up, as they now do, in profound
ignorance.

. . . . . . . . . . . . . . . . . . . . . . . . . . . . . . . . . . . . .
     One of the objections urged against the location of cotton
manufactories in the South, is the deficiency of water-power.
Suppose you have no motive power--make it.  You have plenty of means.
In many Southern places, steam has been long and extensively used as
the driving power for sawmills, and those who use it would hardly
accept water-power as a gift.  Still longer, and more extensively,
the British manufacturer has used steam-power, to work up the cotton
of the American planter, carried near four thousand miles to find a
market.  And his steam has cost him twice as much as it would cost
any southern State.

. . . . . . . . . . . . . . . . . . . . . . . . . . . . . . . . . . . . .
     On looking back to the commencement of the cotton manufacturing
business in New England, and tracing its progress up to the present
period, we shall find that our manufacturers have had difficulties
to contend with, which the people of the South will not have to
overcome.  The business, at that period, was in its infancy, even
in England.  The machinery introduced here was very imperfect in
form, finish, and operation.  From that time to this, there has been
kept up a continual race of improvement, which has rendered the expenditure of vast sums of money necessary to those who have kept up
with the times; while those who have refused to do so, have either
broken themselves down by a spurious economy, or, at best, plod[d]ed
on with little profit.  The southern people will enter the field
with all these improvements ready made to their hands; and, what is
also of vast importance to them, the new and improved machinery can,
at this day, be had at smaller cost than could have been that of
former days, even but a few years since.  Take, also, into account,
the advantage of more than 20 per cent, on an average, which the
manufacturers of the South will have over those of the North, in
the cost of cotton at Lowell, and no good reason can be assigned
why the former should not find the business more profitable than
the latter.  The difference in cost of cotton alone will pay more
than 6 per cent per annum on the capital employed, even if that
difference were but one cent per pound.

. . . . . . . . . . . . . . . . . . . . . . . . . . . . . . . . . . . . .
...the manufacturing spirit is fast gaining strength in the Middle
and Southern States.  Cotton mills are rapidly on the increase.
As their owners begin to handle the profits, you cannot cheat them
out of the evidence of their own senses.  Southern competition must
come.  The South can manufacture coarse goods cheaper, and at greater
profit, than the North.  If the northern manufacturers are wise,
they will, instead of fretting themselves on this account, make all

necessary improvements in their manufacturing establishments, and supply the markets with such fabrics as the South will not find it to its interest to supply for many years to come.

General C. T. James, "The Production and Manufacture of Cotton," Hunt's Merchants' Magazine, November, 1849, pp. 496, 497, 498, 499; (March, 1850), pp. 302, 311.

### 176.  THE FINANCIAL HAZARDS OF COTTON TEXTILE MANUFACTURE IN THE SOUTH (1849)

Lawrence, a New England textile manufacturer and textile merchant, argued that New England textile manufacturing was hardly so profitable as General James claimed, and that therefore Southern haste to duplicate the profits was ill-advised.

But from what source can the labor and the skill be derived, to set in operation an amount of machinery so vast as is here contemplated?  Certainly not from the North, where every good agent, sub-agent, and overseer, is prized and retained, and where operatives are not to be had to run the machinery now built.  Agents and overseers may be brought from England; but unless the Southern men and girls, who are to be under their control, have less independence, or, if one choose to call it so, less prejudice, against obeying foreigners than the girls and men in New England, it will be necessary to bring the operatives also from the manufacturing districts of England; not a desirable population at home, much less so here.

But supposing this difficulty were overcome, from what quarter is to proceed the capital required for the enterprise?  Have our Southern friends such resources of money now at their command as to create these immense works, or are they borrowers?  We have always supposed the latter to be the case.  We sell our fabrics, which are made at the North, to the Southern buyers, on a credit of from six to ten months.  Neither do we receive a similar credit in return, for the reason that they are not in a condition to grant it.  All the great staples sent from the Southern market are sold for cash, or on a credit of sixty days.  It is in this way that the foreign and the home manufacturers supply themselves with cotton.  Though there are many rich men in the large cotton-growing States, the number of moneyed men is very small, and they are not usually the projectors of new enterprises.  The planters are generally in debt, more or less, either from having extended their business beyond their means, or from the habit of anticipating their incomes, by borrowing of their cotton factors, the banks, or by credits at the stores.

A. A. Lawrence, "The Condition and Prospects of American Cotton Manufactures in 1849," Hunt's Merchants' Magazine, December, 1849, pp. 628-629.

177.  SOUTHERN COTTON TEXTILE MANUFACTURE CAN SUCCEED (1849)

Gregg, as a Southern manufacturer of cotton textiles, wished to explain that Southern textile profits were adequate to encourage further investment.  Gregg was the founder of the Graniteville (S.C.) Cotton Manufactory.

While we admit Mr. Lawrence's statement relative to the dividends paid, we cannot but notice the fact, that New England has grown rich and prosperous, beyond all precedent, since her capitalists engaged in this particular field of enterprise.  No one can for a moment doubt that the manufacturing of cotton goods has been chiefly instrumental in producing the great changes wrought in New England, during the last thirty years.
. . . . . . . . . . . . . . . . . . . . . . . . . . . . . . . . .
But it is enough for us, at the South, to know that manufacturing has heretofore paid sufficiently well to induce the continued annual investment of immensely large sums, for thirty years past, both in the Middle and Eastern States, as well as in all parts of Europe--that we have labor, both white and black, at least 20 per cent cheaper than in New England, and with few exceptions, as cheap as in any part of the world--that water-power may be had for almost nothing--that our provisions are as cheap, and, above all, that we have the cotton at hand, sound, bright, and unsullied by the rain, mud, smoke, &c., incident to its transit from the interior of our State, to its final destination.

Letter, William Gregg to editor, December 20, 1849, Hunt's Merchants' Magazine, January, 1850, pp. 107, 108.

178.    EASTERN MANUFACTURERS NEED NOT FEAR SERIOUS
COMPETITION FROM THE SOUTH (1850)

As was usually the case, southern textile manufacturer William Gregg was too optimistic.

I don't think that you Eastern manufacturers need have any
fears of serious competition from the South, for such investments
are slowly made in all countries where manufacturers are introduced,
as the gentleman observes you will build up a town in two years
which will outnumber all the spindles now in the south in motion or
contemplated to be erected for ten years to come, it is now four
years and a half since we commenced Graniteville besides which
there has been but three thousand spindles put in operation in South
Carolina during that period.  Georgia has done more, but all that
has been done in that state in five years will not be equivalent to
the one mill recently started at Hadley falls.  We have however all
the requisets of success, and the business is destined to progress
at the south, it will however be so gradual that we will not be
seriously felt on your heels, you will by imperceptible degrees
have gone onto goods which will not be made here for a half century
to come, we will not probably in our day attempt anything finer than
No. 14.

Letter, William Gregg to Amos A. Lawrence, September 2, 1850,
Thomas P. Martin (ed.), "The Advent of William Gregg and the
Graniteville Company," Journal of Southern History, XI (1945).

179.  A VERY BUSY BUSINESSMAN (1850)

While few men could have had even as many business
connections as A. A. Lawrence, those who did were probably
New Englanders.  Profitable opportunities revolved in a
narrow circle before being opened to the public.  Eight
months after making the following journal entry, Lawrence
wrote to an old schoolmate:  "I am well enough off to
be above the temptation of avarice."

My attention is so much taken up with business during the week
that I find it very difficult to give it to the more important duties
of Sunday.  My mind runs away from its devotions to the plans of

business and various engagements.  I pray God to forgive my frivolty and weakness, and help me to think more of spiritual things.  By way of ascertaining whether I have not assumed more responsibility than is consistent with a proper regulation of the time and the thoughts, I have enumerated them as follows: 1.  My business of commission merchant with a large establishment, clerks, etc., and but one partner.  2.  Office of treasurer of a large manufacturing corporation with a capital of a million of dollars.  3.  Director in ten corporations:  some of them very large, viz.:  Suffolk Bank (eleven years); Massachusetts General Hospital; Cocheco Company; American Insurance Office; Boston Water Power Corporation; Amesbury Company; Middlesex Canal; Massachusetts Bible Society; Massachusetts Board of Domestic Missions; Groton Academy.  4.  I have charge of all my father's property; also Mrs. Luther Lawrence's and Mrs. Seaver's.  5.  Of my own property; including lands in the West, the building of a Seminary and a town (Appleton) in Wisconsin, which is a complicated business.  Then there is the business of receiving and paying visits, which I do only as much of as is necessary.  The membership of various societies requiring some attention; besides my daily duty of giving two hours of daylight to the business of getting exercise enough to keep my body sound.  Some trusts I have given up, but others come in to take their place.  Is not this too much for one who would improve his mind and his heart, and keep himself ready for a change of scene, and an entrance into the spiritual world?  Can one be prepared for higher duties when the mind is filled continually with such thoughts as all these things entail?

Journal entry for February 17, 1850, William Lawrence, Life of Amos A. Lawrence, (Boston, Massachusetts:  Houghton, Mifflin & Co., 1888), pp. 57-58.


180.  INTERNATIONAL PIRATING OF MACHINERY DESIGNS (1851, 1878)


Discussion within the trade concerning piracy of designs suggests that piracy was a well-accepted practice. The tone of the discussion is one rather of entertainment than of condemnation.  A. C. Hobbs who writes this letter was superintendent of the Union Metallic Cartridge Co. of Bridgeport, Connecticut; his correspondent, Robert Grimshaw, was a New York engineer.

Dr. Grimshaw.--I remember calling attention to several cases
of very flat piracy during the Paris Exposition in 1878.  In one
case there were two agricultural machines, one from Canada and one
from Sweden, both of which had the same pattern marks on the castings as the American machines with which they were in competition.
Later on, my attention was called by an exhibitor to some locks
which were exhibited by an Austrian firm in the Austrian Department,
in competition with that exhibitor's American locks.  A careful inspection revealed beneath the enamel--the very sheet marks of the
American firm--the paint marks on the iron sheets.  In other words,
they were American locks, exhibited in competition with our own
locks.  I will speak of another case in which a piece of wood-
working machinery from Cincinnati was purchased by a Manchester
firm, almost with the avowed purpose of copying it.  It was copied
part for part.  It is known that American castings are not usually
much heavier than the law allows.  The fact is, complaint is sometimes made that we do not put quite enough metal in.  This wood-
working machine, which was copied square inch for square inch of
section, went to pieces in about three months' use.  They had not
calculated for the difference in the quality of the iron on the
other side, and on the inexperience of the hands on the other side
in making tough light castings.  It was an awful warning which may
be of use in the future.

Mr. Hobbs.--I happened to be at the exposition in London, in
1851.  Whitworth & Company [of England] had some very nice shaping
machines there and some very nice planing machines, and I have seen
the very same patterns made by Mr. [William] Sellers in Philadelphia.
Mr. Sellers began by copying some very nice machines, and he has
made better machines since.  So I think that Mr. Sellers and Mr.
Whitworth are about even in that particular.

A. C. Hobbs and Robert Grimshaw, Transactions, American Society
of Mechanical Engineers, V (1883), p. 123.


181.  TECHNICAL CHANGE AND FINANCIAL CONSERVATISM (1850's)


John Fritz, the author of this extract, was one of the
most creative technologists in the history of the American
iron and steel industry.  From 1854 to 1860, Fritz was chief
engineer and general manager of the Cambria Iron Works in
Johnstown, Pennsylvania.  In 1860, he joined the Bethlehem
Iron Company.

We had no money, and at that time the iron men were looked upon as paupers. The banks would not loan them any money as long as they could get what they called first-class commercial [i.e., mercantile] paper, and at that time money was not in abundance, as it is today [1912]; consequently the iron men got but little, and that little only for a short time, the bankers fearing they would fail, as in the early days of rail making they were very likely to do. At the time when we were in the midst of our improvements at Cambria, a banker to whom the company owed twenty thousand dollars came into the rolling mill and asked me what we were doing. I told him we were making some changes and improvements. His reply was that any man that would destroy property and spend money as we were doing was a fool or a madman. I told him that I was doing it and it had never occurred to me that I was either. He took the train that night for Philadelphia, and the next morning called at the company's office and demanded his money in such an emphatic manner that they had to pay him that day. I might mention many instances showing the distrust of the bankers toward the iron men, and also what they said about myself and what I was doing. But suffice to say that I passed through a merciless fire of vindictive ridicule to victory, with simplicity and becoming dignity, doubtless to the disgust of some of the wiseacres who had made some direful predictions.

Autobiography of John Fritz, p. 132.


182.  CLOTHING ON THE NORTH IOWA FRONTIER (1850's)


Here Willard Burnap describes fashion under influence of a cash-less economy.


You doubtless notice in the financial statement I have given that there was scant provision made for any comforts or necessities that demanded money to procure. Principal among these was clothing. As new clothing was near the boundary of the impossible, the old was utilized to the limit of its endurance. It is surprising how long a suit will last if so used. Judicious, or even unjudicious, patching will extend its life so that it may even rival the nine assigned the cat. At first it was thought that patches should correspond with the material of the garment, but from lack of material this idea was soon abandoned as unnecessary and as being too much of a concession to eastern style and to the backwoods four hundred. A white patch upon black goods, while not sought for, was permissible; and when time came to patch the patch, if a brilliant red was handy, one's garment might soon rival that ancient and unlucky suit of many colors that Joseph wore. Occasionally in this community might unexpectedly appear a person dressed in fine broadcloth, or rustling silk, according to the sex of its wearer.

Immediately he or she would be surrounded by sympathizing neighbors, who knew only too well the direful fact, that these persons had not achieved wealth, but that everything they possessed was worn out except this suit.  As the saying went, "Poverty had driven them to their best."  The efforts made to preserve this best suit would be pathetic had they not been so amusing.

When we commenced raising wheat, canvas sacks were necessary. As these were hard to keep track of when unlimited borrowing and lending was the rule, each owner branded his own sacks indelibly with his name.  Now two grain sacks make a serviceable pair of pants, and two more a coat, and should a settler appear some morning with a brand new canvas suit bearing one neighbor's name branded on the coat and another friend's initials stamped on the pants, no one was shocked; for it would be a mighty mean man who would begrudge a neighbor a sack or two when he needed a suit of clothes, even though his permission for such reconstruction had not been asked.

. . . . . . . . . . . . . . . . . . . . . . . . . . . . . . . . . . .

The family was largely, if not wholly, clothed in homemade garments.  The wool was sheared, carded, and spun on the farm, woven into cloth by some loom in the community, and cut out and made by the women of the house or some person who went from family to family to do that special work.  Not until the fifties did the young men on the farm commence priding themselves on being the possessors of "store clothes."

Willard A. Burnap, What Happened During One Man's Lifetime, 1840-1920, (Fergus Falls, Minnesota:  The Burnap Estate, 1923), pp. 128-130, 136.

183.  THE CHARACTER OF AMERICAN TECHNOLOGY (1854)

This concrete approach to technology, evaluating it in terms of adaptation, is a valuable way of getting at the heart of the matter.  See also the comments of Montgomery, above.  Sir Joseph Whitworth, the writer here, was a prominent British engineer and manufacturer of machine-tools; Wallis was headmaster of the Birmingham, England school of design and in 1853 joined Whitworth in a visit to the United States to study this country's "arts and manufactures."  (See Sources 169 and 170).

The machinery of a country will naturally correspond with its wants, and with the history and state of its people.  Testing the machinery of the United States by this rule of adaptation, the mechanical appliances in use must call forth much admiration.    A large proportion of the mechanical power of the States has, from its earliest application, been, from the circumstances of the

country, directed to wood, this being the material on which it has
been requisite to operate for so many purposes, and which is presented in the greatest abundance.  Stone, for a similar reason,
has been subdued to man's use by the application of machinery, of
which we have an instance in the fact that one man is able to perform as much work by machinery in stone-dressing, as twenty persons
by hand.  In common with our own and other great manufacturing
countries, the Union presents remarkable illustrations of the
amazingly productive power of machinery, as compared with mere
manual operations.  Into the details of these triumphs of machinery
it is unnecessary here to enter.  It may suffice to refer to the
improvements effected in spinning-machinery, by which one man can
attend to a mule containing 1,088 spindles, each spinning three
hanks, or 3,264 hands a day; so that, as compared with the operations of the most expert spinner in Hindoostan, the American opera-
tive can perform the work of 3,000 men.
. . . . . . . . . . . . . . . . . . . . . . . . . . . . . . . . .
     The comparative density of the old and the new countries,
differing as they do, will account for the very different feelings
with which the increase of machinery has been regarded in many parts
of this country [England] and the United States, where the workmen
hail with satisfaction all mechanical improvements, the importance
and value of which, as releasing them from the drudgery of unskilled
labour, they are enabled by education to understand and appreciate.


     Joseph Whitworth and George Wallis, The Industry of the United
States in Machinery, Manufactures, and Useful and Ornamental Arts,
(London:  George Routledge & Co., 1854), pp. vii, viii.

# D.

# THE ISSUE OF TARIFFS

### 184.  DU PONT REQUESTS TARIFF PROTECTION (1816)

Economists contend about the general economic effects of a tariff.  There can be little doubt, however, of the effects of a tariff on this writer's textile mill.  He is Victor Du Pont who was a partner in a textile mill located on the Brandy Wine River, near Wilmington, Delaware; he writes to Henry Clay, Speaker of the U.S. House of Representatives.

We have been informed that the Committee of ways & means has reduced the tarif [sic] to 20 on Cloth & 25 on Cotton if it passes so, these two branches of industry are _ipso facto_ destroyed never to rise again at least for 50 years--
a french proverb says _aux_ _grands_ _maux_ _les_ _grands_ _remedes_ and in our forlorn desperate situation we are convinced that nothing can save us, nothing can stem the torrent of mediocrity always falling in what is supposed to be a middle course, but the first talents and the greatest influence, if you are so good as to follow the impulse of your patriotic heart and to break a spear or two in our defence probably you may keep the majority straight and we may yet be saved--
if the Committee of ways & means, mean to destroy the manufactures let him [sic] take the shortest way in the name of all the manufacturers on the Brandywine I protest against any extension of the old duty which is so evidently insuficient.  let us die at one blow, honorably & without strugles, do not let us be poisoned or starved and those who do it willfully & knowingly have the credit of having administered remedy & food--

if the tariff passes as it is the probability is that the greatest part of the factories now existing will be destroyed in consequence of the imminse efforts the british are making now in our ports to obtain that desirable end--Congress do not pretend to know I suppose that a considerable number of british shops have been lately established who retail at 25 p% cheaper than the american mercht can import, they are certainly enabled to do so by the British government who pay for the difference--at Savanah [sic] & charleston a number of british vessels are offering to take the Cotton to england for 1/2 pence when the price used to be 2 pence pr. lb and enter into contract that if the cotton do not clear it-self in england, they will take no freight at all,--is it not plain that the object is to drain our factories from the raw material and that the British government is to pays [sic] for that freight,--

in any other country but this, such measures should be retal-iated on, a sum of 3 or 4 millions should be raised to give bounties to the manufacturers or lend them money to enable them to weather the storm--But no--the same spirit of apathy to say nothing more which prevented the last congress to raise men during the war will prevent the present congress to insure the perfect independance of the country in saving their manufactures, and the worse of it is that it will not come altogether from the same side of the house--

a vessel arrived yesterday from Bordeaux has brought 26 manu-facturers german & french Mr. Chaptal & Counsellor Real are coming to this country, and bring with them 25 dyers & other workmen from the famous factory of the Gobelins at paris in the course of 2 or 3 months we shall be able to make in this country colours superior to the english and probably forced to emigrate to South america for there must be factories in this Continent and if the north wont have them the south will find it their interest to give them en-couragement.

there is no doubt that 20 p% will be more than enough after some years when the factories will be perfect well established & the tide of prejudice turned in their favor, but at present under their present difficulties and the formidable opposition of british capital british bounties British habits and british influence 28 is even to [sic] little--

Excuse Sir this last & dying speech of a manufacturer those living on the Brandywine cannot in fact love & honor you more than they do already, but if you can save them. their gratitude will be equal to the importance of the deed.


Letter, Victor Du Pont to Henry Clay, March 11, 1816, James F. Hopkins and Mary W. M. Hargreaves (eds.), The Papers of Henry Clay, II, (Lexington, Kentucky:  University of Kentucky Press, 1961), pp. 173-175.

185.   "ENGLAND SWELLS HER OWN STATUTE BOOKS WHILE SHE WANTS
US TO BE FREE TRADERS" (1817)


The contradiction between England's commercial
pronouncements and her practices was noted by some
historians much after U.S. House of Representatives
member, Thomas Gold, became aware of it.  Gold came
from Oneida County, New York.


It has been a settled course with Englishmen to hold up to
America bugbears to deter from manufacturing.  Her writers on political economy insist that industry should be left to its own course,
and government take no part, while her legislators have swelled
the statute book with regulations on trade.  Those writers proclaim
manufacturing destructive to the human constitution!  While her
historians and war annalists proclaim the British arms, notwithstanding all their manufactures, as invincible, as unpalsied by
manufactures.  In fine, Britain's creed is short:  to manufacture
for the whole world and suffer no nation to manufacture for her;
and I am sorry to see too many Americans bending themselves to
British policy.  It is impossible to shut our eyes on the fact, and
it is time for every friend to his country to rouse himself and
diffuse an American spirit.
    Would our own government do for manufactures one half Great
Britain has done for hers, to raise them to the present pinacle, we
might soon bid defiance to all the efforts to crush our establishments.
    Based on our government is on popular feeling, I behold with
pleasure that manufactures are becoming the people's cause, and I
will never believe that the people will manifest less wisdom and
attachment to manufactures than what we now witness in the continental kingdoms of Europe.  Great as their obligations are to Great
Britain, those governments are not disposed to sacrifice to
English manufactures the interests of their own kingdoms.


Letter, Representative Thomas R. Gold to Charles Shaler,
February 21, 1816, Niles' Weekly Register, March 22, 1817, p. 51.



186.   WE CANNOT LEAVE THINGS TO THEMSELVES (1818)


The laissez-faire argument held that goods would
be produced whenever it became advantageous for an
enterpriser to produce them.  Clay, a Whig leader who
preached national industrial self-suffiency, argued
that social capital--roads, canals, bridges--might never
be built on that criterion.  This view was the basis of

his support of federal expenditures for internal
improvements.


In regard to internal improvements, it did not always follow
that they would be constructed whenever they would afford a competent dividend upon the capital invested.  It may be true generally
that, in old countries, where there is a great accumulation of
surplus capital, and a consequent low rate of interest, that they
would be made.  But in a new country the condition of society may be
ripe for public works long before there is, in the hands of individuals, the necessary accumulation of capital to effect them; and,
besides, there is generally, in such a country, not only a scarcity
of capital, but such a multiplicity of profitable objects presenting
themselves as to distract the judgment.  Further; the aggregate benefit resulting to the whole society, from a public improvement may be
such as to amply justify the investment of capital in its execution,
and yet that benefit may be so distributed among different and distant persons as that they can never be got to act in concert.  The
Turnpike roads wanted to pass the Allegany mountains, and the
Delaware and Chesapeake Canal are objects of the description.  Those
who would be most benefited by these improvements reside at a considerable distance from the scites of them; many of those persons
never have seen and never will see them.  How is it possible to
regulate the contributions, or to present to individuals so situated
a sufficiently lively picture of their real interests to get them to
take exertions, in effectuating the object, commensurate with their
respective abilities?  I think it very possible that the capitalist,
who should invest his money, in one of those objects, might not be
reimbursed three per cent annually upon it.  And yet society, in
various forms, might actually reap fifteen or twenty per cent.  The
benefit resulting from a turnpike road, made by private associations,
is divided between the capitalist who receives his tolls, the lands
through which it passes, & which are augmented in their value, and
the commodities whose value is enchanced by the diminished expence
of transportation.  A combination upon any terms, much less a just
combination, of all these interests to effect the improvement is
impracticable.  And if you await the arrival of the period when the
tolls alone can produce a competent dividend, it is evident that
you will have to suspend its execution until long after the general
interests of society would have authorized it.


Speech in House of Representatives, March 13, 1818, Hopkins
and Hargreaves (eds.), Papers of Henry Clay, II, pp. 486-487.

## 187.  THE BOSTON CAPITALISTS ARE SETTING A
## DANGEROUS EXAMPLE (1827)

A well-defined industrial "lobby" already existed by
the mid-1820's.  Its organizers worked to obtain higher
tariff rates on behalf of specific products.  Spokesmen
for interests which were opposed to the manufacturers--
especially, spokesmen for the cotton South--expressed shock
at this new development.  Matters of simple economic conflict were being interpreted in terms of geographical
interest.  John Calhoun, then Vice President, writes this
comment.

About a year ago, a great excitement was got up in Boston by
the Capitalists, with a view professedly to give an increased duty
on Woollens for their protection.  A Bill was reported to the House
of Rep amounting in fact to a prohibition, and after much heat
passed that body.  It came to the Senate, where it was laid on the
Table by my casting vote.  Since the adjournment, an extensive
scheme, originating as it is thought, with those in power, has been
got up, to have a general convention of the manufacturing interest
at Harrisburgh, avowedly to devise measures for the passage of this
Bill; and thus the dangerous example is set of seperate representation; and association of great Geographical interests to promote
their prosperity at the expense of other interests, unrepresented,
and fixed in another section, which, of all measures that can be
conceived, is calculated to give the greatest opportunity to art,
and corruption, and to make two of one nation.  How far the administration is involved in this profligate scheme, time will determine; but if they be, the curse of posterity will be on their head.
In the mean time, the South has commenced with remonstrating against
this unjust and oppressive attempt to sacrifice their interest; and,
I do trust, that they will not be provoked to step beyond strict
constitutional remedies.  I have given a fuller view on this point,
as I am of the impression, that from it great events will spring.
It must lead to defeat or oppression or resistence, or the correc-
tion of what perhaps is a great defect in our system; that the
seperate geographical interests are not sufficiently guarded.

Letter, John C. Calhoun to James Edward Calhoun, August 27,
1827, Jameson (ed.), Correspondence of John C. Calhoun, pp. 250-251.

188.   THE TARIFF IS A NORTHERN TAX ON THE SOUTH'S
FOREIGN EXCHANGE (1838)

A tariff is one means of redistributing wealth
between classes and section.  Here is a very clear explanation of the process, written by John Calhoun.  Calhoun
was in 1838 a U.S. Senator from South Carolina.  In 1845
he completed an interim term as Secretary of State.  He is
writing to Vethake, an economist at Washington College,
Virginia.  Hammond was a former Congressman and Governor
of South Carolina.

I lay it down as a principle, that to determine where a tax
ultimately falls, we must look not only to the tax, but to its
disbursement.  To seperate them is but to take a half way view.
The one implies the other, and is but its counterpart.  A tax is but
a mode of taking away property, and the appropriation, or disbursement, but a mode of giving it.  The sum abstracted by the tax is not
lost, and to ascertain where the burthen falls, we must not only
ascertain from whom it is taken but also to whom it is given.  They
form parts of one and the same process, and cannot be regarded
seperately without falling into great and dangerous errors.  The
complaint of the South was not, that the planters (the producers of
our staples) bore all of the burthen of the Tariff, but that it was
a tax on their foreign exchange, which in combination with a system
of partial and unequal disbursements transfered annually a large and
exhausting amount of the proceeds of their labour to other sections
of the Union.  To understand the force of this complaint, it is
necessary to look to the state of the facts.
The Tariff of '28 exacted 32 millions out of an importation of
64 millions; that is it passed into the treasury one half of the
value of the whole of the imports estimated at the invoice price
adding thereto ten per cent.  The staple states which constitute
about 2/5 of the population of the Union furnished about 42 millions
of the means by which our foreign exchanges were carried on.
. . . . . . . . . . . . . . . . . . . . . . . . . . . . . . . . . .
Abolish custom Houses and let the money collected in the South
be spent in the South and we would be among the most flourishing
people in the world.  The North could not stand the annual draft,
which they have been making on us 50 years, without being reduced
to the extreme of poverty in half the time.  All we want to be rich
is to let us have what we make.

Letter, John C. Calhoun to Henry Vethake, October 11, 1838,
and to James H. Hammond, August 30, 1845, Jameson (ed.), Correspondence of John C. Calhoun, pp. 402-403, 670,

### 189.  THE PRESIDENT IS NOT IMPRESSED WITH THE MANUFACTURERS'
### PUBLIC RELATIONS (1846)

The next two entries suggest the energy with which
manufacturers hastened to Washington to protect their
interests.  The 1842 Tariff had included some increases,
spurred by the argument that this was the way to recoup
federal finances which were suffering from depression conditions.  Now, four years later, prosperity was under way
but the manufacturers did not want Congress to cut duties
and thus interfere with their prosperity.


A committee of manufacturers accompanied by Mr. Seaton, Mayor
of Washington, called to accompany me to the Manufacturers fair now
holding in this City....I visited the fair accompanied by the Mayor
& committee & the ladies of my family.  There were a great variety
of manufactured articles collected in a very large temporary building erected for the occasion by the manufacturers.  I was informed
that the building alone cost over $6,000, and that as soon as the
fair was over would be taken down.  The specimens of manufacture
exhibited are highly creditable to the genius and skill of our
countrymen.  All must desire that the manufacturing interests should
prosper, but none ought to disire that to enable them to do so heavy
burthens should be imposed by the Government on other branches of
industry.  The manufacturers have spent many thousands of dollars in
getting up this fair, with a view no doubt to operate upon members
of Congress to prevent a reduction of the present rates of duty
imposed by the oppressive protective tariff act of 1842.  To effect
this, lower prices was [were] affixed to & labelled on the specimens
exhibited than they are sold for in the market.  This I know was
the case in reference to some of the articles.  The object of this
is no doubt to impress the public with the belief that [in] the absurd doctrine that "high duties make low goods."  The wealth exhibited at this fair & the expense attending it prove, I think that
the large capitalists owning the manufacturies should rely upon
their own resources not upon the bounty of the Government, (and
especially when that bounty cannot be afforded them but at the
expense of other interests) for their support.  With revenue instead
of protective duties, they have the advantage over all other interests, and with this they should be satisfied.


Entry for May 23, 1846, Milo M. Quaife (ed.), The Diary of
James K. Polk During His Presidency, 1845 to 1849, I, (Chicago,
Illinois:  A. C. McClurg & Co., 1910), pp. 421-422.

190.    "THE CITY IS SWARMING WITH MANUFACTURERS" (1846)


The City is swarming with manufacturers who are making tremendous exertions to defeat it [a bill to decrease tariff rates].
The truth is that such a struggle has rarely been witnessed in
Congress, as that between the Capitalists engaged in manufacturers
on the one hand, and the advocates of moderate and reasonable
taxes.  The deepest anxiety prevails & will continue to prevail....


Entry for July 28, 1846, Quaife (ed.), <u>Diary of James K. Polk</u>,
II, pp. 53-54.

# E.

# ACHIEVING A NATIONAL MARKET

### 191. RAPID TRANSIT ON THE OHIO RIVER (1820's)

An old-style river captain reminisces.

My first sight of the river was from 1823 to 1826; can't recall the date. I was greatly attracted at the sight. At this time only five steamers on the river--names to wit: Pennsylvania, Messenger, Bolivar, Mechanic and Velocipede.

Charley Basham was clerk of Velocipede. After years the great steamboat agent Captain Billy Forsyth said he was the best he ever had, never promised any business or gave any.

The state of morals was low at this time. Simon Girty, the half Indian desperado and terror to the community, had passed away. The run above the city emptying into the Monongahela River, was called Girty's run. He had his headquarters up the run north of the city, where he held carnival with the Indian savages and with devils. After he passed away another type of man--Mike Fink and Mike Wolf, of the keel-boatmen.

At this time no system of transit was inaugurated from Pittsburgh to ports below. The keel-boat, propelled by man, was a model one, 80 to 90 feet long, open hold, with cargo box and running boards, or guards cluted, for to put the foot against with his 12 foot pole. Iron socket at end, and large wood button at top and large sweeps on deck to propel it.

It was a slow system for transit. The time from Philadelphia to Pittsburgh was three weeks with large six horse road wagon, time from Pittsburgh to Cincinnati, Ohio, was three weeks by keel-boat. That was slow transit. Now the age of keel-boating Mike Fink, a type for vulgarity and profanity.

I must not fail to mention the keel-boat propulsion by man-
power was 15 miles per day up stream, and down was paddled about
1 1/2 miles through the water per hour.  The accommodation was not
of the best.  If boat was loaded with pig metal that was the only
bed--unless a board could be found--the living was not likely to
give the gout--a wet tack or pilot bread, side bacon, full of
creepers often, and potatoes, rice, coffee without sugar.  Slow
transit indeed.  Now I drop the keel-boat.

The outfit of the keel-boat was not complete without a barrel
of whisky on deck.

This was the mode, until the great Pennsylvania canal was
built; cost the State fifty millions.  The canal commissioners'
salary twenty thousand dollars yearly.  Now the canal rushed the
goods into Pittsburgh, the commission merchant urging to get goods
to Cincinnati and Louisville.  The keel-boat would not answer any
longer; the rivermen planning ways and means.  Finally it was decided to build light boats, stern wheel, to have capacity for 60
tons and go safe on two foot water.  Now this was the beginning of
light stern-wheel boats, and answered the purpose for a series of
years.  It was schooling a grand lot of rivermen for after use.

Ways and means was employed by the boatmen.  Finally light
water stern wheel-boats were decided would answer.  It was not long
until the river was pretty well supplied.

This system answered for a series of years.  But the cry was
give us, an outlet by railroads.  The Pittsburgh, Fort Wayne &
Chicago was built.  Stock was $50 par, went to $3 per share.  I must
tell of railroad speculation of mine.  A friend came and said there
is to be a road built to Connellsville, then to branch out into
Virginia to the main B.&O. road.  Like Col. Seller's mighty dollar,
there is millions in it.  Well, I bit at the bait and put my name
down for 10 shares, paid in at time of subscription $12 per share.

The road appeared to drop out of sight in a year or two.  I
called at the Treasurer's office and inquired about my railroad to
Connellsville, and the money paid.  He said, your money is all cut
up in oyster suppers; don't know anything about it at present.
Well, in after years I had my steamer loaded for St. Louis, and
ready to leave port.  Law officers come and said there is a judgment against you and execution issued; it must be satisfied now.
How much is the amount.  About $600.  But giving credit for $12 per
share reduced it.  Repudiated the whole matter.  Never went into
railroading again.

The light water stern-wheel boats answered until the Pennsylvania Railroad was completed and finished to Pittsburgh.

And now dawned the great steamboating on the Ohio River.  The
commission merchant wanted more rapid transit.

Your biographer had charge of the finest one of 23.  The owners
said, can you make weekly trips from Pittsburgh to Cincinnati and
return in a week.  I will try.  Started and made 12 consecutive
trips.  It was hard boating, but was found possible.  The owners
said we will build you a fast boat; but I preferred to be so I
could go where and when I pleased.  Now was formed the grandest
packet line of steamers in the world.  We were now up in 1841 and
had full control of river near 10 years, accommodating the Pennsylvania canal.

Pennsylvania Railroad now finished to Pittsburgh.  Cry was
give us, outlet by railroads.  The P.F.W.&C. was pushed to completion, and Panhandle Railroad was being built bee line to Cincinnati.
We had at this time nearly three-quarters of hundred fine steamers
running out of port of Pittsburgh to every port or place below.
(1888 only three stern-wheel boats between Pittsburgh and Cincinnati.)


Letter, William Dean to E. W. Gould, February 4, 1889, E. W.
Gould, Fifty Years on the Mississippi, (St. Louis, Missouri:  Nixon-
Jones Printing Co., 1889), pp. 634-636.


## 192.   ILLINOIS LOOKS IN VAIN FOR NEW YORK INVESTMENT
IN WESTERN CANALS (1832)


At this time, New England capital may have been more
venturesome than New York capital in financing western
canals.  (New York bankers and merchants were hesitant
about financing canals in New York!)  These experiences
helped suggest the soliciting of foreign capital, especially
in England.  During the remainder of the decade, great sums
of English capital were invested in state bonds designed to
supply funds for internal improvements.


I attended a meeting this afternoon at Mr. Bucknor's office,
to confer with Mr. Pugh, one of the canal commissioners of the
State of Illinois, who has been appointed to visit New York in
relation to raising funds to construct a railroad from the head of
navigation on the Illinois river, a distance of ninety miles, to
Chicago, near the southern outlet of Lake Michigan.  This project
would be of great advantage to the State of New York, as it would
divert the trade of the new Western States bordering on the lakes
from New Orleans to our seaport.  The gentlemen present, brokers
and practical money-dealers, did not seem disposed to trust their
funds in an enterprise so far from home, and it is not likely that
Mr. Pugh will succeed in his application.


Entry for January 15, 1832, Bayard Tuckerman (ed.), Diary of
Philip Hone, 1828-1851, I, (New York:  Dodd, Mead and Co., 1889),
p. 45.

193.  BANKING, TRANSPORTATION, AND PENNSYLVANIA
POLITICS (1835)


The federal charter of the second Bank of the United
States was to expire in Pennsylvania.  To achieve this end,
a vast scheme of log-rolling was laid out as follows.  The
writer, William Reed, was chairman of the Inland Navigation
Committee of the Pennsylvania state legislature; Biddle was
president of the Bank of the United States.


I now esteem it especially fortunate that a friend of the Bank
was placed at the head of the Improvement Committee.  That is the
only engine on which we can rely and if it fails we have no chance.
Every one at all acquainted with matters and things here, particularly of late years since the Canal policy has been pursued, knows
that the temptation of a turnpike, or a few miles of canal and rail
road as a beginning on a favorite route is nearly irresistible, and I
am strongly inclined to think that now a few of the many members who
have toiled year after year for branches, and who look to this
session as their last chance could vote against legislation that
would give them their extensions and entrench upon nothing but party
prejudices and antipathies.  If this feeling cannot be operated on,
none other can.  And this applies to those who are here not as
friends of the state administration who perhaps not being unwilling
to see it embarassed could not be operated upon by the measure, if
its effect was to be merely a general relief from taxation.  A reference to the map and the Senatorial Districts will illustrate
this.  The Southern line of Rail Road to connect through York and
Gettysburg with the Baltimore and Ohio Rail Road and thence down
the Younghegany to Pittsbury would of itself affect the votes of at
least three if not four Senators.  So with the Erie extension the
North Branch, the West Branch survey (all that that District wants).
With respect to all these new lines it must be borne in mind that
the commencement of the work is all that will be wanted.  To be able
to go home and boast of having made a beginning is all that is
needed...There is another interest too which must not be overlooked
in the Turnpikes--relief to them no matter how small a pittance,
will be most gratefully received.  By the bye, I understand the
Canal Commissioners, in their Report take up the tune of the Message
and assuming the abundance of funds recommend all the extensions as
a matter of course.
With all these views you will easily understand why I consider
the Improvement Committee, aided as it may be by the Committee of
Ways and Means, a powerful engine to effect our purpose.  I shall
be glad to have your views in strict confidence as to the course
which true policy dictates as respects new banks and increased
capital.  Petitions are rushing in upon us from all quarters.  The
Chairman of the Committee on Banks, Mr. Pennypacker, is one of the
soundest men we have.  His idea is to delay action even in Committee
upon all these new banks, and having ascertained the precise amount

of proposed capital to use it as an argument for the U.S. Bank.
This may do very well so far as our city is concerned but I am inclined to doubt the policy in its general application.  For example
a very strong and respectable application has been made for a new
bank at Pittsburgh where it seems to be conceded since the closing
of the branch that more banking capital is needed.  From what I
learn from third persons I find that all the Pittsburg members and
their friends in the lobby attribute the dilatory action of the
Committee who have refused thus far to report a bill, to a secret
design on the part of the friends of U.S.B. to promote its views.
They are consequently utterly opposed to the charter.  All this I
hear indirectly but still I can depend on it.  Would it not be
better in such a case only, for the friends of the U.S.B. to gain
the Pittsburg influence by aiding their project?


        Letter, William B. Reed to Nicholas Biddle, December 12, 1835,
Reginald C. McGrane (ed.), Correspondence of Nicholas Biddle,
(Boston, Massachusetts:  Houghton Mifflin, 1919), pp. 258-260.


        194.   COMPARISON OF AMERICAN AND BELGIAN RAILROADS (1839)


        While Belgium had built its first railway in 1835,
five years after the first U.S. road, Belgians "took" to
railways faster than did Americans.  Also, Belgian railways
were first constructed to connect up already-populous
places between which a heavy traffic existed.  This was
less true in the United States.
        Gerstner was a prominent Austrian railroad engineer,
builder of Italian and Russian railroads, who visited the
United States for twelve months, 1838-39, and wrote a still-
untranslated two-volume work on the internal communications
of the United States (Vienna, 1842).  While in this country
he is said to have visited every single railroad line either
in operation or under construction.  (There were 178 of
these!)  He also visited the Belgian railroads four times
between 1835 and 1838.  Although the editor of the Journal
of Franklin Institute did not note the fact, evidently the
article was freely translated from a chapter in Gerstner's
book Berichte aus den Vereinigten Staaten von Nordamerica,
(Leipzig:  C. P. Melzer, 1839), pp. 46-55.


We have now the following comparison:
        (a)  Cost of construction.--A mile of Rail Road with a single
track, and the necessary buildings and outfit, costs in America
$20,000; in Belgium $41,300, or more than twice the amount.

(b)  Tariff.--On the American Rail Roads, a passenger pays at an average five cents per mile; on the Belgian Rail Roads, only one cent or five times less; for freight the charge is, in America, at an average seven and half cents per ton per mile.

(c)  Speed.--On the American Rail Roads, passengers are conveyed with a speed of from twelve to fifteen miles per hour, stoppages not included; at the rate of twenty to twenty-five miles.

(d)  Traffic.--There are at an average, 35,000 through passengers, and 15,000 tons of goods carried annually over the American Roads; on the Belgian there have been carried per year 478,783 through passengers, and the transportation of goods only commenced a short time since.

(e)  Gross income.--The same amounts on the American Railroads, at an average per mile and per year,

From 35,000 passengers at 5 cents . . . . . . 1,750 Dollars
From 15,000 tons of goods at 7 1/2 cents  . 1,125 Dollars
From mail and contingencies . . . . . . . .    200 Dollars
                           Total,      5,075 Dollars

On the Belgian Rail Roads the gross income per mile from 478,783 passengers, and the transportation of freight, amounts to 32,000 francs or $6,003.75 per year.

(f)  Expenses per mile of travel.--These amount on the American Rail Roads to one dollar, on the Belgian Roads to one dollar five cents, or they are the same in both countries.

(g)  Number of passengers per trip.--In Belgium there were in each train, at an average of three and a half years, one hundred and forty-three through passengers; on the American roads, a passenger train contains only forty through passengers, at an average.

(h)  Number of trips per year.--In dividing 35,000 by forty, we obtain eight hundred and seventy-five, as the average number of passenger trips per year on the American Rail Roads; and in dividing 478,783 by one hundred and forty-three we get 3,348, which represents the average number of passenger trains passing annually over the Belgian roads.  As at the same time the speed on the latter is greater than on the American Rail Roads, it was necessary to employ rails of forty-five pounds per yard, while their weight is generally less on the American Rail Roads.

(i)  Expenses per passenger per mile.--These are in Belgium only 0.73 cents, and in American two and half cents, or three and a half times less passengers, while the expenses per train per mile are equal in both countries.  It is very nearly the same for a Locomotive to carry forty or one hundred and forty-three passengers in a train.

(k)  Annual current expenses.--In America the annual current expenses for working a Rail Road, are per mile,

For transportation of 35,000 passengers at
      2 1/2 cents,                                   875 Dollars
For transportation of 15,000 tons of goods at
      6 1/2 cents                                    975 Dollars
For transportation of the mail and other
      expenses,                                      100 Dollars
                           Total      1,950 Dollars

Or $63.41 of every one hundred dollars gross income.  On the Belgian
Rail Roads, of every one hundred dollars gross revenue, the expenses
are $65.59, or per year per mile $3,937.86.

(1)  Interest on the capital invested.--In American the annual
average gross income, per mile of Road, amounts to 3,075 dollars,
the annual current expenses to 1,950, leaving $1,125; which com-
pared with the cost of a mile of Road (twenty thousand dollars,)
give five and a half per cent. interest.  On the Rail Roads in
Belgium, the annual gross income per mile, is $6,003.75, the expenses
$3,937.86, leaving $2,065.89 as interest on the cost of $41,300 per
mile, or exactly five per cent.
. . . . . . . . . . . . . . . . . . . . . . . . . . . . . . . . . . . . .
The extremely low charge for passage on the Belgian Rail Roads
has increased the number of passengers in an unparalleled degree,
and produced an intercourse not attained in any other country of
the world.  While the higher prices in the better classes of cars
yields a considerable profit, the price in the last class, or for
the great mass of the people, is so low that it about covers the
expenses only.  The Belgian Rail Roads, are, therefore, throughout,
a great popular, democratic establishment, which must have met the
approbation of the people, and of every intelligent man; the Belgian
Rail Roads afford to the tovernment the greatest facility in the
transportation of troops...the Belgian Rail Roads yield, in con-
formity with the grand idea of their establishment, only the interest and sinking fund of their capital, but the State Treasury has,
by the increase of intercourse, indirectly, gained in all taxes,
in the revenue from tolls on turnpike roads, and from the mail; the
most important gain, however, was...to bring the nation into a
more intimate contact, and to form of it one large family, on which
the actual national device:  "L'Union fait la force," ("Union gives
strength,") becomes realized.


F. A. Chevalier de Gerstner, "Comparison of the Rail Roads of
Belgium with those of the United States," Journal of the Franklin
Institute, whole volume number XXVIII, (September, 1839), pp. 154-
155.  In the above, numerals have been substituted for most of the
amounts which were spelled out in the original article.


195.  DIFFICULTIES OF NAVIGATION ON THE GREAT LAKES (1840's)


Once more is illustrated the pivotal importance
of water transportation to economic development.  Note
the homely politics of internal improvements.  The author,
Isaac Stephenson, became a skilled ship captain on the
Great Lakes.

The problem of transportation was almost as important to the lumber industry as the problem of production itself.  The era of railroads had not yet begun and the isolated mills at the mouths of the rivers emptying into Green Bay, Big Bay de Noc, and Bay de Noquette,--practically the entire northern lake region,--depended upon boats to bring them supplies and to take their output to market.

The importance of navigation on the lakes, although it was the great highway between the East and West over which the grain from the rapidly growing prairie states was carried in exchange for the manufactured products of the older cities along the seaboard, was not generally recognized by the federal government.  The harbors were in wretched condition and lights and buoys to guide the mariner and warn him of dangerous passages were few.

When I came west in 1845 there was only nine feet of water in Milwaukee harbor and conditions at Chicago were just as bad.  Neither were there any tugs to assist a vessel to a safe berth.  In Chicago, for many years, ships were pulled out of the river to the lake by hand, a head wind necessitating the use of a windlass.  What little aid had been extended by the federal government in improving these conditions was withdrawn in 1842 or 1843 when the Democratic administration, then in power, suspended all appropriations for river and harbor work.  As a result every sailor on the lakes became a Whig and afterwards a Republican.

The idea that the lakes were little more than a "goose pond" prevailed in Congress for some years later.  I remember hearing Captain Blake, a veteran of the battle of Lake Erie, who had achieved notoriety in these waters in the early days for his profanity and red waistcoats, expressing the fervent hope, when he had a United States Senator aboard as a passenger, that he might run into a gale to convince the unsuspecting legislator of the hazards of inland navigation.  Even at the "Soo," the great gateway from Lake Superior, no improvements hae been made and freight was transferred around the rapids on a small tramway.

Sailing a ship was not unlike blazing a way through the forest.  With conditions wretched as they were the navigator was practically without charts and the master figured his course as nearly as he could, estimating the leeway and varying influence of the winds.  By comparison with the difficulties that confronted us the lot of the sailors of the present day is an easy one.  With compasses and lights the course of their vessels is as plain as the tracks of a railroad, and the steam-driven propellers keep the ship to it without variation and bring her to harbors equipped with all the aids modern ingenuity has been able to devise.

Among the trips we made in the forties was one, which I still have vividly in mind, from Racine to Escanaba on a vessel laden with hay for the lumber camps.  After setting sail we saw neither light nor land but followed our uncharted course very much as instinct guided us.  Through Death' Door, the narrow passage from Lake Michigan into Green Bay, wo groped, feeling our way with the lead line, and headed cautiously for the mouth of the Flat Rock or Escanaba River.  Proceeding blindly, sounding as we went, we came about in five feet of water, stirring up sawdust from one of the

mills.  From this position we retreated cautiously to deeper water,
lowered a boat, pulled ashore in the dense fog and with the aid of
a compass found our general bearings.  I returned to the ship and
when the fog lifted detected a vessel lying close by.  To our intense relief we discovered that we were in the right anchorage.


Isaac Stephenson, <u>Recollections of A Long Life, 1829-1915</u>,
(Chicago, Illinois:  Privately printed, 1915), pp. 92-94.


### 196.  CARRYING FREIGHT ON EARLY NEW ENGLAND RAILROADS (1840's)


The rudimentary state of goods-shipment by American
railroads can be seen by this comment about what was then
the most industrialized area of the country.


Freight cars in the early days were called "burthen cars"
and trains were known as "brigades."  Freight cars were mere boxes,
a little longer than wide, with a wheel at each corner.  They had
doors on each side, and we trainmen had to walk around the sides on
a footboard, holding on by an iron rod running the whole length of
the car.  Freight cars were so small that we reported two as one,
reporting a train of forty cars, for instance, as twenty.  I remember a freight collision at Sommersworth, in 1849, when the cars were
so small and light that many of them were thrown over a fence and
scattered all over the neighboring farms.


Charles B. George, <u>Forty Years on the Rail</u>, 2nd ed., (Chicago,
Illinois:  R. R. Donnelly, 1887), p. 31.


### 197.  WHAT CANALS HAVE MEANT TO NEW YORK (1840)


An accurate evaluation of the economic advantages
of improved water transportation, made by William Seward,
then governor of New York State.


The navigable waters of the state, open to direct commerce with
the city of New York in 1817, scarcely exceeded three hundred miles
in length.  It is less than forty years since Quebec was generally
regarded as the destined mart of the northern regions of this state,
and Baltimore and New Orleans confidently anticipated the trade of
our southwestern frontier.  The commerce of the state has now its

wharves on the shores of her lakes, rivers, and bays, along an extent of twelve hundred miles, to which must be added four hundred
miles of canals in other states, and three thousand miles of lake
coast, accessible through our artificial channels.  By means of
these improvements, the advantages of navigable communication with
the city of New York have been distributed over a territory of
twenty-five thousand square miles, equal to one half of the surface
of the state, and already sustaining more than one half of its population, per square mile, of the regions thus opened to commercial
intercourse is forty-eight, while that of the regions not thus
accommodated is only seven.  Buffalo and Oswego, Binghamton and
Elmira, which nature seemed to have excluded from commerce with
New York, now enjoy greater facilities of access than Utica did
before the canals were made; and Chicago, a thousand miles distant,
exchanges her productions for the merchandise of the same city, at
less expense and with less delay than Oswego could have done at the
same period.  The wheat of Chautauque county, on the border of
the state, displaces that staple on the shores of the Judson; and
Orange and Dutchess cheerfully relinquish its culture for the more
profitable agriculture required to furnish the daily supplies of a
great city.  Lumber from Tompkins and Chemung, and ship-timber from
Grand Island, supply the wants of the city of New York.  Iron from
the banks of the Au Sable is exchanged for the salt of Onondaga.

Governor's annual message to New York legislature, G. E.
Baker (ed.), Works of William H. Seward, II, (Boston, Massachusetts:
Houghton, Mifflin & Co., 1887), p. 251.


198.  LAND EXPRESS FROM NEW YORK TO NEW ORLEANS (1842)

Virtually all travellers between New York and New
Orleans took a water route, either coastwise or along the
interior rivers aided by a few stretches of land.  The land-
express route was exceedingly expensive and even the
most valuable, compact merchandise could not afford to
bear the expense.  Buckingham who was on the way from
Tuskegee to Montgomery, Alabama writes.


While we were halting here, patching up our broken vehicle,
and lamenting our frequent delays, we were passed by the "Express
Mail," established between New York, and New Orleans.  Letters,
printed slips of news, and prices of goods, of sufficient importance
to warrant the extra expense in their conveyance, are sent by this
mode between the two cities.  A relay of horses is posted all the
way at invervals of four miles, for which it requires a stud of
500 horses, in motion or in constant readiness for mounting.  Each
boy rides only twenty-four miles, twelve onward and twelve back,

changing his horses twelve times in that distance; and for this
purpose, and to supply vacancies by sickness and accidents, about
200 boys are employed, who gallop the whole way, and make good
fourteen miles an hour, including all stoppages.  The expense of
this conveyance is so much greater than its return, that it will
probably be given up.


Buckingham, The Slave States of America, I, pp. 259-269.


### 199.  RAILROADS DESTROY LOCAL HANDICRAFTS (1845)


The very real competition from low-cost manufactured
goods severely affected the southern artisan class which
had, in any event, no very secure base.  Historically,
urbanization in the South had lagged noticeably behind
northern urbanization.


Brother Mechanics of Georgia, and Especially of our own
Village:  The Mechanics of all kinds in this country are injured by
rail roads to some extent.  They are brought single handed to compete with those large manufacturing establishments in the northern
State and foreign countries, where labor is worth comparatively
nothing, brought in opposition by the aid of steam and the rail
roads as it were in your own village, by the transportation of the
manufactured articles of all kinds, and sold at your own shop doors
at reduced prices by your own merchants, and bought by your own
farmers, from who you expected patronage.  Is not this one of the
main causes why your villages are not flourishing, the houses
vacant, and in a dilapidated condition, your academies destitute of
teachers, or if teachers, destitute of pupils?  It certainly is one
of the main causes why Mechanics are reduced to poverty, not being
able to build up our towns and cities or to educate their children
so as to make them respectable members of society.  Brother mechanics, this is not as it should be--then rouse up from your lethargy,
go drooped down and depressed no longer, come forth in your might
and power, and at once, as it were, you will be able to correct the
evil.--You should form yourselves into large and permanent manufacturing companies.  With your skill and enterprise you may soon rear
up in your midst, manufacturing establishments of various kinds to
manufacture those very articles that afford a considerable item in
the commerce of the country, make your towns and villages soon
become flourishing, affording a great market for surplus products,
raised by the farmers in our own midst--and as all classes will
feel the benefit in a short time it will be but a little while
before your business will be profitable to yourselves and the
country in which you live.  I might be asked to suggest some plan
to give the above suggestions a permanent and practical notice to
the community at large.  One that I would mention is that it should

be the business of every mechanic of every branch of business, to
apply himself closely to his business.  Let that be his daily
employment, instead of, as is too often the case, quitting his
shop, taking the streets, becoming a street politician, a dandy, or
a drunkard.  Remedy those three evils and the work is half accomplished.


    Letter to Southern Banner (Athens, Georgia), reprinted in
Federal Union (Milledgeville, Georgia), April 15, 1845, Commons
(ed.), Documentary History of American Industrial Society, II,
pp. 336-337.


### 200.  RAILROAD LEADERS MEET TO REGULATE
COMPETITION (1850-1851)


    During the winter of 1850-1851, New England railroad
managers and directors met in Boston to mitigate the harsh
consequences of competition.  One of the main problems
discussed was passenger and freight rates.  Noteworthy to
the modern reader is the fact that the proceedings of this
price-fixing conference were printed and presumably distributed at large.
    The individuals involved in the debate are Elias Hasket
Derby, who was a prosperous railroad lawyer and director.
He was descended from and named for one of the earliest
millionaires in American history; also Erastus Fairbanks,
who with his brothers founded E. and T. Fairbanks and Co.,
manufacturers of platform scales.  In 1852, he was elected
governor of Vermont.  The last was Thomas Whittemore, a
Universalist preacher, who became, in 1849, president of
the Vermont and Massachusetts Railroad whose tangled financial affairs he successfully unravelled.


    Mr. DERBY, of the Fitchburg Railroad, asked if the last
speaker would go above two and half cents per mile for passengers,
that being higher than the general rates on the New York roads?
    Mr. WHITTEMORE replied that the rates for both freight and
passengers should be raised to a "living" price; high enough to
pay honestly, and well.  If two and half cents would not be enough,
let it be three cents.  He had no special plan to offer, but this
was his theory of the case.
    Mr. [Erastus] FAIRBANKS, of the Connecticut and Passumpsic
Rivers Railroad, supposed the resolution only intended to elicit
discussion.  The two questions, as to freight and passengers,
should be separately considered.  Passengers might so increase in
numbers under low freights as to avoid loss.  No so with freights.

Some freights would decrease in amount if prices were raised, but most would be but little affected.  With certain competing roads--roads competing with water communication--there might be difficulty; freight might be lost by too high a rate.  But in local districts, without such competition, where there was a certain amount of products to go to market, and a certain amount of articles to go from the city for consumption, there would be no loss by a rate decidedly higher than the present, provided it were lower than the price paid before Railroads were introduced.  But the great object now was equalization--people wish to know that all pay alike.

When stockholders invested money, they expected to have a fair remuneration; they expected, in fact, to have more, he believed, be obtained, but only by ample deliberation.  For himself, he had no plan to propose, but thought it more important for the Convention to debate the subject of freight than of passengers.

. . . . . . . . . . . . . . . . . . . . . . . . . . . . . . . . . . . . .

Mr. [Charles] THOMPSON said that to the Sullivan Railroad, they were literally doing business for nothing.  He was for changing the rates with reference to freight and not to passengers.  Freight rates should be increased, and very considerably.  The freight between Boston and White River Junction used to be carried for not less than $20 per ton, and was from four days to a week on the road. Then Railroads were built, and before they were sure of the business, it was well to establish low fares.  But now they were sure of it, and there should be a fairer division between the road and the public.  The question was whether three-quarters of the advantage in time and cost should go to the public, and the roads, in some cases, lost money?  Presidents of roads should see that their stockholders were not robbed for the public convenience.  Rates might be raised considerably, and the public still get full half the benefit; and stockholders had a right to demand their share.

Mr. Gore of the Nashua and Lowell Railroad...we must resolve to change our course of management, or it will be too late.

The main object now seems to be to show a large amount of business done, without regard to the means used to get it, or the profits to be derived from it.  Means are used to get business from other roads, which any one would be ashamed to resort to in the transaction of private business; which shows that the Managers, as well as the Corporations, have but small souls, if any.  We make solemn bargains with each other to be governed by certain principles and rules, and violate them, the same day, by a secret bargain with an individual, to obtain a small pittance of freight from another road.

The people, seeing this, lose all respect for us, as we seem to have none for ourselves; and they approach us to dicker with us, like jockies, without even thinking that we may deem it an insult.  In this way, we have already sunk our characters so low, that the term "Railroad man" is one of reproach, and at once destroys his influence in legislative halls, and jeopardizes his rights, and

the rights of the corporation, even in our courts of justice.    No
merchant or tradesman could live and deal thus with his neighbors.

Proceedings of the Convention of the Northern Lines of Railway, Held at Boston, December 1850 and January 1851, (Boston,
Massachusetts:  J. B. Yerrinton & Sons, 1851), pp. 14-15, 18, 22-23.

### 201.    "THIS RAILROAD HAS MADE LUMBER HIGH" (1851)

When evaluating the economic role of improved
transportation we usually note that railroads brought
increasing supplies of raw materials to the cities with
the result that prices fell.    But we usually forget that
by the same token backcountry users of the now-popular
raw material had to pay rising prices inasmuch as local
demand now competed with demands from urban markets.
(The line in question was the Erie and New York City
Rail Road.)    The writer, Mora Adams, was a farmer in
West Almond, New York.

I built a small house last year--one part two stories high.
The other one thirty-two feet by twenty-four, a stoop on one end
and painted inside and out.    I have a very good cellar, and water
handy.    This railroad has made lumber high.    The best is worth about
twenty dollars per thousand, or more.    The eastern folks are in such
a hurry for lumber, they cannot wait to have it sawed.    Whole trains
go down loaded with nothing but pine logs to New York or near there.

Letter from Mora Adams to "Brother and Sister Fairbanks",
December 26, 1851, George F. Partridge (ed.), "A Yankee [i.e.,
Mora Adams] On The New York Frontier, 1833-1851," New England
Quarterly, X (1937), pp. 771-772.

### 202.    THE SOUTH IS AN ECONOMIC TRIBUTARY
TO THE NORTH (1853)

As producer of the country's single largest
export--cotton--the South sought political power sufficient to protect its institution of slave labor.    To the
North, the South represented a source of raw material,
especially cotton, a market for northwestern farm products,
and northeastern manufactured goods.    Profits from financing

the cotton crop generally drifted northward (and overseas).
In addition, a sizable part of federal revenues came from
the South.  Yet, southern planters and their allies failed
to achieve either economic dominance or political control
in the Union.  Edmund Ruffin, the writer here, was a publisher, an experimental farmer, leader in farm organizations and a defender of slavery.


But there are other and stronger reasons for the prosperity
and success of the Northern States.  Even after negro slavery was
removed from them, its continued existence and extension in the
Southern States served to foster and stimulate, and reward the industry of the Northern States.  Southern products ever since the
existence of the Federal constitution, have been made tributary to
Northern navigation, commerce, and manufactures--and the tribute
has been made more and more oppressive to the South, and profitable
to the North, by means of federal legislations giving bounties,
direct or indirect, to Northern industry, capital, and general
interests.  It will never be known by the South, nor appreciated
by the North, how much tribute has thus been paid by Southern industry and capital, (and all derived from the products of negro
slavery,) to swell Northern profits and wealth, until the existing
union of the Northern and Southern States shall be dissolved.  Should
that contingency occur, then, for the first time, will the Northern
States have to support themselves from their own resources, and without the great and unacknowledged aid to their wealth derived from
the slave labor and the products of the South--and they will then
learn to know the value of all that they have lost.


Edmund Ruffin, The Political Economy of Slavery; or, The
Institution Considered In Regard To Its Influence On Public Wealth
And The General Welfare, (N.P.:  Lemuel Towers, 1853), p. 23.


203.  THE ELECTRIC TELEGRAPH IN AMERICA (1854)


During the same period, both the telegraph and the
railroad reinforced one another in braiding the main
strands of the national market.


The advantages to be derived from the adoption of the Electric
Telegraph, have in no country been more promptly appreciated than
in the United States.  A system of communication that annihilates
distance, was felt to be of vital importance, both politically and
commercially, in a country so vast, and having a population so
widely scattered....

Distances are now to be measured by intervals, not of space,
but of time:  to bring Boston, New York, and Philadelphia into instantaneous communication with New Orleans and St. Louis--to cen-
tralize in Washington, at any given moment, information gathered
simultaneously from the far corners of the thirty-one provinces
of the Union, is to extend throughout the confederacy bonds of the
most intimate connexion.

In the operations of commerce, the great capitals of the North,
South, and West are moved, as it were, by a common intelligence;
information respecting the state of the various markets is readily
obtained, the results of consignments may be calculated almost with
certainty, and sudden fluctuations in price in a great measure provided against.

If, on the arrival of an European mail at one of the Northern
ports, the news from Europe report that the supply of cotton or of
corn is inadequate to meet the existing demand, almost before the
vessel can be moored, intelligence is spread by the Electric Telegraph, and the merchants and shippers of New Orleans are busied in
the preparation of freights, or the corn-factors of St. Louis and
Chicago, in the far west, are emptying their granaries and forwarding their contents by rail or by canal to the Atlantic ports.

There may be, no doubt, similar general advantages derived
everywhere from the introduction of the Electric Telegraph, but they
are such as effect with peculiar benefit a country like the United
States, consisting of confederated provinces, differing one from
another in climate, in productions, in laws, and institutions, and
in some cases in the character of their inhabitants.

. . . . . . . . . . . . . . . . . . . . . . . . . . . . . . . . . .

The most distant points connected by electric telegraph in
North America are Quebec and New Orleans, which are 3,000 miles
apart, and the network of lines extends to the west as far as
Missouri, about 500 towns and villages being provided with stations.

There are two separate lines connecting New York with New
Orleans, one running along the sea-board, the other by way of the
Mississippi, each about 2,000 miles long.  Messages have been trans-
mitted from New York to New Orleans, and answers received, in the
space of three hours, though they had necessarily to be written
several times in the course of transmission.

When the contemplated lines connecting California with the
Atlantic, and Newfoundland with the main continent, are completed,
San Francisco will be in communication with St. Johns, Newfoundland,
which is distant from Galway but five days' passage.  It is, therefore, estimated that intelligence may be conveyed from the Pacific
to Europe, and _vice versa_, in about six days.


Whitworth and Wallis, The Industry of the United States, pp.
35-36, 40.

204.   ROADS FROM IOWA TO PIKE'S PEAK (1857)

Until the transcontinental railroad started operating
regularly in the 1870's, this is how westward travel
proceeded.


Reaching the town of Des Moines, now the capital and metropolis
of our state [Iowa], we found hardly more than a village.  From
there we again went west across another prairie, nearly one hundred
and fifty miles in extent, with houses few and far between, until
we reached the settlement of Council Bluffs on the Missouri River.
Should you examine our route, you would see that from the upper
branch of the Des Moines River to Council Bluffs via Des Moines is
a very long roundabout way.  Deviation was deemed desirable in order
that we might take advantage of the roads that joined the scattering
improvements made in the timber along the river; use the best fords
found through the unbridged streams, and follow the safest and
hardest places across the ungraded sloughs.
The roads we sought would not be recognized as such today.
They were simply trails, unworked wagon tracks, two parallel strips
about twelve inches wide and two feet apart, where the wheels of
wagons and feet of teams had trampled down the grass, leaving the
middle growing as luxuriantly as elsewhere.  This track, or road,
would and twisted across the prairie, following from ridge to
ridge, to find the smoothest land, and going often miles out of the
way to seek a place where an ungraded slough or unbridged stream
might be crossed.
Had we, at that time, attempted to drive the short way between
the two places mentioned, there would have been no track, and we
would not have known where to find crossings of streams and when
to avoid the low, wet and miry land.
. . . . . . . . . . . . . . . . . . . . . . . . . . . . . . . . .
It was almost eight hundred miles from the Missouri River to
our first objective, Fort Laramie, near the foot of the Rocky
Mountains.  In this long distance, there was no mark of white man's
work save Fort Kearney, about half way there, which slightly broke
the monotony.  There was no fear of our losing our way--the road
was plainly marked and deeply worn.  We were now on the old
California Trail, three thousand miles long, composed of many parallel wagon tracks, which here followed the north bank of the Platte
River past Fort Laramie, and thence into South Pass, and onward
through Utah to California.
. . . . . . . . . . . . . . . . . . . . . . . . . . . . . . . . .
There was no danger of our becoming lonesome on our journey
toward the mountains for the California trail was this summer in
the height of its employment and usefulness.  Along some one of its
numerous trails the overland stage drove a three thousand mile trip
from Council Bluffs to Sacramento, and the pony express dashed over
the same route three days to Denver and eight to the last terminal.
. . . . . . . . . . . . . . . . . . . . . . . . . . . . . . . . .

A word about the surprise some of the best outfitted trains received.  Some such, wishing to get to the mines at the earliest date, selected horses or mules to draw their wagons, thinking they could outstrip in travel the slower oxen.  They were disappointed in the final test:  horses and mules had been used to grain; oxen had not, so that when both were compelled to live upon the grass, the grain-fed teams lost all their superiority, and the mileage of both oxen and mules became about the same.

Twenty to twenty-five miles a day was what the average train wanted to make daily when the roads were good and food plentiful. This might be reduced to as little as a mile or two under adverse circumstances.  Some tried to increase this rate by traveling nights during the hot weather and resting days, but stock did not thrive on the schedule, for they wanted their nights to graze and rest. This method was generally given up.

Burnap, What Happened During One Man's Lifetime, pp. 144, 147-148, 151, 158-159.


205.  THE CRUCIAL ADVANTAGE OF NEW YORK CITY
OVER NEW ORLEANS (1860)


A complaint which was made daily in the South is here made by William Seward.  He had been governor of New York State, was now member of U.S. Senate.  In 1860 he lost the Republican nomination for presidency.


The greatest and finest site for commerce on this continent is New Orleans, and in early life I made a pilgrimage there to see whether it was not true that New Orleans was to supersede and supplant New York, the capital of my native state, as the seat of commerce on this continent.  I found that whereas there were some ten times the population in New York that there was in New Orleans, that it was increasing in a ratio of such magnitude that when New Orleans would have a quarter of a million New York would have a million and a half.  Shall I tell you the reason?  I found it in the fact that when I went out in the night in the city of New York, I saw the cobbler's light twinkling in his window in the gray of the morning or late at night.  I saw everything made, as well as sold, in New York; but when I came to the city of New Orleans I found there that everything was sold and nothing was made.  After trying in vain to find any article of human raiment that was made in New Orleans, I did see upon a sign opposite the St. Charles hotel this inscription: "Wagons, carts and wheelbarrows made and sold here."  I said, I have found one thing that is made in New Orleans!

coarse wagons, carts and rough and rude wheelbarrows, but on crossing to inspect the matter a little more minutely, before entering
it in my notes, I found that I had overlooked some words printed
in smaller letters, "at New Haven," and that the sign was rightly
to be read: "Wagons, carts and wheelbarrows made at New Haven and
sold here." Fellow citizens, this is not a reproach. It is not
spoken reproachfully, it would ill become me to so speak it. But
it is their system. They employ slaves, and in New York--I was
going to say that we employ, but I think I will reverse it and say
that freemen employ their masters, the manufacturers. This is but
an illustration. The principle is the same in every department of
industry and manufacture.


     Speech at New York City, November 2, 1860, Baker (ed.),
Works of William H. Seward, IV, pp. 417-418.




              206.  LOSS OF THE SOUTHERN MARKET WOULD
                    CRIPPLE THE NORTH (1860)


     The South was undeniably an important market for
northern manufactures and northwestern farm goods.  To
this extent, Christy's argument, below, was unanswerable.
The immediate economic losses to northern interests following upon secession would be severely felt.  Larger considerations, however, might still make secession acceptable to
the North.  This, Christy did not understand.  If, for
example, secession led to northern control of the federal
government, this outcome would over-balance the immediate
losses.  Further, a national market could be cemented by
compulsion as well as by compromise or cooperation.  The
writer, Christy, was a geologist and a journalist.  (See
Source No. 318).


     It is a fact, not to be questioned, that the productions of
the Northern States amount to an immense sum, above those of the
Southern States, when valued in dollars and cents; but the proportion of the products of the former, exported to foreign countries,
is very significant, indeed, when compared with the value of the
exports from the latter.  And, yet, the North is acquiring wealth
with amazing rapidity.  This fact could not exist, unless the
Northern people produce more than they consume--unless they have a
surplus to sell, after supplying their own wants.  They must,
therefore, find a permanent and profitable market, somewhere, for
the surplus products that yield them their wealth.  As that market
is not in Europe, it must be in the Southern States.  But the
extent to which the South receive their supplies from the North,
cannot be determined by any data now in the possession of the public.

It must, however, be very large in amount, and if withheld, would
greatly embarrass the Southern people, by lessening their ability
to export as largely as hitherto.  So, on the other hand, if the
Northern people were deprived of the markets afforded by the South,
they would find so little demand elsewhere for their products,
that it would have a ruinous effect upon their prosperity.  All
that can be safely said upon this subject is, that the interests of
both sections of the country are so intimately connected, so firmly
blended together, that a dissolution of the Union would be destructive to all the economical interests of both the North and the
South.  Cut off from the South all that the North supplies to the
planters, in such articles as agricultural implements, furniture,
clothing, provisions, horses, and mules, and cotton culture would
at once have to be abandoned to a great extent.  But would the South
alone be the sufferer?  Could the Northern agriculturist, manufacturer, and mechanic, remain prosperous, and continue to accumulate
wealth, without a market for their products?  Could Northern merchants dwell in their palaces, and toll in luxury, with a foreign
commerce contracted to one-third of its present extent, and a domestic demand for merchandize reduced to one-half its present
amount?  Certainly not.


David Christy, "Cotton is King:  or, Slavery in the Light of
Political Economy," in Elliot (ed.), Cotton Is King, p. 221.

# F.

## GROWTH OF THE
## WAGE-EARNER CLASS

207.  THE PROPRIETARY STYLE OF AMERICAN BEGGARS (1818)

Small and middling property ownership was a realistic, widespread condition.  Here is testimony as to the effect of such a condition on the little poverty that existed.  William Cobbett, a well-known English editor with radical political sympathies, writes the comment.  His admiration for American society waxed and waned.

In England a beggar is a poor creature, with hardly rags (mere rags) sufficient to cover its nakedness, so far even as common decency requires.  A wretched mortal, the bare sight of whom would freeze the soul of an American within him.  A dejected, broken down thing, that approaches you bare-headed, on one knee, with a trembling voice, with "pray bestow your charity, for the Lord Jesus Christ's sake have compassion on a poor soul;" and, if you toss a half-penny into his ragged hat, he exclaims in an extacy, "God Almighty bless your honour!"  though you, perhaps, be but a shoe-black yourself.  An American beggar, dressed very much like other people, walks up to you as boldly as if his pockets were crammed with money, and, with a half smile, that seems to say, he doubts of the propriety of his conduct, very civilly asks you, if you can HELP him to a quarter of a dollar.  He mostly states the precise sum; and never sinks below silver.  In short, there is no begging, properly so called.  There is nothing that resembles English begging even in the most distant degree.

William Cobbett, A Year's Residence in the United States of America, II, (London:  Sherwood, Neely and Jones, 1819), pp. 379-380.

208.   DEGRADATION OF MANUAL LABOR IN THE SOUTH (1820)

Identification of slave labor with manual labor was
the rule only in areas of very large plantations.  But
over most of the South white men labored in wheat and corn
fields, and even in cotton fields, without a feeling of
degradation.  Calhoun, it should be noted, came from the
greatest slave state in the South.  He was Secretary of War.

I walked home with Calhoun, who said that the principles which
I had avowed were just and noble; but that in the Southern country,
whenever they were mentioned, they were always understood as applying only to white men.  Domestic labor was confined to the blacks,
and such was the prejudice, that if he, who was the most popular
man in his district, were to keep a white servant in his house, his
character and reputation would be irretrievably ruined.
I said that this confounding of the ideas of servitude and labor was one of the bad effects of slavery; but he thought it attended with many excellent consequences.  It did not apply to all kinds
of labor--not, for example, to farming.  He himself had often held
the plough; so had his father.  Manufacturing and mechanical labor
was not degrading.  It was only manual labor--the proper work of
slaves.  No white person could descend to that.  And it was the
best guarantee to equality among the whites.  It produced an unvary-
ing level among them.  It not only did not excite, but did not even
admit of inequalities, by which one white man could domineer over
another.

Account of conversation with John C. Calhoun; C. F. Adams (ed.),
Memoirs of John Quincy Adams, V, p. 10.

209.   AMERICA IS EAGER FOR ENGLISH MECHANICS (1824)

These days were the dawn of American factory production
when no reserve of skilled workers yet existed here.  This
most valuable resource was almost wholly imported from
England.  This testimony is by Henry Holdsworth, a cotton
spinner and machine worker in Manchester and Glasgow.

I know one gentleman, a highly respectable and extensive
spinner at Glasgow, who has established his son at New York; he told
me, that they are exceedingly anxious to obtain our machinery and
our workmen; and, in proof of it, he mentioned, that at New York,
while he was staying for a ship to bring him home, he met a gentleman who had come 70 or 80 miles; and who had been at New York three

weeks, waiting the chance of a mechanic arriving in some ship from
Greenock or Liverpool.  In America, I understand that three years
ago, the extent of cotton spun there was about 90,000 bags annually;
and I should presume that at that time the consumption of this
country might have been from 450,000 to 500,000:  and my own son,
who was over the last year, told me, there are several new mills
erecting, and there would be a great many more, were it not that
they cannot get mechanics to fit them up.


Testimony of Henry Holdsworth, White (ed.), Committee on
Artizans and Machinery, p. 314.


210.    CHILD LABOR AT PATERSON, NEW JERSEY (1835)


A strike was in progress at the Paterson cotton
mills.  Following are the results of a questionnaire
circulated at the time.


Question 1st.  What number of mills are idle in consequence
of the strike?  Answer.  The number is 19 cotton mills, and 1 woolen
factory.
Question 2d.  What number of children are idle in consequence
of the strike?  Answer.  It would take some weeks to ascertain the
number of minors; the whole number employed in these factories, is
from 19 to 20 hundred; the number of hand-loom weavers and others
dependent on the factories would swell the amount of persons thrown
out of work, much more.
Questions 3 and 4.  What number of children are under 12 years?
What number are over 12 years?  Answer.  We have placed these two
queries together, because, like the question above, we could not
ascertain without an actual personal survey of the town.  Doctor
Fisher, who formerly took the census, and which he has said employed
him nearly six weeks, reported in 1832, the whole number of population under 16 years of age, at 3949; we consider it would be within
compass to take the sixth part as engaged in manufacturing--say 600
under 16 years.
Question 5.  What average compensation for those under 12?
Answer.  From 50 cents to $1.75 per week--average $112 1/2.
Question 6.  What average compensation for those over 12?
Answer.  Many of those work by the piece, as rulers, weavers, war-
pers, &c.  As near as we can learn, the average is $2.12 1/2 per
week.  In reference to this question, we send you two statements on
oath of the wages obtained by the individuals in those two families
(five in each) in one of which you will see they are all over 12
years and average $2.10.  In this statement we do not include
spinners and sub bosses, but only such as may be considered minors
among the male sex; but also includes among the females, many grown
women.

Question 7.  What time do they commence work in summer?
Question 10.  What time do they quit in the evening?  Answer.  From
sun-rise to sun-set from March first to October 1st.
Question 8.  What time is allowed for breakfast?  Answer.
no time allowed.  The hands breakfast by candle-light before going
to work.
Question 9.  What time is allowed for dinner?  Answer.  Three
quarters of an hour, the year round.
Question 11.  The same queries in reference to the winter
season.  Answer.  From October 1st to March 1st, commence at daylight to quit at 8 o'clock; in which some mills are very precise;
others overrun that time, probably on account of the difference of
clocks.
Question 12.  What number are in destitute circumstances?
Answer.  In consequence of the strike, many have left the town.
The whole who remain may be said to be destitute.  Doctor Fisher in
his last census, 1831, stated the numer of widows to be 163, and the
amount of their families to be 834.  Now these are precisely the
class of persons who cannot remove in case of a strike, or of being
thrown out of work from any other cause; and as the town was more
populous as well as more prosperous at the commencement of the
strike, than it was in 1832, being the time of cholera, we believe
we are within compass to say there are 1000 persons in need of
assistance.


John Tilby and John K. Flood in Paterson Courier, reprinted
in National Trades' Union (New York), August 15, 1835, Commons (ed.),
A Documentary History of American Industrial Society, V, pp. 63-65.


211.   COST OF LIVING AND TEXTILE MANUFACTURING
WAGES (1840)


Montgomery's statements about the comparative
cost of foods are not entirely supported by other
evidence.  On the other hand, even by his calculations
American real wages could have exceeded British levels.
At the same time, the high wages were moderated by the
relatively large output per worker.


Now it may be true, that the price of provisions have been
higher in Great Britain than in America; but they are not so now.
I can speak from experience on this subject, and have no hesitation
in asserting, that the price of living is higher in this country
than in Britain; I know of nothing that is cheaper here but spirits,
tea, and tobacco.  I have no doubt but in the interior of the
country, potatoes, Indian corn, butter milk, poultry, &c. may be
much cheaper; but in all the cities and manufacturing places, they

are much higher.  It will be supposed that flour must be considerably cheaper here than in Great Britain; but it is not always so,
as during these few years past, there has been a vast quantity of
wheat imported from Great Britain and the continent of Europe.

House rents are higher here than in Scotland, and fuel is at
least triple the price of what it is in Glasgow.  All kinds of
clothing are higher, and particularly the making of clothes.  The
price of _making_ a coat in Boston is from eight to twelve dollars;
as much as would _purchase_ one complete in Glasgow.
. . . . . . . . . . . . . . . . . . . . . . . . . . . . . . .
That the general rate of wages is higher in the United States
than in Britain is admitted, particularly the wages of females employed in the Factories.  The greater part of these are farmers'
daughters, who go into the Factories only for a short time until
they make a little money, and then "clear out," as it is called;
so that there is a continual changing amongst them, and in all the
places I have visited, they are generally scarce; on that account
the manufacturers are under the necessity of paying high wages, as
an inducement for girls to prefer working in the Factories to
house-work:  and while this state of things continues, it is not to
be expected that wages in this country will be so low as in Great
Britain; and although they have undergone a considerable reduction
during the late depression, still they are higher than in any part
of Britain.
. . . . . . . . . . . . . . . . . . . . . . . . . . . . . . .
The price of living here is higher, and the hours of labour
longer; besides, the greater part of the Factory workers being
connected with farming, whenever wages become reduced so low, as to
cease to operate as an inducement to prefer Factory labour above any
other to which they can turn their attention, then a great many
Factories will have to shut up.  During a stagnation of trade, it
is common for the manufacturers here to stop a part, or the whole
of their Factories, and then the workers retire to their farms:
such was the case in 1837, when a vast number of Factories were entirely shut up.  Yet it seemed not to affect the workers very materially; indeed, many of the girls who had been some time in a
Factory, seemed to rejoice and regard it as a time of recreation....

Montgomery, _A Practical Detail_, pp. 134-135, 135-136, 137.


212.  LENGTH OF WORK WEEK IN LOWELL TEXTILE
FACTORIES (1840)


Montgomery estimated the length of the work week
in Lowell cotton mills at 73 1/2 hours; in the Middle
and Southern states, 75 1/2 hours.

|          | Ho. | Min. |           | Ho. | Min. |
|----------|-----|------|-----------|-----|------|
| January  | 11  | 24   | July      | 12  | 45   |
| February | 12  | "    | August    | 12  | 45   |
| March    | 11  | 52   | September | 12  | 23   |
| April    | 13  | 31   | October   | 12  | 10   |
| May      | 12  | 45   | November  | 11  | 56   |
| June     | 12  | 45   | December  | 11  | 24   |

Montgomery, A Practical Detail, p. 174.

### 213.  THE AFFLUENT SOCIETY (1844)

The truth of the contrast is evident from many
other sources.  This hardly supports the mid-20th century
contention that relative American affluence is only a
recent phenomenon.

No observing American comes from the United States to Europe,
without soon becoming convinced, that economy of living is no where
so little understood as in his own country; and that for nothing are
the Americans more distinguished, than for a reckless waste of the
means of subsistence.  The refuse of many a family, in the United
States, even in moderate circumstances, would often support in comfort a poor family in Europe.  When persons buy tea by the ounce,
and wood by the pound, and hay by the handful, it is quite obvious
that these articles will be expended with far more frugality, than
where the store is less limited and seems inexhaustible.  While
meanness is contemptible, a rigid economy avoiding all waste, is a
great virtue.  The inhabitants of the United States enjoy an abundance for which they cannot be too grateful; but which is very
little understood in Europe, where, with a large portion of the population, including many in the middle condition of life, it is a
constant struggle to live, and to bring even their necessary expenditure within their restricted means; and where the constant inquiry
is, not what they want, but what can they afford,--not what they
will have, but what can they do without.
. . . . . . . . . . . . . . . . . . . . . . . . . . . . . . . . .
American farmers and labourers...are accustomed, even in the
humblest conditions, to sit down daily to a nicely spread table,
covered with a variety and abundance of bread, meat, and vegetables,
to which are often added tea, coffee, and beer.  The diet of the
labouring poor in Europe is chiefly bread; and this is almost always furnished by a professional baker.  During my residence in
Europe, I do not recollect a single instance where bread was made

in the family.  The want of fuel on the continent is a serious
necessity.  There are no labouring people who live in half the
abundance of the labouring people of the United States.

        Colman, European Agriculture and Rural Economy, II, pp. 396,
480.

### 214.  THE DIFFICULTY OF ATTAINING AN INDEPENDENT FOOTING ON THE MILWAUKEE FRONTIER (ca. 1845)

        An accurate and balanced statement about pioneering
made by Isaac Stephenson who became a wealthy lumberman
in the Midwest; Chicago was the center of his operations.
(A "cord" of wood is a pile 8 feet long, 4 feet high
and 4 feet wide, or a total of 128 cubic feet).

For the person who had no capital the difficulty of attaining
an independent footing was almost insurmountable.  Men worked on
the farms for eight dollars a month and board.  Girls and women did
general housework for seventy-five cents a week, the wage rate for
the most proficient, and the measure of luxuries they enjoyed would
put to shame many women of the present day who consider themselves
unfortunate.  In 1846 and 1847 men could be obtained to cut wood
off North Point for twenty-five cents a cord and wages for this
service were traded in at the general store.  From twenty-five to
fifty cents a cord was the rate for cutting, splitting, and piling
hardwood.  The splitting, not infrequently, was done by women.
    The problem, therefore, of establishing a home in the new
country with nothing to start on was a very serious one, and the
fact that lands were cheap offered little encouragement in the
face of the trials and privations and the uncertainty of ultimate
success.  Now that the land has been occupied and brought under
cultivation and the forests for the most part cut, it is a habit
of mind to exaggerate the advantages afforded by the government's
bounty and to minimize the hardships of pioneering.  Having gone
through most phases of this period I am more inclined to the belief
that the government obtained the best of the bargain and that the
returns to the country at large were of incalculable value.

        Stephenson, Recollections, p. 65.

215.  "THE RISK, IF ANY, RESTS WITH THE OWNER
OF THE HANDS" (1852)


Ordinarily, hired slaves were paid a premium wage to
cover the risk to their capital value, as it was then conceived.  Although the law of employers' liability was practically non-existent, North or South, injury to a slave
while he was working for wages usually called for indemnification to the owner.  Now, however, in the 1850's, productive employment for slaves in North Carolina--an old cotton
area--was increasingly rare.  Under such pressure owners of
slaves might well waive their claims, as the leaflet
announced they must.


WE, A PORTION OF THE FISHERMEN ON ALBEMARLE SOUND AND its
tributaries, hereby GIVE NOTICE to the persons from whom we may hire
Hands the ensuing Fishing Season that we shall endeavor to use all
proper care and discretion in the management of our Fishing Opera-
tions, BUT WISH IT DISTINCTLY UNDERSTOOD THAT WE DO NOT HOLD OUR-
SELVES RESPONSIBLE FOR ANY ACCIDENTS WHICH MAY OCCUR, resulting in
LOSS OF LIFE, or in any other injury which the Hands may sustain.
We all adhere to the opinion that the RISK, IF ANY, RESTS WITH THE
OWNERS OF THE HANDS, in consideration of the additional price we
have to pay for such labor, over the price paid for ordinary labor.


Circular, Gatesville, North Carolina, February 16, 1852,
J. G. DeRoulhac Hamilton (ed.), The Papers of Thomas Ruffin, II,
(Raleigh, North Carolina:  Edwards and Broughton Printing Co.,
1918), pp. 320-321.


216.  WHITE WAGE LABORERS ON THE VIRGINIA COUNTRYSIDE (1853)


Frederick Olmsted here makes an informative set of
observations about what many regard as the forgotten class
of the slave South--the poor whites.


I learned that there were not white laboring men here who hired
themselves out by the month.  The poor white people that had to
labor for their living, never would work steadily at any employment.
"They mostly followed boating"--hiring as hands on the bateaus that
navigate the small streams and canals, but never for a longer term
at once than a single trip of a boat, whether that might be long or
short.  At the end of the trip they were paid by the day.  Their
wages were from fifty cents to a dollar, varying with the demand
and individual capacities.  They hardly ever worked on farms except
in harvest, when they usually received a dollar a day, sometimes

more.  In harvest-time, most of the rural mechanics closed their
shops and hired out to the farmers at a dollar a day, which would
indicate that their ordinary earnings are considerably less than
this.  At other than harvest-time, the poor white people, who had
no trade, would sometimes work for the farmers by the job; not
often at any regular agricultural labor, but at getting rails or
shingles, or clearing land.

He did not know that they were particular about working with
negroes, but no white man would ever do certain kinds of work (such
as taking care of cattle, or getting water or water or wood to be
used in the house), and you should ask a white man you had hired,
to do such things, he would get mad and tell you he was n't a
nigger.  Poor white girls never hired out to do servants' work, but
they would come and help another white woman about her sewing or
quilting, and take wages for it.  But these girls were not very
respectable generally, and it was not agreeable to have them in your
house, though there were some very respectable ladies that would go
out to sew.  Farmers depended almost entirely upon their negroes;
it was only when they were hard pushed by their crops, that they
got white hands to help them any.

. . . . . . . . . . . . . . . . . . . . . . . . . . . . . . .

Of course, he did not see how white laborers were ever going
to come into competition with negroes here, at all.  You never
could depend on white men, and you could n't _drive_ them any; they
would n't stand it.  Slaves were the only reliable laborers--you
could command them and _make_ them do what was right.


Frederick L. Olmsted, <u>A Journey in the Seaboard Slave States
in the Years 1853-1854</u>, I, (New York:  G. P. Putnam's Sons, 1904),
pp. 91-92, 93.


### 217.  AN IRISHMAN CAN DO WORK TOO DANGEROUS FOR A SLAVE (1853)


This was a widespread sentiment in the South
during the last twenty years of slavery.


He had had an Irish gang draining for him, by contract.  He
thought a negro could do twice as much work, in a day, as an Irish-
man.  He had not stood over them at work, but judged entirely from
the amount they accomplished:  he thought a good gang of negroes
would have got on twice as fast.  He was sure they must have
"trifled" a great deal, or they would have accomplished more than
they had.  He complained much, also, of their sprees and quarrels.
I asked why he should employ Irishmen, in preference to doing the

work with his own hands. "It's dangerous work (unhealthy?), and a
negro's life is too valuable to be risked at it.  If a negro dies,
it's a considerable loss, you know."


Olmsted, A Journey in the Seaboard Slave States, I, pp. 100-
101.



## 218.   LABOR RELATIONS ON LARGE SLAVE ESTATES (1854)


The impersonality of large-scale agricultural
production.


As a general rule, the larger the body of negroes on a
plantation or estate, the more completely are they treated as mere
property, and in accordance with a policy calculated to insure the
largest pecuniary returns.  Hence, in part, the great proportionate
profit of such plantations, and the tendency which everywhere prevails in the planting districts to the absorption of small, and the
augmentation of large estates.  It may be true, that among the
wealthier slaveowners, there is oftener a humane disposition, a
better judgement, and a greater ability to deal with their depen-
dents indulgently and bountifully, but the effects of this disposition are chiefly felt, even on those plantations where the proprietor resides permanently, among the slaves employed about the
house and stables, and perhaps a few old favorites in the quarters.
It is more than balanced by the difficulty of acquiring a personal
interest in the units of a large body of slaves, and an acquaintance with the individual characteristics of each.  The treatment
of the mass must be reduced to a system, the ruling idea of which
will be, to enable one man to force into the same channel of labor
the muscles of a large number of men, of various, and often conflicting wills.
The chief difficulty is to overcome their great aversion to
labor.  They have no objection to eating, drinking, and resting,
when necessary, and no general disinclination to receive instruction.
If a man own many slaves, therefore, the faculty which he values
highest, and pays most for, in an overseer, is that of making them
work.  Any fool could see that they were properly supplied with
food, clothing, rest, and religious instruction.


Olmsted, A Journey in the Back Country, I, pp. 64-65.

219.  THE ECONOMIC CONTRIBUTIONS
OF IMMIGRANTS (1858)


How much money did immigrants bring with them when
they came?  The latest scholarly study, by Douglass C.
North, The Economic Growth of the United States, 1790-1860,
(Englewood Cliffs, New Jersey:  Prentice-Hall, 1961), uses
an average figure of $75 per immigrant for the period before
1840; and for 1840-1860, $100 per German immigrant, $25 per
Irish immigrant, and $75 per immigrant from all other
countries.  North estimates that from 1820 to 1857 immigrants
brought to this country more than $350 million; this is a
much higher figure than given by Dinsmore, below ($200
million).  Dinsmore, below, estimated total immigration as
"about three millions."  The most recent critical collection
of immigration statistics gives a figure of 4.9 million for
the period 1790-1857!  Thus, the hazards of quantitative
economic history.  Dinsmore was assistant Recording Secretary
of the American Geographical and Statistical Society of
New York.


In 1790 the population of the United States, including whites
and free colored persons, was 3,231,930.  Now the careful calculation of the tables shows that the annual increase of population by
excess of births over deaths is 1.38 per cent (138 in 10,000) in
this country--the largest increase of any country in the world,
the like increase in England and Wales being 1.25, (125 in 10,000,)
in France .44, in Russia .74, in Prussia 1.17, in Holland 1.23, in
Belgium .61, in Portugal .72, in Saxony 1.08.
     At this rate of increase of population, augmented by the excess
of births over deaths alone, we find, availing ourselves of the elaborate tables of Louis Schode, Esq., that we should have had in this
country in 1850, 7,555,423 inhabitants, instead of 19,987,573--a
difference of 12,432,150.  So that, while in the increase of population in this country since 1790 the elements of excess of births
over deaths have given but 4,323,493 of population, the increase
by and through immigration has given over twelve millions--the
proportion being 1 of national increase to 3 of increase through
importation of population.
     If we may measure the value of inhabitants to a State by the
worth of the monuments which industry leaves on the face of the
earth, having meanwhile taken from the earth its daily food, we may
reckon from these data that immigration has given to us three-fourths
of the farm improvements, three-fourths of the cities and towns
built, three-fourths of the miles of railroad constructed, throughout the length and breadth of the land.
     And it will not be forgotten that the kind of population which
immigration has brought us has been mainly of the proletary or productive class.  It is the foreigners who have done the work.  The

natives, born on the soil, have considered themselves the class--
nati consumere fruges--born to consume the fruits of the soil.
Compute, for instance, the actual creating force of the New England
and other native emigration to the West, and omit the consideration
of its capacity in organizing labor, and I think we shall find that
the average amount of real productive toil of each native born
western man, after deducting from his time what the exigencies of
horse-racing, whisky-drinking, attending agricultural fairs, and
speculating in town lots have required of him--his actual productive toil has not exceeded six hours in each week.  But the foreign
emigrant has had no such license granted to him.  The necessities
of his daily life have required an aggregate of fifty hours' labor
per week, spent in adorning and enriching the earth, and in raising
from its bosom the fruits to supply the consumption of the people.

If we may compute the worth of each immigrant and descendant
of immigrants, on the valuation of slave labor--that is, counting
Caucassian blood as worth as much as Ethiopic blood, and assuming
the value of each woman and child at ($400) four hundred dollars,
the aggregate cash value of the immigration since 1790 and its
fruits will be found to be $4,972,860,000, nearly five thousand
millions of dollars.

Another fact, which should not so long have escaped the attention and comment of commercial statistics, is the enormous amount
of coin which has been brought to this country by foreign immigrants.  [A letter was here read from John A. Kennedy, Esq.,
Superintendent at the Castle Garden Immigrant Depot showing, by
careful and systematized inquiry, extending over a period of seventeen months, that the amount of money, almost entirely in coin,
brought on the average by each immigrant man, woman, and child
landing at this port, is ($100) one hundred dollars.]  Taking the
total number of immigrants who have arrived in this country (about
three millions) we may, without hesitation, set down two hundred
millions of dollars ($200,000,000) as the amount in coin which they
have brought to our shores.  That amount is with us now, hoarded
and in circulation among the people.  If it were not tresspassing
on the domain of the society's "Section on Finance," observed the
speaker, it would be curious to calculate of what amount of paper
currency so large a sum of specie might be made the basis at the
rate, for instance, observed in New England banks, of twenty
dollars in bank notes to one dollar in coin.  Fortunately, however,
for the business of the country--annually aggravated and periodi-
cally exploded by undue issues of bank paper and bank credits--
fortunately, the great part of this coin remains hoarded or in
circulation among the people, who wisely prefer to trust themselves
rather than banks of issue.

It was the steady flow of this money, brought by foreign emigrants, as well as of money carried by native emigrants, into the
Western States of the Union, at a rate, perhaps, of ($100,000)

one hundred dollars per day, which, in 1856, sustained the enormously inflated prices of everything in the West, when otherwise
they must have fallen upon the fall of nearly one-half in the
price of breadstuffs, upon which alone the West relied to buy
manufactures and pay debts.

Report of S. P. Dinsmore to the Section on Political Statutes
of the American Geographical and Statistical Society, New York,
March, 1858, Hunt's Merchants' Magazine, May, 1858, pp. 645-646.

# G.

# SLAVERY AND THE ECONOMY

220.  FINANCE EMANCIPATION OF SLAVES BY SALE
OF PUBLIC LAND (1819)

A favorite solution for the slavery problem was
voluntary emancipation followed by colonization in
Africa.  Madison added to this a novel proposal for
financing the solution.

Supposing the number of slaves to be 1,500,000, and their
price to average 400 drs, the cost of the whole would be 600 millions
of doll$^{rs}$.  These estimates are probably beyond the fact; and from
the n$^o$. of slaves should be deducted  1.  those whom their masters
would not part with.  2.  those who may be gratuitously set free
by their masters.  3.  those acquiring freedom under emancipating
regulations of the States.  4.  those preferring slavery where they
are, to freedom in an African settlement.  On the other hand, it is
to be noted that the expence of removal & settlement is not included in the estimated sum; and that an increase of the slaves will
be going on during the period required for the execution of the plan.
On the whole the aggregate sum needed may be stated at about
600 Mil$^s$. of dollars.
This will require 200 mil$^s$. of acres at 3 dol$^{rs}$. per acre; or
300 mil$^s$. at 2 doll$^{rs}$. per acre a quantity, which tho' great in itself, is perhaps not a third part of the disposable territory belonging to the U.S.  And to what object so good so great & so
glorious, could that peculiar fund of wealth be appropriated?  Whilst
the sale of territory would, on one hand be planting one desert with
a free & civilized people, it would on the other, be giving freedom

to another people, and filling with them another desert. And if in
any instances, wrong has been done by our forefathers to people of
one colour, in dispossessing them of their soil, what better atone-
ment is now in our power than that of making what is rightfully
acquired a source of justice & of blessings to a people of another
colour?

As the revolution to be produced in the condition of the
negroes must be gradual, it will suffice if the sale of territory
keep pace with its progress.  For a time at least the proceeds w. be
in advance.  In this case it might be best, after deducting the expence incident to the surveys & sales, to place the surplus in a
situation where its increase might correspond with the natural
increase of the unpurchased slaves.  Should the proceeds at any
time fall short of the calls for their application, anticipations
might be made by temporary loans to be discharged as the land should
find a market.

But it is probable that for a considerable period, the sales
would exceed the calls.  Masters would not be willing to strip their
plantations & farms of their laborers too rapidly.  The slaves themselves, connected as they generally are by tender ties with others
under other masters, would be kept from the list of emigrants by
the want of the multiplied consents to be obtained.  It is probable
indeed that for a long time a certain portion of the proceeds might
safely continue applicable to the discharge of the debts or to other
purposes of the nation.  Or it might be most convenient, in the out-
set, to appropriate a certain proportion only of the income from
sales, to the object in view, leaving the residue otherwise applicable.

Letter, James Madison to Robert J. Evans, June 15, 1819,
Papers of James Madison, Vol. 66, Library of Congress.


221.   THE ILLEGAL SLAVE TRADE (1819)


In 1808, in accordance with Constitutional provision,
Congress outlawed the further importation of slaves into
the United States.  Illegal trade, however, continued,
especially under the spur of burgeoning cotton cultivation.
While because of its nature the precise extent of the illegal trade was unknown, its existence was notorious.  This
statement was made by Joseph Story, an associate Justice
of the U.S. Supreme Court, a teacher at Harvard Law School,
and a writer on legal subjects.


Under such circumstances it might well be supposed that the
slave trade would in practice be extinguished; that virtuous men
would, by their abhorrence, stay its polluted march, and wicked men

would be overawed by its potent punishment.  But unfortunately the
case is far otherwise.  We have but too many melancholy proofs from
unquestionable sources, that it is still carried on with all the
implaceable ferocity and insatiable rapacity of former times.
Avarice has grown more subtle in its evasions; it watches and seizes
its prey with an appetite quickened rather than suppressed by its
guilty vigils.  American citizens are steeped up to their very
mouths (I scarcely use too bold a figure) in this stream of iniquity.
They throng to the coasts of Africa under the stained flags of Spain
and Portugal, sometimes selling abroad "their cargoes of despair,"
and sometimes bringing them into some of our southern ports, and
there, under the forms of the law, defeating the purposes of the
law itself, and legalizing their inhuman but profitable adventures.
I wish I could say that New England and New England men were free
from this deep pollution.  But there is some reason to believe, that
they who drive a loathsome traffic, 'and buy the muscles and the
bones of men,' are to be found here also.

Charge to grand juries of the federal court, October term,
1819 in Boston and November term, 1819 in Providence, William W.
Story (ed.), Life and Letters of Joseph Story, I, (Boston,
Massachusetts:  Charles C. Little and James Brown, 1851), p. 340.

### 222.   ECONOMIC DEVELOPMENT OF THE AUSTIN COLONY
WAITS UPON SLAVERY (1825)

For more than the first half of American history,
economic development was interpreted as the ability to
enter into world commerce.  In part, this expressed the
persistent colonial inability to develop domestic manufactures; in part, it was an attempt to seek a large
market the like of which existed nowhere at home.  Cotton,
the great world product, needed only cheap slave labor
and it could herald the development of Texas even as it was
already developing Alabama and Mississippi.  This letter
was written by Stephen Austin whose father Moses, had
obtained the original land grant from Mexico; Stephen had
the primary responsibility for organizing the colony.

Nothing but foreign commerce, particularly the exportation of
cotton to Europe, can enrich the inhabitants of this section of the
State; and this cannot be expected without an increase of population,
and physical force; for without this, Capitalists will not undertake
to enter into it, with vessels of sufficient size, for European
Commerce; and to obtain these great benefits to the full extent that
would indubitably result to the nation, by the enterprise and industry of these new colonists, it is in my opinion a matter of the

greatest importance, to authorize the emigrants [from the United States] to bring in their Slaves and Servants; and that the right of property in these servants so introduced, as well as their descendants, be guaranteed to them by law; for without this security, we cannot expect colonists with large and competent means, nor can we have hands for the cultivation of Cotton or Sugar; and consequently these fertile lands, instead of being occupied by wealthy planters, will remain for many years, in the hands of mere shepherds, or poor people, who will scarcely raise a sufficiency for the sustenance of their families, without any overplus of sufficient importance to give an impulse to active foreign commerce.

Letter, Stephen F. Austin to Governor Rafael Gonzales, April 4, 1825; Eugene C. Barker (ed.), The Austin Papers, Part 2. (Washington, D.C.:  Government Printing Office, 1924), pp. 1066-1067.  (Annual Report of the American Historical Association for the Year 1919).

223.  CONDITION OF THE SOUTHERN SLAVE WORSENING (1836)

This report by a slave of worsening conditions for slaves is contrary to the weight of the evidence.  It must be said, however, that little of that evidence consists of slaves' testimony.

It has been supposed, by many, that the state of the southern slaves is constantly becoming better; and that the treatment which they receive at the hands of their masters, is progressively milder and more humane; but the contrary of all this, is unquestionably the truth; for, under the bad culture which is practised in the South, the land is constantly becoming poorer, and the means of getting food, more and more difficult.  So long as the land is new and rich, and produces corn and sweet potatoes abundantly, the black people seldom suffer greatly for food; but, when the ground is all cleared, and planted in rice or cotton, corn and potatoes become scarce; and when corn has to be bought on a cotton plantation, the people must expect to make acquaintance with hunger.

Slavery in the United States:  A Narrative of the Life and Adventures of Charles Ball, A Black Man, (Lewiston, Pennsylvania: John W. Shugert, 1836), pp. 6-7.

224.  FREE LABOR IS CHEAPER THAN SLAVE LABOR IN
ATHENS, GEORGIA TEXTILE MILL (1842)


Again and again, the same report by southern apologists
is encountered.  What is usually meant is that less out-of-
pocket cash was needed to pay a white worker.  Apparently
non-existent is a labor-cost calculation which would also
indicate labor-cost-per unit of output as between slave and
free workers.  Complicating the calculation is what costs
to allocate to "depreciation" in the matter of a slave owned
by the factory owner; another, is how to represent the increment in value accruing from children born of slave workers.


On the banks of the Oconee river--one fork of which runs close
by the town of Athens, in a deep valley, the town itself being on a
hill, and the other forks at a distance for a few miles only--are
three cotton factories, all worked by water-power, and used for
spinning yarn, and weaving cloth of coarse qualities for local consumption only.  I visited one of these, and ascertained that the
other two were very similar to it in size and operations.  In each
of them there are employed from 80 to 100 persons, and about an
equal number of white and black.  In one of them, the blacks are
the property of the mill-owner, but in the other two they are the
slaves of planters, hired out at monthly wages to work in the factory.  There is no difficulty among them on account of colour, the
white girls working in the same room and at the same loom with the
black girls; and boys of each colour, as well as men and women,
working together without apparent repugnance or objection.  This is
only one among the many proofs I had witnested of the fact, that the
prejudice of colour is not nearly so strong in the South as in the
North.  Here, it is not at all uncommon to see the black slaves of
both sexes, shake hands with white people when they meet, and interchange friendly personal inquiries; but at the North I do not remember to have witnessed this once; and neither in Boston, New York,
or Philadelphia would white persons generally like to be seen shak-
ing hands and talking familiarly with blacks in the streets.
The negroes here are found to be quite as easily taught to
perform all the required duties of spinners and weavers as the
whites, and are just as tractable when taught; but their labour is
dearer than that of the whites, for whilst the free boys and girls
employed receive about 700 dollars per month, out of which they find
themselves, the slaves are paid the same wages (which is handed over
to their owners,) and the mill-owner has to feed them all in addition; so that the free labour is much cheaper to him than the slave;
and the hope expressed by the proprietor to me was, that the progressive increase of white population by immigration, would enable
him to employ wholly their free labour, which, to him would be more
advantageous.  The white families engaged in these factories, live

in loghuts clustered about the establishment on the river's bank, and the negroes repair to the huts allowed them by their owners when they are near, or stay at the mill, when their master's plantation is far off.

Buckingham, The Slave States of America, II, pp. 111-113.

225.  ENGLAND HOPES TO GAIN BUSINESS FROM AN
ABOLITION OF SLAVERY (1843)

Texas was an independent republic which had seceded from Mexico.  Relations between the two were not good; England often acted as a go-between in relations between Texas and Mexico.  American officials suspected that England was pressuring Texas to abolish slavery in exchange for favorable trade treaties.  Governor Sam Houston denied this, as did the British.  Nevertheless, men representing Southern influence in the American government discussed the issue, if only defensively.  These observations were made by Abel Upshur, the Secretary of State.  He had been a lawyer and was a pro-slave advocate of the annexation of Texas; he wrote to Edward Everett, a former governor of Massachusetts, who, while in Congress, had adopted a compromising attitude toward slavery.

It is impossible to suppose that England is actuated in this matter [of abolishing slavery in Texas] by a mere feeling of philanthropy.  We are forced to believe that she is acting upon motives more in the usual course of policy among great nations, yet equally worthy of her, as a wise and powerful country.  Her objects undoubtedly are to revive the industry of her East and West India Colonies, to find new markets for her surplus manufactures, and to destroy, as far as possible, the rivalry and competition of the manufactures of the United States.  That the abolition of African Slavery throughout the Western World would lead to these results, is altogether probable.  At all events, the plan is sufficiently promising to have engaged the anxious attention of British statesmen; and, for that reason, if for no other, it is worthy of careful consideration by us.

It is well known that the physical constitution of the African is much better adapted to tropical climates than that of the European.  Indeed, in those regions of America which are best suited to the production of sugar, cotton, and rice, the labor of white men cannot be used to any considerable extent.  The soils and climates of the East and West India colonies of Great Britain are

adapted to the production of all these articles; and to these may
be added the finer kinds of tobacco.  If England could produce
these things instead of being compelled to purchase them, it would
be an incalculable relief to her people.  But this she cannot do,
except at a much greater cost than that at which they are now
afforded by the labor of slaves.  Hence, so far as the industry
of her colonies is concerned, she has a direct interest to abolish
slavery in those countries in which the labor of that class now
supersedes the labor of her colonies.

The importance of new markets for her surplus manufactures is
obvious enough.  Nations who are free to make their own contracts,
and able to support their own policy, are not apt to give advantages
in trade, except for fair equivalents.  Texas is not in that condition:  She must make the best terms she can, and be contented even
with the worst, if they be the price of her existence as a nation.
There is no reason to believe therefore that the demands of England
upon that country will be limited to the simple abolition of slavery.  She will expect in return for her interposition and protection, a more substantial advantages;  and that will be a treaty
of commerce granting more favorable terms to her than to other
nations.  This is in the usual course of her policy; and her position as a friendly mediator and protector will give her a fair pretence for such a claim.  Texas will have no alternative but to
allow it.

But the third object which she has in view is still more interesting to us.  Even at this day the United States are her most
formidable rival in commercial enterprize and in manufacturing skill
and industry; and, if we may judge from our rapid advancement hitherto, the time is not distant when we shall surpass her in all these
particulars.  Whatever is calculated to embarrass our movements, or
impede our progress, is a positive advantage to her.  Let us suppose then that her present attempt upon Texas, and through her upon
the United States, will succeed.  We shall thus be the better able
to estimate the influence which that state of things will exert
upon the United States.  The question is not sectional.  Although
the first and most disastrous effects of such a state of things
would be felt in the slave-holding States, they would extend to
and embrace important interests in every other part of the country.
We must contemplate it, therefore, as a national question, and endeavor to ascertain its bearing upon the United States as such, and
upon the several portions of the United States.  It is worthy also
of consideration as a measure of humanity with reference to the
slaves themselves.


Confidential instructions, Secretary of State Abel P. Upshur
to U.S. Minister to England Edward Everett, September 28, 1843,
William R. Manning (ed.), Diplomatic Correspondence of the United
States.  Inter-American Affairs, 1831-1860, VII, (Washington, D.C.:
Carnegie Endowment for International Peace, 1936), pp. 11-12.

## 226.   MEXICAN PEONAGE AND TEXAN SLAVERY (1845)

Unfree labor in Mexico existed principally in the
form of peonage, based on debt slavery arising out of
advances from the landowner to the worker.  The peon was
very much a person under Mexican law; while the slave was a
piece of property under American law.  Still, on the basis of
of day-to-day routine there was probably very little to
favor one mode of servitude over the other.  The writer,
Mayfield, was at the time a member of the Texas Constitutional Convention; Calhoun was Secretary of State.


By the Mexican law of Master and Servant, which I have before
me--(their laws relating to peones) the labouring classes are placed
in a condition inferior to our slaves.  If they work for any one,
as they must do, for the lands are owned by few great proprietors,
they must enter into articles of apprenticeship, and receive their
supplies of food, clothing and otherwise from their Masters, the
owner of the hacienda or rancho, who for that purpose always keep a
store of such things as are necessary or tempting to the peon.  As
long as he remains indebted to his master or the contract lasts, he
cannot quit his master.  He may be punished, imprisoned and
"shackled" by the master, and if he attempts to run away the Alcalde
is expressly directed to apprehend him and punish him by imprison-
ment and shackles.  Such is the language of the law.  He cannot discharge the slave, for he is a slave, even if he is punished to excess
by the master.  If in sickness the master furnishes him with sustenance and medicine, it is charged to the servant, and he remains to
all purposes the slave of the master as long as he owes him one cent.
The contract cannot be rescinded but by consent of both sides.  Such
was the law of Coahuila and Texas under the Mexican rule, before the
Texan Revolution.  How rediculous then to raise an outcry against
establishing and extending slavery there.
    Judge Hemphill the Chief Justice of Texas, a very intelligent
gentleman to whom I am indebted for much information and various
documents on this subject, informed me that after two years residence
at San Antonio, and much intercourse with the Mexicans he came to the
conclusion that the State of Peonage in Mexico, as it existed in
Texas among the Mexicans before the Texan Revolution, was more profitable to the master, and more oppressive to labourers on haciendas
and agricultural ranches than slavery in its worst condition in the
U.S.  Indeed he said that some of the old Mexicans complained to him
of the injury done to them by this lateration of the law of Servitude
and wished it enforced against their peons.


Letter, J. S. Mayfield to John C. Calhoun, February 19, 1845,
Chauncey S. Boucher and Robert P. Brooks (eds.), Correspondence
Addressed to John C. Calhoun, 1837-1849, (Washington, D.C.:  Govern-
ment Printing Office, 1931), pp. 283-284.  (Annual Report of the
American Historical Association for 1929).

227.   PROFITS OF SLAVE-BREEDING IN VIRGINIA (1850)

Whether deliberate breeding occurred has been dis-
puted.  But altogether indisputable is the fact that
slaves produced not only cotton or tobacco but other
slaves as well.  The profits from such slaves-by-slaves
went, of course, to the master.

One of the most melancholy results of the system of slavery in
Virginia, especially since slave-labour ceased to be profitable within the State itself, is the attention which proprietors have been
induced to pay to the breeding and rearing of slaves, and to the
regular sale of the human produce to the southern States, as a means
of adding to their ordinary farming profits—as a branch, in fact,
of common rural industry!
. . . . . . . . . . . . . . . . . . . . . . . . . . . . . . . . . . .
It seems a very cool thing to calculate the actual profits of
such a branch of husbandry, and yet it is necessary to do so, that
the reader may see the nature of the hold it is likely to take on
the planter's mind.
The highest price obtained for Indian corn by the grower in
Virginia may be stated a half a dollar a bushel; and the highest
allowance of food to a grown slave at 16 bushels of this corn a
year.  Suppose a slave to be reared and kept for twenty years with
this large annual allowance, when full-grown, he would have consumed
less than 300 bushels of corn, and would have cost for keep less
than 150 dollars.  His labour, meanwhile, would far more than pay
for the little clothing he obtains, and other small expenses, and
his master would sell him for 200 dollars or more.  Thus he would
obtain the highest price for his corn, work his land with the young
slaves, and receive, besides, a premium of at least 50 dollars a-
head, as interest upon his capital invested.  Hence, if there be a
ready market for slaves, this business will be a most profitable one
to the individual breeder.
Again—the number of slaves in Virginia is diminishing.  In
1830 it was 470,000, while in 1840 it was only 450,000, and it is
probably less now.  The number sold, therefore, exceeds in a small
degree (by 2000 a-year) the natural increase.  Now the annual increase of the whole slave population is about 3 per cent, which,
upon 450,000, is 13,500.  And if only 1500 slaves a-year be sold
beyond this natural increase, about 15,000 will every year go south
to the slave-markets from the State of Virginia.  As these will
generally be sold in the prime of life, they may be reckoned worth
at least 300 dollars a-head, which for the 15,000 gives 4,500,000
dollars as the price received for human stock exported every year
from Virginia.
But Virginia produces yearly 50,000,000 lb. of tobacco, and
2,500,000 lb. of cotton, the value of which, at an average of 8 1/2
cents a lb., is 4,375,000 dollars.  That is to say, the slave-rearing

husbandry brings in more money yearly to Virginia than all its tobacco and cotton do!  Is it surprising, then, that the Virginians,
both individually and as a State, should be anxious to enlarge and
keep up the southern demand.

How profound a moral degradation is implied in such a means of
industrial subsistence, carried out on so large a scale!

It is right, however, to mention, as having an important influence upon the public sentiment in regard to this slave-rearing husbandry, that by far the largest proportion of the slaves are found
in eastern Virginia--east of the Blue Ridge, and are the property of
less than half the white population of the State.  The large income
from this source, therefore, flows into the pockets of this smaller
half of the white inhabitants; and though these are bribed by their
gains to defend the system more warmly, we may hope that the absence
of self-interest in the majority of the State may by-and-by lead to
the entire removal of the evil.

Johnston, Notes on North America, II, pp. 354, 355-356.


228.  COMMERCE AND CAPITAL AFFORD TOLERATION AND SYMPATHY
TO SLAVERY (1850)


The former Governor of New York and now U.S. Senator
from that state knew closely the Northern mercantile partisans of the cotton South.


Slavery has...a more natural alliance with the aristocracy of
the north and with the aristocracy of Europe.  So long as slavery
shall possess the cotton-fields, the sugarfields, and the rice-fields
of the world, so long will commerce and capital yield it toleration
and sympathy.  Emancipation is a democratic revolution.  It is capital that arrests all democratic revolutions.  It was capital that,
so recently, in a single year, rolled back the tide of revolution
from the base of the Carpathian mountains, across the Danube and the
Rhine, into the streets of Paris.  It is capital that is rapidly
rolling back the throne of Napoleon into the chambers of the
Tuilleries.


Speech in U.S. Senate, March 11, 1850, George E. Baker (ed.),
Works of William H. Seward, new ed., I, (Boston, Massachusetts:
Houghton, Mifflin & Co., 1887), pp. 88-89

229.   "THE SUPERIOR RACE HERE IS TRULY FREE" (1852)

Defenders of slavery very often argued that free labor
had been introduced into the North only because it was proved
cheaper than slave labor.  The fact is demonstrable.  (See,
for example, Source No. 50).  From this fact, Ruffin held,
it could be seen that slavery is justice to both the inferior
and superior.  This hardly followed.

The superior race here is truly free.  In the so-called free
countries, the far greater number of the superior race is, in effect,
enslaved, and thereby degraded to a condition suitable only for a
race made inferior by nature.  There exists slavery, or the subjection of man to man, in every country under the sun, except, perhaps,
the most barbarous and ignorant.  In these Southern States we have
the slavery of individual to individual, and of a naturally inferior
to a naturally superior race; which, of all, is the condition best
for both masters and slaves.  In the so-called free countries, in
addition to the sometimes most oppressive rule of a despotic and
grinding government--there is the slavery of class to class--of the
starving laborers to the paying employers.  Hunger and cold are most
exacting of all task-masters.  The victims of hunger and cold are
always, and of necessity, slaves to their wants, and through them,
to those who only can supply their wants.  The great argument urged
by English and Northern advocates for the abolition of our system of
slavery, (while totally regardless of their own,) is that hired labor
is cheaper than slave labor.  And this is unquestionably true, as to
both Old England and New England, and all other countries where the
formerly existing domestic slavery has been abolished, because (and
only because) it had ceased to be the most profitable to the slave-
holders.  Whenever continued severe suffering from hunger and cold,
and the number of the sufferers, compel the destitute class to compete eagerly with each other in lowering the wages of their labor
to obtain bread, then the payment for such labor of so-called free
men necessarily becomes cheaper than would be the support of a domestic slave.  Of course, if domestic slavery then remained in that
country, the owners of slaves would hasten to get rid of them, and
to employ, instead, the cheaper laborers furnished and tasked and
driven by hunger and cold.

Edmund Ruffin, "The Influence of Slavery, Or Of Its Absence,
on Manners, Morals, and Intellect," in The Political Economy of
Slavery, p. 28.

230.   ADVANTAGES OF SLAVE LABOR OVER FREE LABOR
IN PRODUCING COTTON (1854)


The question raised by Olmsted is:  Inasmuch as economies of scale are so extensive in cotton cultivation, could
small-scale, free labor plantations ever be more profitable
than large-scale, slave labor plantations?


It would not surprise me to learn that the cultivation of cotton
by the German settlers in Texas had not, after all, been as profitable as its cultivation by the planters employing slaves in the vicinity.  I should attribute the superior profits of the planter, if
any there be, however, not to the fitness of the climate for negro
labor, and its unfitness for white labor, but to the fact that his
expenses for fencing, on account of his larger fields and larger
estate, are several hundred per cent. less than those of the farmer;
to the fact that his expenses for tillage, having mules and ploughs
and other instruments to use at the opportune moment, are less than
those of the farmer, who, in many cases, cannot afford to own a
single team; to the fact that he has, from experience, a better knowledge of the most successful method of cultivation; to the fact that
he has a gin and a press of his own in the midst of his cotton
fields, to which he can carry his wool at one transfer from picking;
by which he can put it in order for market expeditiously, and at an
expense much below that falling upon the farmer, who must first store
his wool, then send it to the planter's gin and press and have it
prepared at the planter's convenience, paying, perhaps, exorbitantly
therefor; and finally, to the fact that the planter deals directly
with the exporter, while the farmer, the whole profit of whose crop
would not pay his expenses in a journey to the coast, must transfer
his bale or two to the exporter through two or three middle-men,
carrying it one bale at a time, to the local purchaser.  Merchants
will never give as good prices for small lots as for large.  There
are reasons for this which I need now explain.  I consider, in short,
that the disadvantages of the farmer in growing cotton are of the
same nature as I have before explained with those which long ago made
fire-wood of hand looms, and paupers of those who could be nothing
else but hand-loom weavers, in Massachusetts.  Exactly how much is
gained by the application of labor with the advantage of capital and
combination of numbers over its isolated application as directed by
individuals without capital in a slave-holding region, I cannot
estimate, but no one will doubt that it is considerable.  Nevertheless, in all the cotton climate of the United States, if a white
farmer has made money without slaves, it will be found that it has
been, in most cases, obtained exclusively from the sale of cotton.


Olmsted, A Journey in the Back Country, II, pp. 119-120.

231.  WHITE FACTORY LABOR IN SOUTH SUPERIOR
TO SLAVE LABOR (1858)


Broad social-political considerations entered into
the calculations of Southern manufacturers.  Thus, the
following, by a Southern manufacturer, explains how the poor
whites could become identified with slavery by seeing their
economic stake in it.  Manufacturing, by providing poor
whites with a money income—there was no other way to do
this—could also teach them the value of slaves as ultimate
consumers of manufactured goods.  What is more, white factory
labor was more profitable.  James Wesson, who writes, was
president of the Mississippi Manufacturing Company in
Bankston, Mississippi; the firm had been organized eleven
years before, in Columbus, Georgia.  Claiborne, to whom he
writes, was a Mississippi politician and author.


And when all the resources and inergies of the South shall have
been fully developed and improved and diverted, what a large and
prosperous class of population will have been created out of the
very dregs of society (and it may be in some instances worse than
dregs)!
     For if we are permitted to stop here and take a political view
of the Subject and see what an influence a general system of manufacturing in the South would have upon this verry numerious class
of our population, we think it would far accell all pecunary considerations.  It is a debatable question whether they are benefitted by
the peculiar institution, or not.  And as we have some doubts about
their interest, we may doubt their political position upon a direct
issue disconnected from party ties and love of the Union.  A general
system of Manufactoring would raise them above the manual labour performed by the Negro, and identify them with the institution, and
make them the connecting link between the producer and the consumer
(which they would most certainly be in the manufacture of wool hats,
shoes, and the coarser fabrics).  When they become the manufacturers
of the articles produced by the Negro on the other, they are as
clearly identified with him as the owner is, for by him they both
get their bread.


Letter, James M. Wesson to John F. H. Claiborne, August 11,
1858, John H. Moore (ed.), "The Textile Industry Of The Old South
As Described In A Letter By J. M. Wesson In 1858," Journal of
Economic History, XV (June, 1956), pp. 203, 204.

## 232.  AN IRREPRESSIBLE CONFLICT OF TWO ANTAGONISTIC SYSTEMS (1858)

In this contrast of slave and free-labor communities, Seward brilliantly traced the dynamics of a national conflict.  Divest the rhetoric of its cast of inevitability and the statement remains a highly defensible analysis of the essentials.

Hitherto, the two systems have existed in different states, but side by side within the American Union.  This has happened because the Union is a confederation of states.  But in another aspect the United States constitute only one nation.  Increase of population, which is filling the states out to their very borders, together with a new and extended net-work of railroads and other avenues, and an internal commerce which daily becomes more intimate, is rapidly bringing the states into a higher and more perfect social unity or consolidation.  Thus, these antagonistic systems are continually coming into closer closer contact, and collision results.

Shall I tell you what this collision means?  They who think that it is accidental, unnecessary, the work of interested or fanatical agitators, and therefore ephemeral, mistake the case altogether.  It is an irrepressible conflict between opposing and enduring forces, and it means that the United States must and will, sooner or later, become either entirely a slaveholding nation, or entirely a free-labor nation.  Either the cotton and rice-fields of South Carolina and the sugar plantations of Louisiana will ultimately be tilled by free labor, and Charleston and New Orleans become marts for legitimate merchandise alone, or else the rye-fields and wheat-fields of Massachusetts and New York must again be surrendered by their farmers to slave culture and to the production of slaves, and Boston and New York become once more markets for trade in the bodies and souls of men.  It is the failure to apprehend this great truth that induces so many unsuccessful attempts at final compromise between the slave and free states, and it is the existence of this great fact that renders all such pretended compromises, when made, vain and ephemeral.

Speech at Rochester, New York, October 25, 1858, Baker (ed.), Works of William H. Seward, IV, p. 292.

233.   RE-OPENING THE FOREIGN SLAVE TRADE WILL
RUIN THE PLANTER (1859)


A compelling argument based purely on the ground of
commercial self-interest.  Houston, former Governor of
Texas and U.S. Senator from that State, was deeply opposed
to the separatist trend among defenders of slavery.  These
latter, however, regarded re-opening of the African slave
trade as an assertion of the sovereignty of King Cotton,
and pushed it regardless of the strict economics of the
question.


Reopen the African Slave Trade and the South will be deluged
with barbarians.  Your present stock of negroes would fall in value,
and recede in point of intelligence.  Not a poor man would be able
to stay in the country, because labor would be so cheap that he
would not be able to get bread for himself and his family.  The labor
market would be over-done.  The vast army of slaves would be put to
work in your cotton fields, and the vast crop would glut the market
beyond all reasonable demand.  Prices would fall to four or five
cents per pound, and even then, when the demand was supplied, the
greater portion of your crop would lie upon your hands for want of a
purchaser.  Freight would advance to an enormous price, because every
sail that the Yankees could raise--these dear Abolitionist gentlemen
who love the negro so well--would be engaged in the traffic.  Each
vessel that could be bought or pressed into the service would be
upon the coast of Africa.  It would be more profitable than the
carrying trade.  Your cotton would lie and rot upon your wharves or
in your gin-houses, because transportation will not pay, and ruin to
your financial interests will be the consequence.  If negroes would
be cheaper, money would be dearer.  It is easier now to buy a negro
at $1500 than it was 20 years ago at $500.  Increase the production
of cotton at once tenfold, as it would be, and the demand falls off
in proportion.  The yankees would then get your cotton at four cents
per pound, and make it into calico and red handkerchiefs to buy negroes with on the coast of Africa, which they will bring South to
sell for your hard dollars.  To such a ruinous policy I am opposed.
I do not go to the results that will accrue to the African.  I will
not discuss its morality.  That is a question with which I have
nothing to do.  Its practical effects upon us and our posterity are
what we are first to look at.  It may be that the African will be
benefitted; but it will be death to the Whites.


Speech at Nacogdoches, July 9, 1859, Amelia W. Williams and
Eugene C. Baker (eds.), The Writings of Sam Houston, 1813-1863,
VII, (Austin, Texas:  University of Texas Press, 1942), p. 347.

234.    "THE GUILLOTINE IS SUSPENDED OVER YOUR
OWN NECKS!" (1860)

An interesting appeal to Northern rulers, warning
that an attack on slave wealth in the South would spill
over into the North and result in confiscation of property
there, too.  The eventuality was merely plausible.  After
the Civil War, however, this appeal met with a more
sympathetic reception up North, in the matter of Southern
reform.

Many...in the North are engaged in this crusade [against
slavery] in order to divert attention from their own plague-spot--
AGRARIANISM.  We all recollect the Patroon of Albany and the Van
Rensellaer mobs,--the Fourerism and Socialism of the free States,
and the ever-active antagonism of labor and capital.  They are like
the fleeing burglar, who, more loudly than his pursuers, cries stop
thief!  For the time perhaps they have succeeded in hounding on the
rabble in full cry after the South, and in diverting attention from
themselves.  But how will they fare in the end?  It is said of a
certain animal, that when once it has tasted human blood it never
relinquishes the chase; so when the mob shall have tasted the sweets
of plunder and rapine in their raids upon the South, will they spare
the hoarded millions of the money-princes and nabobs of the North?
Are there not thousands of needy and thriftless adventurers, or of
starving and vicious poor, in the free States and cities of the
North, who look with ill-concealed envy, or with gloating rapacity,
on the properity and wealth of the aristocrats, as they term them,
of the spindle and loom, and of the counting-house?  Ye capitalists,
ye merchant princes, ye master manufacturers, you may excite to
frenzy your Jacobin clubs, you may demoralize their minds of all
ideas of right and wrong, but remember!  the guillotine is suspended
over your own necks!!  The agrarian doctrines will ere long be applied
to yourselves, for with whatsoever measure ye mete, it shall be
measured to you again.

Elliott (ed.), Cotton Is King, (Augusta, Georgia:  Pritchard,
Abbott, 1860), pp. 897-898.

235.  A SOUTHERN DEFINITION OF SLAVERY (1860)

The following definition did not describe accurately
the system of rights as it was in fact embraced in American
law.  Under that system, both the slave's person and his
labor were the property of the owner.  The law stipulated no
duty of the owner to the slave, nor any kind of "warrant."

Nevertheless, the following definition, if inaccurate,
was nonetheless of rhetorical value in the debates of
the pre-Civil War decade.


Slavery is the duty and obligation of the slave to labor for
the mutual benefit of both master and slave, under a warrant to the
slave of protection, and a comfortable subsistence, under all circumstances.  The person of the slave is not property, no matter what the
fictions of the law may say; but the right to his labor is property,
and may be transferred like any other property, or as the right to
the services of a minor or an apprentice may be transferred.  Nor
is the labor of the slave solely for the benefit of the master, but
for the benefit of all concerned; for himself, to repay the advances
made for his support in childhood, for present subsistence, and for
guardianship and protection, and to master, as the head of the system, has a right to the obedience and labor of the slave, but the
slave has also his mutual rights in the master; the right of protection, the right of counsel and guidance, the right of subsistence,
the right of care and attention in sickness and old age.  He has
also a right in his master as the sole arbiter in all his wrongs
and difficulties, and as a merciful judge and dispenser of law to
award the penalty of his misdeeds.  Such is American slavery....


E. N. Elliott (ed.), Cotton Is King and Pro-Slavery Arguments,
(Augusta, Georgia:  Pritchard, Abbott, 1860), p. vii.

# H.

## FINANCING ECONOMIC DEVELOPMENT

### 236. "THE ONLY TRUE THEORY OF A BANK OF DISCOUNT" (1818)

Given the historic tendency of frontier areas to be heavy importers of manufactures, underdeveloped areas like the Ohio Valley were further hard-pressed by the need to pay for land. Resort to bank loans become epidemic at times. Senator King, former member of the House of Representatives and failed presidential candidate in 1816, counselled his banker-son to escape infection and to follow a conservative lending policy.

The real, and apparently the insurmountable cause, why money cannot be had, is that adding to the purchase of for. supplies, the purchase of the public Lands, the articles which Ohio sells are of much less value than those she buys: and as money comes in only by selling articles which go abroad, and the sum so recd. is less than that required to be remitted from the State to pay for forn. supplies and for public Lands; neither now, nor next year, if the balances continue the same, will the State be able to make these remittances, unless they anticipate their future means, by borrowing.

The Br.[anch] Bk. may afford some assistance; and if they cd. make a permanent loan, wh. they cannot, they might afford an important Relief. But if they attempt to issue their Paper, upon Landed security, except for a very limited amount, they will throw themselves into great embarrassment. The only and true theory of a bank of discount, or, as yours is, a commercial bank, is this; the security they take must be such as at the period of payment will certainly replace, if required, the loan they shall have made. Now

Land is not of this character, and cannot promptly and adequately be converted into money; notes with sufficient endorsers are, or ought to be, such; notes wh. when due, cannot be collected are no security. I do not mean that the whole mass of discounted Paper could without great distress and even loss, be so converted in any hour.  But there is no safety to a Bk. which cannot rely with entire confidence, that such a proportion of its Debts may at all times be collected, as may be requisite to enable the Bk. to meet its own engagements, or to pay on demand its own Notes Now no Bank, in the great towns even, where the resources are greater, can be sure of doing this, unless it is cautious not to make too great issues; for if a very large excess suddenly returns on the Bank, neither the cash in its vaults, nor the ability of its Debtors, may be sufficient to enable it to meet the demand.

Letter, Rufus King to Edward King, April 5, 1818, C. R. King (ed.), Life and Correspondence of Rufus King, VI, p. 134.

237.  WHY GOOD BANK NOTES MIGRATE TO THE GREAT CITIES (1819)

As Senator King had explained to his son (see the previous document), Clay now pointed out to Cheves that western banking faced some stubborn conditions that worked against conventional ideas of "sound" banking.  Clay was then speaker of the House of Representatives and Cheves was President of the Second Bank of the United States.

When a paper currency is based upon specie it is liable to all the fluctuations of plenty and scarcity to which the metalic basis is liable.  Plenty of specie, plenty of paper.  Scarcity of specie, scarcity of paper.  This is the great defect of our paper system. But specie (and consequently the paper which it sustains) becomes scarce when there is a great foreign demand for it, or when upon one part of the same Country there is a great demand for it to be transported to another part.  The former has been the condition of the Atlantic States in relation to foreign Countries; the latter is the condition of the Western section in relation to the Eastern.  Now I agree with you that the B. of the U.S. has mainly performed this operation, by means of its paper &c, of transfering specie from the West to the Atlantic.  But, my dear Sir, relieve the bank tomorrow from that onerous burthen, and the operation must still be performed, in some other way.  What causes the operation?  the payment of debt to Government and to commerce, but principally the first.  This must be paid.  If the Bank no longer furnishes its instrumentality, some other agency must be employed.  Let me state (which I do from conjecture, that will not be found wide of the truth) that the annual

receipts of Government in the West exceed the disbursements by about
1 1/2 million.  Suppose Govt. were to forbear transfering this
balance to points where it is wanted for only two years, it wd. be
three millions.  But it cannot so forbear for a long time.  And this
transfer produces all the phenomena that we witness in the West.
No modification of the paper system which you can make will enable
us to keep our money in the West, unless you would contrive that we
should not pay our debts.


Letter, Henry Clay to Langdon Cheves, December 13, 1819,
Hopkins and Hargreaves (eds.), Papers of Henry Clay, II,
pp. 729-730.


238.   "THE FROG OF WALL STREET PUFFS HIMSELF INTO THE
OX OF LOMBARD STREET" (1828)


In these days, the attack on the 2nd Bank of the
United States was regarded--correctly, in large part--as
an attempt by the upstart Wall Street financial community
to take national financial-political leadership out of the
hands of the Philadelphia finances.  "Lombard Street" was
the location of the Bank of England.  The writer,
Richard Rush, Secretary of the Treasury, referred to the
old fable about the frog who burst while trying to puff
himself up to the size of an ox.


You have probably as much or more to fear for the Bank, from
New York, as from Virginia, and with even less excuse.  In Virginia,
there are still constitutional scruples.  In New York, none.  But
the frog of Wall Street, puffs himself into the Ox of Lombard
street, and will not have you abuse him.  Hinc ille lacrymae...


Letter, Richard Rush to Nicholas Biddle, December 10, 1828,
McGrane (ed.), Correspondence of Nicholas Biddle, pp. 59-60.


239.   MONIED ARISTOCRACY IN NORTH CAROLINA (1829)


The small farmers and the poor whites of the North
Carolina backcountry provided a ready audience for attacks
on a monied aristocracy.  The complaints were repeated in
state after state:  a small group of large stockholders
controlled the bank, loans were being called in for strategic

rather than economic reasons, bank pressures were forcing
people to emigrate from the state.  These small holder-debtor
views formed an important part of the Jacksonian movement
against the 2nd bank of the United States.


By arts the most designing, the legislature and the people of
the State, for the past ten years, have been held under the spell-
bound influence of the banks; and particularly of that misnamed--the
State Bank.  So great has been this influence, that when a few years
since the Governor of the State had the firmness to call their conduct in question, the Directors at Raleigh boldly stepped out and
hurled the gauntlet of defiance at the Governor and the Legislature;
and all the newspapers in the State sung out--"long live the king."
The number of stockholders in the State Bank we have seen elsewhere
stated to be 495; and of these, it may be said, that at least two-
thirds have been ignorant of the proceedings, and innocent of the
practice of the Bank.  The other one-third say 150 stockholders,
owning more than one million dollars worth of stock are the men who
managed, directed and controlled the affairs of that institution.
These compose the real aristocracy of the land; and of all aristo-
cracies, the most dangerous is a monied aristocracy.  Mammon is
their God--self-interest their polar star.
These Lordly stockholders, dividing a million among 150 of
themselves, have been so long reaping a rich harvest of gains out
of the people of North-Carolina, that they are now dissatisfied with
moderate profits.  Times are changed, and they can no longer divide
8 per cent. with occasionally bonuses of 10 to 35 per cent; and they
have come to the conclusion to call in their debts without any regard
to the condition of the community, but only looking to their own sordid interest.  Let us wind up, say they, at once; let us call in our
debts and get the money into our own hands:--we can make more than
5 per cent. out of it by sharing notes and by buying up property at
sheriff sales.  But, says a whispering spirit, "the people!--you will
ruin the people."  Mammon answers--"What are the people to us!--we
must look to our own interest."  It is better that the people should
suffer; it is better that the poor man, with his wife and his help-
less children, should be turned out of doors; it is better that we
should swell the tide of emigration to the west--than that we should
get only 5 per cent, on our money!  Therefore, let us call in our
debts, and get the capital into our own hands.


Letter to editor, Yadkin and Catawba Journal, February 10,
1829, Hamilton (ed.), The Papers of Thomas Ruffin, I, p. 478.

240.  THE "MONIED MANIA" IN TEXAS (1832)

Some saw the frontier as a promised land of small,
independent farmers who escaped the temptations of commer-
cialism.  Such an escape was always momentary, and ever
disappointing to those who feared the corruption of wealth,
among them Stephen F. Austin in 1832.  He writes to Edward
Livingston, then Secretary of State.


The indians, the Buffalo, the cane breaks and the forests
gradually disappeared--population and civilization soon changed the
face of everything.  They rejoiced and looked forward to the enjoyment of a quiet old age in their once forest homes, surrounded by
their children, and by peace and plenty.  It was all a delusion--
there was nothing real but the pleasure of dreaming that thus it
would be--civilization brought with it the monied mania.  The hostile
indians were replaced by civilized savages of a more brutal and dangerous character, cold hearted unprincipled speculators, men who
considered that to make a fortune, was the great and paramount and
only object of human life--Lawyers, who found in the labyrinths and
abstruse sections of the common law, unexhausted and unexhaustable
arms for the protection of tergifersation quibbling and injustice,
and for the ruin of unsuspecting and ignorant honesty.
. . . . . . . . . . . . . . . . . . . . . . . . . . . . . . . . .
We have a No. of another class--able bodied men, capable of
earning an honest and competent living by labor--but having been
raised in a country where the credit system prevails to such an extent that everything is regulated by it where men of empty pockets
and emptier heads with a little credit to begin with, disdain to
work, and live by their wits, upon the earnings of honest laborers,
they have acquired habits of cunning and the art of imposing by
appearances and fictions, which renders them nuisances to society.
. . . . . . . . . . . . . . . . . . . . . . . . . . . . . . . . .
The mass of the settlers are plain honest farmers, working men
--until within a short time past they have no lawyers amongst them,
and consequently very little litigation.  The monied mania did not
disturb the repose of the wilderness--it enters not the temple of
nature they have had time to contemplate from the peaceful solitudes
of their new homes the war of lawyers the intreagues of speculators,
in short the agonizing th[r]oes of neighborhoods counties and states,
under the high pressure of the credit system.  Having enjoyed a few
years of quietness they dread a change and [wish to] shield themselves from the evils of the monied mania and the expensive laba-
rinths of the old law systems but how prevent it?  Here sir is the
great question which we all wish to have solved.


Letter, Stephen F. Austin to Edward Livingston, June 24, 1832;
Eugene C. Barker (ed.), The Austin Papers, Vol. II, (Washington,
D.C.:  Government Printing Office, 1928), pp. 794-795.  Annual Report
of the American Historical Association In The Year 1922).

241.  A JACKSONIAN ANALYSIS OF AMERICAN
BANKING (1833)


The criticisms of banking were not the less valid
for Gouge's antipathy to the second Bank of the United
States.  His prescriptions, not here reprinted, ran along
the lines of requiring specie for all payments to the
federal government (import duties and land costs); he would
abolish all federal and state chartered banks and encourage
private banking (i.e., by partners who would have unlimited
liability for their bank note issue).  William Gouge represented a viewpoint that wished to combine the obvious commercial advantages of banks with the safeguards suggested by
persons accustomed to small-scale exchange of physical commodities.  He was a former publisher and popular writer on
economic subjects.


We have maintained:
1.  That real money is that valuable by reference to which the
value of other articles is estimated, and by the instrumentality of
which they are circulated.  It is a commodity, done up in a particular form to serve a particular use, and does not differ essentially
from other items of wealth.
2.  That silver, owing to its different physical properties,
the universal and incessant demand for it, and the small proportion
the annual supply bears to the stock on hand, is as good a practical
standard of value as can reasonably be desired.  It has no variations
except such as necessarily arise from the nature of value.
3.  That real money diffuses itself through different countries,
and through different parts of the country, in proportion to the
demands of commerce.  No prohibitions can prevent its departing from
countries where wealth and trade are declining; and no obstacle,
except spurious money, can prevent its flowing into countries where
wealth and trade are increasing.
4.  That money is the tool of all trades, and is, as such, one
of the most useful of productive instruments, and one of the most
valuable of labor saving machines.
5.  That bills of exchange and promissory notes are a mere
commercial medium, and are, as auxiliaries of gold silver money,
very useful:  but they differ from metallic money in having no in-
herent value, and in being evidences of debt.  The expressions of
value in bills of exchange and promissory notes, are according to
the article which law or custom has made the standard; and the
failure to pay bills of exchange and promissory notes, does not
affect the value of the currency, or the standard by which all contracts are regulated.
6.  That Bank notes are mere evidences of debt due by the Banks,
and in this respect differ not from the promissory notes of the
merchants; but, being received in full of all demands, they become
to all intents and purposes the money of the country.

7.  That Banks owe their credit to their charters; for, if these were taken away, not even their own stockholders would trust them.

8.  That the circulating quality of Bank notes is in part owing to their being receivable in payment of dues to government; in part to the interest which the debtors to Banks and Bank stockholders have in keeping them in circulation; and in part to the difficulty, when the system is firmly established, of obtaining metallic money.

9.  That so long as specie payments are maintained, there is a limit on Bank issues; but this is not sufficient to prevent success-ive "expansions' and "contractions," which produce ruinous fluctua-tions of prices; while the means by which Bank medium is kept "convertible" inflict great evils on the community.

10.  That no restriction which can be imposed on Banks, and no discretion on the part of the Directors, can prevent these fluctua-tions; for, Bank credit, as a branch of commercial credit, is affect-ed by all the causes, natural and political, that affect trade, or that affect the confidence man has in man.

11.  That the "flexibility" or "elasticity" of Bank medium is not an excellence, but a defect, and that "expansions" and "contrac-tions" are not made to suit the wants of the community, but from a simple regard to the profits and safety of the Banks.

12.  That the uncertainty of trade produced by these successive "expansions" and "contractions," is but <u>one</u> of the evils of the present system.  That the Banks cause credit dealings to be carried to an extent that is highly pernicious--that they cause credit to be given to men who are not entitled to it, and deprive others of credit to whom it would be useful.

13.  That the granting of exclusive privileges to companies, or the exempting of companies from liabilities to which individuals are subject, is repugnant to the fundamental principles of American Government; and that the Banks, inasmuch as they have exclusive privileges and exemptions, and have the entire control of credit and currency, are the most pernicious of money corporations.

14.  That a <u>nominal</u> responsibility may be imposed on such cor-porations, but that it is impossible to impose on them an effective responsibility.  They respect the laws and public opinion so far only as is necessary to promote their own interest.

15.  That on the supposition most favorable to the friends of the Banking system, the whole amount gained by the substitution of Bank medium for gold and silver coin, is equal only to about 40 cents per annum for each individual in the country; but that it will be found that nothing is in reality gained <u>by the nation</u>, if due allowance be made for the expense of supporting three or four hundred Banks, and for the fact that Bank-medium is a machine which perofrms its work badly.

16.  That some hundreds of thousands of dollars are annually extracted from the people of Pennsylvania, and some millions from the people of the United States, for the support of the Banks, inso-much as through Banking the natural order of things is reversed, and interest paid to the Banks on evidence of debt due by them, instead of interest being paid to those who part with commodities in exchange for bank notes.

17.  That into the formation of the Bank capital of the
country very little substantial wealth has ever entered, that
capital having been formed principally out of the promissory notes
of the original subscribers, or by other means which the operations
of the Banks themselves have facilitated.  They who have bought the
script of the Banks at second hand, may have honestly paid cent.
per cent. for it; but what they have paid has gone to those from
whom they bought the script, and does not form any part of the capital of the Banks.


William M. Gouge, A Short History of Paper Money and Banking
in the United States, (Philadelphia, Pennsylvania:  T. W. Ustick,
1833), pp. 135-137.


### 242.  IT IS A CONTEST BETWEEN CHESTNUT STREET
AND WALL STREET (1833)


One year after President Jackson vetoed the bill to
recharter the Bank of the United States, bank president
Biddle was rallying his forces.  The old charter still had
three years to run.  Here Biddle is writing to Thomas Cooper,
president of the University of South Carolina.  The main
office of the Second Bank of the United States was located
on Chestnut Street, in Philadelphia.


The truth is, that the question is no longer between this Bank
& no Bank.  It is a mere contest between Mr. Van Buren's Government
Bank and the present institution--between Chestnut St and Wall St--
between a Faro Bank and a National Bank.  You do not perhaps know
that soon after these people came into power, there was a deliberation in Caucus of the most active of the Jackson Party as to the
means of sustaining themselves in place--and the possession of the
Bank was ranked as a primary object.  For this purpose they began in
1829 with an effort to remove an obnoxious President of one of the
Branches--which was to be followed by a systematic substitution of
their creatures throughout the whole institution.  This experiment
failed, owing to the firmness of the Directors who determined that
they would not permit the interference of the Executive Officers...
From that moment they despared of turning the Bank to their political
purposes, and have been intent on breaking it down to substitute some
machinery more flexible.  To that spirit, a new impulse has been
given by a coterie of gamblers who having ascertained the views of
the Executive before the last occion of Congress and believing that
they must be fatal to the Bank, made large contracts on time.  These
executive denunciations not having sufficiently lowered the stock
to render the speculations safe or profitable, the parties are now
endeavoring to force the Executive into the withdrawal of the public

deposits, as a measure that would cover their retreat.  This combination of political gamblers and gambling politicans is the key to
the whole history of the relations between the Bank & the executive.
Against that coalition, all honest men should exert themselves.

Letter, Nicholas Biddle to Thomas Cooper, May 6, 1833, McGrane
(ed.), Correspondence of Nicholas Biddle, pp. 209-210.


### 243.  EARLY PRACTICE OF SELLING SHORT (1833)


Having just seen his own stock holdings fall in value
some $20,000 during the preceding sixty days, Mr. Hone
must have felt particularly sensitive about operators who
profited from falling stock prices.  (See Source No. 713).


The gambling in stocks which has been carried on by the brokers
to an extent disgraceful to the commercial character of the city is
another cause of the distress.  It consists in selling out stocks
ahead, as it is called, where a man buys and sells to the amount of
millions, without owning a dollar of the stock, betting it will fall,
and then taking pains by every lying and chicanery to injure the
reputation of the stock that he may win.  This, the good sense of
the merchants, aided by the endeavours of the honorable part of
the brokers, may remedy in time....

Entry for December 30, 1833, Tuckerman (ed.), Diary of Philip
Hone, I, pp. 85-86.


### 244.  BANKING SHOULD BE FREELY COMPETITIVE (1834)


A statement by one of the prime strategists in the
Jackson war against the Second Bank of the United States.
Note the strong argument on behalf of incorporated banks,
of paper money based on bank credit, and of free competition
in the banking business.  This was "sound" banking, minus
the Second Bank of the United States.  The writer is Roger
Taney, Secretary of the Treasury, and his correspondent
is James Polk, at this time, chairman of the House of
Representatives' Ways and Means Committee.

If there were not State banks, the profitable business of banking and exchange would be monopolized by the great capitalists.
Operations of this sort require capital and credit to a large extent,
and a private individual in moderate circumstances would be unable
to conduct them with any advantage.  Yet there is, perhaps, no business which yields a profit so certain and liberal as the business of
banking and exchange; and it is proper that it should be open, as
far as practicable, to the most free competition, and its advantages
shared by all classes of society.  Individuals of moderate means cannot participate in them, unless they combine together, and, by the
union of many small sums, create a large capital, and establish an
extensive credit.  It is impossible to accomplish this object without
the aid of acts of incorporation, so as to give to the company the
security of unity of action, and save it from the disadvantages of
frequent changes in the partnership, by the death or retirement of
some one of the numerous partners.  The incorporated banks, moreover, under proper regulations, will offer a safe and convenient
investment of small sums to persons whose situations and pursuits
disable them from employing the money profitably in any other mode.
It is not more liable to be lost when vested in the stock of a bank,
than when it is loaned to individuals.  The interest on it is paid
with more punctuality, and it can be sold and converted into cash
whenever the owner desires to employ it in some other way.  And if
a larger portion of the metals is infused into the circulation, the
business of banking will become more sound and wholesome, and less
liable to the disasters from which it has suffered under our extravagant and ill-organized system of paper issues.  It will render
holders, and afford them the almost absolute certainty of a reasonable profit, without endangering the capital invested in it.

For these reasons, it is neither practicable nor desirable to
discountenance the continuance of the State banks.  They are convenient and useful also for the purposes of commerce.  No commercial or
manufacturing community could conduct its business to any advantage,
without a liberal system of credits, and a facility of obtaining
money on loan when the exigencies of their business may require it.
This cannot be obtained without the aid of a paper circulation
founded on credit.  It is, therefore, not the interest of this
country to put down the paper currency altogether.  The great object
should be to give to it a foundation on which it will safely stand.
A circulating medium, composed of paper, and gold and silver, in
just proportions, would not be liable to be constantly disordered
by the accidental embarrassments or imprudences of trade, nor by a
combination of the moneyed interest for political purposes.  The
value of the metals in circulation would remain the same, whether
there was a panic or not; and the proportion of paper being less,
the credit of the banks could not be so readily impaired or
endangered.

Letter, Roger B. Taney to James K. Polk, April 15, 1834,
Elliot, <i>Funding System</i>, p. 886.

245.   MR. BIDDLE WAS A BOLD NAVIGATOR (1836)


Nathan Appleton, who wrote Remarks on Currency and
Banking from which this extract comes, was a pioneer
textile manufacturer on a factory basis.  At the time
of writing, his mills were capitalized at $12 million.
During the early 1830's, Appleton had defended Biddle
against President Jackson's attack.


Our experience under the last [i.e., the 2nd] Bank of the
United States is not such as to give us any great warrant for the
future.  On going into operation [in 1816], it fell into the hands
of speculators, and in less than two years, lost more than ten per
cent of its capital, so that it made no dividends during the succeeding two years.  As a regulator of the currency, its success was not
remarkable.  It was obliged to hire the banks of New York, Philadelphia, and Baltimore, to resume [the redemption of their bank notes
in specie], by agreeing to make large discounts in those cities.  It
thus kept up the inflation of the currency, which was the evil of
the time, and by doing so saddled itself with immense losses.  Under
the energetic administration of Mr. Cheves, the currency was indeed
restored to its true character, by a rigid system of contraction,
but accompanied with intense public suffering, which was indeed
unavoidable, but made the bank and Mr. Cheves exceedingly unpopular,
in extensive portions of the country.  It was during this period
that many of the States attempted to expel the bank from operating
within them, by taxing the branches, and other modes of coercion.
     Mr. Biddle came into the administration of the Bank in 1823,
under the most favorable auspices, after the difficulties of the
currency were, in a great measure surmounted; and it cannot be
denied that his management, was for many years, eminently successful, so far as the interests of the bank were concerned.  It may
however be doubted, whether the country is under any great obligation
to him as the regulator of the currency, so far as relates to fluctuations in the money market.  Severe revulsions took place in 1826,
1829, and 1832, and the Bank of the United States took its full share
in the expansions which preceded them.  It was the general impression
of those who watched Mr. Biddle's course, that he was a bold navigator; that he kept his ship under a press of sail, relying upon his
skil[1] in taking in canvass in case of a squall; of which he has
occasionally given us evidence himself.  Now a regulator should go
for security, rather than profit--with much ballast, carrying light
sail.  No one can doubt that his contractions in 1834, so distressing
to the community, were pushed beyond reasonable measure, for the
purpose, by that means, of effecting the renewal of the charter,
under the pretence of the necessity of preparing for winding up its
concerns, whilst his subsequent expansion had a full share in preparing the mad and wild speculations of 1835 and 6.


Nathan Appleton, Remarks on Currency and Banking, (Boston,
Massachusetts:   Charles C. Little and James Brown, 1841), pp. 26-27.

246.  BACKGROUND OF THE SPECIE CIRCULAR (1836)


If the economic development of a country had strongly
speculative elements in it--as in the case of the United
States--how could one discourage the speculation without
also slowing the development?  The Specie Circular was an
attempt to achieve the former without suffering the latter.
(The Circular, by the way, permitted small purchases of land,
of non-speculative character, to be paid for by paper money;
specie was required for all larger purchases.)


The issue of the Treasury order, known as the "Specie Circular,"
was one of the events which marked the foresight, the decision, and
the invincible firmness of General Jackson.  It was issued immediately after the adjournment of Congress, and would have been issued before the adjournment, except for the fear that Congress would counteract it by law.  It was an order to all the land-offices to reject
paper money, and receive nothing but gold and silver in payment of
the public lands; and was issued under the authority of the resolution of the year 1816 which, in giving the Secretary of the Treasury
discretionary authority to receive the notes of specie paying banks
in revenue payments, gave him also the right to reject them.  The
number of these banks had now become so great, the quantity of notes
issued so enormous, the facility of obtaining loans so universal,
and the temptation to converting shadowy paper into real estate, so
tempting, that the rising streams of paper from seven hundred and
fifty banks took their course towards the new States, seat of the
public domain--discharging in accumulated volume there collected
torrents upon the different land-offices.  The sales were running
up to five millions a month, with the prospect of unbounded increase
after the rise of Congress; and it was this increase from the land
sales which made that surplus which the constitution had been bur-
lesqued to divide among the States.  And there was no limit to this
conversion of public land into inconvertible paper.  In the custom-
house branch of the revenue there was a limit in the amount to be
received--limited by the amount of duties to be paid:  but in the
land-office branch there was no limit.  It was therefore at that
point that the remedy was wanted; and, for that reason, the "Specie
Circular" was limited in its application to the land-offices; and
totally forbade the sale of the public lands for any thing but hard
money.  It was an order of incalculable value to the United States,
and issued by President Jackson in known disregard of the will both
of the majority of Congress and of his cabinet.


Thomas Hart Benton, Thirty Years' View, I, (New York:
D. Appleton & Co., 1886), pp. 676-670.

247.  SOME EFFECTS OF THE SPECIE CIRCULAR (1837)


An accurate enough representation of some immediate
effects of the Circular is made here by Andrew Jackson
writing to Francis Blair, publisher of the influential
newspaper, the Globe, and confidant of Jackson's.


all the people, I mean the speculators and borrowers, in
Mississippi and Alabama are broke, their Bank paper at Neworleans,
and Nashvill as I am informed, are from ten to 15 percent below par
and going down.  negroes at sherrifs sale that cost 1800 and 1000,
a short time since, I am informed, are now selling at $300 women
and $500 for men.  would it not prostrate the Executive Government
to be selling their domain for such trash.  I have been conversing
with David Craighead Esqr. senator in our State Legislature, who
has just returned from Arkansa and Mississippi.  he says that the
Treasury order was a great godsend to the Country, that nothing but
this saved the country from total Bankruptcy and of course the
Banks.  it is very doubtful whether some of the Banks will not
fail--if the House of Hill of Nashville, and Dicks of N. orleans
go, several of the Banks must go with them.  The Banks at Nashville
the other day advanced to Hill $319,000, when the best endorsed
paper by any other could not obtain a discount for $2,500.


Letter, Andrew Jackson to Francis P. Blair, April 18, 1837,
Basset (ed.), Correspondence of Andrew Jackson, V, p. 476.


248.  LET US BREAK THE LAST OF THE SOUTH'S
COMMERCIAL SHACKLES (1837)


Southern dependence on Northern (and British) capital
was a public issue throughout these years.  It arose again
on the occasion of the effort to reform the American banking
system after expiration of the charter of the Second Bank
of the United States.  At this time the writer, John Calhoun,
was Senator from South Carolina; he is corresponding with
Duff Green, an editor.


Such of our friends, who take a different view will be woefully
disappointed in the end.  They may sacrifice their principles in
going with others, but their reward will be scorn and contempt.
M. L. has taken the true view, and no one can do more to effect it
both in and out of the administration party, than himself, and if
he succeeds, he will deserve and receive the lasting praise of the

country.  He also selects the proper state in which to commence
action, and can do more there, than any other man.  He has taken,
the common sense and partriotick view, which opens a glim[p]se of
light, coming from that quarter, in the midst of darkness that
surrounds us.


Letter, John C. Calhoun to Duff Green, July 27, 1837, Jameson
(ed.), Correspondence of John C. Calhoun, p. 377.


### 249.  "A METALLIC CURRENCY" (1837)


Jackson believed that, in the main, specie was the
only safe form of money.  This hard-money view served
as an important brake on over-speculation.  Had inflation
been permitted free rein, values would have been so deranged
that production could not have continued.  Jackson is writing to his factor, Maunsel White, located at New Orleans.


The late perfidy of the Banks must lead to a reduction of the
tariff to the real wants of the government--all cash duties, no
credits--to be received in nothing but gold and silver coin.  this
will be a better protection to our home industry, and our american
capitalist, and to over trading, than any tariff can be--all disbursements in gold and silver coin.  this will keep our specie at
home and give full employ to our mints, and thro the army, Navy,
arsnels, Navy yards, fortifications, and all public works and for
public supplies will give it a circulation throughout the Union,
drive out of circulation all notes under twenty dollars, and leave
the Banks and the commercial community to manage their concerns in
their own way.  Whenever the labour of our country will be freed
from the convulsions of over issues of paper and suden contractions,
then, and only then will we be a prosperous and happy people.  we
must have a metalic currency to cover the labour of our country and
as a standard vallue of property, as well as labour, and I am certain the government, if it adopts this system, will save our country from similar convulsions, as it has hitherto been subject to,
from over trading, speculation, and gambling.  My feebl voice has
hitherto but raised its sound in favour of a metalic currency to
cover the labour of our country; and as long as pulsation beats,
it will continue to support this system.  without labour prospers,
commerce and manufacturers must languish and the country be distressed.  This is a government of the people, for their happiness

and prosperity, and not for that of a few, at the expense of the
many. the people have a constitutional right to a metalic currency;
and they will now have it--this is my opinion, and my ardent wish.


Letter, Andrew Jackson to Maunsel White, July 12, 1837,
Bassett (ed.), Correspondence of Andrew Jackson, V, pp. 498-499.


250.  A LOAN APPLICATION FROM ALBION, ILLINOIS
TO HERTFORDSHIRE, ENGLAND (1842)


George Flower was a larger than ordinary landowner,
and yet, so strained was the money situation in America
that he could not obtain a loan here.  Note the indirect
apology for the repudiation by states of their bonded
obligations.  Flower was one of the founders of Albion,
Illinois in 1817-18, along with his fellow Englishman,
Morris Birkbeck; Wead was an attorney.


My Mother has sustained a loss of all her money in the U.S.
Bank, when that institution failed.  No personal inconvenience has
yet occur'd to her in consequence I am happy to say, as my farm
supplies her houshold with meat, Bread--vegetables fruits & fuel.
A small amount of money yet preserved to her in the rent of two
houses--allows her to keep her servants & furnish her Clothing.
You know the disasters & discredit that has since overtaken
almost every State in the Union.  Illinois had two Banks, viz the
"Bank of Illinois at Shawneetown" & the State "Bank of Illinois".
These institutions furnished 5,000,000 of Dollars circulation.
They have failed.  From these and other causes the utmost pecuniary
difficulty prevails.  Thus the act of prudence (in keeping some
money in what was considered the best institution in the Country)
has been the source to us of some difficulty.  Banks when they fail
here do not die an instant death as with you, but linger long, their
paper getting lower & lower.  From the causes above stated I am
left almost without a dollar, but in the possession of a handsome
property, of 16000 acreas of land on which I reside, town property,
a valuable flock of fine wooled sheep &ct &ct.  I owe as principal
and security to these two Banks 5000 dollars.  Their paper has de-
ciated one half, & had I any good dollars to command by the
purchase of their paper my liabilities would be actually reduced
one half.  It may be asked why not sell some property, simply because there is no money to buy with at this time.  These extraordinary monetary revulsions have overtaken us like a thief in
the night.  I am desirous of preserving my valuable property & not
have it sacrificed to a broken bank.

I wish to borrow £1500 upon a part or even the whole of my property and would consent to give (if needs be) 5 per Cent for the same if the interest is made payable in England, or 6 per Cent for the same if the interest is payable in America. I say annually because the sale of the fleeces of my fine wooled flock would be the fund for the interest.

As interest is so low in England I apply to <u>you</u> and to my <u>Brother</u> to whom I have also written to know if you can find the sum I have named to be loaned on landed Security.

If I were a <u>State</u> or <u>Nation</u> in the Western hemisphere, I should abandon the Idea of borrowing in England—from their utter and deserved discredit. But as Banks & Funds are out of all favour, money individually is now only lent on Bond and Mortgage. The wool growing business is yet a good one and Illinois will soon be a second Australia in the production of that article. I have hitherto kept about 400 fine wooled sheep rather as a Gentleman farmer, now I must extend my flock and make it keep me. The depreciation of all farm produce is so great that I have discharged all hired labour, & my farm & flock are very efficiently conducted by my five Sons.

I have sketched with my pen an outline of my property. The woods surround the prairie & the lands within the <u>squares</u> which are Sections of 160 Acres each are mine. They were the first choice of the Country. No Noblemans park in England can surpass it in beauty, nor approach it in fertility. It is a spot on which I have lived and intended to leave it to my children. But circumstances as I am I shall take the first opportunity of selling a portion of it. Speaking of the loan on Mortgage I would take it paying the principal at 6 Months notice at any time, or for Four years certain. The property has been variously estimated according to the times from eighteen to thirty thousand dollars. My Brother knows it all. The title is new, perfect & Clear.

My attorney in this Country is Mr. E. B. Webb of Carmi White County Ills—a gentleman who stands deservedly at the head of his profession. Should you be so fortunate as to procure this loan for me, I will thank you to be very particular in describing the forms you require, which instruction I should submit to him & leave him to see properly executed. You of (course in this business) are my atty in England and whatever agency or other business charges accre will be cheerfully & thank fully accounted for by me. I shall be in great need of at least £500 of the £1500 by next April.

If you will have the kindness to exchange a line with my Brother & give me an early reply you will much oblige

YOUR OBDT SERVT

GEORGE FLOWER

I have put in nearly the whole of my possession that the most ample security may be offered if so much is desired, tho yet I should prefer leaving out those three qrs marked X as I think I shall sell them in the course of a year or two in the case there would be less difficulty in giving an immediate title.

The property which I offer as security is

|          |      |    |     |       |
|----------|------|----|-----|-------|
|          | N.E. | of | 11  | 100 Acres |
|          | S.E. | of | 11  | 160 |
|          | N.E. |    | 14  | 160 |
|          | N.W. |    | 13  | 160 |
|          | S.W. |    | 12  | 160 |
| also X   | S.W. |    | 14  | 160 |
| X        | S.E. |    | 14  | 160 |
| X        | S.W. |    | 13  | 160 |

1220 Acres

270 of which are in cultivation

Letter, George Flower to Joseph Wead, Royston, Hertfordshire, England, December 22, 1842, Edgard L. Dukes (ed.), "George Flower of Albion Seeks A Loan," Journal of the Illinois State Historical Society, XLIX (1956), pp. 223, 226-227.

251.  BUFFALO, NEW YORK NEEDS NEW ENGLAND CAPITAL (1843)

New England capital, based on land, commerce, and textiles, sought profitable outlets on the Pacific Coast, in the Lake Superior copper areas, and in the middle-western land-mortgage business. The call from Buffalo was no cry in the financial wilderness; New England capitalists needed only to be convinced and the capital would flow. All the more appealing was the stipulation that any direct investment (i.e., for factories) go into goods for which there existed a large and steady market.

Demands like this, for active capital, can only be met, and the profits resulting from them be secured, when, either the community in which they occur has accumulated a surplus equal to the emergency, or when the requisite amount can be obtained through banking facilities, which is not now the case here, or from distant capitalists, who either seek the business as an investment, or for the purpose of directing the produce, in its onward course to the consumer, through some specific and desired channel. The capital of New England, which is seeking business employment, by being placed here, either as bank capital, under the general banking law of the State of New York, or in any other legitimate business form, would, then, it is evident, readily command, for New England, a vast amount of trade, which, if not secured at this point, inevitably finds its way into other channels.

The importance, to New England, of meeting her Western customers at Buffalo, and there securing that trade, which, if suffered to pass this point, will unavoidably be divided, and probably with foreigners, has been fully shown, and the necessity of establishing

warehouses of her manufactured goods, as the feasible method of
accomplishing this, has been no less demonstrated.  But, as forming
exceptions to this method, which, in general, is the only sale, and
will prove the only profitable one, there are three prominent
branches of manufacturing that New England must prosecute, with her
capital, at Buffalo, rather than at home, if she would control the
trade of the West in these.  They are, the manufacture of BOOTS and
SHOES, GLASS, and WHITE LEAD.  The products of each of these
branches of industry pertain to what are now classed among the
necessaries of life; and their consumption, therefore, is of constant and daily certainty.

In regard to the first named of these branches, it is ha[r]dly
probable that the first impressions of the reader will accord with
the position here assumed; for, as it is true of most manufactured
articles, that they can be produced cheaper in New England than
here, such, reasoning only from analogy, would naturally be true
of all.  The rule, however, has its limits, and it finds an exception in the case before us.  The most minute and careful estimates,
by men every way wholly competent, in the case, namely, Shoe
Manufacturers, of New England--estimates, too, made here upon the
spot, and including the prices of rent, provisions, fuel, clothing,
raw material--every thing, in short, that can enter into the cost
of boots and shoes, have shown that such first impression is wholly
erroneous; and that wares of this description may be manufactured,
in Buffalo, from twenty to twenty-five per cent CHEAPER than in
New England.  All that has been exhibited in relation to market,
demand, &c., no less than upon the divergence of trade into other
channels, if not met at this point, from the East, and thus secured,
of course applies equally to this business, if conducted here, as
to those branches which shall be prosecuted in New England, the
products being sent hither for a market.  He, therefore, who under-
standingly invests his funds in this business at Buffalo, will, in
the judicious prosecution of his pursuit, enjoy the advantage of
the entire difference which has been exhibited, in first cost, over
his New England competitors--and which, alone, in an extensive establishment, would constitute a highly satisfactory profit.


R. W. Haskins, New England and The West, (Buffalo, New York:
S. W. Wilgus, 1843), pp. 32-33.



252.  COMMODITY MONEY IN CALIFORNIA (1845)


In pre-gold California, as in much of the rest of
the country, grain, hides, and skins served as money.
Beach was publisher of the New York Sun for which Larkin
was a correspondent.

As wheat is the currency of the country, it will require
quite a Vessel to carry home the payment.  You will admit this kind
of money makes excellent small change, and can not be conterfeted.
...The currency of California is Bullock hides & bags of tallow,
Calf & Elk skins for small change or pocket money.  In our money
market the Californians & the origonians are on a par in the Con-
tefetng way.


    Letter, Larkin to Moses Y. Beach, May 31, 1845, in Hammond
(ed.), The Larkin Papers, III, pp. 216–217.



253.  MISSOURI MANUFACTURES NEED EASTERN CAPITAL (1846)


    Tariffs have international effects.  But they may
also have interregional effects, as between a "protected"
and an "unprotected" section of a country.  Here is a
view that tariffs were discouraging manufactures in the
West by encouraging profitable investments in the East.
(See Source No. 257).


The establishment of manufactories is attended with its difficulties.  To carry them on very successfully, large investments and
a superior population are required.  We are not without capital,
but the high rate of interest, and the many supposed profitable
investments for money, which have heretofore existed, have prevented the appropriation of funds to the erection of manufacturing establishments.  If the rate of interest were lower, capital would
be probably invested in manufactories to a considerable extent.
The tariff also retards the establishment of manufactories in our
State, whether it be a tariff for protection, or a tariff for revenue, for all tariffs are protections to a greater or less extent;
but a high tariff tends more to prevent the establishment of manufactories in our State, than a low one, being a protection to the
eastern manufacturer.  The eastern manufacturer contends that he
cannot succeed without remoteness from the principal ports of
entry, gives the manufacturer in this country a protection which
no tariff can immediately affect.  If, then, the eastern manufacturer was but lightly protected, or not protected at all, he would
find it profitable to remove his capital, and to invest it in manufactures in the West, where nature would always protect him against
the foreign competitor.  No country can manufacture cheaper than
our State.  We have all the necessary ingredients at the lowest
prices.  We have the real estate, the waterpower, the ore to make
the iron to make the machinery, the manual labor, the provisions
to support the hands, the raw material, the flax, hemp, and wool
of our own production, and the cotton in exchange for our wheat,

corn, and tobacco, hogs, horses, cattle, and mules--and these ingredients we have, taken together, cheaper than any other country
on earth.  Even our manual labor is at the lowest price.  But, as
before observed, to manufacture very successfully, a superior population is required.  This we can soon have by fostering the common
school, and developing the genius and mechanical ingenuity of the
youth of our country.


Missouri Governor John C. Edwards to state legislature,
November 16, 1846, Hunt's Merchants' Magazine, April, 1847, p. 424.


254.  BANK PRESSURE TO FORCE REPEAL OF CONSTITUTIONAL
        TREASURY PLAN (1846)


          This extract from the Diary of James K. Polk was
part of a cabinet discussion.


Much conversation took place in regard to the loan which had
been proposed by the Treasury Department.  It was stated, and I have
no doubt truly, that there was a combination of the Banks in New
York and Boston to prevent the loan being taken, with the view
probably to force the Government to repeal the Constitutional Treasury law of the last session.  Mr. Buchanan expressed the opinion
that it would be impossible to conduct the war [against Mexico] upon
hard money, and that although he had been an advocate of the Independent Treasury law he was satisfied that the Government could not
get on during the war under its operations.
        After night Col. Benton called as I had requested him to do
when the Cabinet were about to assemble this morning.  I had a long
and interesting conversation with him on the subject of the Mexican
war & the proper manner of prosecuting it with a view to obtain an
honorable and speedy peace.


Entry of November 7, 1846, Quaife (ed.), Diary of James K.
Polk, II, p. 221.


255.  "FINANCIALLY, WE ARE MORE ENSLAVED THAN
        OUR NEGROES" (1847)


Once more, the theme of Northern economic domination
over the South which is seen in Source Nos. 202 and 298.

Our whole commerce except a small fraction is in the hands of
Northern men.  Take Mobile as an example--7/8 of our Bank Stock
is owned by Northern men--as large a portion of the Insurance Stock
of the Companies chartered by our own Legislature; besides 7 or 8
foreign Companies who do their business by agencies.  Half our real
estate is owned by non residents of the same section.  Our wholesale and retail business--everything in short worth mentioning is
in the hands of men who invest their profits at the North.  The
commercial privileges extended by the Constitution has wholly deprived us of a mercantile class--and thus deprives us (I think) of
the most certain means for the accumulation of wealth.  Instead of
the condition of Ireland being that which we may _expect_ _hereafter_,
it is in fact that which we now suffer.  _This_ _little_ _town_ [Mobile]
_pays_ _2_ _millions_ _annually_ _for_ _the_ _reflected_ _glories_ _of_ _the_ _Union_.
I speak advisedly and from figures.  If a swarm of Locusts should
every fourth year settle upon our fields of Corn Cotton and rice
and lay them waste we should loose less than we do from the causes
I have enumerated--causes not peculiar to this place, but in active
operation from N Orleans to the smallest village to the South.
Financially we are more enslaved than our negroes.

Letter, Joseph W. Lesesne to John C. Calhoun, September 12,
1847, Jameson (ed.), Correspondence of John C. Calhoun, pp. 1134-
1135.


256.  BORROWERS ARE ORGANIZING BANKS (1850)


This extract explains a plain fact of everyday business
experience which often, nevertheless, has escaped notice of
some historians and banking theorists.


The demand for new bank capital springs mostly from "borrowers;" in fact, nearly all new banks are started wtih the names of
business men as stockholders, with the general understanding that
they shall have a larger discount line than the stock, or in most
cases "stock notes" amount to.  It is seldom the case that an
amount of actual surplus capital exists in the hands of merchants,
active or inactive, that seeks investments in new banks; and with
such a state of affairs as existed in Boston during the past three
years, when railroads have "sucked up" every available dollar, such
can by no means be the case.  Nobody believes that it is so.  The
demands of the railroads have undoubtedly greatly interfered with
that class of merchants whose actual capital bears but a very small
proportion to the amount of business they do in a year.  Buying on
credits and selling largely on time, depending upon discounts,
keep good the circle of operations.  It is precisely this class of
men from whom, in a season of scarcity, the demand for new banks

emanates.  It is not that they have money to lend that they want
to take stock in a new bank, but because they want to raise money
for their own business on the credit of the new institution.  It is
then the case that the number of "active business men" among the
stockholders is appealed to as a proof of the commercial character
of the concern.  If the institution succeeds in the course of time,
the stock list becomes purged completely of the "active business
men," they being supplanted by those who have actually money to
lend.

Hunt's Merchants' Magazine, April, 1850, p. 423.


257.  "THERE IS WHICH SCATTERETH AND
STILL INCREASETH" (1856)


A most valuable aspect of Weston's analysis is
his equating of capital exports abroad and capital
investments between regions of a single country.  Both
movements tend to keep up an otherwise declining profit
or interest rate.  This insight forms the basis of that
approach which highlights "internal colonialism" as a
feature of American economic development.  (See Source
No. 253).


The most extraordinary fall in the profits of capital, as
evidenced in the fall of the rate of interest, has happened in
Holland, where interest at one period did not exceed the rate of one
percent per annum.  There was in this case a vast accumulation of
wealth, with a very narrow limitation of the field within which it
could be used.  The home territory of the Dutch was small; their
colonial possessions, although large, were only opened to certain
companies; and at the period referred to, considerable opportunities
for the foreign investment of capital did not exist.  No such fall
in the profits of capital has ever occurred in England.  British
capital--vastly exceeding that of Holland, but reaching its culmin-
ating point at a later period--has found foreign, and especially
colonial outlets, and its profits are certainly not falling.  We
observe the operation of the same causes and the same principles
in our own country.  The rate of interest in the old States is kept
up by constant investment in the new.  Western States, counties and
cities, Western railroad and other companies, are constantly competing with other borrowers of money in our Atlantic emporiums.
Eastern capital, too, secures the Western rate of interest in another form--by investment in Western lands, and a consequent participation in the rapid enhancement of real property at the West.
As a result, the rate of profits upon capital has actually risen

within thirty years, in a marked degree, throughout New England
and the Middle States.

It may be said, that although the foreign employment of capital keeps up the rate of profits, that its transfer abroad does,
nevertheless, reduce the proportion of capital to labor at home,
and so tends to lower wages.  But, without taking into the account
that the income of capital employed abroad is expended at home,
it is only necessary to observe that the foreign employment of
capital increases the rate of profit, both upon the capital so
employed and the capital kept at home; that the increase of capital,
as a whole, is thereby promoted, and that by this increase the
general interests of labor cannot fail to be advanced.  Thus, the
total of British capital has been augmented by the colonial employment of a portion of it; the successive abstractions from home have
been compensated by the more rapid increase of what has been retained; and the new fields for labor, opened and made available by
transferred capital, have raised wages at both points.

New England has furnished incalculable amounts of capital to
the Western States within the past fifty years, but has not been
impoverished thereby.  On the contrary, our present population,
and our present possession and employment of capital, would be impossible, if the Western States did not exist.  There is which
scattereth and still increaseth.

George M. Weston, "Improved Condition of Labor," <u>Hunt's
Merchants' Magazine</u>, April, 1856, p. 406.

258.  "AMERICANS CALCULATE ON THE VALUE OF TIME" (1859)

The Americans are reckless of the present because
they regard their resources as inexhaustible.  Thus,
they regard the working-out of economic problems as just
"a matter of time."

It may be here remarked that the Americans, beyond any other
people on the face of the globe, "calculate" on the value of time--
and time is an element of strength on which they largely depend for
recovery from the late boosters.  In fact, knowing the resources of
the country, and looking to their future development, they are in
a manner, and from a European point of view, reckless of the present.  This, in fact, is the key to the great reactive effects of
those principles which attach to the commercial and trading system
of the United States--principles which have really no limitation
but those resources without which, in any practical sense, credit
must prove utterly worthless.  It could be readily shown that the
credit which America has opened up with this country [England] (not
the credit system, which is always the same) must go on indefinitely

increasing, despite the unsound schemes which are borne along with
it.   Whatever the sum of the phrases "prosperity misused," "stocks
falling in price," "real estate declining," "ships becoming a drug,"
"railroads suspending their dividends," with the declared absence
of any guarantee for the payment of claims--notwithstanding these
expressions, the public may be satisfied that the United States is
not fated to perpetual and over-whelming disasters.   Time alone,
not counting on anything else, will save it.


    David M. Evans, The History of the Commercial Crisis, 1857-
1858 and the Stock Exchange Panic of 1859, (London:   Groombridge
and Sons, 1859), pp. 98-99.

# I.

## ACCEPTANCE OF THE CORPORATION

259.  WHY A CORPORATION CANNOT BE A CITIZEN (1809)

Georgia had levied and collected a tax upon the Savannah branch of the First Bank of the United States. The Bank sued in federal court to recover payment. The state of Georgia denied the existence of a federal question inasmuch as the Bank was not a citizen, holding that no corporation could be. The Court (Marshall wrote the opinion) held that individual citizens acting in a corporate capacity on behalf of the Bank could sue in federal court. The Court, faced with a novel economic institution, failed to follow logically the concept of the corporation as an artificial person. The corporation as such was not a citizen but its officers were citizens and so could sue. (See Source No. 262).

The jurisdiction of this court being limited, so far as respects the character of the parties in this particular case, "to controversies between citizens of different states," both parties must be citizens, to come within the description.

That invisible, intangible, and artificial being, that mere legal entity, a corporation aggregate, is certainly not a citizen; and, consequently, cannot sue or be sued in the courts of the United States, unless the rights of the members, in this respect, can be exercized in their corporate name. If the corporation be considered as a mere faculty, and not as a company of individuals, who, in transacting their joint concerns, may use a legal name, they must be excluded from the courts of the Union.

. . . . . . . . . . . . . . . . . . . . . . . . . . . . . . . . . .

The controversy is substantially between aliens, suing by
a corporate name, and a citizen, or between citizens of one state,
suing by a corporate name, and those of another state.  When these
are said to be substantially the parties to the controversy, the
court does not mean to liken it to the case of a trustee.  A trustee is a real person capable of being a citizen or an alien, who
has the whole legal estate in himself.  At law, he is the real proprietor, and he represents himself, and sues in his own right.  But
in this case the corporate name represents persons who are members
of the corporation.

If the constitution would authorize Congress to give the courts
of the Union jurisdiction in this case, in consequence of the character of the members of the corporation, then the judicial act
ought to be construed to give it.  For the term citizen ought to be
understood as it is used in the constitution, and as it is used in
other laws.  That is, to describe the real persons who come into
court, in this case, under their corporate name.

The Bank of the United States v. Devaux et al. (5 Cranch 61),
Joseph P. Cotton, Jr. (ed.), The Constitutional Decisions of John
Marshall, I, (New York:  G. P. Putnam's Sons, 1905), pp. 209-210,
215.


260.  WHAT IS A CORPORATION? (1819)


The corporate charter granted Dartmouth College in
1769 was ruled still a valid contract fifty years later,
and therefore beyond the reach of unilateral state legislative amendment.  Contract and corporation are the two
focal points of the Dartmouth College case.  Their significance for the development of American capitalism was
fundamental.  In this case, the Court adopted Lord Coke's
classic 17th Century definition of a corporation.  There
still remained a strong distinction between artificial
and natural persons.


A corporation is an artificial being, invisible, intangible,
and existing only in contemplation of law.  Being the mere creature
of law, it possesses only those properties which the charter of its
creation confers upon it, either expressly or as incidental to its
very existence.  These are such as are supposed best calculated to
effect the object for which it was created.  Among the most important are immortality, and, if the expression may be allowed, indi-
viduality; properties by which a perpetual succession of many persons are considered as the same, and may act as a single individual.
They enable a corporation to manage its own affairs, and to hold

property without the perplexing intricacies, the hazardous and endless necessity, of perpetual conveyances for the purpose of trans-
mitting it from hand to hand.  It is chiefly for the purpose of
clothing bodies of men, in succession, with these qualities and capacities, that corporations were invented, and are in use.  By these
means, a perpetual succession of individuals are capable of acting
for the promotion of the particular object, like one immortal being.
But this being does not share in the civil government of the country,
unless that be the purpose for which it was created.  Its immortality no more confers on it political power, or a political character,
than immortality would confer such power or character on a natural
person.  It is no more a state instrument than a natural person,
employed by individuals in the education of youth, or for the
government of a seminary in which youth is educated, would not become a public officer, or be considered as a member of the civil
government, how is it that this artificial being, created by law,
for the purpose of being employed by the same individuals for the
same purposes, should become a part of the civil government of the
country?  Is it because its existence, its capacities, its powers,
are given by law?  Because the government has given it the power
to take and to hold property in a particular form, and for particular purposes, has the government a consequent right substantially
to change that form, or to vary the purposes to which the property
is to be applied?  This principle has never been asserted or recognized, and is supported by no authority.  Can it derive aid from
reason?

The objects for which a corporation is created are universally
such as the government wishes to promote.  They are deemed beneficial to the country; and this benefit constitutes the consideration,
and, in most cases, the sole consideration of the grant.  In most
eleemosynary institutions,  the object would be difficult, perhaps
unattainable, without the aid of a charter of incorporation.  Charitable, or public-spirited individuals, desirous of making permanent
appropriations for charitable or other useful purposes, find it impossible to effect their design securely, and certainly, without an
incorporating act.  They apply to the government, state their beneficent object, and offer to advance the money necessary for its
accomplishment, provided the government will confer on the instrument which is to execute their designs the capacity to execute them.
The proposition is considered and approved.  The benefit to the public is considered as an ample compensation for the faculty it confers, and the corporation is created.  If the advantages to the
public constitute a full compensation for the faculty it gives,
there can be no reason for exacting a further compensation, by
claiming a right to exercise over this artificial being a power
which changes its nature, and touches the fund, for the security
and application of which it was created.  There can be no reason
for implying in a charter, given for a valuable consideration, a
power which is not only not expressed, but is in direct contradiction to its express stipulations.

From the fact, then, that a charter of incorporation has been
granted, nothing can be inferred which changes the character of the
institution, or transfers to the government any new power over it.
The character of civil institutions does not grow out of their incorporation, but out of the manner in which they are formed, and
the objects for which they are created.  The right to change them
is not founded on their being incorporated, but on their being the
instruments of government, created for its purposes.  The same institutions, created for the same objects, though not incorporated,
would be public institutions, and, of course, be controllable by
the legislature.  The incorporating act neither gives nor prevents
this control.


The Trustees of Dartmouth College v. Woodward  (4 Wheat.518),
Cotton (ed.), The Constitutional Decisions of John Marshall, I,
pp. 363-366.


261.  CAN A CORPORATION BE A BANKRUPT?  (1840)


The relative novelty of the corporate form is
underscored by these tentative speculations by a legal
scholar.  On the one hand, Story wished not to disturb
the spread of the corporate form nor endanger existing
investments in corporate stock; on the other hand, legal
responsibility for debts must be lodged in the corporation.
This brought up the matter of limited and unlimited liability, by no means a settled matter in 1840.  Story is
writing to Daniel Webster, a prominent lawyer and Senator
from Massachusetts.


I do not know, that there are any absolutely insuperable objections to bringing corporations within the reach of a Bankrupt
Law; but there are some practical difficulties.  The same machinery
which would be complete as to individuals, would require many complex provisions in cases of corporations.  What would you do as to
Railroads, Turnpike, and Bridge Corporations?  Should Banks be also
entirely subject to the same summary proceedings, as common trading
and manufacturing corporations, considering the sudden changes in
circulation and markets, which may compel them sometimes to suspend
for a short time?  What would be the effect of requiring all debtors
to a Bank, suddenly to pay all their notes and liabilities?  How
would you manage with Insurance Companies, when there are many policies of insurance outstanding on long voyages?  Here again, you
must reach the assets of corporations, not only by examining the
officers thereof on oath, but also the stock-holders on oath; otherwise, in many cases, the remedy would be ineffectual.  Consider what

difficulties would arise in cases of numerous stockholders residing
in different States; some infants, some married women, some trustees.
I see much practical embarrassment in bringing them compulsorily
within a Bankrupt Act.  But if they are brought within such an act,
I think the stockholders should have the benefit of a discharge,
upon surrendering all their stock and the corporation assets, exactly as individuals.  Their sacrifices, otherwise, would be enormous, and the future creation of corporations would be greatly
discouraged.

But one main difficulty with me, is, that if corporations, now
existing, should be brought within a Bankrupt Law, without such a
discharge, it would at once shake all confidence in corporation
stock, and depreciate it excessively.  The corporation capital in
New England would at once lose a large part of its present value,
and be scarcely marketable.  This would be a sad consummation of all
our public calamities, and depress us still more.

I confess, too, I have some doubts as to the constitutionality
of a Bankrupt Law, which should put corporations upon a different
footing from individuals, giving the latter a discharge, and not
the former; and providing different rules of bankruptcy in the one
case from the other.  The act would not be a "uniform act on the
subject of bankruptcy," in the sense of the Constitution.

No Bankrupt Law in England, or, indeed, in any other country,
as far as I know, ever has reached corporations.  Is not this a
strong, practical objection?  Is it quite certain, that State Rights,
as to the creation and dissolution of corporations, are not thus
virtually infringed?  I confess, that I feel no small doubt, whether
Congress can regulate State Corporations by any other laws than the
State laws.  A State Corporation is entitled to just such rights and
powers, as the charter gives it, and I do not well see where Congress can get the power to alter or control them, or to suspend or
extinguish them.

These are first, hasty thoughts.  Pray consider them.


Letter, Joseph Story to Daniel Webster, May 10, 1840, W. W.
Story (ed.), Life and Letters of Joseph Story, II, pp. 330-332.


## 262.  A CORPORATION IS A CITIZEN (1844)


In 1809, the Supreme Court had ruled that a
Corporation was not a citizen (See Source No. 259).
Thirty-five years later, the economic reality of corporations convinced the Supreme Court that corporations
might be citizens, even if not "real" ones.  The immediate
question was whether corporations could sue and be sued in
federal courts inasmuch as their charters were issued by
states.  The long-range question was how to integrate a
new economic institution into the existing structure of
property rights and obligations.  This time Story writes

to James Kent, a well-known jurist.  The case involved
was The Louisville, Cincinnati and Charleston Railroad
Company v. Thomas W. Letson, 2 Howard 497 (1844).
Justice Wayne's opinion contains an extraordinary
glimpse into Marshall's expressed doubts, as well as
those of his successors, about the correctness of the
Deveaux ruling of 1809.


I equally rejoice, that the Supreme Court has at the last come
to the conclusion, that a corporation is a citizen, an artificial
citizen, I agree, but still a citizen.  It gets rid of a great an-
omaly in our jurisprudence.  This was always Judge Washington's
opinion.  I have held the same opinion for many years, and Mr.
Chief Justice Marshall had, before his death, arrived at the conclusion, that our early decisions were wrong.


Letter, Joseph Story to Chancellor James Kent, August 31,
1844, W. W. Story (ed.), Life and Letters of Joseph Story, II,
p. 469.

# J.

---

# WORLD MARKETS AND
# CREDITS

---

### 263. "A MUTUAL BARTER OF MONOPOLY" (1818)

American traders sought entry to Dutch ports in the
East and West Indies on the same terms that obtained in
trade between the United States and metropolitan Holland.
The Dutch refused, arguing that colonies were a special
trade interest of the mother country. John Quincy Adams,
at the time of writing, was Secretary of State; Everett
was American chargé d' affaires at the court of the
Netherlands.

The principles assumed by the Dutch plenipotentiaries in their
note of 10 September, 1817, to Messrs. Gallatin and Eustis, afford
the strongest illustration to these remarks. They recur to the
general monopolizing features of the colonial system, not as just
and proper in themselves, but as founded upon and justified by
established European usage. They affirm that while the Netherlands
in Europe enjoy the privileges of a free constitutional government,
their colonies in the East and West Indies are under the servitude
of absolute subjection to the will of the king. Locked up as an
exclusive possession to be administered, not for their own benefit
but for the benefit of the inhabitants of the Netherlands, that
access to them by foreigners is to be obtained, not upon the broad
and equitable principle of one monopoly in return for participation
of another monopoly. So that the United States, to obtain such
access must begin by establishing some such arbitrary monopoly of
their own, and then by relaxing from it in favor of the Netherlands,
yield an equivalent for a like admission to the Dutch colonies.
When it was observed to them by Messrs. Gallatin and Eustis that

the important commerce of Louisiana, though always closed against
them as colonial, had been opened to them since its annexation to
the United States, and thus by a fair application even of their own
principle gave us a claim of admission to their colonies, they contended that our admission to the Belgian provinces was to be considered as an equivalent for theirs to Louisiana; as if the Belgian
provinces had not been open to us much before their annexation to
the kingdom of the Netherlands as they have been since.

The establishment of this principle by the powers of Europe
possessing colonies, of granting access to the colonies of each
other as a mutual barter of monopoly, is nothing less than a commercial conspiracy against the United States, the only nation whom
it materially injures, and the only nation extensively commercial
and maritime which possesses no colonies.


Letter, John Quincy Adams to Alexander H. Everett, August 10,
1818, W. C. Ford (ed.), <u>Writings of John Quincy Adams</u>, VI, pp. 423-
424.



### 264.    EFFECTS OF BRITISH SELF-SUFFICIENCY ON THE AMERICAN ECONOMY (1819)


After the Napoleonic wars, industrialization was
resumed and initiated in one country after another.
Protective tariffs were adopted in an effort to encourage
new domestic industries.  American manufactures rightly
struck Madison as a certain by-product of British tariffs.
Madison was in retirement.  He writes to Richard Rush,
American Minister to England.


In the mean time the policy of the great nations with which
we have most intercourse, co-operates in augmenting the temporary
difficulties experienced.  Whether it may not in the end have a
more salutary operation for us than for themselves remains to be
seen.  G. B. is endeavoring to make herself independent of us & of
the world for supplies of food.  In this she is justified by cogent
views of the subject; altho' with her extensive capital & maritime
power, she w. seem in little danger of being unable at any time to
supply her deficiency; whilst the tendency of this policy is to
contract the range of her commerce, on which she depends for her
wealth & power.  If agricultural nations can not sell her the products of their soil, they cannot buy the products of her looms.
They must plough less, and manufacture more.  The fall in the
price of our Wheat & flour is already re-animating, the manufacturing spirit, and enforcing that of economy.  She is endeavoring also
to make herself independent of the U.S. for the great article of

Cotton wool, by encouraging E. Ind.$^a$ substitutes.  If she pays that
part of her dominions for its raw material by the return of it in
a manufactured State, the loss of our Custom may be balanced, perhaps for a time, overbalanced.  But a proportional loss of our
Custom great & growing as it is, must be certain.  One-half of our
ability to purchase British manufactures is derived from the Cotton
sold to her.  The effect of her Ind.$^a$ importations in reducing the
demand & the price of that article, is already felt, both in the
necessity & the advantage of working it up at home.
. . . . . . . . . . . . . . . . . . . . . . . . . . . . . . . . . . . .

        Neither G. B. nor F[rance]. seems sufficiently aware that a
self-subsisting system in some nations must produce it in others,
and that the result of it in all must be most injurious to those
whose prosperity & power depend most on the freedom & extent of
the commerce among them.


        Letter, James Madison to Richard Rush, May 10, 1819, Papers
of James Madison, Vol. 66, Library of Congress.


        265.  "WE HAVE NO HORROR OF FOREIGN CAPITAL" (1835)


        The 1830's were a decade of very high capital imports.
But the greater part of these imports were exchanged for
government securities rather than bank or canal stock.
(See Source No. 274).


        Ten times the amount of foreign capital has been introduced
into the United States, that was invested in the bank of the U.S.
at the time of the veto [1832]--and more than ten times that amount
had been introduced before.  We do not complain of that.  Capital
is wanted in a new and rapidly growing country.  Pennsylvania "is
sold to the British," as Washington city is to the Dutch--but the
money, if rightfully expended, was rightfully borrowed.  In New
York there are very large investments of English capital; one of
the deposit banks belongs, "body and breeches," to a most noble
marquis"--except about a sufficiency to form a board of directors.
This is all well.  And we see that at New York a loan is authorised
of two millions and a half of dollars to bring in tha Croton river,
which is to be raised in Europe--and we say that this is well,
also.  Louisiana is said to have a banking capital of 50,000,000
dollars--(15 millions incorporated since the last year), a large
part of which is foreign.  We have no horror-of FOREIGN CAPITAL--
if subjected to American management.


        Niles' Weekly Register, May 2, 1835, p. 145.

266.  PRICES OF STATE STOCKS IN LONDON (1840-1843)

   In 1839 occurred the first defaults by American
states on interest payments.  Thereafter, bond prices
fell swiftly.  By 1843, a number had recovered; some
never did.  For banker Rothschild's view of the matter,
see Source No. 268.

| Stock | Rate | | July, 1840 | Sept. 15, 1843 |
|-------|------|---|-----------|----------------|
| Alabama | 5 | dollar | -- | 67 to 68 |
| Do. | 5 | sterling | 78 to 80 | 68 to 70 |
| Illinois | 6 | 1860 | 75 to 77 | 29 to 30 |
| Indiana | 5 | 1861 | 78 to 80 | 29 to 30 |
| Louisiana, M. | 6 | 1844 | 89 to 90 | 87 to 88 |
| Do.  Ill. | 6 | 1844 | 88 to 89 | 75 to 76 |
| Massachusetts | 5 | sterling | 101 to 102 | 100 to 101 |
| Maryland | 5 | do. | 82 1/2 to 83 1/2 | 50 to 55 |
| Michigan | 5 | do. | -- | 20 to 25 |
| New York State | 5 | do. | 87 to 87 1/2 | 90 to 92 |
| Do.  City | 5 | do. | 81 to 81 1/2 | 90 to 92 |
| Ohio | 6 | do. | 90 to 91 | 84 to 85 |
| Pennsylvania | 5 | do. | 81 to 83 | 52 to 55 |
| Kentucky | 6 | do. | 85 to 87 | 88 to 89 |
| Tennessee | 6 | do. | -- | 84 to 85 |

Elliot, Funding System, p. 1184.


267.  INTEREST IN DIRECT TRADE WITH EUROPE VARIES BETWEEN
SEACOAST AND INTERIOR (1842)

   Although a visitor from England, Buckingham observed
a significant split in the planter interest that had escaped the notice of many contemporary (and later) commenta-
tors.


   The subject of direct trade between the Southern States and
Europe, without the intervention of the Northern States, through
which that trade is now almost entirely carried on, has been recently agitated in Augusta, as well as in Charleston, and is still
indeed under discussion in most private circles, having already
been the subject of a public convention.  The planters and merchants
of the interior, however, are not so eager on this subject as those
of the seaports, because their interests are not so deeply involved.

They dispose of their cotton to buyers here, or at the ports on the coast, and trouble themselves no further, as they find all the supplies they want in the stores of the towns at which their sales are made; but the ship-owners and merchants of the coast naturally look with jealousy on a state of things which leads to the importation of all their European supplies through the ports of the North.

Buckingham, The Slave States of America, I, pp. 184-185. Buckingham was in Georgia when he made these remarks; presumably then, by "the coast" he meant the Atlantic Coast.

### 268.  BARON ROTHSCHILD EVALUATES AMERICA'S FOREIGN CREDIT (1842)

The credit rating of American states was at a low ebb at this time because of the widespread repudiation of state obligations since 1839.  Federal bonds, however, were rated highly.  Here, the "head of the finances of Europe" gives a momentarily pessimistic judgment.  Mr. Green was writing from Paris where he served as an unofficial representative of the United States.  At this time, Anglo-American tensions existed over a boundary dispute in the Maine area.

I was introduced to Baron Rothschild by Gen. Cass at a diplomatic dinner and speaking of the question which now absorbs all circles, the probability of war between England and America, he said to me, "But how can you go to war? you can get no money.  I received a letter to-day from my correspondent in London inquiring to know, whether the United States could borrow money on the Continent and my reply was not a dollar."  He proceeded to say to me "You may tell your government, that you have seen the man who is at the head of the finances of Europe and that he has told you--that they cannot borrow a dollar, not a dollar."

I then explained to him that there had been a systematic effort on the part of England to depreciate the credit of the United States --that her purpose was to compel those continental powers of Europe, as well as the United States, who are engaged in rival manufactures, to depend on her East India Colonies for the raw materials; and therefore the war with us would be a war on the manufacturing states of Europe, that we had within ourselves all the elements of war, that we had six hundred steamboats on a single river, and that so far from having anything to fear from England, we did not fear to go to war with England with Europe at her back, but that Europe would have a common interest with us, that by the use of Exchequer bills, convertable into six per cents we could command men, ships and munitions of war, he said, "yes you may get men and ships, but such is the character of your state debts, that the United States

cannot borrow a single dollar in Europe"--this was before dinner.
After the dinner was over, he came to me and urged me to come and
see him and converse with him on this subject. He said, "You may
be able to go to war, but you must get the means at home."


        Letter, Duff Green to John C. Calhoun, January 24, 1842,
Jameson (ed.), Corrspondence of John C. Calhoun, pp. 842-843.



        269.  THE COMMERCIAL POLICY OF OLDER AND MORE
                  ADVANCED NATIONS (1843)


        At mid-19th century, England dominated the commerce
and manufactures of the world.  To maintain that dominion,
potential competitors must be controlled.  Old commercial
laws like England's Corn Laws--which laid a duty on the
importation of foreign grain into England--must be re-
considered.


        In the advanced state of commerce and the arts, the great
point of policy for the older and more advanced nations is to
command the trade of the newer and less advanced; and that cannot
be done, but by opening a free trade in provisions and raw materials with them.  The effect of the contrary policy is not only to
cripple their commerce and manufactures, by curtailling exchanges;
but to force the newer and less advanced portion to become prematurely their competitors.  This England now sees and feels, and
that to remedy the evil, the corn law...in favour of her colonies,
must be repealed, or that she must resort to force to maintain
her commercial and manufacturing superiority.


        Letter, John C. Calhoun to Duff Green, September 8, 1843,
Jameson (ed.), Correspondence of John C. Calhoun, p. 546.



        270.  THREE UNPRECEDENTED OUTBOUND CARGOES (1843)


        Hone, a retired New York merchant, was celebrating
prematurely.  Until the Civil War, cotton dominated
American exports.  Hone's point is significant, but one
should note that even the Northern articles exported were
for the most part raw and semi-finished materials.  The
primacy of cotton was displaced, later on, by the rise
in manufactured exports.

The fine new packet-ship, "Queen of the West," sailed on her first voyage this morning. If John Bull is not "knocked in half" by this specimen of Yankee Naval magnificence and extravagance he has no sensibility. He will begin to think by and by that there may be some truth in the prediction of Monsieur De Tocqueville that "the Americans were born to rule the seas as the Romans were to conquer the world."

A state of things exists in the commerce of this country unprecedented, and worthy to be noted down among the notable accurrences of the day. This ship has taken out to England a cargo consisting of articles all (with the exception of the naval stores) of Northern production, and the "Ashburton," which sailed a day or two since, has not a Southern article on board. Not a single bale of cotton in both cargoes. The "Stephen Whitney" has only one hundred and nineteen bales of cotton. This fact, which may be the forerunner of important commercial change, is so extraordinary that a list of these three cargoes may prove an interesting subject of reference. The large shipments of provisions may be accounted for by Sir Robert Peel's new tariff. Cotton is higher here than in England, and rising.

The cargo of the "Ashburton" is 3,650 barrels flour, 249 boxes of cheese, 62 bales hemp, 345 casks oil, 19 packages hams, 176 firkins butter, 97 barrels ashes, 8 boxes machinery, 480 barrels lard, 39 packages beeswax, 50 barrels beef, 96 packages tallow.

Of the "Stephen Whitney:" 3,200 barrels flour, 1,234 packages lard, 4 packages beeswax, 1,900 barrels turpentine, 1,137 pacakages cheese, 119 bales cotton.

Of the "Queen of the West:" 4,173 barrels flour, 274 barrels lard, 81 hogshead and 30 cases merchandise, 2,400 barrels naval stores, 19 tierces beeswax, 212 tierces rice, 360 boxes cheese.


Entry for September 16, 1843, Tuckerman (ed.), Diary of Philip Hone, II, pp. 193-194.


### 271.    AMERICAN MANUFACTURERS MUST GET POSSESSION OF THE FOREIGN MARKET (1845)


The American tariff on foreign manufactures penalized those who purchased abroad--the Southern cotton planters. One response to this penalty was to fight against a high tariff. Another response, illustrated below, was to call for an alliance of planters and manufacturers. The Calhoun argument was weak in its prematurity rather than its logic since few American industries were sturdy enough to resist English competition. Calhoun is writing to Abbott Lawrence, a prominent New England textile manufacturer.

It is impossible for manufacturers, in their present advanced
state to attain high prosperity, if exclusively dependent on the
home market.  The great point for that purpose is to get possession
of the foreign market; but for that purpose, high duties instead of
aiding, is a great impediment to that.  The relation between imports
and exports is so intimate that the one depend on the other.  This
the manufacturers of England begin to understand and hence the immense exertions which they are making in favour of reducing duties
and free trade.  They have already succeeded in repealing the duty
on cotton, in order that they may get the raw material as low as you
do and will not stop until they repeal them on food when they shall
be able to feed their operatives as cheaply as you do yours.  In
repealing they look to the foreign trade; and when it shall be
fully effected and low duties and free trade become the established
policy, they will successfully compete with you in the general market of the world with high duties and a restricted commerce.  No one
can be more desirous than I am that you should be successful in
commanding the foreign market.  I would much rather see our cotton
go abroad in the shape of yarn and cloth than in the raw state; and
when the price instead of being ruled by the foreign shall be ruled
by the home market.  When that is accomplished all conflict between
the planter and the manufacturer would cease, but until then every
measure which restricts our foreign exchanges acts as a burthen on
the former.  I object to high duties, among other reasons because
they are, in my opinion, the great impediment to bringing about so
desirable a state of things.  I am no opponent to manufactures or
manufacturers, but quite the reverse.  I rejoice in their prosperity.

Letter, John C. Calhoun to Abbott Lawrence, May 13, 1845,
Jameson (ed.), Correspondence of John C. Calhoun, pp. 655-656.


272.  "FRIENDSHIP, COMMERCE, COAL AND PROVISIONS,
AND PROTECTION...." (1852)


Internal events in Japan were already preparing
the way for a fundamental change in Japanese state policy.
The rise of a merchant class, the need to put down a few
feudal lords who ruled over regional domains, the increasing interest in western science and economy, discontent
with the ruling military government, the pilling up of sentiment for a centralized state and a unitary monarch--all
these factors helped lay the basis for those events--Perry's
visit is one of them--which goes by the phrase: "the
opening of Japan."

GREAT AND GOOD FRIEND:  I send you this public letter by
Commodore Matthew C. Perry, an officer of the highest rank in the
navy of the United States, and commander of the squadron now visiting your imperial majesty's dominions.

I have directed Commodore Perry to assure your imperial
majesty that I entertain the kindest feelings toward your majesty's
person and government, and that I have no other object in sending
him to Japan but to propose to your imperial majesty that the
United States and Japan should live in friendship and have commercial intercourse with each other.

The Constitution and laws of the United States forbid all
interference with the religious or political concerns of other
nations.  I have particularly charged Commodore Perry to abstain
from every act which could possibly disturb the tranquility of your
imperial majesty's dominions.

The United States of America reach from ocean to ocean, and our
Territory of Oregon and State of California lie directly opposite
to the dominions of your imperial majesty.  Our steamships can go
from California to Japan in eighteen days.

Our great State of California produces about sixty millions of
dollars in gold every year, besides silver, quicksilver, precious
stones, and many other valuable articles.  Japan is also a rich and
fertile country, and produces many very valuable articles.  Your imperial majesty's subjects are skilled in many of the arts.  I am
desirous that our two countries should trade with each other, for
the benefit both of Japan and the United States.

We know that the ancient laws of your imperial majesty's government do not allow of foreign trade, except with the Chinese and
the Dutch; but as the state of the world changes and new governments
are formed, it seems to be wise, from time to time, to make new
laws.  There was a time when the ancient laws of your imperial majesty's government were first made.

About the same time America, which is sometimes called the New
World, was first discovered and settled by the Europeans.  For a
long time there were but a few people, and they were poor.  They
have now become quite numerous; their commerce is very extensive;
and they think that if your imperial majesty were so far to change
the ancient laws as to allow a free trade between the two countries
it would be extremely beneficial to both.

If your imperial majesty is not satisfied that it would be
safe altogether to abrogate the ancient laws which forbid foreign
trade, they might be suspended for five or ten years, so as to try
the experiment.  If it does not prove as beneficial as was hoped,
the ancient laws can be restored.  The United States often limit
their treaties with foreign States to a few years, and then renew
them or not, as they please.

I have directed Commodore Perry to mention another thing to
your imperial majesty.  Many of our ships pass every year from
California to China; and great numbers of our people pursue the
whale fishery near the shores of Japan.  It sometimes happens, in
stormy weather, that one of our ships is wrecked on your imperial
majesty's shores.  In all such cases we ask, and expect, that our

unfortunate people should be treated with kindness, and that their property should be protected, till we can send a vessel and bring them away. We are very much in earnest in this.

Commodore Perry is also directed by me to represent to your imperial majesty that we understand there is a great abundance of coal and provisions in the Empire of Japan. Our steamships, in crossing the great ocean, burn a great deal of coal, and it is not convenient to bring it all the way from America. We wish that our steamships and other vessels should be allowed to stop in Japan and supply themselves with coal, provisions and water. They will pay for them in money, or anything else your imperial majesty's subjects may prefer; and we request your imperial majesty to appoint a convenient port, in the southern part of the Empire, where our vessels may stop for this purpose. We are very desirous of this.

These are the only objects for which I have sent Commodore Perry, with a powerful squadron, to pay a visit to your imperial majesty's renowned city of Yedo: Friendship, commerce, a supply of coal and provisions, and protection for our shipwrecked people.

Letter, President Millard Fillmore to the Mikado of Japan, November 13, 1852, Frank H. Severance (ed.), Millard Fillmore Papers, I, (Buffalo, New York: Buffalo Historical Society, 1907), pp. 393-395.

273. "YOU ARE A CHIP OF THE OLD BLOCK" (1853)

The immediate occasion of these remarks was a discussion of American expansion in Central America.

In the course of this conversation, I [Buchanan] told him [Clarendon] whilst our good mother had been all the time engaged, for one hundred and fifty years, in annexing one possession after the other to her dominions, until the sun now never set upon her empire, she raised her hands with holy horror, if the daughter annexed territories adjacent to herself, which came to her in the natural course of events. His Lordship replied;--"Well, you must admit, that in this respect, you are a chip of the old block". Very true, I observed; but we could not imagine why England should object to our annexations;--we extended the English language, christianity, liberty, & law wherever we went upon our own continent, & converted uninhabited regions into civilised communities from the trade with which they derived great advantages.

Conversation, British Foreign Minister Lord Clarendon and U.S. Minister to England James Buchanan, November 12, 1853, Manning (ed.), Diplomatic Correspondence...Inter-American Affairs, VII, p. 515.

274.  FOREIGN HOLDINGS OF AMERICAN SECURITIES (1853)

Foreign investors owned over one-third of all government securities but only one-twelfth of all private U.S.
securities issued.  Foreign investors favored the railroad
industry of all available forms of investment, and preferred bonds to stock by a ratio of 5 to 1.  Altogether,
this would not suggest a very daring policy by foreign
investors.

|  | Total. | Held by foreigners. |
|---|---|---|
| United States stocks . . . . . . . | $    58,205,517 | $ 27,000,000 |
| State stocks . . . . . . . . . . . | 190,718,221 | 72,931,507 |
| 113 cities and towns (bonds) . . . | 79,352,149 | 16,462,322 |
| 347 counties (bonds) . . . . . . . | 13,928,369 | 5,000,000 |
| 985 banks (stocks) . . . . . . . . | 266,724,955 | 6,688,996 |
| 75 insurance companies (stocks). . | 12,829,730 | 378,172 |
| 244 railroad companies (stocks). . | 309,893,967 | 8,244,025 |
| Do......do......(bonds) . . | 170,111,552 | 43,888,752 |
| 16 canal and navigation companies (stock) . . | 35,888,918 | 554,900 |
| Do......do......(bonds) . . | 22,130,569 | 1,967,547 |
| 15 miscellaneous companies (stocks). . | 16,425,612 | 802,720 |
| Do......do......(bonds) . . | 2,358,323 | 265,773 |
| Total | $1,178,567,882 | $184,184,714 |

U.S. Congress, 33rd, 1st session, Senate, Executive Document
No. 42, Serial No. 698, Report of the Secretary of the Treasury,
p. 53.  United States "stocks" and state "stocks" were what we
know today as "government bonds."

275.  HOW FINANCIAL PAPER AROSE OUT OF AN AMERICAN PURCHASE
IN LYONS, FRANCE (1857)

Whatever the transaction and the principals involved,
if it was a credit sale then in all likelihood the credit
rested ultimately on the ability of the London money market
to find the funds.  When funds were tight in London, the
world market was strained to find means of payment and
crises in world trade might appear.  George Train, the author
of this extract, at the age of 28 already had commercial
experience in England, Australia, the Far East and the Middle
East.

An [American] importer of good standing, who has paid cash before--always prompt, good customer &c., &c.--calls upon the manu-facturer at Lyons.  Not wishing to pay for goods at once, he says to seller, "Sixty days after you have made the shipment from Havre, draw upon your banker at four months, and I will send out a credit of mine to pay the bills at maturity."  All right.  The contract is signed.

The importer in due time sends to his banker a letter of credit at four months, payable in London, which the banker discounts, and pays the manufacturer's bills.  Therefore, ten months after the goods were bought at Lyons, the four months acceptances must be met.  The importer goes to his New-York banker, and gives his accep-tance at sixty days, for a sixty day bill on England, which he re-mits to his London banker to pay the Paris draft.

Recapitulation.

No drafts made till sixty days after shipment from Havre.. 2 months.
Manufacturer draws on his banker at...................... 4    "
Importer sends his agent letter of credit to pay
    manufacturer's draft................................. 4    "
Buys acceptance in New York to meet bill in England....... 2    "
Bill sixty days........................................... 2    "
    (Course of mail fifteen days each way.)                 __
                                    Total                   14   "

Here you have an old-fashioned cash transaction, worked out to a twelve months credit, over and above the time the bills are on the ocean; each party receiving a slice of the commissions, and the Fifth Avenue consumer, or the bonded proprietor in the fashion-able watering place of Cairo (located at the junction of the Mississippi and Ohio river for the express purpose of finding a good terminus for the Illinois Central Railway), gets credit for the whole--when, Presto!  the Ohio Life and Trust Company shows that when people appear to have the most life, they are least to be trusted!  And, to trace the operation to a conclusion, the creditors of the London banker are surprised to find that there's a difference between banker's paper and hard currency!

This simple transaction between a New-York merchant and a Lyons manufacturer, may appear complicated, but 'tis the simplest thing imaginable.  The system covers the world.

Apply the same analysis to every other interest, and you will realize the signification of a "long credit."  Now, if you can fly the kite so high in the North Atlantic, contemplate for a moment what the shrewd financier can accomplish in India, China, and Australia!  No well-organized house on those seas pretend to manage their "extensive operations" without a dozen partners, in about as many firms, in different parts of the world.

Canton on Calcutta--Calcutta on Shanghai--Shanghai on Batavia--Batavia on Melbourne--Melbourne on Colombo--then Glasgow, and Manchester:--till at last it strikes the banker in London between

the eyes, who is obliged to go over to the Bank of England to get
their "promises to pay" (in the absence of sovereigns), and should
the bank of England happen to be short the whole pile of bricks
tumbles in together.

George F. Train, <u>Young America in Wall-Street</u>, (New York:
Derby & Jackson, 1857), pp. 260–262.

# K.

# IMPERIAL EXPANSION
# WEST AND SOUTH

276. A COLOMBIAN INITIATIVE FOR AN "AMERICAN SYSTEM" (1820)

        Latin America was in revolution and wanted to avoid
a simple change in masters.  It was felt that England,
which had looked benevolently on the revolts against Spain,
was about to dominate Latin America.  The Colombians
appealed to American pride and profit--a powerful pair of
motives.  John Quincy Adams was reporting on a conversation
he had with Mr. Manuel Torres, Chargé d'Affaires from
Colombia.

        But, he [i.e., Torres] said, the views of his Government ex-
tended further.  They were jealous of the European alliance; they
were, above all, jealous and fearful of Great Britain.  They were
desirous of combining an American system to enbrace this whole
hemisphere in opposition to that of Europe, and especially in opposition to England.  They were willing and desirous that the United
States should take the lead in the system, and to be governed entirely by their advice, and, as it would be an object with his
Government to substitute the use of the cotton manufactures of
China and of India for those of England among the people, and as
they had no shipping or seamen, they were disposed to make a treaty
with us, by which the traffic between them and the Asiatic regions
should be carried on exclusively in vessels of the United States.
He had no doubt that this would be resented by Great Britain--
probably by war; but they expected such a war from other causes.
Great Britain had designs upon them which must produce a war.  The
whole Holy Alliance had invariably been, and would continue to
be, against them.  They expected that England would take and destroy

some of their sea-port cities--for all this they were prepared;
but nothing less than the independence of all South America would
satisfy them, and in nothing less could they acquiesce.

Entry for May 13, 1820, C. F. Adams (ed.), Memoirs of John
Quincy Adams, V, p. 115.


277.   ENGLAND'S ADVANTAGE IN SOUTH AMERICAN TRADE (1822)


Adams saw a limited future for inter-American
economic relations.  The narrow perspective resulted
from Adams projecting into the future the existing
transportation difficulties as well as the relative
industrial backwardness of the United States.


As to running a race with England to snatch from these new
nations some special privilege or monopoly, I thought it neither a
wise nor an honest policy.  Do what we can, the commerce with South
America will be much more important and useful to Great Britain
than to us, and Great Britain will be a power vastly more important
to them than we, for the simple reason that she has the power of
supplying their wants by her manufactures.  We have few such
supplies to furnish them, and in articles of export are their
competitors.  Yet I was not apprehensive that England would obtain
from them any exclusive advantages to our prejudice.

Entry for June 20, 1822, account of a Cabinet discussion,
C. F. Adams (ed.), Memoirs of John Quincy Adams, VI, p. 25.


278.   THE FUTURE OF UNITED STATES-COLOMBIAN TRADE (1823)


The future of United States trade was not yet conceived in terms of investments, nor even mainly in terms
of exporting manufactures, but as this country serving
as carrier of goods.  American traders could not forget
the high prosperity during 1797-1807 when the United States
served as carrier of the world's goods.  Here Adams writes
to Richard Anderson, American minister plenipotentiary
to Colombia.

The materials of commercial intercourse between the United States and the Colombian republic are at present not many. Our exports to it hitherto have been confined to flour, rice, salted provisions, lumber, a few manufactured articles, warlike stores and arms, and some East India productions, for which we have received cocoa, coffee, indigo, hides, copper and specie. Much of this trade has originated and is continued only by the war in which that country has been engaged and will cease with it. As producing and navigating nations, the United States and Colombia will be rather competitors and rivals than customers to each other. But as navigators and manufacturers, we are already so far advanced in a career upon which they are yet to enter, that we may for many years after the conclusion of the war maintain with them a commercial intercourse highly beneficial to both parties, as carriers to and for them of numerous articles of manufactures and of foreign produce.

Letter, John Quincy Adams to Richard C. Anderson, May 27, 1823, Ford (ed.), Writings of John Quincy Adams, VII, p. 469.

### 279.  THE ECONOMIC VALUE OF CUBA TO THE UNITED STATES (1823, 1825)

During the colonial period, the British West Indies were a major outlet for American exports. After the Revolution England alternately opened and closed that once-lucrative trade to Americans. America needed sorely to increase its foreign earnings to help pay for industrial imports from England and elsewhere. Shut out from the British West Indies, the prospect of sales to Cuba grew in attractiveness.

These islands [Cuba and Puerto Rico], from their local position, are natural appendages to the North American continent; and one of them, Cuba, almost in sight of our shores, from a multitude of considerations has become an object of transcendent importance to the political and commercial interests of our Union. Its commanding position with reference to the Gulf of Mexico and the West India seas; the character of its population; its situation midway between our southern coast and the island of San Domingo; its safe and capacious harbor of the Havana, fronting a long line of our shores destitute of the same advantage; the nature of its productions and of its wants, furnishing the supplies and needing the returns of a commerce immensely profitable and mutually beneficial; give it an importance in the sum of our national interests, with

which that of no other foreign territory can be compared, and
little inferior to that which binds the different members of
this Union together.

. . . . . . . . . . . . . . . . . . . . . . . . . . . . . . . . . .

The commerce between the United States and the Havana is of
greater amount and value than [our trade] with all the Spanish
dominions in Europe.  The number of American vessels which enter
there is annually several hundreds.


Letter, John Quincy Adams to Hugh Nelson, April 28, 1823,
Ford (ed.), Writings of John Quincy Adams, VII, pp. 372, 421, and
Charles Francis Adams (ed.), Memoirs of John Quincy Adams, VII,
(Philadelphia, Pennsylvania:  J. B. Lippincott & Co., 1875), p. 10.
Nelson was United States Minister to Spain; Adams was Secretary
of State.



280.    "THE TIDE OF CENTRAL AMERICAN COMMERCE...WILL
SET TOWARDS EUROPE" (1850)


The New England industrialist-turned-diplomat kept
a sharp eye on Latin-American markets.  Though it was
barely a year since the discovery of California gold,
Lawrence saw some larger commercial implications of that
discovery.


The great changes taking place in the Commerce of the World
from our occupation of the Shores of the Pacific, the large products
of Gold in California, and the prospect of a ship canal connecting
the Atlantic with the Pacific Ocean [in Nicaragua], greatly increase
the importance of all the Central American States.  Our people will
find their way into all of them; particularly into those through
which the canal will pass.  The proximity of the United States to
this fertile country cannot fail to create intimate personal relations between us--such as, rightly cultivated, will be greatly to
the advantage to both Countries.  The tide of Commerce, under the
impetus that must be given to it almost immediately, will set
towards Europe unless we take speedy measures to carry it to our
borders.  In this connection I beg most respectfully to ask the
special attention of the President to our Commercial Relations with
these States.


Letter, U.S. Minister to England Abbott Lawrence to U.S.
Secretary of State John M. Clayton, July 25, 1850, Manning (ed.),
Diplomatic Correspondence...Inter-American Affairs, VII, p. 401.

281.  AN ISTHMIAN CANAL MIGHT BRING COTTON TO
MANCHESTER (1857)

The problem of land transport from the east to
California was not solved prior to the Civil War.  Meanwhile, by far the largest part of such shipments went on
ships around the Cape Horn which has been called perhaps
"the longest domestic trade route in the world."  In 1855,
the Panama Railway was completed and was found useful for
passengers and light freight.  In the following letter,
Dallas, the U.S. Minister to England, writes to Cass, the
Secretary of State.

I suppose we cannot have too many lines of Isthmian transit.
Until some thirty years hence, when a direct communication with the
shores of the Pacific shall run upon the surface of our own soil,
it will not be wise to rely on a single road at Panama, or San
Juan, or Tehuantepec.  We cannot perhaps have too many strings
to our bow.  Still, the extent to which we will co-operate with
others, either governments or companies, in projects for opening
these passages, deserves careful consideration.  I think it quite
obvious that the commercial interest of England is contemplating
an extensive settlement on the cotton-yielding lands of Southern
China, and looks to hold direct and rapid intercourse across the
Isthmus.  As peaceable competitors, our merchants, with the advantage of location, would distance them in this trade, as they are
fast distancing them everywhere:--yet it might not be prudent to
facilitate their selling cheap China cotton to the manufacture
Manchester.

Letter, George M. Dallas to Lewis Cass, May 26, 1857, George
M. Dallas, A Series of Letters From London Written During The
Years 1856, '57, '58, '59 and '60, I, (Philadelphia, Pennsylvania:
J. B. Lippincott and Co., 1869), p. 169.  (Edited by Julia Dallas).

282.  THE TIDE OF EMIGRATION TO OREGON AND
CALIFORNIA IS UNPARALLELED (1846)

During the mid-1840's, the possible acquisition of
California and Oregon excited the commercial-imperial
appetites of many Americans.  Contemporaries saw the
westward movement as traditional but, as the closing
sentence of the letter below indicates, the federal government did not care to depend solely upon the slow workings
of migrational forces.  Here, Hastings, an enthusiast for
western expansion who dreamt of a separate western empire

based on California, writes Thomas Larkin, American
consul in Monterey. (See introduction to next
Document.)

The tide of emigration to both, this country and Oregon, is
unparalleled in the annals of history.  The eyes of the American
people are now turned westward, and thousands are gazing with the
most intense interest and anxiety upon the Pacific's shores, with
a full determination to make one more, one last more move, to the
"far West," then to make a final, a permanent location.  The emigration of this year to this country and Oregon, will not consist
of less than twenty thousand human souls, a large majority of whom
are destined to this country.  Our friend Farnham, and many other
highly respectable and intelligent gentlemen will accompany the
emigration of this year.  Among them are also many wealthy gentlemen
and capitalists, who design to make large investments in California,
in both agricultural and commercial pursuits.  The house of Bensons
& Co. is about to establish an extension commercial house, in some
portion of this country.  One of the ships of that house is
expected in a few weeks, and another will arrive in the month of
May or June, both of which, are bringing out large cargos of merchandise, suitable to the trade of this country.  Such arrangements
are now made, by that house, that its ships will sail annually,
for this country, one in June, and another in November of each
year.  By these ships also, thousands of emigrants will find their
way thither, especially, as that house proposed to bring all emigrants to this country, and to Oregon, free of charge, they furnishing their own provisions.  Here I will remark, (but I wish it to
be understood that it is confidential,) that this latter arrangement is a confidential, governmental arrangement.  The expense
thus incurred is not borne by that house, but by our government,
for the promotion of what object, you will readily perceive.

Letter, Lansford Warren Hastings to Thomas O. Larkin, March
3, 1846, in Hammond (ed.), The Larkin Papers, IV, pp. 220-221.

### 283.  AMERICAN AGENTS AND AMERICAN CAPITAL
IN CALIFORNIA (1845)

Men like Hastings who were in touch with the most
influential political and commercial circles could speak
authoritatively, if vaguely, about forthcoming events.
Larkin arrived in California in 1832 and soon became one
of the wealthiest merchants in that Mexican province.
During the following 16 years he was, at one time or
another, U.S. Consul in Monterey, Confidential Agent of
the United States, U.S. Navy Agent for the Territory of
California, and U.S. Naval Storekeeper.  He was a prime

organizer of the pro-U.S. movement in California which
culminated in the admission of California as a state in
1850.


Carry on your business exactly as you would if you had been
in Texas 10 years since & knew at that time things would turn out
as they have.  There is some considerable capital that will be
expended in filling up the country round St Francisco with
Americans that I know and eventually you will have another
Revolution like 1836, with this exception instead of setting the
Mexican ensign it will either be an American one or a new one &
American Agents & American capital will be at the bottom of it.
You have no idea of the feeling there is here with regard to
California & Oregon which by the bye is only used as a blind for
the settlement of St Francisco.  The egg is already laid not a
thousand miles from Yerba Buena & in New York the chickens will
be picked.


Letter, Samuel J. Hastings to Thomas O. Larkin, November
9, 1845, George P. Hammon (ed.), The Larkin Papers, IV, (Berkeley,
California:  University of California Press, 1951-1960), p. 92.


284.   ECONOMIC DEVELOPMENT IN EVERY DIRECTION (1845)


Sutter, who was born in Baden, Germany and grew up
in Switzerland, at the age of 31, in 1834, came to the
United States.  In the letter below, his list of projects
is a catalogue of nearly all there was to do on the pre-
gold California frontier.  Sutter was an entrepreneur-of-
all-trades.  As of the date of this letter, however, he
had not yet made any of them profitable.


In the Case you arrange the Affaire with Messrs Wiggins &
Cook, you would do me a great favour to assist me with the most
necessary Articles to drive on well my business; inclosed I give
you a list of them.
My plan is now to sow here 600 fanegas of Wheat and on the
farm on feather River 200 Do.  I will force the Affaire once and
when it turns one year good out, not only all my debts will be paid,
but I will have a very large Amount over.  For make this business
sure, it is necessary that I take the Water from the American fork
to Water my Wheat fields.  If Capt. Grimes would assist me to
build the dam it would be the same benefit for him.  He is coming
here in a few days.  I will propose it to him.  Perhaps he agree
to it.  If not I will do it alone.  Great advantages will come
from this business.  I can build on the same Canal a Grist and Saw

Mill, and the Ditch will enclose the whole rincoan, so that no
Cattle can passe over and go in the fields.  I experienced now how
a tolerable good Crop can be raised, if it is not a very wet year;
but I like to be sure that I can depend on.  I am tired to labour
in vain.  It is a great advantage that I have such a good and sure
Market of the Wheat to the Russians.  They would take any Quantity
of Wheat which I furnish them, because their Colonies in the North
are increasing very rapidly.  Don Pedro told that if I could give
them a full Cargo for four, 400 Tonne Ships they would take it.
In a few years their Contract with the Hudsons Bay Compy. is expired.
The promised me also to give me the preference of this Contract.
It is 7000 fanegas of wheat every Year.  The demand will be stronger
every Year, because the Russian American Comp. made a Contract with
the Emperor to supplie Kamtchatka with Wheat etc Not Only Wheat
any Quantity of flour they would take, the same time a large Quantity
of Beans, Peas, Soap, Manteca and other Articles.  And what a good
pay, in Notes or Bills of San Petersburg.  If I have now in the time
Assistance with the propre Articles for an Amt. of about 4 a 5000
Dollars worth, I am certain that in two years from Now I am able to
make a fortune, because every thing is now arranged and prepared.
In one Word the Establishment is here to produce the demands of the
Russians.

I wish you could come here and convince yourself of the whole
situation.  I looke upon you as the only person in this Country
who assist and encourage enterprise.  My Enemy's Flugge & Weber
perhaps a few others more do their best to ruin my Credit, and so I
labor under a great many disavantages, and for one of my branche
business it is very injurious to me that I am not all time a little
supplied with some Necessary Articles, that is particular for my
Trappers.  Mr. Sinclair got a good Dean of furs from my boys, so did
Mr. Cordua and a good Many others for some Articles which I have
none; but any how it is not right that my Neighbours act in this
Manner, knowing that this boys are hired by me, furnished with the
complet equipement, and all of them in debt to me.  Dr. Marsh is
the badest of all.  He give the Grog for furs and robed me in this
Manner of a large Amount; but I shall take other Measures about
this.

This Year I pay a considerable Amount of my debts, the half
to the Hud. Bay Compie., a good Amount to the Russians.  Mr. Thompson
and others I shall be abble to pay them at least half in furs.  It
is no doubt my Trappers are doing well this time.  I the Month of
September I fit out the Canoes for the Rivers, lakes and Bay, and a
small party in the Mountains where Lieutt fremont passed.  There
are yet plenty of Beaver and never disturbed before by trappers.

A great Advantage for this Establisment is that we have the
best quality's of timber so close by.  It is only 30 Miles from
here where I have 9 white Men and 10 Indians employed, sawing the
best Kind of pine, making shingels of pine and Cedar.  The pump-
maker is making pumps up there.  The Capper get some staffs out, an
an other is getting the lumber out for three flat boats which will
be used as ferry boats, and the next year the have to take heavy
Cargos of Wheat on the Mouth of the River, that the Launches can
make quick voyages to Yerba buena.  In this Cedar and pine Wood I

intend to build a sawmill.  I think this kind of lumber would sell
better as red wood.
    You will have a good many of the new Comers down in Monterey.
    Some of them have a great deal to say against the Country,
before they have seen somthing, and run her down.  I think they are
very poor judges.


    Letter, J. A. Sutter to Thomas O. Larkin, July 22, 1845, in
Hammond (ed.), The Larkin Papers, III, pp. 281-283.



285.  ADVANTAGES TO AMERICAN OWNERSHIP OF CALIFORNIA (1845)


        Although Oregon and California are treated as separate
    episodes, here is a contemporary explanation of the inti-
    mate interconnections joining them.  The writer overstresses
    somewhat the relative importance of California.


    There are many owners of large tracts of land in C. who hold
them under the idea of the Country chang owners, having no preset
use for thm, as the Indians tame & wild steal several thousand head
of Horses yearly from the Rancho.  Most of these horses are stole
for food.  The Indins cut up the meat in strips and dry it in the
sun.  While this continue Grazing of Cattle can not be profitable
conducted.  There is no expectiation that this Govt. will find a
prevntive--nothng but the fear of the Indian for the American
Settlers will prevent it.  They steal but a few horse from Foreigner
as there is to much danger of bng followed.  Mexico may fret and
treatent as much as she pleases but all her Cal. Gov & Gen. give
Cal land to all who apply for thm and from the nature of thigs will
continue to do so.  Foreignrs arring here expect to live & die in
the Country, Mexican officers to remain 2 or 3 years & be shipt off
by force unless they choose to marry a Native and becone a Californian, Body & Soul.  This Ports in C. wil the exceptin of Mazalan
are the only Mexican Pacific Ports that are flourishing.  All othrs
are fallig & fallig fast.  Here there is much advance in every thng
and the Country present each year a bolder front to the world.
It must change owners.  Its of no use to Mexico. .To hir its but a
eye sore a shame and bone of Contentin.  Here are many fine Ports,
the land produces wheat over 100 fold.  Cotten & hemp will grow
here and every kind of fruit there is in New Eng--granes in abundance of the furst qualuty.  Wine of many kinds are made, yet there
is no facyluty of making.  Much of it will pass for Port.  The Bays
are full of fish, the Woods of game.  Bears, and Whales can be seen
from ono viow.  Tho lattor aro offon in tho way of tho Boato noar
the Beach.  Finaly there is San Francisco with its rivers.  This
Bay will hold all the ship in the U.S.  The entranc is verry narrow

between two mountains easly defended and prehaps the most magnuficnt
Harbour in the World and at present of as much use to the civilized
world as if it did not exist.  Some day or other this will belong to
som Naval power.  This every Native is prepared for....Words can not
express the advantag and importance of San F. to a Naval power.
There is 500 to 1000 Am Whaelers with 20000 Amm Seamn in the Pacific.
Half of them will be withen 20 day sail of San F. While the port
belogs to Mex. its a safe place for whale ship in a war with England
fran or Russian.  Should one of these Native own the port and at some
future day declare war aganst the U.S. what the results.  It require
not the discruptin from the writer nor from anyone.  If Congres
wishes the extention[?] of the Navy, our Naval power or our commerce
St F. must be obtaind, or the Origon & Cali must becone a Nation
withn themsefs.  Time is continually brngng this into notice, and
one of the two must soon be consumated or if the Origon dispute
continues let E. take 8 degres N of the Colunbia and purchase 8
Degres S. of 42 of Mex. and exchange.

The Origon will never be a benefit to the U.S. if England owns
St. F.  Vessels sometimes lay withen the bar of the Columbia 30 to
40 days waiting an opportunity to go out.  When once out they can
reach St. F. in 4 days, a Steam Boat in less than two days.  The
time will soon arrive when by steam a person will go from the Columbia to Mont. & back in less in 4 days.  For Navagation of the
Columbia is of little use.  A few English Vessel could prevent any
vessels gong in--even if the wind allowed them.  Whalers now from
the N.S. pass the place for C.

The Settlers of the Origon anticipate the supplying of California.  Under present curcumstances they may.  A California will not
work if he can avoid it.  The time will come, must come, when this
Country is peopled by another race.  This is as fully expected here
as any other natual course of events.  Many children have been sent
to the Oahu English School to learn the Eng language to prepare
them for the coming events, be the visit from John Bull or Uncle
Sam.  One of the two will have the Country.  When once this is
accomplished, the place will team with a busy race.  As I before
observed all fruits will grow here.  Hemp, Cotten every Variuty of
grain, timber from the tender Willow to Tress 17 feet in diamater.
The Natives now expecting Troops from Acupulco to reconquer the
Country are drilling many young men in preparation intended to
surround the first port the Mexicans arrive at, drive away the
Cattle, prevent all intercours with the Ranchos, and by this mean
drive them out of C.  If they can not succeed in this manner take
to the mountains and worry them out.


Letter, Thomas O. Larkin to Journal of Commerce, July, 1845,
in Hammond (ed.), The Larkin Papers, III, pp. 294-295.

286.   AMERICAN TRADE WITH MEXICAN CALIFORNIA (1844)


The weak central government of Mexico was unable
to police its shores against both British and American
traders who violated Mexican prohibitions on coastal
trade.  The prospects of such trade attracted the Hudson's
Bay Company to San Francisco.  American interests felt
threatened by the British competition.  A weak Mexico was
as much a prospective British domain as it was an
American one.


The law of Mexico does not allow coasting by Foreign Vessels.
The California Goverment do allow it on this coast.  This infraction of Law is not noticed by the Supreme Goverment in Mexico.
Its allowance is on very fluctuating terms by the local Authorities
here.  Most of the U.S. Vessels have a hide house in San Diego,
where they always keep a Mate & some men to cure their hides as they
collect them from different Ports in California.  There is no
Foreigners belongs to San Diego nor many Natives.  Our American
Vessels leave this part of the coast last, when bound home.  Withen
three months 40,000 raw Hides have been exported from San Diego for
Boston.  Withen the same time (55000$) Fifty five thousand dollars
has been paid in Monterey for duties on goods from Boston.  There
are Five American Ships now on the Coast.


Letter, Thomas O. Larkin to Secretary of State, April 16, 1844,
in Hammond (ed.), The Larkin Papers, II, pp. 96–97.


287.   ECONOMIC REASONS WHY THE UNITED STATES SHOULD
ANNEX TEXAS (1844)


During the opening years of the 1840s, the American
government pressed Texas to join the Union.  Early in
1844, former president Andrew Jackson joined the campaign
and more or less convinced Houston that annexation was
desirable.  Meanwhile, England, eager for Texas cotton,
wished Texas to remain independent of the United States.
Many cotton producers in East Texas, virtually all
Americans, favored annexation in order to guarantee the
legality of slavery which was outlawed under Mexican rule.
In this unofficial letter are rehearsed the compelling
economic arguments which were being carefully considered
in American councils.  Houston was President of the Texas
Republic; Jackson was in retirement from the American
presidency.

Situated in Texas is in point of locality, with peace she has
nothing to apprehend for years to come.  Other nations would not
dread her rivalry, but rather court her friendship for commercial
advantage.  Her people would have nothing to divert them from their
agricultural pursuits.  Her advancement in the arts of peace and
commerce would be inevitable.  With a government requiring trifling
expenditure, and a tariff much lower than that of the United States,
she would invite the commerce of all nations to her ports, (as is
already to some extent the case;) and while she thus increased the
demand for her productions she would drive the manufactures of the
United States from her markets, from the fact that American manufacturers could not so well compete with those of Europe.  In this
way, the immense trade of the Northern Mexican States as well as
Texas would fall into the hands of European merchants and pass
through our ports and territory.  In a few years the loss to the
American manufacturer would not be a small amount.  But, on the
other hand, by annexation, these advantages would be secured to the
American merchant to the exclusion of the European; for we should
then be but on government, and co[n]sequently in the markets of
Texas no duties could be levied upon home manufactures.  The tariff
of the U. States would operate then to ensure to their own citizens
a valuable market, which must otherwise inevitably be lost to them:
not to say anything about the embarrassments to their revenues by
the smuggling which would certainly be carried on.

Letter, Sam Houston to Andrew Jackson, February 16, 1844,
Bassett (ed.), Correspondence of Andrew Jackson, VI, p. 261.


288.  MEXICO MUST BECOME A PROTECTORATE OF THE
UNITED STATES (1859)


On February 16, 1858, Houston introduced a resolution
in the U.S. Senate calling for the setting up of an
American protectorate over Mexico and Central America.
While the resolution did not pass, it became an issue in
the Texas elections of 1859.  The sentiments expressed by
Houston illustrate the proposition that Mexico had the
poor fortune to gain independence at a time when military
weakness rather than economic underdevelopment was by far
the greater curse.


The object in view in establishing a protectorate over that unhappy country, needs but little explanation to convince all of its
utility.  Mexico has been for near a half century torn by distract-
ing elements.  Her situation appeals to us as her near neighbor to
interpose in the name of humanity and good government.  The crisis
in her affairs has been approaching, it is even now at hand, when her

people mad with anarchy and misrule, will disgrace the character of this century, by bloodshed, debauchery, and riot. Unable to maintain a stable government for herself, she is powerless to protect the rights of our citizens in her limits. Our commercial relations with her are subject to unjust restrictions and our citizens engaged in her trade at the mercy of brigands or rival chieftains. Unable to rest[r]ain the Indians on her borders, they make incursions upon us, and when they have plundered and murdered our frontier settlers, return to her limits and are beyond the reach of punishment. Our slaves flee from their masters and find refuge among her people and we are unable to reclaim them. The destiny of the American people too points in that direction. My object was to create a protectorate which would be self-supporting. The resources of Mexico are immense. Establish peace within her limits, protect her people in their homes, rid them of ruinous exactions, and no country upon God's earth would smile more bounteously to reward industry. The infusion of American energy would develop her incalculable stores of wealth. Her mines would pour out untold millions, and gradually under the influence of our institutions, the country would become Americanized and prepared for incorporation into our Union. Avoid the result as we may, it is bound to come. Would it not be wisdom to exercise the sagacity of statesmen and before the land is destroyed amid the flames of civil war, stretch forth our land to save it. Those who prate about free-soil, with reference to Mexico, know nothing of the character of the institution of slavery. The institution too has its destiny. Wherever it may be profitable, there will it go, and who will pretend to say that the great valley of Mexico is not fitted to slave labor. But apart from this, whether Mexico remains intact or becomes consolidated with us, should we not pursue such a course with regard to her as will ensure protection to our citizens, and enable us to maintain commercial relations with her? If we do not interpose to keep her on her feet and in the exercise of the qualities of government, her overt acts in violations of our rights and the sanctity of our flag will become so flagrant that we will be compelled to seize upon her for "indemnity for the past and security for the future." Or shall we wait until she becomes the prey of foreign powers, who would make her the means of annoying us and threatening our security? Statesmanship and humanity alike dictate our course. The protectorate would not only be self-sustaining, but it would afford a revenue. Beyond that the benefits to our people at large, from an increased commerce, would be great. In her present condition the wealth of Mexico is squandered. Neither herself nor the world without is benefitted. Let her have a good government and the most beneficent results would ensue. It was to promote these ends that I advocated this protectorate.

Speech at Nacogdoches, July 9, 1859, Williams and Barker (eds.), The Writings of Sam Houston, VIII, pp. 360-362.

# L.

## GOVERNMENT'S BROAD ROLE

289. TAXATION IN THE UNITED STATES AND ENGLAND (1818)

A central government existed alongside decentralized markets. Being as yet neither able nor obliged to spend heavily on creation of a national market, the federal government required extremely little revenue. To an Englishman, the situation was noteworthy. (See Source No. 295).

But, you will ask, "are there <u>no taxes</u> "in America?" Yes; and taxes, or public contributions of some sort, there must be in every civilized state; otherwise <u>government</u> could not exist, and without government there could be no security for <u>property</u> or <u>persons</u>. The taxes in America consist principally of <u>custom duties passed on goods imported into the country</u>. During the late war, there were taxes on several things in the country; but, they were taken off at the peace. In the cities and large towns, where <u>paving</u> and <u>lamps</u> and <u>drains</u> and <u>scavengers</u> are necessary, there are, of course, <u>county rates</u> and <u>road rates</u>. But, as the money thus raised is employed for the immediate benefit of those who pay, and is expended amongst themselves and under their own immediate inspection, it does not partake of the nature of <u>a tax</u>. The taxes or duties, on goods imported, yield a great sum of money; and, owing to the persons employed in the collection being appointed for their integrity and ability, and not on account of their connection with any set of bribing and corrupt boroughmongers, the whole of the money thus collected is fairly applied to the public use, and is amply sufficient for all the purposes of government. The <u>army</u>, if it can be so called, costs but a mere trifle. It consists of a few men, who are absolutely necessary to keep forts from crumbling down, and guns from rotting with rust.  The navy is an object of care, and its support and increase a cause of considerable expence.  But the government, relying on the good sense and valour of a people, who must hate or disregard themselves before they can hate or disregard that which so manifestly promotes their own happiness, has no need to expend much on any species of war-like preparations.  The government could not stand a week, if it were hated by the people; nor, indeed, ought it to stand an hour.  It has the hearts of the people with it, and, therefore, it need expend nothing in blood-money, or in secret services of any kind.  Hence the cheapness of this government; hence the small amount of the taxes; hence the ease and happiness of the People.

. . . . . . . . . . . . . . . . . . . . . . . . . . . . . .
I have had living with me an Englishman, who smokes tobacco; and he tells me, that he can buy as much tobacco here for three cents; that is, about three English half-pence, as he could buy in England for three shillings.  The leather has no tax on it here; so that, though the shoe-maker is paid a high price for his labour, the labouring man gets his shoes very cheap.  In short, there is no excise here; no property tax; no assessed taxes.

Cobbett, A Year's Residence in the United States of America, II, pp. 408-409, 412.


290.  BANK INFLUENCE IN THE TREASURY DEPARTMENT (1828)


The Second Bank of the United States, chartered by Congress in 1816, was under a moderate degree of governmental supervision.  The Treasury Department, which banked its funds with the BUS and utilized BUS as a fiscal agent, was a crucial place for BUS influence.  Political influence by bankers was, of course, a rather general thing.  Smith, the writer here, was cashier of the Washington, D.C. branch of the Second Bank of the United States, where Biddle was president.  Dickins was Chief Clerk in the Treasury Department; and general S. Smith, a Senator from Maryland.


Mr. Asbury Dickins, who has had an accommodation of about $2500 in this office, has been lately called upon by our Board [of Directors], either to reduce this debt by curtailments, or to give additional security therefore.  This demand has placed Mr. Dickins in a very unpleasant situation, & he will not be able to comply with the call, unless at very great inconvenience to himself & to his family, & without being unjust to his other creditors.  In a confidential conversation with him, I have learned that there are pressing claims hanging over him to the amount of about $2500, &

that every dollar which he can spare from the economical support of his family, & from the interest on his debts in this office, is applied to the liquidation of his debts.  If, in addition to the sum already loaned to him, the Bank would lend him $2,500, he would pay off the claims pressing upon him, & would leave a standing order to be filed in the Treasury, & to be recognised by the Secretary, to pay us $1,000 annually out of his salary, until his whole debt should be paid off.  The security which he could give would not be adequate to cover this sum; but if he lived, and continued in office, the Bank would be sure to receive the whole amount of his debt.

There are other considerations of a delicate nature, which would induce me [to] accede to this proposition.  They cannot be communicated to the Board of Directors, perhaps, but must readily occur to you.  Mr. Dickins fills the confidential station in the Treasury, which has the management of the Bank Accounts.  He has already evinced the most friendly disposition towards the Bank, & has in many instances, to my certain knowledge, rendered services materially important to its interests.  I do not say, nor do I believe, that he has in a single instance, gone contrary to his duty to the Treasury; but I know that it is very important to have the person filling his station, well disposed to the Bank, as the view which may be taken of the subjects referred to him, may be materially affected by the feelings by which he is governed.  The report on the subjects of Government deposits in the Bank, made to the Senate last winter by Gen. Smith, was in a great measure made from materials furnished by Mr. Dickins, from suggestions obtained from me.  This of course must not be talked of, nor should I have mentioned it, but to illustrate the idea of Mr. Dickins usefulness. Such is my opinion of the services rendered by him, I should think it good policy to give up entirely, the whole $5000, sooner than not to retain his friendly disposition...

Letter, R. Smith to Nicholas Biddle, September 22, 1828, Reginald C. McGrane (ed.), The Correspondence of Nicholas Biddle Dealing With National Affairs, 1807-1844, (Boston, Massachusetts: Houghton Mifflin Co., 1919), pp. 53-54.


291.    "LET GEN. HARRISON BE SILENT--ABSOLUTELY AND
INFLEXIBLE SILENT" (1835)


The Jacksonians could not benefit from more lectures on banking theory, so Biddle now advised meeting them on their own ground--an election battle.  But even here there should be a pure contest of personal popularity rather than political theories and programs.  Later, after the electoral victory, there would be time to chart economic reforms.

My theory in regard to the present condition of the country is in a few words this. For the last few years the Executive power of the Gov. has been weilded by a mere gang of banditte. I know these people perfectly--keep the police on them constantly--and in my deliberate judgment, there is not on the face of the earth a more profligate crew than those who now govern the President. The question is now to expel them. I believe that a very large majority of our countrymen, are disposed to expel them. It remains to see how that majority can be concentrated so as to be effectual. As yet the opinions of the opposition are unformed. No man as yet combine them: they are not fixed on any one man. But they are fixed on several men who are acceptable to various sections. Then the obvious course is, to make these several men in the first instance embody under them the force of these various sections--and when the common enemy approaches to rally under a leader of their own choice. It is manifestly advantageous to let Mr. Webster lead the New England forces, Mr. White the Southwest, or South--and wherever in any one State there is a strong opposition man--to vote for him as such--and settle the pretensions of the chiefs afterwards. I have said again and again to my friends, I have said it this very morning, "This disease is to be treated as a local disorder--apply local remedies--if Gen. Harrison will run better than any body else in Penns., by all means unite upon him." That as far as I understand the case, is the feeling very generally of the opposition & Gen. Harrison must not suppose that there is in this quarter any unwillingness to give him fair play. On the contrary, he is very much respected, and if our friends are satisfied that he can get more votes in Penns. than any other candidate of the opposition they will take him up cheerfully & support him cordially.

I have but one remark more to make. If Gen. Harrison is taken up as a candidate, it will be on account of the past, not the future. Let him then rely entirely on the past. Let him say not one single word about his principles, or his creed--let him say nothing--promise nothing. Let no Committee, no convention--not town meeting ever extract from him a single word, about what he thinks now, or what he will do hereafter. Let the use of pen and ink be wholly forbidden as if he were a mad poet in Bedlam. Gen. Harrison can speak well & write well--but on this occasion he should neither speak nor write--but be silent--absolutely and inflexible silent...

Letter, Nicholas Biddle to Herman Cope, August 11, 1835, McGrane (ed.), Correspondence of Nicholas Biddle, pp. 255-256.

292.    GALLERY OF INDIAN AGENTS ON THE MISSOURI
(1830's AND 1840's)


The author of one of the most authoritative books
on the subject catches the essence of the problem: The
federal Indian agents knew little about and cared less
for the Indians, they soon came under the influence of the
American Fur Company and protected the Company in their
reports to Washington, and wars resulted from this combination of ignorance and avarice.


Major Sanford was very much of a gentleman, but cared more for
the interests of the American Fur Company than for Indian affairs.
He afterward married Mr. Pierre Chouteau's daughter, and one can
judge in whose favor his reports would be likely to be made.
Major Ferguson, the greenest of all agents I ever saw, was paid
$1500 for a pleasure trip from St. Louis to Fort Union. He came up
in the steamer, saw no Indians, and left what few annuities he had
to be divided among them by the Company. What report could that
agent make in regard to his Indians? None, of course. That was the
last of him.
Major More was a great drunkard, who came up to Union in the
steamer, remained 24 hours, and returned to Fort Pierre. It was
reported by a person whom I believe, that the Indians there kicked
his stern, taking him for a dog, when he was crawling out of the
room where they had been sleeping, and laughingly said they were
very sorry that they had kicked their father.
Major Matlock was a drunken gambler. The last I saw of him
was at Trading Point, opposite Bellevue, where he was drinking and
gambling, and kept several Mormon women. I was informed that he
died, shortly afterward, in poverty.
Major Dripps was, I believe, a good, honest old beaver trapper.
He was sent to examine the trading posts, to find out about the
liquor trade. He sent his interpreter ahead to let us know he was
coming. On his arrival he looked in all places except in the cellar, where there was upward of 30 barrels of alcohol. The major was
afterward equipped by the American Fur Company, and went on the
Platte, where he died.
Major Hatting was a young man about 27 or 28 years old, a
drunkard and a gambler, almost gone up by the bad disorder. He was
of no earthly account. I could say much more, but decency forbids.
Major Norwood, instead of being with his Indians, kept himself
about Sergeant's Bluffs, attending balls and parties given by whites
and half-breeds, and was finally killed by William Thompson, who
knocked his brains out with the butt of a rifle. This was the last
of the major.
Major Redfield went 50 miles up the Yellowstone, on his way to
the Crows, was taken sick, and returned to the States in the fall;
his goods were left to be divided by the Company. I knew nothing
regarding his personal character.

Major Vaughan was a jovial old fellow, who had a very fine
paunch for brandy, and, when he could not get brandy, would take
almost anything which would make drunk come.  He was one who remained most of his time with his Indians, but what accounts for that
is the fact that he had a pretty young squaw for a wife; and as he
received many favors from the Company, his reports must have been in
their favor.

I have but little to say about Major Schoonover, who remained
one winter at Union, powerless, like all others, being dependent on
the American Fur Company.

Major Latta was a pretty fair kind of a man, but the less said
of him the better.  He came up to Union, put the annuities out on
the bar, and next day was off.

Major Mahlon Wilkinson came as near doing the right thing as
was in his power, but he was too lazy to do much of anything.

Major Clifford was a captain of the regular army, which rendered him unfit for such an office, not caring a fig about Indians.
I could say a great deal more if I felt so disposed.  From what I
have been able to learn I fully believe that all the Indian agents
were of the same material; and had those men been ever so well qualified to fill their office, they could not have done it under the
existing rules and regulations.  Once in the Indian country they
came entirely under the influence of the American Fur Company, and
could not help themselves.

Those gentlemen were appointed by the Indian Department not
only as agents, but as fathers to the Indians; to remain with their
children, and to make true reports to their Great Father at Washington of the behavior of the Indians and of all transactions in their
country that come to the agent's notice, thus keeping the department
well posted.  The question is, Was that done?  No; evidence shows
the contrary.  In consequence of this bad state of affairs, the
department remained ignorant of the true conditions of the country,
and could never hold the proper kind of council with the Indians;
and, finally, war broke out.  Of all the councils I attended, I
never saw one properly held, according to my knowledge of Indian
character and customs.

Charles Larpenteur, Forty Years A Fur Trader On The Upper
Missouri....Personal Narrative....1833-1872, (Chicago, Illinois:
The Lakeside Press, 1933), pp. 344-348.

293.   SOME LOANS TO CONGRESSMEN, FEDERAL OFFICIALS, AND EDITORS BY
        THE BANK OF THE UNITED STATES (ca. 1837)

The following incomplete list, drawn up by Biddle,
himself, includes a former President, two former Vice-
Presidents, Cabinet members, Senators, Representatives,
and official government printers.  Party lines were
crossed by borrowers.  That a part of these loans were

designed to purchase support was widely
acknowledged.

| New Hampshire | |
|---|---|
| Isaac Hill | 3,800 |

| Massachusetts | |
|---|---|
| W Appleton | 10,000 |
| Dan. Webster | 17,782.86 |
| N Silsbee | 8,000 |
| James Lloyd | 8,000 |

| New York | |
|---|---|
| D. D. Tompkins | 40,000 |
| Jas. W Webb | 18,000 |
| Sam. Beardsley | 4,900 |

| Pennsylvania | |
|---|---|
| Joseph Hamphill | 10,500 |
| Wm. Ramsay | 8,000 |
| Philander Stevens | 3,500 |
| Jno G. Watmough | 1,700 |
| Wm. Wilkins | 6,460 |
| Henry Baldwin | 35,819 |
| Louis McLane | 5,150 |
| R Walsh | 6,541.72 |
| Edw Livingston | 1,000 |
| George A Waggaman | 4,800 |
| H.A. Bullard | 9,050 |
| Joseph R Chandler | 2,000 |
| Jasper Harding | 37,434.81 |

| Maryland | |
|---|---|
| S Smith & Buchanan | 1,540,000 |
| Wm Graydon (?) | 9,800 |

| Washington | |
|---|---|
| James Monroe | 10,596 |
| John C Calhoun | 4,400 |
| James Barbour | 16,000 |
| Tho. Hinds | 6,000 |
| W H Overton | 6,000 |
| Jno H Eaton | 9,000 |
| Jno Branch | 5,100 |
| J L Southard | 1,000 |
| W H Crawford | 1,500 |
| W. B Lewis | 10,765 |
| Henry Clay | 7,500 |
| Gales & Seaton | 32,360 |
| Duff Green | 15,600 |
| Josiah R Johnston | 28,405 |
| Jno McLean | 6,733.30 |
| Amos Kendall | 5,375 |

Virginia
| Andrew Stevenson | 2,000 |
|---|---|
| Wm. C Rives | 5,500 |
| Wm. L Archer | 2,500 |
| Hugh Nelson | 1,000 |
| Robt. S Garnett | 1,500 |
| Dan. Sheffey | 5,000 |
| Thomas Ritchie | 10,900 |

North Carolina
| Wm B Sheppard | 5,000 |
|---|---|

South Carolina
| Ja. Hamilton Jr | 15,400 |
|---|---|
| Joel R Poinsett | 13,100 |
| H Middleton | 6,000 |

Georgia
| R H Wilde | 6,000 |
|---|---|
| Jno Forsyth | 20,000 |

Kentucky
| R M Johnson | 10,820 |
|---|---|
| Wm J Barry | 5,503 |
| George M Bibb | 7,500 |

McGrane (ed.), Correspondence of Nicholas Biddle, pp. 357–359.


294.  BOTH PAUPERISM AND PROPERTY WILL SUCCEED IN
THE UNITED STATES (1837)


Like all bourgeois societies, America was based
on private property.  Inequalities in ownership laid
the basis for social conflict.  Would these inequalities
also lead to fundamental conflict in America?  The writer
of the following comment is Harriet Martineau, an English
popular writer who toured the United States in 1835–36.


One of the most painful apprehensions seems to be that the
poorer will heavily tax the richer members of society; the rich
being always a small class.  If it be true, as all parties appear
to suppose, that rulers in general are prone to use their power for
selfish purposes, there remains the alternative, whether the poor
shall over-tax the rich, or whether the rich shall over-tax the
poor:  and, if one of these evils were necessary, few would doubt
which would be the least.  But the danger appears much diminished

on the consideration that, in the country under our notice, there
are not, nor are likely to be, the wide differences in property
which exist in old countries.  There is no class of hereditary rich
or poor.  Few are very wealthy; few are poor; and every man has a
fair chance of being rich.  No such unequal taxation has yet been
ordained by the sovereign people; nor does there appear to be any
danger of it, while the total amount of taxation is so very small
as in the United States, and the interest that every one has in the
protection of property is so great.  A friend in the South, while
eulogizing to me the state of society there, spoke with compassion
of his northern fellow citizens, who were exposed to the risks of
"a perpetual struggle between pauperism and property."  To which a
northern friend replied, that it is true that there is a perpetual
struggle everywhere between pauperism and property.  The question
is, which succeeds.  In the United States, the prospect is that
each will succeed.  Paupers may obtain what they want, and proprietors will keep that which they have.  As a mere matter of convenience, it is shorter and easier to obtain property by enterprise and
labour in the United States, than by pulling down the wealthy.  Even
the most desponding do not consider the case as very urgent, at
present.  I asked one of my wealthy friends, who was predicting that
in thirty years his children would be living under a despotism, why
he did not remove.  "Where," said he, with a countenance of per-
plexity, "could I be better off?"--which appeared to me a truly
reasonable question.


    Harriet Martineau, Society in America, I, (London:  Saunders
and Otley, 1837, 2nd ed.), pp. 22-23.


### 295.  THE TAX BURDEN IN RURAL INDIANA (1846)


    To Europeans, the very light taxes of the
United States were a source of amazement.  (See Source
No. 289).  Johann Wolfgang Schreyer whose family had
emigrated from Bavaria, Germany to the farm area of
Plymouth, Indiana in 1843, writes the following three
years later.


Concerning the taxes, these are not the same in all states
because the debts of one state may exceed those of another, on
account of the canals and railroads and other enterprises that are
carried on by the state government with the assent of the inhabitants.  Here in the state of Indiana, we have first, for men from
twenty-one to fifty years, the poll tax.  This takes the place of
military service.  Then there is a tax on livestock and furniture
which is assessed each year, but not high, perhaps for half of its
value, and the rate is not the same each year; usually it is sixty

or sixty-two cents on the hundred dollars.  The first hundred
dollars are at present free and likewise the things most essential
to keeping house.  It is a large household that pays sixty to
sixty-two cents household tax.

Public land is free from taxation for five years after purchase; after the expiration of this time, the tax is one cent an
acre.  This tax can be paid by working on public roads, and besides
each man between the ages of twenty-one and fifty must work two days
additional on the roads.  If the taxes are not paid within the
period allowed by law, there is no collector sent until after two
years; and if the taxes are not paid then, the land is advertized
for sale at the county court house by the county officials and sold
to the highest bidder at any price.  Landowners are very careful
and always pay for the previous year if they cannot pay every year.
Trademen pay no taxes on their trade, simply on their stock and
other property.  Capitalists must pay taxes on their capital and
the proprietors of inns and saloons must pay taxes and buy a
license besides.

Letter, Johann Wolfgang Schreyer to Jon. Melchior and Mr.
Neihardt, June 22, 1846, Donald F. Carmony (ed.), "Letter Written
by Mr. Johann Wolfgang Schreyer," Indiana Magazine of History,
XL (1944), pp. 292-293.

### 296.  "WITHOUT THAT PROTECTION THE UNION IS OF
NO USE TO US" (1850)

Being an operator of one of the South's most
profitable industrial enterprises did not prompt Gregg
to avoid the social-political views of his planter-
contemporaries.  Southern manufacturing was seen as com-
patible with its slave base.  Many northern manufacturers,
on the other hand, regarded planter-control of the federal
government as pernicious.  Clearly, the issues that even-
tuated in the Civil War could not be summarized as planter
versus manufacturer.  The issue related to control of the
government by conflicting ruling groups.  The lines were
much broader than simple immediate interest.

A reasonable tariff of protection would set evry thing right
at this time, but unfortunately for the country, just when the
south was ready to receive reasonable propositions on this head,
you people of the North, East, & West, raise up a bone of contention
which has spoiled all, it is mere phathom, an abstraction to you
New England people, who I had hoped had too much hard common sense
to run mad about.  Universal freedom is a hacknied theme with you,

& the people seem to be boiling over with partriotism,, it is a great pity that your emancipators had not turned their efforts of philanthropy to the relief of the poor oppressed Irish & English where great good can be done without invading the right of property. With us, slaves are property, and it amounts to Many Millions, the protection & free use of which is guaranteed to us by the Constitution, without that protection the Union is of no use to us. I am sorry to confess to you that among our best men here, a severance of the Union is desirable, & I believe this sentiment to be almost universal in South Carolina & Georgia, the old substantial men who stood up for union during Nulification, are now on the other side. We are under the impression here, that the spirit of abolition is becoming so rife with you that it will over ride the politicians and wise men of the country, and that the day is not distant when it would be a hopeless case with us to look for redress should a vessel belonging to any other nation land on our coast & take away five hundred or a thousand of our Negroes. I fear that many years of negociations would be resorted to before the Eastern people would be willing to cripple their commerce by war in such a cause particularly if it were with such a powerful nation as England, while the invasion of a yankee fishing smack would set you in a flame. Our distrust does not end here, we look forward to the possibility that the mad spirit of abolition may lead to still more disastrous results, that the money which we contribute to the support of government may in time be used against us to take away our property, a lawless majority is seldom governed by principles. We all know that laws are only binding when sanctioned by public opinion. Constitutions are but ropes of sand when their provisions are contrary to the dictates of a sense of justice, and the consciences of those who have the power to trample them under foot.

Letter, William Gregg to Amos A. Lawrence, September 2, 1850, Martin (ed.), "The Advent of William Gregg," pp. 422–423.

## 297.    SOUTHERN PLANTER DOMINANCE IN THE UNITED STATES SENATE (1856)

In this part of a famous speech, "The Dominant Class in the Republic," Seward painted a picture of overwhelming planter dominance over the Senate. That the leading personnel of important committees were southern is undeniable; and that they used their positions on behalf of the cotton interest is also clear. But missing from Seward's picture is an analysis of the sprouting economic and political role of Northern industry, commerce, and commercial agriculture.

We see prudence, if not jealousy, visibly manifested in the constitution of the committee on the army and the navy, the two great physical forces of the republic. The first of these consists of Mr. Weller of California, Mr. Fitzpatrick of Alabama, Mr. Jones of Tennessee, Mr. Iverson of Georgia, and Mr. Pratt of Maryland, all of whom favor the largest liberty to the slaveholding class; and the other is composed of Mr. Mallory of Florida, Mr. Slidell of Louisiana, Mr. Thompson of New Jersey, Mr. James of Rhode Island, all reliable supporters of that class, together with the independent, upright, and candid John Bell of Tennessee.

The slaveholding class is a careful guardian of the public domain. Mr. Stuart, of Michigan, is chairman of the committee on public lands. He is, as you well know, of the opinion that the agitation of slavery is the prolific cause of the unhappy overthrow of freedom in Kansas, and his associates are Mr. Johnson of Arkansas, Mr. Clayton of Delaware, Mr. Mallory of Florida and Mr. Pugh of Ohio, who all are tolerant of that overthrow, and Mr. Foot, who so faithfully represents the ever-reliable freemen of Vermont.

Mr. Benjamin, of Louisiana, presides over the committee on private claims upon the public domain, supported by Mr. Biggs of North Carolina and Mr. Thompson of Kentucky, with whom are associated Mr. Foster, a senator of redeemed Connecticut, and Mr. Wilson of Massachusetts.

Negotiations with the Indian tribes are continually required, to provide room for the migration of the slaveholder with his slaves. The committee on Indian affairs, excluding all senators from free states, consists of Mr. Sebastian of Arkansas, Mr. Rusk of Texas, Mr. Toombs of Georgia, Mr. Brown of Mississippi, Mr. Reid of North Carolina and Mr. Bell of Tennessee.

Two representatives of the interests of freedom, Mr. Wade of Ohio, and Mr. Fessenden of Maine, hold places on the committee on claims against the government; but they are quite overbalanced by Mr. Brodhead of Pennsylvania, Mr. Geyer of Missouri, Mr. Iverson of Georgia, and Mr. Yulee of Florida.

The post office in its transactions is more nearly domestic and municipal than any other department of the government, and comes home to the business and bosoms of the whole people. Mr. Husk of Texas, is chairman of the committee on the post office and post roads, and his associates are Mr. Yulee of Florida, Mr. Adams of Mississippi, Mr. Jones of Iowa, balanced by Mr. Collamer of Vermont, and Mr. Durkee of Wisconsin.

No inconsiderate legislation favorable to freemen must be allowed in the senate, no constitutional legislation necessary to the security of slavery must be spared. The committee on the judiciary, charged with the care of the public jurisprudence, consists of Mr. Butler of South Carolina, Mr. Bayard of Delaware, Mr. Geyer of Missouri, Mr. Toombs of Georgia, Mr. Toucy of Connecticut,, and Mr. Pugh of Ohio. It was the committee on the judiciary which, in 1845, reported the bill for removing from the state courts into the federal courts private actions brought against federal officers for injuries committed by them under color of their authority.

The slaveholding class watches with paternal jealousy over the slaveholding capital of the United States. The committee on the District of Columbia consists of Mr. Brown of Mississippi, Mr. Pratt of Maryland, Mr. Mason of Virginia, and Mr. Reid of North Carolina, together with Mr. Allen of Rhode Island.

The committee on territories has care of the colonization, organization, and admission of new states, and so is in fact the most important of all the committees in the senate. Mr. Douglas, of Illinois, is its chairman, and his associates are his willing supporters, Mr. Jones of Iowa, Mr. Sebastian of Arkansas, Mr. Biggs of North Carolina, together with Mr. Bell of Tennessee, and the able and faithful Mr. Collamer of Vermont.

Finally, the science and literature of the country must not be unduly directed to the prejudice of the interests of slavery. The committee on the library take charge of this great intellectual interest, and it consists of Mr. Pearce of Maryland, Mr. Cass, the eminent senator from Michigan, and Mr. Bayard of Delaware.

Speech at Detroit, October 2, 1856, Baker (ed.), Works of William H. Seward, IV, pp. 261-263.

## 298.  ECONOMIC ADVANTAGES OF SECESSION (1857)

There are two separate questions here:  (1)  Would secession harm the North?  Economically, this could not be denied.  (2)  Would secession release vast amounts of capital to be invested in Southern industry and commerce? Most likely, not.  The slave-plantation regime regularly absorbed the bulk of available capital.  Secession alone would not produce industrial capital, nor skilled mechanics, nor factory managers, nor supplies of unskilled wage labor.

The revenue and resources of the Southern States, heretofore contributed mainly to aid Northern interests, foster Northern industry and trade, and increase Northern wealth and power, would thenceforward be retained and used to sustain and build up our own commerce, and cities, and general prosperity.  In twenty-five or thirty years our population and wealth will be doubled, and the value of our products and their demand by the commercial world will be increased in still greater proportion.  There will probably be no community of more vigorous and healthy growth, or with better prospects of stable prosperity.  With the aid of our own annual profits of industry and capital, and the encouragement that the new condition and demands of the Southern States will create manufactures, and navigation and commerce will increase rapidly, even if

the growth was stimulated and maintained by Southern resources only.
But in advance of this natural and slower growth, these branches of
industry, and the men to carry them on, and the capital to sustain
them, will be transplanted to any amount that may be desired and
permitted, from the Northern to the Southern States, as soon as they
shall have become separate political communiites.  Plenty of manufacturing capital, and also of capitalists and laborers, and plenty
of ships and sailors, will come to obtain the benefits of an establishment in the South.  There would be nothing more wanting for
this speedy and extensive transferrence of capital, industry, and
also of (at least) professed allegiance, than the sure and simple
operation of greatly reduced employment and profits in the Northern
States, and the great increase of both in the independent and flourishing Southern Confederacy--then just beginning to use its own
funds and resources to build up and sustain its own cities, manufactures, and navigation.


    Edmund Ruffin, Consequences of Abolition Agitation, (Washing-
ton, D.C.:  Lemuel Towers, 1857), p. 36.

# PART III

# A CAPITALIST ECONOMY, 1860-1900

# A.

# NATURAL RESOURCE DEVELOPMENT

### 299. EARLY OIL TRADE IN PITTSBURGH (1861)

Pittsburgh, because of favorable water and rail connections, became the country's first oil shipping center. All the other advantages of a large industrial city lay at the command of the new industry.

No one who does not make an effort to ascertain for himself can conceive the gigantic proportions which the business of producing petroleum has assumed or the vast benefit our city is reaping and will continue to reap from this new and important branch of trade. To form an idea of the reality it is only necessary to pay a visit to the Allegheny wharf, as we frequently do. We think we are are rather under than over the mark when we say that yesterday morning there were at least fifteen thousand barrels of crude petroleum upon and at the wharf. The most general means of transportation is in flats, and the wharf is completely lined with these, full and partially unloaded, while a line of barrels, almost unbroken, extends from Pitt street to about midway between the old Aquduct and the Mechanics' street bridge. In addition to this we observed several boats filled with oil in bulk, which is pumped into barrels and hauled away. Innumerable empty barrels are also piled higher up on the wharf. It has been the custom to make the Allegheny wharf one vast storehouse for oil, but if some of the large quantity now lying there is not removed we cannot see where that yet in the boats is to be unloaded--and, as for future arrivals they must seek landings above or below the lines designated. Indeed it is frequently with great difficulty that consigners and owners find and identify their oil.

Yet, notwithstanding this immense supply of the crude oil,
there is no decline in price.  On the contrary the recent advance
is well maintained and five hundred barrels were yesterday sold at
fifteen cents per gallon.  There is a large demand by refiners, who
are driving a profitable business and daily erecting new refineries.
--Go where you will into the suburbs (and, indeed, within the city
limits) and you will see extensive refiners in full blow and new
ones being erected or just going into operation.  Refined oil has
now advanced to forty and forty-two cents per gallon for the best
qualities, and at this figure the orders of all our refineries are
far in advance of their capacity to fill them.  It is thought by
many that the business is overdone here, but twice the number of
refineries now in operation in this vicinity (the number is variously estimated at thirty-five to fifty) would not supply the demand.
In the East figures are even higher than here and if transportation
to New York could be easily procured a still further advance would
be the result.

The production and refining of this oil gives employment to a
vast number of persons who could otherwise, in the present condition
of affairs, find no labor for their hands.  It is a valuable and
permanent branch of business and must yield a handsome profit to
all who embark in it systematically and with sufficient capital, and
to a great extent overcome.  This trade will ere long be a leading
feature in our city and we should take every measure to promote and
encourage it.

The Pittsburgh Post, December 18, 1861, reprinted in Paul H.
Giddens (ed.), Pennsylvania Petroleum 1750–1872, A Documentary
History, (Titusville, Pennsylvania:  Pennsylvania Historical and
Museum Commission, 1947), pp. 219–220.

### 300.  DIVINING OIL WELLS (1865)

From a scientific point of view, the use of
divining rods in petroleum fields was no cruder
than technical processes then used in many industries.
It was with this semi-magical technology that production of crude oil in the United States, principally
Pennsylvania, rose from 2,000 barrels in 1859 to
nearly 2,500,000 barrels in 1865, the date of the
following story.

The use of the divining rod in the locating of oil wells is
now being generally practiced by those mining for petroleum.  The
mode of operation is exceedingly simple.  The expert uses a forked
twig of witch hazel.  This he takes by the two prongs, or ends,

walks slowly over the ground where he intends to prospect, holding
it in a vertical position.  The theory is, that in passing over a
vein of oil the existence of the same is indicated by the action
of the twig thus held, as the larger end points down toward the
ground.  By this mode of operating, experts claim that they cannot
only discover the existence, but can trace the vein of oil in any
direction, and locate the spot where it is most desirable to drill
an oil well with great certainty of success.  Many wells located by
this means have proved to be good producing ones.  We are not a
believer in the efficacy of the divining rods, as indicating with
any degree of certainty the existence of a productive oil vein.
But as many of the most practical oil men we [know] have practiced
this mode of locating their wells, even if they don't believe in
it, their opinions are entitled to respect.

The sticks used will only operate in the hands of certain
persons, and with these only in places where oil exists beneath the
surface.  At least so it is alleged by the experts.  The reason
given for the vibration and turning of the divining rod is this:
The party operating being possessed of an undue amount of positive
electricity, this electricity acts upon the sticks as above described, and has consequently some affinity with minerals beneath
the earths surface.  Now the sum and substance of the whole matter
is simply this:  As there are no certain indications by which to
locate an oil well that will prove productive, it is just as well
to try the divining rod.  The investment is generally moderate.
And this view is the one taken by most of those boring wells.

Oil City [Pennsylvania] Register, September 7, 1865, reprinted
in Paul H. Giddens (ed.), Pennsylvania Petroleum, 1750-1872, A
Documentary History, (Titusville, Pennsylvania:  Pennsylvania
Historical and Museum Collection, 1947), pp. 296-297.


301.   HAND-UNLOADING IRON ORE AT CLEVELAND (1869)


Note the primitive state of materials-handling
in a raw materials industry that was auxiliary to the
rapidly-mechanizing steel industry.  Cox, who founded
the Cleveland Twist Drill Co., wrote his autobiography
in 1905 but it remained unpublished until 1951.


The iron ore was brought down from Lake Superior in two-masted
schooners.  The two finest schooners on the lakes that season were
the Eliza Gerlach and the Oliver H. Perry.  Their maximum load was
500 tons.  When the boat was ready to be unloaded, a block was suspended by ropes from the mastheads over each of the two hatches.
A rope passed over this block and down into the hold, and on the
end was suspended a wooden bucket, holding from 500 to 1000 pounds.

The other end of the rope passed under a snatch block attached to the edge of the dock.  To this end of the rope a horse was hitched. A boy led the horse back and forth, up and down the dock, lifting the bucket as he led the horse forward, and dropping it into the hold as he backed up.  A staging was erected on the edge of the dock on which two men were stationed to dump the buckets into wheelbarrows.  A runway of planks was built from the staging on the dock runway.  This arrangement entailed the labor of four men on each runway and a horse and boy on the dock, making ten men altogether. Besides the men in the hold who shoveled the ore into the buckets there were also two horses.  All the men working in each hatchway were called a gang, and the two gangs working ten hours a day under favorable conditions could unload a 500-ton schooner in from five to six days.

Jacob Dolson Cox, Sr., <u>Building an American Industry...An Auto</u>biography, (Cleveland, Ohio © The Cleveland Twist Drill Co., 1951), pp. 49-50.


302.  A NEW COAL-CUTTING MACHINE (1873)


The cutting capacity of the machine far outstripped the ability to load its output.  This disproportion set a low limit (25%) to the operation of the machine.  Alexander, the writer of the following letter, was a partner in a firm --Niblock, Zimmerman & Alexander--which operated the Coal Brook Mines in Brazil, Indiana.  The machine was the Brown "Monitor Coal Cutter."


The Coal Cutter has been working pretty much all summer in our No. 3 mine, and has proved itself a practical success.  Not merely experimental cuts have been made, but it has been in operation day after day, and has already mined hundreds of tons.  Like all novelties, it will require increased experience on the part of the operators handling it, before its best results can be brought out.

Owing to the limited space prepared for its operations, it, as yet, has only been running about one-fourth of its time, as it must wait till the coal is taken away.  More room, however, is being prepared, and in a short time it is hoped that its full capacity will be tested.  It is expected that each machine, with seven men, will mine fifty tons each shift of ten hours, or about the output of twenty miners working with the pick.

I have been gathering some facts together with the intention
of preparing a paper to be read before the Am. Inst. of Mining
Engineers, at the Easton meeting, but fear I will hardly be able
to do so now, as my time is much occupied.  It will, however, afford
me pleasure to keep you posted from time to time as to the workings
of the cutter.


Letter, John S. Alexander to editor of the Journal of the
Franklin Institute, October 9, 1873; Journal of the Franklin
Institute, whole volume 96 (1873), p. 295.


303.  GETTING RICH ON SILVER IN NEVADA (1875)


A classic picture of people actually "getting
rich quick."  In 1873, four miners, organized as the
Consolidated Virginia, struck Big Bonanza, a lode 54
feet wide, consisting of gold and silver that brought
them $200 million.  Wright was the editor of a Nevada
newspaper and had spent the past 16 years in that state.


In the Winter of 1874-75, owing to the wonderful developments
made in the Consolidated Virginia and California mines, there was
a grand stock excitement throughout the towns of the Pacific Coast.
San Francisco and Virginia City, however, were the two great centres
of this excitement.  As the vast and astonishingly rich deposits of
ore in the California mine began to be drifted into and opened to
view, the stock of the company rapidly and steadily advanced from
about fifty dollars per share to nearly one thousand dollars.  Consolidated Virginia stock advanced in about the same ratio, as in
the mine of that company the width and richness of the ore was far
beyond anything that had ever before been seen on the Comstock lode.
In the Ophir mine, the next north of the California, large and rich
bodies of ore were being opened, and the stock of that company advanced with almost bewildering rapidity.  Persons who happened to
have twenty, fifty, or one hundred shares in either of these mines
suddenly found themselves rich.  The investment of a few hundreds
of dollars had brought them tens of thousands of dollars.
   The great strike in the "bonanza: mines started up the stocks
of all the adjoining mines, and, indeed, of all the mines along the
Comstock range.  The stock of mines that were rich in "great
expectations" only were as eagerly sought for and as briskly dealt
in, as were those in which ore was already being extracted, for
many said: "It is just as well for us to double our money in a
stock that costs but one or two dollars per share as in stocks that

cost from one to five hundred dollars." And many did double and
more than double their money in such stocks; indeed, in some instances they sold for five or ten times what their stocks cost
them.


    Dan de Quille (William Wright), History of the Big Bonanza,
(Hartford, Connecticut: American Publishing Co., 1877), pp. 402-
403.



    304.  SILVER SPURS ECONOMIC DEVELOPMENT (1877)


    An excellent view of the stimulation afforded
    by discoveries of silver. The point is that such
    discoveries and stimulation were not at all rare in
    nineteenth-century America.


    The mines of the Comstock give life to the whole Pacific Coast,
and are the main-spring, so to speak, of all kinds of trades and
every kind of business. They furnish to the California mechanic
that employment which gives him his bread. The army of workmen
of all kinds, who were employed in the building of the famous Pal-
ace Hotel, of San Francisco, the largest and most costly structure
of the kind in the world, were all paid with money taken out of the
mines of the Comstock. Washoe money also reared the Nevada Block,
and scores more of the finest and most costly buildings in San
Francisco--buildings which are the pride of the city.
    All the foundries and machine-shops of San Francisco and other
large towns on the Pacific Coast are running day and night to fill
orders from Nevada for engines, boilers, pumps, and all manner of
mining machinery; but for the Washoe siler-mines nearly all the
workmen employed in these foundries and machine-shops would be
obliged to migrate to some other land. The ranchmen and fruit-
growers of California would find times very dull with them but for
Nevada, as in the towns of the silver-mines, they always find a
market for all their products at high prices in ready coin. Without the "big bonanza," and the many other silver-mines of all
classes in Nevada, times would be very different from what they
now are in San Francisco, and, indeed, throughout California and
over the whole Pacific Coast.
    The influence of the Washoe silver-mines does not stop on the
Pacific Coast, but extends throughout the United States and is also
felt in Europe. Not only are manufacturing establishments in
California running to fill orders for machinery for the mines of
Nevada, but many establishments in the Atlantic States and a few
in European countries are also at work on certain kinds of machinery required in the silver-mines; as steel-wire cables, air-
compressure power-drills, and the like. Not alone to the deposit

of ore in one or two mines, but to the whole Comstock lode should
be given the name of the "Big Bonanza."

Dan de Quille (William Wright), History of the Big Bonanza,
pp. 494-495.


### 305. TIMBER DEPREDATIONS IN COLORADO (1879)


At this time wood was the preeminent construction
material for residences, factories, and other business
structures, as well as a prime material for heating.
Rapid industrialization, expanding urbanization, and the
growing immigration created an enormous demand for lumber.
Much of this valuable resource was found on land consti-
tuting the public domain and was subject to politically
connected acquisitions or depredations by corporations
and individuals. In many ways, the following analysis
could have applied to numerous earlier and later American
timber frontiers. Thompson, who testifies in the following, was a special agent of the Department of the Interior
and stationed in Leadville, Colorado.


The effects upon the general welfare of the country I conceive
to be mainly of two kinds. In the first place, the destruction of
forests is proceeding far more rapidly than their restoration by
growth. The amount of standing timber in the State has largely and
very visibly decreased during the last ten years, and before many
years have passed the State will be disforested unless the present
tendency is checked. The second effect is very serious. The great
accumulations of snow, which by its melting feeds the streams, are
at those altitudes where timber grows most abundantly. During the
early summer the forests by their shade retard the melting of the
snow, and the streams are fed gradually and slowly and usually keep
up a good flow of water throughout the summer. Where the forests
are stripped off or burned the snow rapidly melts in early summer,
the water runs off in large volume, and then the streams dry up.
Streams which now yield a good body of water for irrigation throughout the summer and pasturage in the lower altitudes would suddenly
become dry or so much depleted as to be practically useless for
irrigating purposes.
The forests are heavier usually upon the western mountain
slopes than upon the eastern. The fires also are more destructive
on the western slopes, partly because there is more wood to feed
them and partly because of the prevalent west winds.

In answer to the inquiry what has been my experience and the
results of my efforts in carrying out the instructions of the
Interior Department, I may say that I have found the owners of sawmills and timber-cutters very indifferent and regardless of the
possible consequences of their depredations either to themselves
or to the community, while they profess themselves desirous of
acquiring rights to timber, they seem to look upon it at present
as a kind of spoil sanctioned to them by local practice and have
little fear of prosecution.  They have apparently the conviction
that even if prosecuted they will not be convicted, because the
local sentiment is entirely favorable to them and no jury would
convict them.  Personally I have nothing to complain of, having
always received civil treatment and found them willing to discuss
the subject.  But they evidently feel secure against any legal consequences and rather despise the law.  They argue, and justly, that
timber is an absolute necessity, and it is undoubtedly true that
the greater part of what has been taken has been put to the most
necessary uses.  In a word, the taking of this timber is regarded
by them as one of those "necessities which know no law."  They are
undoubtedly sustained by public sentiment.

Testimony, James B. Thompson, U.S. Congress, 46th, 2nd
session, House of Representatives, Exec. Doc. No. 46, Report of the
Public Lands Commission, serial number 1923, (Washington, D.C.:
Government Printing Office, 1880), p. 309.

### 306.   THE ANTHRACITE POOL MEETS AT J. P. MORGAN'S (1886)

Ninety-five percent of the best anthracite coal
is located in five Pennsylvania counties.  By controlling
transportation routes from this compact area, several
railroads of J. P. Morgan & Company, in turn, controlled
a few of the most crucial roads and could sometimes thus
act as the effective policy-maker of the anthracite industry.
Harris, president of the Lehigh Coal and Navigation Company
and vice-president of the Lehigh and Hudson River Railroad
Company, served as secretary of the pool and was present
at the meeting of March 22, 1886.

A number of gentlemen, representatives of the anthracite
interests, met Monday evening, March 22d, 1886.  Mr. Morgan stated
that the object in asking the gentlemen to assemble was that they
might take counsel as to the possibility of preventing further
injury to the interests they represented by some concerted action
looking to an arrest of the demoralization of business which
resulted from the existing want of harmony.  The meeting organized

by calling Mr. John King, jr., to the chair, and Mr. J. S. Harris
was appointed secretary.  Upon the call of the roll of the different
interests, it was found that they were represented as follows:
The Philadelphia and Reading interest by George deB. Keim; the
Lehigh Valley interest by E. P. Wilbur; the Delaware, Lackawanna
and Western interest by Samuel Sloan; the Delaware and Hudson
interest by R. M. Olyphant; the Pennsylvania Railroad interest by
George B. Roberts; the Pennsylvania coal interest by George A.
Hoyt; the New York, Lake Erie and Western interest by John King,
jr.; the New York, Susquehanna and Western interest by F. A. Potts;
the Lehigh and Wilkesbarre coal interest by W. T. Tillinghast; the
Lehigh Coal and Navigation interest by J. S. Harris.

"After a very general discussion of all the interests involved
and the best result that it was desired to attain, it was moved by
Mr. Sloan as follows:

"The representatives of the anthracite interests agree upon a
pool of the anthracite to be mined between March 31st, 1886, and
March 31st, 1887.  The output for the year just named is, for the
purposes of this agreement, estimated at 33,500,000 tons.  The percentage of each interest is to be determined hereafter.  Any party
shipping over its percentage shall account to the pool for the
amount by which it may be found on the 31st of March, 1887, to have
exceeded its percentage at the rate of fifty cents per ton.  This
motion, being seconded by Mr. Olyphant, was agreed to by a unanimous vote.  On motion the meeting estimated that the market would
require for the month of April 2,000,000 tons of anthracite.  On
motion the meeting resolved that the price of coal should be immediately advanced twenty-five cents per ton f.o.b. at New York.  On
motion the meeting adjourned to meet at the office of the
Pennsylvania Coal Company in New York on Monday, March 29, 1886,
at 12 o'clock noon."


Testimony, J. S. Harris, quoting minutes of meeting of March
22, 1886, extract from testimony in an injunction suit filed by
the State of Pennsylvania against various anthracite interests,
No. 98, Equity Docket, Court of Common Please of Dauphin County;
reprinted in U.S., Congress, 50th, 2nd session, House of Representatives, Report No. 4147, Labor Troubles in the Anthracite Regions
of Pennsylvania, 1887-1888, (Washington, D.C.: Government Printing
Office, 1889), pp. 649-650.  Serial Number 2676.


307.  THE PETROLEUM SHUT-IN (1887)


Private regulation of production was widely practiced
in the industry.  Lee was president of three oil companies,
lawyer for the Pure Oil Company, he had been an oil attorney
in Venango County, Pennsylvania since 1869 and he was formerly a state senator and Mayor of Franklin, Pennsylvania.

Q. (By Mr. PHILLIPS.) Senator Lee has referred several times
to what was called the "shut-in" movement in oil, or limiting the
production.  It might be interesting and profitable if he would
state what led to that "shut-in" movement, and what action, if
any, was taken in regard to the labor employed throughout the oil
fields?--A.  The price of oil was below the cost of production
during the year 1887.  The average price that year was about 66
cents a barrel.  The Standard Oil Company said that they wanted to
treat the producers fairly, but that they had an excessive stock of
oil on hand--31,000,000 barrels--deteriorating in value, and that
if we wanted to have a better price production must be decreased,
so that they could use up that stock of oil, and take it off the
market, and save loss by wastage.  A number of the leading producers
met a number of the Standard people at Niagra Falls and, after discussing the subject, the producers agreed to limit their production,
in order that the Standard might dispose of that excessive stock of
oil.  I met with them, and I remember the contract by which the
producers purchased from the Standard Oil Company 6,000,000 barrels
of oil, to compensate them for limiting the production, and also to
compensate the labor they employed; because it would cut off the
revenue of the men who were engaged in that industry.  Mr. Phillips,
who was in that movement, insisted that we should set aside
2,000,000 barrels of oil to compensate the laboring men who were
in the industry, and who would be thrown out of employment by
cutting off the drilling of wells.


Testimony, James W. Lee, United States Industrial Commission,
I, p. 284.


308.  LUMBERING WITHOUT HEED OF THE FUTURE (1888)


Mohr predicted the exhaustion of southern timber
in less than a quarter of a century.  He was largely
correct.  Mohr came from Mobile, Alabama and was one of
five vice-presidents of the American Forestry Congress.


...The timber lands in the southern lumbering districts fronting on the water-courses and railroad lines have to a great extent
become exhausted within the distance to render the hauling of the
timber by teams to these lines of transportation any longer profitable.  In order to overcome this difficulty canals and ditches have
been dug wherever practicable, and many miles of transways were
constructed, equipped with iron rails and steam power, penetrating
the forests to the very divides which separate the basin of our
river from another.  Enterprises of the later kind require the
outlay of vast sums of money and are costly to maintain.  Temporary

as they are, to render them profitable they must be kept working
to their fullest capacity and without loss of time.  Consequently,
wherever they have been introduced the depletion of the timber lands
within reach is effected at a rate never existing before.  The
resulting production under the high pressure of capital is unavoidably leading to its concentration and is carried on with the sole
object of speediest returns, without heed of the future.

Charles Mohr, American Forestry Congress, Proceedings...at its
Meeting Held at Atlanta, Georgia, (Washington, D.C.:  Gibson Bros.,
1889), p. 36.

### 309.  BUYERS OF FEDERAL TIMBERLANDS IN LOUISIANA (1880-1888)

Much of the southern timberlands purchased by
absentee owners were held for future profits, and
for some purchasers the idle timberlands served to
minimize competition with their northern holdings.

#### BY NORTHERNERS

| Name | Residence | Acres |
|---|---|---|
| Avery, G. E. | Detroit, Mich. | 6,520 |
| Barnard, E. T. | Greenville, Mich. | 7,882 |
| Barker, S. B. | Chicago, Ill. | 28,380 |
| Birkett & McPherson. | Livingston Co., Mich. | 19,178 |
| Brackenridge & Wasey | Wayne Co., Mich. | 49,325 |
| Bradley, N. B. | Bay City, Mich. | 111,188 |
| Brown, A. C. | Marinette, Wis. | 42,842 |
| Chesbrough, A. M. | Lucas Co., O. | 11,785 |
| Comstock, C. C. | Grand Rapids, Mich. | 33,139 |
| Culver, L. S. | Bay City, Mich. | 9,526 |
| Cummer, J. & W. | Wexford Co., Mich. | 14,897 |
| Eddy, J. F. | Bay City, Mich. | 17,613 |
| Fairbanks & Harvey | Chicago, Ill. | 86,159 |
| Gay, G. W. | Grand Rapids, Mich. | 13,097 |
| Gould, J. | New York, N.Y. | 27,464 |
| Hackley, C. H. | Muskegon, Mich. | 89,743 |
| Hake & Coach | Grand Rapids, Mich. | 6,768 |
| Hamlin, B. C. | Snithport, Pa. | 26,907 |
| Hamlin H. | Snithport, Pa. | 18,002 |
| Head, F. H. | Chicago, Ill. | 109,645 |
| King, H. W. | Chicago, Ill. | 5,640 |

```
Lamport, Alway, et al. . . . . . . Ontario, Canada . . .      23,554
Leatham & Smith. . . . . . . . . . Door Co., Wis.. . . . . -   6,343
Morley, W. B.. . . . . . . . . . . St. Clair Co., Mich..     41,014
Nason, R. H. . . . . . . . . . . . Saginaw Co., Mich.. .     19,276
Penoyer, W. C. & W. V. . . . . . . Iosco Co., Mich.. . .     13,574
Prentice, S. R.. . . . . . . . . . Oakland, Cal. . . . .     18,525
Reinhart, H. . . . . . . . . . . . Sac Co., Iowa . . . .      5,660
Rice, W. M.. . . . . . . . . . . . Somerset Co., N.J.. .     48,608
Robinson, Lacey et al. . . . . . . Grand Rapids, Mich. .     60,025
Silliman, J. R.. . . . . . . . . . New York, N.Y.. . . .     23,843
Smith, M. J. . . . . . . . . . . . Wayne Co., Mich.. . .     10,080
Van Schaick & Carpenter. . . . . . Chicago, Ill. . . . .     70,274
Wasey & Winchester . . . . . . . . Detroit, Mich.. . . .     18,581
Watkins, J. B. . . . . . . . . . . Douglas Co., Kan. . .    145,335
Wetmore, L. C. . . . . . . . . . . Warren Co., Pa. . . .      8,460
Wetmore & Jefferson. . . . . . . . Warren Co., Pa. . . .      6,660
Winchester, C. . . . . . . . . . . Ashburnham, Mass. . .     15,100
Woods, J. L. . . . . . . . . . . . Cleveland, O. . . . .     84,279
Woods & Pack . . . . . . . . . . . Cleveland, O. . . . .      9,650
Yawkey, W. C.. . . . . . . . . . . Bay City, Mich. . . .      5,790
    TOTAL  . . . . . . . . . . . . . . . . . . . . . . . . 1,370,332
```

## THE SOUTHERNERS

| Name | Resident | Acres |
|---|---|---|
| Bradford, J. L. . . . . . . . . . . | New Orleans, La.. . . . | 17,338 |
| Beer, H. & B. . . . . . . . . . . . | New Orleans, La.. . . . | 17,807 |
| English & Drew. . . . . . . . . . . | Calcasieu Parish, La. | 13,475 |
| Forest Land Co. . . . . . . . . . . | Little Rock, Ark. . . | 14,832 |
| Lutcher & Moore . . . . . . . . . . | Orange Co., Texas . . | 108,051 |
| Perkins & Moore . . . . . . . . . . | Calcasieu Parish, La. | 6,097 |
| Poitevant & Favre . . . . . . . . . | Hancock, Miss.. . . . . | 39,771 |
| Thomson & Knapp . . . . . . . . . . | Calcasieu Parish, La. | 24,681 |
| Violett, A. . . . . . . . . . . . . | New Orleans, La.. . . . | 19,880 |
| TOTAL. . . . . . . . . . . . . . . . . . . . . . . . . . | | 261,932 |

Paul W. Gates, "Federal Land Policy in the South, 1866-1888," *Journal of Southern History*, VI (August, 1940), pp. 319-320.

### 310.   LUMBERING AND FORESTRY HAVE LITTLE
IN COMMON (1893)

Toward the end of the 19th century, systematic training for forestry began to take hold in American higher education. With the closing of the frontier, the disappearance of the bounty of timbered lands became a realistic prospect for the first time in American history.

Here, the editor of the leading trade journal, <u>North
Western Lumberman</u>, warns against the shortsightedness
endemic in the commercial practice of lumbering.

The 'Relation of Forestry to the Lumbering Industry' is practically, so far, very meagre....Forestry...as I understand it, means
the handling of timber to the best possible advantage, due attention
being paid to the matter of selection, the prevention of waste, and
the preservation of young trees.  Any one acquainted with American
lumbering methods knows they are not hampered with any such conditions.
 Between the great bulk of lumbering business and forestry there
is at present no actual relation, and it may be readily seen why
there is none....The saws are run strictly on business principles
and for the purpose of putting the last dollar possible into the
pockets of the men who operate them....He is not in the business for
a lifetime, much less for the benefit of future generations.  Ask
the majority of manufacturers, and they will say that in five,
eight, ten, or a dozen years, as the case may be, their timber will
be exhausted and that they will then retire....
 In the future there will be a decidedly intimate relation
between forestry and the lumbering industry, but it will be when the
hum and clatter of the great commercial mills will have nearly died
away, as then there will be but few great bodies of timber from
which such mills may be fed.

Met. L. Saley, American Forestry Association, <u>Proceedings...
of the World's Fair Congress</u>, (Washington, D.C.:  The Association,
1894), pp. 147, 148, 150.

311.  "A NEAT PROFIT OF $36,000,000" (1893)

Here is an excellent example of financiering
that required a booming stock market for its culmina-
tion.  Upshur had been a business associate of John D.
Rockefeller, J. P. Morgan, and James Stillman.  His
book is dedicated to Morgan.

The National City Bank has always been regarded as the metal
merchants' bank.  A group consisting of H. H. Rogers, William
Rockefeller and James Stillman, commonly known as the Standard Oil
gang, which got its start in the panic of 1893, bought the Anaconda
Copper Company from Marcus Daly for $39,000,000.  The gave him a
check for the amount, and this was to be held for a stated time.
Meanwhile the group organized the Amalgamated Copper Corporation,
which took over all of the mines of Anaconda at $75,000,000, paying

for it with all of its capital stock, but no cash.  The National
City Bank undertook to sell the $75,000,000 issue and did so.
This took care of the $39,000,000 check and left a neat profit
of $36,000,000.


George L. Upshur, <u>As I Recall Them</u>, (New York:  Wilson-
Erickson, Inc., 1936), p. 168.

# B.

# DIVISION AND EXTENSION OF THE LAND

312.  CRIPPLING THE HOMESTEAD ACT (1862)

After a generation of agitation, Congress enacted
the Homestead Law of 1862 which offered settlers a free
homestead selected out of federally-owned land.  Some
of its shortcomings are suggested below.  For long a member
of the U.S. House of Representatives from Indiana, the
writer, Julian, was a political descendant of the land
reformers of the 1840's.

One of the great compensations of the war was the passage of
the Homestead Act of the 20th of May [1862].  It finally passed the
House and Senate by overwhelming majorities.  Among the last acts
of Mr. Buchanan's administration was the veto of a similar measure,
at the bidding of his Southern masters; and the friends of the
policy had learned in the struggle of a dozen years that its success
was not possible while slavery ruled the government.  The beneficent
operation of this great and far-reaching measure, however, was
seriously crippled by some unfortunate facts.  In the first place,
it provided no safeguards against speculation in the public domain,
which had so long scourged the Western States and Territories, and
was still extending its ravages.  Our pioneer settlers were offered
homes of one hundred and sixty acres each on condition of occupancy
and improvement, but the speculator could throw himself across their
track by buying up large bodies of choice land to be held back from
settlement and tillage for a rise in price, and thus force them
further into the frontier, and on to less desirable lands.

In the next place, under the new and unguarded land-grant policy, which was simultaneously inaugurated, millions of acres fell into the clutches of monopolists, and are held by them to-day [1884], which would have gone to actual settlers under the Homestead law, and the moderate land-grant policy originated by Senator Douglas in 1850. This was not foreseen or intended. The nation was then engaged in a struggle for its existence, and thus exposed to the evils of hasty legislation. The value of the lands given away was not then understood as it has been since, while the belief was universal that the lands granted would be restored to the public domain on failure to comply with the conditions of the grants. The need of great highways to the Pacific was then regarded as imperative, and unattainable without large grants of the public lands. These are extenuating facts; but the mischiefs of this ill-starred legislation are none the less to be deplored.

In the third place, under our new Indian treaty policy, invented about the same time, large bodies of land, when released by our Indian tribes, were sold at low rates to individual speculators and monopolists, or to railway corporations, instead of being conveyed, as before, to the United States, and thus subjected to general disposition, as other public land. These evils are now remedied, but for nearly ten years they were unchecked. The title to Indian lands was secured through treaties concocted by a ring of speculators and monopolists outside of the Senate, and frequently ratified by that body near the close of a long session, when less than half a dozen members were in their seats, and the entire business was supervised by a single Western senator acting as the agent of his employers and the sharer in their plunder. These fatal mistakes in our legislation have made the Homestead law a half-way measure, instead of that incomplete reform in our land policy which was demanded, and they furnish a remarkable commentary upon the boasted friendship of the Republican party for the landless poor.

George W. Julian, Political Recollections, 1840 to 1872, (Chicago, Illinois:  Jansen, McClurg and Co., 1884), pp. 216-218.

313.   CONFISCATE AND PARCEL OUT THE PLANTATIONS (1864)

The Radical Republicans wished to revolutionize southern life by destroying the economic basis of the Southern aristocracy--the large plantation. Neither Congress nor the President, however, reached this point of view. In the end, such hesitancy led to a fatal weakness of Reconstruction policy.

During the latter part of January [1864] I reported from the
Committee on Public Lands a proposition to extend the Homestead Law
of 1862 to the forfeited and confiscated lands of Rebels.  It was
a very radical proposition, proposing to deal with these lands as
public lands, and parcel them out into small homesteads among the
poor of the South, black and white.

. . . . . . . . . . . . . . . . . . . . . . . . . . . . . . . . . . . .

On the 12th of May the House passed my Southern Homestead Bill
by the strictly party vote of seventy-five to sixty-four.

. . . . . . . . . . . . . . . . . . . . . . . . . . . . . . . . . . . .

The passage of the Southern Homestead Bill, however, could
only prove a very partial measure without an enactment reaching the
fee of rebel land owners; and I confidently anticipated the endorsement of such a measure by the Republican National Convention, which
was to meet in Baltimore, on the seventh of June.  I was much gra-
tified when the National Union League approved it, in its Convention
in that city the day before; and a resolution embodying it was also
reported favorably by the sub-committee on resolutions of the
National Republican Convention the next day.  But the General
Committee, on the motion of McKee Dunn of Indiana, always an incor-
rigible conservation, struck it out, much to the disappointment of
the Republican masses....

Having understood that Mr. Lincoln had changed his opinion respecting the power of Congress to confiscate the landed estates of
rebels, I called to see him on the subject on the 2d of July, and
asked him if I might say to the people that what I had learned on
the subject was true, assuring him that I could make a far better
fight for our cause, if he would permit me to do so.  He replied
that when he prepared his veto of our law on the subject two years
before, he had not examined the matter thoroughly, but that on further reflection, and on reading Solicitor Whiting's law argument,
he had changed his opinion, and thought he would now sign a bill
striking this statement, which was of service to the cause in the
canvass; but, unfortunately, constitutional scruples respecting such
legislation gained ground, and although both Houses of Congress at
different times endorsed the principle, it never became a law, owing
to unavoidable differences between the President and Congress on the
question of reconstruction.  The action of the President in dealing
with rebel land owners was of the most serious character.  It para-
lyzed one of the most potent means of putting down the Rebellion,
prolonging the conflict and aggravating its cost, and at the same
time left the owners of large estates in full possession of their
lands at the end of the struggle, who naturally excluded from the
ownership of the soil the freedmen and poor whites who had been
friendly to the Union; while the confiscation of life estates as a
war measure was of no practical advantage to the Government or
disadvantage to the enemy.

Julian, Political Recollections, pp. 238, 240, 242, 245-246.

314.   "THE NEGROES WERE ALL ANXIOUS TO PURCHASE LAND" (1866)

The most basic yearning of the freed slaves was
to own land.  During the Civil War, in various parts of
the South, the freedmen succeeded in becoming landowners
although many were dislodged from this role at war's end.
While a minority of Radical Republicans in Congress during
the late 1860s pressed for a division of the plantations
among the ex-slaves, a majority of both parties refused to
make such a decision.  This left individual freedmen on
their own in their efforts to buy land.

The negroes were all anxious to purchase land.  "What's de use
of being free," said one, an old man of sixty, who was begging permission to plant cotton; "What's de use of being free if you don't
own land enough to buried in?  Might juss as well stay slave all
yo' days."  "All I wants," said another, explaining what he was going to do with his money, of which he had already saved four or
five hundred dollars; "All I wants is to git to own fo' or five ac-
cres of land, dat I can build me a little house on and call my
home."  In many portions of the Mississippi Valley the feeling
against any ownership of the soil by the negroes is so strong, that
the man who should sell small tracts to them would be in actual personal danger.  Every effort will be made to prevent negroes from acquiring lands; and even the renting of small tracts to them is held
to be unpatriotic and unworthy of a good citizen.  Through such
difficulties is it that the subject-race is called upon to prove,
by its prosperity, its fitness for freedom.

Whitelaw Reid, After the War:  A Southern Tour.  May 1, 1865
to May 1, 1866, (London:  Sampson Low, Son, and Marston, 1866),
pp. 564-565.

315.  MR. ASTOR'S CORNER LOTS (1870)

Mr. William Astor, the eldest son of John
Jacob Astor, was surely a chip off the old block.

In the upper part of New York hundreds of lots can be seen enclosed by dilapidated fences, disfigured by rocks and waste material, or occupied as gardens; mostly corner lots.  These are eligibly
located, many of them surrounded by a fashionable population.  They
give an untidy and bankrupt appearance to the upper part of the
city.  Mr. Astor owns most of these corner lots.  He will sell the
centre lots, but keeps the corners for a rise.  He will neither sell

nor improve them.  Frequently men call, and announce some great
improvement in the vicinity of his up-town property.  They are
about to build a church, or put up some public institution, and ask
of him a subscription.  He usually gives nothing.  He knows that no
parties can improve the centre of the block without benefiting
the corners.  He knows the improvements will go on whether he gives
or not.  He leaves the giving to others, while he enjoys the profit.
. . . . . . . . . . . . . . . . . . . . . . . . . . . . . . . . . .
      In the upper part of the city can be seen, in fashionable
localities, large tracts of unoccupied land.  Goats graze on them,
or at best, market sauce is raised, fences are down or dilapidated.
These lands belong to the Astors,--they are held for a rise.  The
scraggling look of upper New York is owing to the same cause.  A
house here and there,--a small row of houses in the center of a
street,--while corner lots are vacant every where.  If the Astors
sell, they sell in the middle of the block.  Every course of brick
laid enhances the value of the property.


Matthew Hale Smith, Twenty Years Among the Bulls and Bears of
Wall Street, (New York:  American Book Company, 1871), pp. 101-102,
103.


### 316.  BLACK LAND OWNERSHIP IN THE SOUTH (1870)

      The writer, who was General Superintendent of
Education of the Freedmen's Bureau, was anxious to show
how freedmen were succeeding in becoming landowners and
thus economically self-sufficient (he had recently completed a tour of the South).  Why they did not become so
is partly explained by Source Nos. 339 and 340.


South Carolina appropriated last year $200,000 to buy land in
the upper part of the State which has been sold to Freedmen for
homesteads.  Upwards of 40,000 acres of this land have been actually
sold during the year to poor men of all colors.  The Governor says
he intends this year to recommend for the same purpose an appropriation of $400,000....
      The Freedmen are very eager for land.  The savings they have
placed in our Banks, and the profits of cotton this year, are
enabling them to make large purchases.  In Orangeburg County, South
Carolina, hundreds of colored men have bought lands and are building
and settling upon them.  In a single day, in our Charleston Savings
Bank, I took the record of seventeen Freedmen who were drawing their
money to pay for farms they had been buying, generally forty or
fifty acres each, paying about $10 per acre.  I met at a cotton
merchant's in that city ten Freedmen who had clubbed together with

the proceeds of their crop and bought a whole Sea Island plantation
of seven hundred acres.  The merchant was that day procuring their
deed.  He told me that the entire purchase price was paid in cash
from the balance due them on the crop of the season.  Here, then,
besides supporting their families with provisions raised, these men
had each, by the profits of a single year, bought a farm of seventy
acres.  What northern laborer could do better?

I found on the Islands other clubs forming to do the same
thing, and this in a season when the caterpiller has destroyed one-
half their cotton.  A leading cotton broker in Charleston told me
that he thought nearly half the cotton on the Islands belonged to
colored men.  He had himself already 126 consignments from them,
and the amount of his sales on their account had reached over
$30,000.  As I learned, the average of the Freedmen's crop, or
share of crop, of Sea Island cotton is from three to six hundred
pounts each.

Just out of the city [of Atlanta, Georgia] is a settlement of
about one hundred families--something like the Barry Farm at
Washington--where small homesteads have been purchased and are
being paid for; average value of each from $100 to $500.  These
families are joyously cultivating their own gardens and provision
grounds, also finding work in the city.  The Bureau has erected for
them a convenient house, now used for a school and chapel.

Further in the interior the Freedmen are buying or renting
land and raising their own crops.  A community of such families,
about thirty miles out (in South Carolina), came in, a few days
since, to market their crops for the season.  They had chartered
a railroad car for $140 the round trip, and loading it with cotton,
corn, &c. exchanged the same for clothing, furniture, implements
of husbandry, and supplies for putting in their next crop.

I find the following history of the Freedmen's labor [in Macon,
Georgia]:  The first year they worked for bare subsistence; second
year they bought stock-mules, implements, &c.; third year many
rented lands; and now, the fourth year, large numbers are prepared
to buy.  This is the record of the most industrious, others are
following at a sowwer pace.  In this process difficulties have been
encountered--low wages, fraud, ill-treatment, &c., some becoming
discouraged, but the majority are determined to rise.  As illustrations:  Several Freedmen in Houston county have bought from 100 to
600 acres of land each.  One man is now planting for fifty bales of
cotton.  A colored company (called Peter Walker's) own 1,500 acres.
Two brothers (Warren) saved in the bank $600, and with it obtained
a title to 1,500 acres, having credit for the balance, and both are
now building houses and preparing to make a crop which they expect
will clear off their whole debt.  In Americus fully one hundred
houses and lots belong to colored people....

I still find evidence of thrift among the Freedmen.  From
returns, made at the capital, it appears that in nearly every county
of Georgia they have purchased land and commenced farming on their
own account....

Mr. Harris, our inspector, who resides at Beaufort, S.C. and
whom I find earnestly examining the freedmen's banks in this
region, has given me the record of nearly two thousand families now
settled on Sea Island lands owned by themselves.  For these purchases most of them had saved their money in the savings bank,
at Beaufort.

Letters from the South Relating to the Condition of the
Freedmen, Addressed to Major General O. O. Howard by J. W. Alvord,
(Washington, D.C.:  Howard University Press, 1870), pp. 5, 9-10,
15-16, 19, and 28.

317.  RESTRICTION ON LAND OWNERSHIP IN MISSISSIPPI (1871)

Land ownership meant economic independence which
would mean higher wages for the remaining laborers.
Mississippi planters forestalled the latter by precluding
blacks from owning land.  Powers was Lt. Governor of
Mississippi, having been elected on December 1, 1869.

Question.  Has there been, so far as your information extends,
any disposition on the part of the white class to prevent the
colored race from becoming the owners of lands--cultivating them?
Answer.  There was a very manifest disposition to prevent
them from owning lands in 1866 and 1867, at the time the legislature of those years passed the law forbidding them to own or lease
lands.  There was such a law passed by this State by the legislatures in 1865 and 1867.
Question.  What did you understand to be the reasons that
induced that legislature?
Answer.  Well, sir, the planters had an idea at the time, and
the prevailing idea was that it was impairing their efficiency as
laborers; that the good of the country required that they should
be kept in such a condition that they could be controlled as they
had formerly been.
By Mr. BUCKLEY:
Question.  Was that a democratic legislature?
Answer.  Yes, sir, it was a democratic legislature.  The idea
of the planters at first was to keep large plantations; to run
large plantations the same as they had done prior to the war.  It
was a long time before they could give up the idea of planting on
a large scale.  At that time it was thought that if the colored
men were allowed to lease or buy lands, it would demoralize the
labor of the entire country.  It was necessary, they thought, to
control the labor in order to do anything at all to prosper.

By the CHAIRMAN:

Question. Did they apprehend a scarcity of labor to run
their plantations in case the negroes generally became independent
freeholders?

Answer. Yes, sir; that was one of the motives, undoubtedly.


Testimony, Ridgeley C. Powers, November 8, 1871; U.S.
Congress, Joint Select Committee to Inquire into the Condition of
Affairs in the Late Insurrectionary States, Testimony, XI,
(Washington, D.C.: Government Printing Office, 1872), p. 590.


318.  DIFFICULTIES OF BLACK LAND OWNERSHIP IN FLORIDA (1871)


Privately-owned farm land was not sold to blacks
and they had difficulty buying small parcels of government land. Fortune, an ex-slave, had been a member of the
Florida legislature and a member of the state constitutional
convention.


Question. How do they regard your people getting land and
owning it for themselves?

Answer. Well, they generally do not interfere with them much,
not in that line.

Question. Are they ready to sell them land?

Answer. No, sir; they will not sell land; we have to purchase
land from the Government, or from the State, otherwise we cannot
get it. They do not sell our people any land; they have no disposition to do so. They will sell them a lot now and then in a
town, but nothing of any importance.

. . . . . . . . . . . . . . . . . . . . . . . . . . . . . . . . . . . . .

Question. You spoke of the difficulty of obtaining land; is
it not very abundant in Florida?

Answer. Yes, sir.

Question. And cheap?

Answer. Not very cheap.

Question. If you wanted to buy a farm what could you get a
pretty good farm for here; how much an acre?

Answer. Cultivable land over there was generally worth from
ten to fifteen dollars an acre.

Question. You could get a good piece of land for that?

Answer. Yes, sir.

Question. What did you get Government land for?

Answer. I think the State lands were one dollar and a quarter
an acre.

Question. And you could obtain lands for how much under the
homestead law?

Answer. I have forgotten the terms of the homestead law; but
a great many of our people take up homesteads.

Question. Can you buy all the good lands you want for ten or fifteen dollars an acre?

Answer. Very poor people cannot afford that.

Question. You can get it if you have the money?

Answer. They will not sell it in small quantities. I would have bought forty acres there if the man would have sold me less than a whole tract. They hold it in that way so that colored people cannot buy it.

Question. Do you think it is held so that they cannot buy it, or does the set of buildings on a farm make too big a piece for a poor man to buy?

Answer. No sir; the quarters are excluded from the cultivable land. The lands we cultivate, generally, are swamp, or hommock, or lowlands.

Question. There is an objection to selling small quantities of land?

Answer. Yes, sir; and that is really the great obstacle in the way of colored people getting land.

Question. Is there not plenty of other land to buy?

Answer. Not that is worth anything in that county. I do not know of any Government land there that will raise cotton.

Question. How about other parts of Florida?

Answer. I do not know about other parts; I believe in some other counties they do better. For instance, in Marion County and in Alachau County they get better lands there as homesteads than in other counties. But the homesteads in Jackson County are of no account at all--very poor.

Question. The good lands are all occupied?

Answer. Yes, sir; all taken up.


Testimony, Emanuel Fortune, November 10, 1871; U.S. Congress, Joint Select Committee to Inquire into the Condition of Affairs in the Late Insurrectionary States, Testimony, XIII, (Washington, D.C.: Government Printing Office, 1872), pp. 95, 96-97.


319.  FRAUDULENT LAND ENTRIES IN THE UNITED STATES (1883)

These years saw the final foreclosing of the historic dream of a nation of independent farmers. Concentration of land-ownership and outright fraudulent acquisition of the remaining public lands combined to bring about the end of free land on the frontier. McFarland was Commissioner of the General Land Office and Teller was Secretary of the Interior.

The rapid absorption of public lands under the various acts
for their appropriation and disposal has brought the remaining
lands into great request, and the marketable price of unimproved
land in many parts of the country much exceeds the government
price.

This fact stimulates entries for speculative purposes, and
the exceedingly liberal legislation of Congress designed to favor
actual settlers, has become an instrumentality for the fraudulent
acquirement of titles and claims by means of which the actual
settler is prevented from making settlement unless he enters into
an expensive contest to clear the land from a fraudulent claim,
or purchases at a speculative price the relinquishment of some
claim of that character.

My information is that desirable agricultural lands in new
States and Territories are, in many instances, and in some portions
of the country apparently in all instances, covered with claims
simultaneously with the filing in the local land office of the
plats of township surveys.

These claims consist of pre-emption filings, soldiers' homestead filings, timber culture entries and homestead entries. Such
filings and entries are frequently made by professed agents or
attorneys, who in many cases immediately thereafter advertise
relinquishments in this wholesale manner is _prima_ _facie_ evidence
of the fraudulent character of claims proposed to be so relin-
quished. And yet such claims hold the land until the parties controlling the relinquishments can find customers in the persons of
actual settlers or other parties who will buy the relinquishments
from them, unless the fraudulent claims are removed by individual
contests, or by an investigation and hearing at the instance of
the government.

. . . . . . . . . . . . . . . . . . . . . . . . . . . . . . . . . .

Under the desert-land act entries are procured to be made in
the interest of others than the professed entryman, in violation
of the restriction to one entry by any one person, and large tracts
of land are thus unlawfully secured.

Desert entries are also frequently made upon good grass or
agricultural lands which are leased for grazing or other purposes,
or held for speculation. Such entries are also used to control
the water supply upon which larger areas of country are dependent,
when no intention of complying with the law exists, or little or
no attempt at such compliance is made.

Forged soldiers' additional homestead certificates have been
located on a large belt of the most valuable timber land in
California, and the timber cut and removed.

In the grazing districts of Western Kansas, in Colorado,
New Mexico, Arizona, California, Nevada, Idaho, Wyoming, and
Montana, the title to agricultural lands and water rights is in
large classes of cases obtained by perjury and fraud, followed or
preceded by the unlawful inclosure of tracts of public lands,
varying from some thousands to several thousand acres each, over
which dominion is exercised by private parties to the exclusion of
valid settlement rights under the laws of the United States. It

appears also, in some cases, that lands so fenced in are parcelled
out according to the number of the cattle possessed by individual
ranchmen, and the right to herd upon such public lands leased to
them for a money consideration.

In California, Oregon, and Washington Territory collusive
entries are made under the timber-land act for the purpose of procuring or controlling the timber in large quantities, contrary to
the restrictions of the law.  It is also represented that lands
valuable for agriculture, as well as for timber, are entered under
the timber-land act, and that titles to large bodies of timbered
farming lands are thus illegally obtained by single individuals.

Valuable timber lands, and lands unfit for anything but timber,
are fraudulently entered under the homestead and pre-emption laws
in the above and other States and Territories.

Timber lands in Northern Minnesota have been so largely entered
by false affidavits of settlemen under these laws that I felt compelled during the past year to place 3,000,000 acres on the market
at the minimum price on agricultural land to avoid such wholesale
criminality.

A partial investigation in Alabama has disclosed the fact that
the government has been defrauded out of some millions of dollars
through the unlawful entry of coal and iron lands under agricultural
laws.  Information of similar frauds committed in Colorado and elsewhere, has been pressed upon my attention; but not investigated
for want of means.

. . . . . . . . . . . . . . . . . . . . . . . . . . . . . . . . . .
There are now before this office claims in some initiative
or progressive stage covering titles to more than 200,000,000 acres
of land, of which some 50,000,000 acres are embraced in individual
entries under general laws.

That a very considerable proportion of these claims are without
validity or merit is indisputably true.  Yet this office has been
compelled for years past to treat doubtful claims as valid, and to
pass over to claimants the title of the United States because it
could not investigate the facts.


Letter, N. C. McFarland to H. M. Teller, February 3, 1883,
U.S. Congress, 47th Congress, 2nd session, Exec. Doc. No. 61,
Violations of Laws Relating to Public Lands, serial number 2076,
pp. 3, 4 and 5.



320.   ACQUIRING LAND IN ABERDEEN, DAKOTA TERRITORY (1884)


Here is a candid view of the land business on the
plains.  During the 1880s, Humphrey was a Boston farm
mortgage firm's land inspector in Dakota Territory.

It was a great game, this settling of the new country, and as
full of tricks as the frontier gambling house.  Many a man working
or clerking in town was "holding down a claim" by going out to
live in his little sod shack over Sunday.  If it was too far away,
he would go out even less often and take the risk of having his
claim "jumped"--that is, occupied and filed on at the local government land office by someone else.  Human scavengers were always on
the lookout for such opportunities to get a good claim for themselves or, more frequently, to bleed the lax settlers for a stiff
sum as the price of moving off.  But if the settler happened to be
a bit stern in his notions and free with his gun, this coy little
trick often resulted in a dead jumper.

Sometimes the settler, knowing that he would be "in wrong" at
the land office in the event of a lawsuit, would sell out to the
jumper and "relinquish"--that is, cancel his own filing and thus
make the jumper's filing good.  Contests before the land commissioner involved tall swearing, both in and out of court and by both
contestants, since it was rarely possible to get impartial witnesses
or, for that matter, any witnesses at all.  Delays of a year or
more were not uncommon, and even then justice was often largely a
matter of guesswork.  It was usually the part of wisdom for either
settler or jumper to relinquish to the other for a consideration.

Often a settler who was ill prepared for the long tough job
of getting his land into shape to yield a living, having acquired
wisdom from experience, would accommodatingly sell out his uncom-
pleted right to some newcomer whose enthusiasms were still fresh
and unspoiled.  "Relinquishing" in this way before acquiring title
to the land, although it was frowned upon by the land office,
became quite a business, and land traders frequently took a hand
in bringing the two parties together.  There was no standard consideration for these relinquishments; they varied from several
hundred dollars to a pair of boots, depending on how desperate was
the one and how optimistic the other.

These were only a few of the ways to defeat the government's
purpose in its distribution of land to settlers.  A man of some
means once came to us in the mill with an offer of good wages and
little work for six months if we would join his crowd, who were
going to exercise their "preemption rights" in one big group,
"prove up" and take titles in their own names, and then deed the
lands at a very reasonable cost.  But government spotters were
always on the alert for just such frauds as this.  And it happened
that they caught, among others, this too clever individual.

A great game it was and a crooked one.  Much of the land went
at first to a "fly-by-night" crowd; the real pioneer farmer was the
big Swede who came in afterward with his family, bought his land
"on time," and settled down to a life of hard work....

Many a settler who tried honestly to succeed was doomed to
failure because he had never learned in advance the biggest lesson
of this or any other prairie frontier, that one hundred and sixty
acres of tough prairie sod do not constitute a farm; they are the
raw material out of which a farm can be made with proper equipment
and years of hard labor.

The government encouraged this delusion when it failed to require anything more than a shack, the breaking of ten acres, and a well; not a line as to personal qualifications and equipment. This policy of giving away land to anybody and everybody not only defeated the one sane purpose of the distribution, but wrecked thousands of well-intentioned men and women with the belief that getting a piece of governmental land was all they needed to become successful farmers.

Of course these pathetic failures were in a small minority. By far the greater number of landseekers took up government land with the intention of unloading it on somebody else, the loan companies offering themselves as the easiest possible marks. It was the few who stayed and tried and failed that made the tragedy of the Dakota prairies; and the failure bore heaviest on the women.

Seth K. Humphrey, Following the Prairie Frontier, (Minneapolis, Minnesota: University of Minnesota Press, 1931), pp. 82-85, 132.


321.  FOREIGN HOLDINGS OF WESTERN LANDS (1886)


In 1795, Talleyrand had advised Dutch capitalists to invest in American land (see Source No. 7).  A century later, over 30 million acres were owned by British and other investors.  Here is one of the few contemporary statistical inquiries into the subject.


The extent of this foreign holding of lands here is illustrated by the following list and amounts in acres, not complete by any means, but illustrative of the situation:

An English syndicate, No. 3, own in Texas................3,000,000
The Holland Company, New Mexico..........................4,500,000
Sir Edward Reid and a syndicate in Florida...............2,000,000
English syndicate in Mississippi.........................1,800,000
Marquis of Tweeddale.....................................1,750,000
Phillips, Marshall & Co., London.........................1,300,000
German syndicate.........................................1,000,000
Anglo-American syndicate, London.........................  750,000
Byron A. Evans, of London................................  700,000
Duke of Sutherland.......................................  425,000
British Land Company in Kansas...........................  320,000
William Whalley, M.P., Peterborough, England.............  310,000
Missouri Land Company, Edinburgh, Scotland...............  300,000
Robert Tennet, of London.................................  230,000
Dundee Land Company, Scotland............................  247,000
Lord Dunmore.............................................  120,000
Benjamin Newgas, Liverpool...............................  100,000

Lord Houghton, in Florida.............................    60,000
Lord Dunraven, in Colorado...........................    60,000
English Land Company in Florida......................    60,000
English Land Company in Arkansas.....................    50,000
Albert Peal, M.P., Leicestershire, England...........    10,000
Sir J. L. Kay, Yorkshire, England....................     5,000
Alexander Grant, of London, in Kansas................    35,000
English syndicate, Wisconsin.........................   110,000
M. Ellerhansen, of Halifax, in West Virginia.........   600,000
A Scotch syndicate in Florida........................   500,000
A. Boysen, Danish consul, Milwaukee..................    50,000
Missouri Land Company, of Edinburgh..................   165,000
          Total....................................20,747,000

This list could be greatly enlarged. Only the more important cases are given. Cases of like character are numerous, but small in area, aggregating over 30,000,000 acres.

U.S. Congress, 49th, 1st session, House of Representatives, Committee on Public Lands, Report No. 3455, Ownership of Real Estate in the Territories, p. 2.


322.   OPENING OF THE CHEROKEE OUTLET (1893)


        Starting in 1889, the federal government opened the first of a number of Oklahoma ex-reservation-areas to homesteaders. These areas had been purchased by the government from the Indian tribes. Mossler lived near Corydon, Indiana and left for the Cherokee outlet in Oklahoma early in September 1893. He was 31 years old at the time.


        About five minutes before 12:00 o'clock, when a pistol was to be fired by a soldier as a signal to start, we noticed the lines to the west of us moving, not leisurely but at full speed. Someone shouted to the soldier to let us go, but before he did someone gave a whoop and away the crowd dashed, taking everyone along. Just as we passed the soldier he fired the gun, then turned his attention toward keeping from being run over and trampled by the crowd. As far as one could see east and west, people were going at full speed. After about the first mile the crowd began to widen out, giving more room. Dust was thick and stifling, but luckily there was a little side wind and the horses were able to keep abreast of the thickest of it.
. . . . . . . . . . . . . . . . . . . . . . . . . . . . . . . . .

Now we could see on either side of the trails men and women
on horseback and vehicles slowing up, dismounting, and driving
stakes, signifying their choice in a home site.  Since we had not
yet found the kind of land we wanted, we rode on.  Ahead of us
suddenly was plainly visible a cloud of smoke, and we soon came to
a prairie fire.  Because of the short grass and the side wind the
horses jumped it easily.  It was generally supposed that the men
who came into the territory the night before the run and who bore
the name of "Sooners" set the fire.

. . . . . . . . . . . . . . . . . . . . . . . . . . . . . . . . . . . . . . . .

When we arrived in Perry the town site was teeming with people
from all parts of the United States.  There stood a tent city of
ten thousand population, where the day before had been only prairies.  Filing companies were formed which took several hours.  It
was necessary to stay close together in order to file when the
company was called.  If you weren't there when called, you had to
go to the end of the line and join another company, which caused
delay.

Louis A. Mossler, "Opening of the Cherokee Outlet," <u>Indiana
Magazine of History</u>, edited by Mrs. Grace M. Smith, 50 (1954),
pp. 169, 170, 172.

### 323.  "HE'S ONE OF OUR KIND, TOM" (1893)

Obtaining part of the valuable public domain,
as the English colonists learned, was partly a matter
of political influence.  It was no different in the
Far West.

In February, 1893, I went to Washington to get the patents on
iron claims and lands for townsite purposes I had applied for.  The
morning following my arrival, Senator Francis E. Warren went personally with me to the General Land Office and introduced me to
Thomas H. Carter of Montana, the General Land Commissioner, and with
his hand on the commissioner's shoulder said sotto voce "He's one
of our kind, Tom, see what you can do for him."  This was of value
to me then and years later in another matter.
...The day I received what I came after, never having mentioned
the matter in the meantime to the Senator, though we were together
more or less every day and night, I went to say good-bye to him.
He was at his desk in his committee room at the Capitol, writing,
and without turning said: "Well, Charlie, have you got what you
came for?"  "Yes."  "What have you got?"  "I have seventy-two
mineral and twenty-three agricultural patents, ninety-five in all,

in my own name." He whirled his swivel chair around and facing me said earnestly: "Don't tell anybody that. It's more than anyone has got since the government was formed." He had pressed the button, and I had done the rest.

Just ten years later, on another trip to Washington, I brought back patents for forty-six iron claims.


Charles A. Guernsey, <u>Wyoming Cowboy Days</u>, (New York:   G. P. Putnam's Sons, 1936), pp. 155-156.

# C.

# THE TRANSPORTATION
# NETWORK

### 324.  BUILD A ST. LAWRENCE SEAWAY (1863)

The obvious commercial advantages of the
St. Lawrence Seaway were understood a century ago.
Especially interesting is the fact that the propo-
nent, below, was neither a midwesterner nor a
representative of water-transport interests.  Poor
was a lawyer and promoter of railroads in New England;
his youngest brother was Henry Varnum Poor.


Great as is now the internal trade of the country, it is tithe
only of what it will, in a few years attain to.  The production of
food is not, at this time, equal to one tenth of the capacity of
the Northwestern states, without resort to the artificial stimu-
lants that are common in the British Isles.  Besides this, one half
of all the grain raised in the United States is produced at points
so remote from market that its value would be consumed in the mere
cost of transportation by the ordinary channels.  With the aid of
all existing canals and railroads, a bushel of wheat in the Northwest is only worth one half its value in Liverpool, so enormous is
the cost of present transportation.  The question is:  How shall
this difficulty be overcome?  And it is this question alone that
will engage the time and thoughts of the members of the convention.
It has seemed to me that the great difficulty lies in the way
of outlets from Chicago, Milwaukee, and other lake ports, rather
than in the lack of means to bring produce to the lake shores.

Cheaply built and economically worked lines of railway, with other means of transit, bring into these great granaries--the lake ports--more produce than the outlets can economically take away.

What are wanted are cheap and expeditious means of transit from the upper lakes to the open sea. To secure these most effec- tually, we must make the St. Lawrence waters an open Mediterranean Sea; so that, from the head of Lake Superior and from Chicago, ships of useful size for navigating the ocean can pass, free of duty and with despatch, to the Atlantic ports and Europe, and backward to the same places, fully laden. By this means, you could diminish by one half, the cost of transit, for the benefit of the farmers of the Northwestern states; and indirectly, for the advantage of the entire population of the country.

Ships should load at Chicago for any port into which an Atlan- tic sailer can enter, and by as many routes as can be created: from the St. Lawrence, by the way of Lake Champlain into the Hudson, by the Ottawa, and by Lake Ontario. The advance in the price of a single crop of wheat would pay for making all these routes, from Chicago to the Atlantic, navigable for ocean-going sailing-ships and steamers.

Montreal harbor could be made for the trade of New York what Albany is now; and that, too, while the St. Lawrence basin, below the Victoria Bridge, would be crowded, like the Thames in our day, from London to the sea, when this continent is as fully peopled as Europe.

From Chicago to the Atlantic, for nearly the whole distance, navigation is as cheap as on the ocean. Short canals and lockage would not detain ships more than the average adverse winds of the Atlantic, so that the transit of goods, to and from Chicago and Liverpool, would be nearly as cheap as to and from New York. At one tenth of the cost of transportation by railway, such a line of navigation would supply an outlet to the trade of the Northwest. To transport a ton of goods, by ordinary highways, costs on an average of twenty dollars per hundred miles. The railroads will perform this service for two dollars, the sailing-vessel for one tenth of this, or twenty cents, per ton. Open a ship-canal by the way of the St. Lawrence to Chicago, and the cost of freight per mile will scarcely, if at all, exceed the cost of transit on the ocean, or the lakes.

John A. Poor, The First International Railway and the Colonization of New England. Life and Writings of John Alfred Poor, ed. Laura E. Poor, (New York: Putnam's, 1892), pp. 212-213, 213-214.

325.  HAULING PETROLEUM (1865)

A graphic example of the incompatability of modern industrial materials being transported by antiquated means.

But few persons realize the extent of the business carried on in the Pennsylvania Oil Regions, unless they visit here and judge for themselves. The number of teams required for the transportation of petroleum from the wells to the different shipping points in seasons when both river and creek are low, and navigation suspended, is immense. For several days during the recent good order of the roads, there have been an almost continuous train of wagons loaded with oil, traveling on the road from Cherry Run to Franklin, a distance of over twelve miles. Just think of it, reader. A train of wagons loaded with the product of one single township in this State, over twelve miles in length. And this too only from a portion of the producing locality of this same township. For it is reasonable to suppose that the amount of oil shipped to the Shaffer Farm, and other railroad points, is equally as great. The load for these wagons is generally seven barrels, and the daily traffic carried on by means of wheeled vehicles, is it any wonder that our roads here soon become impassable? No road could long stand such wear and tear, without constant extensive repairs. If, therefore, our roads, and even the main street of Oil City, which is the great thoroughfare, should appear almost impassable to the denizens of other places, they must take into consideration that a good reason exists for it.

Oil City Register, January 26, 1865, reprinted in Giddens (ed.), Pennsylvania Petroleum, pp. 256-257.

326.  THE EARLIEST PIPE LINES (1863-1866)

The pipe line was a daring invention when you keep in mind the obstacles that stood in its way: topography, inadequate pumping power, rudimentary pipe-making capacity, and lack of sufficient knowledge about pressures. But it was a brilliant invention, simple in principle and extraordinary in economic impact. The oil is said to have moved at the same speed as a person walking.

The first pipe used for the transportation of oil within the oil regions, was laid during the summer of 1863 by Messrs. Hutchins and Foster from the Tarr Farm on Oil Creek to the Humbolt Refinery

at Plumer, a distance of about two miles.  It was of wrought iron,
two inches in diameter.  A force pump at Tarr Farm and two at intermediate stations forced the oil through the tube over intervening
high land, an elevation of over 400 feet above Oil Creek.  Owing
to the faulty machinery used for forcing, the enterprise was only
partially successful.

During the winter of 1863-64 the same parties laid a cast iron
pipe three inches in diameter from the then famous "Noble" well to
Miller Farm station on the Oil Creek R.R., a distance of about 3
miles--with an elevation of about 50 feet above the point at which
oil was received.  The undertaking proved a failure, disastrously so
to its projectors.  The pipe used was of good quality, provided with
Robbins patent lead joint, of the superiority of which there is no
question.  As in the proceeding case the failure is attributed to
the faulty machinery used for forcing the oil; the constant vibration of the pipe, resulting from suddenly varying the velocity of
the oil caused the joints to leak and occasionly the pipe to
rupture.  Good mechanics are of the opinion that these difficulties
are not insurmountable, yet prudence will dictate the use of wrought
iron, except when the oil is to flow by gravitation only.

Simultaneously with the failure of the Oil Creek pipe Mr.
Warren then a refiner at Plumer, laid and successfully operated a
two-inch wrought iron tube for forcing "distilate" or distilled
petroleum from Plumer to the Allegheny river--a distance of about
three miles.  In October last Messrs. Van Syckle, Noble and others
brought into successful use a line of two-inch wrought iron tubing
from Pithole City to the Miller Farm on the Oil Creek R.R., a distance of less than 5 miles.  Immediately thereafter, Mr. Warren
brought into use a similar line, constructed by himself from Pithole
City to Henry's Bend, on the Allegheny river, about five miles distant.  Each of the two lines have a capacity of about 1,000 barrels
in 24 hours.  Messrs. Van Sycle & Col, in Dec., last, laid a second
line to the Miller Farm, thereby doubling their ability for transportation.

The works of the "Penn. Tubing Transportation Co." projected
by Col. Thomas C. Bates, of Rochester, N.Y., were completed and
brought into successful use about the 1st of Dec., last.  Their
"Tube" is constructed of cast iron pipe, six inches internal diameter, laid with Robbins joint, and extends from Pithole City to
Oleopolis, on the Allegheny river, seven miles in length, having
an average fall of nearly sixty feet per mile--every part of it
being laid on a descending grade.  It has a capacity of 7,500
barrels per day, by force of gravitation only.

Two lines of two-inch wrought iron tubing having a capacity
of 1,000 barrels per day each, have just been laid from Pithole
City to Titusville, having two pumping stations--a distance of
9 1/4 miles, by Messrs. Philpot, Sherman, Picket and others, and
will be opened to the public within a few days.

Two lines of similar capacity have just been completed by
Messrs. Henry Harley & Co., from Bennehoff Run to Shaffer Farm on
the Oil Creek R.R., a distance over the hills of only two miles.

The construction of lines of pipe from Petroleum Centre to
Titusville, and from the same point to Oil City is but a question
of time; more than one party is in the field for each line.

In all the lines heretofore successfully laid for forcing oil,
two-inch wrought iron tubing has been used, partly because it can
be more promptly obtained and partly because of less depreciation
in its value should it ever be wanted for other purposes.  If a
greater capacity than can be obtained through a single two-inch
tube is required, economy will dictate the using of a single tube
of sufficient capacity rather than increasing the number of smaller
ones, because the prime cost does not increase with the capacity
and because the power necessary to overcome friction decreases
directly as the diameter increases.  It requires a pressure of 52
lbs. per square inch to force 1,000 barrels of oil in 24 hours
through a straight horizontal pipe one mile long and through a
straight horizontal pipe one mile long and through a 3-inch tube
34 2/3 lbs., a 4-inch tube 26 lbs. per square inch.  The pressure
necessary to overcome friction will also vary as the square of the
quantity delivered, for example in the case supposed for a two-inch
pipe one mile long to deliver 1,000 barrels requires a pressure of
52 lbs. per square inch; 50 barrels would require but 13 lbs;
2,000 barrels 208 lbs.

The pressure must increase substantially as you increase the
length of pipe to accomplish the same result.

In all cases there must be added a force sufficient to overcome the resistance due to curves (generally 10 to 30 per cent,
according to circumstances), and also a force sufficient to overcome
the pressure due to the difference in the level between the point of
receiving and the highest point on the line, amounting for oil to
40 lbs. per square inch for each 100 feet difference in level.  For
descending grades a corresponding deduction will be made.

The cost of lap welded tubing (the only kind which should be
used) fluctuates with the value of iron and with the supply of and
demand for the same.  At present it can be bought at the manufacturers for about 40¢ per lineal foot for 2-inch tubing--delivered
and distributed say 45¢.  Cost of trenching and laying, to the
usual depth of thirty inches varies with circumstances.  Under
favorable circumstances about $1,000 per mile.  Force pumps and
steam engines combined cost about $800 each.  Steam boiler capable
of running two pumps $2,000.  Pumping stations should not generally
be more than 5 miles apart.

Tankage costs 65¢ per bbl. for wood and $1.00 for iron.

The weight and cost of different sizes of tubing increase
nearly as the square of the diameter to-wit:  2 inch, 40¢, 3 inch
90¢, 4 inch 160¢, &c., &c.

The cost of forcing oil after works are completed will not
generally exceed 5¢ per bbl. for each pumping station, when a
constant supply is furnished.

Titusville, Pennsylvania Morning Herald, March 6, 1866,
reprinted in Giddens (ed.), Pennsylvania Petroleum, pp. 308-311.

327.   RAILROADS WIDEN THE MARKET FOR FARM GOODS (1868)

America's outstanding railroad expert of the day explains graphically how vastly the railroads expand the market for farm goods.  Poor was editor of the American Railroad Journal and publisher of the annual Manual of the Railroads of the United States.  He was the youngest brother of John A. Poor.  (See Source No. 324).

Railways, unlike canals, are everywhere practicable.  Nothing retards their progress.  They traverse lofty ranges of mountains with the same ease, almost, that they do wide extended plains. The reduction they effected in the cost of transportation gave a market at his door, to the producer, in every portion of our vast domain.  A familiar illustration will give the best possible idea of the value of this new method over the old.  The cost, for example, of transporting Indian corn and wheat over ordinary high-ways will equal 20 cents per ton per mile.  At such a rate the former will bear transportation only 125 miles to market, where its value is equal to 75 cents per bushel.  The latter only 250 miles, when its value is $1.50 per bushel.  With such highways only, our most valuable cereals will have no commercial value outside of circles having radii of 125 and 250 miles respectively.  Upon a Railroad the cost of transportation equals one and a quarter cents, per ton, per mile.  With such a work, consequently, the circle within which corn and wheat, at the prices named, will have a mar-ketable value, will be drawn upon radii of 1,600 and 3,200 miles respectively.  The area of a circle with a radius of 125 miles is 46,875 square miles; that of a circle drawn upon a radius of 1,600 miles is nearly 200 times greater, or 7,680,000 square miles. Such a difference, enormous as it is, only measures the value of the new agencies employed in transportation, and the results achieved, compared with the old.
     The commerce of our Railroads may be said to date from the same great event that gave such a stimulus to their construction. The earlier roads were rude and unsubstantial structures compared with the permanent and finished work of the present day.  They were adaped neither to high speed nor to a heavy tonnage traffic.  The lines built were chiefly those between the more important cities in the Eastern States, for the accommodation of their passenger traffic.  The commerce between them was still carried on almost wholly by water.  No great lines expressly designed as outlets for the interior basin of the continent were constructed till 1851, when the Erie Railway was opened.  The links comprising the New York Central had been opened at an earlier day, but they were not designed for freight, and were restricted in its transportation for the benefit of the Erie Canal.  These restrictions were not removed till the opening of the Erie Railroad.  The other great lines connecting the West with the East were not opened till a still later date; the Baltimore and Ohio not till 1853, the Pennsylvania not

till 1854.  Of the great interior lines, the Illinois Central was
not completed till 1856; the Pittsburg, Fort Wayne and Chicago was
not fully opened in 1858; the Chicago and Rock Island, which was
the first line to unite Lake Michigan with the Mississippi, was
opened in 1854; the Michigan Central and Southern Railroads, connecting Lake Erie with Lake Michigan, were opened in 1852.  The
great bulk of their tonnage traffic, as will be hereafter shown,
has been the creation of the last ten years.  The rapidity of its
growth and its present extent is even more wonderful than that
of their mileage.

Henry V. Poor, Influence of the Railroads of the United States
in the Creation of its Commerce and Wealth, (New York:  Journeymen
Printers' Co-operative Association, 1869), pp. 11-13.

### 328.  DIFFICULTIES OF FINANCING SOUTHERN RAILROADS (1870)

Despite these difficulties, shipment of cotton by
railroad increased sharply in the years after this.
Robert Somers, a British traveller, describes the process.

Many of the planters of North Carolina send down their cotton
to Wilmington, bale by bale as they gather it, under heavy charges
of transit, which, in a state of declining prices, may one day turn
the scale against production.  As it is, there is much grumbling
this season.  The growers say that 15 cents per lb. at the gin is
the lowest price at which they can produce cotton, as 15 cents go
at present in the United States.  The cheapest access to market
is thus of the most vital importance.  Yet the promoters of the
Wilmington and Rutherford Railroad, notwithstanding all the outlay
and substantial progress they have made, are met by great difficulty.  Three years ago they were authorized by their charter to
borrow 2,500,000 dollars on first mortgage bonds, than which there
is no better security; but there would seem to be little hope of
getting the money on this Continent unless the company sell its
bonds at 50 for 100 at 8 per cent. interest, or, in other words,
borrow at 16 per cent. and pay at last in principle 100 for every
50 borrowed!  New York, which is the chief centre of these financial
operations, has probably no great disposition to promote railways
which threaten in some degree its own imperial monopoly, or it may
not have funds enough for all the projects of this kind urged on
its attention; but such things might surely somehow be better and
more easily accomplished.

Robert Somers, The Southern States Since the War, 1870-1,
(London:  Macmillan & Co., 1871), pp. 34-35.

329.   "LET US BUILD A RAILROAD, I HAVE
TWENTY-FIVE CENTS" (1871)


An all-too common example of an uneconomic railroad
yielding gains to some promoters but losses to the investors.  (See the following source).  McMaster had been a
trader, a railroad man, and a steamboat operator.  His
field of operations lay in the area between Rock Island,
Galena, and St. Louis.


About 1871 L. Abbott, of Cordova [Illinois] and some of his
neighbors were sitting around the stove one winter evening discussing the hard times and the little they could find to do in the
quaint dull old town.  Abbott says let us build a railroad, I have
twenty-five cents in my pocket as a cash capital on which to
commence operations.  This quiet talk between these few men led to
the building a railroad from Barstow [Illinois] to St. Louis
[Missouri] by the way of Rock Island.  A company was organized and
a charter obtained.  Some parties who had some capital, enough to
set the project in motion, took hold with Abbott.  They leased a
large tract of coal lands on the line of the road in Rock Island
and Henry counties.  Had maps and drawings made of the route showing
grades and the towns lying along the route, all gotten up in a very
attractive form, accompanied with a glowing description of the
beautiful productive country through which the projected road was
to pass.  A shrewd agent was employed to go to Europe and despose
of the bonds issued for the construction of the road.  He succeeded
in making an agreement with some capitalists of Holland to take the
bonds of the road to the amount of $20,000 for each mile built and
equipped.  Subscriptions to the stock were solicited from towns
along the line of the road, and quite a large amount of available
means were obtained by selling the bonds issued by these towns and
counties, enough to start the road on its legs.  Work was commensed
on the eastern end.  The coal banks were opened, which was easily
done, as the outcrop was near the surface and only required a
little stripping.  The right of way was purchased at normal prices
and generally without the costs of arbitration until the canvassers
reached Moline and Rock Island.  Here wherever the right of way
passed through private property the appraisers gave the owners a
fair price for the same.  They obtained the right of way on some of
the streets in Moline and Rock Island and from Rock Island used the
track of the Peoria, under a running arrangement, to Coal Valley.
The dutch capitalists advancing money on the bonds as the work
progressed until the road reached East St. Louis [Illinois].  It
was a splendid successful scheme, if any enterprise founded on gas
and fraud can be called successful.  Some of the subcontractors and
the many men employed to puff and work up the credit of the road
may have made something.  It was run a short time by the original
projectors, and then the deceived bondholders sent over an agent
to see after the delayed interest due on the bonds.  This agent of

the bondholders took charge of the road....The poor deceived bondholders were compelled finally to sell the road which cost them ten
million of dollars, for one and a half million.


S. W. McMaster, 60 Years on the Upper Mississippi, (Rock
Island, Illinois:  J. B. Brown, printer, 1893), pp. 245-247.


330.  FOREIGN CAPITAL BUILT ILLINOIS RAILROADS (1873)


Testifying at the twilight of a gigantic railroad-
building boom, financed significantly by foreign capital,
an industry leader stressed some realistic factors in the
railroad situation.  Newell was president of the Illinois
Central Railroad.


In 1868 this State [Illinois] had about 3,300 or 3,400 miles of
railroad.  It has now 6,400.  This gain of 3,000 miles of road has
been made chiefly in this wise:  In 1868 the legislature authorized
municipalities to vote aid to new railroads.  The municipalities all
over the State, led on by speculators--people in the business of
building railroads--voted aid to a large extent, generally, all over
the State, the aid ranging in one case as high as $8,000 a mile in
local bonds, for which the railroad companies were to give the stock.
Now, these gentlemen say:  "Here is a railroad wanted; we can go on
and get this local aid; we will go along the route and get the vote,
and if we can get $5,000 a mile in local aid, that is very well."
They go to work and do it, and then go to a railroad contractor and
say, "Here is this large profit to be made in the building of this
line."  The contractor goes to a banker in New York, with whom perhaps he is associated, and says:  "If you can place the bonds of
such a railway to a sufficient extent to build that line, we can
pocket the profit of this local aid--these local bonds."  They do
it; and European capitalists five or six years ago, not having acquired as much experience as they have now with the value of this
property, were eager to take these bonds at a low figure.  They were
placed at a low figure, and money enough was raised to construct the
line out of bonds, and the contractors simply took as a profit the
local aid.  Now, that, really, to my mind, is the reason why these
roads have been multiplied to such an extent.  The individual profit
made by the contractors in building them has urged the construction
of them....
I will say...that if any gentleman goes to Europe, and raises
any money on any railway that is not paying interest, he will do
better than I think.  In other words, you cannot raise money to
build a railroad in Illinois on the basis I have named; you cannot
do it.  The money for the construction of these railways has not
been raised in this State, nor in this country.  It has been raised
from the bonds sold abroad.  Very few of those bonds have been sold

in this country.  There was one road particularly, in the southern
part of the State, that was constructed on bonds placed in New
York.  The party who took those bonds has got them yet, cannot sell
them, and has to carry them.  I refer now to the Springfield and
Illinois Southeastern road.  There are other roads; the Cairo and
Vincennes road was built on bonds placed in London.  They are now
in the hands of the banker.  Now, the reason they have been able to
build these roads is this:  some of the lines in Illinois were
making 10 per cent. dividends, as was the Illinois Central.  The
prospectus of the parties selling the bonds shows there is a population in the county and a traffic which will justify earnings
equal to those of the Illinois Central, for instance.  That road is
well known in England and Holland.  They go there and say, "There
is a line that can do as well as the Illinois Central, and there
are the figures to prove it."  They can sell these bonds, for the
reason that the surplus capital, getting only 2 1/2 or 3 per cent.,
was willing to go where it could take 10 per cent.  Now, in
Amsterdam they say they will not take anything except on a railroad
making an interest at the present time.  In other words, they have
become completely loaded with these bonds to such an extent that
they won't touch any other, and are entirely dissatisfied.  But a
year and a half these lines have not extended half so rapidly as
they did previously.  We have paid 10 per cent. dividends on the
stock since 1871.  We actually earned last year less than 8 per
cent.; but we had a reserve from the land-grant, and we thought
last year was an exceptional one, and the directors, as the stockholders were foreigners and might be disturbed at a reduction, said
we had better take the chance of continuing the 10 per cent. and
make it so as to prevent a feeling of dissatisfaction or panic
among small holders abroad.


        Testimony, John Newell; U.S. Congress, 43rd, 1st session,
Senate, Report 307, part 2, Report of the Select Committee on
Transportation-Routes to the Seaboard, serial number 1589,
(Washington, D.C.:  Government Printing Office, 1874), pp. 291, 292.


        331.  RAILROADS FORCE OHIO CANALS OUT OF BUSINESS (1873)


        It was the same the country over.  In 1860, railroads
and canals carried roughly equal amounts of freight.  Ten
years later, railroads had taken the lead, although not
uniformly.  The Erie Canal, for example, did not reach its
peak traffic until 1880.


        The Ohio Canal, from Cleveland to Portsmouth, three hundred
and nine miles, for many years brought pretty much all the goods
that came from New York to Cincinnati, and all the West, through

the Erie Canal from Buffalo to Cleveland, in that way.  The building
of the different railroads kept cutting it off, but finally they got
this canal built from here to Toledo.  Then the price of transportation on the lake from Buffalo up to Toledo was no more than it was
to Cleveland.  This canal was shorter than the other, and this
canal became a competitor for the through business both ways,
against the Ohio Canal, down to Portsmouth.  It did a very large
business until the railroad would put down its rates from here to
Toledo very low; they would carry wheat as cheap as by canal; but
the moment that is came cold weather, and the fall came in, they
would put up their rates.  The canal would freeze up, up North, and
the rates would go up.  The result was that owners of boats would
not replenish them.  They let them gradually die out.  It would not
pay them, as they had the railroad to compete with in the summer,
and the boats began to decay, and there were no parties here who
would fight the railroads from here to New York any more.  They
would make through rates from here to New York 45 to 50 cents a
hundred, and by the lake route, although we could carry to Toledo
very cheaply, and from there East, yet the difference in the time
of getting the property to New York, and these low through rates,
gradually drove the business from the canal.  The boats began to
decay, and they are building hardly any.  I think business last
year was just about the same as it was the year before, but there
is no through business on either of the canals at all.  I do not
suppose that there is a ton of freight that starts from Cincinnati
and goes to the sea-board by either of the canals during the whole
season, but yet there is quite a large local business done.

Testimony, Benjamin Eggleston; U.S. Congress, 43rd, 1st
session, Senate, Report 309, part 2, Report of the Select Committee
on Transportation Routes to the Seaboard, serial number 1589,
(Washington, D.C.:  Government Printing Office, 1874), p. 538.


332.  AIR BRAKE DEVELOPMENT AND THE RAILROADS (1870's)

Note that while railroad men showed no interest
during the earliest stages, they became very cooperative once the finished air brake was demonstrated to be
practical.  Here is an account by the inventor and
innovator of the device.


Prior to the construction and practical test of the air
brake [in 1868], I had opportunities while traveling to present the
subject to numerous railway officials and to endeavor to secure
their cooperation in the development of the apparatus.  None of
those approached appeared to have faith in the idea, though I
afterwards found that the acquaintances made and the many

discussions I had had with railway people were of great advantage
in the introduction of the air brake upon the railways with which
they were connected.
. . . . . . . . . . . . . . . . . . . . . . . . . . . . . . . . . . . . .
     The next event of importance was the application of the brakes
in November 1869, to a longer train of ten cars upon the Pennsylvania
Railroad, which was taken to Philadelphia for the purpose of demon-
strating to the directors of that railway the success of the apparatus.  I may say at this point that the Pennsylvania Railroad had
been using for some years a chain brake similar to the one applied
by Mr. Ambler, but had found that its use was limited to short
trains and that it was not a satisfactory contrivance for the purpose intended.  There were invited to witness these trials in
Philadelphia a large number of railway people and the papers gave
extended notices of the tests made, which brought to the train on
the next day Mr. George L. Dunlop, the General Superintendent of
the Chicago & North Western Railway, who was desirous of having the
whole apparatus fully explained to him.
. . . . . . . . . . . . . . . . . . . . . . . . . . . . . . . . . . . . .
     My story would be incomplete without a reference to the splen-
did assistance which the railways of this and many other countries
have rendered.  They have been lavish in providing those facilities
for making the thousands of tests which were necessary to progress
in the developments I have recited; to the Pennsylvania Railroad
especially, upon which the most important experiments were first
made, the other railways of the country, as well as the traveling
public, owe a debt of gratitude.  When a railway (as did the Southern Pacific two years ago) provides a new train of 100 steel cars
to be fitted with the newer form of automatic brake, in order to
carry on, with a staff of skilled men under the direction of the
chief officers of the company, a series of experiments upon its
heaviest gradients, requiring several weeks, for the purpose of
securing greater safety and an increased carrying capacity per
train, with the consequent lessening of the cost of transportation,
it is just that the managers of such a corporation should receive
credit for their farsighted policy.  To name the railways and merely
to state chronologically the tests of brakes which have been made
during forty years would require several volumes.


     George Westinghouse, "Presidential Address," Transactions,
American Society of Mechanical Engineers, XXXII (1910), pp. 1094,
1097, 1107.



                333.  THE QUESTION OF REBATES (1870's)


     Railroads made a reality of the national market.
The largest shippers forced rebates from the roads, and
often received rate information about their competitors.
Following is a benign portrayal of rebates.

Of all the subjects which seem to have attracted the attention of the public to the affairs of the Standard Oil Company, the matter of rebates from railroads has perhaps been uppermost. The Standard Oil Company of Ohio, of which I was president, did receive rebates from the railroads prior to 1880, but received no advantages for which it did not give full compensation. The reason for rebates was that such was the railroads' method of business. A public rate was made and collected by the railroad companies, but, so far as my knowledge extends, was seldom retained in full; a portion of it was repaid to the shippers as a rebate. By this method the real rate of freight which any shipper paid was not known by his competitors nor by other railroad companies, the amount being a matter of bargain with the carrying company. Each shipper made the best bargain that he could, but whether he was doing better than his competitor was only a matter of conjecture. Much depended upon whether the shipper had the advantage of competition of carriers.

The Standard Oil Company of Ohio, being situated at Cleveland, had the advantage of different carrying lines, as well as of water transportation in the summer; taking advantage of those facilities, it made the best bargains possible for its freights. Other companies sought to do the same. The Standard gave advantages to the railroads for the purpose of reducing the cost of transportation of freight. It offered freights in large quantity, car-loads and train-loads. It furnished loading facilities and discharging facilities at great cost. It provide regular traffic, so that a railroad could conduct its transportation to the best advantage and use its equipment to the full extent of its hauling capacity without waiting for the refiner's convenience. It exempted railroads from liability for fire and carried its own insurance. It provided at its own expense terminal facilities which permitted economies in handling. For these services it obtained contracts for special allowances on freights.

But notwithstanding these special allowances, this traffic from the Standard Oil Company was far more profitable to the railroad companies than the smaller and irregular traffic, which might have paid a higher rate.

To understand the situation which affected the giving and taking of rebates it must be remembered that the railroads were all eager to enlarge their freight traffic. They were competing with the facilities and rates offered by the boats on lake and canal and by the pipe-lines. All these means of transporting oil cut into the business of the railroads, and they were desperately anxious to successfully meet this competition. As I have stated we provided means for loading and unloading cars expeditiously, agreed to furnish a regular fixed number of carloads to transport each day, and arranged with them for all the other things that I have mentioned, the final result being to reduce the cost of transportation for both the railroads and ourselves. All this was following in the natural laws of trade.

Rockefeller, Random Reminiscences, (New York: Doubleday, Page & Co., 1909), pp. 107-110.

334.  WAUSAU, WISCONSIN GETS TELEPHONES (1881)

In 1876, Alexander Graham Bell patented the telephone
and opened the first telephone exchange two years later
in New Haven.  Over 300,000 telephones were in use by 1895.
During the early years, the telephone was in part an adven-
ture, in part a convenience.  Here is a delightful sketch
of the elements in that combination as recounted by the
superintendent of operations of the Wisconsin Telephone
Company.


There was congratulations on the new service and assurances
that Wausau had the very latest thing in telephone exchanges.  As I
listened in and heard them say how good they felt about it, please
be sure that I felt twice as good for I realized that the system
had come to life, after less than three weeks of hard work, and had
set the town to talking, a telephone line of talk that will continue
as long as people live in Wausau and have anything to talk about.
     As one call begets another so, within an hour, the city was
full of "Hellos" and everyone who could get at a telephone tried to
call someone else with greetings of every possible kind.  "Isn't
this wonderful?"  "My, but you sound just like yourself."  "No,
I ain't got nothing to say.  I just wanted to try the darned thing."
"Nothing slow about Wausau!" etc., etc.  There were, of course, the
man who shouted:  "By yimminy, she talks Swedish!" and others as-
tounded to hear words in their native tongues come out of the small
black rubber hand piece.
     Very few had seen or used a telephone before and the principal
task was to start them off right.  We used the Blake transmitter,
the little square wooden box with the hole in the center, and the
speaker must speak to it and at it in just the right way to get the
best results.  Operating on such a day, therefore, was accompanied
by a succession of suggestions.  "Please!  Not so loud; don't
stand so near; that's it, about three inches away; just speak in a
natural voice; no, you're too far away; get closer; that's better;
listen!  of course you hear him; tell him who you are; when you are
through hang up the telephone and give a short ring; the telephone
is the instrument you hold against your ear; no, not your head,
your ear; yes, hold it tight and listen"; and so on and so on.  Some
people were so nervous they could scarcely talk at all.  Some yelled
in their excitement but after a while things began to settle down.
Papa said:  "Well, if it ain't Mama," and Mama said "Ain't it
wonderful?" for the last time and then they began to do business--
order railway cars, send telegrams and even to ring up "the house"
to say how sorry they were they would be late for dinner.


Angus Hibbard, Hello Goodbye.  My Story of Telephone Pioneering, (Chicago, Illinois: A. C. McClurg & Co., 1941), pp. 16-18.

335.  RIDING TO WORK IN PHILADELPHIA   (1883)


At this time, horse-drawn cars and a few newly-
introduced cable cars carried some 100 million passengers
a year in Philadelphia.  Lines were owned by numerous separate small firms and there was a minimum of municipal regulation.  Horse cars -- when they moved at all -- covered
some five miles an hour; their runs could thus only extend
some three to four miles from the center of town.  Expenditures on horses consumed two-fifths of capital investment.
Here is a rare account by a consumer of these meager services, Fred H. Colvin.


Getting to work in those dim romantic days was often a minor
achievement in itself.  You must imagine a world without subways,
trolley cars, busses, automobiles, or taxicabs.  When I made my
inauspicious debut as a machine-shop apprentice on July 5, 1883,
the very last word in public conveyances was the horse-drawn omnibus, a poky sort of stagecoach that averaged 5 miles to the quart
of oats.  Due apparently to a shortage of Percherons on the Race
and Vine Street route, the cars that served the Rue mechanics were
drawn by lowly mules.  These went much slower.  To get to work on
time in the winter meant rising in the middle of the night, waiting
on a deserted street corner for the half-frozen mules to put in
appearance, and then burrowing molelike into one corner in order to
keep warm during the hour-long trip across the city.
     For there was no heat in the cars for either passengers or
crew.  A few years before, some of the more prosperous lines had
gallantly installed potbellied stoves in the front end of each car
to temper the wintry breeze, but this public-spirited gesture was
short-lived indeed.  It seems that a certain conclave of medical men
ventured the opinion that heat was unhealthy in the horsecars, being
a leading factor in the spread of pulmonary congestions and similar
disorders.  The potbellied stoves were forthwith removed, leaving
the occupants once more exposed to the healthy arctic night.  By
the time I had become a regular customer on the Rue and Vine Street
line, a concession had been made to the popular demand for warmer
vehicles.  The car-line operators caused several layers of bedding
straw to be spread on the floor of each car, as a kind of thermal
insulation.  When it snowed or rained this straw became nice and
soggy, and the steamy atmosphere inside the omnibus reminded me of
an old-fashioned livery stable.  But it was still cold.
     This Toonerville Trolley of my younger days also provided me
with a modicum of outdoor exercise such as I did not get working
over the lathes in the Rue Manufacturing Company.  Every so often,
in fair weather or foul, the diligence I happened to be riding would
casually leap its traces and founder in the soft earth alongside the
tracks.  When this happened, all able-bodied male passengers were
expected as a matter of course to get out and push.  The frequency
with which this diversion occurred caused the route to be known as
the "G.O.P. Line," which had nothing to do with party affiliations.

Transportation in those days was not limited to the horse car,
however.  Well-to-do businessmen rode to work in their own
carriages, drawn by a spanking pair of trotters.  For the less
affluent workaday journeyman, there was the high-wheeled bicycle or
"ordinary," which was a distinct improvement over the "boneshaker"
velocipede of the 'sixties, but a daredevil contraption on cobble-
stone pavements.  Without gears, the ordinary was strictly a tall
man's vehicle in any contest of speed, but despite my 5-foot 5-inch
stature I managed to get about fairly well on a high-wheeled
Columbia on Sundays and holidays when traffic was at a standstill.

Fred H. Colvin (with D. J. Duffin, <u>60 Years with Men and</u>
<u>Machines</u>, (New York:  McGraw-Hill Book Co., 1947), pp. 12–13.


336.   THE VIRTUES OF RAILROAD POOLING (1885)


A pool is an agreement among business enterprises
to allocate exclusive territories or establish identical
rates in common territories.  Railroad pools were a common
form of collusive price-fixing during the 1880's.  Here
is a defense of pooling by the president of the Union
Pacific Railroad.


I should unhesitatingly say that the pooling system has been
of great service to the public, so far as it has gone.  Indeed, it
has been of far more service to the public than to the railroads.
I think it has prevented in some degree the terrific work of competition.
It may produce good in the end; but railroad competition, as
necessarily practiced, causes for the time being the wildest discrimination and utmost individual hardship.  That is, under its
operation you will always find certain points, when there is a war
of rates going on, which have enormous advantages conferred upon
them, which advantages are not and cannot be extended to other
points.  The point, therefore, which is not influenced by the war
of rates suffers terribly.  Its business is destroyed.  How the
business community, under the full working of railroad competiton
can carry on its affairs I cannot understand.  I had not been able
to understand how it could do it before I became president of a
railroad, and I do not understand now.  The business man never
knows what railroad rates are going to be at other places, or at
different times.  He cannot sit down and say "I can count upon such
a transportation rate for such a period of time, and make my
arrangements accordingly."  He has to say, "I cannot tell to-day
what the transportation rate is going to be to-morrow, either for
me or my competitor."  This must be just so long as uncontrolled
competition exists.  It cannot be avoided.

The effect of pooling has been to equalize and steady rates. It has never been able to hold the rates up. Owing to the natural force of competition here, there, and elsewhere, as the history of railroads will show, a steadily decreasing rate has been the rule year after year, until now the rate of transportation in this country is unquestionably lower than in any other country in the world; and the rate has been coming down and down, until I do not see how any further considerable reductions can be made and the machine be kept running.

Testimony, Charles Francis Adams, U.S. Congress, 49th, 1st session, Senate, Select Committee on Interstate Commerce, Report...Testimony, serial number 2357, Report 46, part 2, pp. 1205-1206.

### 337.  RAILROADS DELIVER MORE OR LESS THE CORRECT AMOUNT (1885)

Business dissatisfaction with railroads powered the movement for federal regulation. Here is an example of one specific business complaint against railroads. Kemble was a Boston commission merchant specializing in breadstuffs, grain, and flour; he was a member of the Boston Board of Trade and a member and former president of the Commercial Exchange.

One of the first great evils, it appears to me, which is troubling the mercantile community, in connection with inter-State commerce, is the want of responsibility, or rather the shirking of responsibility, on the part of the railroads. This is done in various ways, and systematically. Here is one form. It is the custom of many railroads to insert in bills of lading the words "more or less." Of course I do not refer now to the main trunk lines running between the great cities.

I would also say right here that I am not here to complain of railroad rates at the present time. Of course nobody would think of doing that. But this shirking of responsibility which I refer to comes in the way I am about to mention.

These railways are in the habit of inserting in the bills of lading the words "more or less" or "shipper's account." This is done systematically. It is not done exceptionally. It is done regularly where it is possible to do it; and there are thousands of places in this country where the shipper cannot help himself. He is obliged to accept the bill of lading or not do business. Of course under bills of lading of this kind, when the merchandise arrives at the point of destination, the consignees are obliged to receive whatever is delivered to them, and they have no remedy.

If the consignee makes a claim for deficiency, the bill of lading
is referred to, and the clause "more or less," very often obscurely
written, is seen, and he has no claim or standing.

The CHAIRMAN.  Does that clause "more or less" refer to the
quantity of stuff shipped, or what does it refer to?

Mr. KEMBLE.  "More or less" or "shipper's account" are put on
the bill of lading for grain; so far as my experience goes, mostly
for grain.  I have often found the words "shipper's account" on
bills of lading for cargoes of flour.  Now, it seems to me that the
railroads should be responsible to the extent that they shall know
what they receive from the shipper, and that they shall assume a
proper liability while transporting, which they do not now in very
many cases.

Senator HARRIS.  You mean the bill of lading provides or sets
forth that the transportation company has received so many hundred
pounds or so many bushels of wheat, "more or less"?

Mr. KEMBLE.  Yes, sir.

Senator PLATT.  Which they agree to deliver?

Senator MILLER.  In other words, they do not guarantee the
amount to be delivered.


Testimony, Edward Kemble, U.S. Congress, 49th, 1st session,
Senate, Select Committee on Interstate Commerce, Report...Testimony,
serial number 2357, Report 46, part 2, pp. 371-372.


### 338.  THE MYSTERY OF RAILROAD ACCOUNTING (1885)


Corporate fraud was facilitated by loose railroad
accounting practices.  Worse, so inadequate were these
practices that corporate officers themselves not infrequently were in the dark about the financial condition
of their firms.


The system of railway accounts has been a mystery even to
railway accountants; that is to say, a Pennsylvania railway accountant was, until recently, absolutely in the dark as to how the New
York Central kept its accounts.  The Reading's accountant could not
tell how the Jersey Central kept its books.  The books of each
railway company were a sealed mystery to all save the head of its
bookkeeping department.  Each particular road had its own system
of accounts.  Indeed, it was testified before a railway committee
that some $700,000 expended during one particular year by the Erie
Railway as a corruption fund and for legal expenses was carried to
the India-rubber account, and thus found its way into the construction account.  So that part of the construction account of some of
these railways is what they expend annually upon legislative
committees, or in influencing or preventing legislation, and in the

law courts.  The New York Central Railway Company in 1869 doubled
it  stock, watered its stock by 50 per cent., on the amalgamation
or consolidation of the New York Central and Hudson River roads,
issuing $2 for one of the entire stock of these several companies.
They had, therefore, after this consolidation, a stock account
which was out of all harmony with their construction account, and,
for ten years following, every year varying from 3 to 8 per cent.
of this water was artificially carried into the construction
account, so that eventually the construction account and the capital
account balanced; and there is therefore a construction account
wholly fictitious as to a trifle of $40,000,000 or thereabouts in
the New York Central books.  As a system of book keeping it had to
balance, and therefore the balance was forced by carrying some
years 3, some 5, and some 8 per cent. of this water into the construction account, as though so much construction had been carried
on that year, and eventually the two accounts balanced.  In the
same way the balances were forced in the Erie Railway Company when
Mr. Gould took $40,000,000 of the stock of the Erie Railway Company
out of its books, sold it on the street, and appropriated the
money to his own use, and there was not a dollar's worth of construction to represent it, and when a reorganization took place the
balance of the Erie Railway Company was forced to meet that violence
done to the stock account.  So that in some of these railway corporations their system of keeping accounts is a mystery to everybody outside of the corporation.

Testimony, Simon Sterne, U.S. Congress, 49th, 1st session,
Senate, Select Committee on Interstate Commerce, Report...Testimony,
serial number 2357, Report 46, part 2, pp. 78-79.


339.  THE STEVEDORE SYSTEM ON THE GREAT LAKES (ca. 1885)


The stevedore system placed heavy reliance on the use
of physical violence for an employment advantage.  It contributed to a tradition of violence in the industry.
Barter was Secretary-Treasurer of the International
Longshoremen's Association, Detroit, Michigan.


Q.  Since your organization has had a foothold on these ports
of the lakes have wages of this class advanced or are they stationary?--A.  Oh, yes; advanced materially, especially during the
last 3 years.  In the old days men did not know what they were
getting--under the old stevedore system.  Ten years ago or 15 years
ago it was worse yet  A good many of the men were hired for their
being pretty good, stout, husky fellows, so that in case of necessity they could fight for the stevedore.  In those old days competition was in vogue, and the stevedore backed by a good strapping

band of fighters could necessarily drive the stevedore with a monopoly of the work, and then when he was successful, he would charge
all kinds of fancy prices for loading and unloading.  But while the
competition existed, the stevedores would cut prices with one another, and sometimes would do the work quite reasonable, but the
men were made to suffer for it.  In the old days there were bunks
in the saloon, or in a barn or shed which was adjacent to the
saloon, and the men lived there in the summer season, stayed there,
and most of their pay was bad whisky.  Since our organization has
taken hold, a better class of men work at the business more sober
men.  In fact, drunkenness is not permitted.  The organizations
take that matter up themselves, and in many ports when a man becomes
drunk he is fined $5 and is not permitted to work until that fine
is paid.  In a good many of the ports the men prohibit liquor from
going aboard a vessel.
     Q.  During working hours?--A.  During working hours.  In that
way we have gained favors from the lake carriers, and they have
become our friends instead of fighting us as an organization.
Our wages have increased 100 per cent since the abolishment of the
contract system.


     Testimony, Henry C. Barter, United States Industrial
Commission, IX, p. 310.



     340.  SELLING LONG-DISTANCE TELEPHONE (ca. 1886)


          Few signs showed so well the development of the
     national market as did long-distance telephony.  Five
     years after the Bell patent was obtained, in 1876, the
     first long-distance telephone call was made from Boston
     to Providence.  In 1884, New York and Boston were connected.
     Long-distance telephony served admirably to interconnect
     the rapidly expanding national market of the United States.
     Hibbard, author of the following, was general superinten-
     dent of the American Telephone and Telegraph Company, in
     charge of operations, engineering, and development.
     The company was founded in 1880 and owned all the Bell
     patents.


On to Boston and through New England, up the river to Albany,
on to Buffalo and the many cities between, through and over the
mountains to Pittsburgh and cities of the coal country went the
new long distance lines.  Problems there were, of whom to serve and
how to serve them, factories of New England or upstate, miners and
millers, steel men and spinners, telephones were to bring them to
market and each to the other, a service entirely new.
. . . . . . . . . . . . . . . . . . . . . . . . . . . . . . . . .

The task was to show the public the value of long distance service, and its great field of operations made possible by the construction of our lines of copper wire and the development of improvements in telephone instruments.

It was more than a means of sending messages--it was a means of conversational intercommunication between individuals in points widely separated which practically brought them together.

Its greatest value was to customers of a special class having interests in points distant from each other, and to them it must be demonstrated and sold at rates warranted by the cost.

. . . . . . . . . . . . . . . . . . . . . . . . . . . . . .

It was not easy at first to convince a customer that, by paying a dollar to carry on a conversation with someone he wanted in Philadelphia, he could save a day's time and the cost of the journey. We claimed that a long distance call might be made the equivalent of a trip "there and back," wherever the "there" might be and, increasingly, we proved it.

. . . . . . . . . . . . . . . . . . . . . . . . . . . . . .

When the lines reached out over Pennsylvania, special "periods of service" from coal mining companies to their New York offices were quite popular. In a few cases their officials brought me (not for publication) the suggestion that the "periods" should not begin so early in the morning. It was hinted that the "Old Man" up at the mines, (who was not infrequently the president of the company) began to call them up at eight o'clock in the morning and it was embarrassing, sometimes, to have to explain that nine or nine-thirty o'clock was a usual starting time of office hours in New York.

Soon after the completion of the lines to Boston various public demonstrations of the service were made at one of which I met the New York representatives of a large firm of cotton mill operators and brokers having offices in both cities. After some tests and preliminaries I was asked to call at their New York office and secured their order for an all-day private wire service between the two cities. This was our largest contract, up to that time, and I was so excited about it that I ran most of the way from their offices in Wall Street to show it to Mr. Hall and others.

Hibbard, Hello Goodbye, pp. 82, 83, 84-85.


341.  CHARGES AGAINST UNREGULATED RAILROADS (1885)


For its first half-century, the U.S. railroad industry remained unregulated by the federal government. Rate discriminations and other inequalities were thus solidly rooted by the mid-1880's. This report led to passage of the Interstate Commerce Act two years later.

The complaints against the railroad system of the United States expressed to the committee are based upon the following charges:

1. That local rates are unreasonably high, compared with through rates.

2. That both local and through rates are unreasonably high at non-competing points, either from the absence of competition or in consequence of pooling agreements that restrict its operation.

3. That rates are established without apparent regard to the actual cost of the service performed, and are based largely on "what the traffic will bear."

4. That unjustifiable discriminations are constantly made between individuals in the rates charged for like service under similar circumstances.

5. That improper discriminations are made between articles of freight and branches of business of a like character, and between different quantities of the same class of freight.

6. That unreasonable discriminations are made between localities similarly situated.

7. That the effect of the prevailing policy of railroad management is, by an elaborate system of secret special rates, rebates, drawbacks, and concessions, to foster monopoly, to enrich favored shippers, and to prevent free competition in many lines of trade in which the item of transportation is an important factor.

8. That such favoritism and secrecy introduce an element of uncertainty into legitimate business that greatly retards the development of our industries and commerce.

9. That the secret cutting of rates and the sudden fluctuations that constantly take place are demoralizing to all business except that of a purely speculative character, and frequently occasion great injustice and heavy losses.

10. That, in the absence of national and uniform legislation, the railroads are able by various devices to avoid their responsibility as carriers, especially on shipments over more than one road, or from one State to another, and that shippers find great difficulty in recovering damages for the loss of property or for injury thereto.

11. That railroads refuse to be bound by their own contracts, and arbitrarily collect large sums in the shape of overcharges in addition to the rates agreed upon at the time of shipment.

12. That railroads often refuse to recognize or be responsible for the acts of dishonest agents acting under their authority.

13. That the common law fails to afford a remedy for such grievances, and that in cases of dispute the shipper is compelled to submit to the decision of the railroad manager or poor commissioner, or run the risk of incurring further losses by greater discriminations.

14. That the differences in the classifications in use in various parts of the country, and sometimes for shipments over the same roads in different directions, are a fruitful source of misunderstandings, and are often made a means of extortion.

15.  That a privileged class is created by the granting of passes, and that the cost of the passenger service is largely increased by the extent of this abuse.

16.  That the capitalization and bonded indebtedness of the roads largely exceed the actual cost of their construction or their present value, and that unreasonable rates are charged in the effort to pay dividends on watered stock and interest on bonds improperly issued.

17.  That railroad corporations have improperly engaged in lines of business entirely distinct from that of transportation, and that undue advantages have been afforded to business enterprises in which railroad officials were interested.

18.  That the management of the railroad business is extravagant and wasteful, and that a needless tax is imposed upon the shipping and traveling public by the unnecessary expenditure of large sums in the maintenance of a costly force of agents engaged in a reckless strife for competitive business.

It will be observed that the most important, and in fact nearly all, of the foregoing complaints are based upon the practice of discrimination in one form or another.  This is the principal cause of complaint against the management and operation of the transportation system of the United States, and gives rise to the questions of greatest difficulty in the regulation of interstate commerce.

It is substantially agreed by all parties in interest that the great desideratum is to secure equality, so far as practicable, in the facilties for transportation afforded and the rates charged by the instrumentalities of commerce.  The burden of complaint is against unfair differences in these particulars as between different places, persons, and commodities, and its essence is that these differences are unjust in comparison with the rates allowed or facilities afforded to other persons and places for a like service under similar circumstances.

The first question to be determined, apparently, is whether the inequalities complained of and admitted to exist are inevitable, or whether they are entirely the result of arbitrary and unnecessary discrimination on the part of the common carriers of the country; and the consideration of this question suggests an inquiry as to the proper basis upon which rates of transportation should be established.

Senator S. M. Cullom, U.S. Congress, 49th, 1st session, Senate, Select Committee on Interstate Commerce, Report No. 46, serial number 2356, volume 2, pp. 180–182.

342.  RAILROAD VALUES DEPEND ON FUTURE PROSPECTS (1887)

Jay Gould explains why future profit prospects
excelled past achievements as an indication of the
value of a railroad property.  Gould controlled the Union
Pacific and Missouri Pacific lines and made them the
basis of a Southwestern railroad empire.


THE WITNESS.  I have been all my life dealing in railroads--
that is, since before I was of age--and I have always bought them
on the future and not on the past.  That is the way I have made my
money.  The first railroad I ever bought in I bought the bonds at
10 cents.  Afterwards I took the property and built it up, that is,
the future of it.  Not only my bonds became good but I sold my stock
out at 125.  It was just so in the Union Pacific.  I say, when I
went in, that there was a future coming there.  That is the reason
I went into it.  And just so in the Kansas Pacific, but I saw that
the Kansas Pacific was going to develop faster than the other,
because it ran through a better country.

Q.  Do you not think there is any difference between determining just terms of consolidation representing the rights of stockholders and creditors, by the tests of the past, and the cases
which you cite from your own experience, which are individual
speculations, where a man has a right to make his own adventures?--
A.  Yes; there is a better test than any of these, and that is the
future.  What was the effect of it?  There is a test that you have
not at the time you make it.  That is the test you have now got
here....

Q.  I want now to call your attention to this, and ask your
judgment respecting the comparative values of the Kansas Pacific,
including the Denver Pacific, properties, and the Union Pacific
property at the date of the consolidation in January, 1880?--A.
The Kansas Pacific properties were the most valuable.

Q.  Will you give your reasons?--A.  In the first place, the
road [referring to a map] is about 50 miles farther east.  It begins
farther east.  That is, it has 50 miles more of the rich agricultural country.  You see, when you get out about here [about 300 miles]
you get out of agricultural land.  To explain that, when you commence at Kansas City and Omaha and go west you gradually climb up.
In every mile you pull up about 15 feet, until you get to Cheyenne,
and you are then as high as at the top of Mount Washington; and
Cheyenne is right at the foot of the Rocky Mountains.

Q.  Give the number of feet of elevation.--A.  Over 6,000
feet.  When I first went over the Union Pacific they stopped me
at Columbus, 100 miles west of Omaha, to show me the line between
the agricultural country and the great desert.  They said there
was nothing west of that.  No agricultural products would grow.
But I had noticed that the original line was moving west about 20
miles a year, so that gradually it was working up.  But this country
was then already good agricultural land, so much farther east of it.

Then this road [the Kansas Pacific] lies about 2,000 feet lower
than the Union Pacific, so that it is a better agricultural country
all the way up.  As the result has shown, the land grant that went
with the Kansas Pacific has already netted $150 on the stock, and
when it is all closed up it will have netted $200, an asset outside
of the road.  That is one asset.  Out between Cheyenne and Denver,
if you go through there, you will find it a perfect garden.  They
raise the finest wheat in the country there.  The reason is it lies
at the base of the Rocky Mountains, where the snow is constantly
melting, and they have those streams with which they irrigate that
country.  The Union Pacific has nothing of that kind.  When they
strike the mountains here [at Cheyenne] it is out of the region of
snow and water.  The result is that they never got over about 250
miles of agricultural land from their land grant.  The Kansas
Pacific got a great deal more.

Then, again, the Kansas Pacific country was filling up.  Of
course I saw, with my knowledge of the Union Pacific, that the day
of through business, which had been their golden harvest, was
gradually being taken away by other roads south and north, and I
saw that it was only a question of time when that, the great element on which the road would live, would disappear, and it would
have to come down to local business.  I judged these properties
by their merits, locally, from the best light I could get.  The
six or seven years since this amalgamation was made, on the
practical tests, will demonstrate whether I was right or wrong.

There was another thing that governed me.  The terminal properties of the Kansas Pacific in Kansas City and Denver are perfectly magnificent.  I think them worth $2,000,000 in Kansas City
and $1,000,000 in Denver.  The Union Pacific had no such terminals.

Then the Kansas Pacific had these branches.  They had been
using their earnings and had built these feeders, and had kept the
bonds and stock.  They had strained themselves to do it, but they
had managed to keep the stocks and bonds of these feeders in their
treasury, and they passed under the trust that Mr. Sage and I
represented.  These feeders are very valuable.


Testimony, Jay Gould, May 17, 1887, U.S. Congress, 50th,
1st session, Senate, Executive Document No. 51, part 2, serial
number 2505, Testimony Taken by the United States Pacific Railway
Commission, pp. 479, 583-584.


343.  A TOWN MOVES TO A RAILROAD (1888)


This account answers the question:  What happened
when one town--Clayton, Kansas--lost out in the competition for a railroad?

At the time of which I write, even Oberlin, our County seat, had no railroad. Every settler in Decatur county had to haul his farm produce to Norton, before it could be shipped by rail. ...This handicap is hard to appreciate by those whose farms have always been close to a convenient railroad. Our isolation not only narrowed our market, but also enabled shrewd cattle buyers from Nebraska and Iowa to take advantage of us. Doing their own hauling, they would induce the farmer to sell to them well below market prices, on the strength of a cash deal based on "well come and get it." In our extremity, while the drought was on, it was hard to resist this form of trading, badly as it hurt us through reduced revenue.

The drought years had made us realize more than ever that if Clayton was to survive and grow, a convenient, close-at-hand rail connection was imperative. Teams, wagons, and farm help were needed for full-time farm work, without being diverted to long-distance hauling. As long as this transport problem remained, no settler could make his farm fully productive.

This agitation for rail facilities continued all through 1888. Had we been better organized as a group, we might possibly have influenced the Rock Island definitely in our favor. Be that as it may, an extension beyond Norton had been decided, but its exact direction was still a question. With our County seat at Oberlin, we of course concluded that this would be the new terminus. Clayton would then be an intermediate station, and would have suited us well. Basing on this, our little community went ahead with its surveys. Lots were staked off, to include a rail depot and water tank, with adjacent yards for team tracks and warehouses. We all felt that our transportation problem was at last solved.

But, once again, we were doomed to disappointment. Instead of Oberlin, the railroad finally decided to make Colby, in Thomas County, its next objective. Its last survey, under this plan, carried the line south of Prairie Dog creek, leaving Clayton a mile and a quarter to the north.

Once this decision became final, we knew that our existing town-site was doomed. The railroad having refused to come to us, our only recourse was to move to it....

Now, with the coming of the railroad, we Claytonites had a new outlook. At last we were to be on the railroad map of the United States. Our produce would now find its market anywhere we could compete. Likewise, our farm and home needs would be met in a way hitherto impossible. One single carload of lumber, brought by rail, would fill at least a dozen farm wagons. Attractive frame houses would now gradually displace our crude dugouts and soddies.


Roderick Cameron, Pioneer Days in Kansas, (Belleville, Kansas: Cameron Book Co., 1951), pp. 107-109, 114.

344.  DECLINE OF MISSOURI RIVER FREIGHTING (1880's)


A not-entirely sentimental story of river freighting.
The dedication to Heckman's book reads:  "To Mrs. J. W.
Riley, the author's eldest Daughter, who, wherever she
went, said, 'My Daddy is the best pilot on the Missouri
River'"


In the eighties the mountain trade was about played out and by
the end of the decade the railroads had whipped most of the boats
off the river.  The old school of pilots were getting scarcer as
there was no business on the river and hence no call to learn the
profession.  In those early days a pilot's berth was a gift from
the gods.  For a period of twenty years of desolation along the
rivers the Heckman family with the Thompson family had boys who
upheld the river by learning the profession and becoming first
class pilots and staying with it until the river traffic increased
and our new school of pilots, who are piloting today, came along.
. . . . . . . . . . . . . . . . . . . . . . . . . . . . . . . .
In the latter seventies, Kansas City, known as the gateway to
the West, was still a great shipping point by way of the river.
The Star line steamers were then making their last stand against
the railroads with their tactics of taking freight boats in
the St. Louis-Kansas City trade, but along about 1877 these boats
gave up the ghost.  Some of the captains and pilots in this line
were:  Ralph Whitledge, George and Henry Keith, Bill and John
Massie, Jim and John Gonsols, Ed Waldwin, Tony Swope, Tony Burbank
and Bill Lingo.  Most of these men had served as "mountain" pilots
before the great Star line had been dreamed of.
After this company had failed in its big fight against the
railroads one might have thought steam-boating was at an end in
Kansas City, but this was not the case.  Col. Hunter Ben Jenkins
with others, secured three large, light-draught sternwheel steamers:
the Wyoming, the Dacotah and the Montana.  These boats, designed
and built by Captain Joe Todd near Pittsburgh, were the largest
and best boats of their class ever built for the Missouri river.
They were really built for the mountain trade but came in about
ten years late and made only a few trips in this dying trade.  Built
ten years sooner they would have made a million dollars for Captain
Todd.
From 1877 until 1882 these boats put up one of the greatest
freight and rate wars ever staged on western rivers against the
iron horse, but by encountering ever-increasing bad river, rebating,
cut rates and propaganda that did everything to kill the river
traffic, they had to quit.  They were forced to carry nails and
fourth class freight for six cents per hundred pounds.
In 1882 when these boats went out of the picture on the
Missouri river, Col. Jenkins said that it was not the bad river nor
the railroads that made him quit but that steel hull compartment
boats were not yet in use on the rivers and every time they got

twenty or thirty thousand ahead, one of the three boats would sink
and it took all of the profits to raise and repair her....
    These boats were 48 foot beam, 250 feet long and 5 feet depth
of hull.  They could carry 1000 tons on 4 1/2 feet of water.  Boats
of this kind in the year 1937, if given the amount of freight they
got in 1878 would carry freight in the Kansas City trade on our
improved rivers for one half of what our railroads are now charging,
and make 25 per cent on investment.
    When these boats quit in 1883 Kansas City had little if any
river traffic from St. Louis.  It is presumed that railroad rates
then went up until the big business men of Kansas City decided to
give the river another whirl.  In the latter eighties they made up
some $200,000 and went over to the Ohio river and contracted for
three large wooden sternwheel boats named:  the A. L. Mason, the
State of Kansas and the State of Missouri.  These boats were
supposed to be duplicates of the Wyoming, Dacotah and Montana.
For some reason they were altered slightly by the makers and they
did not handle as well, being heavier draught, too short-hulled and
incorrectly chained.  They ran between Kansas City and St. Louis
for three years when it was reported that the large shippers had
made a ten year agreement with the railroads on rates.  When this
happened these boats were sold down the Mississippi.


    William L. Heckman, Steamboating.  Sixty-five Years on
Missouri's Rivers, (Kansas City, Missouri:  Burton Publishing Co.,
1950), pp. 147, 148-149, 150-151.



### 345.  THE MISERABLE COUNTRY ROADS (1894)


    The good-roads movement originated in the efforts
of bicyclists but it laid the basis for large economies
for farmers.  (See Source No. 556).  Potter was a leader
in the League of American Wheelmen, formed to advance the
interest of bicyclists in good roads and highways.


    Let us admit that these country roads are about as bad as
roads can possibly be; that they are laden and wet and soft and
soggy in Spring and Fall, dry and dusty in Summer, and rough the
year round....Let us admit that these bad roads keep us away from
town and from each other; that we can't get to market when prices
are good; that we are hauling scant loads, racking our wagons,
killing our horses and rasping our tempers; that they keep our
wives shut up like cattle in a pen; that they increase our solitude,
keep our children from school and send our young men to the cities
with a solemn oath upon their lips that they will never till the
soil....Everybody except the farmer measures distance by time and
cost....Think of waiting for the mud to "dry up."  Sixteen million

horses and mules idle in the stable.  Four million dollars a day
for horse feed; twenty-eight millions a week.  Think of the loss of
time and labor; the dwarfed and shrunken values of our farms; of
the slack supply and good prices when the roads are impassable;
think of the procession of farmers that rush to town and glut the
market in the first days of dry weather, and think of the paltry
prices they get when everybody is trying to sell to an overstocked
merchant.  From the standpoint of profit, in dry weather and wet,
the badly kept dirt road is much the same.  There is little difference between selling a full load at half price and half a load at
full price....A good road shortens distance, saves time, wagons,
horse flesh, harnesses, increases the load and lessens the burden
and makes it possible to haul two tons to market with the same power
that now leaves one ton stuck in the mire.  It brings us closer
together, drives out gloom, makes neighbors of hermits, discounts
every farm mortgage and brings joy and contentment to every community.  Imagine a man, knee deep in the mud, trying to look cheerful!

Isaac B. Potter, Country Roads, (Boston, Massachusetts:
League of American Wheelmen, 1894), pp. 5-6, 8-9.


346.  FREIGHTING IN OKANOGAN, WASHINGTON (1890's)

The history of frontier transportation was being
rehearsed once more.  The irony was that just hundreds
of miles away the most modern trains and ships were in
use.  The geographical gap between frontier and settled
economy was very narrow but functionally the two were
distant.


In the early days the business of hauling freight from railroad terminals and steamboat landings to mining camps and commercial
centers was an indispensable occupation.  The men who engaged in it
were known as freighters.  As a rule they drove four horses, but,
when necessary, they used six or eight to haul two wagons.  In a
six-horse outfit the first team was known as the "leaders," the
middle team as the "swing," and the team next to the wagon as
the "wheelers."  It is interesting to note that while each horse
knew its own name, each team responded to the team name.  Most
teams became expert in their respective places in the outfit, but
some were so well broken that they could work interchangeably.
Freighters never considered any distance too great, regardless
of the condition of the roads.  There were no graded highways; the
drivers started out for their destinations by either making new
tracks or by following in the ruts of old ones.  Since other travelers followed these same routes, regardless of rocks, roots, and
deep chuckholes, they soon became the paths of common travel.  In
the spring of the year the ruts were full of mud and in summer they

were deep with dust.  And because different freighters tried to
avoid the worst places, there were often as many as fifty of these
improvised roads running side by side across a flat....

During the late nineties, I freighted my own produce to the
boom town of Republic, a mining center in Ferry County.  When I
did not have a full load of my own produce, such as potatoes, vegetables, butter, and fresh pork, I would buy enough apples, peaches,
tomatoes, and melons from other settlers to fill out my load.  The
freight rate from Brewster to Republic, which were, roughly, a
hundred miles apart, was about one and one-fourth cents a pound,
but I could not make as much money by charging that rate as I could
by buying produce and selling it.  I have bought fifty-pound boxes
of apples for a dollar and then sold them for two and half dollars
a box—and sometimes for as much as four dollars.  My loads averaged
three thousand pounds, and I drove twenty-five to thirty miles a
day.  I made the round trip of two hundred and ten miles in seven
days.  This period included one day spent in selling my produce.

...The autumns of 1898 and 1899 were unusually rainy, and
there was mud wherever a person drove.  The ground was so soft
that it was a common thing to find freight wagons mired to the
axle.  This always necessitated complete unloading so that the
wagon could be pulled out.  Then the freight would have to be
carried across the mudhole to be reloaded.  At such times, freighters freely helped one another out of their difficulties.


Ulrich E. Fries, From Copenhagen to Okanogan.  The Autobiography of a Pioneer, ed. Grace V. Stearns and Eugene F. Hoy,
(Caldwell, Idaho:  The Caxton Printers, Ltd., 1951), pp. 251, 253.

# D.

# AGRICULTURAL GROWTH AND ORGANIZATION

347.  OVERPRODUCTION OF CORN IN IOWA (1862)

> Market problems on the corn frontier during the
> Civil War are described here by Isaac P. Roberts, a
> farmer in Iowa at this time.  Later, he became dean
> of the faculty and director of the agricultural experi-
> ment station at Cornell University.

At the time I settled near Mount Pleasant, Iowa, the condition
of the farmers was most unfortunate; although in the midst of
plenty they were really very poor.  Little hamlets were strung over
those fertile prairies along the railway like tiny beads on a
string.  The village was usually on one side of the track and corn
cribs without number on the other side.  You might suppose that I
would glory in those ample graneries filled to overflowing with the
golden harvest, the result of making a thousand bushels of corn grow
where only one buffalo grew before; but did you ever realize what it
means to a farmer to sell a bushel--70 to 75 pounds--of corn in
the ear for ten cents?....Imagine...such a farmer, out in the field
by sunrise some frosty morning, with a span of horses and wagon,
husking a load of corn, which means thirty bushels, and which would
keep him at work all of the short autumn day.  The next day he must
take the corn to one of those only fence-board cribs at the station,
ranged parallel with the railroad track--another day's work!  And
for all this labor of man and team--growing, harvesting, and
delivery--he received only three paper dollars!....
The corn cribbed at the station was not shipped for many months
after it was produced but was held for speculative purposes.  The
owners sold it many times but as it could not be stored in Chicago

the difference in price between the first day of the month and the
last, was paid when the corn was resold.  If a part of the corn was
really wanted in Chicago it could be shelled and delivered in less
than a week.  By the end of harvest in 1864 corn had advanced to
twenty cents per bushel....I had left some cribs of corn in Indiana
which I ordered shelled and marketed in the fall of 1863; the returns gave me eighteen cents per bushel net, while it had cost me
between thirty and fifty cents to raise that corn!


Isaac P. Roberts, Autobiography of a Farm Boy, (Albany, New
York:  J. B. Lyon Co., 1916), pp. 129–132.


## 348.  FREEDMEN STREAM TO THE MISSISSIPPI (1865)


Very soon after the War, the freedmen learned how
to move about freely in pursuit of economic advantage.
The planters in Mississippi seem to have understood the
efficacy of higher wages.  Trowbridge, a Boston literary
man, was a prolific contributor to magazines and was
serving as an editor of Our Young Folks.


A tide of negro emigration was at that time flowing westward,
from the comparatively barren hills of Northern Georgia to the rich
cotton plantations of the Mississippi.  Every day anxious planters
from the Great Valley were to be met with, inquiring for unemployed
freedmen, or returning home with colonies of laborers, who had been
persuaded to quit their old haunts by the promise of double wages
in a new country.  Georgia planters, who raise but a bale of cotton
on three, four, or five acres, could not compete with their more
wealthy Western neighbors:  they higgled at paying their freedmen
six or seven dollars a month, while Arkansas and Mississippi men
stood ready to give twelve and fifteen dollars, and the expenses
of the journey.  As it cost no more to transport able-bodied young
men and women than the old and the feeble, the former were generally selected and the latter left behind.  Thus it happened that an
unusually large proportion of poor families remained about Atlanta
and other Georgia towns.


J. T. Trowbridge, The South, (Hartford, Connecticut:  L. S
Stebbins, 1866), p. 460.

349.  FINANCIAL STRINGENCY IN COTTON MARKETS (1870)

Following are some excellent analytical comments
by a British traveler, Robert Somers.


[S. Carolina]  The cotton speculators at New York push over
the heads of the local merchants and factors, and, by cutting before
the point, do little good probably to themselves, while impoverishing the trade of the Southern seaports and muddling and confusing
the market.  Instances have occurred in which they have bought
cotton in the interior, cash on the spot, upon which advances had
already been made by Southern merchants; but this, of course, is a
practice which cannot extend, and immediately checks itself.  Yet
the excessive activity of speculation in buying and moving cotton
is very apparent, and is of doubtful benefit either to the planter
or to the consumer.  The poverty to which the cotton dealers of
Charleston were reduced by the war, and the ruin which fell upon
all her financial resources, made an opening for the capital of
speculators of which they have availed themselves, and which only
closes up as the profits of trade once more accumulate and the town
becomes richer.  Before the war Charleston had a banking capital of
only 1,892,000 dollars.  The State of South Carolina, outside of
Charleston, had a banking capital before the war of 3,000,000
dollars, but now of only 300,000 dollars.  The crippled capacity of
planters and merchants to raise and move such large crops of expor-
table produce as those of South Carolina may be inferred from these
facts.  The charges for the use of money are enormous.  The banks
turn over money at the rate of 18 to 24 per cent., on a class of
business which presents little or no risk.  In the country districts
the rates are still more exorbitant, so that it is with money as
with everything else that enters into the production and transport
of cotton--it is loaded with a costliness in dollars of now all but
par value with gold, which to an Englishman or Scotchman appears
simply unbearable.  Hence the cry for a high price; hence the
difficulty and discontent into which every fall seems to plunge the
producer; and hence the struggling condition of the Southern States
despite their natural advantages and hold on the commercial world.
Until capital be more largely established on the spot for the trading purposes of the country, and substantial reductions of the
tariff permit a more direct trade between the South and Europe, and
bills on England become saleable in the great depots of Southern
produce, the cotton trade can hardly be in a sound condition, while
it is impossible that such cities as Charleston can be enriched
by the vast inland countries behind them, or be to them in return
the strength, support, and ornament they might well be.
. . . . . . . . . . . . . . . . . . . . . . . . . . . . . .
Complaints of the usurious rates charged for money are general
among the farming community.  Twenty-five and even thirty per cent.
is taken by banks and people who have money to lend as a quite
ordinary rate; and it is doubtful whether the planters are as thriving as the commercial interests around them.
. . . . . . . . . . . . . . . . . . . . . . . . . . . . . .

[Georgia] Augusta is an extensive cotton market. Since the
lifting of this year's crop began, the receipts have been about
1,500 bales a day. The railroads place Augusta in rapid communication with the adjoining counties of South Carolina, and with all
parts of Middle Georgia, and the cotton collected from these wide
districts is poured down by rail to Savannah for shipment. The
telegraph works all day betwixt Augusta and Savannah, and betwixt
Augusta and towns farther inland, telling what cotton can be bought
or is selling for; while prices at New York and Liverpool are eagerly scanned, and form the basis of the day's transactions. The local
factors and merchants deal freely in cotton, though the former operate chiefly on order from Savannah, Charleston, and New York. Seldom has cotton been brought more rapidly to market than this season,
which is to be ascribed not only to the favourable weather, but to
the activity of buyers and speculators, and the necessity, rather
than the interest, of the planters; for under the heavy fall of
prices, generally attributed here to the war in Europe, and scarce
at all to the yearly expansion of the crop, the planter might be
tempted, with the stock of American at Liverpool still low, and the
return of peace probably not distant, to hold back in expectation
of better prices. But the growers of cotton, though restoring
rapidly their plantations and their stock of implements, are, for
the most part, still poor in purse, and have to draw heavy advances
on the growing crop. Paying from 2 to 2 1/2 per cent. for money
per month, with storage and insurance charges to boot, the planter
finds that to hold is a costly business, and that it is better to
sell at once than to extend his borrowings and charges in the expectation of an advance of two or three cents per lb. The crop,
save in so far as it may be interrupted by the action of middlemen
and speculators, is therefore rolled from the field, over hundreds
of miles of railway and thousands of miles of ocean, to the great
markets with marvellous despatch. Though insurance in the South
was swept away during the war, yet it is growing up again with
great rapidity; and statemen and generals, whose names were famous
in the war, preside over local companies or act as agents of New
York or British corporations.


Somers, The Southern States Since the War, pp. 45, 57, and 63.


350.  WHITE LABOR ENTERING COTTON CULTIVATION (1870)


     An unusual contention that the cotton crop was less
a "Negro crop" after the war than before, primarily
because white labor had entered cotton cultivation under
varying circumstances.

The ad captandum mode of arguing the superior efficiency of
free negro labour—viz. that so many negroes perished in the war,
that negro women do not now work in the field, that negro children
are put to school, and that nevertheless the crop being all but
equal to what it was under slavery, it follows that the negroes
free must produce greatly better than when slaves—is superficial,
and does not touch the substantial merits of the question.  It does
not embrace the fact that scarcely any of the plantations on which
cotton was grown under slavery are nearly up to the mark of production before the war; and it leaves out of view the great number of
small white farmers who, under the disability of the former growers,
have begun for the first time to raise cotton, the numerous bands
of white labourers who have availed themselves of the abundant
opportunities of renting and cropping from year to year, the white
villages who have thrown their sickles into the common harvest—
though small their patches individually, yet considerable in the
aggregate—and the cloud of white planters and their families reduced to poverty, who have been the foremost to go down into the
Western bottoms, and there and elsewhere have bent with noble for-
titude and ardour to labour in the fields.  It would be a misapprehension to take the cotton crop now as the product of negro labour
in the same sense as it was before the war.  The intermixture of
white labour in the cotton culture of the South is already large,
and though the forms under which the lands are cultivated are
various yet the general distinction betwixt large plantations
wrought by negroes under white employers, and small farms wrought
chiefly by white people, remains a prominent feature of the new
state of things, the practical force of which is felt more year
by year.

Somers, The Southern States Since the War, pp. 272-273.


351.  AMERICAN FARMING IS HIGHLY SPECULATIVE (1871)


The American farmer produced for the world market
and was always under the threat of overproduction.


The Tennesseean farmers began some time ago to grow broom-corn
—a wild grass of great length and tenacity of fibre, requiring a
strong soil, of which house brooms, very neatly got up, are made—
and found it profitable a year or two, while there were comparatively few growers.  But this season there has been an over-supply of
broom-corn, and the price has fallen below the remunerative point.
The circumstances cannot be much different in the great agricultural
regions of the West, where wheat grows luxuriantly, but grows
luxuriantly in so many other vast spaces of the globe that in
meeting the changes of the foreign market and the expenses of

transportation it often yields to the Western farmer only a petty
return.  The superabundance of land in America, and the ease with
which, under its now advanced stage of occupation, any ordinary
product may be supplied beyond the limits of profit, from the great
difficulty of agriculture in the United States; and the British
farmer, with a rent to pay, but with a demand round his steading
for everything he produces always in excess of his supply, labours
under but a milder form of the evil which besets the American
farmer, with the soil of his own or given to him for his staple
produce, and uncertain whether he will find one that will repay him
anywhere.  The cultivation of the soil in the United States has
thus a much more speculative character than in Europe; and as the
American farmer is not content by hard manual labour to earn a
rough livelihood only, but seeks to grow richer as he works on,
there is more changing from one system of crops and from one tract
of land to another than, and probably quite as much dissatisfaction
in the result as, in most other countries.


Somers, The Southern States Since the War, pp. 271-272.



352.   ONE-SIDED SHARECROPPER CONTRACTS (1871)


     When it came to drawing up or enforcing a legal
contract, the sharecropper suffered a fatal weakness
in bargaining power.  Robert Meacham, an ex-slave, was a
Florida state senator and a register of the United States
Land Office (at Monticello?).


     Question.  How has it been with regard to their contracts for
employment; have they had much trouble in settling up fairly and
getting their pay?
     Answer.  A great deal.
     Question.  What has been the difficulty?
     Answer.  In the first place a majority of them do not know how
to make a contract for their interests.  The farmers who make the
contracts with them draw up the contracts in writing and read it
to them.  The colored people are generally uneducated, and when a
contract says this or that they hardly know what it means.  A
great many of the contracts give the farmer a lien upon what portion
of the crop is coming to them for any debt they incur.  Another
reason why they do not get much is, that in the months of August
and September mostly, when the crops are laid by, the slightest
insult, as they call it, or the slightest neglect, is sufficient
to turn them off, and according to the contract they get nothing.
The contracts are made in this way:  articles of agreement are
drawn up which provide that if either one of the parties of the
first part or the second part violate any of the articles they are

to be turned off and get nothing.  Now that is remedied a little;
there is a law now in this State that allows a man to get what he
works for, unless it is proven fairly that he has willfully neglected or violated any of the articles of agreement.  In a great
many instances about my portion of the country--I know this person-
ally--you will find that for the slightest offense the laborers
are turned off and get nothing.

Question.  Does that occur before the crop is made, or after
it is made?

Answer.  In the months of August and September generally, when
the crop is made; sometimes in July.

Question.  When there is nothing to do about the crop except
to gather it?

Answer.  Yes, sir; in the month of July the corn is made, and
they pull fodder here then.


Testimony, Robert Meacham, November 10, 1871; U.S. Congress,
Joint Select Committee to Inquire into the Condition of Affairs
in the Late Insurrectionary States, Testimony, XIII, (Washington,
D.C.:  Government Printing Office, 1872), pp. 101-102.


### 353.  COTTON FINDS NEW MARKETING CHANNELS (1876)


The rise of the railroad set the stage for extreme
changes in the marketing of the cotton crop.  Here is an
authentic summary of these changes made by Henry Hester,
secretary of the New Orleans Cotton Exchange.


A glance at the table of cotton-receipts at New Orleans will
show a marked falling off in the percentage of receipts of the total
crop at that port.

Various causes have been assigned for this decrease, the principal of which, however, is the opening up of new channels of trade,
developing points which, prior to the war, were comparatively un-
important as cotton-receivers.  New railroads have been built and
old ones completed, permeating every section of the cotton-belt,
and a strong competition between the various routes of transportation has resulted in a marked curtailment of the shipments of
cotton by river and a corresponding increase by rail.  In 1855,
according to the annual-crop statement of the New York Shipping
List, the overland shipments to eastern delivery-ports direct from
producers were only 7,661 bales out of a crop of 2,847,339.  Five
years late, (1860,) this movement had increased to 10,676 out of a
crop of 4,669,770, the largest ever grown.  And ten years subsequent
to the latter, (1870), with a crop of 4,347,006 bales, 580,813 were
transported overland to delivery ports and to mills north and east
of the Ohio and Mississippi Rivers.

Wherever a section is tapped by railroads with through connections it can hardly be said to be entirely tributary to any particular port.  In other words, the movement of cotton every year becomes
more and more governed by the cost of transportation and contingent
charges en route from the producer to the consumer.  A variation of
1/8 to 1/4 of a cent per pound is sufficient to turn the course of
almost the entire shipments of an interior point from their accustomed channels.  The movement via Norfolk is an exemplification of
these facts.  In 1855 the entire quantity of cotton handled at
Virginia ports was 31,000 bales, this including amount manufactured
in Virginia taken from sea-ports; 1861 it had increased to 78,132,
but fell back in 1866, the year subsequent to the war, to 37,531
bales.  The repair and extension of the various rail-routes from
the interior increased the cotton-movement via Norfolk from 123,627
in 1867 to 505,866 in 1874.

A large part of the cotton shipped via Norfolk, the produce
of Tennessee and Arkansas, formerly went to New Orleans by river,
besides a considerable portion of that which is now included in
the "overland movement."
. . . . . . . . . . . . . . . . . . . . . . . . . . . . . . . . . . .
It will be observed that, of the total movement from Memphis
in 1865, 197,990 bales, or 60 per cent, sought the northern seaboard
or eastern mills by overland rail-routes, while 58,491 were transported by river to points in the West, from whence all but a small
fraction consumed were transported east by rail, as with the 60
per cent, above stated, and leaving but 68,782 shipped to New
Orleans.

. . . . . . . . . . . . . . . . . . . . . . . . . . . . . . . . . . . .
We thus find a growing tendency, controlled by a strong competition which has cheapened freights from many interior points by
rail, in addition to the desire to escape the charges of middle-men
at delivery-ports or elsewhere, to transport cotton direct from
the producer to the consumer.

Not only are the agents of American mills to be found in almost every interior town of importance, a custom which was not
established until within a few years back, but buyers also for
Great Britain and Europe, whose purchases are shipped on through-
bills of lading avoiding all unnecessary delays, to the final
point of destination.

It would be a work of supererogation to follow the ramifica-
tions of the staple from the interior of the various Cotton States,
the mere statement that nearly one-fourth of the crop finds an outlet to domestic and foreign consumers by overland routes across the
Ohio and Mississippi Rivers and through Norfolk, Va., (which is
really only a point of transit,) combined with the facts above set
forth, being sufficient to furnish a clear conception of the manner
in which the American cotton-crop is now marketed.


Henry G. Hester; U.S. Congress, 44th, 2nd session, House of
Representatives, Exec. Doc. No. 46, part 2, Joseph Nimmo, Jr.,
First Annual Report on the Internal Commerce of the United States,
serial number 1761, (Washington, D.C.: Government Printing Office,
1877), Appendix No. 14, pp. 175-176, 176-177.

354.  MACHINE-THRESHING WHEAT IN KANSAS (1877)

Here is an unusually detailed account of mechanical
threshing of wheat.

We have been threshing three days, and it is no easy work.
Threshing here is different from what it is in the East.  The
machine is put together so that the grain is fed in at one end,
and the straw is carried out at the other, while the clean grain
comes out at one side of the machine.  The horsepower requires ten
horses to run it.
    Threshing machines here thresh as much as 500 or 600 bushels a
day, when they do not have to travel too far between jobs, which is
not often, for these machines sometimes pull ten miles between jobs,
and jobs are not very big because most men's acreage is small.
Some days the thresher will knock out several jobs without being
much richer, even though the price is five cents a bushel where
the quantity is a hundred bushels or more.  When there is less than
a hundred bushels it is a "set" job, and costs the grain raiser
$5, besides board for the machine men and their teams and the
neighbors who help.
    The machine owner furnishes three teams for the power and the
farmer supplies all the other teams needed as well as the helpers.
Cooking for the crowd is no little work, but the woman of the house
always has enough help, for on such occasions most of the men who
help bring their families along, and the women folks have a real
good visit while preparing the meals....When the machine pulls
in to a set all the neighbors have been notified in advance--for
they go with the machine while it is in the neighborhood.  Every
man gathers up all the sacks he owns and takes them along, for
the grain being sacked when it is taken to the granary, many sacks
are in use for a short time and no one man has enough for the
occasion.  After the rounds are made, it takes a lot of sorting to
get each man's property out of the pile, often considerably the
worse for wear.
    A threshing crew, besides the machine men, consists of two or
three pitchers, generally three.  The sheaves are bound with straw
bands.  Three boys are put at the end of the ten-foot carrier to
pitch the straw away from the machine, and it is no snap, for the
straw rolls out fast enough to keep them very busy.  Then there is
the measure man, who sees that the grain does not slop over the
edge of the half bushel measure.  The grain comes out of a V-shaped
sheet iron spout slipped through the wheel, between the spokes.
The measure man has to keep his wits about him, to keep track of
the bushels.  He has a bit of board filled with gimlet holes on
each side of the machine, and with little pegs keeps count of the
number of bushels.  There are four rows of holes, ten in a row.
The upper row is for half-bushels:  when the peg has been moved,
a notch at a time, from the left end of the row to the right, five

bushels have been tallied and the peg in the right hand end of the
second row is stuck in the first hold on the left, marking five
bushels.  The same process is used in the other tow rows of holes,
only in the third row a tally stands for 50 bushels, and in the
fourth for 500.

The measure man has an assistant, whose duty is to hold sacks
for the grain--considered an easy job....The grain hauler has an
assistant, too, because the granaries are small and unhandy to fill.
When the bin is nearly full the sack emptier has to wriggle along
on top of the pile of grain and empty the sack as best he can, which
under the circumstances is no easy task.

The band cutter, an important member of the crew, stands on top
of a pile of sheaves placed at the table on which the bundles are
pitched.  Sometimes the grain is stacked, but when it is not, two
pitchers are needed in the field, to pitch the sheaves onto the
wagons, and two men with a wagon each.

We had nine teams and thirteen men at work--five teams attached
to the horsepower, three hauling grain from the field, and one hauling the clean grain to the granary.

It took two days threshing to get all Henry's grain away, and
we threshed nearly 1000 bushels altogether.  The oats averaged 62
bushels per acre, and if we had not fed any from the sheaf, it
would have averaged about 70.


Howard Ruede, Sod-House Days.  Letters from a Kansas Homesteader, 1877-78, ed. John Ise, (New York:  Columbia University
Press, 1937), pp. 119-122.


355.  SOIL DRAINAGE ON PRAIRIE FARMS (1878)


Low land prices could create a reluctance to invest
in drainage measures.  (See Source No. 151).  But lack of
knowledge also played a part.  Cleveland, a landscape architect, who lived in Chicago and published various works on
agriculture and forestry, writes this account.


The general topography and character of the soil of the
prairies is so much like, that for the greater portion of the
farms in Illinois the rules for drainage are identical.  Almost
every farm is intersected more or less by low, wet tracts, known as
sloughs, the intervening uplands being generally only gentle eleva-
tions, and rarely obtaining the dignity of hills.  The subsoil is
generally clay, which is not unfrequently compressed into "hard
pan," which is nearly impervious to water, but speedily becomes
ameliorated by drainage, which necessarily causes alternate disten-
tion and shrinkage, and after a time works a complete change in its
character.  The sloughs, except during the heats of summer, are

impassable beds of mire, and are incapable of cultivation; but when
drained become at once the richest portion of the farm.

It is in the sloughs, of course, that the main drains must be
laid, beginning at the outlet, or lowest point, and working upward,
preserving always the longest possible stretches of straight lines,
and making angles, or curves, only where it is absolutely necessary.

And it is of the utmost importance that these mains should,
from the outset, be large enough to carry all the water that may be
brought to them by side drains or by future extension.

Comparatively few farmers have yet extended their lines of
tiles beyond the sloughs and wet grounds which demand immediate
attention.  They follow the course of the slough from the outlet to
the head, or to the highest point within their own bounds, laying a
four, six or eight-inch tile for a main, and then connecting any
outlying pools, or wet places with it by a lateral or smaller size.
The day is not distant, however, when the beneficial effect of
drainage of uplands will be as universally acknowledged as that of
the sloughs has already become.

The effect of drains in ameliorating the soil and preserving
an equal degree of moisture, by means of the ventilation they
afford, is but imperfectly comprehended by the mass of farmers, who
think only of the necessity of removing standing water.  They think
it unnecessary to provide artificial means for removing the water
when it is not seen to stand upon the surface; but in reality it
(in the great majority of cases) is held in the soil to such an
extent as to be greatly injurious to the growing crops.  If drain
tile are laid at intervals of forty or fifty feet, the effect will
be that the water from heavy rains will speedily pass off, and the
soil, instead of remaining soggy and dead, will become friable and
easy to cultivate, and as the water runs off its place is supplied
by air, which keeps it light and porous, and in times of drought
imparts to it the moisture with which, even in the dryest times, it
is laden, and thus prevents its ever becoming baked in clods, as
clay land is sure to do if undrained.  The most obstinate clays are
so affected by drainage that they crack and crumble, and become
annually more loose and friable.


H. W. S. Cleveland, The Great Want of Illinois.  Farm and
Road Drainage, (Chicago, Illinois:  Hazlitt and Reed, 1878), pp.
13-14.



356.  IRRIGATION IS PRACTICABLE IN CALIFORNIA (1879)


The progress of irrigation waited upon a solution
of the legal problem of water rights.  In California,
at least, there was hardly a problem of an absolute shortage
of water.  The writer, W. T. Haywood, described himself as
being engaged in the irrigation business.

412    A Capitalist Economy, 1860-1900

I have had some experience in the matter of irrigating lands
for five or six years.  In my judgment the public lands and waters
should never be separated.  In Spain, Italy, and all other countries
except India, the waters and the land are not separated.  In India
all the canals are owned by an English company and the waters sold
to the natives who lease the lands.  This is an interesting question
to every man in this State who has lands.  The difficulty of securing water rights permanently depreciates the value of this kind of
property to a very great extent.  There are thousands of acres of
lands, not only in San Bernardino County but in other parts of the
State, that could be made available, and would be made so at once
and be occupied, provided there was a certainty of getting a title
to the land and water alike; for title to the land alone is of no
value.  Now the difference in valuation of land with water over
that without, in the same neighborhood and having the same soil
precisely, will be from fifteen to twenty dollars per acre.  For
instance:  I have been president and superintendent of the Riverside
Company, and we have spent $230,000 in furnishing water and irrigat-
ing about twelve thousand acres of land.  Now this land was put
upon the market with other large bodies of land as early as 1853 by
proclamation of the President.  It laid there unoccupied as government land until 1865, when in consequences of greenbacks being at a
low figure it was bought up by men in California at $1.25 per acre
from the government.  It laid there idle from 1853 to 1865, and
then it was held from 1865 to 1874, when I purchased it.  Now that
land was apparently of no value, not worth ten cents per acre.
Without water it could not have been beneficial in any way.  Having
put water upon it we have sixteen hundred people occupying that
tract of land, who have four hundred thousand orange trees growing,
and one hundred thousand fruit trees, and we have a very prosperous
and thrifty class of people there.  That is the result of one irrigation scheme.  I do not believe extensive irrigation is possible
without organization.  There should be a government system of irrigation, and there must be some organization, or else you must leave
the matter to work itself out.  We understand that the law by which
we have acquired our water rights from the State has been confirmed
by Congress and that we are safe.  Other people have different views
and they are contesting the matter with us in the courts.  All such
actions have a tendency to depreciate that property, to prevent
its sale and settlement.


Testimony, W. T. Haywood; U.S. Congress, 46th, 2nd session,
House of Representatives, Exec. Doc. No. 46, Report of the Public
Lands Commission, serial number 1923, (Washington, D.C.:  Government
Printing Office, 1880), pp. 65-66.

## 357.  FENCE THE COLORADO STOCK RANGES (1879)

The larger cattle ranchers argued for fencing
the range and thus for being allowed to buy extensive
tracts of the range.  Illegal fencing abounded despite
government prohibitions.  McCaskill, of Pueblo, Colorado,
was president of the Southern Colorado Cattle Growers'
Association.  The following is his testimony.

There are in this State about 400,000 sheep, and I think that
about 250,000 of them are in this land district, and they are worth
at least half a million dollars.  It is very injurious to a cattle
range to feed sheep upon it.  The sheep nibble very close and their
feet are so sharp that they cut the grass and the wind blows the
grass away; then, too, the grass being eaten down so close it does
not come up again readily.  They also destroy the winter range.
While the cattle are gone up on the summer range the sheep come
along and eat up the winter range.  If the ranges were fenced this
would be obviated.  There is much trouble with jumpers.  The Texas
cattle man will come along, and, if he finds water, he will locate
on your range and eat it all off, just as the sheep men do.  When
the time comes to pay taxes they move off.  There is a row between
the cattle and sheep men all the time on account of the inroads of
the sheep upon the cattle pastures.  This could all be stopped by
fencing.  If the land could be purchased in large tracts this would
settle the whole matter; of course giving both an equal chance to
buy.  The jumpers and Mexicans do not wish to have fences, because
then, if they owned the land, they would have to pay taxes and could
not roam where they please.  On account of the dry climate sheep
require a great deal of water, differing in this respect from the
Eastern States.  Because of the inroads upon the ranges, sheep men
are fighting among themselves.  Owing to the fact that the ranges
are overstocked with sheep, the grass is being eaten out completely
and the ranges entirely destroyed.  Some men on the Chico are
commencing to fence the public domain.  As a result of this, some
of their neighbors are having their ranges taken away from them.
If the opportunity was offered they would buy this land at low
prices, but as they cannot buy it there will be trouble.
   The difficulty about fencing the public land is this:  One
man fences and another fences and another, and when it comes to be
entered properly in the land office the person making the entry will
be resisted by the persons who are in possession, when he goes to
take up his land.  This causes a great deal of difficulty and often
bloodshed, inaugurating a sort of "squatters' war."  If the lands
could be purchased from the government in large tracts and fenced,
a better class of cattle could be produced.  One half of the cattle
that we now have would then produce as great a profit.  The grass is
running out so that the cattle will not get fat enough for market,
and they will be compelled to take their beef cattle off to fatten
them.  Last winter and this winter too we buried in Pueblo County
3,500 head of cattle that died from starvation.  By taking the beef

off and fattening them in Kansas, you can support just that many
more stock cattle.  If the stockmen could buy their ranges they
would build good houses, make permanent improvements, and live
there; but as it is now, they do not make homes there.  If you go
into the country now, you will see only one-story log-cabins,
because they do not know how long they will be able to live there.

Testimony, John McCaskill; U.S. Congress, 46th, 2nd session,
House of Representatives, Exec. Doc. No. 46, Report of the Public
Lands Commission, serial number 1923, (Washington, D.C.:  Government
Printing Office, 1880), pp. 292-293.

### 358.   OXEN ON THE FARM (1870's)

Oxen are usually associated with the earliest,
slowest-moving of pioneer days.  Here is why.  The
writer, Edson Mudge, grew up on a farm in northern
Newaygo County.

There were several reasons why oxen were preferred to horses
in pioneer days, the principal one being their practical use in
clearing land.  In the clearing process the timber was cut and
allowed to lay for some months, then the slashing was fired and
everything burned away except the bare logs with the larger limbs.
Then with ax and saw these were cut into such lengths as could be
hauled about.  The ox team was universally used for "snaking" the
logs into position where they could be rolled into heaps for burning.  A long, stout chain was the only attachment needed, with a
driver who could yell "Gee!" "Haw!" or "Giddap!" with sufficient
vigor.  Horses on the other hand would require one man to hold the
lines and another to manipulate the whippletrees as the team was
turned about among the stumps.  Besides, an ox team was a far more
suitable target for the driver's profanity.  I have heard of people
who could "swear like a sailor," but I think few sailors could
compete with the average ox teamster in the use of original and
expressive swear words.
For plowing among the stumps the ox team was far preferable.
One man could hold the plow and drive the team, while a horse team,
bound up in harness with tugs and whippletrees, was something of a
nuisance.  A single horse, however, was sometimes used quite satisfactorily.  The first plowing was usually done with a single shovel
plow combined with a coulter set on a slant, which carried the plow
over the roots.  Oxen were not only useful for all sorts of work
around the backwoods farm, but when not in use they could be turned
out into the woods along with the other neighborhood cattle.

On most farms the reign of the ox was of short duration.
Within a few years, when the stumps had rotted away or had been
pulled (more commonly the former), so that plowing in a more modern
way was possible, he was relegated to the regions still in the early
pioneer stage, and the horse team took over.  The ox was too slow,
and driving him on the road was tedious.  It was difficult for him
to make the trip to the nearest town and return in a single day,
while a horse could do it easily.  The first horses on a pioneer
farm were likely to be ancient nags, far past their prime, which
the hopeful settler picked up from somewhere at a price he could
afford to pay.  Naturally such animals, often without adequate food
and housed in primitive stables, did not survive many years.
Veterinarians were practically unknown, and the ailing horse had to
depend on his own recuperative powers.


Edson H. Mudge, "From the Oxcarts Up," _Michigan History_, XXXV
(1951), pp. 216-2818.


359.  DROUGHT AND IGNORANCE ON THE KANSAS FRONTIER (1880)


A farmer schooled in the ways of Ohio or Illinois
agriculture soon found that he had to start learning
all over again.  This problem arose continually during
the westward movement.


The average annual rainfall for Norton and Decatur counties is
less than twenty inches.  For a country such as ours this is altogether too little.  Dry, hot winds from the south, prevailing during
much of the summer, soon absorb top soil moisture, making the ground
hard and powdery.  The July and August sun does a thorough job of
baking it.  Obviously, irrigation is needed to supplement the scant
rainfall.  Our principal creek, the Prairie Dog, would almost run
dry as the summer advanced.  To reach underground springs, Artesian
wells were needed, sinking them to at least a hundred and thirty
feet....The digging of these wells began in 1880, and was continued
all through the drought years.  But had the rainfall been sufficient, it is doubtful whether these wells would ever have been put
in.  But they were urgently needed, and once water was obtained
from them, were of enormous benefit.  So the drought, in forcing us
to sink the wells, was really a disguised blessing.
Almost as damaging as the lack of water, was the average
settler's lack of farming knowledge suited to the locality.  In his
ignorance, he thought that the same methods he had found successful
elsewhere would be equally so in northwest Kansas.  Instead of
sowing hard wheat, which would have been drought and frost resis-
tant, he sowed soft wheat, which is neither.  Also, in cultivating
the soil, he showed equal ignorance.  Could he have known and

practiced dry farming methods, he would in many cases have been successful.  The proof of this is to be seen in the case of the Mennonites, from southern Russia, sowing Turkey red hard wheat, after an early deep plowing, and thorough surface cultivation, came successfully through the drought years, and suffered little loss. They used the same methods they had found successful in southern Russia, which has a climate almost identical with that of Kansas.

Had the homesteaders who abandoned their claims, adopted the same methods as the Mennonites, they would have had a different story to tell.

Cameron, Pioneer Days in Kansas, pp. 91-92.

360.  OPEN-KETTLE SUGAR MAKING (1880's)

Following is a rare description of a technological process which has now disappeared.  The plantation described was near Plaquemine, Louisiana, facing the Mississippi River.

My earliest recollection of sugar making on the plantation was of a little mill that had run for many "grinding" seasons during the time of my father and grandfather.  The Clement mill, however, was dismantled in later years, and the cane sold to larger mills nearby.  But when I was a little boy the old fashioned sugar mill operated in all its glamour, and for the last two or three months of the year it was the momentous concern of all the plantation people, white and black, young and old.  Big slabs of wood, from nearby stacked cords of this home-produced fuel, thrown or pushed into blazing fires under the big old-fashioned boilers, was a spectacle in itself.  A cane "carrier" brought the great piles of juicy looking "ribbon" cane to the crushing rollers.  The cane juice flowed in a small river to the row of "batteries" where the boiling and "skimming off" of impurities took place.

These batteries of "open" kettles or cauldrons with steam coils underneath were arranged in order.  The transfer of the hot juice from one to the other was done by a hand-operated ladling process, amid a steamy surrounding, with much sampling and testing to find when the point of proper cooking had been reached.  Great long sweeps with wooden buckets were the ladles that carried the boiling cane juice from one cauldron to the other and to the final-process vat before it was transferred to coolers in the "cooling room." There the soft sugar mass was left to solidify into the brown sugar, the finished product.  Later, men with ordinary spades dug the brown sugar out of the coolers and filled sugar barrels and hogsheads for shipping to New Orleans.  Some of the juice ended up as

our Retreat Plantation <u>Delectable</u> brand of molasses.  Molasses of
course was handled differently, and was poured into a tighter
barrel.  After each boiling when the molasses was cooled off there
remained at the bottom of the kettle a thick substance called
<u>cuite</u>.  This ropey, taffy-like confection was a table delicacy with
the flavor of sugar cane and was much enjoyed during the season.
It could not be kept long without turning into sugar.  Cuite is now
almost a system such as ours is now extinct.  At one time there
were hundreds, now only one or two left--if that.

All these little old-time mills, one on practically every
sugar plantation--some horse operated, some steam--making the simplest form of plain brown sugar, had their own cooper shop attached.
There barrels were made and put together.  The work was done by
home-trained expert Negro coopers.  After the barrels were filled
four-mule carts hauled them out along the road in front of our
house, over the levee and down to the boat landing where they were
loaded on a steamboat to be taken to New Orleans.

The transport of the weighty hogsheads of sugar was effected
by a special lifting apparatus, which hoisted the great casks and
hung them under and between two big wheels to form a novel conveyance.  Queer looking rigs these were, generally pulled by oxen,
travelling at a slow pace with the big barrel-shaped container
hanging only a few feet from the ground.  In bad weather, when the
roads were deep with mud, hauling entailed great difficulties.  But
there was no trouble in getting steamboats to take on this freight
as it stood on the bank of the river.  I remember freight agents
from the boats coming to our home and pestering our people for
business.

The forest in rear of our plantation did not supply quite all
the wood that was needed to "take off" the river crop.  So each
spring, when the river-rise brought great logs down the river, a
gang of our colored workers using four-oared skiffs would go out
into the stream and bring to shore some of the largest of the
constantly passing uprooted trees.  These logs, some of them of
great size, were drawn from the waters edge to the working area
high on the bank by means of hand-wind-lasses.  Round and round the
men went pulling out the logs.  Sometimes a small horse was used to
pull the big lever around.  The logs were then sawed in proper
lengths by hand, two men with cross-cut saws.  By using axes and
wedges, the sawed sections were split into "slabs" for the sugar-
house furnaces.  They were then piled to dry for the coming "grinding" season....In talking recently with former U.S. Senator Edward
Gay about this rather primitive fuel operation of the sugar making
process of many years ago, when compared to modern oil burning
equipment now used in most all the big sugar mills, he said, "Yes,
I remember the old method."  "But in those days," he said, "The
Sugar mills made a lot more money than they do at present."

William Edwards Clement and Stuart Omer Landry, <u>Plantation
Life on the Mississippi</u>, (New Orleans, Louisiana:  Pelican
Publishing Co., 1952), pp. 13-15.

361.  THE TEXAS CATTLE TRAIL (1880's)


The following description contains enough
work-a-day detail and romance to convince us that
it is typical if not entirely accurate.


In the morning the herd might be fifteen or twenty miles from
camp and it would take all day or longer to get them on the trail
again and all the cowpunchers would be kept in the saddle without
rest or food until all were moving along again.  If a cowboy was
killed in a stampede his comrades dug a shallow grave, wrapped
the trampled form in his blankets and laid him to rest.
    The greatest responsibility rested on the trail boss.  He had
to know where water was a day ahead and the drive made according.
There was one dry drive forty miles long.  When there was a long
dry drive the cattle would be watered and then pushed on away into
the night.  Cattle can smell water for a very long distance and if
the wind was from the north next morning, the herd would travel
along all right, but if there was no wind they would travel slow.
If the wind blew up from behind late in the afternoon when they were
suffering for water, there was trouble.  They would "bull," that is
try to turn and go back to water and it required all the skill and
best efforts of every cowpuncher in the outfit to keep the herd
moving forward and then it could not always be done.
    I have seen a herd traveling along only a few miles from where
they were going in to water, when the wind would suddenly blow from
a river behind them.  The cattle would turn as one cow, start for
that water, possibly ten miles distant, and nothing could stop
them.
    A herd cannot be made to swim a large river if the sunshine
on the water reflects in their eyes; nor will they go into a river
if the wind is blowing and the water ripples.  In 1885 John Lea,
one of the experienced trail bosses, struck the Yellowstone river
with a herd.  The wind blew hard for three days and kept the water
rippled, and nothing would induce those cattle to cross the river
until the water was smooth.
    A day's drive on the trail is from ten to fifteen miles, but
it is always governed by water.  A herd of steers make much better
time than a mixed herd.  There was never any such thing as "resting
up" or "laying over;" the herd was kept moving forward all the time.
. . . . . . . . . . . . . . . . . . . . . . . . . . . . . . . . . . . . . . . . .
    Trailing cattle came to be a profession and the trail men a
distinct class.  They came north with a herd in the spring and
returned south in the fall, worked in the chaparral, gathering
another herd during the winter and then drove north again in the
spring.  They took a great pride in their work and were never so
happy as when turning a fine herd on the range at the end of the
trail.
    It was a pleasing sight to see a herd strung out on the trail.
The horses and the white-covered mess wagon in the lead, followed
by a mass of sleek cattle a half mile long; the sun flashing on

their bright horns and on the silver conchos, bridles, spurs, and pearl-handled six shooters of the cowpunchers. The brilliant hand-kerchiefs knotted about their necks furnished the needed touch of color to the picture.

Paul C. Phillips (ed.), <u>Forty Years on the Frontier as Seen in the Journals and Reminiscences of Granville Stuart</u>, II, (Cleveland, Ohio: Arthur H. Clark Co., 1925), pp. 191-193.


362. AMERICAN COTTON IN RUSSIA (1880's)


During the 1880's, under stimulus of the Russian government, an American variety of upland cotton was grown in Tashkent. Between 1884 and 1889 Russian acreage sown with American upland cotton expanded from 810 to 120, 150. This extract is from a report by J. M. Crawford, U.S. Consul-General at St. Petersburg.


At first the introduction of American seed was looked upon as a mere speculation which tempted only the more venturesome farmers; the success, however, of the initiators in this matter was very marked, in that they received a hundred per cent of clear profit on their invested capital, in other words, ten dollars per acre. Such a success brought about a genuine cotton fever in the country and the aristocracy and even military men hastened to rent land for cotton plantations. The growing of American cotton increased incredibly fast. The 300 pounds of American cotton seed imported in 1884 yielded after six years a crop of 45,600,000 pounds of clean fibre and in 1891 the shipment of cotton from Central Asia to the interior amounted to 108,000,000 pounds. Such an increase in the cotton industry in Central Asia must be looked upon, how-ever, as abnormal and to some extent as the result of the cotton fever. Such a forced cultivation to the very limits of the northern boundary of the cotton zone (Tashkent for example being 41$^{o}$N.), shows the instability of the entire movement. It will be easily seen that however rich the local soil, it must soon succumb to such irrational methods of cultivation. If the success of the Govern-mental efforts to grown American cotton in Russia depended upon the results of the unreasonable demands of the speculators, the entire scheme would undoubtedly fail. However, independent of the cotton speculators, different sorts of American cotton are being grown by the local farmers who are more reasonable in their demands of the soil. Due to this fact, American cotton is gradually and surely driving out the local varieties. The regular farmers in the cotton-growing districts are introducing more or less generally, American cotton along with other crops, thus giving the industry

a stable position in the agriculture of the country, inasmuch as
cotton yet occupies not more than one-tenth of the total of ploughed
fields.


Report of J. M. Crawford, May 25, 1893, U.S. Congress, 53rd,
3rd session, Senate, Report 986, part 1, Committee on Agriculture
and Forestry, Report...on the Condition of Cotton Growers, II,
serial number 3290, (Washington, D.C.:  Government Printing Office,
1895), p. 167.


### 363.  A MANUFACTURER DISCUSSES RAW MATERIALS (1893)


A Congressional committee was inquiring into the
connection between low cotton prices and the rise of
the cotton futures system.  Following is a statement by
a textile manufacturer denying the existence of any such
connection.  He was Arthur T. Lyman, treasurer of the
Lowell Manufacturing Company of Lowell, Massachusetts.


The Lowell Carpet Company uses very little cotton (chiefly for
the back of certain goods), but I am a stockholder and director in
most of the cotton mills in Lowell, and in other mills in Massachusetts, so that I know all about their methods of doing business.
All kinds of materials are arranged for in advance.  We contract
for a year's delivery of soda ash, for instance, and although we
do not advance money directly to the woolgrower in Russian or South
America, the people with whom we deal do.  We have to sell according
to fixed habits of the trade (for good reasons) carpets for delivery
ahead at fixed prices and for six months in advance for carpets we
might, of course (if it were in the market), buy the wool needed
for the orders, but we should save often a large amount in interest
by buying for future delivery.  Of course we might think that wool
was to fall in price, and so take the risk of the market and buy
only from week to week.
I am glad to answer any questions about the sale of cotton for
future delivery, which being comparatively new in the regular manufacture of cotton goods, is perhaps not fully understood.  I refer
of course to the purchase of cotton for future delivery for actual
use and to make goods which have either been sold at fixed prices,
or which it may seem best to a mill manager to secure at a fixed
price with a view to make goods for sale at prices which he expects
to get.
There can be, I think no question that such an operation is
perfectly legitimate and useful to all branches of the trade.
Business is nowadays very largely done on orders, i.e., I can get
an order for cotton yarn or cloth to run over many weeks or months
in the delivery if I can name a definite price--the buyer can then
sell woven fabrics or clothing, etc., at fixed prices, and the whole

transaction is carried on through many lines and many people on fixed and known conditions. To secure this result, I must be able to know what the cotton will cost me. I say must, because now, though the quantities are often immense, the margins are almost always very small. I think the system is of as much benefit to the cotton-planter as to the spinner or weaver, or converter of cloth into garments, etc. I have no hesitation in saying that I consider the system legitimate, useful to all, harmful to no one, and in accord with requirements, and almost necessities of modern business.

Of course, I refer to real deliveries, and not to merely speculative purchases. The prohibition of sales for use would be very injurious to the planter and manufacturer and the consumer. There is no justification of it. Speculative sales are difficult to control--so are many other foolish acts that are beyond the practical reach of the law, and even speculative sales have a value in adjusting and equalizing the market. I do not see that the cotton-planter suffers from them unless he dabbles in them himself, which, I believe, he is more apt to do than a manufacturer. It is, perhaps, impossible to prohibit speculative sales of cotton without interfering with legitimate and regular business.

As to the low price of cotton, I might ask in reply why have cotton goods and carpets and wheat and iron and nearly all manu-factured goods fallen enormously in the past ten or twenty years? Chiefly, certainly, on account of increased areas worked or culti-vated and opened to the world by new railways, and by the extra-ordinary changes and improvements in methods and machinery. The making of steel by the Bessemer, and similar processes, illustrates fully a reduction of cost to an extraordinary extent, evidently quite independent of any question of wages (which are higher per day and per man) or of silver or paper. Cotton spindles run twice as fast as they did. Carpet looms weave twice as many yards. The weaver is paid less per yard, but gets a great deal more per day.

Of course, there was an enormous crop of cotton two years ago, and this, with some other cause operating to a small extent, natur-ally reduced the price. During the past year, although the crop was much reduced, there was a decidedly poorer trade in manufactured goods, as was most pointedly shown by the enormous stoppage of spindles in England.

Arthur T. Lyman, August 5, 1893; U.S. Congress, 53rd, 3rd session, Senate, Report 986, part 1, Committee on Agriculture and Forestry, Report...on the Condition of Cotton Growers, I, serial number 3290, (Washington, D.C.: Government Printing Office, 1895), pp. 441-442.

364.   THE SOUTHERN DEMAND FOR COTTON (1893)


A Congressional committee asked, among other things, whether "the establishment or increase of cotton mills in your State tended to increase cotton culture and caused better home prices to the producers"?


Has not tended to increase the acreage in cotton but has improved the price of cotton locally.
. . . . . . . . . . . . . . . . . . . . . . . . . . . . . . . . . . .
The establishment of mills has not increased cotton culture, but has caused better prices.  The reason why better prices has not increased cotton culture is that part of the labor of each locality has gone in the mills and part of the labor on the farms is employed to grow crops for mill operatives.
. . . . . . . . . . . . . . . . . . . . . . . . . . . . . . . . . . .
Wherever factories are located I find the market is better.
. . . . . . . . . . . . . . . . . . . . . . . . . . . . . . . . . . .
The location of cotton mills in this section does not materially stimulate the cultivation or price of cotton, as the freight rate to the mills from here, a distance of 40 to 70 miles is 25 cents per 100 pounds, and the rate to Boston, a distance of near 1,000 miles, is only 70 cents.
. . . . . . . . . . . . . . . . . . . . . . . . . . . . . . . . . . .
I do not think the establishment of cotton mills in this State has increased the cultivation of cotton or caused better home prices to the producers.  I base this opinion on this fact.  The Mississippi mills at Wesson are large cotton and woolen mills and are not more than 50 miles from this place, yet it is very rare that any cotton from this district is sold to the Mississippi mills. So far as I can learn cotton sells at Wesson for the same price it does at other towns near by.


W. E. Ardrey, Charlotte, N.C.; W. L. Durst, Greenwood, S.C.; S. Y. Stribling, Senaca, S.C.; W. E. Dargan, Darlington, S.C.; T. B. Ford, Columbia, Miss.; U.S. Congress, 53rd, 3rd session, Senate, Report 986, part 1, Committee on Agriculture and Forestry, Report...on the Condition of Cotton Growers, I, serial number 3290, (Washington, D.C.:  Government Printing Office, 1895), pp. 285, 290, 291, 303-304, 338-339.


365.   BUSINESS METHODS ON THE LARGE PLANTATION (1893)


It is often forgotten that the southern plantation after the Civil War became a thoroughly capitalistic form of agriculture.  By the 1890's, the South accounted for

the majority of all hired farm workers. Field workers
were shuttled from wage status to share cropper, depending
on the level of cotton prices. The writer here, J. F.
Frank, was a cotton factor, merchant, and planter, with
headquarters in Memphis, Tennessee. He was 73 years old
and had been doing business for 47. He was a member of the
Memphis Cotton Exchange and he owned up to ten plantations
in Tennessee, Arkansas, and Kentucky which he had acquired
through bankruptcy proceedings he had initiated.

The Southern planters are not farmers; that is their own curse,
because if they would plant what they need to use, corn, or hay, or
things like that--millions of dollars goes away every year in this
country for that--they could hold their cotton. I plant myself.
I am the first man in the Mississippi River Valley that planted
with hired labor. I had planted on shares, I had fed the negroes,
they worked when they wanted to, and consequently what little they
made they would not pick out, left it in the field, and I said, if
I can't have control of my labor, I quit. I hired labor. I am
working now about 1,500 or 2,000. My main place is at Bledsoe. I
had all the laborers I wanted. I pay my laborers up every Saturday
night what I owe them; but if the men don't work, I don't feed
them. But if I have got share hands, they come and look to me, I've
got to feed them. Every share hand is a boss. If any of you gentlemen has planted any, you know that. The great fault is in the
low price of cotton. I have held my cotton; in 1872, in place of
getting 10 cents, I got 20 cents, because the cotton was mine, did
not belong to a merchant. Last year I sold my cotton for 10 cents.
If this was the merchant's that owned it, I couldn't hold it,
because the merchant is not able to hold it for everybody. I get
10 cents now for my cotton before the 1st of May....
    And when you generally see a fellow down on futures, you
generally know he has been in and the other fellow made the money.
But you see, those fellows that talk so much about it never raise
the cotton. They talk a heap, and don't know nothing about it.
Now, in my planting, I will show you that a man can make money if
he works it right. You can raise corn in the Mississippi River
bottom at 10 cents, and I keep count myself how much it cost me to
work labor, because if you work by hired labor you get more work
out of a negro in one day than in three days if he is his own boss.
Now, here, gentlemen, you can see what I spent since 1881; I just
drew it off my ledger. Take my new "Hope" farm; I had to take that
from a man that owed me $15,000, and I had to take the farm. He
hadn't a ditch on the farm; hadn't a house on it; hadn't a plank to
make a coffin when I took it first; I took my wagon body and made
a coffin of it. The consequence is, I have spent $194,958 to
November 10 since 1881 on that place; but I sold $199,254.55 in
that time; but I got my crop for this year on hand yet. At the
same time I cleared, I suppose, 1,200 acres of land on that place.
I got fifty mules on that place; I got seventy-odd buildings, which
I got since I commenced--negro houses and gins, and tool houses.
I just wanted to show that it is not the future[s] business, but
is the management of the farmers.

Now, according to what they say, I got the finest improvements
on my place on the Mississippi River.  If I had worked on shares
I wouldn't have no place and would have been broke, because I would
have had to sell my cotton for whatever I could get for it.  I sold
my cotton seed last year for $25 a ton.  I have my own scales and
everything that way.  But this future business, that has nothing in
the world to do with the cotton; it is only the people ought not to
spend their cotton or products until they make it, and ought to
make everything they need for their home consumption.  If a man has
to buy everything he needs he is a broke man in a short time in his
planting.  I suppose I have got now in cultivation about 1,600 acres
in corn and cotton, and so on; but when I started I hadn't more than
200 or 300 acres.  I used to talk from experience myself, what I
made and what it cost me to farm; I counted it up.  And the reason
so many people get broke is because they are buying everything and
selling their crops before they make it, and then they have to take
whatever they get.


Testimony, J. F. Frank; U.S. Congress, 53rd, 3rd session,
Senate, Report 986, part 1, Committee on Agriculture and Forestry,
Report...on the Condition of Cotton Growers, I, serial number 3290,
(Washington, D.C.:  Government Printing Office, 1895), pp. 144-145.


366.  THE BENEFITS OF COTTON FUTURES (1893)


The most common defense of the futures system was
that it:  (1) assured manufacturers a steady supply of
cotton at a foreseeable price, and (2) stimulated cotton
buying and thus raised prices to the grower.  This testimony was made by C. P. Hunt, of Memphis, general manager
of the Mississippi Cotton Company, and a former cotton
factor.


I have been connected with the New York and New Orleans future
boards, and also been a factor here a great many years prior to my
present business, and also in New York.  Now, a large proportion of
the cotton sold in Memphis is sold to exporters, most of whom represent Liverpool houses, Lancashire mills, and continental firms.
These people all need a certain character of cotton adapted to the
peculiar requirements of the people they buy for.  They buy this
cotton wherever they can find it, and pending the sale of the cotton
which they have bought they sell contracts against it to protect
themselves against any decline.  This method of doing business furnishes a demand for cotton at all times, even when the mills and
spinners generally are out of the market, and brings out a competition that would not exist were the seller and speculator to be done
away with.  It is the opinion of the best informed men of our market

that a variety of demand, no matter what its source, no matter whether speculative or consumptive, brings about a competition that facilitates the sale of cotton and enhances its value.  I might mention an instance, and would like you gentlemen to know this.

For the purpose of illustration we will suppose, for instance, that a spinner walking down Broadway meets an old acquaintance from the far West, say a large merchant in Santa Fe, or Denver, or some other thriving town.  After having exchanged greetings, the spinner proposes to sell the merchant 500 or 1,000 bales of osnaburgs.  The merchant regrets not being able to buy it at the moment, because he has just supplied all his needs, but states that in a few months he will need some, and asks the spinner at what price he will sell him 1,000 bales of osnaburgs, to be delivered six months hence.  The spinner at once takes out his pencil, takes the cost of the raw materials, adds to it the cost of manufacture, adds also his percentage of profit, and makes a price on the goods to be delivered at the time named.  The merchant thinks it is a bargain and accepts his offer.  Now, the spinner has figured on the cost of cotton the day upon which he makes the sale.  Should the market advance, the transaction upon which he expects to make a profit will make a loss. In order to protect himself, and not wishing to invest $5,000 or $6,000 in actual cotton to be carried over for a period of six months, he goes into the future market and buys 1,000 bales of cotton, to be delivered to him during the month in which he is to deliver his goods.  By so doing he insures and consolidates the profit which he has just figured out.  In other words, spinners, dealers, and planters can profitably use the future market as an insurance, and to good profit, and in the interest of commerce.

Testimony, C. P. Hunt; U.S. Congress, 53rd, 3rd session, Senate, Report 986, part 1, Committee on Agriculture and Forestry, Report...on the Condition of Cotton Growers, I, serial number 3290, (Washington, D.C.:  Government Printing Office, 1895), p. 100.

### 367.  DEPRESSION ON THE NEW YORK COUNTRYSIDE (1894)

The Depression of the 1890's hit hard in New York City.  One aggravating factor was the inflow of rural workers.  A civic association sponsored a study to determine whether farm areas could not absorb city workers or at least, retain their own people in the first place.

From the answers received by him, Mr. Powell calculated the average depreciation [of farm land during the preceding twenty-five years] at 48 per cent....It may be noted here that the "deserted" farm is a misnomer.  It is quite true that a large number of farmers have failed agriculturally and left their property to the mortgagee, and there are far too many deserted farmhouses, barns and other outbuildings, but the land itself has been absorbed by some more prosperous farmer or business man of the neighborhood. The land, therefore, and its empty buildings are not to be had for the mere asking....[Mr. Powell writes:]  "The farmer's wife rebels at longer providing food, washing and shelter for foreign laborers, who receive every cent the farmer earns.  He cannot live on the basis of the foreigner, who furnishes his wife and daughters with but one calico dress a year.  His sons refuse to take the farm as a gift if they must work it.  Heartbroken and discouraged, he moves to town and rents his farm to the foreigner.  Lack of adequate remuneration for labor, and the isolation of the farm home.  No provision for satisfying the cravings of the young people for having good social times.

"It is more than a tendency [towards tenancy]; in some sections, almost an exodus, as for example, I count on the old Genesee Turnpike, on which I live, fifty farms, a little over one-half of which are rented, worked on shares for some other way, by tenants. The farmers are getting tired of this struggle....The best farm laborers leave the country for cities to obtain yearly work, which most farmers do not furnish in late years; also to perform less hours of labor."

....Tenant farming is on the increase.  This has been known to be the case for a number of years past throughout the New England States, but it is apparently spreading rapidly....

Your committee believe at the same time it is the universal experience, that, generally speaking, the poor countryman is better off than the poor citizen.  Certainly there is very little of that suffering in the country which we so commonly meet here.  The farmer or farm laborer who has enough land to enable him to keep chickens and to raise a few potatoes, can generally manage to get through the winter without earning anything by labor.  It is true that he frequently runs up a bill at the village store, but the practical certainty of employment with the early spring gives him abundant credit at the grocery.  Now while the direct effort on any scale to bring together the unemployed or semi-employed of the city and the unused land of the country would be attended by almost insuperable difficulties, some attempt should at least be made to check that tide of migration to the city that threatens to make the condition of multitudes there quite intolerable.


New York Association for Improving the Condition of the Poor, Inquiry into the Causes of Agricultural Depression in New York State, (New York:  The Association, 1895), pp. 6-7, 8-9, 10.

368.  VAST WHEATLANDS OF THE MISSOURI VALLEY (1898)


     The agricultural development of the Missouri Valley
enabled the United States to pay for large imports of
manufactured goods and to repay foreign investments.
The writer, C. Wood Davis, a wheat grower and statistician,
lived in Peontone, Kansas.


West of the Mississippi, and lying mostly within the drainage
basin of the Missouri River (for convenience, called "the Missouri
Valley"), are the political divisions of Minnesota, Iowa, Missouri,
Kansas, Nebraska, South Dakota, North Dakota, and Oklahoma, having
an area, exclusive of an arid western border of about 100 miles in
width, of some 300,000,000 acres, or something less than a sixth
of the area of the United States, not counting Alaska and the
recently acquired islands.
. . . . . . . . . . . . . . . . . . . . . . . . . . . . . . . .
     This region is three times the extent of all the actually or
potentially wheat-bearing lands of South America, and is probably
the largest continuous body of equally fertile land in either
temperate zone.  Being almost a treeless plain over which population
could move with the greatest facility, this region was susceptible,
as few others are, of the rapid development which here took place
since 1865.
. . . . . . . . . . . . . . . . . . . . . . . . . . . . . . . .
     In 1870 the Missouri Valley, as a whole, was very sparsely
inhabited, and grew but 47,000,000 bushels of wheat on some
3,500,000 acres.  Since 1870, however, development has been so
rapid, that in 1898 this district had no less than 22,700,000 acres
under wheat, yielding 326,000,000 of the 675,000,000 bushels grown
in the United States.  It comprises more than half the nation's
wheat lands, grows 40 per cent. of the oats, more than half the
maize entering commercial channels, has 33 per cent. of all the
farm horses, and 28 per cent. of the cattle and swine, although
it possesses less than 16 per cent. of either the population of
land of the Republic.
. . . . . . . . . . . . . . . . . . . . . . . . . . . . . . . .
     Thus a region which thirty years ago was in large part a
hunting ground of the untutored savage has become the granary of the
nation, and grows more wheat, nearly as much oats, and twenty times
as much maize as the 112,000,000 inhabitants of all that part of
the Russian empire lying north of the Caucusus and west of the
Urals; and this with an industrial, commercial, and agricultural
population probably less than 12,000,000....Therefore, it is to
this remote mid-continent district that Western Europe is indebted
for that enormous volume of bread-making and feeding grains which
has kept want from its doors for at least a decade.


     C. Wood Davis, in Sir William Crooks, The Wheat Problem,
(London:  John Murray, 1899), pp. 150-153.

369.   HAND CRADLING CHEAPER THAN MACHINE REAPING (1899)


Extremely low labor costs discouraged the wider
use of machines in Southern agriculture.  Here J. Pope
Brown, president of the Georgia State Agricultural Society,
testifies.


Representative BELL.  Mr. Brown, is not labor at a cost of $8
a month cheaper than machines?
Mr. BROWN.  Well, I argue that, too.  I say I can take my hands
in the neighborhood there--for instance, I give my cradlers, as I
figure it, $1 a day and feed them.  When I cut oats, if I have 100
acres of oats, I want five or six men; if I have 200, I want to
double up; and if I have 400, I double up, and keep doubling up.
Representative BELL.  It is really cheaper, is it not, than
the machinery?
Mr. BROWN.  I am inclined to think it may be.  After I count
up the expense and the interest, the repairs, and wear and tear,
I would just as soon have the negro cradlers.  There is one thing
about it--you can not cut it quite so clean, but I try to fix that
this way:  I let the hogs follow the cradlers, and they get what is
left.
Representative BELL.  It costs about $1 an acre with a machine?
Mr. BROWN.  I can cut it cheaper than that.


Testimony, J. Pope Brown, United States Industrial Commission,
X, p. 80.



370.   AGRICULTURAL TRUSTS IN CALIFORNIA (1899)


The agricultural trusts concentrated on a coordinated
selling program rather than a merger of physical properties.
Their aim was to raise prices.  This time George Holmes,
statistician of the U.S. Department of Agriculture,
testifies.


To give another instance of an agricultural trust, let me
mention the comprehensive and successful one of the California fruit
growers.  They were compelled to form a trust for the purpose of
getting remunerative prices, for the purpose of suppressing
competition among themselves, for the purpose of getting lower
freight rates, and for the purpose of finding responsible customers
in the East and elsewhere.

As the matter stood, an orange buyer, for instance, would go
to an orange grower and offer him a certain price for the pick of
his crop.  The fruit grower, not being satisfied with the offer,
would decline to do, because they were able to go to neighboring
orange growers and obtain the oranges they wanted at the low offer
that they had made.  The result was that the fruit growers, without
knowing what the market was or was to be, without knowing trade
conditions and through freight rates, and without being able to
obtain low freight rates on small shipments, were eventually compelled, in their own interest, to form what are known as
"exchanges."

The fruit growers of Santa Clara Valley, for instance, have
formed a trust for the purpose of suppressing competition among
themselves as well as for the purpose of having an expert manager
to become acquainted with the conditions of the market and make
their sales for them.  And so there have grown numerous fruit
associations all along the Pacific coast, embracing oranges, lemons,
various citrus fruits, grapes, and English walnuts, and all the
other fruits for which California has become famous; and these
associations are coordinated by a central exchange in San Francisco,
so that the entire fruit business of California is of a trust.  It
is not called a trust, but it has the essential elements of a trust,
its objects being among other things, to suppress competition among
fruit growers and to regulate and perhaps raise the price of fruit.


Testimony, George K. Holmes, United States Industrial
Commission, X, pp. 158-159.


371.  TELEPHONES FOR LONELY COUNTRY PEOPLE (1890's)


"Harkin'" became a rural hobby in these days.
Hibbard (see Source No. 334) was now general manager
of the Chicago Telephone Company.


On a visit...to a "farm line" exchange in Grundy County, I
took the place of the operator at the switchboard at six o'clock
on the morning of a summer day, and there were many calls at that
hour.  At first when I responded I was asked who I was and what
had become of Mary, the well-liked operator.  With the assurance
that Mary was still on the job, I completed the connections and
listened in often enough to find out what the farmers did with the
telephone at that time of day.  There was enough "doing" in the
first hour to convince me that the farmer's telephone had come to
stay.  Jones called Brown to ask if he might borrow his hay cutter--
he would send over for it; Olson called Swenson to ask the loan of
his hired man for the afternoon--his hay must be brought in;
Rodinski called Smith to say that he would be over after breakfast

and bring the hay rake.  And so it went, plans for many things of
immediate necessity for the day.  A little later the calls were
from the farmers' wives to ask who was going to town; what was the
price of eggs; could they borrow or lend this, that, or the other
thing; would Mary stop and take little Anna to school; had the
baby come at the Jones'?  Of course, there were "party" lines; that
is, eight, ten, and sometimes more farmhouses would be connected
on one wire.  When anyone was called, the bells would ring all along
the line and there might be an unanimous answer, because everybody
wanted to know what was going on.  In the evening there was general
conversation up and down the line.  Little Willie would play on his
new harmonica and Bennie would sing "Silver Threads Among the
Gold," or take a crack at it.  I recall a country store, in the
rear of which was located the farmers' exchange switchboard.  One
cold day in the fall, a circle of men sat around the stove.  The
wooden box filled with sawdust was their target, as usual (there
were tobacco chewers in those days).  An old man with a bushy
beard, and much bundled up, entered and was accosted:
    FARMER:  "Say Bill, I hear you got a telephone--are you going
to call up anybody?"
    BILL:  "Nope."
    FARMER:  "Is anybody going to call you?"
    BILL:  "Nope."
    FARMER:  "Well, what you got the telephone for?"
    BILL.  "I got it because I just want to hark."
    And that was really the word that revealed the entertainment
function of the telephone to these lonely country people.


Hibbard, Hello Goodbye, pp. 194-195.

# E.

# THE RISE OF MODERN MACHINE INDUSTRY

372. THE WEST MEETS NEW ENGLAND COMPETITION (1863)

Following are extracts from a highly perceptive discussion of the industrial future of the West.

In the past ten years the West has, as we have shown, exceeded all other sections of prosperity. Population and capital have flowed in upon her, developing productions which have found a ready sale at good profits, while by means of the railroads the whole Western country has participated in the general prosperity. Now the population has grown somewhat in excess of the number which can readily be supported from agriculture, even if possessed of a large foreign market, and, as formerly in the East so at present in the West, manufactures are growing up and are succeeding, even in spite of the advantages of capital and long experience of the East.
. . . . . . . . . . . . . . . . . . . . . . . . . . . . . . . . . .
Thus it appears that the value per head of manufactures at the West is $46, and at the East $122, and that the West produces nearly one-third as much as the Eastern and Middle States. But the productions are of a coarser description, as is evident from the fact that at the West the raw materials are 60 per cent of the value produced, while at the East they are but 50 per cent. These manufactures at the West, it must be remembered, have grown up without any protection from the vast competition of New England capital, although that competition has been far more direct and effective than was that of foreign goods against New England at the close of the war in 1812.
. . . . . . . . . . . . . . . . . . . . . . . . . . . . . . . . . .

Thus, articles like shoes and clothing have not as yet flour-
ished at the West under the severe competition of the East, although
the West has the advantage in respect to raw materials.  But in the
heavier articles, like iron, furniture, agricultural implements,
steam engines, etc., which are protected at the West by the cost
of transportation of the materials, the increase there has far outstripped the progress of the same branches at the East.  These
figures also indicate that all branches of manufactures are
organized and ready for expansion.  At such a moment war supervenes
and closes the door to much of the usual trade of that region, by
cutting off the Southern outlets.  The employments of Western capital come to an end, and enterprise is turned in the direction of
manufactures at the very moment when cotton, the raw material for
$106,000,000 of Eastern manufactures, is no longer available, and
the flax and wool of the West are becoming the materials for
clothing.
      Thus the golden period for the West has arrived; the East hav-
ing no longer the advantage over her, and the usual employment for
capital being cut off to a great extent, we shall soon find her
expanding in this new direction and furnishing not only food but
clothing for the world.  Her fertile soil, aided by machinery, can,
with the same amount of manual labor, furnish a larger surplus of
food than any other region; while her raw materials, her minerals,
her water-courses, and her railroads all combine with cheap food to
make the West the region for the cheapest possible production of m
manufactures.  The fruits of her rich soil will then find a market,
not only directly but also in the shape of goods.  England now imports food and material from the West, and, combining them with
English labor, furnishes goods for the supply of the world.  The
Eastern States have also in the same way gained great wealth.  But
now the West is about to do that business for herself--combining her
her own labor, material, and food, and thereby becoming the center
of manufactures.


Hunt's Merchants' Magazine, April, 1863, pp. 279-280.



373.  INDUSTRY MUST CURTAIL OUTPUT (1867)


      In general, manufacturing industries were marked by
extensive price competition.  A slump during the latter
half of 1867 brought a response of lower prices but sustained output.  Here a business journal lectures manufacturers on the advantages of reducing output rather
than prices.


Time fails to bring relief to our manufacturing industries.
The depression which, for a time, was confined to one or two
branches is now becoming general, and some anxiety is felt as to

the result of the ordeal through which manufacturers are passing.
We have repeatedly urged the importance of a limitation of production as the best means of bringing down the prices of labor and
raw materials, and thereby enabling producers to meet the demand
for goods at lower rates; but manufacturers appear to have regulated
their production by the capacity of their works rather than by the
capability of consumers; and the result has been that the supply
of goods has been so far in advance of the demand as to place the
determination of prices in the hands of buyers, causing upon many
descriptions of goods very heavy losses.  The current high prices
of agricultural products, and the comparatively low prices of manufactures, suggests the conclusion that the war has left us with an
undue proportion of the capital and labor of the country employed
in manufactures, and an inadequate proportion engaged in the culture
of the soil.  Breadstuffs and animal food are essential to subsistence; and, though scarce and dear, they have had to be brought in
about the usual quantity; but under such circumstances a large portion of the community are compelled to forego the supplying of
other wants which contribute rather to comfort, luxury or adornment.
This condition of things ought to have had its due weight with
manufacturers, inducing them to produce with a moderation corresponding to the ability of consumers.  They had, however, profited
largely through a special demand for war purposes, and, without
making due allowance for the cessation of this special consumption,
have regarded the past consumption as the measure for the present.

Hunt's *Merchants' Magazine*, December, 1867, p. 419.


### 374.  SUPERIOR BRITISH TOOLS (1868)

The condition described here did not continue for
long.  (See, for example, Source No. 586).  Charles
Porter, who writes here, had completed a period of
training in England.  He returned to the United States
and became an engine designer and manufacturer.


At that time [1868] toolmaking in this country, which has since
become so magnificently developed, was in many important respects
in a primitive condition, and I proposed to introduce into my shop
every best tool and method, adapted to my requirements, that I could
find in England.  For this purpose I visited and carefully studied
all the tool works of good standing, and my final conclusion was
that the best tools for design, strength, solidity, facility of
operation and truth of work were those made by Smith & Coventry....
So I prepared a careful list of tools that I proposed to order from
them in time to be ready for use as soon as my shop should be
completed.  I found also the remarkable fact that I could obtain

these tools, duty and freight paid, decidedly cheaper than corresponding inferior tools could then be got from American makers.


        Charles T. Porter, Engineering Reminiscence, (New York:  Wiley,
1908), pp. 169-170.



                    375.  MAKING SOAP AT HOME (1860's)


        While machine industry was rising in the Northeast
and Middle West, pioneer communities in Texas and elsewhere lived at primitive levels.  This contrast can be
found throughout American history of which it is an important economic characteristic.  Frank S. Gray is the author.
His home was located near Cherokee Creek in San Saba County,
Texas.


    Mother, and most all pioneer housewives, had an ash hopper for
making lye which they used to make soap.  A log about five feet
long was obtained and hewn out into a trough.  Two short legs
were fastened to one end of the trough which mounted it higher than
the other end.  Two large flat rocks the length of the trough and
about four feet high were placed in the trough with the top edges
flaired out in a V shape.  This V shaped opening between the rocks
was then filled with strong ashes.  Water was then poured on top
which filtered through the strong ashes and made lye.  When it
reached the lower end of the trough it ran into a bucket which was
placed there to catch the liquid.
    From this lye the pioneer housewives made great washpots of
lye soap.  It was the only kind of soap the women had in those days.
Being made from ash-hopper lye, it was a very strong soap and was
about as thick as heavy sorghum molasses.  The workmen and the
entire family used it to wash their face and hands before going to
the family table.  Housewives also used it to wash clothes.  In
later years manufacturers made a concentrated lye that was used in
making laundry soap.  It was a hard soap and not as strong as the
soft lye soap which was formerly used.


        Frank S. Gray, Pioneer Adventures, (Cherokee, Texas:  The
Author, 1948), pp. 30-31.

376.   COST ACCOUNTING IN IRON PRODUCTION (1860's)


Profit margins in the iron industry were kept low
through extreme competition.  Cost accounting permitted
management to raise margins by reducing costs.  This
practice was one of Carnegie's few personal innovations
in the industry.  (For a different evaluation of cost
accounting, see Source No. 588).


As I became acquainted with the manufacture of iron I was
greatly surprised to find that the cost of each of the various processes was unknown.  Inquiries of the leading manufacturer of
Pittsburgh proved this.  It was a lump business, and until stock
was taken and the books balanced at the end of the year, the manufacturers were in total ignorance of results.  I heard of men who
thought their business at the end of the year would show a loss and
had found a profit, and vice-versa.  I felt as if we were moles
burrowing in the dark, and this to me was intolerable.  I insisted
upon such a system of weighing and accounting being introduced
throughout our works as would enable us to know what our cost for
each process and especially what each man was doing, who saved
material, who wasted it, and who produced the best results.
To arrive at this was a much more difficult task than one
would imagine.  Every manager in the mills was naturally against
the new system.  Years were required before an accurate system was
obtained, but eventually, by the aid of many clerks and the introduction of weighing scales at various points in the mill, we began
to know not only what every department was doing, but what each one
of the many men working at the furnaces was doing, and thus to
compare one with another.  One of the chief sources of success in
manufacturing is the introduction and strict maintenance of a perfect system of accounting so that responsibility for money or
materials can be brought home to every man.  Owners who, in the
office, would not trust a clerk with five dollars without having
a check upon him, were supplying tons of material daily to men in
the mills without exacting an account of their stewardship by
weighing what each returned in the finished form.


The Autobiography of Andrew Carnegie, edited by John C.
VanDyke, (Boston, Massachusetts:  Houghton Mifflin Co., 1920),
p. 135.



377.  THE SUSPECT SCIENTIFIC ENGINEER (1860's)


The following is a sobering reminder of the
recency of mechanical engineering in the United States.

One of the most recent developments of the experts has been that of the Science of Engineering. So recent is this development that I can remember distinctly the time when an educated scientific engineer was looked upon with profound suspicion by practically the whole manufacturing community.

The successful engineers of my boyhood were mostly men who were endowed with a fine sense of proportion--men who had the faculty of carrying in their minds the size and general shape of parts of machinery, for instance, which had proved themselves successful, and who through their intuitive judgment were able to make a shrewd guess at the proper size and strength of the parts required for a new machine.

It was my pleasure and honor to know intimately one of the greatest and one of the last of this school of empirical engineers-- Mr. John Fritz,--who had such an important part in the development of the Bessemer process, as well as almost all of the early elements of the steel industry of this country. (See Source No. 181).

When I was a boy and first saw Mr. Fritz, most of the drawings which he made for his new machinery were done with a piece of chalk on the floor of the pattern room, or with a stick on the floor of the blacksmith shop, and in many cases the verbal description of the parts of the machines which he wished to have made were more important than his drawings. Time and again he himself did not know just what he wanted until after the pattern or model was made and he had an opportunity of seeing the shape of the piece which he was designing. One of his favorite sayings whenever a new machine was finished was, "Now, boys, we have got her done, let's start her up and see why she doesn't work."

The engineer of his day confidently expected that the first machine produced would fail to work, but that by studying its defects he would be able to make a success of his second machine.

Do not for a moment misunderstand me. I am not in the smallest degree belittling Mr. John Fritz. He was one of the greatest men of his time--a man of remarkable originality, force of character, and general engineering ability. What I am endeavoring to do is to make it clear to you that the Science of Engineering is a very recent development, as are, in fact, the sciences of chemistry, physics, and even astronomy.

The Science of Engineering started only when a few experts (who were invariably despised and sneered at by the engineers of their day) made the assertion that engineering practice should be founded upon exact knowledge of facts rather than upon general experience and observation.

Frederick W. Taylor, address, "Laws versus Private Opinion as a Basis of Management," 1914, reprinted in Frank B. Copley, Frederick W. Taylor. Father of Scientific Management, 2 vols., (New York: Taylor Society, Harper & Bros., 1923), I, pp. 100-102.

378.  "THREE GREAT INVENTORS, YET UNKNOWN" (1881)


Electricity, light, and flight were three great
technological challenges to the age; so wrote Robert H.
Thurston, professor of mechanical engineering at Stevens
Institute of Technology and president of A.S.M.E.

I have sometimes said that the world is waiting for the appearance of three great inventors, yet unknown, for whom it has in store
honors and emoluments far exceeding all ever yet accorded to any one
of their predecessors.

The first is the man who is to show how, by the consumption of
coal, we may directly produce electricity, and thus, perhaps, evade
that now inevitable and enormous loss that comes of the utilization
of energy in all heat engines driven by substances of variable volume.  Our electrical engineers have this great step still to take,
and are apparently not likely soon to gain the prize that will yet
reward some genius yet to be born.

The second of these greatest of inventors is he who will teach
us the source of the beautiful soft-beaming light of the firefly and
the glow-worm, and will show us how to produce this singular illum-
inant, and to apply it with success practically and commercially.
This wonderful light, free from heat and from consequent loss of
energy, is nature's substitute for the crude and extravagantly
wasteful lights of which we have, through so many years, been fool-
ishly boasting.  The dynamo-electrical engineer has nearly solved
this problem.  Let us hope that it may be soon fully solved and by
one of those among our own colleagues who are now so earnestly
working in this field, and that we may all live to see him steal
the glow-worm's light, and to see the approaching days of Vril
predicted so long ago by Lord Lytton.

The third great genius is the man who is to fulfill Darwin's
prophecy, closing the stanza:
"Soon shall thy arm, unconquered steam, afar
Drag the slow barge or drive the rapid car,
Or, on wide-waving wings expanded bear
The flying chariot through the fields of air."
The quotation may excite a smile to-day, but when first pub-
lished, just one hundred years ago, the last lines must have seemed
hardly more extravagant than the first.


Robert H. Thurston, "Our Progress in Mechanical Engineering,"
Transactions, American Society of Mechanical Engineers, II (1881),
p. 447.

### 379.  "THE BEST IS THE CHEAPEST" (1881)

In 1881, steel had not yet conquered, and so many
industrial items were still made of wood.  At the same
time, wood-working was becoming more mechanized.  Thus,
it was of broad industrial significance when, increasingly,
the lesson of "the best is cheapest" was being learned.
This report was made by F. R. Hutton, assistant in mechanical engineering, School of Mines, Columbia College,
New York.

But it is difficult to leave the class of wood-working machinery without referring to two points, which are indicative of recent
progress.  The first is the change by which the manufacture of this
class of machine has passed from the hands of wood-working operatives into those of mechanical engineers.  The first machines were
built with wood frames, and were open to all the objections which
follow from the use of a material which is elastic and is susceptible to atmospheric influences.  The newer machines are more deserv-
ing of their name.  They are built of steel and iron, by specialists
in their manufacture, and with the same care in fitting which is
called for in metal-working tools.  A much higher grade of work
must result, which will favor successful competition in critical
markets.  The second point to be noted is in part a consequence of
the first.  It is the gradual increase in speed of feed, and the
capacity for enlarged output, due to that increased speed and to
better construction.  The increased output makes it possible for
the purchaser to pay for a better machine, and the better machine
cheapens the product by a wider distribution of the interest account
and of the diminished repair account.  In the earlier days the excuse for the purchase of cheap machinery was that new improvements
would make it necessary to exchange old tools before they had paid
for themselves.  Tool-builders must always meet the demand for the
grade of machine wanted, and these two causes interacted.  But of
later years, the better judgment of consumers, and the more advanced
skill of specialist builders, has given an impulse in the direction
of true progress, and the engineering community is realizing more
fully the truth of the old aphorism, "the best is the cheapest".

F. R. Hutton, "Report on Machine Tools and Wood-Working
Machinery," U.S. Congress, 47th, 2nd session, Miscellaneous Document No. 42, part 22, serial number 2152, p. 290.

### 380.  MASS PRODUCTION REQUIRES A STANDARD MEASURE (1882)

Since Hall's revolutionary demonstration of
practical interchangeability, mass production had

been applied to a number of fields of manufacture.
Its general applicability, however, waited upon a
system of universal standard measures.

   In my last address, I referred very briefly to the modern
Method of Manufacturing Machinery in quantity for the market as
distinguished from the old system, or lack of system, of making
machines.  This method compels the adaptation of special tools to
the making of special parts of the machines and the appropriation
of a certain portion of the establishment to the production of each
of these pieces, while the assembling of the parts to make the
complete machine takes place in a place set apart for that purpose.
But this plan makes it necessary that every individual piece of any
one kind shall fit every individual piece of another kind without
expenditure of time and labor in adapting each to the other.
   This requirement, in turn, makes it necessary that every piece,
and every face and angle, and every hole and every pin in every
piece, shall be made precisely of this standard size, without comparison with the part with which it is to be paired, and this last
condition compels the construction of gauges giving the exact size
to which the workman or the machine must bring each dimension.
   Finally:  In order that this same system which has introduced
such wonderful economy into the gun manufacture, into sewing-machine
construction, and into so many other branches of mechanical business, may become more general, and in order to secure that very important result, a universal standard for gauges and for general
measurement, we need an acknowledged standard for our whole country
--one that shall be an exact representation of the legal standard
measure, and one which shall be known and acknowledged as such, and
as exactly such.
   It could hardly be expected that private enterprise would
assume the expense and take the risk involved in this last work.
Such work has heretofore only been done by governments.  Yet among
our colleagues are found the men who have had the intelligence,
the courage and the determination to accept such risks and to meet
such expense, and the men who have the knowledge and the skill
needed in doing this great work.  I think that the report of our
committee on gauges and the paper of our colleague, Mr. Bond, will
show that this great task has been accomplished, and we shall find
that we are indebted to the Pratt & Whitney Co., to Prof. Rogers
and to Mr. Bond for a system of measurement and a foundation system
of gauges that will supply our tool makers and other builders with
a thoroughly satisfactory basis for exact measurement and for
accurate gauging.
   It is encouraging to observe that this subject is attracting
the attention of men of science, and that so distinguished a body
as the British Association for the Advancement of Science is
taking action regarding it.

   Robert H. Thurston, "The Mechanical Engineer--His Work and His
Policy," Transactions, American Society of Mechanical Engineers,
IV (1882-1883), pp. 79-81.

381.  MACHINE SHOP METHODS ARE CHANGING (1882)


The direction of mechanical change was towards
facilitating repetitive operations.  Note the large
savings obtainable from re-arrangement of work.  (For
savings derived from economies of actual machine tooling,
see Source No. 592).  Charles Fitch, who writes here,
was a special agent of the Census Bureau.


Old machine-shop methods are in process of change, and the
improvements are usually less suitable to the requirements of small
makers and for single pieces of mechanism than to the wholesale
fabrication of uniform work.  Already methods which suggest those
of the watch factory are in use at some of our large engine-shops,
and engines of considerable size are built in lots of 10 with the
employment of standard gauges and templates.  Workmen are employed
to repeat a given operation upon great numbers of parts, and where
this can not be done the work is classified by its likeness, and
one workman is kept upon one class of work.  For example, let us
consider the work of planing.  There are in a room, say, 20 or 30
planers operating upon a much greater number of different parts of
machines.  If the manager or foreman be unable to keep one planer
running at one speed on one class of work and under one man, he
exerts his ingenuity to come as near this desideratum as possible.
The better he is able to succeed in such matters the more exact is
the workmanship and the more profitable the manufacture.  Further
than this, the machinery so made, other things being equal, commends
itself to a greater number of purchasers, and under enterprising
oversight the large demand reacts to insure better facilities for
uniform work.
    The attempt to gain valuable time by systematizing work is an
attempt to diminish the time, not of actual machine tooling, but of
setting, waiting, and preparation; and an inquiry into the actual
time of machine operations reveals the great amount and importance
of the portion of time not occupied by the actual tooling.  In
machining gun components we may easily estimate by number of parts
turned out in a day, and such estimates are made the basis of wages;
but in the large work of machine-shops there must be a large and
ill-defined allowance of time for setting and waiting.  Making an
estimate of time spent in actual machine tooling upon work, we find
that it must be doubled, trebled, or quadrupled in many cases, in
order to account for the total time.  Herein lies the value of
handy tools in which American shops excel, and of which many examples might be cited.  I will mention one.  Messrs. William Sellers
& Co. [in Philadelphia] build a lathe in which the screw and hand-
wheel motions are displaced by a device which does the setting by a
single motion of the hand.  Such a device may at first sight seem
trivial and of no great advantage, but when we estimate the number
of times in a day a machinist has to perform this motion, and the
aggregate saving of time, we find that upon some classes of work
it has a money value which is not to be despised.  Such handy

appliances also help the spirit of the workman, and stimulate him
to alarcity in the performance of his work.

In time of setting and waiting, also, lies the great difference
in cost between large work, or work which can be done piece after
piece of the same kind, keeping one workman on one job, and work
which involves a new essay of preparation, adjustment, and experiment for every successive piece.  Thus in making pulleys of one
size in large lots, and in making various parts of engines in small
lots, there is a vast difference in cost of work by the pound.  The
value and productive power of labor can best be maintained by close
attention to shop system, and a convenient tool, kept in good working order, may involve as great a saving as a rapid-acting tool.


Charles J. Fitch, "Report on the Manufacture of Engines and
Boilers," U.S. Congress, 47th, 2nd session, Miscellaneous Document
No. 42, part 22, serial number 2152, p. 22.


382.   UNEVENTFUL AMERICAN WOOL TECHNOLOGY (1882)


Conservatism and caution characterized the American
textile machinery industry.  For a great exception, see
Source No. 769.  This report was written by Knight Neftel,
special agent of the Census Bureau.


The greater part of the machinery in our mills is of American
manufacture.  In some of the older mills foreign machines are still
in use, but are invariably replaced when new ones are wanted by
domestic appliances.  In many mills the reason for retaining old
machines is either the conservative spirit of proprietors (this is,
however, rare in face of competition), or more often the fact that
a profitable business is carried on and the first cost of new
machinery a bugbear.

In most cases all American wool machinery is but improved
foreign design.  For many years no very notable new mechanical contrivance has been introduced which would have a revolutionary
effect.  The English loom has been greatly improved, but does not
differ essentially in principle from the first power-loom.  The
Jacquard attachment for figured goods has likewise been increased
in efficiency, but is the same machine.  The spindle now running
in our mills with remarkable speed and steadiness is but an improved
form of the first spindle brought to this country.

There have been many new inventions, which have improved the
various machines and greatly assisted in the general advance of the
mechanical efficiency, yet there has not been any new departure or

novel idea of transforming effect, such as there has been in many
other industries, since 1776.


Knight Neftel, "Report on Wool and Silk Machinery," U.S.
Congress, 47th, 2nd session, Miscellaneous Document No. 42, part
22, serial number 2152, pp. 1-2.


383.  SPECIALIZING-OUT OF MACHINE TOOL MANUFACTURE (1883)


As mechanized agriculture and mining and railroad
equipment were increasingly located to the West, the
machine-tool industry moved westward.  Also, machine-tool
manufacture became less a side-line and tended to become
the sole occupation of a shop.  Specializing-out was the
shedding of a side-line in favor of concentrating on a
single major line.  Cox, the writer here, had his plant
in Cleveland, Ohio.


I had felt for a long time that we were making a mistake in
devoting so much of our time and capital to the manufacturing of
machinery to sell.  In order to satisfy myself fully as to the advisability of making any change, I had for a year or more kept close
account of the cost of manufacturing machinery and the income from
the same, as compared with the cost of manufacturing twist drills
and the income from their sale.  I satisfied myself that it would
be greatly to our advantage to drop the manufacture of machinery
and devote our entire attention to twist drills.  Upon the return
of Mr. Prentiss from one of his trips, I laid before him figures
which showed that we were diverting the profits received from the
manufacture of twist drills to the building of machinery, which did
not yield us nearly so much profit for the capital and time invested.  We therefore decided at once to abandon the manufacture of
machinery.
When we announced this decision, a Mr. Eynon, who was the
foreman in the machine shop, said he would like to buy our patterns
and start in the machine business himself.  The arrangement was soon
completed and we sold to W. R. Eynon & Son all the patterns of
machinery which we had bought for building these machines.  The
remainder of our large and heavy machinery, such as we did not now
need for our own work, was sold to other parties, and with the
money thus obtained we greatly increased our facilities for making
twist drills.


Cox, Building an American Industry, © The Cleveland
Twist Drill Company, pp. 115-116.

### 384.  AUTOMATIC SUPPLY OF MACHINE COOLANT (1883)

Great heat was generated at the point where several
milling cutters were revolving rapidly as they removed
metal from a part.  They had to be cooled as they revolved.
By 1918, all milling machines had a built-in tank and pump
that supplied coolant automatically.

One day in the summer of 1883, as I went into the milling
machine room, I noticed that one of the operators was just about to
pour the soda water from a large pail under his machine into the
receptacle over the machine.  This was common practice whereby the
lubricant could run back over the cutters and down into the pail
again.  It struck me that this operation alone consumed a good deal
of his time, so I waited about in the room until it was necessary
for him to repeat the operation.  In the meantime, I had noted by
my watch how long it took the same man to take out of the machine
a completed drill and put in a fresh blank.  When he again changed
the water on his machine, I timed him with my watch and found that
it took longer to change the water than it did to change the blanks
in the machine.  I immediately figured out a system of pipes and
tanks which, by means of a pump operated from the line shaft,
could handle the water for the entire room.  This was installed as
rapidly as possible, and in a short time we were able to reduce
materially the number of men required to run the milling machines.
This system of supplying lubricant to milling machines has been
favorably commented upon by many manufacturers who have seen it,
and it has been adopted by many of them.

Cox, Building an American Industry,© The Cleveland
Twist Drill Company , pp. 116-117.

### 385.  FACTORIES BRING A NEW CIVILIZATION TO THE SOUTH (1886)

While essentially correct, those who hailed southern
industrialization were also prone to underestimate the
resilience and resistance of old ways of life even under
industrialization.

The rapid growth of this new civilization is evidenced by the
increase in number of small farmers and their general prosperity,
and in the rapidly multiplied factories in both the cotton and iron
sections of the State.  With forty cotton-factories and the cease-
less hum of nearly two hundred thousand spindles, and with nearly
one hundred furnaces and iron-mills to diversify industry and open
new markets for the farmers, there must be progress.  The factory

and the school are the great civilizers of the age in the South,
and they are now doing a grand work in Georgia.  Here the cotton
is grown; here labor is cheaper than in the North; here it can be
fed and clothed better than on the bleak hills of New England or in
the crowded cities, and here the cotton-spindle should answer the
song of the cotton-gin.  And wherever the factory is reared, there
is a new civilization planted in the desolation of slavery.  The
shade, the vine, the flower, the tidy fence, and the tasteful home
about the cotton-mill, tell the story of the future South, and the
uniform prosperity of the mills of this State must speedily multiply their numbers.  They have invaded South Carolina across the
Savannah from Augusta, and Augusta has built a vast canal to furnish
water-power to invite capital, while South Carolina exempted from
taxation for ten years all factories erected in the State.  Columbus, in this State, is one of the most prosperous towns in the whole
country, solely because of the many factories which nestle in and
around it, and some of the mills divide from fifteen to thirty per
cent. to their shareholders, while all of them are earning profits.


A. K. McClure, The South:  Its Industrial, Financial, and
Political Condition, (Philadelphia, Pennsylvania:  J. B. Lippincott
Co., 1886), pp. 62-63.


386.   THE NORTHERN IRON INDUSTRY WILL INVEST IN THE SOUTH (1886)


    Preaching the gospel of southern industrialism,
reconciliation with the North, and an inferior status
for blacks, the Atlanta publicist Henry W. Grady had
helped create an ideology of the New South.  Business
considerations could now overcome political and sectional
hesitations and bring about an economic unification in
which both North and South would be equals.  A. K. McClure,
who writes the following, was a Pennsylvania publisher,
politician, and lawyer.


Tennessee has over five thousand square miles of the great
Appalachian coal-field of the continent; it has four thousand square
miles containing rich red and brown hematite ores, and, like
Alabama, it has the iron, coal, and limestone in close proximity.
The highest estimate I have had from experienced iron men as the
average cost of producing iron in this State is eleven dollars and
fifty cents per ton, and many claim that every well-appointed and
managed furnace produces it as low as ten dollars and sixty cents.
Birmingham now ships iron to Philadelphia, Pittsburgh, and New
England, as I saw by the books of leading furnace men there; but
Birmingham and Tennessee now control the iron markets of the large
iron-consuming States of Indiana and Illinois.  Birmingham can ship

to Philadelphia or New York by rail to Charleston or Savannah, and
thence by water, for three dollars and eighty cents per ton; it can
reach Indianapolis for three dollars and seventy-five cents, and
Tennessee can reach the West for a little less.  These are the rates
with the present necessarily expensive transportation; and what will
be increased advantage of Tennessee and Alabama in coal and iron,
when multiplied capital and riper experience and largely increased
product shall cheapen both the product and its transportation?
These facts present a grave problem to the great coal and iron
industries of the North, and they must and will be squarely and
intelligently looked in the face.  I do not fear that the South will
destroy the coal and iron industries of Pennsylvania, for that is
impossible; but I am convinced that it will speedily revolutionize
both.  Business follows natural laws as surely as the stars follow
their appointed courses in the heavens, and I look for the North to
hasten the transfer of much of its capital and business experience
to the virgin and more inviting coal- and iron-fields of Tennessee
and Alabama.  It will be done because the obstacles of slavery, of
civil war, and of lingering distrust, which have hitherto been in-
surperable, are about to perish, and North and South will be bound
together by the indissoluble ties of business interest.

     A. K. McClure, The South:  Its Industrial, Financial, and
Political Condition, (Philadelphia, Pennsylvania:  J. B. Lippincott
Co., 1886), pp. 146-148.


     387.  THE SOUTHERN IRON INDUSTRY IS GROWING RAPIDLY (1887)


          From the '70's to the '90's, the Birmingham iron
     industry came to produce one-third of national pig iron
     output.  In time, high transport costs to Northern markets
     and the unsuitability of Southern pig iron for use in
     Bessemer steel slowed down this rapid growth.


     As one company after another commenced the erection of addi-
tional furnaces, and as the shipments of pig iron North steadily
increased, Northern iron makers were forced to admit that they had
underestimated the iron possibilities of the South.  Mr. Samuel
Thomas, of the great Thomas Iron Company, of Pennsylvania, after
thoroughly investigating the advantages of Alabama for the cheap
production of iron, concluded to build furnaces near Birmingham,
and he and his associates organized a $1,000,000 company which is
now putting up one furnace, with the plant so arranged that others
can be added after this is finished   This move attracted wide
attention, for it was the strongest possible endorsement of what
the press and the people of the South had so persistently claimed.
During 1886 new companies organized to build furnaces were formed

so rapidly as to fairly bewilder one who attempts to keep the run
of new enterprises, and at this writing there are no indications
of any let-up in the stupendous developments that each day brings
forth in the South.  The Center of the greatest activity has been
in Alabama and Tennessee, but in Virginia plans are being matured
for gigantic iron enterprises that promise to make the Southwestern
part of that State, so rich in mineral resources, rival to some
extent the first two States in the manufacture of iron and steel.

The vast developments that are now being made in the iron
interests of the South will be best appreciated by a summary of some
of the most important enterprises now under way.  The Pratt Coal &
Iron Company, and the Tennessee Coal, Iron & Railroad Company, which
were consolidated in 1886 with a capital stock of $10,000,000, have
five furnaces in operation, are now building five more, and will
also erect steel works.  Four of these furnaces and the steel works
will be located at the new town of Ensley, near Birmingham, and one
will be added to the three owned by this company at South Pittsburgh.  The magnitude of the business carried on by this great corporation is seen from a recent letter from the manager to the
Manufacturers' Record, in which it is stated that with their five
furnaces they are now turning out more iron than the Thomas Iron
Company, of Pennsylvania, with its twelve, and that they are
shipping iron to Canada, Connecticut, Massachusetts, Rhode Island,
New York, New Jersey, Pennsylvania, California, Utah, Nevada,
Montana, Texas, and all the intervening States and Territories.


M. B. Hillyard, The New South, (Baltimore, Maryland:   The
Manufacturers' Record Co., 1887), p. 23.



388.   ARTICLES MADE WITHOUT BENEFIT OF A STANDARD (1889)


Enthusiasts about the rapid progress of interchangeability should be shown this list.


Street-Car Gauge.--No established standard.
Nails.--A system of sizes fairly adhered to, but not of record.
Braces and Bits.--No system of interchange.  Custom leaves the
shanks of bits to be filed to form by the carpenter incapable of
doing it.
Tool Sockets, Tool Eyes, and their Handles Generally.--An
intelligent desire for a system of standards, hopeless in the ab-
sence of places of record.
Machine Tool Posts.--Ditto.
Matches and Match Boxes.--No established length of matches.
Match boxes on the market to-day will not receive the matches of
yesterday.

Sections of Rolled Iron.--No uniformity in shapes substantially alike, and no community of dimension of iron from different mills. Established standards of common shapes are much needed.

Electric Light Carbons and their Holders.--No standard, and every premonition of trouble in the future.

Door Knobs and Spindles.--A sort of common following, with just sufficient recognition to result in exasperation.

Doors and Door-Frames.--These are now market articles, emanating from different factories. There is no established system of sizes.

Picture-Frames.--There is in the market a line of what are called "ordinary sizes," and pictures and glass are also marketed in a line of "ordinary sizes." The line of ordinary sizes started out with something of an understanding, on the part of the trade, by reason of the number of sizes being limited, but as the list was added to, the original understanding was lost sight of, and all is now in confusion.

Stove Pipe.--No standard ever adopted which will enable pipe sections to interchange. The standing joke.

Panes of Glass.--"Ordinary sizes" not based on any common understanding.

Washers.--No standards.

There never seems to have been any community of thought between the candlestick-maker and the chandler. Candles will go into candle-sticks, but have never been known to fit....

There is no uniformity in sizes of beds, and everything is at sixes and sevens regarding bedsteads, mattresses, blankets, quilts, and sheets. The mattress of one room should certainly fit at least one other bedstead.

Pins.--Pins have their length specified by an arbitrary system of symbols. Such as "D C," "B C," "F 3 1/2," "D B," "S"." These symbols mean double corkey, big corkey, short corkey, and so on.

Manufacturers and dealers have no mutual understanding of the system employed. The system is not used alike by any two makers. In addition to the lengths, pins are specified in classes, as "Class A," which refers to brass pins of the largest size, stuck in papers in twelve rows, thirty pins to the row, and 360 pins to the paper, etc. There is no uniform understanding of the system, but all use it.

James W. See, "Standards," Transactions, American Society of Mechanical Engineers, X (1889-1890), pp. 550-556.


389.  THE MEAT POOL IN CHICAGO (1889)


Perfection of the refrigerated railroad car permitted large-scale shipments over long distances from giant marketing centers. Control of this invention directly led to concentrated meat production in Chicago.

By the 1880's, several meat packers effectively
monopolized a goodly part of the supply of meat.
Baurmann, who testifies, had served for 3 years
as the head of the dressed beef department of
Nelson Morris & Co.


Q.  State whether you know of any combination between dressed-
beef concerns in Chicago.--A.  Yes, sir; there is a combination.
Q.  How long has it existed?--A.  Since last May a year ago.
Q.  Were you in the employ of Nelson Morris & Co. prior to
that time?--A.  Yes, sir; I had been in their employ for a year
previous.
A.  Did you know the extent and nature of their business?--A.
Yes, sir.
Q.  State whether there has been any increase in their business
after that combination was made?--A.  They have increased since I
first went in their employ about three times the dressed-beef
business alone.
Q.  Who constitute this combination; who are in it?--A.  Armour
& Co., Swift & Co., Nelson Morris & Co., and George H. Hammond & Co.
Q.  Do they all live in Chicago?--A.  The three first firms
are in business in Chicago.  Hammond is in Hammond, Ind., just over
the line, with head offices at Detroit.
Q.  What is the nature of this combination?  What are the terms
of it?--A.  They have a pool which is based on the business that
each firm had done from the first day of January until the first
day of May.  They make out weekly statements of the total amount of
the weight of beef on each Saturday night.  This is taken Monday
morning to the headquarters down town.  The packers' representatives
say Frank Vogel, of Nelson Morris & Co., or Eddie Morris, of Nelson
Morris & Co., Mr. Armour, or some representative of his, the secretary of Swift & Co., or Mr. Louis Swift, and a representative of
Hammond & Co., meet each Tuesday in the Grand Pacific Hotel, in
Chicago.  These meetings have been held since the agreement between
them up to the present day.  They take statements with them of the
price of beef received in the different cities, telegrams, etc.,
which are submitted and gone over at this meeting.
Q.  Do they bid against each other for beef that is sold in
Chicago?--A.  No, sir.  They have a combination in Chicago.  They
set the price of beef.  It is killed, say, to day, and the cost of
it is figured the same day.  The next morning a certain price is
put upon it.
Q.  If a man takes a lot of beef cattle to Chicago and offers
them for sale at the stock-yards, does he get more than one offer
from these concerns?--A.  No; there is no competition in the purchase.  If one of the firms sees a bunch of cattle which he wants
he immediately notifies any other firms if they should come there
and attempt to purchase them.
Q.  He tells them he has a bid on the cattle?--A.  Yes, sir;
that he has a bid on them; and they frequently wait until after
3 o'clock before making any purchases in order to break the price.
Q.  Then the man who brought the cattle there has to keep them
over night at great expense in order to sell them?--A.  Yes;

he has to pay another day's yardage and also for feeding them,
which is very expensive.  They charge very high, a dollar a bushel
for corn and a dollar a hundred for hay.

    Q.  At the yards?--A.  At the yards, and you can not buy out-
side of the yards at all.

    Q.  Why not?--A.  They are not allowed to buy hay outside of
the stock-yards or to feed cattle outside the yards.  If the cattle
are in the yards they have to buy from the stock-yards company,
and these packers are all stockholders in this company--the Union
Stock-yards and Transit Company.

    Q.  These packers are all interested in the yard?--A.  Yes,
sir.  Mr. Nelson Morris, I think, has the biggest amount of the
stock.

    Testimony, G. Baurmann, U.S. Congress, 51st, 1st session,
Senate, Report No. 829, <u>Testimony Taken by the Select Committee...</u>
<u>on the Transportation and Sale of Meat Products</u>, (Washington, D.C.:
Government Printing Office, 1889), pp. 182-183.

390.  DEVELOPMENT OF IRON PRODUCTION IN ALABAMA (1880's)

    During these years there was a veritable rage
about the industrial future of Birmingham.  Part of
the excitement was soundly based on raw materials
accessibility.  The rest was based on the hope for
booming real estate values.

Twelve years ago the total coal product of Alabama was ten
thousand tons a year; now nearly half that amount is sent to market
each day, the total tonnage of 1885 being over one million five
hundred thousand.  Twelve years ago the total pig-iron product of
the State was sixty thousand tons; now it is six hundred thousand.
These two sentences speak volumes to the iron and coal interests
of the whole country.

. . . . . . . . . . . . . . . . . . . . . . . . . . . . . . . . .

    It is idle for Pennsylvania and other great iron- and coal-
producing States to close their eyes to the fact that we have
reached the beginning of a great revolution in those products.  No
legislation, no sound public policy, no sentiment can halt such a
revolution when the immutable laws of trade command it; and the
sudden tread of the hordes from the Northern forests upon ancient
ome did not more surely threaten the majesty of the mistress of
the world, than does the tread of the iron- and coal-diggers of
Alabama threaten the majesty of Northern iron- and coal-fields
I do not credit the common saying that iron can be produced here
for nine dollars per ton.  There are many here who will tell you
so; but after careful inquiry in the most intelligent and reliable
circles, I fix an entirely safe limit of average cost at eleven

dollars and fifty cents.  There is iron produced here at less than
that cost; but eleven dollars and fifty cents is as just an estimate for Birmingham as seventeen dollars is for Pennsylvania; and
it must be remembered that Pennsylvania has reached the minimum
cost in the production and marketing of her iron, while Alabama can
and will greatly cheapen the delivery of her iron in the great
centres of the trade.

McClure, The South, pp. 98 and 103.


### 391.  HAND-PUDDLING IRON (1880's)


Until the age of cheap steel, wrought iron was
the most generally acceptable mass-metal.  It was tough,
and it was easy to work into a variety of simple tools
and implements.  The puddler, the cook of the wrought
iron brew, became of pivotal importance in the industry.
Until a new technical stage was reached in the industry,
puddlers drew the highest wages and were relatively
heavily unionized.


But the working door of a puddling furnace is the door through
which the puddler does his work.  It is a porthole opening upon a
sea of flame.  The heat of these flames would wither a man's body,
and so they are enclosed in a shell of steel.  Through this working
door I was put in the charge of "pigs" that were to be boiled.
Six hundred pounds was the weight of pig-iron we used to put
into a single hearth.  Much wider than the hearth was the fire
grate, for we needed a heat that was intense.  The flame was made
by burning bituminous coal.  Vigorously I stoked that fire for
thirty minutes with dampers open and the draft roaring while that
pig-iron melted down....  There were five bakings every day and this
meant the shoveling in of nearly two tons of coal.  In summer I was
stripped to the waist and panting while the sweat poured down
across my heaving muscles.
What time I was not stoking the fire, I was stirring the charge
with a long iron rabble that weighed some twenty-five pounds.  Strap
an Oregon boot of that weight to your arm and then do calisthenics
ten hours in a room so hot it melts your eyebrows and you will know
what it is like to be a puddler.  But we puddlers did not complain.
There is men's work to be done in this world, and we were the men
to do it.
After melting down the pig-iron as quickly as possible, which
took me thirty minutes, there was a pause in which I had time to
wipe the back of my hand on the dryest part of my clothing (if any
spot was still dry) and with my sweat cap wipe the sweat and soot
out of my eyes.  For the next seven minutes I "thickened the heat
up" by adding iron oxide to the bath.  This was in the form of roll

scale.  The furnace continued in full blast till that was melted.
The liquid metal in the hearth is called slag.  The iron oxide is
put in it to make it more basic for the chemical reaction that is
to take place.  Adding the roll scale had cooled the charge, and it
was thick like hoecake batter.  I now thoroughly mixed it with a
rabble which is like a long iron hoe.

The puddler's hand-rag is one of his most important tools.  It
is about the size of thick wash-rag, and the puddler carries it
in the hand that clasps the rabble rod where it is too hot for bare
flesh to endure.

The melted iron contains carbon, sulphur and phosphorus, and
to get rid of them, especially the sulphur and phosphorus, is the
object of all this heat and toil.  For it is the sulphur and
phosphorus that make the iron brittle.  And brittle iron might as
well not be iron at all; it might better be clay.

My purpose in slackening my heat as soon as the pig-iron was
melted was to oxidize the phosphorus and sulphur ahead of the
carbon.  Just as alcohol vaporizes at a lower heat than water, so
sulphur and phosphorus oxidize at a lower heat than carbon.  When
this reaction begins I see light flames breaking through the lake
of molten slag in my furnace.

The flames are caused by the burning of carbon monoxide from
the oxidation of carbon.  The slag is basic and takes the sulphur
and phosphorus into combination, thus ending its combination with
the iron.  The purpose now is to oxidize the carbon, too, without
reducing the phosphorus and sulphur and causing them to return to
the iron.  We want the pure iron to begin crystallizing out of the
bath like butter from the churning buttermilk.

More and more of the carbon gas comes out of the puddle, and
as it bubbles out the charge is agitated by its escape and the
"boil" is in progress.  It is not real boiling like the boiling of
a teakettle.  When a teakettle boils the water turns to bubbles of
vapor and goes up in the air to turn to water again when it gets
cold.  But in the boiling iron puddle a chemical change is taking
place.  The iron is not going up in vapor.  The carbon and the
oxygen are.  This formation of gas in the molten puddle causes
the whole charge to boil up like an ice-cream soda.  The slag over-
flows.  Redder than strawberry syrup and as hot as the fiery lake
in Hades it flows over the rim of the hearth and out through the
slag-hole.  My helper has pushed up a buggy there to receive it.
More than an eighth and sometimes a quarter of the weight of the
pig-iron flows off in slag and is carted away.

Meanwhile I have got the job of my life on my hands.  I must
stir my boiling mess with all the strength of my body.  For now is
my chance to defeat nature and wring from the loosening grip of
her hand the pure iron she never intended to give us.

For twenty-five minutes while the boil goes on I stir it
constantly with my long iron rabble.  A cook stirring gravy to
keep it from scorching in the skillet is done in two minutes and
backs off blinking, sweating and choking, having finished the
hardest job of getting dinner.  But my hardest job lasts not two
minutes but the better part of half an hour.  My spoon weighs

twenty-five pounds, my porridge is pasty iron, and the heat of my
kitchen is so great that if my body was not hardened to it, the
ordeal would drop me in my tracks.

Little spikes of pure iron like frost spars glow white-hot and
stick out of the churning slag.  These must be stirred at once; the
long stream of flame from the grate plays over the puddle, and the
pure iron if lapped by these gases would be oxidized--burned up.

Pasty masses of iron form at the bottom of the puddle.  There
they would stick and become chilled if they were not constantly
stirred.  The whole charge must be mixed and mixed as it steadily
thickens so that it will be uniform throughout.

The charge which I have been kneading in my furnace has now
"come to nature," the stringy sponge of pure iron is separating
from the slag.  The "balling" of this sponge into three loaves is
a task that occupies from ten to fifteen minutes.  The particles
of iron glowing in this spongy mass are partly welded together;
they are sticky and stringy and as the cooling continues they are
rolled up into wads like popcorn balls.  The charge, which lost
part of its original weight by the draining off of slag, now
weighs five hundred fifty to six hundred pounds.  I am balling it
into three parts of equal weight.  If the charge is six hundred
pounds, each of my balls must weigh exactly two hundred pounds.

But the iron worker does not guess his pigs.  He knows exactly
how much pig-iron he put into the boil.  His guessing skill comes
into play when with a long paddle and hook he separates six hundred
pounds of sizzling fireworks into three fire balls each of which
will weigh two hundred pounds.

The balls are rolled up into three resting places, one in the
fire-bridge corner, one in the flue-bridge corner, and one in the
jam, all ready for the puddler to draw them.

My batch of biscuits is now done and I must take them out at
once and rush them to the hungry mouth of the squeezing machine.
I have to use long-handled tongs, and each of my biscuits weighs
twice as much as I weigh.

One at a time the balls are drawn out on to a buggy and wheeled
swiftly to the squeezer.  This machine squeezes out the slag which
flows down like the glowing lava running out a volcano.  The
motion of the squeezer is like the circular motion you use in
rolling a bread pill between the palms and squeezing the water out
of it.  I must get the three balls, or blooms, out of the furnace
and into the squeezer while the slag is still liquid so that it can
be squeezed out of the iron.

From cold pig-iron to finished blooms is a process that takes
from an hour and ten minutes, to an hour and forty minutes, depending on the speed and skill of the puddler, and the kind of iron.


James John Davis, The Iron Puddler, (Indianapolis, Indiana:
Bobbs-Merrill, 1922), extracted from pages 97-113.

392.  CHEMISTRY, GUIDE TO INDUSTRIAL PROFIT (1870)


Inadequacies of chemical and metallurgical knowledge
combined with financial conservatism retarded the development of applied science in the iron and steel industry.
Carnegie was one of the few leaders in the industry who
made some room, at least, for applied science.  (For the
persistence of artisan technology in blast furnace practice,
see Source No. 770).


Looking back to-day it seems incredible that only forty years
ago (1870) chemistry in the United States was an almost unknown
agent in connection with the manufacture of pig iron.  It was the
agency, above all others, most needful in the manufacture of iron
and steel.  The blast-furnace manager of that day was usually a rude
bully, generally a foreigner, who in addition to his other acquire-
ments was able to knock down a man now and then as a lesson to the
other unruly spirits under him.  He was supposed to diagnose the
condition of the furnace by instinct, to possess some almost super-
natural power of divination, like his congener in the country districts who was reputed to be able to locate an oil well or water
supply by means of a hazel rod.  He was a veritable quack doctor
who applies whatever remedies occurred to him for the troubles of
his patient.
The Lucy Furnace was out of one trouble and into another,
owing to the great variety of ores, limestone, and coke which were
then supplied with little or no regard to their component parts.
This state of affairs became intolerable to us.  We finally decided
to dispense with the rule-of-thumb-and-intuition manager, and to
place a young man in charge of the furnace.  We had a young shipping
clerk, Henry M. Curry, who had distinguished himself, and it was
resolved to make him manager.
Mr. Phipps had the Lucy Furnace under his special charge.
His daily visits to it saved us from failure there.  Not that the
furnace was not doing as well as other furnaces in the West as to
money-making, but being so much larger than other furnaces its
variations entailed much more serious results.  I am afraid my
partner had something to answer for in his Sunday morning visits to
the Lucy Furnace when his good father and sister left the house for
more devotional duties.  But even if he had gone with them his real
earnest prayer could not but have had reference at times to the
precarious condition of the Lucy Furnace then absorbing his
thoughts.
The next step taken was to find a chemist as Mr. Curry's assistant and guide.  We found the man in a learned German, Dr. Fricke,
and great secrets did the doctor open up to us.  Iron stone from
mines that had a high reputation was now found to contain ten,
fifteen, and even twenty per cent less iron than it had been credited with.  Mines that hitherto had a poor reputation we found to
be now yielding superior ore.  The good was bad and the bad was
good, and everything was topsy-turvy.  Nine tenths of all the

uncertainties of pig-iron making were dispelled under the burning
su.1 of chemical knowledge.

At a most critical period when it was necessary for the credit
of the firm that the blast furnace should make its best product, it
had been stopped because an exceedingly rich and pure ore had been
substituted for an inferior ore--an ore which did not yield more
than two thirds of the quantity of iron of the other.  The furnace
had met with disaster because too much lime had been used to flux
this exceptionally pure ironstone.  The very superiority of the
materials had involved us in serious losses.

What fools we had been!  But then there was this consolation:
we were not as great fools as our competitors.  It was years after
we had taken chemistry to guide us that it was said by the proprietors of some other furnaces that they could not afford to employ
a chemist.  Had they known the truth then, they would have known
that they could not afford to be without one.  Looking back it
seems pardonable to record that we were the first to employ a chemist at blast furnaces--something our competitors pronounced extravagant.

The Lucy Furnace became the most profitable branch of our
business, because we had almost the entire monopoly of scientific
management.

Autobiography of Andrew Carnegie, pp. 181-183.


393.  THE TRADE PRESS DIFFUSES TECHNICAL KNOWLEDGE (1880's)


The writer of this article, Fred Colvin, published
his first article in American Machinist, a trade journal.
During the next sixty years he was associated with the
journal in various capacities, including editor.  While
a trade journal editor might tend to overstress the importance of his work, the fact is that his contribution
is generally overlooked.


It is a curious fact that the printing press, which owes its
present existence to the development of machine tools, was itself
responsible for the tremendous growth of the machine-tool industry
during the past half century.  Before the coming of trade publications and technical magazines, machinists and tool designers in
widely separated shops all over the world had no means of knowing
what progress was being made in their field except through occasional letters between individuals, or through the reports of itinerant
millwrights or journeymen mechanics who had the opportunity to
observe methods and conditions in a number of different plants.

Consequently when new tools or improved shop practices were developed independently in a particular plant or locality, it might be months or even years before the industry as a whole got wind of them, with the result I mentioned earlier in connection with the primitive gas buggy that there were at least eight or ten inventors working at the same thing at the same time in almost complete ignorance of each other's failures or successes. Something like this was true of the machine-tool industry before the days of such technical magazines as the Northwest Mechanic, the Practical Mechanic, the American Machinist, Machinery, the Locomotive Engineer, and other trade papers that appeared during the last two decades of the past century.

With the publication and circulation of such periodicals, however, it became possible for the owners and operators of machine shops, the designers, engineers, shopworkers, apprentices, and buyers of machinery to get an over-all picture of the latest improvements, applications, and possibilities for development, as well as a share in the total experience of thousands of fellow workers in the field, plus a knowledge of their typical troubles and the remedies that they had found to be of practical use. Most important of all, the trade journal and technical publication made possible the concept of standardized practice and standardized measurement, without which it is safe to say our present machine-age civilization would be a great deal more chaotic than its severest critics can imagine. It has been through such mediums that the recommendations of the various engineering societies concerning the subject of standardization have been brought to the attention of everyone in the machine-tool industry.

Colvin, 60 Years with Men and Machines, pp. 37-38.


394.   TRADE SECRECY IN THE RUBBER INDUSTRY (1896)


Aside from Edison's enterprises, there was not a single industrial research laboratory in the United States whch concerned itself primarily with research, applied or pure. Industrial technology was of an artisan and empirical nature. Modern industry was virtually unacquainted with chemistry and physics. P. W. Litchfield, who writes here, later became president of the Goodyear Rubber Company.


I went through the various other departments after that until I was familiar with all the processes, then was promoted to compounder. That was much more interesting. The rubber we got in then varied widely, so I had to make up a batch from each shipment, experiment with it until I found the best combination of compounds, curing times, and temperatures.

Compounding was a position of trust.  The compounds were in
code, company secrets to be guarded from competitors.  In some
plants the owner of the business himself was compounder, the only
one who knew what specifications were being used--and he might
carry these in his head, not trust them to paper.

Morrison, who seemed to have taken a liking to me, passed on
what information he had accumulated about the reactions of rubber,
and one night called me in for a long talk.

"Right now rubber is a backward industry," he said.  "It
doesn't attract the right kind of men.  You probably would not have
taken this job if you could have found anything else.  But it is
an industry with great possibilities.  There's much to be done.
Little scientific research has gone into rubber since Charles
Goodyear's day.  We've been mixing various compounds with rubber
without knowing why, only because someone had found out they improved it.  One of these days people will go into the field more
scientifically.  With your technical training that might be a good
opportunity."

I appreciated his interest, but had no intention of spending
my life in a laboratory.


P. W. Litchfield, Industrial Voyage.  My Life as an Industrial
Lieutenant, (Garden City, New York:  Doubleday and Co., 1954),
p. 59.



395.  THE ADVANTAGES OF INDUSTRIAL COMBINATIONS (1899)


A rather bland discussion by a prime authority
on industrial combinations by John D. Rockefeller,
founder of the Standard Oil Company.


Q.  What are, in your judgment, the chief advantages from
industrial combinations--(a) financially to stockholders; (b) to
the public?--A.  All the advantages which can be derived from a
cooperation of persons and aggregation of capital.  Much that one
man can not do alone two can do together, and once admit the fact
that cooperation, or, what is the same thing, combination, is
necessary on a small scale, the limit depends solely upon the
necessities of business.  Two persons in partnership may be a
sufficiently large combination for a small business, but if the
business grows or can be made to grow, more persons and more
capital must be taken in.  The business may grow so large that a
partnership ceases to be a proper instrumentality for its purposes,
and then a corporation becomes a necessity.  In most countries, as
in England, this form of industrial combination is sufficient for
a business coextensive with the parent country, but it is not so
in this country.  Our Federal form of government, making every
corporation created by a State foreign to every other State, renders

it necessary for persons doing business through corporate agency
to organize corporations in some or many of the different States in
which their business is located.  Instead of doing business through
the agency of one corporation they must do business through the
agencies of several corporations.  If the business is extended to
foreign countries, and Americans are not to-day satisfied with home
markets alone, it will be found helpful and possibly necessary to
organize corporations in such countries, for Europeans are pre-
judiced against foreign corporations as are the people of many of
our States.  These different corporations thus become cooperating
agencies in the same business and are held together by common ownership of their stocks.

It is too late to argue about advantages of industrial combinations.  They are a necessity.  And if Americans are to have the
privilege of extending their business in all the States of the
Union, and into foreign countries as well, they are a necessity on
a large scale, and require the agency of more than one corporation.
Their chief advantages are:

(1)  Command of necessary capital.
(2)  Extension of limits of business.
(3)  Increase of number of persons interested in the business.
(4)  Economy in the business.
(5)  Improvements and economies which are derived from know-
     ledge of many interested persons of wide experience.
(6)  Power to give the public improved products at less prices
     and still make a profit for stockholders.
(7)  Permanent work and good wages for laborers.


Statement, John D. Rockefeller, December 30, 1899, United
States Industrial Commission, I, p. 796.


### 396.  PATENTS, COMPETITION AND PROFIT (1899)


Here is a straightforward argument made by John
Gates, chairman of the American Steel and Wire Company
of New Jersey, that bestowal of a patent entitles the
patentees to receive an extraprofit on the patented
item.


Q.  About what proportion do you have of the output of wire
nails?--A.  I should say about the same proportion as of plain wire.
Q.  (By Representative LIVINGSTON.)  What is that?--A.  Sixty-
five to 80 or 95 per cent, somewhere; I can not tell you.
Q.  Is it not a fact that competition has kept the price of
wire nails down, while the smooth wire has gone higher?--A.  No; I
do not think so.
Q.  Do you not know it to be a fact that the farmers and the
mechanics object to the price of wire nails, and will take the

other nails just as soon as you put up the price?--A.  I think
every advance that we have made in the last year has affected wire
nails and smooth wire about the same.

Q.  The price of wire nails has not gone up, while the price
of smooth wire and barbed wire has doubled almost.--A.  We claim a
perfect right to put any price on barbed fence wire that would seem
justifiable on the ground that we have paid out hundreds of thousands of dollars for patents.  We do not claim that right on the
others.

Q.  You have acquired a patent monopoly, and you justify it
then?--A.  Yes.  The granting of a patent gives a man a monopoly,
as I understand, if he has a good patent.

Q.  (By Mr. CONGER.)  Do you make as much profit on the manufacture of nails as you do on the manufacture of barbed wire?--A.
No, I think not.

Q.  Why do you not?  Why do you not ask a price that will bring
you as much profit on the nails as on the barbed wire?--A.  Because
there are no patents on nail machinery that we know of, and there
are patents on barbed-wire machinery producing this product.

Q.  There is some competition, then, in the manufacture of wire
nails?--A.  Yes; there is some in the manufacture of barbed wire,
but not very much.  It is limited to two or three, probably three
more concerns that have licenses.

Q.  (By Mr. JENKS).  Is there as much profit at the present
time for your concern in the manufacture of wire nails as there is
in the manufacture of smooth wire?--A.  Why, I think about the same.

Q.  Do you have agreements with independent manufacturers of
wire nails, more or less formal, as regards the prices at which
the nails shall be marketed?--A.  No; we do not; we have no agreement whatever.

Q.  You furnish to those manufacturers of wire nails in various
cases the smooth wire from which the nails are manufactured?--A.
Yes; sometimes we do.

There is a great deal of woven wire fencing made in this country.  We claim a monopoly under patents of most of the woven wire
fencing.  We made the past year about 25,000 miles of woven wire
fencing under patents that we purchased, and we get a very much
larger profit on that than we do on the plain fence wire or even
barbed wire or wire nails, for the reason that we own the patents
on the machines and the patent on the product.


Testimony, John W. Gates, United States Industrial Commission,
I, p. 1010.


### 397.    MACHINERY IN THE GLASS TRADE (1899)


Very few operations were mechanized in the glass
industry; exclusively, so far, in the manufacture of
glass jars.  Bottle-making remained untouched by machinery.

(See Source No. 622).  This comment was made by
Denis Hayes, president of the Glass Bottle Blowers'
Association of America.


The glass trade has been free from machinery until within the
last couple of years.  Machinery has now been invented to make
fruit jars, and they are made successfully, in a factory in Indiana
especially.  They had 273 of our members employed last year; now
they have only 83 of these men, and they are now working for 45
per cent less than before the machine came in....
     This machine question brings up a few points that are not
noticed by the average statistician, I think.  Most mechanics are
what we call specialists.  Ten or fifteen years ago if you met a
glass blower he could make anything from a 1-ounce to a gallon
bottle; to-day you meet a 1-ounce blower, 16-ounce, demijohn, and
fruit-jar blowers.  They are kept on one class of work; their
muscles and intellect are drilled into one line of work.  They get
larger production out of a man when kept on one kind of work.  Now
they had, up to the introduction of machinery, 500 men that could
make fruit jars.  They were specialists, yet their indentures say
"they shall be taught the art of glass blowing," but they
were only taught a part of the trade, and were kept on fruit jars,
and could scarcely make anything else.  They might make an effort
at other kinds of work, but if they did not come up to the standard of production they would have to get out.  A machine comes
along that could make fruit jars; it displaces men who have made
certain preparation for their children's future.  We move with such
regularity and precision that when a machine comes in, that man is
useless for any other kind of work.  After a man passes middle life
he can not adapt himself to other lines of work, statisticians to
the contrary notwithstanding, even if he is not a specialist.  The
machine being covered by patent, and other manufacturers not being
able to get it, we found out to the best of our ability what the
product of that machine could be sold for; then we cut wages, what
we call the jar scale, to 45 per cent less than it was before the
introduction of machinery.  That enabled manufacturers who did not
have machines to employ a certain part of our jar blowers for the
present, but they must eventually give way to the machine.  The
result of the introduction of machinery, owing to the conditions
which I have stated, is that there will be a certain number of men
thrown out of work, who must be supported by the union, or their
children.  Usually their children go to work; women also work to
support the men displaced by machinery.  Remember, I am not saying
this now because I am opposed to machinery.  Trades unions are not
opposed to the introduction of machinery, as is usually supposed,
but we do want to bring out some of the facts which are usually
ignored when it is said the introduction of machinery makes more
work.  It may make more work for coming generations, but machines
always reduce wages, and force women and children to work.  Take

conditions of industry where men are only a part of the machine,
they are displaced promiscuously, and that is one of the things
that gives such an incentive to the necessity of child labor.


Testimony, Denis A. Hayes, United States Industrial Commission,
VII, pp. 111-112.


398.  UNEMPLOYMENT EFFECTS OF THE LINOTYPE MACHINE (1899)


An interesting example of a union taking direct
financial responsibility for retraining and relocating
workers who were displaced by technological advance.
Note that the union looked toward an increase in business
as the long-run factor which would revive the demand for
printers.  Here the speaker is Samuel Donnelly, president
of the International Typographical Union, an organization
of 38,000 members.


Q.  What has been the effect on the printer of the introduction of the Mergenthaler linotype machine?--A.  At the time of the
introduction of the machine and for 3 years after its introduction
the printers of the country suffered; the journeymen securing employment on the machine and 3 being displaced.  The policy adopted
by the typographical union was not to oppose the machine, but to
admit of its success and make the best of it; to try and master it.
The spirit that was manifested by the members was something of this
kind:  "Here is something that will take my bread and butter away
from me and I must try and become its master."  They endeavored to
learn the machine as quickly as possible, and after 5 years the
trade has about adjusted itself to normal conditions, and the
membership of the printers' union is to-day greater than its membership of compositors ever was.
    Q.  Do you think there are as many printers employed to-day as
there was before the introduction of the Mergenthaler linotype?--
A.  Not as many to-day, but with a continuation of present conditions one year from now there will be as many.
    Q.  By reason of the increase in the printing business?--A.
By reason of the increase in the trade.  At the time the machines
were introduced the local typographical unions through the country--
I should say from 1892 to 1896--expended $500,000 for supporting
members displaced.  The New York typographical union, the largest
in the country, had at one time 680 men on its unemployed list,
principally men who were displaced by the introduction of machines.
Of the number on the unemployed list today who were displaced by
the introduction of machines, 50 per cent are men who were, by
reason of their age, not competent to operate or considered competent to operate the machine, as compared with the younger men.

The introduction of machines had this effect on the trade:  In 6
years after the first machine was introduced the trade will have
again reached the same condition in regard to the number of men
employed as before the introduction of the machine; but of the men
displaced there is an army of old men who are to-day unemployed,
whose places in the trade have been taken by younger men; and of
the men displaced by the introduction of machines at least 25 per
cent will never be again employed in a printing office at the particular department in which they worked when the machines were introduced.  The unions are taking care, to a great extent, of these
men by relieving them and assistant them to other situations.


        Testimony, Samuel B. Donnelly, United States Industrial
Commission, VII, p. 276.


        399.  "CHANGES IN THE WORKMAN'S SOCIAL HABITS" (1899)


        How distant were the days of the tiny shop is
shown by the fact that it was already time to collect
momentoes about them!  Horace Eaton, general secretary-
treasurer of the Boot and Shoe Workers' Union, describes
the past.


        Q.  (By Mr. RATCHFORD.)  You have been in a position to observe
the effect of this change on the workman as compared with the older
system I have referred to.  What effect, if any, has it had on the
social habits of the workman, or have you noticed any?--A.  I think
it has had quite an effect.  In Lynn [Massachusetts] to-day--I speak
of Lynn as illustrative of other shoe centers--the city government
is trying to agree upon a site for one of the old-time shoe factories.  They are going to preserve it as an heirloom; a little
factory about 10 by 14, a little shop.  In these old shops, years
ago, one man owned the shop; he took in work and 3, 4, 5, or 6
others, neighbors, came in there and sat down and made shoes right
in their laps, and there was no machinery.  Everybody was at liberty
to talk; they were all politicians.  Those were the times when
Henry Wilson, who was also a shoemaker, said that every shoemaker
in Lynn was fit to be a United States Senator.  Of course, under
these conditions, where there was absolute freedom and exchange of
ideas, they naturally would become more intelligent than shoe workers can at the present time, when they are driving each man to see
how many shoes he can handle, and where he is surrounded by noisy
machinery.  And another thing, this nervous strain on a man doing
just one thing over and over and over again must necessarily have
a wearing effect on him; and his ideals, I believe, must be lowered.


        Testimony, Horace M. Eaton, United States Industrial
Commission, VII, p. 363.

# F.

## EVOLVING WAGE LABOR

400.  FREEDMEN DO ALL THE PHYSICAL LABOR OF THE SOUTH (1865)

> An interesting eyewitness account of the situation
> in the South; it was written by Colonel Samuel Thomas
> who was Assistant Commissioner of the Freedmen's Bureau
> for Mississippi and northeastern Louisiana.  He writes
> to General Carl Schurz who, at the request of President
> Johnson, had just toured the states of South Carolina,
> Georgia, Alabama, Mississippi, and Louisiana.

It is nonsense to talk so much about plans for getting the
negroes to work.  They do now, and always have done, all the physical labor of the south, and if treated as they should be by their
government, (which is so anxious to be magnanimous to the white
people of this country, who never did work and never will,) they
will continue to do so.  Who are the workmen in these fields?  Who
are hauling the cotton to market, driving hacks and drays in the
cities, repairing streets and railroads, cutting timber, and in
every place raising the hum of industry?  The freedmen, not the
rebel soldiery.  The southern white men, true to their instincts
and training, are going to Mexico or Brazil, or talk of importing
labor in the shape of Coolies, Irishmen--anything--anything to
avoid work, any way to keep from putting their own shoulders to the
wheel.
The mass of the freedmen can and will support themselves by
labor.  They need nothing but justice before the courts of the land,
impartial judges and juries, to encourage them in well-doing, or
punish them for the violation of just laws, a chance to own the land
and property they can honestly obtain, the free exercise of their
right to worship God and educate themselves, and--let them alone.

The delegates to Washington think that it is their duty, peculiarly, to see the President and arrange the affairs of the negro. Why don't they attend to their own business, or make arrangements for the working of the disbanded rebel army in the cotton fields and workshops of the south? There are to-day as many houseless, homeless, poor, wandering, idle white men here as there are negroes in the same condition, yet no arrangements are made for their working. All the trickery, chicanery and political power possible are being brought to bear on the poor negro, to make him do the hard labor for the whites, as in days of old.

To this end the mass of the people are instinctively working. They steadily refuse to sell or lease lands to black men. Colored mechanics of this city, how have made several thousand dollars during the last two years, find it impossible to buy even land enough to put up a house on, yet white men can purchase any amount of land. The whites know that if negroes are not allowed to acquire property or become landholders, they must ultimately return to plantation labor, and work for wages that will barely support themselves and families, and they feel that this kind of slavery will be better than none at all.

Letter, Colonel Samuel Thomas to General Carl Schurz, September 28, 1865, U.S. Congress, 39th, 1st session, Exec. Doc. No. 2, Condition of the South, serial number 1237, p. 82.

### 401. EMPLOYMENT OF ONE'S FORMER SLAVES (1865)

Written at the very end of the Civil War, the terms of employment closely resemble the situation under slavery; this document was drawn up in April, 1865 by Paul C. Cameron to cover freedmen on his own and his family's farms in Orange County, North Carolina.

That for this year 1865 the negroes shall have the 4th of wheat--the 3rd of corn--the 3rd of molasses, and the 4th of sweet potatoes and pease--all the seed wheat to be returned to proprietor before a division of the crop. Rye and oat crops to be sown for the use of farm stock, which with the shucks of the corn crop and chaff of the wheat crop, and wheat straw shall all be put up for the use of the cattle and stock of the farm without any division. The negroes to feed and clothe themselves and their families. The negroes to have firewood to be cut as shall be ordered by the proprietor or his agent. House quarters, garden ground with the use of such milch cows as may be on the plantation to be allotted by lot, provided that they shall not be used to the destruction of the young cattle, and provided that the proprietor may at any time withdraw any he may need for the use of himself and family.

The proprietor to provide land--teams of mules, horses, oxen, carts and wagons and tools, with all the proper machinery (except cotton gins) for the proper farm work.  There shall be on the plantation a Depot for all farm tools and gear at which all tools and gear shall be delivered on the order of the proprietor or his agent, and any one failing to return his tools or gear, shall repay the value of the same to the proprietor or account to him satisfactorily for the loss or failure for the delivery.

The whole business of the farm to be directed by the proprietor, or by his agent who shall make his home on the place--who is to furnish all his own supplies except firewood, which shall be put out at his own door from wagons and carts as heretofore and his compensation shall be made from the undivided crop.

The whole matter to be set out in a written contract, with full specifications as to the time and amount of labour to be performed-- 10 hours of labour the year round--on each and every day--Sunday excepted.  If any one or number of negroes shall commit any theft or destruction of any property by killing stock--or stealing grain from the store houses or barns or mills he or they shall be required to leave the plantation instanter, with their families, and the proprietor shall have restitution for all property so lost or destroyed from the products of the crop at market prices.  No use shall be allowed of the farm stock except for farm purposes, but by permission of the proprietor.  No sales shall be made of any species of property by the negroes, but with the consent of the proprietor or his agent, and delivery thereof shall at all times be in the presence of the proprietor or his agent, and the person violating shall, if required, leave the plantation without claim for compensation and if he sells the property of any other person, such person shall have restitution out of the crop of the offender.

All shall promise to be perfectly respectful in language and deportment to the proprietor and his agent or agents, and to one another and the persons so offending shall be required to leave the plantation without claim for services.

The proprietor or his agent to detail such men as he or they may think best for the care of the stock, and for any other farm duty, and such service shall be considered as a part of the farm work.  The contract to continue until the 20th. of December 1866, and during all that time all the usual work of the farm, according to seasons, shall be faithfully and cheerfully performed, by all whose names shall be registered and laborers on the farm including the repairs of inclosures, house quarters, barns, mills and ditching, except in cases of sickness, and any refusal to perform any manner of work, shall be regarded as a violation of the contract, and the party shall be required to leave with his family, without claim for compensation.

The Sabbath shall be observed as a day of rest and quiet and no large assemblage of negroes shall take place on the plantation for any other religious purposes, and no visitors shall be allowed, and no person shall be introduced as a preacher, except with the approval of the proprietor.

J. G. deRoulhac Hamilton (ed.), The Papers of Thomas Ruffin, III, (Raleigh, North Carolina: Edwards & Broughton Printing Co., State Printers, 1920), pp. 449-450.

### 402. PLANTER CONTROLS OVER FREEDMEN'S WAGES (1865)

Were labor costs under freedom lower than under slavery? Here is some evidence, written by J. T. Trowbridge --there is more--that the answer is "yes."

Before the war, it was customary to pay for ordinary able-bodied plantation slaves, hired of their masters, at rates varying from one hundred and ten to one hundred and forty dollars a year for each man, together with food, clothing, and medical attendance. After the war, the farmers in many counties of Virginia entered into combinations, pledging themselves to pay the freed slave only sixty dollars a year, exclusive of clothing and medical attendance, with which he was to furnish himself out of such meagre wages. They also engaged not to hire any freedmen who had left a former employer without his consent. There were private leagues instituting measures similar to those which South Carolina and some other States afterwards enacted as laws, and having in view the same end, namely, --to hold the negro in the condition of abject dependence from which he was thought to have been emancipated.

Trowbridge, The South, p. 229.

### 403. NEGRO CRAFTSMEN IN RICHMOND, VIRGINIA (1865)

Before the Civil War, many slaves had been craftsmen. The tendency remained in the immediate post-War period. Over the years, however, the Negro was eased out of the crafts. Again Trowbridge reports.

The work of rebuilding the burnt district had commenced, and was progressing in places quite vigorously. Here I had the satisfaction of seeing the negroes, who "would not work," actually at

their tasks.  Here, as everywhere else in Richmond, and indeed in
every part of Virginia I visited, colored laborers were largely
in the majority.  They drove the teams, made the mortar, carried
the hods, excavated the old cellars or dug new ones, and, sitting
down amid the ruins, broke the mortar from the old bricks and put
them up in neat piles ready for use.  There were also colored masons
and carpenters employed on the new buildings.  I could not see but
that these people worked just as industriously as the white laborers.  And yet, with this scene before our eyes, I was once more
informed by a cynical citizen that the negro, now that he was free,
would rob, steal, or starve, before he would work.


     Trowbridge, The South, p. 150.



     404.  LIVING STANDARDS RISING AMONG FREEDMEN (1865)


          Emancipation meant the ex-slave could live for more
than work.  To outsiders, this appeared as laziness.  The
following observer saw more deeply.  Whitelaw Reid, Washington correspondent for various Cincinnati newspapers and
librarian of the U.S. House of Representatives, had just
surveyed the South on a trip with Chief Justice Salmon P.
Chase.  While in Louisiana, Reid invested in cotton lands
there.  Here Reid was visiting St. Helena Island, South
Carolina.


     Withal, they work less, and have more time for self-improve-
ment, or for society, than when slaves.  It is the common testimony,
on those islands where white men have bought the plantations, and
employed the negroes as laborers, that the old task, which the
slave worked at from sunrise to sunset, is now readily performed by
the freedman in six or seven hours.  Still, the exports from the
sea islands will not be as great as during the existence of slavery.
Then, they were mere machines, run with as little consumption as
possible, to the single end of making money for their masters.  Now,
as it was in the West Indies, emancipation has enlarged the negro's
wants, and, instead of producing solely to export, he now produces
also to consume.  Then he ate with his fingers from the hominy pot,
in the fireplace; now he must have plates, knives and forks, with a
table on which to spread them.  Then he wore the scant summer and
winter suits of negro cloth; now he must have working suits and
Sunday suits, and each must be cut with some vague reference to
prevailing fashions, and made up by hands that, under the old
regime, would have been busy beside his own in the cotton field.


     Reid, After the War, pp. 115-116.

405.  IT IS A STRUGGLE FOR AND AGAINST COMPULSION (1865)


    Free or slave, the Negro did much of the South's
work.  Would the freedmen work only under compulsion?
The following account, written by Sidney Andrews,
contradicts a widely-held misconception.  During
September-October, 1865, Andrews visited North Carolina,
South Carolina, and Georgia as correspondent of the
Boston Advertiser and the Chicago Tribune.


    Three fourths of the people assume that the negro will not
labor except on compulsion; and the whole struggle between the
whites on the one hand and the blacks on the other hand is a
struggle for and against compulsion.  The negro insists, very
blindly perhaps, that he shall be free to come and go when he
pleases; the white insists that he shall only come and go at the
pleasure of his employer.  The whites seem wholly unable to comprehend that freedom for the negro means the same thing as freedom
for them.  They readily enough admit that the government has made
him free, but appear to believe that they still have the right to
exercise over him the old control.
. . . . . . . . . . . . . . . . . . . . . . . . . . . . . . . . . . .
    It is a cruel slander to say that the race will not work except
on compulsion.  I made much inquiry wherever I went, of great numbers of planters and other employers, and found but very few cases
in which it appeared that they had refused to labor reasonably well
when fairly treated and justly paid.  Grudgingly admitted to any
of the natural rights of man, despised alike by Unionists and
Secessionists, wantonly outraged by many and meanly cheated by more
of the old planters, receiving a hundred cuffs for one helping hand
and a thousand curses for one kindly word, they bear themselves
toward their former masters very much as white men and women would
under the same circumstances.


    Sidney Andrews, The South Since the War:  As Shown by Fourteen
Weeks of Travel and Observation in Georgia and the Carolinas,
(Boston, Massachusetts:  Ticknor and Fields, 1866), pp. 398, 399.


406.  CONTEMPT FOR MANUAL LABOR PERSISTS (1865)


    The great mass of southerners, white and black,
worked with their hands.  Contempt for manual labor was
concentrated in the southern white upper class, as during
slavery and especially in areas of large plantations.
(See Source No. 208).  Again Andrews comments.

I believe the contempt for labor and the laborer is at least
quite as strong in Georgia as even in South Carolina.  In the office
of headquarters at Americus I met an ex-colonel, a man of forty-
five years, who had a plantation and worked thirty-four negroes.  I
asked him how he and his neighbors were getting on with the fall
work.  "I know nothing about the work, sir," said he with a lofty
air, in which there was a fine sneer.  At Macon I found a man who
mourned for the State because her "gentlemen" had all been ruined,
and she must hereafter be the home of "greasy workingmen."

It has not been held degrading to "be in trade," and accordingly hundreds of men are opening little stores in localities where
those already existent find but precarious support.  Since the war
it has not been held degrading to superintend to plantation, and
accordingly many men are looking for easy supernumerary places
among the planters.  But woe to the upper-class white man who proposes to come down from his proud idleness and put his own hand
into farm work!  And woe to him of that class who talks of learning
a trade!--"What, work with niggers and Yankees!"

Andrews, The South Since the War, pp. 375-376.


407.  A STRIKE INTERFERES WITH PROVIDENCE (1866)


A ship-caulkers' strike was in progress in New York
City and signs pointed to an employers' victory.  The
country's leading commercial magazine drew a moral.


The power to conquer is unquestionably in the hands of the
employers; and the result of the well planned and desperately
supported strike of the calkers is an evidence that if the employers are united they have the power of enforcing their own settlement.

The calkers must have already suffered to an extent calculated
to cool their ardor for strikes.  For several weeks they have been
absolutely idle, their principal reliance being a weekly pittance
from the funds of their association, and such charity as other organizations chose to bestow upon them.  In hundreds of cases the
father has eaten the bread earned by the sweat of his wife and
children, driven to some form of cheap labor, and to compete with
some branch of that common organization of labor which it was
supposed the strike was calculated to support.  In the mean time,
the place vacated by the idle striker was being filled.  The ship-
builders were putting raw hands upon their vessels and training them
to efficiency; so that the calkers, on returning to work, find they
have created a large addition to their trade, who will be future
competitors for employment, tending to depress wages even below
the rates at which they refused to work.  Thus will strikes ever
result in the ultimate injury of those who engage in them.  They may

meet, and have met, with apparent success for a time, but being
against reason, and opposed to that community of interest which
Providence has instituted between the workman and the employer,
they must in the end bring the sure penalty that attends every
infraction of natural law.  They are a suspension of that process
which connects existence and enjoyment with the sources of susten-
tation; and consequently they result in injury to the most vital
interests of society.

Hunt's Merchants' Magazine, July, 1866, pp. 64-65.


### 408.  A FREE LABOR CONTRACT (1867)

A South Carolina planter contracts with five
former slaves, two adults and three minors.  (Dink
and Barnet were the adults; Dal, Wade, and John the
minors).  The agreement was made by planter, D. T.
Crosby.

State of South Carolina
Fairfield District

Article of agreement between D. T. Crosby and the following
freedmen whose names are hereunto attached.

1st The Said freedmen agree to hire their time as labouring
on the plantation of D. T. Crosby from Jan 1-1867 to Jan 1-1868 to
conduct themselves faithfully, honestly, civilly and diligently,
to perform all labor on Said plantation, or such as may be connected therewith that may be required by the Said D. T. Crosby nor to
leave the premises during working hours, without the consent of
the proprietor.  The Said freedmen agree to perform the daily tasks
hitherto usually allotted on Said plantation.  In all cases where
tasks can not be assigned they agree to labor diligently ten hours
a day.

For every days of labor lost by absence, refusal or neglect
to perform the daily task or labor Said servants shall forfeit fifty cents (50cts)  If absent voluntarily or without leave, two
dollars a day.  if absent more than one day without leave to be
subject to dismissal from the plantation and forfeiture of Share
in the crop or wages as the case may be.

Said freedmen agree to take good care of all utensils tools
or implements committed to their charge and to pay for the same if
injured or destroyed also, to be kind and gentle to all work animals under their charge and to pay for any injury which they may
sustain while in their hands through their careless ness or neglect.

They agree to be directed in their labor by the foreman,
to obey his orders, and that he shall report all absences, neglect
refusal to work or disorderly conduct to the employer.  Said
employer agrees to treat his employees with justice and kindness,
and to divide the crop with them in the following proportions, vis.
Dink and three boys gets a portion of the crop one-third of the
corn peas and potatoes gathered and prepared for market, and one-
third nett proceeds of the ginned cotton or its market value, and
Dink agrees to pay Barnet fifty five dollars in currency and a
pair of shoes at the end of the year  Dink also agrees to furnish,
Barnet, with one peck of meal 2 1/2 lbs of meat a week during the
year....
     And I further agree to give Dink (one fifth) of the wheat crop
harvested by them.
     Said employer agrees to furnish animals, and to feed them,
also waggons carts, plantation implements such as cannot be made by
the laborers on...the plantation.  All violations of the terms of
this contract, or of the rules and regulations of the employer,
may be punished by dismissal from the plantation with forfeiture of
his or her share of the crop or wages, as the case may be.
     The employer or his agent shall keep a book, in which shall be
entered all advances made by him, and fines and forfeitures for
lost time, or any cause, which book shall be received as evidence
in same manner as merchants books are now received in Courts of
Justice, and shall have a right to deduct from the share of each
laborer all his or her fines and forfeitures also all advances
made by him.
     The laborer shall not sell any agricultural products to any
person whatever without the consent of the employer until after the
divission of the crops.
     The laborer shall commence work at sunrise and be allowed from
one to two hours each day for their meals, according to season of
the year.
     Witness our hands &c this
     14 April 1867


     Agreement, D. T. Crosby, planter, with five freedmen; Jessie
M. Fraser (ed.), "A Free Labor Contract, 1867," Journal of Southern
History, VI (1940), pp. 547-548.


          409.  "THE EVILS OF PIECE-WORK" (ca. 1868)


     A union leader, William Sylvis, examines a growing
practice and suggests it will work against the solidarity
which underlies unionism.  Sylvis was a far-sighted labor
leader, president of the Iron Molders Union and the National
Labor Union.

The evils of piece-work begin to assume an alarming shape, and must become fearful in their magnitude, if the present condition of trade be an index to that of the future.  If so seriously felt at the very commencement of the dawning depressions, what mischief will it not work ere we witness a revival of trade, or behold our social equilibrium restored after the disbanding of the army? We admire industry, we commend prudence and economy, and love to see a man provide for his own household, so long as his efforts are marked by a due consideration for the welfare of others; but we do object to the overstraining of these virtues, until honest ambition is transformed into the basest kind of selfishness.

When work is plenty and workmen few, there may be some pretext for working to the utmost tension of a man's physical endurance, whether suggested by sordid motives or a desire to oblige the employer.  Under such circumstances, none are injured but those who violate the laws of nature; but when the reverse is the case--the many idle and the few employed--we hold it to be ungenerous, if not inhuman, for half a dozen men to transcend their physical abilities by working late and early, to monopolize all the work in the shop, when that labor divided would give as many more employment, and furnish food for their destitute families.  Such a course can result in but temporary advantage to those who pursue it, because they know not how soon "the tables may turn."  If they were guaranteed life-long employment in the same shop, they might escape the consequences of their folly; but no employer will do this.  Promising as their prospects may be, a mistake, a neglect, a hasty word, or a capricious whim of the employer, at any moment, may send them adrift on the sea of uncertainty, where they will meet those to whom they denied a helping hand.  In turn, the outs may get in, and how hard it will be for them to encounter the very selfishness of their own creation.  The maxim, "Get all you can, and keep all you get," is one against which journeymen mechanics have never ceased to declaim; but it seems that piece-workers have learned to overcome their scruples, and are carrying it out to the most selfish extreme.  Surely, were they to reflect upon the danger, and consider the evil tendency of this flagrant abuse of piece-work, they would speedily abandon it.  For what do we combine, but to establish rules and regulations for the observance of a uniform system, which was designed for the good of all.  The aim of our unions is to secure equal advantages to every member; and, to retain the power of self-protection, we must be a unit in heart and purpose, tolerating no innovation which secures a benefit to one at the expense of another.  Least of all should we suffer avarice or selfishness to wean us from an association of interest, to band in half-dozen squads or more, for the purpose of robbing our companions in toil of their share of work.  When employers find us conflicting, and set the example of "every man for himself," can we blame them for dosing us with our own medicine?  In short, piece-work must eventually lead to the monopoly of labor by a few to the detriment of the many.  This will produce heart-burning, and arouse a spirit of retaliation, which will induce men to work for what they can get. It will destroy confidence, render our unions weak and impotent

by contention, and leave us at the mercy of employers. We need not
name the advantages which an abandonment of the practice would secure to us.  It is enough to say that, by abridging the hours of
labor when work is scarce, and sharing it with our needy brethren,
we take the initiatory step towards legalizing, by precedent, the
eight-hour system.  We strengthen the bonds of union and friendship
by acknowledging our mutual dependence.  We establish harmony in our
unions, and invest them with a strength and power which render them
doubly strong for our defence.  We win the esteem of workingmen of
all trades and give them hope by the force of example.  We convince
employers that "we know our rights, and knowing, dare maintain
them."  We might add, that the magnanimity of sharing employment and
sustenance with our associates, in times of great depression, must
exalt the workingmen of America to the highest standard of refine-
ment and humanity.  Reader, gaze on both sides of the picture--see
what we must eventually lose by piece-work, and look at what we will
surely gain by its abandonment.


    William H. Sylvis, in James C. Sylvis (ed.), The Life,
Speeches, Labors and Essays of William H. Sylvis, (Philadelphia,
Pennsylvania:  Claxton, Remsen and Haffelfinger, 1872), pp. 434-436.


    410.  FREE LABOR WILL BE CHEAPER THAN SLAVE LABOR (1868)


        The conversion of slave into free, wage labor is
    seen as the guarantee that capitalist industry, especially
    an iron industry, will prosper in the South.


    The labor system of the South under its new conditions, in-
deed, promises to become a source of progress which in a few years
will compensate the South for all the material disasters of the War.
Negro labor is already proving to be cheaper under freedom than it
was under slavery; and this fact foreshadows an early development of
industries in that section which hitherto have barely existed.  The
peculiar physical qualifications of the negro for labor in hot climates, together with his limited wants as compared with the white
laborer, enable him to render a given amount of work for a lower
compensation than will be accepted by the white workman; nor does
there appear to be any good reason for supposing that the competition
for colored labor will early modify its cheapness.
    It is easy to see how this fact is likely to conduce to the
development of those industries which require muscle rather than
skill in the laborer.  There is, for instance, a broad basis for a
profitable iron trade, which is already in course of successful
development.  Iron ore of excellent quality exists in the South
in abundance, and is easily obtainable on prominent thoroughfares;

while the requisites to its manufacture are available at a very low
cost.  Charcoal can be produced there at 5 cents per bushel, while
Northern manufacturers are at an expense of about 15 cents for the
same material.  Negro labor for mining and reducing the ore can be
procured at the rate of 75 cents per day, or about one third the
wages paid in the North.  Considering that charcoal and labor are
the main elements of the cost of producing iorn, it is evident that
there is here an ample basis for successful competition with the
iron trade of other sections.  Nor has the South been slow to discover the strength of its position in this respect, for even now
they have a number of furnaces in full blast producing profitably
a superior quality of iron, which is readily sold in our markets.
Their coal deposits also afford similar inducements to that branch
of mining.  The large forests afford a foundation for the production
of lumber at a cost much below that produced by white labor at the
North.  So long as the negro population were under the absolute control of a class devoted almost wholly to planting and disinclined
to manufacturing, colored labor was practically unavailable for
developing the resources of the mine and the forest; now, however,
the negro is free to use his labor wherever it may be most wanted;
and there can be little doubt that capitalists will be found ready
to employ it largely in the development of these hitherto neglected
resources.

. . . . . . . . . . . . . . . . . . . . . . . . . . . . . . . . . . .
    It may, we think, be regarded as a fact already demonstrated
by experience that free labor will be cheaper to the planter than
that of the slave.  The negroes, as a rule, even now work with
much regularity, and as the country becomes more settled politically, and the reward of industry will, without doubt, stimulate
them to render an amount of effort greatly in excess of all former
experience.

Hunt's Merchants' Magazine, October, 1868, pp. 290-291,


411.  THE BLACK AND LABOR (1869)


    Emancipation threw hundreds of thousands of newly-
freed black workers onto the labor market.  Almost alone,
the National Labor Union welcomed local unions composed of
freedmen.  At the 1869 national convention of the N.L.U.,
black delegate Isaac Myers arose to remark on the significance of the N.L.U. action.  Myers, a member of the
Colored Caulkers' Trade Union Society of Baltimore, was
one of the five black delegates to the N.L.U. convention,
and was later elected president of the National Colored
Labor Union, affiliated with N.L.U.

GENTLEMEN:  It would be an act of great injustice to your Godlike charity should I allow the deliberations of this Convention to close without returning you the thanks of four millions of our race for your unanimous recognition of their right to representation in this Convention....Gentlemen, silent but powerful and far-reaching is the revolution inaugurated by your act in taking the colored laborer by the hand and telling him that his interest is common with yours, and that he should have an equal chance in the race for life.  These declarations of yours are ominous, and will not only be felt throughout the length and breadth of this great Republic, but will become another great problem in American politics for the kings and dynasties of Europe to solve.  It is America, and it is only Americans that can work up and work out such great revolutions in a day.  God grant that it may be as lasting as the eternal hills.  I speak today for the colored men of the whole country...when I tell you that all they ask for themselves is a fair chance; that you shall be no worse off by giving them that chance; that you and they will dwell in peace and harmony together; that you and they may make one steady and strong pull until the laboring man of this country shall receive such pay for time made as will secure them a comfortable living for their families, educate their children and leave a dollar for a rainy day and old age. Slavery, or slave labor, the main cause of the degredation of white labor, is no more.  And it is the proud boast of my life that the slave himself had a large share in the work of striking off the fetters that bound him by the ankle, while the other end bound you by the neck.

The white laboring men of the country have nothing to fear from the colored laboring man.  We desire to see labor elevated and made respectable; we desire to have the highest rate of wages that our labor is worth; we desire to have the hours of labor regulated, as well to the interest of the laborer as the capitalist.  And you, gentlemen, may rely on the support of the colored laborers of this country in bringing about this result.  If they have not strictly observed these principles in the past, it was because the doors of the workshops of the North, East and West were firmly bolted against them, and it was written over the doors:  'No negro admitted here.' Thus barred out, thus warned off, his only hope was to put his labor in the market, to be controlled by selfish and unscrupulous speculators, who will dare to do any deed to advance their own ends.

...American citizenship with the black man is a complete failure, if he is proscribed from the workshops of this country--if any man cannot employ him who chooses, and if he cannot work for any man whom he will.  If citizenship means anything at all, it means the freedom of labor, as broad and as universal as the freedom of the ballot.  I cannot tell how far your action in admitting colored delegates on this floor is going to influence the minor organizations throughout the country....The question being today asked by the colored men of the country is only to be answered by the white men of the country.  We mean in all sincerity a hearty co-operation.

You cannot doubt us. Where we have had the chance, we have always
demonstrated it. We carry no prejudices. We are willing to forget
the wrongs of yesterday and let the dead past bury its dead.


Clipping found in the Ely Clippings in the John Crerar
Library, Chicago; the original apparently was taken from the
Workingmen's Advocate.


412. STRIKES AND SUSPENSIONS IN ANTHRACITE (1871)


"There is too much coal going to market"--the eternal
complaint of the industry. Suspensions were facilitated by
the close control of the anthracite industry by a few firms.
Benjamin James , a Welsh miner who now lived in St. Clair,
Pennsylvania, writes this description.


The miners here in the anthracite fields of Pennsylvania
have been idle for about six weeks. Everything throughout these
five counties--that is Schuylkill, Cumberland, Northumberland,
Carbon, and Luzerne--is at a standstill at present. All the miners
in the above counties have been on suspension from the time mentioned and hundreds of them had been idle for a long time before
that. Many of the works have been idle since before Christmas and
with little hope of them restarting. Many of the works have not
been open for more than four months in the past year and, when
working, the miners have not earned wages corresponding to the high
prices of everything in this country. Hundreds of families are as
poor here as ever they were in the Old Country.
. . . . . . . . . . . . . . . . . . . . . . . . . . . . . .
    We are all on suspension at the moment and not on strike. The
name suspension is more "genteel" than strike; suspension does not
create bad feeling between masters and workmen because on both sides
they are suspending work until the coal on the market has been
bought up by the merchants. The trust is that there is too much
coal going to the market to meet the demand. As a result the price
of coal falls until the coal operator is unable to pay the basis of
the regular wages for the miners. So he prefers to stop working
rather than pay money out of his pocket, and on the other side,
the miner prefers to be idle in the house rather than working underground in the gas, sulphur, and coal dust for next to nothing. So
it develops into a general suspension on both sides. Before a
family can pay off the debts from the previous strike there is a
suspension again. So it is to a similar degree with the iron-
workers who are at a standstill because they need coal. The owners
of the ironworks want the coal for six dollars a ton and the coal

operatives refuse to sell it under seven and a half dollars.  So
the furnaces are blown out, the forges stop, trade becomes stagnant,
and the workmen suffer.


        Letter, Benjamin James, February 8, 1871; Alan Conway (ed.),
The Welsh in America.  Letters from the Immigrants, (Minneapolis,
Minnesota:  University of Minnesota Press, 1961), pp. 189-190.



        413.  FORCE AND FREE LABOR IN GEORGIA (1871)


        Here is testimony on some economic aspects of mob
violence.  Alfred Richardson, an ex-slave and a carpenter
who had served in the Georgia legislature, testifies.  He
had been attacked twice, once by the Ku Klux Klan, and
once by an anonymous group.


Do these bands make the negroes work for whomever they please?
Answer.  Do you mean the Ku Klux?
Question.  Yes, sir.
Answer.  Well, they go sometimes so far as this:  When a man
is hired, if he and his employer have any dispute about the price,
and there are hard words between them about the amount of money to
be paid, they whip the colored men for disputing the white man's
word, or having any words with him.
        Question.  They whip the colored man for having any dispute
with his employer about what shall be paid him?
        Answer.  Yes, sir.
        Question.  Is that common?
        Answer.  Yes, sir; that has been done several times.  Sometimes
colored people are working for a part of the crop.  They work on till
the crop is nearly completed and ready for gathering.  Then a fuss
arises between them and the employer, and they are whipped off by
these men in disguise.  If they do not whip a man, they come and
knock his door down and run him out, and he gets scared and moves
away, leaving his share of the crop.  He will sometimes go to the
employer, and the man will say, "Your crop in the field is worth
such and such a price, and that is all I will give you."  The man
will have to take what he can get and move off.  Some of the colored
people swear that they do not intend to farm any more, excepting
they can have peace to gather what they plant.  Now, they work a
part of the year and then get run off and make nothing.  So they
conclude it is best to go to some city and work by the day for what
they can get.  Every town in our State where there is any protection
is overrun with colored people.  Many of the farm lands are there;
and there is a great mass of loafers who stand round town because
they have got no work to do.  Yet people's fields around in the

country are running away with grass.  Some men go to town and try
to get hands.  The colored men will ask, "In what part of the
country do you live?"  The man will mention such and such a place.
They will say, "We can't go down there; the Ku Klux is down there.
If it wasn't for the Ku Klux we would go down and work for you."


Testimony, Alfred Richardson, July 7, 1871; U.S. Congress,
Joint Select Committee to Inquire into the Condition of Affairs in
the Late Insurrectionary States, Testimony VI, (Washington, D.C.:
Government Printing Office, 1872), pp. 12-13.


### 414.  A MACHINIST'S TRADE MARKS (1874)


A graphic reminder of the great importance of
skilled hand-labor in American industry during the
1870's, written by Jacob Cox.


At some time during my apprenticeship in the machine shop of
the Cleveland Iron Company, I received what the men at the time
called my "trade mark."  I was grinding a planer tool on a badly
worn out and cracked grindstone.  The point of the tool caught in
the crack of the grindstone and carried my left hand down into the
frame of the machine, pinching off the ends of two of my fingers.
This made it impossible for me to work for some time and those
days of idleness I spent at Oberlin.
....I have still another "trade mark" evidence of my apprenticeship as a vise hand.  Before I had become skillful with the
hand hammer and chisel, I quite frequently used to miss the top
of the chisel, the hammer hitting the thumb of my left hand.  This
was repeated at such frequent intervals that it produced a permanent red spot on my thumb.


Cox, Building an American Industry, © The Cleveland Twist
Drill Company , p. 72.


### 415.  INSIDE CONTRACTING IN CLEVELAND (1874)


The system of inside contracting was a transition
from skilled craft shop to full-scale factory.  Under it,
a skilled mechanic hired helpers or journeymen and was
responsible for their wages and working conditions.  In
turn, the mechanic contracted with the factory management
an agreement covering price.  (For the later development of
this system in Philadelphia, see below, Source No. 623.)

When I went to work for McCusker in December 1874, I ceased
to be an employee of the company, as the puddler's helpers were
responsible to no one but the puddler.  The same was true of the
mill gang.  They were hired and they were paid by the roller, and
in this way their names did not appear on the mill payroll.

Cox, Building an American Industry, © The Cleveland Twist
Drill Company , p. 77.


416.  "FREE LABOR IS AN UNDOUBTED SUCCESS IN THE SOUTH" (1875)


After the Civil War and the end of slave labor,
planters tried wage labor, tenancy, and share-cropping.
The last-named form of labor system proved most durable.
It required little cash outlay and was largely self-
financed as the planter was able to recoup on many
expenses by charging excessive prices on supplies and
food advanced to the sharecropper.  The plantation
regimen precluded independent political action by blacks
and insecurity of person was extreme throughout the
newer cotton areas more in search of livelihood than
a haven.  Charles Nordhoff, a former seaman and short-
story writer, had been managing editor of the New York
Evening Post and was now Washington correspondent for
the New York Herald.  His positive evaluation of share-
cropping was at odds with much daily reality.


The negro, in the main, is industrious.  Free labor is an
undoubted success in the South.  In Georgia he owns already nearly
four hundred thousand acres of farming real estate, besides city
property.  The negro works; he raises cotton and corn, sugar and
rice, and it is infinitely to his credit that he continues to do
so, and, according to the universal testimony, works more stead-
fastly and effectively this year than ever before since 1865, in
spite of the political hurly-burly in which he has lived for the
last ten years.
    For ought we of the North to forget that a part of the credit
of the negroes' industry to-day is due to the Southern planters,
who have been wise enough to adapt themselves to the tremendous
change in their labor system, and honest enough not to discourage
the ignorant free laborer by wronging him of his earnings or by
driving unjust bargains with him.
    The system of planting on shares, which prevails in most of
the cotton region I have seen, appears to me admirable in every
respect.  It tends to make the laborer independent and self-helpful,
by throwing him on his own resources.  He gets the reward of his own
skill and industry, and has the greatest motive to impel him to
steadfast labor and to self-denial.

I have satisfied myself, too, that the black man gets,
wherever I have been a fair share of the crop he makes.  If anywhere
he suffers wrong, it is at the hands of poor farmers, who cultivate
a thin soil, and are themselves poor and generally ignorant.  It is
a curious evidence of the real security of the negro, even in the
rudest parts of the South, that some thousands of them have emigrated from Alabama and Georgia into the Yazoo Bottom in
Mississippi, and into the cotton regions of Arkansas and Louisiana--
parts of the South where, if we might believe the general reports
which have been spread through the North, no negro's rights and
life are safe.

    C. Nordhoff, The Cotton States in the Spring of 1875,
(New York:  Appleton-Century-Crofts, 1876), pp. 20-21.


    417.  "THE AMERICAN STYLE OF WORKING" (1875)


    The swift pace of shop work in this country had
often been remarked, but the observer had seldom linked
it to style of working.  The author here, Frank Roney,
was an Irish immigrant iron molder who became active in
the American labor movement.


The Pacific Iron Works job lasted only a few months.  I then
went to the Union Iron Works and secured a job, although I had
been advised of the tyranous reputation of Mr. Dimmick, the foreman.
I was a total stranger in the shop, which gave me a splendid opportunity to observe and study the men.  The American style of working,
which I had noticed in New York, St. Louis, and Chicago, consisted
of competing to secure the favor of the foreman and through that
means retain steady employment.  It was carried to the limit in the
Union Iron Works.  No foreman was needed to urge these men to work
to the point of exhaustion.  They labored hard of their own voli-
tion and displayed an eagerness most discouraging to one who wished
to see each of them occupy the niche of a man.
    It looked as if my stay would be brief in such a place working
among men so utterly selfish and slavish.  I did not and would not
descend to their level if I never worked at moulding.  When business
did slacken somewhat I was surprised at my good fortune in being
retained when many of the other workers were allowed to go.  I
never hurried and always suppressed any disposition that I might
have had to take work away from others.  Strangely enough I seeming-
ly prospered although others, exhibiting the traits mentioned,
were set aside.


    Frank Roney, Irish Rebel and California Labor Leader.  An
Autobiography, ed. by Ira B. Cross, (Berkeley, California:
University of California Press, 1931), pp. 262-263.

418.  AGAINST AN ARISTOCRACY OF LABOR (1881)

At a time when labor unions comprised almost exclusively skilled craftsmen, it was highly unusual for
a labor leader to champion the common interests of all
workingmen.  Roney was now president of the San Francisco
Trades Assembly, a central body of local unions in the
city.

The Riggers and Stevedores Union...action disgusted me.  Its
membership included three employers.  The initiation fee had been
placed at $100.  If the person seeking membership was favorably
regarded the entrance fee could be paid in installments, and if he
were not so regarded it had to be paid in a lump sum.  During rush
period outsiders were employed at the same rates as members, i.e.,
$5 per day for eight hours' work.  If business became slack the out-
siders were laid off and members only were employed.  This organization refused to send delegates to the Trades Assembly or to become a distinctive trade union by ousting the employer-members.
The commerce of San Francisco was increasing at such a rate that
about as many outsiders were as steadily employed as union members,
but only a few members were admitted to the union from time to time.
I finally got the outsiders to organize a union, and they took from
the consignees the contract of loading and unloading the ships at a
cheaper rate than was charged by the bosses in the older organization.  As the men of the new union worked cooperatively their pay
was always much more than that of those of the older organization.
In addition, as the new union sent delegates to the Trades Assembly
they were recognized as the representatives of the only body of
union stevedores on the wharves.  The hoisting engineers employed
along the docks also organized and sent delegates to the Trades
Assembly.  They gave their support to the new stevedores' union
because of the failure of the older union to affiliate with the
Trades Assembly.  A stiff, short fight ensued with the result that
the bosses withdrew from the older union of stevedores, the entrance
fee was reduced, and harmony prevailed.  This also ended the attempt
of the stevedores to establish an aristocracy of Labor.
A certain aloofness or feeling of superiority exists even today
among the members of certain trades, but not so markedly as was
formerly the case.  Mechanics thought themselves superior to the
laborers who helped them and the latter tacitly admitted the superiority.  I personally desired to destroy that sentiment.  It was
difficult of accomplishment because it was in a measure recognized
by both sides.  Talking of the folly of the claim of the mechanics
on the one hand and on the other urging the laborers to assert their
demand of equality and recognition was, I felt, the most direct
method of bringing about a correct understanding.
The injustice of placing men upon a footing of inferiority
because of their poverty was repugnant to my sense of justice and
appeared to me to be destructive of the democracy which should prevail among laborers of every degree.  The laborer was usually the

son of poor parents whose necessities compelled him at an early age
to seek such employment as afforded him a fair living.  The mechanic
was the son of parents in more favorable circumstances who could
afford to board him during the whole period of his apprenticeship
without feeling the pinch.  There were and still are other contri-
buting causes to this disparity, but this I considered the main
one, and it was sufficient for me.  There was another which appealed
to the selfishness of the mechanic more forcibly than the first,
and that was that in case of a strike the young intelligent helper
might in his resentment take the place of the not always too skillful striker.  I wanted every worker, skilled and unskilled, organized into a union of the craft or industry in which he was employed.

Roney, _Irish Rebel and California Labor Leader_, pp. 349-351.


### 419.  PULLMAN:  A COMPANY TOWN (1894)

    The Pullman Strike of 1894 publicized living
conditions inside what was up to then widely regarded
as a model paternalistic community.  The model turned
out to be less than ideal.  This is the testimony of
Thomas Heatcoate, who had been a car builder for 30
years, the last five at Pullman; he was president of
Local No. 208 of the American Railway Union.  Miss Curtis,
who also testifies, was a seamstress in the repair shop
sewing room and served as president of the girls' union,
Local No. 209.


    (Commissioner WORTHINGTON).  Do I understand you to say that
all the operatives who live in Pullman and are housekeepers live
in houses owned by the Pullman company?--Ans.  Whenever a man is
employed in the Pullman shops he is supposed to live in a Pullman
house until the Pullman houses are filled; that has been the case
previous to this strike; when a man came to the shops he must live
in a Pullman house.  He could not live in Roseland unless he owned
his own property; he must live in Pullman.  I have known men who
owned property in Roseland who had to leave their property not
rented and come down to Pullman and hire houses in order to fill
up the Pullman houses.
    (Commissioner KERNAN).  How was that rule made and enforced?--
Ans. Suppose you made application to a foreman for a job; if the
houses in Pullman were not filled he would give you a job, provided
you moved into Pullman; that was made a condition of the job.  I
have seen men that lived out of Pullman get jobs when men were out
of employment in Pullman, but that was through the favoritism of
the foremen.

(Commissioner WORTHINGTON).  Do you mean to say that a man
having a job in Pullman and who was living in one of the Pullman
houses, if he saw fit to move to Roseland and rent there, that
would be sufficient cause for losing his job?--Ans.  Yes, sir.
. . . . . . . . . . . . . . . . . . . . . . . . . . . . . . . . .
(Commissioner WRIGHT).  State briefly what you did as a member
serving upon those committees.--Ans.  I was on a committee that
went from Pullman to speak for the girls in May before the strike,
to ask for more wages.
(Commissioner WRIGHT).  Whom did you see?--Ans.  We saw Mr.
Wickes the first time, and the second time we saw Mr. Brown, Mr.
Perant, and Mr. Wickes, and all the head managers of the company
were there; also Mr. Pullman.
·(Commissioner WRIGHT).  State what took place at the first
interview.--Ans.  We went there and asked, as the men did, for
more wages; we were cut lower than any of the men's departments
throughout the works; in 1893 we were able to make 22 cents per
hour, or $2.25 per day, in my department, and on the day of the
strike we could only earn, on an average, working as hard as we
possibly could, from 70 to 80 cents a day.
(Commissioner KERNAN).  Can you give us how the wages changed
from month to month?--Ans.  Whenever the men were cut in their wages
the girls also received a cut.  We were cut twice inside of a week
in November, 1893, and in January our wages were cut again; that
was the last cut we received, and we worked as hard as we possibly
could and doing all we could, too.  The most experienced of us
could only make 80 cents per day, and a great many of the girls
could only average 40 to 50 cents per day.
...(Commissioner WRIGHT).  Do you pay rent in Pullman?--Ans.
No, sir; not now.
(Commissioner WRIGHT).  You pay board?--Ans.  Yes, sir.  My
father worked for the Pullman company for thirteen years.  He died
last September, and I paid the rent to the Pullman company up to
the time he died; I was boarding at the time of my father's death.
He being laid off and sick for three months, owed the Pullman
company $60 at the time of his death for back rent, and the company
made me, out of my small earnings, pay that rent due from my father.
(Commissioner KERNAN).  How did they make you do it?--Ans.
The contract was that I should pay $3 on the back rent every pay
day, and when I did not do so I was insulted and almost put out of
the bank by the clerk for not being able to pay it to them.  My
wages were cut so low that I could not pay my board and given them
$3 on the back rent, but if I had $2 or so over my board I would
leave it at the bank on the rent.  On the day of the strike I
still owed them $15, which I am afraid they never will give me
a chance to pay back.


Testimony, Thomas W. Heathcoate and Jennie Curtis; U.S.
Congress, 53rd, 34th session, Senate, Exec. Doc. No. 7, Report
on the Chicago Strike of June-July, 1894, by the United States
Strike Commission, serial number 3276, (Washington, D.C.:  Government Printing Office, 1895), pp. 425 and 434.

420.  BLACKLIST ON THE ILLINOIS CENTRAL (1894)


The bitter Pullman strike destroyed the American
Railway Union.  Supporters of the strike and union were
penalized by having their names placed on a blacklist.
A number found jobs elsewhere, under assumed names.

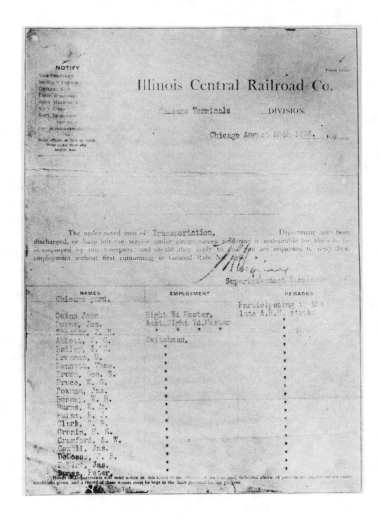

Taken from photoreproduction in Report of the Industrial
Commission on Transportation, IV, (Washington, D.C.:  Government
Printing Office, 1900), facing page 513.

421.    ALTGELD ON THE DEBS INJUNCTION (1895)


Eugene Debs, leader of the American Railway
Union in the Pullman Strike, was silenced by a sweeping injunction.  The Supreme Court, steadfast champion
of propertied interests in the 1890's, gave judicial
approval to what Altgeld here named "government by
injunction."  This interview is with John Peter Altgeld,
progressive governor of Illinois, who had braved the
storms of the vested interests when in 1893 he freed the
Haymarket anarchists.  Within the Democratic party,
Altgeld led the wing that favored cooperation with
populists and labor.


Remanding Debs to jail is in itself a matter of small consequence, but the principle established is of transcendent importance.
This decision marks a turning point in our history.  For it estab-
lishes a new form of government, never before heard of among men,
that is, government by injunction.  Under this procedure a federal
judge sitting in the rear room can, on motion of some corporation
lawyer, issue a ukase, which he calls an injunction, forbidding
anything he chooses to.  Where the law forbids a thing, no injunction is necessary.  In other words, he can legislate for himself,
and having done so he can then turn around and imprison as many
people as he pleases; not for violating any law, but on the mere
pretense that they had disregarded his injunction, and mark you,
they are not tried by a jury according to the forms of law, but
the same judge who issues the ukase, and who claims that his dignity was offended, himself tries the case, and whether anything is
proven or nothing is proven he can send the man to prison at pleasure, and there is no remedy.
The provision of the constitution 'that no man shall be deprived of his liberty without a trial by an impartial jury' is
practically wiped out by this decision of the United States supreme
court.  And the theory that ours was an exclusive government of
law is now at an end.  For every community is now subject to obey
any whim or caprice which any federal judge may promulgate.  And
if any federal judge can do this then it will not be long until
state judges will follow this example.  The constitution declares
that our government has three departments and that no one shall
trench on the other.  But under this new order of things a federal
judge becomes at once legislator, court, and executioner.
For over a century our government moved along the lines of
the constitution, and we became great and powerful.  Life and
property were protected and the laws enforced.  Now we have made a
departure; the bulwark of liberty has been undermined; trial by
jury has been stricken down.  You know there were two separate
proceedings against Debs.  One was according to the established
forms of law; he was indicted by a grand jury for acts alleged to
have been done during the strike, and he was regularly tried by a
jury, and it turned out that there was absolutely no case against
him.

Nothing was proven.  It is true the jury were not allowed to bring in a verdict because near the end of the trial one of the jurors became ill and the prosecution refused to go on.  Debs' attorney offered to proceed with the remaining eleven, or to add a new man and proceed, but the railroad lawyer who also represented the government, seeing that he had no case at all, would not consent, and he thereby prevented a verdict of acquittal and had the case postponed.  The other proceeding was by injunction.  A federal judge on motion of some railroad attorney issued a ukase against the people of all the states in that judicial circuit, in which he forbade nearly everything that the ingenuity of man could think of, and which, the law did not forbid, and having thus legislated he turned around and had Debs and others arrested not for violating any law, but for failing to respect his ukase and injunction.

And the the judge not only refused to give a jury trial, but he himself proceeded to determine whether his own dignity had been offended, and he promptly sent the prisoner to the prison, the judge being legislator, court, and executioner.  Had there been a jury trial the defendents would have been discharged, because it was not proven that they had violated any law.  This would have been in harmony with the constitution, with the law of the land, and with eternal justice.  But the corporations wanted a constitution brushed aside, and the United States supreme court has now approved his acts.

For a number of years it has been remarked that the decisions of the United States supreme court were nearly always in favor of corporations.  Then it was noticed that no man could be appointed to a federal judgeship unless he was satisfactory to those interests.  Over a year ago the New York World talked about a packed supreme court, and that court has within a few days rendered two decisions that unfortunately tend to confirm this charge.  A week ago it did violence to the constitution and laws of this country.  Now it has stricken down trial by jury and has established 'government by injunction.'

George William Curtis described the slave power of forty years ago as follows:  'Slavery sat in the white house and made law in the capitol; courts of justice were its ministers and legislators were its lackeys.  It silenced the preacher in the pulpit; it muzzled the editor at his desk, and the professor in his lecture-room. It set a price upon the head of peaceful citizens; it robbed the mails and denounced the vital principles of independence as treason. Even states whose laws did not tolerate slavery ruled the club and drawing-room, the factory and office.  It swaggered at the dinner table, and scourged with scorn a cowardly society.  It tore the golden rule from school books, and the pictured benignity of Christ the prayer book.'  Now substitute the word 'capitalism' for the word 'slavery' and the above is an exact picture of our condition today.

The American people crushed the slave power; they washed the stain from off our flag and saved our institutions.  Can they rescue them again?  Many say yes, but they have not reflected that the crushing force which now confronts them is greater than was ever the slave power.  Besides, slavery itself was sectional.

And in the end it was possible to unite the rest of the country
against it.  But the corrupt money power has its withering finger
on every pulse in the land, and is destroying the rugged manhood
and love of liberty which alone can carry a people through a
great crisis.

What then is the situation today?  For over twenty years foreign and domestic capitalism had dominated.  'It sits in the white
house and legislates in the capitol; courts of justice are its
ministers and legislators are its lackeys.  And the whole machinery
of fashionable society is its handmaid.'  Just see what a brood of
evil has sprung from the power of capitalism since 1870.  First,
the striking down of over one-third or more of the world, thus
crushing the better class and paralyzing the industries.  Second,
the growth of that corrupt use of wealth, which is undermining our
institutions, debauching public officials, shaping legislation and
creating judges who do its bidding.  Third, exempting the rich from
taxation.  Fourth, the substitution of government by injunction
for government by the constitutional laws.  Fifth, the striking
down of trial by jury.  Never was there so much patriotic talk in
the last twenty-five years, and never were there so many influences
at work strangling the republican institutions.


Text of June 2, 1895 interview with Governor Altgeld,
Chicago Chronicle, June 8, 1895, in Ely Clippings.



422.  FACTORY WELFARE AND THE EFFICIENCY MOTIVE (1898)


The pace and discipline required in a mechanized
factory were far from the informal and homey atmosphere
of the small craft shop.  Ironically, providing some
of "the comforts of home" in the factory resulted in
acclimating workers to factory requirements.  Jacob
Cox writes.


When we commenced the west wing of the factory (No. 4 Bldg.)
in 1898, we decided to furnish it with the most modern and best
sanitary appliances.  We put in ample facilities for washing,
supplying the wash basins with soap and towels.  On the completion
of the building, we opened a restaurant in the top story so that
every noon the men could have hot dinners.  We felt that too many
of the men were going off at noon to the corner saloons for beer
and sandwiches and that better work would be done by them if they
could have a hot lunch with coffee.  We also equipped the factory
with openwork iron lockers so that each man could have a place
for his clothes and lunch basket.

When we served our first lunch on November 29, 1899, it took
us forty-five minutes to serve the tables after the men sat down.
It looked as though we had undertaken something which would be
very difficult to accomplish.  However, by a little planning we
succeeded after a short time in serving the tables promptly.  We
arranged the workmen in groups, assigning nine men to each table,
but placing only eight seats to a table; the odd man, who was
elected by each group, was allowed to leave his work fifteen minutes
before noon.  These men, one from each table, immediately assembled
in the dining room and served the soup, bread and butter and coffee
to the tables.  This consumed about all of the fifteen minutes
allowed them, and they were ready upon the seating of the workmen
to distribute the meat, vegetables and dessert.  This arrangement
worked so satisfactorily that by the end of twenty minutes the
workmen were ready to leave the tables.

In order to keep the men in the factory and to encourage their
desire for reading, we established a reading room in which we placed
all of the popular illustrated magazines, many scientific and trade
papers, besides two copies each of the morning papers.  We also
decorated the walls of the reading room with maps of the world
showing the telegraph, railroad and steamship routes.


Cox, Building an American Industry, © The Cleveland
Twist Drill Company , pp. 166-167.


### 423.  SOUTHERN WHITE AND BLACK RAILWAY LABOR (1899)


Systematic discrimination against black workers
was characteristic.  The discrimination was most serious
with regard to unequal pay for equal work and in closing
off promotions to higher-paying jobs.  Black workers
were thus left in the lowest-paid, most unpleasant jobs.
Samuel Spencer, who was a railroad specialist and partner
in Drexel, Morgan and Company for nine years, and had
headed the Morgan-created Southern Railway since its
founding in 1894, testifies in this extract.


Q.  Are there colored firemen on your system?--A.  Yes,
a great many.

Q.  Is there any trouble between the white labor and colored
labor on that account?  Do the white firemen object to the employment of colored firemen?--A.  They may have some objections.  These
objections do not take any serious form; but the question is sometimes discussed, though there has never been any organized or
real opposition to it.

Q.  No objection of the firemen against the employment of
colored labor in that capacity?--A.  I do not recollect such.  That
thing may have taken place in the general manager's and general
superintendent's offices without my having personal knowledge of it;

not reached a point where action was required. My impression is
that it has not, however.

Q. (By Mr. PHILLIPS.) In what other capacity, if any, are
colored men employed on the system?--A. We employ them on the train
as trainmen, what correspond before the days of air brakes to brakemen.

Q. Are they employed as switchmen?--A. As a rule, not. There
may be some exceptions, but, as a rule, not.

Q. (By Mr. KENNEDY.) The colored fireman can never hope to be
an engineer in your system, can he?--A. Our policy is now not to
make an engineer of him. What the future may develop I do not know,
but we certainly do not now.

Q. (By Mr. RATCHFORD.) Are they promoted as conductors on
your line?--A. No.

Q. Can not rise above the condition of firemen or trainmen?
A. Not in train service.

Q. Is there any discrimination in wages for the same class of
labor, regardless of color?--A. Regardless of color? I am not
sure that I know what you mean by that.

Q. The colored firemen, for instance, and white firemen--do
they receive the same wages?--A. No; but when you said "regardless
of color." I did not know that was what you meant. The colored
fireman is paid less than the white fireman. That would naturally
follow from this circumstance, if not other: There are white firemen always on the road who are candidates for promotion to engineers. These white firemen outrank, so to speak, the colored firemen,
and we keep that line of white firemen moving up all the time, and
they get the higher wages as firemen.

Q. They receive higher wages for their labor and also have the
chance of promotion as against the colored men?--A. Yes.

Q. Is the same true with your trainmen?--A. Yes.

Q. How much difference is there in the wages of firemen and
trainmen?--A. As compared with white, about 10 per cent.


Testimony, Samuel Spencer, Report of the Industrial Commission
on Transportation, IV, (Washington, D.C.: Government Printing
Office, 1900), pp. 266-267.



424.   "MINERS NEVER LOST ANYTHING BY A STRIKE" (1899)


A coal union leader, John Mitchell, president of
the United Mine Workers Union, analyzes realistically
the mechanics of raising wages by strikes.


Q. (By Representative LIVINGSTON.) From your observation and
from statistics you have at your command, have your miners lost as
much by strikes as they would have lost by reduction of wages?--A.
No. I will say the miners never lost anything by a strike. They

never lost anything by being thrown out of employment one month.
It is my opinion, however, that strikes among coat miners, when
they are general in their character, tend to stagnate the business
of the country, increase abormally the cost of coal to the consumer,
and result in extreme hardship to the purchasers of coal, particularly those engaged as wage-earners in other trades.  In the
miners' strike of 1897 they remained on strike 84 days.  The miners
worked as many days in that year as we worked in the preceding
year, a year that had no strikes; and yet the amount of money earned
in 1897 was more than that earned in 1896.  This is accounted for by
the fact that a higher rate of wages was paid after the strike than
prior to it.  The employers suffered heavy losses from the strike
because of the property in repair, etc.  The longest strike that
has ever taken effect in the coal mines--that is, general strike--
was that of 1897, when the miners remained idle for an average of
84 days.  That year they worked more days than they did in the year
preceding, in which there was no strike.  The possible production
or the capacity of the mines of the country is one-third greater,
or 40 per cent greater, than the possible consumption of coal; so it
is impossible for the miner, even under the most favorable circumstances, to work more than two-thirds of the time.  Two-thirds of
the time will produce more coal than is consumed.  Last year, or
1897, the miners worked an average of 185 days.
     Q.  On your theory it is the employer and not the miner who
loses the money by a strike?--A.  Yes, that is true in a general
strike.  In a local strike or sectional strike the miner sometimes
loses money; but to take all the strikes in which the coal miners
have been engaged, the miners have gained increased wages.  When
strikes are only sectional, then the coal is supplied from some
competing district.  Then the miners in that district, those who
have worked, gain money that would have gone to the striking district, and while the miners as a whole, in the aggregate, have lost
nothing, the miners in some particular sections have lost.  In 1897
the miners worked an average of 179 days.  There were employed in
that time 397,701 miners.  They produced in that year 200,221,265
tons.  The capacity of the mines is all of 100,000,000 tons greater
than that.  It would indicate that the capacity of the mines is
about 40 per cent greater than the present output of them, and
that the miners are necessarily thrown out of employment one-third
of the time, or 40 per cent of the time.
. . . . . . . . . . . . . . . . . . . . . . . . . . . . . . . . .
     A general strike is only resorted to when the coal market
becomes so demoralized and chaotic that it is absolutely necessary
to curtail production, so that prices of coal may be restored and
it is possible for employers to pay a higher rate of wages.


     Testimony, John Mitchell, U.S. Industrial Commission, XII,
pp. 36, 37.

# G.

# DEVELOPMENT OF MARKETING

425. "DESTROY THE INDIANS' COMMISSARY" (1875)

In 1875, General Phil Sheridan tried to convince
members of the Texas legislature that buffalo hunters
should be decorated rather than prevented from carrying
out the slaughter.  General Sheridan was commander of the
Southwest military department, with headquarters at
San Antonio.

"These men have done in the last two years, and will do more
in the next year, to settle the vexed Indian question, than the
entire regular army has done in the last thirty years.  They are
destroying the Indians' commissary; and it is a well-known fact
than an army losing its base of supplies is placed at a great disadvantage.  Send them powder and lead, if you will; but, for the
sake of a lasting peace, let them kill, skin, and sell until the
buffaloes are exterminated.  Then your prairies can be covered
with speckled cattle, and the festive cowboy, who follows the
hunter as a second forerunner of an advanced civilization."

General Phil Sheridan, speech to Texas legislature, John R.
Cook, The Border and the Buffalo.  An Untold Story of the Southwest
Plains, (Chicago, Illinois:  The Lakeside Press, 1938), p. 164.

426.   CHANGES IN MERCHANDISING SINCE 1875 (1900)

Large-scale organization first entered the field
of retailing in the form of department stores.  The owner
and his staff became expert buyers, they short-circuited
the jobber, preferring to deal directly with the manufacturer, and they turned to advertising as a means of
stimulating sales.  The testimony here was made by Samuel
Woodward who operated a Washington, D.C. department store
which had annual sales of $2 million.


Q.  What, then, in your opinion, is the reason for the change
that has occurred in the last 25 years in methods of conducting
mercantile business?--A.  First, the fall in prices; and second,
the difficulty of getting any profit at all, have compelled men who
had the ability, means, and capacity to extend their lines; and in
the third place, so many men in business after the panic of 1857
had nothing to do in the early sixties but to go to their places of
business in the morning and mark up the prices of their goods.  When
the great change came in the end of the sixties they did not know
how to do business on a falling market; that is, as we say, they
were not quick sellers enough.  When we think that ordinary cotton
cloths sold for 60 and 70 cents a yard when the war ended--well, I
use cotton cloth as an extreme illustration, but the same was true
in every line of what we call textiles--underwear, outside wear,
and house furnishings in general.  In my experience, on Hanover
street, in those days a good many merchants thought they were worth
a great deal of money, but it was in stock on the shelf, that was
depreciating all the time until prices got down to a level; then
it was too late.
    Q.  You think that stocks of goods are turned over, that is,
converted into cash, more rapidly nowadays than 25 or 30 years
ago?--A.  Immeasurably.
    Q.  That permits the merchant to accept a smaller profit and
still do well, does it not?--A.  Yes, sir.  We would not do business nowadays and carry the stocks that we did 25 or 30 years ago.
    Q.  Is there some credit still given in the business of retail
merchandising?--A.  Yes.
    Q.  How long credits, as a rule?--A.  Baltimore is the only
city that I know of that holds on to the old 6 months' credit
system.  All good merchants that I know of in the North and East
require monthly settlements.
    Q.  That is considered practically cash?--A.  Practically cash,
yes.  They get their money before the 10th of the following month.
It is practically cash, and I am sure that these accounts are not
wanted unless they are paid in that way.


Testimony, Samuel Walter Woodward; United States Industrial
Commission, VII, p. 734.

## 427. THE RISE OF THE TRAVELING SALESMAN (1877)

Another mark of the growth of the national
market was the traveling salesman or "commercial
traveler." Joseph Nimmo Jr., who was Chief of the
Division of Internal Commerce, Bureau of Statistics,
Treasury Department, here reports.

A statement in regard to the competitive forces affecting
commercial movements between different sections of the country
would be incomplete without noticing the results of the system of
employing commercial travelers. This comparatively new agency of
commerce has not only been the means of developing new commercial
movements and of greatly extending the limits of the commerce of
the various cities. Twenty years ago the commercial traveler was
regarded as a sort of privateer upon trade, and this repute undoubtedly caused his operations to be lacking in some of the essential characteristics of legitimate business transactions. But as
the avocation has increased in importance as it has advanced in dignity, and an almost opprobrious appellation at first applied to
those engaging in it, has been exchanged for one more befitting the
occupation. This new agency of commerce is now seen to be a natural
outgrowth of the facilities afforded by railroads and telegraphs.

The soliciting of orders and selling by sample in the hands of
the agents of business houses has become an established method of
intercourse between buyer and seller. The old habits of trade have
been abandoned and the commercial traveler has of necessity become
more closely identified with the interest of the business which he
represents. From the force of competition between those of his own
vocation he has been obliged to acquire a knowledge of the state of
markets in all parts of the country and of other conditions vital
to the interests of trade. Almost every conceivable article of
merchandise is now sold through this agency, and purchases of raw
material are extensively made in the same manner. The economies
of this mode of commercial intercourse are obvious. Buyer and
seller are thus brought closer together, losses through bad credits
are reduced, trade is extended, competition is rendered more
active, collections are more promptly made, interest on capital is
saved, and the expenses of the great body of retail dealers are
reduced.

Every sale made by the commercial traveler tends to promote
the prosperity of the city in which his business house is located,
and to extend the commercial influence of that city. This creates
competition with other commercial cities, and forces transportation-
lines to provide the requisite facilities to meet the new demands
of trade. At the present time there are very few manufacturing
or commercial houses in this country which do not employ one or
more commercial travelers, and it is an indisputable fact that
the energy, tact, and persistency of these men have much to do in
determining the direction of the commercial movements of the day.

Besides, all the railroad companies and freight-lines have in
their employ agents at almost every important commercial point, who
are actively engaged in soliciting freights.  This, also, tends to
multiply and to complicate the elements of competition.


Joseph Nimmo Jr., First Annual Report on the Internal Commerce
of the United States, serial number 1761, (Washington, D.C.:
Government Printing Office, 1877), pp. 66-67, U.S. Congress, 44th,
2nd session, House of Representatives, Exec. Doc. No. 46, part 2.


428.   WHOLESALE GROCERS ENCOURAGE SUGAR MONOPOLY (1888)


Wholesale grocers were cutting sugar prices to
a level where no profit was left.  To create order in
the industry and make room for a profit, the grocers
went to the American Sugar Refining Company, dominated
by the Havemeyers.  G. Waldo Smith was a whole sale grocer
and was president of the Wholesale Grocers Association
of New York City.  He testifies in this extract.


Mr. Nichols, Mr. Seaver, of Boston, Mr. Howard Spur, of
Boston, and others whose names I do not recall, and myself--went to
Mr. Havemeyer and Mr. Searles and asked if some way could not be
invented by which we could get a profit on sugar.  We were closeted
with them discussing the matter for six afternoons, and it was
settled as a result of our talk that they would bill us sugar at
5 3/16 cents and that if we maintained the price at 5 3/16 cents,
say, for 3 months, they, at the end of that time, would give us a
rebate of 18 3/4 cents a hundred.  This was to be uniform to all
buyers, wholesale and retail, manufacturers, and everybody.  It was
simply the terms by which they would sell their sugar.
    Q.  They would sell at the same price to everybody?--A.  Yes,
everyone the same.
    Q.  Regardless of whether or not they were represented by
you?--A.  No; it was no concern to us at all.  It was to cover
New York as far as Poughkeepsie, New England, and New Jersey.
    Q.  How about the grocers who were beyond these limits?--A.
They came in afterwards.  They saw we had a good thing and asked
for the same thing.
    Q.  Will you go further, telling us the nature of the agree-
ment, if there was anything further?--A.  There was never any
agreement.  They simply said to us:  "If you will prove to us that
you want it, why, we may consider the matter."  And we proved to
them by getting all the grocers of that entire territory of New
England and New York, as I have said, and a portion of New Jersey,
all except three, to sign a petition that they would adopt the
system.

Q.  That was considerably over 90 per cent, probably about
99 per cent?--A.  Ninety-five per cent was their ultimatum, and
we got practically the whole.  There were only 3 of them who did
not sign, and they were in Europe, and no one was authorized to
sign for them.  It was practically unanimous.

Q.  Will you please tell again clearly what the nature of the
terms of sale was to be?--A.  In place of granulated sugar being
sold and billed at 5 cents, they would bill the sugar at 5 3/16 and
we would pay 5 3/16, and on condition that we sold at no less than
that they, at the end of 3 months, would give us a rebate amounting
to 18 3/4 cents a hundred pounds.

Q.  When were you to pay for this sugar?--A.  We were to pay
for it in 7 days.  We could get 30 days, but we could get one off
for cash in 7 days.

Q.  Thirty days was the time?--A.  Yes.

Q.  And you got one off for cash in 7 days?--A.  Yes.

Q.  How long did that custom or plan last?--A.  It has lasted
practically until the present time, although there is no enforce-
ment of it in any way.  The wholesale grocers simply buy at a
certain price, and if they sell at less they get what they are paid
and do not get this rebate.

Q.  In case a person was not willing to abide by it, and did
not maintain the price, what would be the penalty?--A.  The penalty
would be the loss of the rebate at that time, but for 4 or 5 years
there has not been any penalty.


Testimony, G. Waldo Smith, June 12, 1899, United States
Industrial Commission, I, p. 56.


429.  DECLINE OF NEW YORK AS A COTTON SALES CENTER (1894)


New York had once been the greatest sales center of
spot cotton.  It was now the location of the greatest
cotton futures market.  Thus, its overall importance in
the industry had not declined.  The situation is discussed
here by E. J. Donnell who represented a New York cotton
firm.


The causes which have reduced the sales of spot cotton in this
market are these:  Formerly cotton was consigned to New York and the
leading markets of Europe to be sold on account of Southern planters
and merchants.  Now, the spinners of America and Europe have their
agents in all the leading Southern markets, through whom they obtain
their supplies direct.  From interior towns in the South they can
send their cotton to Europe, on through bills of lading, at less
cost than it could be delivered at any Northern port.  All the
large spinning establishments are financially independent of New

York.  A few small establishments still buy some cotton here on
account of credits they receive.  Generally there is more or less
demand from spinners whose stocks happen to be exhausted.  The only
reason why any considerable quantity of cotton comes to this market
is because it can be stored here and sold against for future delivery at a premium sufficient to compensate the owners for holding
the cotton in store many months.  The present stock of cotton in
store here is more than 45% of all the cotton in all the ports.
This cotton is never pressed on the market when the price is declining, because it is protected from loss by future sales.  I am
satisfied that if it were not for the system of future deliveries
there would be much less cotton brought here than there is at
present.  Though this cotton is held out of the market a considerable time, it must be sold or delivered on the contracts sold
against it sooner or later.  In this sense the system of future
sales makes much business here in actual cotton that would not exist
without it.  The changes and progress of the last thirty years have
practically left New York out of the trade in spot cotton.  Now
cotton merchants and spinners of the world are in telegraphic
communication with the cotton plantations.  There is no reason
why they should buy cotton here unless it might be to obtain
credit, which much fewer than formerly require.

E. J. Donnell, May 16, 1894, U.S. Congress, 53rd, 3rd session,
Senate, Report 986, part 1, Committee on Agriculture and Forestry,
Report...on the Condition of Cotton Growers, I, serial number 3290,
(Washington, D.C.:  Government Printing Office, 1895), p. 489.


### 430.  THE LITERATURE BUSINESS (1893)

The rise of the magazine after the Civil War
made a commodity of writing as it created a ready
market for industrious if uninspired authors.  William Dean
Howells writes this comment.  Between 1866 and 1892, he
had been assistant editor and editor of Atlantic Monthly,
and had served on the editorial staff of Harper's Magazine
and Cosmopolitan.


I may say that it is only since the [Civil] war that literature
has become a business with us.  Before that time we had authors, and
very good ones; it is astonishing how good they were; but I do not
remember any of them who lived by literature except Edgar A. Poe,
perhaps; and we all know how he lived; it was largely upon loans.
They were either men of fortune, or they were editors, or profess-
ors, with salaries or incomes apart from the small gains of their
pens; or they were helped out with public offices; one need not go
over their names, or classify them.  Some of them must have made

money by their books, but I question whether any one could have
lived, even very simply, upon the money his books brought him.  No
one could do that now, unless he wrote a book that we could not
recognize as a work of literature.  But many authors live now, and
live prettily enough, by the sale of the serial publication of their
writings to the magazines.  They do not live so nicely as successful
tradespeople, of course, or as men in the other professions when
they begin to make themselves names; the high state of brokers,
bankers, railroad operators, and the like is, in the nature of the
case, beyond their fondest dreams of pecuniary affluence and social
splendor.  Perhaps they do not want the chief seats in the synagogue;
it is certain they do not get them.  Still, they do fairly well,
as things go; and several have incomes that would seem riches to
the great mass of worthy Americans who work with their hands for a
living--when they can get the work.  Their incomes are mainly from
serial publication in the different magazines; and the prosperity
of the magazines has given a whole class existence which, as a
class, was wholly unknown among us before the war.  It is not only
the famous or fully recognized authors who live in this way, but
the much larger number of clever people who are as yet known chiefly
to the editors, and who may never make themselves a public, but who
do well a kind of acceptable work.  These are the sort who do not
get reprinted from the periodicals; but the better recognized authors
do get reprinted, and then their serial work in its completed form
appeals to the readers who say they do not read serials.  The multitude of these is not great, and if an author rested his hopes upon
their favor he would be a much more embittered man than he now
generally is.  But he understands perfectly well that his reward is
in the serial and not in the book; the return from that he may
count as so much money found in the road--a few hundreds, a very
few thousands, at the most....

William Dean Howells, "The Man of Letters as a Man of Business,"
Scribner's, October, 1893, reprinted in Clara M. and Rudolf Kirk
(ed.), Criticism and Fiction and Other Essays by W. D. Howells,
(New York:  New York University Press, 1959), pp. 301-302.


431.  MASS PRODUCTION REQUIRES MASS MARKETS (ca. 1895)

During the 1890's, the Rockefeller Standard Oil group
produced one-third of the country's petroleum and refined
over four-fifths of the national output.  Control of
marketing was necessary to seal Standard's dominance
over the entire industry.


This plan of selling our products direct to the consumer and
the exceptionally rapid growth of the business bred a certain

antagonism which I suppose would not have been avoided, but this
same idea of dealing with the consumer directly has been followed
by others and in many lines of trade, without creating, so far as
I recall, any serious opposition.

This is a very interesting and important point, and I have
often wondered if the criticism which centered upon us did not come
from the fact that we were among the first, if not the first, to
work out the problems of direct selling to the user on a broad
scale. This was done in a fair spirit and with due consideration
for every one's rights. We did not ruthlessly go after the trade
of our competitors and attempt to ruin it by cutting prices or
instituting a spy system. We had set ourselves the task of building
up as rapidly and broadly as possible the volume of consumption.
Let me try to explain just what happened.

To get the advantage of the facilities we had in manufacture,
we sought the utmost market in all lands--we needed volume. To do
this we had to create selling methods far in advance of what then
existed; we had to dispose of two, or three, or four gallons of oil
where one had been sold before, and we could not rely upon the usual
trade channels then existing to accomplish this. It was never our
purpose to interfere with a dealer who adequately cultivated his
field of operations, but when we saw a new opportunity or a new
place for extending the sale by further and effective facilities,
we made it our business to provide them. In this way we opened
many new lines in which others have shared. In this development
we had to employ many comparatively new men. The ideal way to
supply material for higher positions, is, of course, to recruit
the men from among the youngest in the company's service, but our
expansion was too rapid to permit this in all cases. That some of
these employees were over-zealous in going after sales it would not
be surprising to learn, but they were acting in violation of the
expressed and known wishes of the company. But even these instances, I am convinced, occurred so seldom, by comparison with the
number of transactions we carried on, that they were really the
exceptions that proved the rule.

John D. Rockefeller, <u>Random Reminiscences of Men and Events</u>,
(New York: Doubleday, Page and Co., 1909), pp. 57-59.


432.  ON DEFRAUDING LIFE INSURANCE COMPANIES (1896)


This catalogue of horrors was designed to expose
"the piratical adventurers who prey upon beneficent
institutions." It made no mention of the companies who,
as the Armstrong Investigation showed in 1906, did much
preying themselves. Note the bitter--apparently, endless--
attack upon popular juries. John Lewis, medical director
and adjuster for the Travelers Insurance Company, writes to

Charles Bombaugh, a medical examiner for life
insurance and editor of the Baltimore Underwriter.


The first edition of this book appeared in 1878.  It was
limited to fifteen hundred copies, and was exhausted soon after
publication.  Subsequent applications for copies were attended with
disappointment, and followed with frequently repeated requests for
a new edition embracing the more important additional cases which
have occurred during the intervening period.  The present revised
and enlarged volume is published in response to this demand, and is
commended as a trustworthy record to those for whose use and
reference it is primarily intended--life insurance companies and
agents, medical examiners, insurance lawyers, and medico-legal
experts.
     Objection has been made that if such a record of ingenious
devices for defrauding the life companies transcends its immediate
design and purpose, it may prove dangerously suggestive.  But it
should be remembered that a double-edged sword cuts both ways, and
if these narratives fall within the range of the evil eye, the
vision is not confined to the exposure of the cunning contrivances
and artifices of this class of schemers and plotters; it includes
picturesque views of the detection and punishment; of the determined
efforts of the companies, at whatever cost, to run them down; of
the machinery of courts of justice; of the gloom of the prison cell;
of the dark outlines of the scaffold.  The cases in this book are
for the most part more suggestive or instructive to detective
agencies than to conspirators.
     To the managers of our life companies whose records furnish an
impressive lesson.  Collectively they emphasize, as never before,
the increasing importance of scrutinizing the moral hazard as
closely as the physical risk, and the need of more watchful attention to the question of insurable interest, and its bearing upon
assignments.  The anxiety of the companies to increase the lines
upon their books, and of the agents to increase their remuneration,
has heretofore been largely responsible for placing aggressive
weapons in the hands of intending assailants.  It is encouraging to
note steady improvement in this direction; to observe that the
companies are substituting quality for quantity, and circumspection
for over-confidence.  They also realize that in their coming en-
counters with this form of human depravity, half-way measures of
repression and compromise settlements must give way to remorseless
pursuit.
     In the cases in which important questions of law are involved,
the opinions of the courts are given at more or less length for
convenient reference.  In addition to the law points, the reader
will find in some of the charges of judges to juries concise and
careful and comprehensive reviewal of the facts, and these are
valuable because of the fairness and the intelligence to which they
bear witness.  There are but few cases in this volume in which the
fairness of the bench is questionable.  It is quite otherwise with
the twelve in the box.  The perverse prejudice of the average jury-
man against corporations too often results in scandalous injustice,
as many of the verdicts herein reported prove.  If their finds

were to end with subversion of justice, with expression of contempt
of the obligations of the companies to honest policy-holders, and
with manifest disregard to the sacredness of trust funds, it would
be deplorable enough, but as these records show, such jurymen serve
as scene-shifters for fresh conspiracies, and tempt the malefactors
they have liberated to the commission of new crimes.

These narratives also show that no community has a monopoly
of the piratical adventurers who thus prey upon beneficent institutions.  They are of all nationalities as well as of both sexes,
and everywhere alike "to no code or creed confined."  A remarkable
instance of their machinations may for a season concentrate attention upon a given locality, but the next startling outbreak may be
thousands of miles away.  The offenders vary in character from the
smooth and polished and educated scoundrel to the coarse and vulgar
and illiterate outlaw; some of the actors in the drama rise to the
higher realms of comedy or tragedy, while others are never lifted
above the low level of the brutal villain of the play.  If this
book shall in any measure be helpful in diminishing the number of
sensational scenes on this stage of action, it will more than
serve its purpose.

John B. Lewis and Charles C. Bombaugh, Stratagems and
Conspiracies to Defraud Life Insurance Companies, 2nd ed.,
(Baltimore, Maryland:  James H. McClellan, Publisher, 1896),
pp. 3-4.


433.  DEPARTMENT STORES BENEFIT THE MANUFACTURER (1899)


The following material is from one of the most
knowledgeable contemporaries in the field of merchandising.  He is John Wanamaker, who was the founder of
Philadelphia's first department store and who operated
another one in New York.


Q.  You speak of the elimination of jobbers and other middle
men.  Is it the practice of the department retail stores to buy
directly from manufacturers?--A.  It is.  No large retail store
could exist at a profit otherwise.

Q.  By buying in that way do you get as low prices as were
formerly given to jobbers, or as are now given to the few jobbers
that are left?--A.  We get very much lower prices for many good
reasons.

Q.  Will you please name some of those reasons?--A.  Well, the
manufacturer, until a very few years ago, took all the risk of
creating his production.  Necessarily, he had to be in advance
of the season from 6 months to 1 year.  It required large capital,

necessitating the mercantile banker, in the shape of the commission
merchant.  His principal business was banking--to receive the goods
and advance upon them.  Generally it was his own paper.  That is
to say, the manufacturer drew bills on his commission man, who
indorsed them.  He charged a commission for that, and then the
manufacturer had to find the facilities to use the paper when he
got it; he had to find the banker to furnish the money, generally
a local banker.  The commission man sold the goods to the jobber,
which necessarily resulted in another building, and the goods were
then sold, scattering them over the country, thus necessitating
two organizations and two risks, the manufacturer's risk and the
commission man's risk.  Mr. Stewart's wholesale business was one
of the best places in the world to buy goods from, because he would
take goods on consignment, and when the interest of his advances
on them counted up too much, he would sell them.  Of course he
would get his money back, but the manufacturer would make the loss.
That is true of the commission man always.  The jobber would make
the loss for himself if he bought the goods.  Now, practically,
the jobber and the commission man are done away with.  I do not
know of any commission house in Philadelphia to-day in general dry
goods.  There is some representation of mills for the purpose of
knowing the market; but when I was a boy we had, I should say,
certainly scores of commission men and jobbers in Philadelphia.
I do not believe you will find in that city of 1,200,000 people
to-day 10 jobbing dry-goods houses.  Yet, there was a time that the
Southern merchants had their offices in Philadelphia and came there
and stayed for weeks  gathering their goods.  Now that is all gone.
The manufacturer does not need the commission men.  To be logical,
through the retailer in touch with the consumer he can find out
exactly what his mills should make and often has the retailer's
order before a thread is in the looms.  This is a large matter from
every point of view.  He can make his goods closer to the time of
distribution; he does not have to prepare them and put them first in
the commission man's hands to find a jobber that will buy them, and
the jobber to find other customers that will take them.  There are
long periods during which interest has to be paid, and the fashions
change, for women's things particularly; so that a man might make
some kind of shawls or some kind of women's wear, and by the time
he got down to the people who wear them they would only sell for
about what they cost.  The manufacturer has less risk, less interest to pay, and less trouble in having his collections made.  While
the jobber might not be able to charge back to the manufacturer,
since he bought his goods from the commissio  merchant, any of
his loss, yet no jobber would buy those goods unless he got them at
a price that would give him an insurance against those losses.  The
manufacturer has not directly or indirectly to meet any such
contingencies now, but he makes the relations with the man that
distributes the goods, who gets the money right away for them from
the people.  It is a wonderful advantage to the manufacturer.  He
saves his risk.  When working for concerns like Marshall Field or
McCreery, or like a number of concerns in New York, they are just
as sure of their money as they would be if they were permitted to
draw on the Bank of England.  They work very low, and especially

for stores that know what their probable output will be, so that
they can give them work through the dull season when, sometimes,
they have had to shut up their mills.  They will often work for
5 per cent where they would otherwise charge 15.  The manufacturer
is sure of the employment of his people.  In a little village, if
the mills shut down for a month, he can not pay his rent, can not
pay his store bills.  So everything tends toward the manufacturer
making a sure thing; and when he can eliminate all risk and get a
sure output for his production, he can make very much lower prices.
And the storekeeper, on his side, if he can offer these goods at
so much less because of the saving that has been created, it is
greatly to his interest to do that, because he increases his
clientele.


        Testimony, John Wanamaker, United States Industrial Commission,
VII, pp. 455-456.

# H.

# EARLY ECONOMIC EXPANSION ABROAD

434.  OCEANIC CABLE UPSETS LIVERPOOL TRADE (1866)

Technology, as the writer demonstrates, loosened
American mercantile dependence upon England.  The growth
of American manufacturing also made British supplies less
necessary for planters and importers in the United States.
More than a shift in merchandising was involved in the
decline of the Anglo-American economic connection.  The
author, John Crosby Brown, was a partner in the far-flung
Brown banking enterprises.

Communication between the Old and New Worlds by cable, successfully established in 1866, revolutionized trade between the two
countries, leaving the Liverpool merchants connected with that
trade without their usual occupation.  In fact, the necessity for
the intervention of merchants gradually ceased.  Manufacturers in
England, France and Germany bought their cotton by cable on samples
previously sent to them from the various places of shipment, i.e.,
New Orleans, Mobile, Charleston, Savannah, Galveston, Memphis, and
other inland towns.  Samples were sent to them from brokers and
merchants in these cities, oftentimes accompanied by a firm offer
price.  These they could examine carefully in their own offices,
make their selection for the style of goods they desired to manufacture, and cable either the acceptance of the offer or a counter-
draw against shipment.  As a consequence warehouse property in
Liverpool, largely built for cotton storage, and which had heretofore brought a good return to the owners, was for a time empty, and
its value greatly diminished.  Consignments of cotton and other

produce to Liverpool for sale practically ceased, and to a great
extent manufactured goods for shipment to this country, which had
heretofore been attended to by Liverpool merchants, were shipped
direct by the manufacturers to the buyers in the United States on
a through bill of lading. The old mercantile firms which were the
pride of Liverpool soon disappeared. They had either to change the
character of their business or close their establishments, and
it is sad to note how many, unable to adapt themselves to changed
conditions, failed. The port of Liverpool, however, still continued
to thrive, and became the centre of the great shipping interest of
the west of England, steamers gradually taking the place of sailing
craft. The foresight of its public officials in providing the
largest and best docks in Great Britain retained for the city a
large part of the foreign and coast trade of England.

John Crosby Brown, A Hundred Years of Merchant Banking,
(New York:  Privately printed, 1909), pp. 123-124.


435.  GOLD PREMIUM AND AMERICAN IMPORTS (1866)


American manufacturers welcomed high prices during
the Civil War. After the war, however, these same prices
became a handicap on the world market. America's competitive position was weakened by high price levels; further
complicating matters was the difference in value between
American paper currency and gold. This is from the report
of a three-man United States Revenue Commission. The author
is Stephen Colwell, an iron master from Philadelphia.


Our home production has seldom been in greater peril than at
this moment. Foreign manufacturers and merchants, never long in
discovering any gap affording them access to our high-priced markets,
now perceive an opportunity of enlarging their trade with the
United States, offering more and greater advantages than they have
enjoyed in this country for many years. Our high prices, the result
of many causes connected with the war, such as the withdrawal of
labor from many avocations, the combinations of speculators, and
the large and incessant government demand, are not the only temptations to the excessive importations with which the country is now
threatened. Foreign merchants, manufacturers, and bankers know
sufficiently well that the bonds of the United States are as good
a security as can be issued by any government in the world. Despite
long-continued efforts to discredit them, they are flowing steadily
into the possession of foreign capitalists, destined to yield a
large profit at no distant day. A bond of the United States is
worth as much intrinsically for investment as that portion of English
consols which will yield in interest the same quantity of gold.

It cannot be doubted that capitalists in England and upon the continent are now willing to take bonds for the United States for the proceeds of all shipments of commodities to this country, as long as the bonds can be had at a price which will yield six per cent. interest, and much more readily when the bonds can be got at a rate, as now, yielding nearly nine per cent.

The reason our national bonds sell at such a large discount in Europe is, that as the foreign purchases can obtain them at the low rate, they are not disposed to give more. Gold being overvalued in this country, having risen in price on account of the special demand for it to pay customs duties to the amount of two millions weekly, they purchase our bonds, intrinsically worth gold at par in London, and pay us in gold at forty per cent. premium. If the merchants and manufacturers, who now threaten to overwhelm a premium of forty per cent. in our currency, and then take the bonds at par; or, if they sell their bonds at our high rates in currency, they take the bonds at par, and one thousand dollars in these bonds are worth more to hold in London than £206 9s., the equivalent, at par, in sterling.

At present these circumstances offer the largest profit ever made on the shipment of foreign goods to this country. Those interested in this movement can now realize high prices for their rivals, and obtain our national bonds at a heavy discount. These great advantages, thus offered to foreign capitalists, are as fully to our detriment as to their benefit. They imperil our productive power, our ability to pay taxes, and, in fact, our whole financial system. They sap our national strength; they continuously damage our domestic industry by substituting the products of their own-- by depriving our laborers of employment, while obtaining in our markets the means of employing their own, besides realizing large profits for the enterprising individuals who engage in the business.

Stephen Colwell, Report of the United States Revenue Commission, February, 1866, U.S. Congress, 39th, 1st session, House of Representatives, Executive Document No. 68, Special Report No. 10, serial number 1256, pp. 16-17.

436.    IMPORTING THROUGH FOREIGN COMMISSION HOUSES (1870)

This changeover had an interesting political aspect. American importers had often identified with the interests of the country from which the imports came; the Federalists, with England, for example. As foreigners took over importing, politics left the field.

The business of importing and jobbing has not changed more in locality, than it has in the style in which it is conducted. After the war of 1812, vessels came rarely to New York. When they did, merchants went on board and bought from twenty to thirty thousand dollars worth of goods at a time. This was an inconvenient mode of doing business and a few merchants began to import goods as they needed them, and the importing trade became large and remunerative.

Almost the entire importing business has passed out of the hands of Americans. This change commenced in 1840. The commercial disasters of 1837, shook the confidence of European manufacturers after the interests of importers of goods in America. Nearly all the great manufacturers in Switzerland, France, and England, now have houses in New York, to which goods are consigned. It is estimated that three-fourths of the imported goods sent to New York are sold on commission. A glance at the names of importing houses will show that they are nearly all foreign.

Smith, Bulls and Bears of Wall Street, pp. 503-504.


437.   CUBA AND LOUISIANA SUGAR (1871)


Potentially, Cuba was the greatest competitor to Louisiana sugar. Only the tariff prevented the latter from being swamped by Cuban sugar. Robert Somers makes this comment.


Were tranquility to be restored to Cuba, or that island to be annexed to the United States, the sugar-planting interest in Louisiana, under its present conditions, would probably be placed in peril. The Cuban insurrection, by disturbing the system of slave labour, can only have been a help to the Louisianian planters, while the duty on Cuban insurrection, by disturbing the system of much money put into their pockets by the Federal Government, which Congress at any hour has the power to withdraw. There may be little time to lose in probing the difficulties of sugar-production in Louisiana to the foundation, and in removing the defects under which it labours, the chief of which appear to be an inefficient extraction of the juice of the cane alike where the fixed capital is small or moderate; greatly too costly machinery and apparatus where the process is more perfect; and the difficulty, not peculiar to sugar-culture here, of attempting to do on the plantations what had better be done, under other capital and responsibility, in the refineries of the large towns.

Somers, The Southern States Since the War, p. 231.

438.   SPECIE RESUMPTION AND THE BALANCE OF TRADE (1874)


Ever since the Civil War, federal currency was irre-
deemable, i.e., not convertible into gold or silver.  Here
is an argument that convertibility--"resumption"--could not
be practiced until a favorable balance of trade permitted
more of our gold to stay here.  (It was during this decade,
in fact, that the U.S. trade balance turned favorable and
pretty much stayed there.  Resumption followed.)


And we ought to go on accumulating more gold in the country,
if we ever expect to resume.  I must come back to what I said in
Chicago, that before we can resume the balance of trade must be
turned in our favor.  It is the only thing which can bring us back--
many sneer about it,--and we are told that the balance of trade is
against England.  The reason is very simple:  England is largely a
creditor nation, and we are largely a debtor nation.  Our bonds are
held to the amount of hundreds of millions on the other side.  We
have a large amount of English money here; we are shipping gold to
England to pay our indebtedness--our interest at least.  England is
building railways, and gas-works, and water-works all over the
world.  Not alone in her possessions; she is doing it in France,
in Italy and in North America.  She sends her money everywhere, but
it flows back to England again, because England is the creditor
nation of almost the whole world.  If we were in that position we
need not mind the balance of trade, up to last year, has been continually against us to the amount of fifty to one hundred millions.
I think last year it was turned in our favor between thirty and
forty millions.  Let us hope to continue in that way, and we shall
certainly and surely come back to specie payments.


Mr. Meissner of New York, Debates and Action on the Subject
of Currency and Finance by the National Board of Trade...1874,
(Chicago, Illinois:  Knight & Leonard, Printers, 1874), pp. 47-48.


439.   AMERICAN BEEF COMPETES IN ENGLAND (1877)


The period 1875-1885 saw a sharp increase in the
shipment of American beef overseas, primarily to England.
In 1875 began the first regular shipment of refrigerated
meat.  Much of this beef was, contrary to this author,
James Macdonald's expectation raised in Kansas.  He was
an authority on Scotch agriculture who visited the United
States in 1877 under commission of a Scotch newspaper to
investigate the competitive threat of American beef in
the English market.

I frankly admit that there is a much larger number of really good cattle (besides shorthorns) in America than I was prepared to find.  In such states as Illinois, Kentucky, Indiana, and Ohio there are a great many more beef cattle that I expected there really were that would rank among the average of Scotch cross steers; but in those large western herds...not a pound of beef is raised that could be placed on an equality with an average pound of Scotch or English beef; there is not one animal in every thousand that could be classed amongst even a second-rate Scotch herd....

But the mistake lies in its being supposed that this quality of beef is being exported to British markets.  It has never been, at least beyond a mere experiment, and is never likely to be....My firm impression is, that until both the class of cattle and the mode of their treatment are greatly improved, the British markets will never be disturbed by the ordinary beef of America, but that the best quality of American beef...will be poured in upon us, and will find a moderately ready sale at a certain price.


James Macdonald, Food for the Far West, (New York:  Orange Judd Company, [1878], pp. 263-265.


### 440.  PLANTING HAWAIIAN SUGAR ON SHARES (1879)


Hawaii, in these years, was a frontier for Americans seeking a "second chance."  With experience and capital, it was possible to make a successful entry into sugar cultivation.  This writer, John Horner, a Californian whose fortune had been lost in the Panic of 1857, became a wealthy planter and rancher in Hawaii; he twice served as Noble in the Hawaiian legislature.


In 1879 my brother and I made a contract with Mr. Claus Spreckels to go to the Sandwich Islands and cultivate sugar cane for him on shares.  In fulfillment of this contract we sold our farms, chartered a schooner and placed therein our families, 18 souls; our household effects, our horses and farming tools, and started for the Islands, where we arrived on the 25th of December, 1879.  We landed on Maui this time, it being a different Island from the one we had stopped at on our wedding tour thirty years before.  The schooner quickly discharged and we commenced hauling our lumber which we had brought with us for building our houses on the land we were to use, about six miles distant.  We erected our houses and soon commenced our plantation work.  We had 500 hundred acres of land allotted to us.  My brother and sons worked the western half, I and my sons the eastern half, under the firm name of "J. M. Horner & Sons."  My boys did all our plowing and team work in preparing for planting and growing our first crop of 240 acres.

From the time we commenced preparing for planting until we got
returns from the sale of our sugars two full years rolled away.  In
consequence of our planting a much larger area than we contracted
to plant the first year J. M. Horner & Sons borrowed $40,000.  Our
crop did well, exceeded our expectations in both yield and the
price for which it sold.  We returned the borrowed money with the
interest and had a net profit from our venture of $25,000.  Mr.
Spreckels could not let us have any more land to cultivate, and as
250 acres was rather a small plantation for five able men to
superintend, seeing it only required replanting once in four years,
and further, Mr. Spreckels' superintendent did not want any planters
on the plantation, he preferred doing the planting as well as the
milling.  So I and one of my boys went prospecting around the Island
of Maui, finding nothing encouraging there I and another boy went
prospecting on the Island of Kauai, openings for cane planting such
as were looking for we did not find on that Island.  We also pros-
pected the cane belt on the large Island of Hawaii.  Here we contracted with owners of the Pacific Sugar Mill Co. to do one-half
of the planters for their mill, and one of my boys took charge of
the business.  Here we made considerable sugar, increasing the
yield on our half of the plantation from 500 tons per year to 2,000.
We had accumulated there a property we valued at $150,000, but the
"McKinley Bill" so effected sugar property here we sold it willingly
for one-half of that sum.

On this same prospecting tour we rented 1,250 acres (since
increased to 2,000) of good wild cane land, with a view of starting
a new plantation.  This was rather a discouraging work to undertake,
as the land, though rich, was covered with a jungle of trees and
brush and had all to be grubed and cleared before it could be used,
at an expense of $33 per acre.  Besides habitations for superinten-
dents, quarters for 150 or 200 laborers and accommodations for
more than half of that number of horses had to be provided, as well
as the horses themselves, and plantation tools, roads, bridges, (a
wagon wheel had never yet turned upon the land), fencing and mill
had all to be built, as well as raising the cane.

John Meirs Horner, National Finance and Public Money...and
Personal History of the Author, (Honolulu, Hawaii:  Hawaiian Gazette
Co., 1898), pp. 271-272.


441.  HIGHLY UNFAVORABLE BALANCE WITH LATIN AMERICA (1882)


To pay for large American purchases in Latin
America this country sold raw materials and food to
Europe.  As explained below by James Blaine in a
letter to President Chester A. Arthur, upon the delicate
balance between Latin American and European trade depended
the entire specie position of the United States.  Blaine

was a former Secretary of State and the most prominent
advocate of U.S. commercial expansion in Latin America.


Beyond the philanthropic and Christian ends to be obtained by
the American conference, devoted to peace and good will among men,
we might well hope for material advantages as a result of a better
understanding and closer friendship with the nations of America.
At present the condition of trade between the United States and its
American neighbors is unsatisfactory to us, and even deplorable.
According to the official statistics of our own Treasury Department
the balance against us in American trade last year was $120,000,000
in coin--a sum greater than the yearly product of the gold and silver mines in the United States.  This large balance was paid by us
in foreign exchange, and a very large proportion of it went to
England, where shipments of cotton, provisions, and breadstuffs
supplied the money.  If any thing should change or check the balance
in our favor in European trade, our commercial exchanges with
Spanish America would drain us of our reserve of gold coin at a
rate exceeding $100,000,000 per annum, and might precipitate the
suspension of specie payment in this country.  Such a result at
home would be worse than a little "jealousy and ill will" abroad.


Letter, James G. Blaine to President Chester A. Arthur,
February 3, 1882, Blaine, Political Discussions, p. 407, reprinted
in James W. Gantenbein (ed.), The Evolution of Our Latin-American
Policy.  A Documentary Record, (New York:  Columbia University
Press, 1950), p. 51.


442.  AMERICAN HANDICAPS IN THE CUBA TRADE (1880's)


During the 1880's, you could not discuss Latin-
American trade without first facing up to the British
presence there.  In Cuba, the lingering Spanish sovereignty constituted another obstacle to American commercial
expansion.  The author, Edwin Atkins, was successor to his
father as head of E. Atkins & Company, of Cienfuegos, a
merchant-banking firm specializing in sugar exports.


Spanish commerce was guarded by the strictest tariff.  That
in force up to the time of the Spanish-American War was arranged
under four heads, namely:
1.  Spanish goods in Spanish bottoms.
2.  Spanish goods in foreign bottoms.
3.  Foreign goods in Spanish bottoms.
4.  Foreign goods in foreign bottoms.
Excessive duties practically wiped out trade under the last
head.  England, always ready to encourage her foreign trade in all

parts of the world, soon built steamships to be operated under the
Spanish flag and manned by Spanish officers and sailors, than whom
there are none better in the world.  Taking advantage of the third
proviso of the Spanish tariff for the English manufacturers, she
loaded the English-owned Spanish steamers at Liverpool for Santan-
der, Cadiz, or Barcelona.  These cargoes discharged, the steamers
were reloaded, under the first proviso, with Spanish merchandise
for Cuba; but this 'Spanish' merchandise was largely the product of
English factories which had been established in Spain, and England
was the gainer still.  These cargoes having been discharged in
Cuba, the steamers proceeded in ballast to some American port--New
Orleans, Savannah, Charleston, or New York--there loaded with cotton
or wheat for Liverpool or Spain, and in due course returned to Cuba
with cotton goods or flour made from these raw materials.  Thus the
United States threw the game into England's hands, and not only
deprived her manufacturers of just so much business, but paid
freight on the raw materials to English-owned Spanish steamers for
a distance of some five thousand miles as against twelve hundred
and fifty had she shipped them direct from New York to Havana.
There were also regular lines of Spanish steamers from Holland,
France, and Belgium, carrying cargoes from those countries, which
were entered under the third proviso of the tariff.  In this way,
for more than a century Spain controlled both the commerce and the
carrying trade for Cuba.  This repressive policy was an important
factor in the decline of the Island's prosperity, which had been
at its height just before the Ten Years' War.  Then Cuba, known
for centuries as the 'Ever Faithful Isle," was still pouring a
stream of gold into the Spanish treasury, and Havana was one of
the commercial centres of the new world.  Its harbor was crowded
with the sail of all nations, but there was good reason for the
United States flag being a small factor in that shipping, as she
assessed such high duties on all imports that here cost of production was raised above that of other countries, and her tariff upon
imports in Spanish bottoms was prohibitive.  As a consequence she
sold little or nothing but coal and lumber to Cuba.


     Edwin F. Atkins, Sixty Years in Cuba, (Cambridge, Massachu-
setts:  Privately Printed, 1926), pp. 78-79.


     443.  BRITISH CONTROL OF FOREIGN EXCHANGE MARKET (1889)


     World banking centered in London because that city
was the greatest point of international payments.  Banking followed trade.  In settling balances with its trading partners, the United States was forced by circumstances to depend upon British banking facilities.  This extract
is from a letter written by William R. Grace to Charles
Flint.  Grace, head of W. R. Grace and Company, was a

successful international merchant then in the process
of negotiating--on behalf of British creditors of Peru--
to reorganize that country's heavy external debt on the
security of extensive Peruvian silver, guano, land, and
oil concessions. Flint, a trade in South America, was
one of ten United States delegates to the first International American ["Pan-American"] Conference.

It is just this way [said the Hon. William R. Grace, of New
York, recently]:  Supposing I want to buy a cargo of goods in any
South American country.  I say nothing about the West Indies, for
I do not trade there, and I know nothing about what the arrangements are there, but of South America I know considerable.  Of
course, if I buy my cargo, I must pay for it.  Now, there is practically only one way in which I can do it.  I must send a draft on
London, or rather I send to my South American correspondent a
written authority to draw on a London bank.  Of course I have to
keep an account in London to do this, and the London banker charges
me a commission for doing this kind of business, so that it is a
constant expense to me.

The obviously simple way for me to pay would be to authorize
the South American merchant to draw on me directly, but I can not
do this for a simple reason.  Europe has the bulk of the trade of
the world, and especially the bulk of the South American trade,
and London is the monetary center of Europe.  The South American
does not buy in the United States a sufficient quantity of goods
to make a draft on New York valuable to him.  He does not want
his money placed here, for it will cost him some trouble and some
expense to transfer it to London, where he has to meet his payments.  Therefore I have to do it for him.

There are Spanish-American products imported into the United
States amounting in the aggregate to $181,000,000.  Products of
the United States exported to the South American nations aggregate
$69,000,000.  Naturally it would be supposed that the value of
all the exports from the United States would be to their extent
an offset in the liquidation of the traffic.  As a matter of fact,
only rather less than more than $45,000,000 is liquidated in this
manner or through North American financial institutions.  The
remainder, $136,000,000, is paid by drafts at ninety days on
North American merchants upon London banks or bankers, which, after
acceptance, become immediately available for the purchase of
European products.  The North American merchants' further responsibility consists merely in having the cash in London before the
date of maturity.  English bankers charge three-quarters per cent.
for this accommodation.  Thus, on the $136,000,000 liquidated in
this manner the English banker's profit is a round million dollars.

William R. Grace and Charles R. Flint in William E. Curtis,
Trade and Transportation between the United States and Latin
America, (Washington, D.C.:  Government Printing Office, 1890),
pp. 290-291.

444.  HAWAII IS IMPORTANT TO AMERICA'S TRADE (1891, 1892)

American sugar planters in Hawaii were planning
the overthrow of the Hawaiian royal government and
the ultimate annexation of Hawaii by the United States.
The prime stake in Hawaii was sugar.  There were also
other economic issues as well as several strategic
considerations.  Stevens, who writes this letter, had
been U.S. Minister to Uruguay, Paraguay, Norway, and
Sweden.  He was Minister to Hawaii from 1889 to 1893 when
he was recalled for having illegally encouraged the
American revolt of that year.  Blaine, Stevens' political
sponsor, was Secretary of State until his resignation in
1892; he had long been an annexationist with respect to
Hawaii.  Foster succeeded Blaine as Secretary of State.


It is also becoming more and more obvious that these islands
are to be of commanding importance in the near future to American
trade in the North Pacific.  Great Britain, France, Germany, and
Spain have taken possession of nearly all of the principal groups
in the South Pacific and of the small isolated islands in the
Central Pacific.  If the Hawaiian group should slip from our control our national rivals would gain great naval and commercial advantage in the North Pacific, whose dominance fairly belongs to the
United States.  Nothing can be plainer than that it is our imperative duty to hold these islands with the firm resolution and the
invincible strength of the American nation.  To ignore their prospective value and to treat them other than with a liberal and fostering policy would be one of those blunders which justly have
their place among the crimes of statesmen.  Nothing should be done
or neglected to be done, which would drive them into the control of
England or Germany.  At the present time the German plantation
owners and the German commercial houses tend strongly towards the
United States and want Hawaii to become an American dependency, and
would even favor annexation.  A majority of the English would yield
readily to the same tendency if our Government should not hesitate.
. . . . . . . . . . . . . . . . . . . . . . . . . . . . . . . . . . . .
The strong inclination of several European powers to gain
possession of all the islands in the Pacific, except such as are
expressly protected by the United States, is plainly shown by what
has taken place in recent years.
The seizure of Gilbert, Johnson, and other islands, in the
past few months, and what recently transpired in regard to Samoa,
emphatically show that England certainly has not moderated her
policy in the indicated regard, to which course the Canadian Government is undoubtedly the inspiring cause.  The enormous cost of the
Canadian Pacific Railway impels its managers to make the most
desperate efforts to secure freight and passengers, and hence its
aggressive plans to secure Pacific commerce and to gain political
and commercial influence in these islands.  The scheme of a British

cable from Vancouver to Honolulu to Australia, as well as to Japan
and China, and of establishing commercial and mail lines of steamers on the same route, is not an idle dream.  Powerful agencies are
already working to these ends, and to effectively safeguard American
interests on the Pacific and in these islands there is no time for
hesitation and delay.  If the United States Government does not
very promptly provide for laying a cable from San Francisco or
San Diego to Honolulu or Hilo, it may be regarded as certain that
a cable will be laid by British capital and be controlled by
British managers.  Pearl Harbor for a coaling station and an
American cable between California and Hawaii are of immediate vital
importance to American commercial and naval interests and to the
maintenance of American influence on these islands.


    Letter, John L. Stevens to James Blaine, September 5, 1891;
letter, Stevens to John Foster, November 20, 1892; U.S. Congress,
53rd, 2nd session, House of Representatives, Exec. Doc. No. 48,
Hawaiian Correspondence, serial number 3224, pp. 85-113.


### 445.  LUXURY RUGS FROM ENGLAND (1893)


    Wealthy Americans were willing to pay extra for
luxuries when these came from overseas.  This was a
lingering evidence of the oft-remarked tendency of the
American wealthy to practice snobishness through identification with things English.  The British adjusted to the
fact.  The writer is Claude Meeker, U.S. consul at
Bradford, England.


    Undoubtedly there is an increasing tendency to mix cotton with
other fibers, especially with wool and silk.  This tendency, it is
quite certain, increases the consumption of cotton enormously.
Cotton is also used in conjunction with mohair, and mixed wool and
cotton combine a staple cloth that is used for a variety of purposes, chiefly in the wearing apparel of men and women.  The largest
carpet manufacturing establishment in the world, employing 5,000
persons, is located in this consular district.  American cotton
purchased chiefly from the Lancashire spinners is used almost
exclusively as a warp in its fine carpet products and as a mixture
in the inferior carpets.  The most elegant carpets it turns out
are for the American trade alone, and the common goods are for the
domestic market only.  The information was elicited in a call upon
this establishment that especially expensive designs were made for

the American market, and that no other country, England not excepted, would buy such high-class goods.


Report of Claude Meeker, July 21, 1893; U.S. Congress, 53rd,
3rd session, Senate, Report 986, part 1, Committee on Agriculture
and Forestry, Report...on the Condition of Cotton Growers, II,
serial number 3290, (Washington, D.C.: Government Printing Office,
1895), p. 147.


## 446.    HOW TO INCREASE OUR ARGENTINE TRADE (1892)


American trade with the rest of the western hemis-
phere was handicapped by poor transportation, inadequate
banking facilities, and inadequate knowledge about markets.
These were true also for trade between Argentina and the
United States.  This report was made by E. L. Baker, then
U.S. consul at Buenos Aires, Argentina.


There is no doubt that one of the first prerequisites to any
very great increase on our cotton trade, and indeed of our trade
generally, with the River Plate, is the adoption, as far as possible, of the methods which have been so successful in the case of
Great Britain.  These should consist, as I have already stated, of
direct lines of steamships, international banking facilities with
the United States, and the establishment down here of American
business houses.  We are at present provided with none of these
facilities.
    (1)  In the first place it is next to impossible for American
manufacturers, even with better goods to sell, to compete with the
European market, on equal terms, without the advantage which sure
and quick intercommunication afford.  The saving of time and the
dispatch with which orders can be filled in England and the other
maritime countries of Europe necessarily give those markets the
preference.  When the fleet of ocean steamers which connects Europe
with the River Plate can put down at this port goods ordered by
cable in from twenty to twenty-five days, merchants here, even if
they were otherwise so disposed, would hesitate about sending orders
to the United States, knowing that they can, in the great majority
of cases, only be filled by sailing vessels which require from
fifty to ninety days to make the passage.  Our commerce with all
this part of South America continues to be conducted through the
slow and uncertain medium of sailing vessels, which are only suitable for heavy cargoes and raw materials.  A line of steamers direct
to the River Plate, in my opinion, would not be long in working
important changes in our trade and especially our textile trade
with the Argentine Republic.

(2)  In the second place, we need more intimate banking relations with the Argentine Republic.  All the exchange business of
this country with the United States, and vice versa, is done through
English banks.  New York as a financial center is hardly known here.
Credits sent out here for the purchase of Argentine produce, and
credits sent from here to the United States for the purchase of our
textile and other manufactures, are nearly all given on London.  And
all remittances on account of sales of merchandise received from the
United States are made by bills on English banks.  The value of
these banking facilities can hardly be over-estimated in the conduct
of a general trade.  The matter of exchange is a most important ingredient in the business of reciprocal commerce, and contributes
very essentially to its success.  With such facilities here, the
settlement of international balances between the United States and
the Argentine Republic would be accomplished directly, cheaply,
and without trouble.

(3)  In the third place, the advantage which would accrue to
our textile trade with this country, if there were distinctive
American business houses here, would be incalculable.  There is, of
course, something gained, in this and other lines of goods by manufacturers obtaining the views and opinions of consular officers, who
being on the spot have an opportunity, in a general way, of watching
the course of trade; and there is probably still more benefit derived from sending agents down here, who, being thoroughly posted
in the details of the cotton manufactures of our country, can intelligently "talk business" with the merchants of the Argentine
Republic, and at the same time obtain exact information in regard
to the wants, demands, and capabilities of the market, the kinds of
fabrics best suited to the trade, and such other points in regard
to make up as experts in the business fully understand.  But, after
all, the surest and most effectual method of placing our textile
trade upon a satisfactory basis in this country is through those
whose especial work it is here on the spot to put such goods upon
the market.


E. L. Baker, June 6, 1893; U.S. Congress, 53rd, 3rd session,
Senate, Report 986, part 1, Committee on Agriculture and Forestry,
Report...on the Condition of Cotton Growers, II, serial number
3290, (Washington, D.C.:  Government Printing Office, 1895), pp.
40-41.



447.  "SUGAR HAS BEEN A CURSE TO THESE FAVORED ISLANDS"  (1893)


In this little-known source, one can sense the
persistent cry of resource-rich but poverty-stricken
colonial areas.  This statement was made by the Hawaiian
Patriotic League, formed in 1893 by Hawaiians, that opposed
both the American-backed Provisional Government which had

taken power by force, as well as annexation by the
United States.


This change in the morality of the missionary descendants
came to its climax through sugar, and it may here be said that sugar
has been a curse to these favored islands, making some few men--
foreigners--immensely rich, but impoverishing the masses, the natives especially, and bringing about corruption and greed, and political venality unknown to the converts of the early missionaries.
The sugar greed was of long and gradual growth, the early
efforts to give it an impetus by appealing to American generosity
having repeatedly failed through the prudence of Congress; and it
can be safely said that just prior to the season of extraordinary
financial prosperity that followed the treaty at last granted in
1876, by the kindness of our great and good friend, the Republic of
the United States of America, all the old foreign complications had
worn out, so that the native Government was running smoothly and
our people at large were living in peace and in greater harmony than
they have ever since.  It was a time when we had less wealth and
less selfishness, but more quiet contentment.
The divergence of sentiment and lack of harmony came about
through the ambition, the sordid desire of foreign residents and
sons of missionaries to accumulate great wealth and grow suddenly
rich.  To accomplish this end the few who had the advantage in
lands, money, and friends saw that the main point for them was to
control the Government, so as to secure the special legislation
necessary to carry out their designs, and especially to procure the
indispensable cheap labor and keep them down under labor laws equivalent to slavery.  To this faction this country owes the undesir-
able and un-American introduction of Chinese, Japanese, and the
still more ignorant and illiterate Portuguese.  Millions of public
money, under the fallacious pretext of "encouragement to immigration," have been spent for the sole purpose of bringing in laborers
for the planters, and even the voyage around the world of King
Kalankaua was made use of to try to obtain Indian coolines under
British jurisdication, which would have made this country practically an English colony, had it not been for the veto of the
American Government, and yet the idea was not entirely abandoned,
for only a year ago Mr. Marsden, one of the commissioners who went
to Washington to beg for annexation, was sent to India to try to
revive the matter, and he reported in favor of it.
This goes to show the reason why so many annexationists in the
country have alternately shifted from loyal Hawaiians to rank annexationists, according to what appeared most expedient for their
purposes or gain; thus it can be safely said that few indeed is the
number of those who want annexation for mere patriotism; for the
majority, it is essentially a question of dollars and cents they
think they can make out of Uncle Sam, and even to-day, many of the
hottest annexationists would turn right over to any other power if
they had any prospect of making more money by such a change.
. . . . . . . . . . . . . . . . . . . . . . . . . . . . . . . . .

Having regained temporary possession of the power, through the revolution of 1887, the sugar missionaries dropped for a time their annexation schemes, and merely tried to use the United States to keep themselves in power, reserving annexation as a desperate expedient. This is proved by the treaty which they attempted to negotiate in 1889-'90, in which a special clause, now known as the "bayonet clause," allowed them to call at any time for the landing of the United States troops, to protect them and any cabinet they might uphold. This treaty was rendered impossible by the turn of the elections in 1890, in which the sugar planters and missionary influence combined were downed by the strong will of the natives, allied with the foreign workingmen and mechanics, who opposed the coolie-labor policy of the wealthy class.

. . . . . . . . . . . . . . . . . . . . . . . . . . . . . . . . . . . . .

To cover their numerical weakness, the annexationists' faction have tried to awaken American sympathies by alluding to the necessity of protecting American capital, which they claim to be so largely invested in these islands. To give plausibility to this assertion, tables have been prepared, purporting (on estimations, not on any positive documents) to show that the total capital engaged in sugar (in corporations and nonincorporated plantations) amounted to $33,420,990, out of which $24,735,610 were claimed to be American, or about four-fifths; $6,038,130 British, $2,008,600 German, $226,280 native, and $299,000 of other nationalities. This fantastic array is contradicted by the mere fact that out of a total of $537,757 for internal taxes, Americans paid only $139,998 (official figures), or one-fourth, while, according to the above statement, American plantation stock alone, outside of commercial firms and other American taxable property, ought to have paid over $247,000. But even allowing that a large portion of the sugar interests may be apparently in American hands, it is far from correct to call it American capital.

It is an undeniable fact that outside of Mr. Claus Spreckels, of California, no American has ever brought into this country any capital worth mentioning, but many have sent away fortunes made here; most of our present American capitalists, outside of sons of missionaries, came here as sailors or school-teachers, some few as clerks, others as mechanics, so that, even if now they do own or manage, or have their names in some way connected with property or corporations, this does not make their wealth of American origin. Those who are now independent run their plantations or business firms on money made here, out of the Hawaiian people and from Hawaiian soil, through coolie labor; the others are simply running on capital borrowed principally from English or German capitalists, and their concern should be more justly called English or German capital because, in case of bankruptcy, such capital would really be lost, not American capital.

The local Croesus, American by birth, the banker, C. R. Bishop, came here poor and started his fortune by marrying the wealthiest native princess, whose lands and income allowed him to duplicate it by banking on Hawaiian capital; surely his can not be termed American capital. The conclusion of all this must then be, that certainly American capital and interests here can be cheerfully

acknowledged as very large and important, and entitled, like all
other foreign capital and interests, to every consideration and
protection; but American annexation can not be justified on the
sole ground of the asserted extreme preponderance of such American
capital, or on the pretension of that capital to be entitled to
special or exclusive protection or favor, not any more than German
or English planters would be entitled to ask for annexation to
their countries on the same grounds.


        Statement of the Hawaiian Patriotic League; U.S. Congress,
53rd, 2nd session, House of Representatives, Exec. Doc. No. 47,
President's Message Relating to the Hawaiian Islands, serial
number 3224, (Washington, D.C.:  Government Printing Office,
1893), pp. 45-451, 453, and 455.


            448.   ECONOMICS OF HAWAIIAN ANNEXATION (1893)


        In 1893, American sugar interests in Hawaii manu-
    factured a revolt for independence and annexation.
    President Cleveland refused to honor the agreement made
    by an American representative there; the latter was recalled
    and a new representative dispatched.  Following is one of
    his first reports.  He was James Blount, a Georgian, who
    was now serving President Cleveland in March, 1893.  Blount
    had been a member of the House of Representatives from
    1872 to 1893, and in his last term had served as Chairman
    of the Committee on Foreign Affairs.  Gresham was Secretary
    of State.


        The controlling element in the white population is connected
with the sugar industry.  In its interests the Government here has
negotiated treaties from time to time for the purpose of securing
contract laborers for terms of years for the plantations, and paid
out large sums for their transportation and for building plantation
wharves, etc.
        These contracts provide for compelling the laborer to work
faithfully by fines and damage suits brought by the planters against
them, with the right on the part of the planter to deduct the
damages and cost of suit out of the laborer's wages.  They also
provide for compelling the laborer to remain with the planter during
the contract term.  They are sanctioned by law and enforced by civil
remedies and penal laws.  The general belief amongst the planters
at the so-called revolution was that, notwithstanding the laws
against importing labor into the United States in the event of their
annexation to that Government, these laws would not be made opera-
tive in the Hawaiian Islands on account of their peculiar conditions.  Their faith in the building of a cable between Honolulu and

San Francisco, and large expenditures at Pearl Harbor in the event
of annexation have also as much to do with the desire for it.

In addition to these was the hope of escape from duties on
rice and fruits and receiving the sugar-bounty, either by general
or special law.

The repeal of the duty on sugar in the McKinley act was regarded a severe blow to their interests, and the great idea of
statesmanship has been to do something in the shape of treaties
with the United States, reducing their duties on agricultural products of the Hawaiian Islands, out of which profit might be derived.
Annexation has for its charm the complete abolition of all duties
on their exports to the United States.

The annexationists expect the United States to govern the
islands by so abridging the right of suffrage as to place them in
control of the whites.

Letter, James H. Blount to Walter Q. Gresham, July 17, 1893;
U.S. Congress, 53rd, 2nd session, House of Representatives, Exec.
Doc. No. 47, President's Message Relating to the Hawaiian Islands,
serial number 3224, (Washington, D.C.: Government Printing Office,
1893), p. 133.

### 449.  CUBAN SUGAR AND AMERICAN TARIFFS (1894)

The Wilson Tariff Bill removed Cuban sugar from
the tariff-free list and cancelled tariff reciprocity
treaties between the U.S. and Spain. American economic
interests in Cuba feared the reappearance of earlier
competitive disabilities. (See Source No. 442). The
following was written before passage of the Wilson Bill.
Edwin Atkins now writes to Senator Aldrich of Rhode
Island, leader of the high tariff men in the Senate.

I view with some alarm the possibility of the abrogation of
the reciprocity treaty with Spain, which I think would be most
unfortunate. The benefits of the treaty have fully equalled the
expectation of those interested in business between the United
States and Cuba. As you are aware, it has very largely increased
the exports to this Island, and has turned the demand for sugar
machinery, flour, coal, lumber, hardware, etc., from Europe to the
United States. It has restricted Spain in the imposition of certain
taxes, thereby reducing cost of production of sugars and cost of
freights, as well as ensuring greater safety upon the investment
of Northern capital. With a few years more of the present treaty
the United States will have the entire control of the markets of
the Island, a condition which is more to be desired than annexation.
Several of the best and largest sugar places here are owned by
Americans, their output being over 100,000 tons, say ten per cent

of the production of the Island.  Our market is New York, Boston,
Philadelphia, and we do not want to be forced to purchase our
supplies from Europe as was the case before the [reciprocity] treaty, and would be again in case of its abrogation....


        Letter, Edwin F. Atkins to Senator Nelson W. Aldrich, 1894;
Atkins, Sixty Years in Cuba, pp. 143-144.


        450.  "CUBA AS AN AMERICAN COUNTRY" (1899)


        The Spanish-American War had just ended and Cuba
was now part of the United States sphere of influence.
What would this mean for the future expansion of American
economic interests in Cuba?  Admiral Robert Porter comments.
He was serving as Special Commissioner for the United
States to Cuba and Puerto Rico.  In this capacity, he had
recently conducted a six months' study of conditions in
Cuba and had received extensive testimony.


        Cuba is no longer a European colony, but an American country,
under the protection of the United States.  So long as the Island
is occupied and governed by the military forces of the United
States, law and order will be maintained and equal rights will be
granted to all the people.  From an industrial point of view Cuba
will have practically obtained what she has been fighting for for
nearly a generation:  namely, industrial and commercial freedom.
The United States will administer the laws for the Cubans in the
interest of Cuba.  The United States asks nothing in return but the
same opportunity for trade and commerce as is accorded to the other
countries of the world.  The Republic will levy no tribute, nor will
it exact a dollar of taxation over and above the revenue necessary
for protecting life and property, and the cost of inaugurating such
works for the improvement of sanitation, or the carrying on of
industries, as may become necessary.
· · · · · · · · · · · · · · · · · · · · · · · · · · · · · · · · ·
        The strongest and uppermost sentiment in the Island, as I have
found it since the close of the war, is for peace and reconstruction
under the guidance of the United States.  Those who have made the
greatest sacrifice for independence are apparently willing to rest
for a while and enjoy the glorious results of industrial and commercial independence and a release for ever from Spanish misrule.
Let the future shape its own political policy, as the desire of all
intelligent Cubans.  In commercial and business circles (and it
must be remembered that the author has, in the course of his inquiries, been very rarely thrown in contact with business people),
the desire for ultimate absorption or annexation by the United
States is almost unanimous.  Those who have property, those engaged

in industrial pursuits, those carrying on commerce, those interested
in affairs, regardless of nationality, see the greatest future for
Cuba in ultimate annexation to the United States, and openly advocate that policy.

Robert P. Porter, Industrial Cuba, Being a Study of Present
Commercial and Industrial Conditions, with Suggestions as to the
Opportunities Presented in the Island for American Capital,
Enterprise, and Labor, (New York:  G. P. Putnam's Sons, 1899),
pp. 14, 32-33.


451.  "RELIEVE THE HOME MARKETS OF OUR SURPLUS" (1899)


In the 1890's the cry for new markets was heard
increasingly.  It was usually tied up with calls for
government shipping subsidies to extend sales of surplus
goods.  F. B. Thurber, president of the United States
Export Association, a former wholesale grocer and publisher
of The American Grocer, writes.

With a consuming power of 75,000,000 we have a producing power
of 150,000,000.  Our problem is to keep our labor and capital continuously and remuneratively employed by preserving our home market
and reaching out for a place to dump our surplus among the other
1,365,000,000, each of whom has some wants.
     Q.  You say our object should be to keep our home markets.
Suppose we produce more than we can consume, what then?  A.  We
then sell it abroad for any price we can get.
     Q.  Does that hurt anybody?--A.  I do not think it does.
     Q.  Does it not hurt the producer?  I want to know your exact
opinion on that.  Suppose we produce more wheat than we can consume,
and throw it on the market anywhere; is the price raised or lowered?
--A.  Undoubtedly, if we produce too much, i.e., if we produce in
excess of the consumptive demand the world over, the price is
reduced, because the price of our wheat is made in Liverpool.
     Q.  If we should limit production at home, would that enable
us to extend our markets abroad?--A.  My answer to that is, that
we should endeavor to preserve our home markets so far as possible
and to extend our foreign markets at the same time, in order to
relieve the home markets of our surplus.  If we produce a surplus,
whether of natural or manufactured products, that surplus presses
down on the market and reduces prices to an unremunerative point,
and in manufactures causes the closing of factories and the discharge of laborers.  The great problem is to keep our labor and
capital both employed.

Q.  In preserving our home markets are we not competing with
foreigners and prejudicing them against us?  Do we not suffer on
that account?--A.  Foreign buyers purchase from us when they can do
so to better advantage than elsewhere.  While trade follows the
flag to some extent, it follows the price list to a much greater
extent, and we must do all that we dan to extend our markets so that
our factories can run continuously.  As the producing capacity of
our factories is  reater than the consuming capacity of the United
States, we must look abroad for our markets, else our factories can
not run and furnish employment.

Q.  Do I understand you to say this, that, as we are an over-
producing country, not only in the manufacturing line but in the
agricultural line, it should be the policy of this country to
extend its markets?--A.  Yes.

Q.  Now, how can that be done and at the same time keep up
our home markets?--A.  Give us an American merchant marine; let
our own ships distribute our own goods.

Testimony, F. B. Thurber, United States Industrial Commission,
I, p. 10.


452.  ATTEMPTED FORMATION OF WORLD WIRE CARTEL (1899)


When the Sherman Anti-Trust Act of 1890 was passed,
domestic monopolization was the sole concern of legislatures.  Most American participation in the world market
consisted of farm products and raw materials.  In some
regional markets, such as Latin America, American manu-
tures were sold.  The idea of American manufacturers
regularly participating in world-wide or even European
monopolies was novel.  Here a principal in the U.S. Steel
Corporation relates straightforwardly how his firm sought
to join in a European monopoly of wire.


Q.  (By Mr. JENKS.)  It was reported some months ago that
there had been in serious contemplation, at any rate, a combination
between the American manufacturers here and corresponding manufacturers in Germany.--A.  I went over there for that purpose.

Q.  Will you kindly explain that to us?--A.  I met all the
wire makers of England, Germany, Belgium, France, and Austria, and
I believe all in Europe, and I advocated an agreement by which we
could get better prices for our product and divide the tonnage on
an equitable basis.  They thought we were entitled--I have no objection to telling you--to about 25 per cent of the business, and
they thought they ought to have 75.  Before I got away they offered
us 45 and wanted 55.  I did offer to take 50 and give them 50, but
they would not do that.
. . . . . . . . . . . . . . . . . . . . . . . . . . . . . . . . .

Q.  (By Mr. CLARKE.)  If you had been able to effect an agreement with them such as was proposed, what would that be--an international trust?--A.  I do not know but we should have infringed a
little bit, as far as that is concerned; but they talked about
putting the prices up pretty high.  The Germans wanted to put them
higher than I did.  I was in favor of putting the prices up about
$10 a ton, and they thought they would stand $30.  The only question was that we could not agree on the percentage.

Q.  If you had an international agreement of that kind, how
could our Government control it?--A.  They could tax us on our
profits.

Q.  They could tax you, but they could not tax the other
fellow?--A.  They could make us get a larger percentage--each firm;
and we would get it, too, if we had any chance.


Testimony, John W. Gates, <u>United States Industrial Commission</u>,
I, pp. 1017, 1018.

# I.

# A NATIONAL FINANCIAL SYSTEM

453. "I'LL PAY YOU IN REAL MONEY" (1862)

Greenbacks--"promises"--circulated at a sharp discount. But gold was "real money."

On a Saturday night we stopped at a quiet farmhouse [in Iowa] and stayed until Monday morning; on asking for my bill my host replied: "Since you have respected the Sabbath day I will charge you but half price--one dollar." For some time I had been carrying one of those foolish but precious little one-dollar gold pieces-- "good for the eyes," we used to call them--and I gave him that cherished coin, remarking: "You have been so liberal I will pay you in real money, not in promises." Ten meals and horse-feed for a day and two-thirds, for one dollar in gold, which was equivalent to two dollars in currency, was certainly liberal.

Roberts, Autobiography of a Farm Boy, pp. 128-129.


454. A NATIONAL BANK IS NEEDED IN NEW YORK CITY (1863)

The newly-created National Banking System needed to become established in the nation's financial center if it was to succeed. The federal government appealed to the financial community in the name of both patriotism and profits. These comments were made by Hugh McCulloch, the Comptroller of the Currency.

In relation to the organization of a large National Bank in
New York, Mr. McCullough said, he trusted that such a Bank would
be organized as the result of this meeting.

He thought there could be no doubt, that if established by
the right kind of men, and conducted in a liberal spirit, it would
be a great success.  There had been already organized upwards of a
hundred National Banks, and others were being duly organized, which
had a deep interest in the organization of a National Bank with
large capital in this city.  All of them needed correspondents in
New York, and the provisions of the act were such, that it was very
desirable, if not absolutely necessary, that these correspondents
should also be National Banks, inasmuch as 3/5 of the lawful money
to be kept on hand by the National Banks might be kept with such
depositaries in New York and certain other cities.  The National
Banks of the interior would constantly have on deposit, with their
correspondents in New York, many millions of dollars, and a Bank
established by such gentlemen as were present, would be very certain
to secure a large portion of these deposits.

. . . . . . . . . . . . . . . . . . . . . . . . . . . . . . . . . .

In regard to the effect upon the State Banks, which would be
produced by the organization of National ones, Mr. McCulloch said
that while there was no necessary antagonism between the two systems, and while the officers of the Government would wage no war
upon the State Banks, many of which had come nobly forward to sustain the National credit in the darkest hours of the terrible trial
to which the Nation is being subjected, the National Banking System
would, nevertheless, gradually supersede the banking system of
the States, because it would provide a bank-note circulation (which
State Banks had failed to do) of unquestionable solvency, and which
would be current throughout the Union.

He believed that the National System would, at no distant day,
absolutely absorb the State systems of banking, because it would
commend itself to capitalists and to the people as the best system
yet presented to them.

The people had demanded of the Government protection against
the impositions to which they had been subjected by local banks,
by being supplied with a circulation which should not only be
secured beyond reasonable doubt, but which should be so nearly uniform in value as to meet the requirements of the "commerce between
the States."

The National Currency Act was passed by Congress to satisfy
this demand.  If it should accomplish what it was intended to
accomplish; if it should furnish a circulation of undoubted solvency, and of nearly uniform value from the Atlantic to the Pacific,
which should meet the wants of trade and commerce, which know no
State lines, and be the means of binding the people to the Government by the strong and enduring ties of pecuniary interest; and if
it should mainly do this, as he believed it would, by a mere transfer into National Banks of the capital now invested in local banks,
and that, too, without any loss to the stockholders of the latter,--
who could doubt that the country will be immensely the gainer by
the financial revolution which it will accomplish?

That State and National Systems would soon be on trial, not
as antagonists, but rather as competitors for the "field of circulation." That system which furnishes to the people the most reliable currency and the most uniform in value, that system which commends itself, in the greatest degree, to the loyalty of the people,
and is the best adapted to the genius of our political institutions, will, in spite of all opposion, be, ere long, the prevailing
system of Banking in the United States.

Report of remarks by Hugh McCulloch, October 21, 1863,
Proceedings of the Meeting in Relation to the Establishment of a
Large National Bank in this City, (New York:  William Cullen
Bryant & Co., : inters, 1863), pp. 4, 6-7.


455.  SKYROCKETING INVESTMENTS IN PETROLEUM (1864)

Five years after the first discovery of Pennsylvania
petroleum and during the Civil War a new industry arose.
Prospective profits attracted large investments.


The capital now being invested for the purpose of developing
the petroleum interest is beyond precedent.  Every week new companies are organized, very many of them giving promise of unusually
favorable results.  Dividends of from 3 to 5 per cent per month are
by no means uncommon.  Of course if such returns could be depended
upon, from year to year, the flow of capital towards petroleum investments would be even much more rapidly increased.  Comparatively
few, however, anticipate so rich a harvest, and yet so long as the
present high prices are maintained, we cannot see how investments
in the good companies can fail to be extremely remunerative.  The
cost of working the land is comparatively small, and when a good
well is struck the returns are enormous, leaving a large balance
of profits.
We have been requested to call attention to the New York and
Liverpool Petroleum Company, (71 Broadway), as one of unusual promise.  Of course we know little with regard to the actual resources
of the land held by that corporation, not having examined it personally.  Yet its list of property, favorably located, is very
large indeed, and the names of its directors are a guarantee of
good faith.  For every five dollars subscribed ten dollars in stock
is received, so that if the comapny is successful the profits must
be very large.  Were we about to make investments of that nature,
we should certainly be favorably inclined towards this company,
and give it a further examination.

Hunt's Merchants' Magazine, December, 1864, pp. 485-486.

456.  SPECULATION IN OIL STOCKS (1864)


Expansion of the market, a series of technical
improvements, and startling profits fed a "rage for
[oil] stocks" during the Civil War.


One of the most singular features of the times is the extraordinary demand that has sprung up for oil stocks.  If this demand
were confined to the stocks of producing companies we could understand it, but applying as well to the stock of organizations which
have not yet commenced boring even, as to the dividend paying
shares, we are at a loss to comprehend it.  Indeed such is the rage
for stocks of this character now here that sales are common in companies where the stock certificates have not yet been issued or the
transfer books opened, and instances are now uncommon where stock
has been sold at an advance of two hundred per cent even before the
company was organized!  Of course in such wild speculation as this
some one is bound to get "burnt."  Many of these organizations will
doubtless pay in the end, it may be that some of them, like the
"Columbia," "Dalzell," "Maple Shade" and other producing companies,
will more than realize the expectations of the stockholders; but it
is equally apparent that many more of them are gotten up wholly for
speculative purposes, and that in a year from now their shares will
not be worth more than the paper on which they are printed.  In view
of this fact too much circumspection cannot be used in making investments of this character.  In purchasing the stock of producing
companies, in which regular dividends are declared, the buyer does
not run so very much risk, but when it comes to the stock of companies which have not yet got fairly into operation, it is different, and great caution should be exercised.  The value of an organization of this kind can generally be judged from the character of
the men at the head of it.  If you find a company with men of
wealth, character and integrity at the head of it you may rest
assured that, however the enterprise may turn out, it will be
prosecuted honestly and for the benefit of the stockholders; while,
on the other hand, where you find an organization under the control
of financial sharpers, ever on the lookout for the easiest way to
"make an honest penny," you may set it down as a kite-flying concern
gotten up for the personal emolument of its originators, who, as
soon as they have got things fairly started, will sell out at a
handsome profit, leaving their dupes to shoulder the loss.


Pittsburgh Evening Chronicle, August 26, 1864, reprinted in
Giddens (ed.), Pennsylvania Petroleum, p. 246.

457.   EACH NEW YORK BANKER ACTS FOR HIMSELF (1864)

Federal fiscal policy was necessarily dominated
by war needs.  But policy makers, as a matter of custom,
kept in close touch with the business community on policy
matters.  (See Source No. 702).  McCulloch, the author
here, resigned as president of an Indiana bank in 1863
and became the first Comptroller of the Currency under
the National Banking Act.

Soon after Mr. [William P.] Fessenden was appointed Secretary
[of the Treasury], he thought he should see his way more clearly if
he knew what the prominent bankers and merchants of New York would,
advise in regard to his policy.  At his request, therefore, I went
to New York, and had a free talk with a number of such men as I
knew to be intelligent and who I thought would give me disinterest-
ed opinions.  I did not ask them to meet together, but in private
interviews I endeavored to obtain from each as much light as he
could shed upon the points which were presented to him.  I did not
expect to gain much by these interviews, but I confess I was disappointed at the want of accord in the opinions that were expressed.
They were all high-toned and able men, but I could not avoid the
conclusion that all viewed the questions in which Mr. Fessenden was
so deeply interested in the light of their own personal interests.
This was natural, for no honorable business man ever supposes that
his own interests can be antagonistic to those of the Government.
There was no accord even among the bankers in regard to what should
be the policy of the Secretary.  I ought not to have been surprised
at this, for I knew that the bankers of New York had always been in
the habit of deciding and acting each for himself in cases of emergency, without reference to the opinions and action of others—that
there was not then and never had been in that city, in times of
financial trouble, a banker of such acknowledged superiority that
the other bankers would look to him for guidance.

Hugh McCulloch, Men and Measures of Half a Century, (New
York:  Scribner's, 1888), pp. 199-200.

458.   OUR NATIONAL DEBT MAY BE A NATIONAL BLESSING (1865)

Eighty-four years before, Alexander Hamilton had
argued for the good effects of a national debt (see
above, Source No. 104).  The newer argument differed
little from the older one.  Most striking is the emphasis
of both upon manufacturing.  Samuel Wilkeson wrote this
pamphlet from which the following comes.  It was done at

the request of Jay Cooke, who, during the Civil War,
served the Union government as general agent to sell
federal bonds.


   It was not the industry, persistency, and frugality of the
British people--it was not their insular position--it was not their
coals nor their iron stone that gave them supremacy on the ocean and
in the money markets and trading exchanges of both hemispheres.
Their insular position was against them.  Their limited island
territory was unfavorable to empire.  Their want of space and their
climate made them dependent upon other countries for their bread.
They became supreme as merchants, manufacturers, and money lenders,
simply because their national debt added four thousand millions of
capital to their previously acquired wealth, and simply because this
vast infusion of wealth, which had every business virtue of standard
coin, spurred the industry of the island, developed its mineral
resources, invented and put in motion a vast mass of machinery which
spun, wove, and hammered for the world, and undersold the world, and
sent the world to London to pay debt and to borrow money.  What
place among the cities of the world would not a permanent American
debt of four thousand millions give New York?
   It is precisely so with the War Debt of the United States.
Seven-Thirties are available for any enterprise to which unoccupied
lands, undeveloped mines, unestablished arts, and unseized commerce,
invite Americans.  They are cash capital, literally, absolutely,
and without figure of speech.  Practically they are cash in bank and
cash in the pocket.  The artificial measures of their value which
Stock Exchanges have succeeded in instituting, at times nominally
gave fluctuation to their worth as they lie in the bureau drawers
of farmers.  But in reality the depreciation of Wall Street does
not whittle off the thousandth part of a hair's breadth from that
worth.  Those farmers know that they are first bond and mortgage
upon all the United States, and on all the people in the United
States, and upon their children, and their children's children.
But whether 3 per cent above par or 1 per cent above par, holders
of this War Debt of Three Thousand Millions can at any day and any
hour, from San Francisco to New York, and from Portland to New
Orleans, convert it into cash.
   The Funded Debt of the United States is the addition of three
thousand millions of dollars to the previously realized wealth of
the nation.  It is three thousand millions added to the available
active capital.  To pay this debt would be to extinguish this capital and to lose this wealth.  To extinguish this capital and lose
this wealth would be an inconceivably great national misfortune.
   This, our National War Debt, should be held forever in place
as the political tie of the states and the bond forever of a fra-
ternal nationality.  It will give a common interest in the Union
between thirty-five millions of people the unity of feeling arising
from a community of interest in a co-partnership capital of three
thousand millions of dollars.  Tied to the Union by the Union debt,
nor Western states, nor Southern states--states beyond the Rocky
Mountains nor states by the Atlantic Sea--states that plant nor

states that weave--states that mine nor states that smelt and
hammer, can ever find inducement in sectional interests to draw
asunder from each other....

Our National Debt should be held firmly in place as the foundation of a system of diversified national industry which shall relieve us from dependence upon Europe--shall give us the near and
cheap home market instead of the distant and costly foreign market--
shall double the profits of farming by doubling the markets for
farm products--shall swell the class that is devoted to Agriculture,
which is the sheet anchor of Democracies--shall free man by freeing
labor, by giving it many markets in which to sell itself to competing bidders.  The maintenance of our National Debt is Protection.
The destruction of it by payment is bondage again to the manufacturers of Europe.

Samuel Wilkeson, How Our National Debt May Be a National
Blessing, (Philadelphia, Pennsylvania:  Jay Cooke, 1865), extracts
reprinted in Charles J. Bullock (ed.), Selected Readings in Public
Finance, 3rd edition, (Boston, Massachusetts:  Ginn and Co., 1924),
pp. 831-832.


459.  THE CIVIL WAR WAS SUCCESSFULLY FINANCED (1865)


During the Revolutionary War, Benjamin Franklin
had remarked on the wonderful capacities of paper
money (see Source No. 103 above).  Nearly a century
later, the same might have been observed of the greenbacks and government bonds.  The writer of the following
is Elbridge Spaulding, who was a member of the House
of Representatives from New York, and during the Civil
War had served as chairman of the Ways and Means Sub-
committee on the National Currency Bank Bill.


...The management of the fiscal affairs of the Government,
both legislative and executive, during the war, was a material
departure from the sound political economy, applicable to ordinary
times of peace.  The demand for money means forced upon the country
by such a gigantic rebellion, was wholly unprecedented--nothing
ever recorded in history equaled this demand--and reached to such
overwhelming amounts, so vastly beyond any former financial
requirements, that the careful observer cannot but look back with
wonder and amazement that the Government was at all able to pass
successfully through such an extraordinary crisis.  The authoriza-
tion of a loan of $900,000,000, in one act, and an increase of
the public debt in one year of over $940,000,000, over and above
custom duties and internal taxes, are matters of history.  The
amount of the issue of paper currency and temporary obligations

in various forms was almost appalling.  Considerably over one
million of men were at one period of the war withdrawn from productive labor.  The strain upon the credit of the Government, with
eleven States practically out of the Union, was very great.  It
would seem that no other country could have borne up under such a
sudden expansion of the credit circulation, and the changing of so
many men from producers to destroyers of life and property.  This
great inflation of the paper medium had, however, some compensating
advantages.  It stimulated into wonderful activity all the productive energies of common labor, skilled labor, and machinery of all
kinds.  War material was produced with amazing rapidity, and in
abundant quantity, for equipping, supporting and moving all the
great armies in the field and navies afloat.  The people never
flagged, hesitated, or faltered in producing and furnishing all
these vast war materials, and receiving in exchange for it the promises issued to them by the Government.  They seemed to be getting
rich by the operation, and although it was to some extent unreal,
yet this stimulus, aided by patriotic determination to maintain the
Union, was great enough to induce the people to furnish every thing
necessary to supply the army and navy to crush the rebellion, at
the mouth of the cannon and point of the bayonet.  No compromise
was made.  Superior force, backed by powerful and abundant resources, accomplished this great achievement.  The army and navy
were powerful and victorious, because they were sustained by all
the vast resources of the country, brought to their aid voluntarily,
and by the superior power of the Government which commanded these
resources.  These bold and decisive financial measures gave power
and dignity to the Government, and although it operated upon the
unwilling as a force loan, the crisis demanded it; it was the price
of the national Union; the national faith is pledged, and every
dollar of this debt must be paid, principal and interest, in gold
and silver.

     The value of the Union and the Government preserved in full
vigor under the Constitution, cannot be estimated in dollars and
cents.  It is above all price.  A vast continent, embracing territory and people, is now held under the control of a mighty central
and consolidated Government, based upon the will of an enterprising
intelligent and powerful people.


     Elbridge G. Spaulding, History of the Legal Tender Paper
Money Issued During the Great Rebellion, (Buffalo, New York:
Express Printing Co., 1869), pp. 209-210.

460.   "THE SOUTH NEEDS CAPITAL" (1865)


Immediately following the Civil War, very little
long-term northern capital entered the South.   The
principal reason for this hesitancy is explained in
the following paragraph in a comment by General Schurz
speaking in Congress.


The south needs capital.   But capital is notoriously timid
and averse to risk itself, not only where there actually is
trouble, but where there is serious and continual danger of trouble.
Capitalists will be apt to consider--and they are by no means wrong
in doing so--that no safe investments can be made in the south as
long as southern society is liable to be convulsed by anarchical
disorders.   No greater encouragement can, therefore, be given to
capital to transfer itself to the south than the assurance that
the government will continue to control the development of the
new social system in the late rebel States until such dangers are
averted by a final settlement of things upon a thorough free-labor
basis.


General Carl Schurz, U.S. Congress, 39th, 1st session,
Exec. Doc. No. 2, Condition of the South, serial number 1237,
p. 41.


461.   NORTHERN CAPITAL IN THE SOUTH (1865-1866)


Northern investors probed investment possibilities far and wide in the South.   Whitelaw Reid writes
about the situation.


[Newbern, N.C.]  Returning merchants find sutlers behind their
counters, reckoning up gains such as the old business men of Newbern
never dreamed of; all branches of trade are in the hands of Northern
speculators, who followed the army; half the residences are filled
with army officers, or occupied by Government civil officials, or
used for negro schools, or rented out as "abandoned property."
. . . . . . . . . . . . . . . . . . . . . . . . . . . . . . . .

[New Orleans, La.]  New Orleans had proved a rich harvest-field
to a crowd of new men and miscellaneous adventurers from the North.
Hundreds had accumulated fortunes since the occupation of the
city.

. . . . . . . . . . . . . . . . . . . . . . . . . . . . . . . . .

Few of these Northerners had yet made permanent investments in
the South.  Plantations had not begun to come into the market.
Southerners had hardly had time to look about them and decide what
to do.  But it was already evident that, provided they could make
titles which were good for anything, plenty of them would soon be
anxious to sell.  Northern capital and energy were likely to have
still finer openings within a few months, than any that the confusion of a captured city and the chaos of constantly shifting military government had afforded.

. . . . . . . . . . . . . . . . . . . . . . . . . . . . . . . . .

[Richmond, Va.]  But business was greatly overdone by Northern
speculators who had rushed down with heavy supplies of goods immediately after the surrender.  The first pressing necessities satisfied, the Virginians were too poor to trade largely.

Thanks to Northern loans, in sums ranging as high (in one or
two cases, at least,) as a half-million dollars, the railroads were
rapidly getting into running order, and old lines of travel were
reopening.

. . . . . . . . . . . . . . . . . . . . . . . . . . . . . . . . .

[Lynchburg, Va.]  The town was swarming with representatives
of Northern capitalists, looking for investments.  Baltimoreans
were also found frequently among them.  The most went further South,
over the Virginia and Tennessee road; but a few had ideas about the
mineral resources of these mountains.  Many seemed to think it
necessary to adopt the coddling policy in their talk wiht the
Virginians.

. . . . . . . . . . . . . . . . . . . . . . . . . . . . . . . . .

[Selma, Alabama]  Northern men were pressing in rapidly.  Many
officers were in Selma in November, arranging for pretty heavy
operations; and soldiers who had gone home, talked about returning
to lease small plantations.  General McArthur, of Illinois, had
leased five in Central Alabama.  Generals Charles and William R.
Woods, of Ohio, were getting some; so were Colonel Gere, of Iowa,
and a number of others.  Their plan was to rent at three to five
dollars an acre, one-third down and the remainder payable 1st
January, 1867.  Then they hire, at liberal salaries, competent
overseers for each plantation.  In this mode of operating, everything, of course, depends on skillful management.  I should judge
it a splendid opening for careless men to lose money.

. . . . . . . . . . . . . . . . . . . . . . . . . . . . . . . . .

[Mobile, Ala.]  Mobile talked, however, rather of plantations and cotton than of politics.  Dozens of Northern men were on the streets, buying cotton on speculation.  Every steamboat swelled the number of Yankees on the lookout for plantations, and of planters anxious to sell or lease.  These planters were entirely honest in the idea which lies at the bottom of their convulsive grasp on slavery.  They did not believe the negro would work without compulsion.  Accordingly, they considered themselves absolutely destitute of reliable labor, and were anxious to be rid of their lands.  The Yankees had faith in Sambo and propose to back their faith with abundant capital.  If they succeed, their cotton fields are better than Nevada mines.  If they fail--but a Yankee never fails in the long run.

. . . . . . . . . . . . . . . . . . . . . . . . . . . . . . . . . .

[Memphis, Tenn.]  General Frank Blair, who engaged in cotton planting on the opposite side of the river, was in town.  Many other adventurous cotton planters from the North made Memphis their head-quarters.  None seemed to suffer the slightest inconvenience from any unfriendly disposition on the part of the people.  On the contrary all Northern men, bringing capital to stock and conduct these great plantations which had hitherto made the prosperity of Memphis, seemed to be sure of a fervid welcome.

. . . . . . . . . . . . . . . . . . . . . . . . . . . . . . . . . .

This flunkeyism of Northern men, who "expected to stay in this country and didn't want to make enemies," was manifest everywhere.  For a genuine toady, commend me to a Northern adventurer, or "runner," in the cotton-growing regions.  Through the winter of 1865-'66, the South was full of them, looking for cotton-lands, soliciting custom for Northern business houses, collecting old debts.  They never spoke of Rebels, but with great caution called them Confederates.

. . . . . . . . . . . . . . . . . . . . . . . . . . . . . . . . . .

Nothing but the prevalent sense of the insecurity attending all Southern movements, during the political and social chaos that followed the surrender, prevented a large immigration from the North in the winter of 1865-'66.  That the openings which the South presents for Northern capital and industry are unsurpassed, has been sufficiently illustrated.  With a capital of a few thousand dollars, and a personal supervision of his work, a Northern farmer, devoting himself to cotton-growing, may count with safety on a net profit of fifty per cent. on his investment.  With a good year and a good location he may do much better.  Through Tennessee and the same latitudes, east and west, he will find a climate not very greatly different from his own, and a soil adapted to Northern cereals as well as to the Southern staple.  The pine forests still embower untold riches; the cypress swamps of the lower Mississippi and its tributaries, only await the advent of Northern lumbermen to be converted into gold-mines; the mineral resources of Northern Georgia and Alabama, in spite of the war's developments, are yet as attractive as those that are drawing emigration into the uninhibited wilds across the Rocky Mountains.  But capital and labor--especially agricultural labor--demand security.

Along the great highways of travel in the South, I judge
investments by Northern men to be nearly as safe as they could be
anywhere.  The great cotton plantations bordering the Mississippi
are largely in the hands of Northern lesees; and few, if any of
them have experienced the slightest difficulty from any hostility
of the inhabitants.  So, along the great lines of railroad, and
through regions not too remote from the tide of travel and trade,
there are no complaints.  It is chiefly in remote sections, far
from railroads or mails, and isolated among communities of intense
Southern prejudices, that Northern men have had trouble.


Whitelaw Reid, After the War, pp. 30, 240-242, 324, 332, 382,
405-406, 426, 560, 578-579.



462.  MANUFACTURERS SHOULD BE SOFT-MONEY MEN (1866)


While the American money supply was inflated by
Greenbacks, foreigners could exchange valuable gold for
less valuable paper money.  When they spent the paper
money here, they received more goods for it than they
would have gotten in Europe for their gold.  The greater
the difference in value between gold and paper, the
larger the American sales abroad.  Conversely, the less
the difference in value between gold and paper, the
smaller the American sales abroad.  Jonathan Sturges, a New
York merchant and director of a bank and railroads,
writes to John Sherman, a U.S. Senator from Ohio and a
specialist in financial legislation.


There are some elements operating against our manufacturers,
which are not generally understood, and they will continue to act,
so long as money is cheap in Europe, and Gold is dear here.  All
articles manufactured in Europe, are purchased upon a Gold basis,
labor is paid for at Gold rates, so that all these manufactures are
laid down here on a Gold basis.  They are sold here on a Currency
basis, which has been forty or fifty per cent above Gold.  When
sold for the account of European manufacturers, remittances are not
made while Gold is up, but the money is borrowed in Europe at their
low rates, until Gold falls here; this gives them a great advantage
over our manufacturers, and I have no doubt, is a serious cause of
our present embarrassment.  As soon as Gold falls twenty or thirty
per cent, the foreign houses rush in and buy for remittances; and
this puts gold up and enables them to go through the same operation
again.
Our own manufactures are all on a Currency basis, (materials
and labor) and are sold for Currency.  When Gold falls, the manufacturer loses the difference on the stock on hand.  Gold has fallen

20 per cent in 60 days.  The foreign manufacturer, all things being
equal, can sell 20% cheaper than we can goods manufactured before
Gold fell.  This may be remedied by increasing the duty on foreign
manufactures until Gold falls, say for two years, and Foreigners
will lose the advantage which they now have, just so soon as Gold
is permanently lower.


Letter, Jonathan Sturges to Senator John Sherman, December 29,
1866, in Robert P. Sharkey, Money, Class, and Party, (Baltimore,
Maryland:  Johns Hopkins Press, 1959), pp. 172–173.


463.  RIOTING WILL SET OFF AN EXODUS OF NORTHERN CAPITAL (1866)


On July 30th, 1866, a riot against blacks broke out
in New Orleans.  Evidence strongly suggested the mayor
and police force aided the attack.  Note the warning of
Gen. Sheridan against frightening away northern capital.


The more information I obtain of the affair of the 30th in this
city the more revolting it becomes.  It was no riot; it was an absolute massacre by the police, which was not excelled in murderous
cruelty of that of Fort Pillow.  It was a murder which the mayor
and police of this city perpetrated without the shadow of a necessity; furthermore, I believe it was premediated, and every indication points to this.  I recommend the removing of this bad man.  I
believe it would be hailed with the sincerest gratification by two-
thirds of the population of the city.  There has been a feeling of
insecurity on the part of the people here on account of this man,
which is now so much increased that the safety of life and property
does not rest with the civil authorities, but with the military.
...I have the honor to report quiet in the city, but considerable excitement in the public mind.  There is no interference on
the part of the military with the civil government, which performs
all its duties without hindrance.
I have permitted the retention of the military governor
appointed during my absence, as it gives confidence and enables the
military to know what is occurring th the city.  He does not interfere with civil matters.
Unless good judgment is exercised there will be an exodus of
Northern capital and Union men, which will be injurious to the city
and to the country.  I will remove the military governor in a day
or two.  I again strongly advise that some disposition be made to
change the present mayor, as I believe it would do more to restore

confidence than anything that could be done.   If the present governor could be changed it would not be amiss.


        Telegrams, General P. H. Sheridan to General U.S. Grant,
August 2 and 3, 1866; U.S. Congress, 57th, 2nd session, Senate,
Exec. Doc. No. 209, serial number 4430, (Washington, D.C.:  Govern-
ment Printing Office, 1903), p. 141.



        464.   "WHO MAKES MONEY ON WALL STREET?" (1870)


        A comprehensive catalogue of winners:   it is
    followed by a section--not reproduced here--entitled:
    "Who Lose Money on Wall Street."   The writer, Mathew
    Smith, wrote for the Boston Journal under the name of
    "Burleigh."


        1st.   Those who trade legitimately in stocks.   A commission
house in Wall Street, that buys and sells stocks, as a trade, and
does nothing else, must make money.   It cannot be otherwise.   Such
men run no risks.   A legitimate house never buys stocks without
a margin.   The operator holds the stocks, watches the market, and
can protect himself when he will.   The great temptation is to speculate.   Why make a paltry commission, when by a nice investment,
thousands may be secured?   Few houses are successful, because few
adhere to the rule, rigidly, not to touch any thing as a speculation, however tempting the offer.   One of the heaviest houses in
New York, that went down on the Black Friday, failed because it
added speculation to a commission business.   For years the house
refused to speculate.   It became one of the most honored, and trus-
ty, as well as one of the most successful.   While the principal
partner was absent in Europe, his associates ventured on a little
speculation.   It proved successful, and the house became one of the
largest operators in Wall Street.   The crash came, as it comes to
all such, and the ruin was terrible.   Had the house been content
to follow the legitimate business that made it, it would have
stood to-day.
        2d.   Operators make money who buy in a panic.   Few men in Wall
Street can invest during a panic.   When Stocks are low, and growing
lower, and the bottom seems to be knocked out of everything
speculators are at their wits' end, like men in a storm at sea.
Then, cool, shrewd, careful captitalists buy.   Men in California
Chicago, Baltimore, Boston, Buffalo, have standing orders with
their brokers, to buy when stocks are low.   These are quiet men,
that know that the law of the street is sure and stocks will recover.   They never buy on what is called a Bull market, but always when
Stocks are low, and buy for a rise.   Millions change hands by
telegraph, when the Street is in a war.

3d.   Another class that make money buy without any reference
to the street.  They select a line of stocks, with the value of
which they are well acquainted.  They buy the stock and pay for it.
They take it home and lock it up.  It is their own.  No broker can
sell them out.  They have no margin to lose, and none to keep good.
If the stock goes down twenty per cent. they are not alarmed.  They
know that the street will repeat itself, and that the stock will
come up.  They bide their time, and sell out when they please.

4th.   Another class of operators make money who average their
stocks.  These operators buy a line of stocks—a thousand shares of
Lake Shore at ninety.  An order is left with the broker to buy Erie
as it goes down, and so keep purchasing three hundred.  Lake Shore
falls, as other stocks go down, but the party is securing other
lines at a lower rate.  When the market rises, they all go up together.  It takes capital and pluck to do this.  Operators must
have money to hold the thousand shares, and secure other lines of
stock to average the decline.  The wealthy operators on the street—
the old heads, who are sure of a rise if they wait for it, are the
men who average their stock.

5th.   Men make money on the street who are content to do a
small business; who are statisfied with small profits.  Such men
are not bold operators, but they are very safe ones.  Five hundred
dollars profit is very satisfactory.  Most operators want to make
money at a blow; making five hundred, they reinvest it at once,
like a gambler, who having made fifty dollars, is in a glow of
excitement to make a hundred.  Such men often buy the same stock
over, that they have just sold, and but it at a higher price.  Instead of taking their little gains out of the street and waiting,
then try another battle with fortune, and continue till all is
swept away.  Henry Keep, called "Henry the silent," on the Street,
was one of the most successful operators that ever dealt in stocks.
He said to a friend one day, "Would you like to know how I made my
money?  I did it by cooping the chickens; I did not wait till the
whole brood was hatched.  I caught the first little chicken that
chipped the shell, and put it in the coop.  I then went after more.
If there were no more chickens, I had one safe at least.  I never
despised small gains.  What I earned, I took care of.  I never per-
illed what I had, for the sake of grasping what I had not secured."

6th.   Men who can control the street are sure to make money.
Vanderbilt, Drew, Law, and men of their capital can do this when
they please.  When they combine, they can make the nation reel.  If
they want to control stocks, they buy them up, and lock them up.
They can keep them as long as they please, and sell them when and
as they please.  They can run the price up to any height.  These men
not only make a fortune in a day, but they make fortunes for all
their friends whom they choose to call in.  The permanent success
among operators and speculators is found in the classes named.

Smith, Bulls and Bears of Wall Street, pp. 549–552.

465.  THE WALL STREET LAWYERS (1870)

A money market existed on a base of financial
paper.  That meant that considerations of legal obligation and liability were crucial.  The Wall Street lawyers
became a necessity and they prospered from that necessity.


Wall Street lawyers like Wall Street bankers, are the men who
give character to their profession.  Out of three thousand who
practice law in New York, a very small part get their living by
practicing that profession.  They are brokers in a small way, dabble
in real estate, become literary critics, and eke out a living in
various ways.  About a dozen lawyers have a national reputation,
and these will be found in and around Wall Street.  These form a
select society--socially and legally.  They are high toned,
gentlemanly and genial; among whom the espirit de corps of the profession is found.  The rest of the profession have very little in
common.  New York lawyers have seldom occasion to meet, except they
are engaged in the same individual cause.  The manner in which suits
are brought is very peculiar.  Till the trial, every thing is done
out of court, and done by clerks, students and subordinates.  When
the calendar is called it is watched by mere boys, and leading counsel are seldom seen in court unless an important motion is to be
argued, or the cause is actually on.  Lawyers of note have junior
partners who attend to all the preliminary details of the suit.
     The legal business of New York is broken up into departments
and eminent counsel have specialties.  One class devote themselves
wholly to criminal practice; others confine themselves to the
Federal Courts; some are commercial lawyers, others conduct
Admiralty cases; one class are Patent lawyers; but the most successful and remunerative practice is that connected with real estate.
A chain of titles from certain lawyers would pass all the parks in
the city.
     Charles O'Connor stands at the head of the profession without
controversy.  James T. Brady was his successful rival.  Since his
death, no one has arisen to take his place.  Mr. Evarts is the
attorney for the highest toned bankers, merchants, and insurance
offices in the street.  He is one of the ablest lawyers in New
York, and one of the safest counsellors.  David Dudley Field leads
in a certain kind of practice.  He is the shrewdest and most successful counsellor at the New York bar.  His income is probably
larger than that of any lawyer in New York.  He is very successful
in heavy railroad suits, patents and other intricate cases.  He
would not be taken in court by a stranger for a man of any mark.
He has a sleepy, indifferent sort of look when he is in repose,
as if he had no interest in any matter at all.


Smith, Bulls and Bears of Wall Street, pp. 465-467.

### 466.   FINANCE IN MOBILE, ALABAMA (1871)

The early insurance companies were state-chartered
and restricted by law to investments in land mortgages
and government securities; savings banks were under the
same limitation.  During the 1870s and 1880s, however,
the capital needs of American industry prevailed and
such restrictions were greatly moderated or abolished
altogether.

But Mobile, like the other Southern seaports, labours, after
the huge losses of the war, under a disability in want of capital.
There are only three banks, and these of very limited means, in
the city--the Bank of Mobile with a capital of 500,000 dollars,
the Southern Bank of Alabama and the First National Bank, with
capitals respectively of 300,000 dollars.  But for the insurance
companies, which have prospered greatly since the war, and which
invest their surplus means in commercial paper to an amount exceeding the total capital of the banks, trade would have been much
more crippled than it has been; and, of course, a commodity, so
scarce in proportion to the work to be done as money here, is only
obtainable on very high terms.

Somers, The Southern States Since the War, p. 184.

### 467.   SHORTAGE OF CAPITAL IN NEW ORLEANS (1871)

The following correctly subdues the then-current
idea that Northern capital was eagerly flowing Southward.
Some was, but not much according to Robert Somers.

The deficiency of capital in New Orleans for the commercial
demands and resources of the port can only be referred to with a
certain reserve; and it must be remarked, both in justice to the
relative merits of the case and in legitimate reduction of a too
inflated idea abroad as to what Northern capital and enterprise
may now be expected to do in the South, that deficiency of capital
is written over all parts of the Union as well as the South, and
that, save in some few localities where a long course of almost
fanatical Protectionist policy has developed an outlay of hard
money and entailed a perennial public sacrifice disproportioned
to their natural value, there is scarcely any section of this
immense continent in which land, labour, and productive resource
are not greatly in excess of the capital necessary to employ and

cultivate them.  There has never been any great country so hostile
in its commercial legislation to other countries, while so dependent on other countries for its most essential means of progress,
as the United States.  But in the South, so lately desolated by
war, the deficiency of capital is more marked than elsewhere.  The
British and other European houses that deal in exchange, bring
great resources to bear on moving the cotton crop.  The effective
purchasing power at the other end overcomes all obstacles to its
purpose.  Yet it is observable that from September to January, when
this movement is at its height, the pressure for funds is usually
severe, and in the course of the present season, aggravated somewhat probably by the war in Europe, as much as two per cent. per
month has been paid on good mercantile paper.

Somers, The Southern States Since the War, pp. 209-210.


468.   RUDIMENTARY BANKING IN RURAL MISSISSIPPI (1871)


Perhaps one could not blame planters for dallying
when it came to pay a note bearing 20 to 30 percent
interest.


There is no banking accommodation in this and many other
districts of the State of Mississippi worthy of the same.  Yet planters of means and substance can sometimes obtain loans on their personal notes at an interest of 20 to 30 per cent. per annum; and,
deplorable as this may seem, until country gentlemen in the South
show more attention to their notes when due by personal appearance,
even at the expense of a ten or fifteen miles' ride on horseback,
it must be vain for them to think of coming under the reign of
ordinary monetary usance.  Complaints of bank and note collectors
as to the cavalier indifference of the onerous parties are very
common, even where no doubt is entertained of ultimate payment.

Somers, The Southern States Since the War, pp. 243-244.


469.   HOW TO CREATE A TIGHT MONEY MARKET (1871)


The following is an apt illustration of some negative
consequences of a relatively inelastic supply of currency.

Large dealers in stocks have power to create a panic by making what is called a tight money market. They lock up greenbacks and gold, and produce general distress and ruin. It requires a large combination to do this. Men of heavy capital, of great resources, who watch the market and strike together when the right time comes. Ten men combining, who could control ten millions, would agitate the street. But a combination, able to control twenty millions, would tighten the money market and produce a panic. Money is limited. The clearing house daily indicates the amount of cash in circulation. All banks are required to keep 25 per cent. of their deposits and circulation in the bank. The cliques who propose to tighten the money market understand that. Some banks are wicked enough to lend themselves to such a combination. When the scheme is ripe a well known party goes to a bank and enquires, "how much money have you got?" "Two hundred thousand dollars" is the reply. "I want to borrow a million." A million is borrowed of a bank that has but two hundred thousand dollars to loan. The interest is paid on this million for one, ten, or thirty days. A certified check is taken by the borrower and is locked up. A million is taken from circulation, for the bank can make no loans as the certified check may turn up at any minute. Nineteen men are doing the same thing with nineteen other banks. Twenty millions of greenbacks are locked up. The money is not taken from the bank; it is understood that it shall not be. The bank, with two hundred thousand dollars receives the interest of a million of dollars, keeps the money in its own vaults and has parted with nothing but a certified check. Speculators who have bought stocks cannot hold them, for they have no money; the banks cannot discount, money cannot be borrowed except at ruinous rates. The cliques who have tightened the market often ask as high as one per cent. a day. for money. Speculators have to throw their stock on the market, the market tumbles and the combination buy at their own prices.

Another method of tightening the money market is, by a combination which wears a different phase, though the result is the same. In this combination, fifty thousand dollars control a million. Twenty or thirty men conspire to make money scarce. A party borrows of a bank $50,000 on one, or ten days. Interest is paid and a certified check taken. The money remains in the bank--it is effectually locked up, the bank cannot loan it, for the certified check may be presented at any moment. This check is taken to another bank and $50,000 borrowed upon that. No money is removed, but a certified check taken and placed in another bank with like results. So the party moves from bank to bank, till he has locked up a million with his fifty thousand. Each member of the clique is doing the same thing, and a panic in stocks follows. A third method is, to draw greenbacks from the bank, and seal them up and keep them till the market is ripe for taking off the pressure.


Smith, Twenty Years Among the Bulls and Bears of Wall Street, pp. 57–59.

470.    SOUTHERN AGENCIES OF NORTHERN BANKING FIRMS (1870's)


The need of British industry for raw cotton, and
the need of New York bankers and merchants for customers
created a close bond between British cotton buyers,
New York financiers and shippers, and Southern planters.
The latter, lacking domestic carrying and banking facilities, constituted a rich source of earnings for North and
overseas.  (See Source No. 434).  Again John Crosby Brown
writes.


In the early days of the firm and during the lifetime of
Alexander Brown, cotton raised in the South was shipped mainly from
New Orleans, Mobile, Savannah and Charleston, and in all these
places the firm had its correspondents and later its own agents.
The business of these correspondents and afterward of the agents
was to advance a safe amount of money on cotton consigned to the
Liverpool house for sale and also to buy bills of exchange against
shipments of cotton to England and the Continent usually with bills
of lading attached.
    A few years after the [Civil] war the business of the agencies
grew less and less, and, with the exception of New Orleans, they
ceased to be important factors in the transactions of the firm.
The rapid and improved railway communication between the North and
the South, the shortening of the time for the transit of the mails
and the almost universal use of the telegraph by merchants and
bankers more and more concentrated the market for exchange in New
York, and there was no longer any need to maintain an agent in the
Southern ports to secure a good supply of commercial bills.  They
could be purchased in New York through brokers at almost the same
rates as by our own agents, and in addition, for a very slight advance in price, they often carried a bank endorsement.  The agencies
therefore came to a natural end, and one after the other was abandoned.  New Orleans was continued longer than the others, and for
a long time there were earnest discussions among the partners both
in New York and England about the advisability of strengthening and
maintaining the agency there; but after a careful examination of the
field it was found that unless it should be so enlarged and stren-
thened that the house there could compete for a share of the good
local business of the place and adjoining country,--a policy which
would have required not only additional capital, but also in all
probability, the presence of a resident partner--it would not pay
to maintain it solely as a centre for the purchase of sterling
exchange.  As the business of the firms, both in the North and in
London, was constantly increasing, and demanded all the time and
strength of the partners, it was determined to abandon that field
and to concentrate more and more in New York and adjacent cities,
which were in daily and hourly contact with the head office.


Brown, A Hundred Years of Merchant Banking, pp. 255, 276-277.

471.   THEORIES ARE GOOD FOR AFTER DINNER (1874)

Following is a westerner's argument that an elastic
currency will serve the interests of all sections but
that it is crucial for the further economic development
of the West.

You eastern men gave us a panic last September; you call it a
currency panic.  We call it a gambler's panic in Wall street, that
the honest men of the country had nothing to do with; it was not a
depreciation of the currency.  I do not pretend to account for it.
I want you gentlemen to account for it, for there are a great many
things I cannot account for.  One thing is this everlasting adher-
ence to the idea of a specie standard, when there is not a specie-
paying civilized country on the globe to-day.  If I had time to give
you a lecture on my political economy, as these gentlemen have on
theirs, I could convince you of the fact that there is not, to-day,
a civilized country, and has not been since commerce attained what
it is, that has not cured all its financial troubles by what we call
suspension and by a paper currency.  Now, if the medicine is good
for a sick patient what is the use of dosing him with other medicine.
    Last September your bankers and your papers cried out, we did
not have money enough.  I remember a remark by the President of
the Metropolitan Bank of New York, that was quoted with great favor
in our country, as the remedy for the evil.  I have not heard from
the President of the Metropolitan Bank lately, but he expressed the
western idea exactly; and the New York and eastern press, at that
time, expressed the western idea exactly, because they then understood the condition of affairs.  They understood that this panic
was the result of a vicious system, and that we must cure the system; that it was not for want of specie payment or anything of
that kind, but it was from the vicious system of gambling; and
they demanded exactly the same cure that we gentlemen from the
West are demanding here to-day.  And if you had another panic to-
morrow, you would demand the same thing.  Theories are good things,
gentlemen, when you have eaten good dinners.
. . . . . . . . . . . . . . . . . . . . . . . . . . . . . . . . . . .
    Gentlemen, we are all bound together in a common interest, in
this country; the West is simply a colony of the East, to which
your eldest and best boys go; and when you help us, you help them;
and when you help us you help the country.  We have got to feed you.
You know it.  We are able to do it.  But we are ambitious to emu-
late the example of our ancestors, and our relatives in the east.
We want to do a little manufacturing; we want to make iron; we
want to make cotton cloth; we want to make woolen goods; we want
to build railroads, and we want to get a little money out of the
Treasury for the improvement of rivers and harbors.  I do not
blame you, gentlemen, for wanting to get all the interest you can
on your money, because you have accumulated wealth by years of
industry and intelligence, and the honest pursuit of business; it

is your just due.  But I do not want you, from that fact, to conclude that you are the country, by any means, and that all legislation, and particularly legislation affecting the finances and
money of this country, should be from your standpoint alone.


Mr. Van Horn of Kansas City; <u>Debates and Action on the Subject
of Currency and Finance by the National Board of Trade...1874</u>,
(Chicago, Illinois:  Knight and Leonard, Printers, 1874), pp. 74,
75.


472.  WHO ARE THE DEBTORS AND CREDITORS?  (1874)


The virtue of the following is that it points
out business borrowers as the source of much agitation against currency contraction.


Much has been said here, and elsewhere, about the efforts of
the creditor class to bring about specie payments, and the wrong
of so doing inflicted upon the debtor class.  Who constitute these
classes?  The producing classes, that is, those who work for hire
and those small proprietors who work their own shops or farms, are
supposed to own no very large part of the wealth of the country in
any form.  Yet they own about two hundred millions of hoarded
currency; they own the greater part of the seven hundred and eighty
millions deposited in the savings banks, and they own some part of
the stock and deposits in the National banks.  Altogether they hold
about one thousand millions of the capital in the country which is,
or should be, loaned.  (The total loans of the National banks are
only nine hundred and forty millions.)  In respect of aggregate
capital, to say nothing of numbers, what other class holds so large
a part of its capital in loanable wealth, or could profit so much
by the improvement of the currency, if that will make money dearer
to hire?  There is none approaching to it.  Aside from their savings
deposited, or hoardings, hearly all of them have more money due to
them than they owe.
The great body of the workers in this country belong to the
creditor class.  Who, then are the debtors?  First, there is the
mercantile body, who are legitimately debtors, constantly making
and constantly paying debts, to their own average profit and the
good of the whole country, whose prosperity they largely promote.
There is the large class of mortgage debtors, owing long debts well
secured.  The greater part of these find profit in borrowing money
on security of their estates, large or small.  If prudent in their
engagements, they do well, and in making the long debt they took
the risk of changes in the currency.  The rates they pay range from
seven per cent. in the East, to fifteen or eighteen per cent. in

the Far West and South.  Given two years of sound currency and specie payment, they would then find it easy to borrow at lower rates
on the same security, if originally good.

But the great, importunate and noisy debtor class consists of
men of great wealth, real or imputed, who are constantly trying to
float enormous loans on the market for themselves, or for corporations whose offered security is not too good among lenders, and of
needy speculators and adventurers.  These last, whether in or out
of Congress, have much to say of the wrong to debtors threatened
by a contraction of currency and its rise to specie par.


Statement, B. F. Nourse of Boston; Debates and Action on the
Subject of Currency and Finance by the National Board of Trade...
1874, (Chicago, Illinois:  Knight and Leonard, Printers, 1874),
pp. 60-61.



473.  WORKING CAPITAL THROUGH MONTHLY PAY DAYS (1877)


This might be regarded as forced lending at a zero
rate of interest.  Jacob Cox is the author.


In the latter part of 1877 we were very much embarrassed for
funds and one Saturday reached a point where it was impossible for
us to raise enough cash to pay the few hands we had working for us.
Therefore, on Saturday afternoon I went to see father in Toledo,
hoping to borrow more money, and explained to him the difficulties
we were in.  Father said he could let us have more money if it was
absolutely necessary, but he did not feel that we had reached that
point yet.  He told me it was a bad plan for us to get into the
habit of borrowing money every time we felt a little pinched and
that, if I found after getting back to Cleveland that I must have
more money, I could draw on him for such a sum as was necessary
to tide us over the difficulty.  I felt a little hurt at this, but
at the same time could not but believe his advice was sound.

In the mill where I had worked so many years the custom had
always been to pay about the 15th of the month, wages and salaries
earned during the previous month.  This was necessary in an institution as large as the rolling mill, where there were many hundreds
of men employed, whose wages had to be figured per ton of output.
This delay in pay gave the bookkeepers and timekeepers sufficient
time after the closing of the month's business to figure out the
payroll.  I knew that most of the men working in Cleveland were
accustomed to this method of payment.  I therefore reluctantly
announced on returning to the factory that hereafter Newton & Cox

would pay in this manner.  This left us a full two weeks longer in
which to accumulate funds enough to pay the men the amounts due,
and we got along without borrowing any more money at that time.


    Cox, Building an American Industry, © The Cleveland Twist
Drill Company , pp. 95-96.


    474.  CONDITIONS LEADING TO MORTGAGES IN KANSAS (mid-1880's)


        The following story was re-enacted up and down the
    great wheat belt where the mortgage burden moved commer-
    cial wheat growers into politics.


    Our land boom was like an incoming spring tide; it advanced
beyond the natural limits imposed by the conditions.  Its only justification was a rising market for farm products.  When our prosperity began, wheat was at a dollar a bushel, and corn at fifty-
five cents, with livestock prices up in proportion.  Of course
these prices stimulated the cultivation of larger acreages.  The
settler aimed to produce bigger and bigger crops, trusting that
the good prices would continue.
    But in due course the market gradually became glutted, and
prices on cereals and livestock slowly began to sag.  To offset
this, the settler attempted to increase his total crop, by bringing
still more land under cultivation.  However, to do this, he needed
more farm help, which was not available.  So he naturally turned
to the one source of help remaining--modernized farming implements
displacing hand labor...
    The first McCormick reaper [was] followed later by the Marsh
Harvester and automatic binder.  There were also other settlers
adopting the latest farming implements then coming on the market.
These included the steam-driven threshing machine, the grain-drill,
the disk harrow, the gang plow, the corn cutter and husker, and
similar labor and time-saving devices.
    At the time of which I write, labor-saving farm machinery such
as here mentioned involved a heavy cash outlay.  Mass production
in manufacture had not then developed; nor were there any time-
payment plans.  So the progressive farmer of the middle eighties,
in his eagerness to improve his land, became a good prospect for a
farm mortgage.  Unwittingly, he then entered a "vicious circle."
To produce more, he had to increase his acreage.  To do that profitably, he needed labor-saving implements.  To acquire these, he
had to have more cash capital, and that meant--a farm mortgage.
 . . . . . . . . . . . . . . . . . . . . . . . . . . . . . . .
    When the collapse came, as eventually it had to, many of
the settlers lost their land.


    Cameron, Pioneer Days in Kansas, pp. 98-100.

475.  FARM LOAN COMPANIES IN DAKOTA TERRITORY (1880's)

The following account by Seth Humphrey contains
an unusual mixture of concern for the settler and
for the mortgage company's loans.

All through the eighties, while the settlement of government
land was going forward in Kansas, Nebraska, and Dakota Territory,
farm loan companies throve enormously in the business of making
first mortgage loans to settlers and selling the paper to small
investors in New England, New York, and eastern Pennsylvania.  The
demand for these western investments often exceeded the supply, and
loan companies competed with each other to get mortgages; in fact,
through their local agents they would persuade settlers to borrow
and borrow generously.  It thus became really too easy for settlers
to cash in on their western venture and "go back to their wives'
folks."  They borrowed more than the land was worth and fled.
Naturally the companies began to stagger under their loads of de-
faulted mortgages.
. . . . . . . . . . . . . . . . . . . . . . . . . . . . . . . . .
In the middle of October, 1889, the clouds gathering over the
western farm mortgage business broke violently.  The failure of one
of the biggest companies engaged in it revealed to the public for
the first time the incredible extent to which western farms had been
deserted, and carried with it the implication that the affairs of
all other companies must be in the same unhappy state.  Down
slumped the sales of western farm mortgages, almost overnight.
. . . . . . . . . . . . . . . . . . . . . . . . . . . . . . . . .
On sending me to Nebraska the company had suggested that I
indicate all delinquents on my charts, so that I might collect
interest past due as I drove about; particularly in this county so
heavily mortgaged I might make it my business to canvass it, township by township, and do a thorough job in interviewing our nonpay-
ing farmers.  In reply I sent in a report on my first four days of
inspecting in the county.  Of forty-one pieces of land visited
three were occupied by the original mortgagers and three by squatters; on the remaining thirty-five there was not so much as a board
to show that claim shacks had once adorned them.  This settled for
all time any prospect of collecting delinquent interest by canvass-
ing.
Yet in this county of deserted claims I saw evidence of honest
failure, in a great amount of broken ground and in signs of repeated
cropping by settlers who had been determined to try to the limit to
make good; settlers perhaps misguided by that biggest fallacy of
the prairie frontier, that one hundred and sixty acres of raw land
constitute a farm.
Because of a peculiar psychological twist, settlers everywhere
had more or less feeling against outside loan companies.  These
companies were really their saviors at times, lending them money
at ten per cent a year; yet they tolerated as necessary evils the
local bankers who charged three per cent a month and were as

merciless as crocodiles in cases of failure to pay.  The only
reason for this was that the local men robbed them with a personal,
sympathetic touch, while outside companies doing legitimate business
represented, in a vague, impersonal way, aggregations of great
wealth preying on the farmers.  In this view they were steadily
encouraged by the political mountebanks.

Humphrey, Following the Prairie Frontier, pp. 95, 153,
146-165, and 171.


### 476.  CREDIT CRUCIAL IN RURAL AREAS (1893)

Commercialization of farming outpaced the development
of rural banking facilities.  The need for credit, however,
could not be repressed.  Here is a description of the use
of bank-substitutes in commercialized farming areas made
by Thomas Shearman, a prominent New York corporation lawyer
whose clients had included James Fisk, Jr., Jay Gould, and
James J. Hill; he spent much of his fortune in the service
of charity and "good causes."


The bulk of transactions in the rural districts, especially in
the South and Southwest, are carried on with even less use of money
than is usual in the great cities of the North and East.
In the cities and large towns it is quite true that most retail
transactions are settled by the use of actual money, but in strictly
agricultural districts and mining regions, which together cover
nine-tenths of the area of the United States, it seems to be universally conceded that very few transactions of any kind, whether
wholesale or retail, are settled by immediate cash payments.  Everybody keeps an account at the country store, and everything is done
upon credit.  Generally speaking, a farmer or planter opens a credit
at the nearest store, upon the faith of which he draws, not money,
but plows, tools, seed, provisions, clothing, and everything else
which he needs.  Against this he deposits no money, but when his
crop is gathered he delivers the crop itself to the storekeeper, or
sells it to some traveling agent who pays its price to the storekeeper.  In this manner, it is believed, nine-tenths of the small
farmers conduct their business; and their retail transactions,
without the use of money.  Even farm laborers, it is said, receive
by far the greater part of their wages in the same way.  The farmer
advances to them the things which they want, which he in turn
obtains from the storekeeper; or else he guarantees an account which
the laborer keeps at the store.  In one way or another the entire
business of the agricultural districts, we are assured, centers in
the country stores, and is conducted with less literal money than
the business of cities and towns.

That this must be so would seem to follow inevitably from the well-known fact that the great bulk of money is always to be found in the cities and towns, and from the never-ending complaints of the lack of momey in all agricultural districts.  Farmers would not complain so bitterly of the absence of money if there was in circulation among them an amount of all corresponding with that which is in circulation in the cities.  The proof seems conclusive that in reality a smaller proportion of business is done upon a cash basis in the country than in the cities.

If the facts are as here stated, does it not follow that nine-tenths of all our commercial transactions, whether in city or country, are conducted through banking operations?  Are not the small farmers of the South and West actually more dependent upon bankers than are even the merchants of the East?  True, the store-keepers of the rural districts are not called bankers, but names do not change the nature of things.  Their business is as truly a banking business as is that of any national bank on Wall street.  But their methods are clumsy and inconvenient, and their charges are enormous.  They maintain a permanent suspension of specie payment, and properly enough, because they never receive actual money on deposit, and therefore never ought to be asked for it.  They unite the business of banking with the business of merchandising, and they do not perform either function well or cheaply.

Testimony, Thomas G. Shearman of New York; U.S. Congress, 53rd, 1st session, House, Committee on Banking and Currency, Hearings, (Washington, D.C.:  Government Printing Office, 1893), pp. 219-220.

### 477.  THE PREFERRED STATUS OF NATIONAL BANKS (1893)

Under the National Banking Act of 1863, federally-chartered banks could issue bank notes--i.e., currency--on the basis of federal bonds they bought and deposited with the Comptroller of the Currency.  By 1865, state banks were required to pay a prohibitive tax on the circulation of their own bank-notes.  Partisans of state banks fought a long battle against their privileged national brethren.  Davis, the writer here, was a Populist Congressman from Kansas who had been a farmer in that state since 1872.  He was also secretary of the Central Kansas Horticultural Society, and had served as the first president of the Farmers' Cooperative Association.

Suppose that, under the laws as they now exist, five men shall become organized into a corporation for business purposes.  They unite their funds and purchase $50,000 of United States bonds with

the intention of borrowing money from the United States Government
at 1 per cent per annum, on twenty years' time. Their agent proceeds to Washington, and having found the office of the Secretary
of the Treasury, the following dialogue might naturally occur:

Agent: "You have money to loan, I believe, Mr. Secretary, on
United States bonds at 1 per cent per annum?"

Secretary: "Plenty of it. How much do you want?"

Agent: "I have $50,000 in Government bonds which I desire to
deposit as security for a loan of $45,000 in currency to be used
by our corporation in opening and operating its farming lands."

Secretary: "Stop! Stop! You need say no more. This Government has no money to loan for farming purposes. That would be
'paternalism,' such as President Cleveland condemns in his inaugural
address."

Agent: "I am surprised, Mr. Secretary, that I can not borrow
money for agricultural purposes; but, since the lands our corporation own are underlaid with valuable mineral deposits, if I may be
allowed to use the money for the purpose of opening and working our
mines it will answer our purpose quite as well."

Secretary: "You can not sir. The Government has no money to
loan for mining purposes."

Agent: "Can we have this 1 per cent money, then, for the
purpose of operating the plant in which our ores will be refined by
the use of coal from our mines? If not, by your leave, we will
take the loan for the purpose of building a steamer in which to
transfer the products of our mines and farms to distant markets."

Secretary: "You can not have the money for any such purposes.
A law authorizing such loans as you mention would be one of those
class laws, 'the unwholesome progeny of "paternalism,"' which is
'the bane of Republican institutions.' The doctrines of paternalism which you seem to have imbibed 'ought to be unlearned, and the
better lesson taught, that while the people whould patriotically and
cheerfully support our Government, its functions do not include the
support of the people.'"

Agent: "Thank you, Mr. Secretary, for your kind advice. I
know that I and my people are not very wise, but by keeping ourselves in a receptive frame of mind we may learn something. Perhaps
I may venture to assert that just now I am learning very fast. The
information you have just imparted gives me a wonderful insight
into the philosophy of government. The members of our corporation
knew of an instance wherein a certain banking corporation was granted a loan of $45,000 in currency for twenty years, at 1 per cent
per annum, on deposit of $50,000 in United States bonds as security,
and we innocently supposed that our corporation, for the same security, would be granted an equal sum to be used in industrial pursuits
which will give employment to labor and develop the resources of
the country."

Secretary: "That is entirely a different matter, sir. For
banking purposes you can have all the money you desire (up to 90
per cent of the bonds you deposit) at 1 per cent per annum, on
twenty years' time. I will pay you gold interest on the face value
of your bonds, while they are on deposit, one year in advance,
exempt your currency from all State or local taxation, and renew

your currency when old bills become mutilated, without extra charge.
Your bonds are already exempt from all taxation.  Your currency,
which costs you 1 per cent here, can be loaned in most of the
Western States at 10 per cent, compounded from four to twelve times
per annum.  Your taxes will be light, and the profits on the cost
of your currency will be approximately $10 to $1; or, a protection
of about 1,000 per cent.  No business in this country is guaranteed
by the Government such profits as banking."

Agent:  "Again, Mr. Secretary, I thank you.  But is there no
paternalism about this?"

Secretary:  "You will get all needed information regarding
details of the loan from the Comptroller of the Currency, who will,
in due time, forward you the money.  I will be much pleased to see
you at any time you are in Washington.  Good day, sir."


Testimony, Hon. John Davis, representative from Kansas; U.S.
Congress, 53rd, 1st session, House, Committee on Banking and
Commerce, Hearings, (Washington, D.C.:  Government Printing Office,
1893), pp. 82-83.



478.  BANKING AND CURRENCY IN COTTON ALABAMA (1893)


The depression in cotton was blamed by some on a
currency shortage.  Under the National Banking system a
shortage seemed built-in.  Critics like the following one
did not explain how periods of prosperity could occur
under the contractive banking system.  The writer, Colonel
Hiram Hawkins, was a planter in Hawkinsville, Alabama,
president of the Alabama State Agricultural Society and
Master of the Alabama State Grange.


The action of Congress making U.S. bonds payable in gold,
taxing State banks out of existence, thereby making the credit of
the Government the basis of its banking currency, and permitting
but 90 per cent of the face value of the bonds to be issued as
banking capital, has had the effect of contracting the currency.

It has also had the effect of forcing the money of the country
to the great commercial centers, leaving the more remote sections,
especially the cotton-raising districts, without sufficient money
circulating to transact the necessary business.  To have this money
to return, as it must, to enable the cotton raiser to make his crop,
he must give mortgage on the crop and other property to his commission or advancing merchant.  This paper (mortgage) is taken by the
commission merchant to some bank.  The bank with these collateral
and its own credit borrows money from these great money centers.
The circulating medium necessary for the growing districts comes
from a distant State for hire.  When the cotton crop is harvested

all this money, together with what it has earned, flows back to
the commercial center; and the last state of many cotton raisers
is worse than the first.  This annual drain upon the cotton growing
section has added millions to the great money centers, build up
towns and cities far in advance of the rural districts.  In this
connection it is also worthy of remark that the action of Congress
prohibiting national banks from loaning money on real estate has
greatly impaired the value of land by debasing it as a means of
credit.  This crime against the farmer has forced thousands of
free holders (however unwise and unnecessary it may have been) to
make terms with land syndicates at ruinous rates, many of whom are
now but tenants at will under alien landlords, and Congress is
responsible for its share of the distress referred to.  While it
is not the duty of Congress to provide easy terms to money borrowers, it is no more its duty to throw obstacles in their way by
legislating in the interest of the banks and money lenders--as
though money could not take care of itself.

        Col. Hiram Hawkins, August 1, 1893; U.S. Congress, 53rd,
3rd session, Senate, Report 986, part 1, Committee on Agriculture
and Forestry, Report...on the Condition of Cotton Growers, I,
serial number 3290, (Washington, D.C.:  Government Printing Office,
1895), p. 309.


                479.  PREMIUM FOR ACTUAL CASH (1893)


        The stock market crash of 1893 led to runs on
banks for cash.  So short did the supply of cash
become that member banks of the New York Clearing
House Association resorted widely to extra-legal
certificates to settle clearing balances.  Cash
became a very valuable commodity.  At this time
Noyes, the author here, was financial editor of
the New York Evening Post.


        It must be remembered that in 1893 there was no Federal Reserve
to issue currency quickly under the law, on pledge of banking assets,
and that the taking out of new bank notes, under the National Bank
Act, was a long and tedious process.  That was the curious situation
which was met by the equally curious expedient, applied by one or
two Wall Street money brokers, of offering through newspaper adver-
tisement a premium for actual cash.  The premium was paid by large
employers who had to meet their weekly payrolls.  It meant that the
hoarder of $100 silver or paper money could obtain for it from the
money broker a certified bank check, at first for $101.50, later on
for $104.  I had the curiosity to visit the offices of these brokers,
which were mostly situated in basement or ground floor on New Street.

It was a miscellaneous crowd which was bringing actual money to
sell; many of them were unkempt and dirty individuals, who evidently had the hoarded cash of themselves and their neighbors.    The
currency delivered was dirtier than the bearers.    It had apparently
been kept under mattresses or between sole and stocking, and the
long line of clerks behind the counter were equipped with sprays of
disin ectant which were in constant use.    No doubt much larger sums
of hoarded cash changed hands in the back office, to which it was
brought in satchels by wealthy hoarders.    Since no immediate limit
was placed upon the purchases, American gold coin was obtained
abroad, to be sold on arrival at the 4 per cent premium to the
brokers.    One singular result of this was that the banks, whose
paper-money holdings had been withdrawn by hoarders, began as soon
as they received the gold from abroad to pay it out to depositors.


Alexander Dana Noyes, The Market Place.    Reminiscences of a
Financial Editor, (Boston, Massachusetts:    Little, Brown, 1938),
pp. 109-110.


### 480.    THE RITUAL IMPORTANCE OF GOLD (1898)

Earlier in the decade men had considered it a
matter of life and death whether gold or silver was
the country's monetary standard.    By 1898, and probably
much earlier, this question was shown to be an unreal
one.    Lyman Gage, who testifies here, was then Secretary
of the Treasury; he had been president of the First
National Bank of Chicago.


Mr. PRINCE.    Will you please state, if you can, how many
dollars in greenbacks you have been called upon to redeem in gold
since you have taken the office of Secretary of the Treasury?
Secretary GAGE.    I could not tell you how many.    I could make
a guess, if you wanted me to.
Mr. PRINCE.    Well, please give it to me as nearly as you can.
Secretary GAGE.    I think an average of $75,000 to $100,000
per day.    That is all.
Mr. PRINCE.    That is to say, greenbacks are being brought to
the Treasury of the United States and to the subtreasuries in an
amount equal to $75,000 a day, and gold is asked in exchange?
Secretary GAGE.    Yes, sir; but more than that in gold is
coming in.
Mr. PRINCE.    I was going to ask you that question.    Now please
state how much gold is brought daily to the Treasury or subtreasury,
and greenbacks asked to be given in exchange for gold.

Secretary GAGE. It does not work exactly in that way. I will tell you how we get gold. We buy gold at the assay offices of the United States, giving a check on the subtreasuries in payment. These checks are payable in gold, but many of the holders are indifferent whether they get gold or not, and they do not draw the gold. They come in as current funds, and we get the gold. It is a disbursement, you may say, of paper money, indirectly. Still, a larger part of them take the gold on those checks. They would cease utterly to do it if the habit could be broken up, which would be done by some action which would give no doubt as to the continued action of this Government as to gold payments. I should add, further that this drawing of from $75,000 to $100,000 a day, which is somewhere near the true amount, is drawn not for hoarding, I think, but for investment purposes; not from any mistrust.

Mr. PRINCE. That was the point I was getting at. Whether it was drawn from distrust, as matters are now running in this country. Further, will you please state whether we have now more gold on hand than we had on the first of March, when you took your office, coming in in the course of business, and for which no bonds have been issued or required to be issued?

Secretary GAGE. If I remember rightly, when I came into the Treasury, there was $155,000,000 of gold belonging to the Government.

The CHAIRMAN. Besides the gold certificates?

Secretary GAGE. The net gold. Afterwards an outward movement set in to foreign countries, in the payment of balances, which reduced it to about $141,000,000. I may not be speaking with strict accuracy. Since then it has gradually grown until it is $162,000,000 to-day. In fact, at the present time the Government is indifferent about taking gold, and has refused to take it for some time past at points where, some time ago, they would have been glad to have taken it and given greenbacks in exchange. For instance, we were lately offered in San Francisco $500,000 in gold in exchange for greenbacks at that point, and we declined the offer because it involved the expense to the Government of transporting that gold from San Francisco to where we would want it. And if the gold continues to come in in the same general ratio as it has, it will be only a question of time when we will be obliged to force gold out on our creditors, whether they want it or not.


Testimony, Lyman J. Gage; U.S. Congress, 55th, 2nd session, House of Representatives, Committee on Banking and Currency, Hearings and Arguments, (Washington, D.C.: Government Printing Office, 1898), pp. 146-147.

481.  PROMOTING MERGERS (1899)

A promoter organized a large-scale merger and
took his commission out of receipts from a super-issue
of stock in the new firm.  William H. Moore testifies.
He was promoter of industrial mergers and had initiated
the following:  American Tin Plate Company, National Steel
Company, American Steel Hoop Company, National Biscuit
Company, and Diamond Match Company.


A.  It is comparatively a simple matter and yet a difficult
thing to do.  At that particular time these modern organizations--
there were very few of them, and capitalists did not understand
them, and, therefore, it was very difficult--next to an impossi-
bility--to get this organization through....
A.  Practically the same thing applies to the American Tin
Plate Company as to the other organizations.  If I recall, there
were 35 or 40 different plants....
In a nutshell, I found it necessary to deal with each one of
the manufacturers individually and to buy their property on a cash
basis.  I found it was going to be necessary to have a very large
amount of money, not only for working capital, but also to pay each
individual manufacturer, because they did not know me; they did not
know much of the organization.  They were afraid they would get into
some company where they would be much worse off than before.  I
finally prepared myself with the proper amount of capital to pay
them the cash and also to furnish the working capital for expenses.
Then I organized the company, and I said to the manufacturers, "Here
are so many plants--35 or 40 plants.  I propose to pay you cash for
all these plants if you want it, each or any one of them, and I
propose to put in so much working capital."
Q.  How much did you put into the Tin Plate Company?--A.  I
think it has been stated here.
Q.  Five million?--A.  Four and a half or five.  You have it
already stated in the testimony.
That amount of money I furnished.  In other words, I practically bought and owned the plants personally, and the manufacturers
did not compensate me for organizing the company.  In other words,
I was the lawyer and the banker as well.  I obtained money from
many different sources.  I borrowed large amounts of money myself
in order to carry it through, and, as stated, there was no prospectus issued.  I did not think it the proper thing to issue a prospectus, but it was stated in the subscription paper, mentioning the
number of plants:  "Whereas it is proposed by a syndicate to organize a company known as the American Tin Plate Company, with a certain number of plants"--mentioning the names of the plants--"and
with so much capital, and for that amount of capital the syndicate
shall receive so much stock, which is all preferred stock"--you have
heard it here--"and also all the common stock."  So it went together in one lump sum.  There was an extra amount of common stock

over preferred stock.  You gentlemen know that it is necessary to
pay commissions, and the expenses run up very largely, and sometimes
you are in danger of falling down.  You will find on investigation
that hundreds of organizations have fallen down in th   last few
months.

Q.  If I understand the plan with reference to the American
Tin Plate Company, it was this:  It was stated here that there were
$46,000,000 of capital stock issued altogether, $18,000,000 of
preferred and $28,000,000 of common, in payment for all these plants
and a certain amount of cash, and there were $10,000,000 extra left.
Do I understand this extra $10,000,000 would be considered the cost
of promoting the organization?--A.  The cost of promotion and organization.  I have in mind a case where it was necessary to give away
all the common stock and a good deal more to get it through.  In
other words, in order to organize a company of this kind you must
prepare in advance for an amount of money sufficient to carry it
through.  The tin-plate men were anxious to have this company organized.  If I handled it I wanted it to go through; I could not
afford to have it fail.  Therefore I had to have sufficient compensation to distribute as I saw fit in obtaining money necessary to
carry it through.  The manufacturers change their minds, often at
the last minute.  The manufacturers say to you, "I do not care to
have any stock in the organization;" but at the last moment, when
they find it is to be a success and the capital is there, they
believe in its success and come in and subscribe for the stock.
But you must provide for all of the capital you need to put it
through.


Testimony, William H. Moore, United States Industrial
Commission, I, pp. 959-960.



482.  CLEARINGHOUSES CONTROL BANK COMPETITION (1899)


On April 3, 1899 the New York Clearing House
Association passed a rule requiring that all member
banks charge a minimum amount for the service of
collecting out-of-town checks.  With the growth of
New York as a trade center, the city's banks wished to
create greater stability in their business; one way was
by discouraging undue competition for out-of-town business.
A. Barton Hepburn, chairman of the board of Chase National
Bank, testifies in the following.


Mr. UNTERMYER.  At the time of the promulgation of these regu
lations, in 1899, the various bank members of the clearing house
were dealing entirely independently with their customers in the
collection of out-of-town checks, were they not?

Mr. HEPBURN.  They were.

Mr. UNTERMYER.  Each bank was making its own arrangements?

Mr. HEPBURN.  Yes.

Mr. UNTERMYER.  If a customer was worth it, and they thought his account was sufficiently valuable, they were collecting these checks without compensation?

Mr. HEPBURN.  They were.

Mr. UNTERMYER.  Some were and some were not?

Mr. HEPBURN. Yes.

Mr. UNTERMYER.  That created a condition of active competition for business between the banks, did it not?

Mr. HEPBURN.  Why, yes; I think there were some banks that made gratuitous collections of those items as a source of getting business.

Mr. UNTERMYER.  That was a very general custom, was it not, just before this rule was promulgated?  It was that which led to the rule, was it not?

Mr. HEPBURN.  What led to the rule, primarily, was this:  The people all over the country buying goods in New York used to remit in payment for those goods in New York funds, and then they began to remit by checks on their local banks; which was agreeable to the local bankers, because the funds remained there until the checks traveled to New York and back.  Very soon the customer found that he need not make his deposits as against these checks drawn until about the time that they took to travel to New York and back, and the result was that all New York bills from all over the country were being paid in local checks; and it involved a very severe loss, and especially to those banks----

Mr. UNTERMYER.  Loss to whom?

Mr. HEPBURN.  To the banks that had large mercantile accounts.

Mr. UNTERMYER.  You mean to the New York banks?

Mr. HEPBURN.  Yes; they were in the habit of taking them as cash.

Mr. UNTERMYER.  Yes; but they could have taken them for collection, could they not?

Mr. HEPBURN.  Not without losing their accounts.  That is where that account business came in.

Mr. UNTERMYER.  It was because of the competition that they took them for cash instead of for collection?

Mr. HEPBURN.  Yes.

Mr. UNTERMYER.  In order to prevent that keen competition, this rule was passed, was it not?

Mr. HEPBURN.  Well----

Mr. UNTERMYER.  Well, was it not?

Mr. HEPBURN.  No; the primary object----

Mr. UNTERMYER.  No, no.  I think it is fair I should get an answer.  I think you will admit it.  It was in order to prevent that keep competition that the rule was passed, was it not?

Mr. HEPBURN.  It was to prevent the loss.


Testimony, A. Barton Hepburn, U.S. Congress, Subcommittee of the House Committee on Banking and Currency, Money Trust Investigation, (Washington, D.C.:  Government Printing Office, 1913), p. 306.

483.  BANKING IN KERN COUNTY, CALIFORNIA (1900)


Small-town banking was marked by informality of
business practices.  Here are several examples, noted by
Arthur Crites, who, at the time, was the bank's bookkeeper.


Through a bank of that character and at that time passed the
financial transactions of the entire county and everyone in the bank
knew something, if not all, about every transaction that went
through.

It was before the present California Banking Law and before
the day of the bank auditor and bank examiner.  There was a Banking
Commission of three members appointed by the governor.  They came
around once a year and counted your cash and glanced through your
notes and that was about all.  The standing of the various borrowers
was not substantiated by statements, or written evidence.  The
statement of the cashier, as to the value of the note or security,
was accepted as sufficient.  Many of the practices of the bank of
that time would not be permitted for an instant today, in fact some
of them are felonies under the present banking law.

The bank had about $1,000,000 in deposits at that time.  Over-
drafts today are almost prohibited, but in those days overdrafts on
accounts were not only permitted, it was a common practice.  Many
customers of the bank did all their borrowing through overdrafts.
Much of time one-quarter of the bank's deposits were loaned out on
overdrafts.  Many times one overdraft would equal more than ten per
cent of the bank's total deposits.  However, there was no record
of overdrafts on the bank's general books.  The deposit account
showed the total deposits less the total overdrafts.  At the end of
each month a charge for interest on the overdrafts was made, the
general rate charged being ten per cent.  There were quite a number
of overdrafts that had no charges made against them year after year
except the charge for interest.

Upon inquiry I learned these overdrafts were really owed by
someone associated with the bank.  Sometimes it was a case of a
firm going out of business and when the firm finally wound up its
affairs and closed its account at the bank, it was allowed to draw
the amount owed as an overdraft and to stand in the firm's name as
an overdraft year after year.  This was an indirect way of borrowing
money and under present-day banking law is a felony.  It was, of
course, strictly unethical at that time, although not a criminal
act.


Arthur S. Crites, Pioneer Days in Kern County, (Los Angeles,
California:  The Ward Ritchie Press, 1951), pp. 167-168.

# J.

# BUSINESS AND GOVERNMENT

### 484.  THE IRRESISTIBILITY OF GRAFT PAYMENTS (1866)

The leading commercial monthly advises acceptance of
the practice of political graft as one of the infirmities
of human nature.

Moralising upon the subject is of little use; declamation
about it, as we often notice in the daily newspapers, is more than
idle.  The root of the evil is not well understood; and, if it was,
there is hardly a public journal that would dare expose it to public
reprehension.  The evil of corruption at elections, and of dishonesty in the lobbies of legislative bodies, is incidental to the infirmities of mankind; and, like other offenses, can only be checked
in some of its outbreakings, but not eradicated till human nature
itself shall have undergone renovation.
We may expect that close organizations, like political committees, lobbies and legislatures, rings in common councils, and other
municipal bodies, will arise as quickly as mushrooms and with greater tenacity of life.  We regret that legislation should be made
mercenary, or that peculation on the bench should be suspected.
We would not have the idea of official honesty treated as a very
jest.  But we are disposed to be.  It has been the rule for many
centuries, and yet the world has lasted; nations have lived out
their time, and there has been general prosperity.  Statesmanship
appears to be little else than judicious employment of human motives
in the business of governing, and he is the wisest who is best able
to maintain the due equilibrium of human passions and ambitions.
Still the whole world moves, and will continue to move.

We have to expect to be often deceived.  Politicians are pro-
verbially inconstant.  Good legislation is often defeated if its
supporters do not pay the fees of a ring and lobby.  We shall de-
nounce this whenever we detect it, and shall delight to see princes
of the lobby arraigned before courts of justice.  But these are
only checks to the offense.  Instead, therefore, of predicting all
manner of calamities, and making ourselves unhappy and dyspeptic
over the matter, we shall be wiser to go on with our business, pay
our "backshish" to the lobby-chief whom we meet, rejoice that it is
no higher, and regard it as one of the conditions of human society
to which it becomes us to submit with as good a grace as possible.
It ought to be better; it is fortunate for us that it is no worse.

Hunt's Merchants' Magazine, August, 1866, pp. 92-93.


485.   "WHITE AND BLACKS MARCHING TOGETHER" (1867)


In western North Carolina, the end of the Civil War
gave rise to a political movement of freedmen and lower-
class whites.  The shock that such a movement produced
among the former ruling class may be judged from the
following account, written by Randolph Shotwell, co-
publisher of the New Bern, N.C. Journal of Commerce which
had just become defunct, ran for a place in the state
convention of 1867 but was defeated.


Tongue nor pen can describe the condition of things when in
1867.8, I first went to Rutherford to reside; hoping to get rid of
Ague and Fever chills contracted during my residence in the East.
Politically there was but one class--the Red Strings!  For the
Democrats and decent people were so hopelessly in the minority
that few of them even took the trouble to go to the polls, while
at least 250 of the wealthiest citizens (being required to go a
full day's journey to Morganton and take the oath of allegiance
before an insolent Freedmen's Bureau officer) had never registered.
On the first Saturday after my return to Rutherfordton I was
surprised at seeing long processions of countrymen entering the
village by the various roads, mounted and affot, whites and blacks
marching together, and in frequent instances arm-in-arm, a sight
to disgust even a decent negro.  These proved to be the members of
the Red String League, which had gradually enlisted in its ranks
a large majority of the small farmers, tenants, laborers, and
rougher classes of the region.  There were local meetings at the
oohool houses, and other places, in different townships, but the
county conclave convened at the Courthouse once or twice amonth,
besides called meetings.  These meetings were strictly secret, and

were conducted behind closed doors, with armed guards posted outside to prevent approach of any save the Elect.  All that could be
learned by casual passers-by was that the negroes, and low-whites,
often became worked up to a frenzy of fury as the shrewd wire
pullers, for whose benefit the Leagues were devised appealed to
their passions and prejudices by inflammatory declarations as to
their wrongs at the hands of the "White Aristocracy," and by declaring that the Democrats were plotting to re-enslave the Freedmen,
and renew the Rebellion, etc.  Such speeches, interspersed with
vulgar anecdotes, and personal denunciation (safely uttered behind
the pledge of secrecy which bound their auditors) stirred up the
meeting to uproarious applause, shouts, yells, and cursing that
forced all decent people in the vicinity to close their windows.
As not one in twelve of the Leaguers could read or write, and most
of them were embittered by the dissensions of the War period, it
was easy for the leaders to obtain credence for the most abominable
falsehoods, all of which tended to bind more firmly the bonds of
ignorance and prejudice by which the organization was sustained.
The League, indeed, has now become all-powerful throughout the
greatest portion of Western Carolina.

J. G. deR. Hamilton and Rebecca Cameron (eds.), The Papers of
Randolph Abbott Shotwell, II, (Raleigh, North Carolina:   North
Carolina Historical Commission, 1931), pp. 295-296.


486.   HIGHWAYMAN'S NOTION OF TAXATION (1869)

A bill was introduced into the New York state
legislature to tax all brokers $50 a year; and to collect
a duty of 1/20th of 1 per cent of par value on all bullion,
foreign exchange, and securities handled by brokers.  The
high moral tone of the editorial below may have occasioned
merriment among the Vanderbilts, Drews, Goulds, and other
Wall Streeters.


It is high time, however, that this highwayman's notion of
taxation--to seize money where it happens to be most abundant--were
unlearned at least among men holding the responsible position of
law makers.  An idea very generally prevails that the business of
Wall street is merely a system of demoralizing speculation, to be
tolerated in much the same way as we should tolerate gambling; but
which cannot be overtaxed, simply because so far as taxes may injure
its interests they repress a public evil.  This vulgar notion finds
countenance too much among our legislators; and they are all the
readier to embody it into a law from the fact that such laws awaken
a responsive chord in popular prejudice.  This hostility, however,
is simply the result of misconception as to the part that bankers

and brokers play in the vast system of commercial and financial
exchanges.  There is doubtless a certain amount of speculation there
based upon factitious occasions, as there is in every branch of
business where values are subject to frequent fluctuations.  But,
at the same time, there is much speculation that is legitimate and
wholesome in its results.  The perpetual changes in the affairs of
corporations are reflected in the fluctuating value of their shares;
and how is it to be shown that the purchase or sale of stocks, in
accordance with these fluctuations, is illegitimate.  The holders
of shares are the owners of the properties represented by the stock;
and what objection can be urged to the transfer of proprietorship,
according to the varying estimate of value between buyers and
sellers?

Hunt's Merchants' Magazine, April, 1869, pp. 244-245.


487.  BRIBING OFFICIALS IS LIKE TRADING HORSES (1871)


A South Carolina white leader, Matthew Butler,
complained that the Negro-dominated legislature was
corrupt, and that the state land commission accepted
bribes.  The leader was asked whether the corruptor
was not as guilty as the corrupted.  Here is his answer.
Butler had been a major-general of Confederate cavalry and
now was a lawyer and active in politics.


If I had 10,000 acres of land to sell, and a senator would
come to me and say, "I will buy that [in the name of the state] if
you will give me $500," I would buy him up as I would buy a mule.
Question.  Has the impression been made on the public mind
that the corruption existing in the South Carolina legislature and
through the negroes is attributable entirely to these bad men who
come from the North?
Answer.  I don't think it has.
Question.  Nor that the disturbed condition of your State is
attributable to them?
Answer.  No, sir.  I think some of the natives of the State
are as responsible as men from the North; but there is this difference, that one is invested with a trust, a public trust, and the
other is not.  He is simply a private individual making a trade,
like trading horses.  But here stands a man clothed with a public
trust, and, of course, the obligation rests upon him to discharge
that trust honestly and faithfully, and there is no excuse for him.
Question.  Certainly not; but is the moral atmosphere of this
State of such a character that it holds that the public servant
who is corrupted is to be any more reprobated than the man who
corrupts him?

Answer.  I think so, clearly so; because if a man who has a
public trust is susceptible of being corrupted, there are corrupt
men everywhere; he only wants an excuse.  It is far more reprehen-
sible in a man who is invested with a public trust.  I do not
apologize for the morality of cheating in a horse trade, or anything
else; but the public servant never could have been corrupted if he
had not been approachable.

Testimony, Matthew Colbraith Butler, July 21, 1871, U.S.
Congress, Joint Select Committee to Inquire into the Condition of
Affairs in the Late Insurrectionary States, Testimony, IV,
(Washington, D.C.:  Government Printing Office, 1872), pp. 1207-
1208.

488.   RAILROADS TRIED PRIVATE REGULATION LONG AGO (1874)

Federal regulation often aims to accomplish a
business goal that businessmen desire but are unable
to attain.  Recalling events of eleven years before,
the speaker regards this as happening in the area of
railroad regulation.  Isaac Sturgeon, a St. Louis
railroad man, had been since 1855 a railroad president
and superintendent, and under President Grant had served
as a railroad commissioner to inspect federally-aided
railroads.  He submitted this statement in 1885 to the
Cullom Committee.

In 1874 the New York and Erie, New York Central, and Pennsylvania Central Railroads, together with many of the leading Western
railroads, met through their representatives at Saratoga, N.Y., and
appointed three commissioners to represent the three Eastern trunk
lines named and seven commissioners for the Western railroads, and
without my knowledge I was selected as the Western commissioner
for Saint Louis.  The object of the roads in establishing this
Eastern and Western commission was to regulate rates and make them
uniform, leaving shippers to select the route by which they would
ship and to do away with the system of rebates and drawbacks, &c.,
the object seeming to be to do that which a national commission
established by Congress might do.  But after six months of trial
the commission was dissolved and the effort abandoned.  The
commission found their efforts opposed very generally by the general
freight and ticket agents of the roads, and the press at that time
generally seemed inimical to the effort.  But since that time and
at the present day there seems quite a unanimity of sentiment in
favor of the Government establishing a national board, with power
to enforce that which the roads then voluntarily made an effort
to do.  I might say that the managers of the fast freight lines

were evidently opposed to the commission, and it seemed to me did
all in their power to have the railroads abandon the effort to regulate rates through a commission.


Isaac H. Sturgeon, U.S. Congress, 49th, 1st session, Senate,
Select Committee on Interstate Commerce, Report, Appendix, Report
No. 46, serial number 2356, volume 2, pp. 161-162.



489.   A RESPONSIBLE AND REGULATED MONOPOLY (1886)


        Private centralization of railroad capital and
the prospect of government regulation were developing
together.  Here is one prediction by an industry insider,
Charles Adams, president of the Union Pacific Railroad,
of the probable course of these two tendencies.


The period of indecisive railroad wars is drawing to a close.
The development in these cases is moreover made with ready money;--
that is, the earnings of the combinations are continually accumulated
in the business.  There is no toppling super-structure of debt.
Those earnings aggregate millions a year.  In view of these facts
there would seem to be some ground for supposing, as was suggested
in another connection, that the railroad system of this country is
now on the threshold of a most active and unprecedented consolidating
development, and that the question of the survival of the fittest
among railroads may here be decided at a less remote day than is
usually supposed.
. . . . . . . . . . . . . . . . . . . . . . . . . . . . . . . . .
        Owing to the extremely complicated character of the American
railroad system, rendering anything like a territorial division
among corporations impossible, results here work their way out
slowly.  When they do work their way out, however, it is apt to be
on a large scale and in a way not easily susceptible of change.  So
far as any progress has yet been made, it is obviously in the
direction indicated,--the development of government supervision on
the one side, and the concentration of railroads to escape competition on the other.  The manner, indeed, in which, starting from
different stand-points of interest and opposite sections of the
country, the Massachusetts commission and the Southern Railroad and
Steamship Association have unconsciously worked towards a common
ground, is noticeable.  On the one hand the whole effort of the
commission has been to develop a tribunal which, in all questions
affecting the relations of the railroad system to the community,
should secure publicity and that correct understanding of the principles upon which only legislation of any permanent value can be based,
and which is reached through intelligent public investigation.  That
secured, all else might safely be left to take its own course.  A

sufficient responsibility would be secured to afford a guarantee
against abuse.  On the other hand the fundamental idea of the
association, without the realization of which it remains incomplete,
is to so confederate the railroad system that the members of it
should be amenable to control and that responsibility should attach
to it.  Could the two results be brought about, the machinery would
be complete.  The confederated railroad system would confront the
government tribunal, and be directly responsible to public opinion.

Charles Francis Adams, Jr., Railroads.  Their Origin and
Problems, rev. ed., (New York:  Putnam's, 1888), pp. 196-197 and
214-215.


490.  GOVERNMENT GAINED FROM LAND GRANTS (1887)

The Union Pacific Railroad was one of the largest
recipients of federal land grants.  What did the government gain from the grants?  Here is an answer by an
interested party, Charles Adams.


People are apt to forget the past.  They look upon things in
the light of the present; and in the case of the Union Pacific they
are disposed to insist that the private parties concerned in the
construction of the road saw perfectly clearly what the course of
future events was to be, and, seeing it clearly, succeeded somehow
in swindling a confiding Government.  Meanwhile, what did this
"confiding" Government itself get out of the enterprise?  It went
into what was at the time regarded as one of the maddest material
ventures ever suggested.  It went into it as a political necessity,
during a period of war.  The chances were large that, after the road
was constructed, it would have to be operated by the United States
Government as a military and political necessity.  The Government
never expected to get back one dollar it advanced to aid the construction of the Pacific roads.  That is simply a matter of record.
It runs through all the debates of Congress preliminary to the
passage of the charters.  Meanwhile, what was the result?  Instead
of losing its entire advances and finding a military road on its
hands to be operated at the public expense, it in the first place
saved for the national Treasury several times the entire cost of
the road through reduced rates in carrying its mails.  Second,
it saved several times the entire cost of the road through the
economy with which it transported its material and general supplies.
Third, through the rapidity with which it was able to move troops
and munitions it put an end to a most costly and unending series
of savage wars.  Fourth, it filled up a desert country with a producing and tax paying population.  Fifth, it solved the problem of
transcontinental transportation, rendering it possible to develop

a mineral region of unsurpassed richness among mountains before
considered inaccessible.  I hold, therefore, I am clearly justified
in saying that from a merely business point of view this transaction
was a monumentally successful one.  It would have been monumentally
successful, and so considered universally, had private parties alone
been concerned in it; and it does not cease to be such because the
Government was concerned in it.  I confidently submit, therefore,
that there is no good reason for the Government of the United States
to turn upon the company in this matter and insist upon it that the
transaction has been one of fraud from which the Government has sustained nothing but loss.  The Government, I say again, made at
least five dollars in this enterprise to every single dollar that
was either honestly or fraudulently made in it by private parties,
from the year 1863 to this day.


Testimony, Charles Francis Adams, June 4, 1887, U.S Congress,
50th, 1st session, Senate, Executive Document No. 51, part 2, serial
number 2505, Testimony Taken by the United States Pacific Railway
Commission, p. 987.



491.  "HUMAN NATURE IS HUMAN NATURE ALL THE WORLD OVER" (1888)


      If Senator Allison could raise the tariff rate against
foreign steel rails from $14.00 to $15.68, the American
steel rail manufacturers would all the more readily add
nearly $40,000 to their Republican campaign contribution.
This letter was written by James Swank, general manager of
the American Iron and Steel Association who edited the
Association's Bulletin.  He writes to William Allison,
Republican U.S. Senator from Iowa.  He served as chairman
of the Senate Committee on Finance which had reported out
favorably the high-tariff Allison bill of 1888.


The announcement in the Philadelphia Press this morning that
its correspondent had been "officially" advised that the duty on
steel rails had been fixed at $14 in your bill created a great deal
of consternation among our steel-rail friends.  I earnestly hope
that the statement was unauthorized and untrue.  I have my own reasons for begging you and our friends in the Committee to keep the
rate at $15.68, and these reasons I will frankly state to you.  I
would go to Washington immediately instead of writing to you but
I can not possibly get away.
My reasons are these:  I have worked hard in this office for
many years to promote the interests of the Republican party, collecting money and distributing documents in every campaign since
1872.  Our Association has been especially active in this work
since 1880.  I have personally raised large sums of money for the
National and Congressional Committees, and in addition to this we

have every year for many years printed and distributed large quantities of tariff documents.  I inclose you a statement of our work for
this year down to the 1st instant.  This year we have undertaken
to raise more money than in any previous campaign.  I have personally appealed for financial aid for the National Committee to the
Bessemer steel rail manufacturers, assuring them at every turn I
have made that their interests were safe in the hands of the Republican party.  I have particularly assured them that the duty on
steel rails had been fixed in your bill at $15.68.  Upon the
strength of the assurances I have given these friends they have
agreed to help Chairman Quay's Committee to a considerable sum of
money, which I have hoped would reach about $75,000 or $80,000.
I have already collected and paid over to the Committee $37,000,
all contributed by the steel rail manufacturers, $2,000 of which
were sent to Dr. Beardsley.  I am just making arrangements to call
on the steel-rail manufacturers to duplicate the checks they have
already paid.

All this is <u>strictly</u> <u>confidential</u>.  How can I go ahead with
this work if the impression should be generally created that your
bill fixes the duty on steel rails at $14?  Human nature is human
nature all the world over.

We would not for one moment think of using any improper means
to secure the favorable consideration by your Committee of the
steel-rail duty.  But our friends on the Committee are Republicans,
striving for the success of our party in the coming election.  I
beg you, therefore, to make it easy for me, and not difficult or
maybe impossible, to secure the $35,000 or $40,000 of additional
collections which I hope to make from the steel-rail manufacturers.

If I have seemed in this letter to be over-anxious I know
that you will put yourself in my place and imagine the position
which I sustain toward the people who have money to give for the
success of Republican principles.


Letter, James M. Swank to William B. Allison, September 26,
1888; A. L. Volwiler (ed.), "Tariff Strategy and Propaganda in
the United States, 1887-1888."  <u>American Historical Review</u>, XXXVI
(1930-1931), pp. 95-96.


492.   WORKING OUT THE ROAD TAX (1889)


The sparsely settled Pacific coast was little
more than a series of isolated, rural communities.
In economic and political organization, they resembled
closely a frontier Wisconsin settlement of 1850 or one
in Minnesota in 1870.  Ulrich Fries describes the
settlements.

When Okanogan County was first organized and a full set of
officers appointed by the governor, there were not buildings in
which they could meet to transact business.  So they agreed to come
together in a centrally located homesteader's cabin at the head of
what was known as Johnson Creek.  Of course there were no funds in
the treasury because no treasury had been established.  There were
no roads and no funds with which to build them.  But at that time,
according to territorial law, all persons over twenty-one years of
age had to pay a road and a poll tax, each calling for four dollars.

When the county officers held their meeting they agreed to
give the taxpayers a choice of paying in cash or of performing work
on the road, allowing two dollars a day in wages, no board, lodging,
or tools furnished.  To help increase the road fund, it was also
agreed to apply the property tax to the road fund.

I plainly remember that the road question was the one which
puzzled the board the most, since there were no roads in existence.

One of the first roads in the county was built from the mining
camp at Ruby up the mountain to the Loop mining camp.  It was paid
for in county warrants, drawing interest from the time of issue.

In the fall of 1889, we were called upon either to pay or work
out the above-mentioned taxes.  Those who wished to work were told
to come to one of the worst bottlenecks in the county, a place
commonly known as Rattlesnake Point.  This mountain, by which the
Okogan River follows dangerously close for a quarter of a mile,
was about in the middle of our district, which at that time covered
a distance of approximately thirty miles between the towns of
Okanogan and Pateros.

We who lived within five or six miles of the place took our
own lunches, with a cup, a skillet to fry venison in, and a coffee-
pot, which was a baking-powder can to which a wire bail had been
attached.  But the settlers from the extremities of the district
brought pack horses carrying provisions and bedding.  We worked
ten hours a day, and those from a distance remained until all their
tax was paid.

Our road equipment consisted of what we brought along, mostly
shovels.  I remember plainly we had but one pick and only two axes
in the crowd.  When our tax was paid, the supervisor, Mr. Watson,
handed us our receipts.  Mine were dated November 23, 1889, and
showed that I had worked out four dollars in road tax, four dollars
in poll tax, and ninety-two cents in property tax.

Fries, From Copenhagen to Okanogan, pp. 432-433.


493.  DIVISION OF THE INSURANCE LOBBYING MARKET (1899)


Uniformly, state governments regulated the insurance
business.  It became a business necessity, therefore, to
be prepared to lobby in every state legislature.  The

insurance industry approached the matter in the
following way.  Warren Thummel was a lawyer-lobbyist
employed by the Mutual Life Insurance Company.  He was
testifying before the Armstrong Committee in 1905 and
was being questioned by Committee Counsel Charles
Evans Hughes.


Q.  What department of legal work receives your attention?
A.  Taxes.
Q.  Anything else?  A.  Legislation.
Q.  Generally throughout the United States?  A.  Generally.
Q.  And that has been so for some time?  A.  Always; since I
have been with them.
Q.  We have had some evidence from a representative of the
Equitable Life Insurance Society with regard to arrangements that
are made between you and Mr. Hamilton and Mr. Mayne with regard to a
division of territory.  Will you please state just what was done in
that respect?  A.  That arrangement existed before my connection
with the company and has been continued up to the present time, so
far as I know.  Certain portions of the United States that required
attention were divided so as not to multiply effort.  The balance
of the states were what we called open; anybody attended to them
that could most coveniently.
Q.  What was the actual division of territory between you and
the New York Life and the Mutual, the last division made?  A.  I
will have to give that from memory because I haven't any list of it.
The Mutual Life had Virginia, North Carolina, Alabama, Kentucky,
Ohio, Michigan, Minnesota and Washington, Oregon and New Mexico.
The Equitable had Maryland, South Carolina, Georgia, Louisiana,
Mississippi, Texas, Colorado, Arkansas, California and Nevada.  The
New York Indiana, Illinois, Wisconsin, Iowa, Nebraska, Kansas,
Missouri, Tennessee, Indian Territory I don't mean Indian Territory,
Oklahoma.  The rest of the territory was regarded as open.  We
looked particularly after--when we conveniently could--anything
that happened up in the New England States, and I think the Middle
States.  Affairs in the District of Columbia I usually attended to,
although that was not supposed to be in the general arrangement.
I had nothing to do personally with the direction of affairs except
in Massachusetts until I got down to Virginia.  Of course, if I was
directed by the general solicitor to do any particular act in any
place I would do it, but I didn't take any initiative in any of
them except there.
Q.  Does that also refer to New York, include New York?  A.
Oh, yes, sir.  I had nothing whatever to do with New York at any
time.
Q.  Who did?  A.  Well, I don't know any more about it than
was in the papers yesterday.  I never had anything to do with it,
and was never consulted in regard to it and I have no personal
knowledge in regard to that matter.
Q.  How was the matter of expenses adjusted between the
companies?  A.  Why in a general way--the general plan was that
each paid their own expenses, and from time to time we adjusted
and paid differences.

Q.  If the Mutual Life, for example, had general supervision over certain states, the amounts expended, would be expended through the Mutual Life's representative, would they not?  A.  I presume so.

Q.  And you mean that then there would be a clearing of expenses in the different territories and balances would be paid? A.  Well, if I understand your meaning by that word "clearing," yes, sir, it would be true.

Q.  Well, to avoid any possibility of misapprehension, if you will explain just what was done.  A.  Well, for instance, if at any time we got--when it was convenient we found--of course, these figures are merely arbitrary--that we had expended say $10,000, I would charge the Equitable with one-third of that $10,000 when we came to settle up, if I was doing that part of it.  If they had in the same time expended $12,000 they would charge us with one-third of that $12,000, and, of course, we would pay them the difference between our one-third and their one-third.

Testimony, Warren F. Thummel; New York State Legislature, Joint Committee on Investigation of Life Insurance, Testimony, II, (Albany, New York:  Brandow Printing Company, 1905), pp. 1535-1540.

# BIBLIOGRAPHY

1 Henretta, James A. "Economic Development and Social Structure in
    Colonial Boston." William and Mary Quarterly (January
    1965).
  Rutman, Darrett B. Winthrop's Boston (1965).

2 Perkins, Edwin J. The Economy of Colonial America. New York:
    Columbia U. Press, 1980.
  Sosin, Jack M. Whitehall and the Wilderness: The Middle West in
    British Colonial Policy 1690-1775. Lincoln, NB: U. of
    Nebraska Press, 1961.

3 Davis, A. M. The Confiscation of John Chandler's Estate (1903).
  Yoshpe, Harry B. The Disposition of Loyalist Estates in the
    Southern District of the State of New York (1939).

4 Malone, Joseph J. Pine Trees and Politics. The Naval Stores and
    Forest Policy in Colonial New England, 1691-1775. Seattle,
    Wa: U. of Washington Press, 1964.
  Volwiler, Albert T. George Croghan and the Westward Movement,
    1741-1782 (1926).

5 Main, Jackson T. "The Distribution of Property in Post-Revolu-
    tionary Virginia." Mississippi Valley Historical Review XLI.
  Morris, Richard B. "Primogeniture and Entailed Estates in
    America." Columbia Law Review XXVII.

6 Bliss, Willard F. "The Rise of Tenancy in Virginia." Virginia
    Magazine ot History XVIII.
  Treat, Payson J. The National Land System, 1785-1820 (1910).

7   Bidwell, Percy W. and Falconer, John I.  History of Agriculture
    in the Northern United States, Chapters 5 and 11 (1925).
    Gray, Lewis C.  History of Agriculture in the Southern United
    States to 1860 I, II, Chapters 7 and 27 (1933).

8   Hibbard, Benjamin H.  A History of the Public Land Policies
    (1924).
    Nettels, Curtis P.  The Emergence of a National Economy, 1775–
    1815, Chapter 7 (1962).

9   Kinney, J. P.  A Continent Lost--A Civilization Won.  Indian Land
    Tenure in America (1937).
    Wallace, Anthony F. C.  "Political Organization and Indian Land
    Tenure Among the Northeastern Indians, 1600-1830."  South-
    western Journal of Anthropology XIII.

10  Carrier, Lyman.  The Beginnings of American Agriculture (1923).
    Rutman, Darrett B.  Husbandmen of Plymouth:  Farms and Villages in
    in the Old Colony, 1620-1692.  Boston, MA:  Beacon Press,
    1967.

11  Bridenbaugh, Carl.  Myths and Realities.  Societies of the Colon-
    ial South (1952).
    Middleton, Arthur P.  Tobacco Coast:  A Maritime History of the
    Chesapeake Bay in the Colonial Era.  Mason, G. C., ed. (1953).

12  Beatty, Richard C.  William Byrd of Westover (1932).
    Morton, Louis.  Robert Carter of Nomini Hall (1941).

13  Gray, Lewis C.  History of Agriculture in the Southern United
    States to 1860 I, Chapter 8 (1933).
    Sharrer, G. Terry.  "Indigo in Carolina, 1671-1796."  South
    Carolina Historical Magazine 72 (April 1971):  94-103.

14  Gray, Lewis C.  History of Agriculture in the Southern United
    States to 1860 I, Chapter 18 (1933).
    Sioussat, St. G. L.  "Virginia and the English Commercial Sys-
    tem."  American Historical Association Report (1905).

15  Fussel, G. E.  "Ploughs and Ploughing Before 1800."  Agricultural
    History 40 (1966).
    Rothenberg, Winifred B.  "The Market and Massachusets Farmers,
    1750-1855."  Journal of Economic History 41 (June 1981):
    283-314.
    Walcott, R. R.  "Husbandry in Colonial New England."  New England
    Quarterly IX.

16  Masterson, William H.  William Blount (1954).
    Nettels, Curtis P.  The Emergence of a National Economy, 1775–
    1885, Chapter 8 (1962).
    Szatmary, David P.  Shays' Rebellion:  The Making of an Agrarian
    Insurrection.  Amherst, MA:  U. of Massachusetts Press, 1980.

17  Bassett, J. S. "Virginia Planter and London Merchant." American
      Historical Association Report I (1901).
    Gray, L. C. "Market Surplus Problems of Colonial Tobacco."
      Agricultural History II.

18  Jefferson, Thomas. Farm Book. Betts, E. M., ed. (1953).
    Washington, George. Letters on Agriculture...with Statistical
      Tables and Remarks, by Thomas Jefferson, Richard Peters...
      on the Economy and Management of Farms in the United States
      (1847).

19  Baldwin, L. D. Whiskey Rebels (1939).
    Whitten, David O. "An Economic Inquiry Into the Whiskey Re-
      bellion of 1794." Agricultural History 49 (1975).

20  Mirsky, Jeanette and Nevins, Allan. The World of Eli Whitney
      (1952).
    Oliver, John W. History of American Technology (1956).

21  Gray, Lewis C. History of Agriculture in the Southern United
      States to 1860 II, Chapters 29-30 (1933).
    Kelsey, Darwin P. (ed.). Farming in the New Nation -- Inter-
      preting American Agriculture, 1790-1840. Washington, D.C.:
      Agricultural History Society, 1972.
    Mirsky, J. and Nevins, The World of Eli Whitney (1952).

22  Buck, Solon J. "Frontier Economy in Southwestern Pennsylvania."
      Agricultural History X.
    Loehr, Rodney C. "Self-Sufficiency on the Farm." Agricultural
      History XXVI.
    Primack, Martin L. "Land Clearing Under Nineteenth-Century
      Techniques." Journal of Economic History 22 (December
      1962): 484-497.

23  Gray, Lewis C. History of Agriculture in the Southern United
      States to 1860 II, Chapter 30 (1933).
    Martin, Thomas P. "Some International Aspects of the Anti-
      Slavery Movement, 1818-1823." Journal of Economic and
      Business History I.

24  Bridenbaugh, Carl. Cities in the Wilderness. (Rev. ed., 1955).
    Crittenden, Charles C. "Means of Communication in North Caro-
      lina, 1763-1789." North Carolina Historical Review VIII.

25  Jensen, A. L. The Maritime Commerce of Colonial Philadelphia
      (1963).
    Nettels, C. P. "Economic Relations of Boston, Philadelphia,
      and New York, 1680-1715." Journal of Economic and Business
      History III.

26  Scharf, John T. History of Maryland from the Earliest Period
      to the Present Day. 3 vols. (1879).
    _____ and Westcott, Thompson. History of Philadelphia, 1609-
      1884. 3 vols. (1884).

27  Caruso, John A.  The Appalachian Frontier:  America's First
      Surge Westward (1959).
    Dunaway, Wayland F.  History of the James River and Kanawha
      Company (1922).

28  Harrell, J. S.  Loyalism in Virginia:  Chapters in the Economic
      History of the Revolution (1926).
    Low, W. A.  "Merchant and Planter Relations in Post-Revolutionary
      Virginia, 1783-1789."  Virginia Magazine of History and
      Biography LXI.

29  Hedges, James B.  The Browns of Providence Plantations (1952).
    Peterson, Arthur G.  "Commerce of Virginia, 1789-1791."  William
    and Mary Quarterly X, 2nd ser.

30  Alvord, Clarence W.  The Illinois Country, 1673-1818 (1920).
    Vaccaro, Leopold S.  "Frencesco Vigo, Financier of the Northwest
      Territory."  General Magazine and Historical Chronicle LIV.

31  Armstrong, Ellis L. and others (eds.).  History of Public Works
      in the United States, 1776-1976.  Chicago, IL:  American
      Public Works Association, 1976.
    Ludlum, David M.  Early American Hurricanes, 1492-1870 (1963).
    Snow, Edward R.  Famous Lighthouses of America (1955).

32  Cole, Arthur H.  "The Tempo of Mercantile Life in Colonial
      America."  Business History Review XXXIII.
    Earle, A. M.  Stage-Coach and Tavern Days (1900).

33  Callender, Guy S.  "The Early Transportation and Banking Enter-
      prises of the States in Relation to the Growth of Corpora-
      tions."  Quarterly Journal of Economics XVII.
    Ransom, Roger L.  "Interracial Canals and Economic Specializa-
      tion in the Antebellum United States."  Explorations in
      Entrepreneurial History N.S., 5 (Fall 1967):  12-35.
    Taylor, George Rogers.  The Transportation Revolution, 1815-
      1860, Chapter 3 (1951).

34  Handlin, Oscar and Mary F.  "Origins of the American Business
      Corporation."  Journal of Economic History V.
    Sanderlin, Walter S.  The Great National Project (1946).

35  Nettels, Curtis P.  The Emergence of a National Economy, 1775-
      1815, Chapter 12 (1962).
    Rockwood, Nathan C.  One Hundred Fifty Years of Road Building
      in America (1914).

36  Atherton, Lewis E.  "The Problem of Credit Rating in the
      Ante-Bellum South."  Journal of Southern History XII.
    Mair, John.  "Book-Keeping Modernized [1784]."  William and Mary
      Quarterly XIV, 1st ser.

37  Jenkins, Stephen.  The Old Boston Post Road (1914).
    Wood, F. J.  Turnpikes of New England (1919).

38  Atherton, Lewis E.  "John McDonough--New Orleans Mercantile
        Capitalist."  Journal of Southern History VII.
    Galpin, W. F.  "The Grain Trade of New Orleans, 1804-1814."
        Mississippi Valley Historical Review XIV.

39  Dumbell, Stanley.  "The Cotton Market in 1799."  Economic
        Journal Supplement, Economic History Series, I.
    Rowland, Mrs. Dunbar (ed.).  Life, Letters and Papers of William
        Dunbar (1930).

40  Albjerg, Victor L.  "Internal Improvements Without a Policy."
        Indiana Magazine of History XXVIII.
    Baldwin, L. G.  Keelboat Age on Western Waters (1941).

41  Reiser, Catherine E.  Pittsburgh's Commercial Development 1800-
        1850 (1951).
    Wade, Richard C.  The Urban Frontier:  The Rise of Western
        Cities, 1790-1830 (1959).

42  Hulbert, A. B.  The Cumberland Road (1904).
    Jordan, Philip D.  The National Road (1948).

43  Lippincott, Isaac.  A Century and a Half of Fur Trade at St.
        Louis (1916).
    Phillips, Paul C.  The Fur Trade. 2 vols. (1961).

44  Lippincott, Isaac.  "Internal Trade of the United States."
        Washington University Studies III.
    Taylor, George R.  "Agrarian Discontent in the Mississippi
        Valley Preceding the War of 1812."  Journal of Political
        Economy XXXIX.

45  Bishop, A. L.  State Works of Pennsylvania (1907).

46  Bridenbaugh, Carl.  The Colonial Craftsman (1950).
    Rose, Walter.  The Village Carpenter (1939).

47  Galenson, David W.  "White Servitude and the Growth of Black
        Slavery in Colonial America."  Journal of Economic History
        41 (March 1981):  39-47.
    _____.  White Servitude in Colonial America:  An Economic
        Analysis.  New York:  Cambridge U. Press, 1981.
    Gray, Ralph and Wood, Betty.  "The Transition from Indentured
        Servant to Involuntary Servitude in Colonial Georgia."
        Explorations in Economic History 13 (October 1976):  313-
        370.

48  Ballagh, J. C.  White Servitude in Virginia (1895).
    Smith, Abbott E.  Colonists in Bondage (1947).

49   Siebert, W. H.   "Slavery and White Servitude in East Florida,
         1726-76."  Florida Historical Quarterly X.
     Wallace, David D.  The Life of Henry Laurens (1915).

50   Abernethy, Thomas P.  Three Virginia Frontiers (1940).
     Edwards, C. R.  Frontier Policy of the Colony of Virginia (1915).

51   Lasansky, Jeanette.  To Draw, Upset, and Weld:  The Work of the
         Pennsylvania Rural Blacksmith 1742-1935.  Lewisburg, PA:
         Union County Historical Society, 1980.
     Tunis, Edwin.  Colonial Craftsmen and the Beginnings of American
         Industry.  Cleveland, OH:  World, 1965.

52   Bridenbaugh, Carl.  The Colonial Craftsman (1950).
     McKee, Samuel.  Labor in Colonial New York (1935).

53   Belknap, Henry W.  Trades and Tradesmen of Essex County,
         Massachusetts (1929).
     Morris, Richard B.  Government and Labor in Early America (1946).

54   _____.  Government and Labor in Early America (1946).
     Swank, James M.  History of the Manufacture of Iron in All Ages.
         2nd ed., Chapter 11 (1892).

55   Clark, Victor S.  History of Manufactures in the United States
         I, Chapters 7 and 15 (1929).
     Commons, John R.  History of Labour II.
     Goldin, Claudia and Sokoloff, Kenneth.  "Women, Children, and
         Industrialization in the Early Republic:  Evidence from the
         Manufacturing Censuses."  Journal of Economic History 42
         (December 1982):  741-774.

56   Carey, Lewis J.  Franklin's Economic Views (1928).
     Wetzel, W. A.  Benjamin Franklin as an Economist (1895).

57   Bining, A. C.  Pennsylvania Iron Manufacture in the Eighteenth
         Century (1938).
     Boyer, A. S.  Early Forges and Furnaces in New Jersey (1931).

58   Clark, Victor S.  History of Manufactures in the United States
         I, Chapter 8 (1929).
     Thompson, Mack.  Moses Brown:  Reluctant Reformer (1962).

59   Boyd, Julian K.  Anglo-American Union:  Joseph Galloway's Plans
         to Preserve the British Empire, 1774-1788 (1941).
     Nettels, Curtis P.  The Roots of American Civilization.
         Chapter 16 (1938).

60   Bishop, J. Leander.  A History of American Manufactures from
         1608 to 1860 I, Chapter 16 (1866).
     Weiss, Harry B. and Grace M.  Early Tanning and Currying in New
         Jersey (1959).

61  Clark, Victor S.  History of Manufactures in the United States
        I, Chapter 11 (1929).
    Huebner, G. G.  "The First Quarter Century, 1790 to 1815," in
        Johnson, Emory R. et al., History of Domestic and Foreign
        Commerce of the United States II, Chapter 23 (1915).

62  Bruce, P. A.  Economic History of Virginia in the Seventeenth
        Century II.
    Clark, Victor S.  History of Manufactures in the United States
        I, Chapter 7 (1929).

63  ____.  History of Manufactures in the United States I, Chapter
        16 (1929).
    Woodbury, Robert S.  "The Legend of Eli Whitney and Interchange-
        able Parts."  Technology and Culture II.

64  Bishop, J. Leander.  A History of American Manufactures from
        1608 to 1860 I (1866).
    Rezneck, Samuel.  "The Rise and Early Development of Industrial
        Consciousness in the United States, 1760-1830."  Journal of
        Economic and Business History IV.

65  Bishop, J. Leander.  A History of American Manufactures from
        1608 to 1860 I (1866).
    Weeden, William B.  Economic and Social History of New England,
        1620-1789 II, Chapters 22-23 (1891).

66  Clark, Victor S.  History of Manufactures in the United States
        I, Chapter 11 (1929).
    Jeremy, David J.  Transatlantic Industrial Revolution:  The
        Diffusion of Textile Technologies between Britain and
        America, 1790-1830s.  Cambridge, MA: M.I.T. Press, 1981.
    Smith, Adam.  The Wealth of Nations.  Book 4, Chapter 8 (1776).

67  Paskoff, Paul F.  "Labor Productivity and Managerial Efficiency
        against a Static Technology:  The Pennsylvania Iron Indus-
        try, 1750-1800."  Journal of Economic History 40 (March
        1980):  129-135.
    Temin, Peter.  Iron and Steel in Nineteenth-Century America.
        Cambridge, MA: M.I.T. Press, 1964.

68  Prime, A. C.  Arts and Crafts in Philadelphia, Maryland and
        North Carolina, 1721-1785.  2 vols. (1929).
    Swank, James M.  History of the Manufacture of Iron in All Ages.
        2nd ed., Chapters 23 and 30 (1892).

69  Green, Constance M.  Eli Whitney and the Birth of American
        Technology (1956).
    Mirsky, Jeannette and Nevins, Allan.  The World of Eli Whitney
        (1952).
70  Clark, Victor S.  History of Manufactures in the United States
        I, Chapter 11 (1929).
    Sears, Louis M.  Jefferson and the Embargo (1927).

71  Kidwell, Claudia B. and Christman, Margaret C.  Suiting Everyone:
      The Democratization of Clothing in America.  Washington,
      D.C.:  Smithsonian Institution Press, 1974.
    McGouldrick, Paul F.  New England Textiles in the Nineteenth
      Century: Profits and Investment.  Cambridge, MA: Harvard
      U. Press, 1968.
    Ware, Carolina F.  The Early New England Cotton Manufacture
      (1931).

72  Tryon, R. M.  Household Manufactures in the United States, 1640-
      1860 (1917).
    Van Wagenen, Jared.  The Golden Age of Homespun (1953).

73  Bezanson, Anne, Gray, Robert D. and Hussey, Miriam.  Wholesale
      Prices in Philadelphia, 1784-1861 (1936).
    Nettels, Curtis P.  The Emergence of a National Economy, 1775-
      1815, Chapter 15 (1962).

74  Ransom, Roger L.  "British Policy and Colonial Growth:  Some
      Implications of the Burden from the Navigation Acts."
      Journal of Economic History 28 (September 1968):  427-435.
    Thomas, Robert Paul.  "British Imperial Policy and the Economic
      Interpretation of the American Revolution."  Journal of
      Economic History 28 (September 1968):  436-440.

75  Bining, Arthur C.  British Regulation of the Colonial Iron
      Industry (1933).
    Cochran, Thomas C.  Frontiers of Change:  Early Industrialism
      in America.  New York:  Oxford U. Press, 1981.
    Hartley, E. Neal.  Ironworks on the Saugus (1957).
    Hatch, Charles E., Jr. and Gregory, Thurlow G.  "The First
      American Blast Furnace, 1619-1622:  The Birth of a Mighty
      Industry on Falling Creek in Virginia."  Virginia Magazine
      of History and Biography 70 (July 1962):  259-296.
    Price, Jacob M.  "The Economic Growth of the Chesapeake and
      the European Market, 1697-1775."  Journal of Economic
      History 24 (December 1964):  496-511.

76  Goldin, Claudia D. and Lewis, Frank D.  "The Role of Exports in
      American Economic Growth during the Napoleonic Wars, 1793 to
      1807."  Explorations in Economic History 17 (January 1980):
      6-25.
    Shepherd, James F.  "Commodity Exports from the British North
      American Colonies to Overseas Areas, 1768-1772:  Magnitudes
      and Patterns of Trade."  Explorations in Economic History
      8 (Fall 1970):  5-76.

77  Billias, George A.  The Massachusetts Land Bank of 1740 (1959).
    Sosin, Jack M.  "Imperial Regulation of Colonial Paper Money,
      1764-1773."  Pennsylvania Magazine of History and Biography,
      (April 1964).

78  Bining, Arthur C.  British Regulation of the Colonial Iron
    Industry (1933).
    Johnson, Keach.  "The Baltimore Company Seeks English Markets...
    1731-1755."  William and Mary Quarterly XVI.

79  Barrow, Thomas C.  Trade and Empire:  The British Customs Service
    in Colonial America, 1660-1775.  Cambridge, MA:  Harvard U.
    Press, 1967.
    McClellan, W. S.  Smuggling in the American Colonies at the
    Outbreak of the American Revolution (1912).
    Pares, Richard.  Yankees and Creoles:  The Trade between North
    America and the West Indies before the American Revolution
    (1956).

80  Greene, Jack P. and Jellison, Richard M.  "The Currency Act of
    1764 in Imperial-Colonial Relations, 1764-1776."  William
    and Mary Quarterly (October 1961).
    Price, Jacob M.  Capital and Credit in British Overseas Trade.
    The View from the Chesapeake, 1770-1776.  Cambridge, MA:
    Harvard U. Press, 1980.

81  Morgan, Edmund S. and Helen M.  The Stamp Act Crisis:  Prologue
    to a Revolution (1953).
    Sosin, Jack M.  Agents and Merchants.  British Colonial Policy
    and the Origins of the American Revolution, 1763-1775
    (1965).

82  Bailyn, Bernard and Lotte.  Massachusetts Shipping 1697-1714.
    A Statistical Study (1959).
    Thomas, Robert P.  "A Quantitative Approach to the Study of the
    Effects of British Imperial Policy Upon Colonial Welfare."
    Journal of Economic History (December 1965).

83  Harper, Lawrence A.  "Mercantilism and the American Revolution,"
    in Saveth, Edward N. (ed.), Understanding the American Past
    (1954).
    Schlesinger, Arthur M. [Sr.].  The Colonial Merchants and the
    American Revolution (1918).

84  Bemis, Samuel F.  Jay's Treaty:  A Study in Commerce and Diplo-
    macy.  2nd ed. (1962).
    Gipson, Lawrence H.  "The Triumphant Empire:  Thunder-Clouds
    Gather in the West, 1763-1766."  Vol. X of The British Em-
    pire Before the American Revolution, Chapter 8 (1961).

85  Nettels, Curtis P.  The Emergence of a National Economy, 1775-
    1815.  Chapter 3 (1962).
    Sheridan, Richard B.  "The British Credit Crisis of 1772 and
    the American Colonies."  Journal of Economic History XX.

86  Evans, Emory G.  "Planter Indebtedness and the Coming of the
    Revolution in Virginia."  William and Mary Quarterly
    (October 1962).

Price, Jacob M.   "The Rise of Glasgow in the Chesapeake Tobacco
   Trade, 1707-1775."  William and Mary Quarterly XI.

87  Burnett, Edmund C. (ed.).   "Observations of London Merchants on
      American Trade, 1783."  American Historical Review XVIII.
   Peabody, Robert E.   Merchant Venturers of Old Salem (1912).

88  Keith, Alice B.   "Relaxations in the British Restrictions on
      the American Trade with the British West Indies, 1783-1802."
      Journal of Modern History 20 (March 1948):  1-18.
   Setser, V. G.   Commercial Reciprocity Policy of the United
      States, 1774-1829 (1937).

89  Bjork, Gordon C.   "The Weaning of the American Economy:  Inde-
      pendence, Market Changes, and Economic Development."
      Journal of Economic History (December 1964).
   Nettels, Curtis P.   The Emergence of a National Economy, 1775-
      1815, Chapter 10 (1962).

90  Jones, Chester L.   The Consular Service of the United States:
      Its History and Activities (1906).
   Nichols, Roy F.   "Trade Relations and the Establishment of the
      United States Consulates in Spanish America, 1779-1809."
      Hispanic American Historical Review XIII.

91  Horner, J.   The Linen Trade of Europe During the Spinning Wheel
      Period (1920).

92  Adams, Donald R., Jr.   "American Neutrality and Prosperity,
      1793-1808:  A Reconsideration."  Journal of Economic
      History 40 (December 1980):  713-737.
   Ritcheson, Charles R.   Aftermath of Revolution:  British Policy
      Toward the United States, 1783-1795.  Dallas, TX:  Southern
      Methodist U. Press, 1969.

93  Crouzet, Francois.   "Wars, Blockade, and Economic Change in
      Europe, 1792-1815."  Journal of Economic History 24
      (December 1964):  567-588.
   Spivak, Burton.   Jefferson's English Crisis:  Commerce, Embargo,
      and the Republican Revolution.  Charlottesville, VA:
      U. Press of Virginia, 1979.

94  Goebel, Dorothy B.   "British Trade to the Spanish Colonies,
      1796-1823."  American Historical Review XLIII.
   Muller, Herman J.   "British Business and Spanish America, 1700-
      1800."  Mid-America (January 1957).

95  Huebner, G. G.   "The First Quarter Century, 1790 to 1815," in
      Johnson, Emory R. et al., History of Domestic and Foreign
      Commerce of the United States II, Chapter 23 (1915).
   LaTourette, K. S.   The History of the Early Relations between
      the United States and China, 1784-1844 (1917).

Perkins, Edwin J. "Financing Antebellum Importers: The Role of Brown Brothers and Company of Baltimore." Business History Review 45 (1971): 421-451.

96 Crosby, Alfred W., Jr. America, Russia, Hemp, and Napoleon: American Trade with Russia and the Baltic, 1783-1812 (1965).
Hildt, J. C. Early Diplomatic Relations of the United States with Russia (1906).
Perkins, Edwin J. Financing Anglo-American Trade: The House of Brown, 1800-1860. Cambridge, MA: Harvard U. Press, 1975.

97 Chadwick, John W. Cap'n Chadwic, Marblehead Shipper and Shoemaker (1906).
Hall, John P. "Shoemaking in the Post-Revolutionary Period." Business Historical Society Bulletin XXV.

98 Clark, V. S. History of Manufactures in the United States I, Chapters 6 and 15 (1929).
Davis, A. M. Currency and Banking in the Province of Massachusetts Bay (1900-1901).

99 East, Robert A. Business Enterprise in the Revolutionary Era (1938).
"The Commerce of Rhode Island." Massachusetts Historical Society, Collections, Ser. VII, Vol. IX.

100 Brock, Leslie V. The Currency of the American Colonies, 1700-1764: A Study in Colonial Finance and Imperial Relations. New York: Arno Press, 1975.
Myers, Margaret G. A Financial History of the United States. New York: Columbia U. Press, 1970.
Weiss, Roger W. "The Issue of Paper Money in the American Colonies, 1720-1774." Journal of Economic History 30 (December 1970): 770-784.

101 Ferguson, E. James. "Currency Finance: An Interpretation of Colonial Monetary Practices." William and Mary Quarterly (April 1953).
Nettels, Curtis P. "The Origins of Paper Money in the English Colonies." Economic History III.

102 "Counterfeiting in New York during the Revolution." New York Historical Society Quarterly XLII.
Scott, Kennth. "New Hampshire Tory Counterfeiters Operating from New York City." New York Historical Society Quarterly XXXIV.

103 Bullock, C. J. Finances of the United States, 1775-1789 (1895).
Norton, W. B. "Paper Currency in Massachusetts during the Revolution." New England Quarterly VII.

104 Ferguson, E. James. The Power of the Purse: A History of American Public Finance, 1776-1790 (1961).

Ver Steeg, Clarence.  Robert Morris, Revolutionary Financier
     (1954).

105  Jensen, Merrill M.  The New Nation...1781-1789 (1950).
     Nettels, Curtis P.  The Emergence of a National Economy, 1775-
     1815, Chapter 3 (1962).

106  Van Fenstermaker, J.  "The Statistics of American Commercial
     Banking, 1782-1818."  Journal of Economic History 25
     (September 1965):  400-413.
     Wilson, Janet.  "The Bank of North America and Pennsylvania
     Politics:  1781-1787."  Pennsylvania Magazine of History
     and Biography LXVI.

107  Crittenden, Charles C.  The Commerce of North Carolina, 1763-
     1789 (1936).
     Giddens, Paul H.  "Trade and Industry in Colonial Maryland,
     1753-1769."  Journal of Economic and Business History IV.

108  Cowan, Helen I.  Charles Williamson,--Genesee Promoter--Friend
     of Anglo-American Rapprochement (1941).
     Evans, Paul D.  The Holland Land Company (1924).

109  Hammond, Bray.  Banks and Politics in America, Chapter 5 (1957).
     Nettels, Curtis P.  The Emergence of a National Economy, 1775-
     1815, Chapter 6 (1962).

110  Beard, Charles A.  Economic Origins of Jeffersonian Democracy
     (1915).
     Wetterau, James O.  "The Branches of the First Bank of the
     United States."  Journal of Economic History II.

111  Holdsworth, John T. and Dewey, Davis R.  The First and Second
     Banks of the United States (G.P.O., 1910).
     Mai, Chien Tseng.  The Fiscal Policies of Albert Gallatin
     (1930).

112  Dodd, William F.  "The Effect of the Adoption of the Constitu-
     tion upon the Finances of Virginia."  Virginia Magazine of
     History X.
     Main, Jackson Turner.  The Antifederalists.  Critics of the
     Constitution, 1781-1788 (1961).

113  Burt, A. L.  The United States, Great Britain, and British
     North America from the Revolution to the Establishment of
     Peace after the War of 1812 (1940).
     Thomas, G. M.  American Neutrality in 1793 (1931).

114  Ferguson, E. James.  The Power of the Purse (1961).
     Konkle, Burton A.  Thomas Willing and the First American Finan-
     cial System (1937).

115  Ferguson, E. James.  "Speculation in the Revolutionary Debt:
       The Ownership of Public Securities in Maryland, 1790."
       Journal of Economic History XIV.
     Nettels, Curtis P.  The Emergence of a National Economy, 1775-
       1815, Chapter 6 (1962).

116  Hackett, Homer C.  Constitutional History of the United States
       I (1939).
     Hughes, Jonathan R. T.  The Governmental Habit:  Economic Con-
       trols from Colonial Times to the Present.  New York:  Basic
       Books, 1977.
     McLaughlin, Andrew.  Constitutional History of the United
       States (1935).

117  Forsythe, Dall W.  Taxation and Political Change in the Young
       Nation, 1781-1833.  New York:  Columbia U. Press, 1977.
     McCoy, Drew R.  The Elusive Republic:  Political Economy in
       Jeffersonian America.  Chapel Hill, N.C.:  U. of North
       Carolina Press, 1980.

118  Guiness, R. B.  "The Purpose of the Lewis and Clark Expedition."
       Mississippi Valley Historical Review XX.
     Wilson, C. M.  Meriwether Lewis (1934).

119  Jackson, Donald (ed.).  Letters of the Lewis and Clark Expedi-
       tion:  With Related Documents, 1783-1854 (1962).
     Young, F. G.  "The Higher Significance in the Lewis and Clark
       Exploration."  Quarterly of the Oregon Historical Society
       VI.

120  Anderson, F. M.  "Opposition to the War of 1812."  Mississippi
       Valley Historical Association, Proceedings VI.

121  Benton, Elbert J.  The Wabash Trade Route in the Development
       of the Old Northwest (1903).
     Gates, Paul W.  "Land Policy and Tenancy in the Prairie Counties
       of Indiana."  Indiana Magazine of History XXXV.

122  _____ and Swenson, Robert.  History of Public Land Development.
       Washington, D.C.:  GPO, 1968.
     Rohrbough, Malcolm J.  The Land Office Business:  The Settle-
       ment and Administration of American Public Lands, 1789-
       1837.  New York:  Oxford U. Press, 1968.

123  Gates, Paul W.  "Frontier Estate Builders and Farm Laborers,"
       in Wyman, Walker D. and Kroeber, Clifton B. (eds.), The
       Frontier in Perspective (1957).
     Zahler, H. S.  Eastern Workingmen and Land Policy, 1829-1862
       (1941).

124  Hicks, William and Ross, John.  Address by chiefs of Cherokee
       Nation, October 13, 1828, Cherokee Phoenix I (October 22,
       1828) in Dunbar, Seymour, A History of Travel in America IV,
       appendix J (1915).

Prucha, Francis P.  American Indian Policy in the Formative
    Years:  The Indian Trade and Intercourse Acts, 1790–1834
    (1962).

125  Silver, James W.  "Land Speculation Profits in the Chickasaw
        Cession."  Journal of Southern History X.
    Soltow, Lee.  "Inequality Amidst Abundance:  Land Ownership
        in Early Nineteenth Century Ohio."  Ohio History 88 (Spring
        1979):  133–151.
    Young, Mary E.  "The Creek Frauds:  A Study in Conscience and
        Corruption."  Mississippi Valley Historical Review
        (December 1955).

126  Clawson, Marion.  The Land System of the United States.
        Lincoln, NB:  U. of Nebraska Press, 1968.
    Stephenson, George M.  The Political History of the Public
        Lands from 1840 to 1862 (1917).
    Wellington, Raynor G.  The Political and Sectional Influence
        of the Public Lands, 1828 to 1842 (1914).

127  Gates, Paul W.  "The Role of the Speculator in Western Develop-
        ment."  Pennsylvania Magazine of History and Biography
        (July 1942).
    Sakolski, A. M.  The Great American Land Bubble (1932).

128  Davies, Pearl J.  Real Estate in American History (1958).
    Dillon, Richard H.  J. Ross Browne:  Confidential Agent in Old
        California (1965).

129  Easterby, James H. (ed.).  The South Carolina Rice Plantation
        as Revealed in the Papers of Robert F. W. Allston (1945).
    House, Albert V. (ed.).  Planter Management and Capitalism in
        Ante-Bellum Georgia; the Journal of Hugh Fraser Grant, Rice
        Grower (1954).

130  Craven, Avery O.  Soil Exhaustion in the Agricultural History
        of Virginia and Maryland, 1606–1860 (1926).
    Gray, Lewis C.  History of Agriculture in the Southern United
        States to 1860 II, Chapters 27, 33, and 38 (1933).

131  Fletcher, Stevenson W.  Pennsylvania Agriculture and Country
        Life, 1640–1840 (1950).
    Gates, Paul W.  The Farmer's Age:  Agriculture, 1815–1860,
        Chapter V (1960).
    Rasmussen, Wayne D. (ed.).  Agriculture in the United States:
        A Documentary History.  4 vols.  New York:  Random House,
        1975.

132  Buck, Solon Justus.  Illinois in 1818 (1918).
    Danhof, Clarence H.  Change in Agriculture.  The Northern
        United States, 1820–1870.  Cambridge, MA:  Harvard U.
        Press, 1969.

Gordon, Leon M., II. "The Price of Isolation in Northern Indiana, 1830-1860." Indiana Magazine of History XXXXVI.

133  Bidwell, Percy W. "The Agricultural Revolution in New England." American Historical Review XXVI.
Gates, Paul W. The Farmer's Age: Agriculture, 1815-1860, Chapter 13 (1960).

134  Anderson, Russell H. "New York Agriculture Meets the West, 1830-1850." Wisconsin Magazine of History XVI.
Atkinson, Edward and Powers, L. G. "Farm Ownership and Tenancy in the United States." American Statistical Association, Quarterly Publications V.

135  Baldwin, Arthur D. A Memoir of Henry Perrine Baldwin, 1842 to 1911 (1915).
Moody, V. A. Slavery on Louisiana Sugar Plantations (1924).

136  Flanders, Ralph B. Plantation Slavery in Georgia (1933).
Sellers, James B. Slavery in Alabama (1950).

137  Atherton, Lewis E. The Southern Country Store, 1800-1860 (1949).
Haskins, Ralph W. "Planter and Cotton Factor in the Old South: Some Areas of Friction." Agricultural History XXIX.
Woodman, Harold D. King Cotton and His Retainers: Financing and Marketing the Cotton Crop of the South, 1800-1925. Lexington, KY: U. of Kentucky Press, 1968.

138  Gould, C. P. "Economic Causes of Rise of Baltimore," in Essays Presented to C. M. Andrews (1931).
Livingood, J. W. Philadelphia-Baltimore Trade Rivalry (1947).

139  Gates, Paul W. "Land Policy and Tenancy in the Prairie States." Journal of Economic History I.
McNall, N. A. First Half Century of Wadsworth Tenancy (1945).

140  Ellis, David M. Landlords and Farmers in the Hudson-Mohawk Region, 1790-1850 (1946).
Hedrick, U. P. A History of Agriculture in the State of New York (1933).

141  David, Paul A. "The Mechanization of Reaping in the Ante-Bellum Midwest," pp. 3-39 in Rosovsky, Henry (ed.), Industrialization in Two Systems: Essays in Honor of Alexander Gerschenkron. New York: Wiley, 1966.
Frederico, P. J. "Arbitration of Early Patent Disputes." Arbitration Journal II.
Rogin, Leo. The Introduction of Farm Machinery in its Relation to the Productivity of Labor in the Agriculture of the United States during the Nineteenth Century (1931).
Vaughn, F. L. The United States Patent System: Legal and Economic Conflicts in American Patent History (1956).

Wik, Reynold M.  Steam Power on the American Farm (1958).

142  Craven, Avery O.  Soil Exhaustion as a Factor in the Agricul-
        tural History of Virginia and Maryland, 1606-1860 (1925).
     Gates, Paul W.  The Farmer's Age:  Agriculture, 1815-1860,
        Chapter 19 (1960).

143  Craven, Avery O.  "The Agricultural Reformers of the Ante
        Bellum South."  American Historical Review XXXIII.
     Phillips, Ulrich B.  "Plantations with Slave Labor and Free."
        American Historical Review XXX.

144  Parker, William N.  "The Slave Plantation in American Agricul-
        ture," in First International Conference of Economic
        History (1960).
     Schlesinger, Arthur M., Sr.  "Was Olmsted an Unbiased Critic
        of the South?"  Journal of Negro History XXXVII.

145  Eaton, Clement.  "Class Differences in the Old South."
        Virginia Quarterly Review (Summer 1957).
     Yoder, Paton.  "Private Hospitality in the South, 1775-1850."
        Mississippi Valley Historical Review XLVII.

146  Bogue, Allan G.  From Prairie to Corn Belt:  Farming on the
        Illinois and Iowa Prairies in the Nineteenth Century
        (1963).
     Kohlmeier, A. L.  The Old Northwest as the Keystone of the
        Arch of American Federal Union:  A Study in Commerce and
        Politics (1938).

147  De Voe, Thomas.  The Market Book, Containing a Historical
        Account of the Public Markets in the Cities of New York,
        Boston, Philadelphia, and Brooklyn... (1862).
     Schmidt, Louis B.  "The Internal Grain Trade of the United
        States, 1850-1860."  Iowa Journal of History and Politics
        XVIII.

148  Davidson, Philip G.  "Industrialism in the Ante-Bellum South."
        South Atlantic Quarterly XXVII.
     Rezneck, Samuel.  "The Rise and Early Development of Industrial
        Consciousness in the United States, 1760-1830."  Journal of
        Economic and Business History IV.

149  Porter, Kenneth W.  The Jacksons and the Lees.  2 vols.  (1937).
     Smith, Merritt Roe.  "John H. Hall, Simeon North, and the
        Milling Machine:  The Nature of Innovation among Antebellum
        Arms Makers."  Technology and Culture 14 (October 1973):
        573-591.
     Wooster, Harvey A.  "Manufacturer and Artisan, 1790-1840."
        Journal of Political Economy XXXIV.

150  Burchard, John and Bush-Brown, Albert.  The Architecture of
        America:  A Social and Cultural History.  Part I (1961).

Fitch, James M.  American Building (1948).

151  Barber, Edwin A.  American Glassware, Old and New (1900).
     Watkins, Lura W.  Cambridge Glass, 1818 to 1888 (1930).

152  Appleton, Nathan.  The Introduction of the Power Loom (1858)
     Baird, R. H.  The American Cotton Spinner (1851).
     Jeremy, David J.  "British Textile Technology Transmission
        to the United States:  The Philadelphia Region Experience,
        1770-1820."  Business History Review 47 (Spring 1973):
        24-25.

153  Nesson, Fern L.  Great Waters.  A History of Boston's Water
        Supply.  Hanover, N.H.:  U. Press of New England, 1982.
     Redlich, Fritz.  "The Philadelphia Water Works in Relation
        to the Industrial Revolution in the United States."
        Pennsylvania Magazine of History and Biography LXIX.
     Taylor, Elbert J.  "The Beginnings of Philadelphia's Water
        Supply."  American Water Works Association Journal XXXXII.

154  Stevens, H. R.  "Bank Enterprisers in a Western Town [Cincinna-
        ti], 1815-1822."  Business History Review XXIX.

155  Mantoux, Paul.  The Industrial Revolution in the Eighteenth
        Century, introduction to first edition (1928).
     Marx, Capital I, Chapter 14 (1867).

156  Fitch, Charles H.  "Report on the Manufacture of Interchange-
        able Mechanism," in U.S. Census Office, Tenth Census:
        Manufactures II (G.P.O., 1883).
     Uselding, Paul J.  "Technical Progress at the Springfield
        Armory, 1820-1850."  Explorations in Economic History 9
        (Spring 1971):  291-316.
     Woodbury, Robert S.  "The Legend of Eli Whitney and Inter-
        changeable Parts."  Technology and Culture II.

157  Clark, Victor S.  History of Manufactures in the United States
        I, Chapter 17 (1929).
     Van Wagenen, Jared, Jr.  The Golden Age of Homespun (1953).

158  Knowlton, Evelyn H.  Pepperell's Progress:  History of a Cotton
        Textile Company, 1844-1945 (1948).
     Zevin, Robert B.  "The Growth of Manufacturing in Early Nine-
        teenth Century New England."  Journal of Economic History
        (December 1965).

159  Bathe, Greville and Dorothy.  Jacob Perkins (1943).
     Flinn, M. W.  Men of Iron:  The Crowleys in the Early Iron
        Industry (1962).

160  Ernst, Robert.  Immigrant Life in New York City, 1825-1863
        (1949).
     Marburg, Theodore F.  "Aspects of Labor Administration in
        the Early Nineteenth Century Century."  Bulletin of the
        Business Historical Society XV.

161    Taylor, George R.   The Transportation Revolution, 1815-1860,
         Chapter 12 (1951).
       Ware, Norman.   The Industrial Worker 1840-1860 (1924).

162    Cameron, E. H.   Samuel Slater--Father of American Manufactures
         (1960).
       White, George S.   Memoir of Samuel Slater (1835).

163    Burke, John G.   "Bursting Boilers and the Federal Power."
         Technology and Culture (Winter 1966).
       Calhoun, Daniel H.   The American Civil Engineer:   Origins
         and Conflict (1960).

164    Kauffman, Henry J.   The Gunsmith (1959).
       Sturt, George.   The [English] Wheelwright's Shop (1923).

165    Atack, Jeremy and others.   "The Regional Diffusion and Adoption
         of the Steam Engine in American Manufacturing."   Journal
         of Economic History 40 (June 1980):   281-308.
       Dickinson, H. W.   A Short History of the Steam Engine (1939).
       Hunter, Louis C.   A History of Industrial Power in the United
         States, 1780-1930:   Waterpower in the Century of the Steam
         Engine.   Vol. I.   Charlottesville, VA:   U. Press of
         Virginia, 1980.
       Stowers, A.   "The Stationary Steam-Engine, 1830-1900," in
         Singer, Charles et al. (eds.), A History of Technology V,
         Chapter 6 (1958).

166    Appleton, Nathan.   Introduction of the Power Loom and Origin
         of Lowell (1858).
       Draper, George O.   Labor-Saving Looms, 3rd ed. (1907).
       Jeremy, David J.   "Innovation in American Textile Technology
         during the Early 19th Century."   Technology and Culture 14
         (January 1973):   40-76.

167    Hayes, John L.   American Textile Machinery (1879).
       Strassman, W. Paul.   Risk and Technological Innovation, Chapter
         3 (1959).

168    Copeland, Melvin T.   The Cotton Manufacturing Industry of the
         United States (1912).
       Folsom, Michael B. and Lubar, Steven D. (eds.)   The Philosophy
         of Manufactures:   Early Debates over Industrialization in
         the United States.   Cambridge, MA:   M.I.T. Press, 1981.
       Murphy, W. S. (ed.)   The Textile Industries.   3 vols.   (1910).

169    Dodd, G.   The Textile Manufactures of Great Britain (1851).
       Nasmith, J.   Modern Cotton Spinning Machinery 1890).

170    Bryant, L. S. and Rae, J. B. (eds.)   Lowell, An Early American
         Industrial Community (1950).
       Shlakman, Vera.   Economic History of a Factory Town:   Chicopee
         (1935)

171  Durfee, William F.  "The History and Modern Development of the
     Art of Interchangeable Construction in Mechanism."  Ameri-
     can Society of Mechanical Engineers, Transactions XXII.
     North, Simon N. O. and North, Ralph.  Simeon North:  First
     Official Pistol Maker of the United States (1913).

172  Parsons, R. H.  A History of the Institution of Mechanical
     Engineers, 1847-1947 (1947).
     Roe, Joseph W.  English and American Tool Builders (1916).

173  Bateman, Fred.  A Deplorable Scarcity:  The Failure of Indus-
     trialization in the Slave Economy.  Chapel Hill, N.C.:
     U. of North Carolina Press, 1981.
     Griffin, Richard W.  "The Origins of the Industrial Revolution
     in Georgia:  Cotton Textiles, 1810-1865."  Georgia Histori-
     cal Quarterly (December 1958).
     _____.  "Manufacturing Interests of Mississippi Planters,
     1810-1832."  Journal of Mississippi History (April 1960).

174  Allen, Robert C.  "The Peculiar Productivity History of
     American Blast Furnaces, 1840-1913."  Journal of Economic
     History 37 (September 1977):  605-633.
     Bining, Arthur C.  Pennsylvania's Iron and Steel Industry
     (1954).
     Carlsen, Carl (pseud.) [Arthur W. Fey].  Buried Black Treasure:
     The Story of Pennsylvania Anthracite (1954).

175  Bateman, Fred.  "Large-Scale Manufacturing in the South and
     West, 1850-1860."  Business History Review 45 (1971):  1-17.
     Lander, Ernest M., Jr.  "Manufacturing in South Carolina,
     1815-1860."  Business Historical Review XXVIII.
     Mitchell, Broadus.  Rise of Cotton Mills in the South (1921).

176  Bateman, Fred and others.  "Profitability in Southern Manufac-
     turing:  Estimates for 1860."  Explorations in Economic
     History 12 (July 1975):  211-231.
     Gregg, William.  Essays on Cotton Manufacture.  Graniteville,
     S.C.:  Graniteville Company, 1941.
     Griffin, Richard and Standard, D.W.  "The Cotton Textile
     Industry in Ante-Bellum North Carolina."  North Carolina
     Historical Review XXXIV.

177  Fries, Adelaide.  "One Hundred Years of Textile in Salem
     [North Carolina]."  North Carolina Historical Review XXVII.
     Mitchell, Broadus.  William Gregg, Factory Master of the Old
     South (1928).

178  Bateman, Fred and others.  "The Participation of Planters in
     Manufacturing in the Antebellum South."  Agricultural
     History 48 (April 1974):  277-297.
     Paskoff, Paul F. and Wilson, Daniel J. (eds.).  The Cause of
     the South:  Selections from De Bow's Review, 1946-1867.
     Baton Rouge, LA:  Louisiana State U. Press, 1982.

179  Hill, Hamilton A. Memoir of Abbott Lawrence, 2nd ed. (1884).
     Wildes, Harry. Lonely Midas: The Story of Stephen Girard
          (1943).

180  Nasmyth, J. An Autobiography (1833).
     Strassmann, W. Paul. Risk and Technological Innovation,
          Chapter 4 (1959).

181  Mack, Edward C. Peter Cooper: Citizen of New York (1949).
     Strassman, W. Paul. Risk and Technological Innovation,
          Chapter 6 (1959).

182  Earle, Alice M. Customs and Fashions in Old New England (1893).
     Parsons, Elsie C. Old Fashioned Woman (1913).

183  Clark, Victor S. History of Manufactures in the United States
          I, Chapter 16 (1929).
     Habakukk, H. J. American and British Technology in the Nine-
          teenth Century. The Search for Labour-Saving Inventions
          (1962).

184  Elliott, Orrin L. The Tariff Controversy in the United States,
          1789-1833 (1892).
     James, John A. "The Welfare Effects of the Antebellum Tariff:
          A General Equilibrium Analysis." Explorations in Economic
          History 15 (July 1978): 231-256.
     Stanwood, Edward. American Tariff Controversies in the Nine-
          teenth Century. 2 vols. (1903).

185  Robbins, Lionel. The Theory of Economic Policy in English
          Classical Political Economy (1952).
     Walker, Kenneth O. "The Classical Economists and the Factory
          Acts." Journal of Economic History I.

186  Hartz, Louis. Economic Policy and Democratic Thought:
          Pennsylvania, 1776-1860 (1948).
     Taussig, F. W. The Tariff History of the United States (1892).

187  Clark, Victor S. History of Manufactures in the United States
          I, Chapter 12 (1929).
     Eiselen, Malcolm R. The Rise of Pennsylvania Protectionism
          (1932).

188  Bancroft, Frederic. Calhoun and the South Carolina Nullifica-
          tion Movement (1928).
     Edwards, Richard C. "Economic Sophistication in Nineteenth
          Century Congressional Tariff Debates." Journal of Economic
          History 30 (December 1970): 802-838.
     Peterson, Merrill D. Olive Branch and Sword--The Compromise
          of 1833. Baton Rouge, LA: Louisiana State U. Press, 1982.
     Russell, R. R. Economic Aspects of Southern Sectionalism
          (1924).

189  Eiselen, M. R.  The Rise of Pennsylvania Protectionism (1932).
     McCormac, E. I.  James K. Polk (1922).

190  Clark, Victor S.  History of Manufactures in the United States
       I, Chapter 12 (1929).
     Taylor, George R.  The Transportation Revolution, 1815-1860,
       Chapter 16 (1951).

191  Downes, Randolph C.  Canal Days (1949).
     Haites, Erik F. and Mak, James.  "Ohio and Mississippi River
       Transportation 1810-1860."  Explorations in Economic
       History 8 (Winter 1970-71):  153-180.
     Klein, Benjamin F. and Klein, Eleanor W.  The Ohio River Hand-
       book (1949).
     Mak, James and Walton, Gary M.  "Steamboats and the Great
       Productivity Surge in River Transportation."  Journal of
       Economic History 32 (September 1972):  619-640.
     Scheiber, Harry N.  Ohio Canal Era:  A Case Study of Govern-
       ment and the Economy, 1820-1861.  Athens, OH:  Ohio U.
       Press, 1969.

192  Goodrich, Carter (ed.).  Canals and American Economic Develop-
       ment (1961).
     Krenkel, John H.  Internal Improvements in Illinois, 1818-1848
       (1937).

193  Jenkins, H. M.  Pennsylvania...1608-1903 II (1903).
     Klein, Philip S.  Pennsylvania Politics, 1817-1832 (1940).

194  Flint, Henry M.  The Railroads of the United States:  Their
       History and Statistics (1868).
     Taylor, George R.  The Transportation Revolution, 1815-1860,
       Chapter 7 (1951).

195  Fletcher, Daniel O.  "The Decline of the Great Lakes Package-
       Freight Carriers."  Business History Review 36 (1962):
       387-407.
     Hatcher, Harlan.  The Great Lakes (1944).
     Plumb, Ralph G.  History of the Navigation of the Great Lakes
       (G.P.O., 1911).

196  Transportation and the Early Nation:  Papers Presented at an
     Indiana American Revolution Bicentennial Symposium.  Indiana-
     polis, IN:  Indiana Historical Society, 1982.

197  Miller, Nathan.  The Enterprise of a Free People.  Aspects of
       Economic Development in New York State During the Canal
       Period, 1792-1838 (1962).
     Shaw, Ronald E.  Erie Water West:  A History of the Erie Canal,
       1792-1854 (1966).

198  Abbott, Carl.  "The Plank Road Enthusiasm in the Antebellum
       Middle West."  Indiana Magazine of History 67 (June 1971):
       95-116.

Fishlow, Albert.  American Railroads and the Transformation
    of the Ante-Bellum Economy (1965).
Phillips, Ulrich B.  A History of Transportation in the Eastern
    Cotton Belt to 1860 (1908).
Shumway, George and others.  Conestoga Wagon, 1750-1850:
    Freight Carrier for 100 Years of America's Westward Expan-
    sion.  Second edition.  York, PA:  G. Shumway and Early
    American Industries Association, 1966.
Taylor, Morris F.  First Mail West:  Stagecoach Lines on the
    Santa Fe Trail.  Albuquerque, N.M.:  U. of New Mexico
    Press, 1971.

199  Phillips, Ulrich B.  Life and Labor in the Old South, Chapter
        8 (1929).
     Taylor, George R.  The Transportation Revolution, 1815-1860,
        Chapter 10 (1951).

200  Chandler, Alfred D., Jr.  "The Railroads:  Pioneers in Modern
        Corporate Management."  Business History Review 39 (1965):
        16-40.
     Kirkland, Edward C.  Men, Cities and Transportation, A Study
        in New England History, 1820-1900.  2 vols.  (1948).
     MacGill, Caroline et al.  History of Transportation in the
        United States before 1860.  Meyer, B. H., ed., Chapter 12
        (1917).

201  Cleaveland, Dorothy K.  "The Trade and Trade Routes of Northern
        New York from the Beginning of Settlement to the Coming of
        the Railroad."  Quarterly Journal of the New York State
        Historical Association IV.
     Fox, W. F.  A History of the Lumber Industry in the State of
        New York (1902).

202  Callahan, Colleen M. and Hutchinson, William K.  "Antebellum
        Interregional Trade in Agricultural Goods:  Preliminary
        Results."  Journal of Economic History 40 (March 1980):
        25-31.
     MacGill, Caroline E. et al.  History of Transportation in the
        United States before 1860.  Meyer, B. H., ed., Chapter 15
        (1917).
     Wender, Herbert.  Southern Commercial Conventions (1930).

203  Du Boff, Richard B.  "Business Demand and the Development of
        the Telegraph in the United States, 1844-1860."  Business
        History Review 54 (1980):  459-479.
     Hindle, Brooke.  Emulation and Invention.  New York:  U. Press,
        1981.
     Reid, James D.  The Telegraph in America (1879).
     Thompson, Robert L.  Wiring a Continent, The History of the
        Telegraph Industry in the United States, 1832-1866 (1947).

204  Jackson, W. Turrentine.  Wagon Roads West.  A Study of Federal
        Road Surveys and Construction in the Trans-Mississippi West,
        1846-1869 (1952).

Jervis, John B.  Railway Property (1861).
MacGill, Caroline E. et al.  History of Transportation in the
    United States before 1860.  Meyer, B. H., ed., Chapter 12
    (1917).
Majors, Alexander.  Seventy Years on the Frontier (1893).
Walker, Henry P.  The Wagonmasters:  High Plains Freighting
    from the Earliest Days of the Santa Fe Trail to 1880.
    Norman, OK:  U. of Oklahoma Press, 1966.

205  Puckett, Erastus P.  "The Attempt of New Orleans to Meet the
        Crisis in Her Trade with the West."  Mississippi Valley
        Historical Association, Proceedings X.
     Van Metre, T. W.  "Expansion of Internal Commerce, 1830 to
        1860," in Johnson, Emory et al., History of Domestic and
        Foreign Commerce in the United States I, Chapter 13 (1915).

206  Kettel, T. P.  Southern Wealth and Northern Profits (1860).
     Way, R. B.  "The Commerce of the Lower Mississippi in the
        Period, 1830-1860."  Mississippi Valley Historical
        Association, Proceedings X.

207  Klebaner, Benjamin J.  "Poverty and Its Relief in American
        Thought, 1815-61."  Social Service Review (December 1964).
     Schneider, D. M.  History of Public Welfare in New York State
        (1938).

208  Eaton, Clement.  The Growth of Southern Civilization, 1790-
        1860, Chapter 7 (1961).
     Owsley, Frank L.  The Plain Folk of the Old South (1949).

209  Berthoff, Rowland T.  British Immigrants in Industrial America
        (1953).
     Yearley, C. K.  Britons in American Labor...1820-1914 (1955).

210  Field, Arthur S.  "The Child Labor Policy of New Jersey."
        American Economic Association Quarterly XI.
     Josephson, Hannah.  The Golden Threads (1949).
     Matthies, Susan A.  "Families at Work:  An Analysis by Sex of
        Child Workers in the Cotton Textile Industry."  Journal of
        Economic History 62 (March 1982):  173-180.

211  Adams, Donald R., Jr.  "Some Evidence on English and American
        Wage Rates, 1790-1830."  Journal of Economic History 30
        (September 1970):  499-520.
     Layer, Robert G.  Earnings of Cotton Mill Operatives, 1825-1914
        (1955).
     Lebergott, Stanley.  "Wage Trends, 1800-1900," in Trends in the
        American Economy in the Nineteenth Century (1960).
     Zebler, Jeffrey F.  "Further Evidence on American Wage Differ-
        entials, 1800-1830."  Explorations in Economic History 10
        (Fall 1972):  109-117.

212   Foner, Philip S.   History of the Labor Movement in the United
          States I, Chapter 11 (1947).
      Ginger, Ray.   "Labor in a Massachusetts Cotton Mill, 1853-60."
          Business History Review XXVIII.

213   Martin, Edgar W.   The Standard of Living in 1860 (1942).
      Williamson, Harold F.   "An Appraisal of American Economic
          Progress."   American Economic Review XL.

214   Bidwell, Percy W. and Falconer, John I.   History of Agriculture
          in the Northern United States, 1620-1860, Chapter 22
          (1925).
      Lippincott, Isaac.   History of Manufactures in the Ohio Valley
          up to 1860 (1914).
      Walsh, Margaret.   The Manufacturing Frontier:   Pioneer Industry
          in Antebellum Wisconsin, 1830-1860.   Madison, WI:   State
          Historical Society of Wisconsin, 1972.

215   Eaton, Clement.   "Slave-Hiring in the Upper South:   a Step
          toward Freedom."   Mississippi Valley Historical Review
          XLVI.
      Stampp, Kenneth.   The Peculiar Institution (1956).

216   Buck. Paul H.   "The Poor Whites of the Ante-Bellum South."
          American Historical Review XXXI.
      Morris, Richard.   "The Measure of Bondage in the Slave States."
          Mississippi Valley Historical Review XXXXI.
      Terrill, Tom E.   "Eager Hands:   Labor for Southern Textiles,
          1850-1860."   Journal of Economic History 36 (March 1976):
          84-99.
      Wright, Gavin.   "Cheap Labor and Southern Textiles before
          1880."   Journal of Economic History 39 (September 1979):
          655-680.

217   Morris, Richard.   "Andrew Jackson, Strikebreaker."   American
          Historical Review LV.
      Phillips, Ulrich B.   American Negro Slavery, Chapter 15 (1918).

218   _____.   Life and Labor in the Old South, Chapter 15 (1929).
      Stampp, Kenneth.   The Peculiar Institution (1956).
      Sutch, Richard.   "The Treatment Received by American Slaves:
          A Critical Review of the Evidence Presented in Time on the
          Cross."   Explorations in Economic History 12 (1975):   335-
          438.
      Vedder, Richard K.   "The Slave Exploitation (Expropriation)
          Rate."   Explorations in Economic History 12 (1975):   453-
          457.

219   Blegen, Theodore C.   "The Competition of the Northwestern
          States for Immigrants."   Wisconsin Magazine of History III.
      Walter, Mack.   Germany and the Emigration, 1816-1885 (1964).

220   Richardson, Eudora Ramsay.   "The Virginian Who Made Illinois
          a Free State."   Illinois State Historical Society Journal
          XXXXV.

Staudenraus, P. J.  The African Colonization Movement, 1816-1865 (1961).

221  Du Bois, W. E. B.  Suppression of the African Slave Trade (1896).
     Dunne, Gerald T.  Justice Joseph Story.  New York:  Simon & Schuster, 1971.
     Howard, Warren S.  American Slavers and the Federal Law:  1837-1862.  Berkeley, CA:  U. of California Press, 1963.
     Stephenson, Wendell H.  Isaac Franklin, Slave Trader and Planter of the Old South (1938).

222  Bugbee, Lester G.  "Slavery in Early Texas."  Political Science Quarterly XIII.
     Rather, E. Z.  "Influence of Slavery in Colonization of Texas."  Mississippi Valley Historical Review XI.

223  Fogel, Robert W. and Engerman, Stanley L.  Time on the Cross. 2 vols.  Boston, MA:  Little, Brown, 1974.
     Henry, H. M.  The Police Control of the Slave in South Carolina (1914).
     Wiley, Bell I.  "The Movement to Humanize the Institution of Slavery During the Confederacy."  Emory University Quarterly V.

224  Lander, Ernest M., Jr.  "Slave Labor in South Carolina Cotton Mills."  Journal of Negro History XXXVIII.
     Moss, John E.  "The Absorption of Capital in Slave Labor in the Ante-Bellum South and Economic Growth."  American Journal of Economics and Sociology XX.

225  Adams, E. O.  British Interests in Texas (1910).
     Barker, E. C.  "The African Slave Trade in Texas."  Texas Historical Association, Quarterly VI.

226  Billington, Ray A.  The Far Western Frontier, 1830-1860 (1956).
     Curlee, Abigail.  "The History of a Texas Slave Plantation, 1831-63."  Southwestern Historical Quarterly XXVI.

227  Conrad, Alfred H. and Meyer, John R.  "The Economics of Slavery in the Ante Bellum South."  Journal of Political Economy LXVI.
     Phillips, Ulrich B.  "The Economic Cost of Slaveholding in the Cotton Belt."  Political Science Quarterly XX.

228  Albion, Robert G.  The Rise of New York Port, 1815-1860 (1939).
     Foner, Phillip S.  Business and Slavery (1941).

229  Craven, Avery O.  Edmund Ruffin, Southerner (1932).
     Skipper, Otis C.  J. B. De Bow, Magazinist of the Old South (1958).

230   Russel, Robert R.   Ante Bellum Studies in Slavery, Politics
         and the Railroads (repr. 1960).
      Taylor, Paul S.   "Plantation Labor Before the Civil War."
         Agricultural History XXVIII.

231   Bruce, Kathleen.   "Slave Labor in the Virginia Iron Industry."
         William and Mary Quarterly VI.
      Griffin, Richard W.   "Poor White Laborers in Southern Cotton
         Factories, 1789-1865."   South Carolina Historical Magazine
         (January 1960).

232   Conrad, Alfred H. and others.   "Slavery as an Obstacle to
         Economic Growth in the United States:  A Panel Discussion."
         Journal of Economic History 27 (December 1967):  518-560.
      Genovese, Eugene D.   The Political Economy of Slavery (1965).
      Stampp, Kenneth M.   The Peculiar Institution.  Slavery in the
         Ante-Bellum South (1956).

233   Carnathan, W. J.   "Proposal to Reopen African Slave Trade."
         South Atlantic Quarterly XXV.
      Du Bois, W. E. B.   The Suppression of the African Slave Trade
         to the United States of America, 1638-1870 (1896).

234   Grayson, William J.   The Hireling and the Slave (1856)
      Fitzhugh, George.   Cannibals All (1857).

235   Hurd, J. C.   The Law of Freedom and Bondage in the United
         States.  2 vols.  (1858, 1862).
      Moore, Wilbert E.   "Slave Law and Social Structure."   Journal
         of Negro History XXVI.

236   Knox, John Jay.   A History of Banking in the United States
         (1900).
      Summer, William G.   A History of Banking in the United States
         (1896).

237   Adams, Donald R., Jr.   Finance and Enterprise in Early America:
         A Study of Stephen Girard's Bank, 1812-1831.  Philadelphia,
         PA:  U. of Pennsylvania Press, 1978.
      Hinderliter, Roger H. and Rockoff, Hugh.   "The Management of
         Reserves by Ante-Bellum Banks in Eastern Financial Centers."
         Explorations in Economic History 11 (Fall 1973):  37-53.

238   Hammond, Bray.   Banks and Politics in America from the Revolu-
         tion to the Civil War (1957).
      Shannon, Fred A.   "Bankers in Politics."   Science and Society
         XXIV.

239   Hundley, Daniel R.   Social Relations in Our Southern States
         (1860).
      Johnson, G. G.   Ante-Bellum North Carolina, A Social History
         (1937).

240   Barker, Eugene C.  "Land Speculation as a Cause of the Texas
          Revolution."  Texas State Historical Association, Quarterly
          XVIII.
      Williams, Elgin.  The Animating Pursuits of Speculation:  Land
          Traffic in the Annexation of Texas (1949).

241   Martin, David A.  "Metallism, Small Notes, and Jackson's War
          with the B.U.S."  Explorations of Economic History 11
          (Spring 1974):  227-247.
      McFaul, John M.  The Politics of Jacksonian Finance.  Ithaca,
          N.Y.:  Cornell U. Press, 1972.
      Redlich, Fritz.  The Moulding of American Banking, Men and
          Ideas.  2 vols.  (1947, 1951).
      Smith, Walter B.  Economic Aspects of the Second Bank of the
          United States (1953).

242   Boyles, W. Harrison and Alleben, Frank.  "A History of Banks
          and Banking in the City of New York."  Journal of American
          History XVI.
      Hammond, Bray.  Banks and Politics in America, Chapter 12
          (1957).
      Scheiber, Harry N.  "The Pet Banks in Jacksonian Politics and
          Finance, 1833-1841."  Journal of Economic History 23
          (June 1963):  196-214.
      Sushka, Marie E.  "The Antebellum Money Market and the
          Economic Impact of the Bank War."  Journal of Economic
          History 36 (December 1976):  809-835.

243   Hedges, Joseph E.  Commercial Banking and the Stock Market
          Before 1863 (1938).
      Meeker, J. Edward.  Short Selling (1932).

244   Brantley, William H.  Banking in Alabama, 1816-1860 I (1961).
      Van Fenstermaker, J.  The Development of American Commercial
          Banking, 1782-1837 (1965).
      Wilburn, Jean A.  Biddle's Bank:  The Crucial Years.  New York:
          Columbia U. Press, 1967.

245   Fraas, Arthur.  "The Second Bank of the United States:  An
          Instrument for an Interregional Monetary Union."  Journal
          of Economic History 34 (June 1974):  447-467.
      Hammond, Bray.  "Free Banks and Corporations:  The New York
          Free Banking Act of 1838."  Journal of Political Economy
          XLIV.
      Redlich, Fritz.  The Molding of American Banking I (1947).
      Walton, Gary M. and Shepherd, James F.  The Economic Rise of
          Early America.  New York:  Cambridge U. Press, 1979.

246   Macesich, George.  "Sources of Monetary Disturbances in the
          United States, 1834-1845."  Journal of Economic History XX.
      McGrane, Reginald C.  The Panic of 1837, Chapter 6 (1924).
      Timberlake, Richard H., Jr.  "The Specie Circular and Sales of
          Public Lands:  A Comment."  Journal of Economic History 25
          (September 1965):  414-416.

247   Hammond, Bray. _Bank and Politics in America_, Chapter 15 (1957).
      Timberlake, Richard H., Jr.  "The Specie Circular and Distribu-
         tion of the Surplus."  _Journal of Political Economy_ LXVIII.

248   Jordan, Weymouth T.  _Rebels in the Making:  Planters' Conven-
         tions and Southern Propaganda_ (1958).
      Russel, Robert R.  _Economic Aspects of Southern Sectionalism,
         1840-1861_ (1924).

249   Callender, G. S.  "The Early Transportation and Banking Enter-
         prises of the States in Relation to the Growth of Corpora-
         tions."  _Quarterly Journal of Economics_ XVII.
      North, Douglass C.  _The Economic Growth of the United States,
         1790-1860_, Chapters 9 and 10 (1961).

250   Boewe, Charles.  _Prairie Albion:  An English Settlement in
         Pioneer Illinois_ (1962).
      Jenks, Leland H.  _The Migration of British Capital to 1875_
         (1927).

251   Erickson, Erling.  _Banking in Frontier Iowa, 1836-1865_.
         Ames, IA:  Iowa State U. Press, 1971.
      Johnson, Arthur M. and Supple, Barry E.  _Boston Capitalists
         and Western Railroads:  A Study in the Nineteenth-Century
         Railroad Investment Process_.  Cambridge, MA:  Harvard U.
         Press, 1967.
      Sylla, Richard.  _The American Capital Market, 1846-1914_.
         New York:

252   Coman, Katherine.  _Economic Beginnings of the Far West_.
         2 vols. (1925).
      Hittell, T. H.  _History of California_ II (1897).

253   Norris, James D.  _Frontier Iron:  The Maramec Iron Works, 1826-
         1876_ (1964).
      Primm, James N.  _Economic Policy in the Development of a
         Western State, Missouri, 1820-1860_ (1954).

254   James, Marquis.  _Life of Andrew Jackson_ (1938).
      Taus, Esther R.  _The Central Banking Functions of the United
         States Treasury, 1789-1941_ (1943).
      Timberlake, R. H., Jr.  "The Independent Treasury and Monetary
         Policy Before the Civil War."  _Southern Economic Journal_
         (October 1960).
      _____.  "The Specie Standard and Central Banking in the United
         States before 1860."  _Journal of Economic History_ XXI.

255   Stone, Alfred H.  "The Cotton Factorage System in the Southern
         States."  _American Historical Review_ XX.
      Van Deusen, J. G.  _Ante-Bellum Southern Commercial Conventions_
         (1926).

256  Conant, Charles A. and Nadler, M.  History of Modern Banks of
     Issue.  6th ed. (1927).
     Klebaner, Benjamin J.  Commercial Banking in the United States:
     A History.  Hinsdale, IL:  Dryden Press, 1974.
     Schultz, W. J. and Caine, M. B.  Financial Development of the
     United States (1937).

257  Gates, William B., Jr.  Michigan Copper and Boston Dollars
     (1951).
     Horton, John T.  History of Northwestern New York (1947).
     Kane, Lucile M.  "Hersey, Staples, and Company, 1854-1860:
     Eastern Managers and Capital in Frontier Business."
     Bulletin of the Business Historical Society XXVI.
     Rapp, Marvin A.  "Buffalo's First Harbor."  Inland Seas (Fall
     1956).

258  Van Vleek, George.  The Panic of 1857 (1943).
     Veblen, Thorstein.  The Higher Learning in America, Chapter 2
     (1918)

259  Davis, Joseph S.  Essays in the Earlier History of American
     Corporations.  2 vols.  (1917).
     Livermore, Shaw.  "Advent of Corporations in New York."
     New York History, XVI.
     Williamson, Oliver E.  "The Modern Corporation:  Origins,
     Evolution, Attributes."  Journal of Economic Literature 19
     (December 1981):  1537-1568.

260  Cadman, John W., Jr.  The Corporation in New Jersey.  Business
     and Politics 1791-1875 (1949).
     Dodd, Edwin M.  American Business Corporation Until 1860:  With
     Special Reference to Massachusetts (1954).
     Seavoy, Ronald E.  The Origins of the American Business Corpora-
     tion, 1784-1855:  Broadening the Concept of Public Service
     during Industrialization.  Westport, CT:  Greenwood, 1982.

261  Noel, F. Regis.  A History of Bankruptcy Law (1919).
     Warren, Charles.  Bankruptcy in United States History (1935).

262  Dodd, Edwin M. and Baker, Ralph J.  "The Evolution of the
     Business Corporation."  Cases on Business Associations,
     Corporations I (1940).
     Spear, Samuel T.  "The Citizenship of Corporations."  Albany
     Law Journal (1877).

263  Hamilton, Earl J.  "The Role of Monopoly in the Overseas Expan-
     sion and Colonial Trade of Europe before 1800."  American
     Economic Review XXXVIII.
     Westermann, J. C.  The Netherlands and the United States, Their
     Relations in the Beginning of the Nineteenth Century (1935).

264  Fay, C. R.  The Corn Laws and Social England (1932).

Potter, J.  "The Atlantic Economy, 1815-60:  The U.S.A. and the Industrial Revolution in Britain," in Pressnel, L. S. (ed.), Studies in the Industrial Revolution (1960).

265  Buck, Norman S.  The Development of the Organization of Anglo-American Trade, 1800-1850 (1925).
Hidy, Ralph W.  The House of Baring in American Trade and Finance (1949).

266  McGrane, Reginald.  Foreign Bondholders and American State Debts (1935).
Ratchford, B. U.  American State Debts (1941).

267  Eaton, Clement.  The Growth of Southern Civilization, Chapter 9 (1961).
Wender, Herbert.  Southern Commercial Conventions, 1837-1859 (1930).

268  Dorfman, Joseph.  "A Note on the Interpenetration of Anglo-American Finance, 1837-1841."  Journal of Economic History XI.
McGrane, Reginald C.  Foreign Bondholders and American State Debts (1935).

269  Rabbens, Ugo.  The American Commercial Policy.  2nd ed. (1895).
Smith, Edward.  England and America After Independence...1783-1872 (1900).

270  Albion, Robert G. and Pope, Jennie B.  The Rise of New York Port (1939).
Taylor, George R.  The Transportation Revolution, 1815-1860, Chapter 9 (1951).

271  Huebner, G. G.  "The Foreign Trade of the United States since 1789," in Johnson, E. et al., History of Domestic and Foreign Commerce of the United States II (1915).

272  Miyamoto, Mataji, Sakudo, Yotaro and Yasuba, Yasukichi.  "Economic Development in Preindustrial Japan, 1859-1894."  Journal of Economic History (December 1965).
Sansom, George.  A History of Japan, 1615-1867 (1963).

273  Cecil, Algernon.  British Foreign Secretaries, 1807-1916 (1927).
Weinberg, Albert K.  Manifest Destiny (1935).

274  Robertson, W. S.  Hispanic-American Relations with the United States (1923).
Rutter, F. R.  South American Trade of Baltimore (1897).

275  Finkelstein, Herman N.  Legal Aspects of Commercial Letters of Credit (1930).
Klein, Joseph J.  "The Development of Mercantile Instruments of Credit in the United States."  Journal of Accountancy XII, XIII.

276   Bernstein, Harry. Origins of Inter-American Interest (1945).
      Tanner, Earl C. "Caribbean Ports in the Foreign Commerce of
         Providence, 1790-1830." Rhode Island History (October
         1955).

277   Goebel, Dorothy B. "British-American Rivalry in the Chilean
         Trade, 1817-1820." Journal of Economic History II.
      Rippy, J. Fred. Rivalry of United States and Great Britain
         over Latin America (1929).

278   Chandler, Charles L. "United States Commerce with Latin Ameri-
         ca at the Promulgation of the Monroe Doctrine." Quarterly
         Journal of Economics XXXVIII.
      Gray, William H. "Early Trade Relations between the United
         States and Venezuela." Estudios de historia de America.
         Mexico: Pan American Institute of Geography and History,
         1948.

279   Ely, Roland T. "The Old Cuba Trade." Business History Review
         (Winter 1964).
      Rauch, Basil. American Interests in Cuba (1948).

280   Buck, Norman S. The Development of the Organization of Anglo-
         American Trade, 1800-1850 (1925).
      Hidy, Ralph W. and Muriel. "Anglo-American Merchant Bankers
         of the Old Northwest, 1848-1860." Business History Review
         XXIV.

281   Kennedy, Crammond. "Comparison of the Relative Interests of
         the United States and Great Britain in the Western Hemis-
         phere at the Different Stages of Negotiations [for the
         Panama Canal]." American Society for International Law,
         Proceedings VII.
      Williams, Mary W. Anglo-American Isthmian Diplomacy, 1815-
         1915 (1916).

282   Merk, Frederick. "The Genesis of the Oregon Question."
         Mississippi Valley Historical Review XXXVI.
      Winther, Oscar O. The Old Oregon Country, A History of Frontier
         Trade, Transportation and Travel (1950).

283   Parker, Robert J. "Larkin, Anglo-American Businessman in
         Mexican California," in Greater America: Essays in Honor
         of Herbert Eugene Bolton (1945).
      Underhill, Reuben L. From Cowhide to Golden Fleece (1939).

284   Wilbur, Marguerite E. (ed.) A Pioneer at Sutter's Fort (1941).
      Zollenger, James P. Sutter: The Man and His Empire (1939).

285   Callahan, J. W. "The Mexican Policy of Southern Leaders under
         Buchanan's Administration." American Historical Association
         Annual Report (1910).
      Rippy, J. Fred. The United States and Mexico (1931).

286  Cleland, Robert G.  "The Early Sentiment for the Annexation of
        California:  An Account of American Interest in California,
        1835-1846."  Southwestern Historical Quarterly XVIII.
     Lawrence, Eleanor.  "Mexican Trade between Santa Fe and Los
        Angeles, 1830-1848."  California Historical Society
        Quarterly X.

287  Barker, Eugene C.  "President Jackson and the Texas Revolution."
        American Historical Review XII.
     Smith, Justin.  The Annexation of Texas (1911).

288  Graebner, Norman.  Empire on the Pacific (1955).
     Winther, Oscar O.  "California as a Factor in the Pacific
        Northwest Trade, 1829-69."  Huntington Library Quarterly
        VI.

289  Adams, H. C.  Taxation in the United States, 1789-1816 (1884).
     Ratner, S.  A Social History of American Taxation (1942).

290  Powell, J. H.  Richard Rush (1942).
     White, Leonard D.  The Jacksonians...1829-1861 (1954).

291  Poage, G. R.  Clay and the Whig Party (1936).
     Schlesinger, Arthur, Jr.  The Age of Jackson, Chapters 22-23
        (1945).

292  Gallaher, Ruth A.  "The Indian Agent in the United States
        before 1850."  Iowa Journal of History and Politics XIV.
     Seymour, Flora W.  Indian Agents of the Old Frontier (1941).

293  Catterall, Ralph C. H.  The Second Bank of the United States
        (1903).
     Hammond, Bray.  Banks and Politics in America, Chapter 14
        (1957).

294  Adams, Donald R., Jr.  "The Standard of Living During American
        Industrialization:  Evidence from the Brandywine Region,
        1800-1860."  Journal of Economic History 42 (December
        1982):  903-917.
     Hartz, Louis.  The Liberal Tradition in America (1955)
     Main, Jackson T.  "Trends in Wealth Concentration Before 1860."
        Journal of Economic History 31 (June 1981):  445-447.
     Smith, J. Allen.  Growth and Decadence of Constitutional
        Government (1930).

295  Buley, R. C.  The Old Northwest...1815-1840.  2 vols.  (1950).
     Hedrick, W. O.  "The Financial and Tax History of Michigan."
        Michigan History Magazine XXII.
     Ratner, Sidney.  Taxation and Democracy in America.  Rev. ed.
        New York:  Wiley, 1967.

296  Craven, Avery O.  The Growth of Southern Nationalism (1953).
     Nevins, Allan.  The Emergence of Lincoln. 2 vols.  (1950).

297  Bancroft, Frederick. *Life of W. H. Seward*. 2 vols. (1900).
     Phillips, U. B. *Life of Robert Toombs* (1913).

298  Lord, Daniel. *The Effect of Secession on the Commercial Rela-
     tions Between the North and South*, Secession Pamphlets VIII
     (1861).
     Mitchell, Betty L. *Edmund Ruffin, A Biography*. Bloomington,
     IN:  Indiana U. Press, 1981.

299  Butt, John. "Legends of the Coal-Oil Industry (1847-64)."
     *Explorations in Entrepreneurial History* NS., 2 (Fall 1964):
     16-30.
     Darrah, William C. *Pithole, the Vanished City:  A Story of
     the Early Days of the Petroleum Industry*. Gettysburg, PA:
     The Author, 1972.
     Enos, John L. *Petroleum Progress and Profits* (1962).
     Giddens, Paul H. *Birth of the Oil Industry* (1938).

300  De Golyer, Everette L. "How Men Find Oil:  The Dean of Oil
     Geologists Recalls When Wildcatting Was All Luck."
     *Fortune* XL.
     Tait, S. W., Jr. *The Wild Catters* (1946).

301  Bridges, Hal. *Iron Millionaire--Life of Charlemagne Tower*
     (1952).
     Evans, H. O. *Iron Pioneer:  Henry W. Oliver, 1840-1904* (1942).
     Lesy, Michael. *Bearing Witness:  A Photographic Chronicle of
     of American Life, 1860-1945*. New York:  Pantheon, 1982,
     pp. 46-47.

302  Marovelli, Robert L. and Karnak, John M. "The Mechanization
     of Mining." *Scientific American* 247 (September 1982):  90-
     102.
     "Mining and Processing Coal." *Automation* VIII.
     Ritson, J. A. S. "Metal and Coal Mining, 1750-1875," in
     Singer, Charles et al. (eds.), *A History of Technology* IV,
     Chapter 3 (1958).

303  Lewis, Oscar. *Silver Kings* (1947).
     Smith, Grant H. *History of the Comstock Lode* (1943).

304  Hagedorn, Hermann. *The Magnets:  William Boyce Thompson and
     His Time (1869-1930)* (1935).
     Lyman, George D. *Ralston's Ring:  California Plunderers of
     Comstock Lode* (1937).

305  Appleman, Roy E. "Timber Empire from the Public Domain."
     *Mississippi Valley Historical Review* XXVI.
     Defebaugh, J. E. *History of the Lumber Industry of America*.
     2 vols. (1906-1907).
     Libecap, Gary D. and Johnson, Ronald N. "Property Rights,
     Nineteenth-Century Federal Timber Policy and the Conserva-
     tion Movement." *Journal of Economic History* 39 (March
     1979):  129-142.

Robbins, William G. Lumberjacks and Legislators: Political
    Economy of the U.S. Lumber Industry, 1890-1941. College
    Station, TX: Texas A & M U. Press, 1982.

306  Carlsen, Carl. [Arthur W. Fey]. Buried Black Treasure: The
        Story of Pennsylvania Anthracite (1954).
     Hoffman, John N. "Anthracite in the Lehigh Region of
        Pennsylvania, 1820-45." U.S. National Museum Bulletin Paper
        72 (1968): 90-141.
     Jones, Eliot. The Anthracite Coal Combination in the United
        States (1914).
     Powell, H. Benjamin. Philadelphia: First Fuel Crisis: Jacob
        Cist and the Developing Market for Pennsylvania Anthracite.
        University Park, PA: Pennsylvania State U. Press, 1978.

307  Hidy, Ralph W. and Muriel E. Pioneering in Big Business, 1882-
        1911 (1955).
     Miller, Ernest C. This Was Early Oil: Contemporary Accounts
        of the Growing Petroleum Industry, 1848-1885. Harrisburg,
        PA: Pennsylvania Historical and Museum Commission, 1968.
     Williamson, Harold F. and Daum, Arnold R. The American Petrol-
        eum Industry...1859-1899 (1959).

308  Pinchot, Gifford. Breaking New Ground (1947).
     Johnson, Ronald N. and Libecap, Gary D. "Efficient Markets and
        Great Lakes Timber: A Conservation Issue Reexamined."
        Explorations in Economic History 17 (October 1980): 372-
        385.
     Rodgers, Andrew D., III. Bernhard Edward Fernow, A Story of
        North American Forestry (1951).
     Smith, David C. "The Logging Frontier." Journal of Forest
        History 18 (October 1974): 96-106.

309  Hickman, Nollie. Mississippi Harvest: Lumbering in the Long-
        Leaf Pine Belt, 1840-1915 (1962).
     Hidy, Ralph W. and others. Timber and Men: The Weyerhaeuser
        Story. New York: Macmillan, 1964.
     Le Duc, Thomas. "The Historiography of Conservation." Forest
        History 9 (October 1965): 23-28.
     Woodward, C. Vann. Origins of the New South, Chapter 11 (1951).

310  Clepper, Henry. Professional Forestry in the United States.
        Baltimore, MD: Johns Hopkins Press, 1971.
     Everest, D. C. "A Reappraisal of the Lumber Barons." Wisconsin
        Magazine of History XXXVI.
     Gates, Paul W. The Wisconsin Pine Lands of Cornell University:
        A Study in Land Policy and Absentee Ownership (1943).
     Polenberg, Richard. "Conservation and Reorganization: The
        Forest Service Lobby, 1937-1938." Agricultural History 39
        (1965).

311  Cleland, R. G. A History of Phelps Dodge, 1834-1950 (1952).

Navin, Thomas R.  Copper Mining and Management.  Tucson, AZ:
    U. of Arizona Press, 1978.
O'Connor, Harvey.  The Guggenheims (1937).

312  Gates, Paul W.  "The Homestead Act in an Incongruous Land
        System."  American Historical Review XLI.
     Riddleberger, P. W.  "George W. Julian:  Abolitionist Land
        Reformer."  Agricultural History XXIX.

313  Abbott, M.  "Free Land, Free Labor, and the Freedmen's Bureau."
        Agricultural History XXX.
     Bleser, Carol K. R.  The Promised Land:  The History of the
        South Carolina Land Commission, 1869-1890.  Columbia, S.C.:
        U. of South Carolina Press, 1969.
     Clarke, G. J.  George W. Julian (1923).

314  Cox, La Wanda.  "The Promise of Land for the Freedmen."
        Mississippi Valley Historical Review XLV.
     Gates, Paul W.  "Federal Land Policy in the South, 1866-1888."
        Journal of Southern History VI.
     Ransom, Roger and Sutch, Richard.  "The Impact of the Civil
        War and of Emancipation on Southern Agriculture."  Explora-
        tions in Economic History 12 (January 1975):  1-28.

315  Morgenthau, Henry [Sr.], in collaboration with Strother,
        French, All in a Life-Time (1923).
     "The Astors."  Fortune (October 1933).

316  Bentley, George R.  A History of the Freedmen's Bureau (1955).
     Brooks, R. B.  Agrarian Revolution in Georgia (1914).
     Reid, Joseph D., Jr.  "White Land, Black Labor, and Agricultural
        Stagnation.  The Causes and Effects of Sharecropping in the
        Postbellum South."  Explorations in Economic History 16
        (January 1979):  31-55.
     Sutch, Richard and Ransom, Roger.  "The Ex-Slave in the Post-
        Bellum South:  A Study of the Economic Impact of Racism
        in a Market Environment."  Journal of Economic History 33
        (March 1973):  131-148.

317  Brandfon, Robert L.  Cotton Kingdom of the New South:  A
        History of the Yazoo Mississippi Delta from Reconstruction
        to the Twentieth Century.  Cambridge, MA:  Harvard U.
        Press, 1967.
     Du Bois, W. E. B.  The Negro Landholder of Georgia (G.P.O.,
        1901).
     Highsmith, William E.  "Louisiana Landholding during War
        and Reconstruction."  Louisiana Historical Quarterly
        XXXVIII.

318  Aptheker, Herbert.  To Be Free.  Studies in American Negro
        History, Chapter 6 (1948).
     Davis, W. W.  Civil War and Reconstruction in Florida (1913).

319  Dunham, Harold H.  Government Handout.  A Study in the Admin-
        istration of the Public Lands, 1875-1891 (1941).

320  _____.  Government Handout (1941).
     Robbins, R. M.  Our Landed Heritage (1942).

321  Brayer, Herbert O.  William Blackmore.  A Case Study in the
        Economic Development of the West.  2 vols.  (1949).
     Clay, John.  My Life on the Range (1924).

322  Foreman, Grant.  Oklahoma (1942).
     Rister, C. C.  Land Hunger (1942).

323  Dunham, H. H.  "The Crucial Years of the General Land Office,"
        Agricultural History XI.
     Hibbard, B. H.  A History of Public Land Policies (1924).

324  Stephens, George W.  The St. Lawrence Waterway Project (1930).
     Willoughby, William R.  The St. Lawrence Waterway:  A Study
        in Politics and Diplomacy (1961).

325  Maybee, Rolland H.  Railroad Competition and the Oil Trade,
        1855-1873 (1940).
     Williamson, Harold F. and Daum, Arnold R.  The American Petrol-
        eum Industry...1859-1899 (1959).

326  Johnson, Arthur M.  The Development of American Petroleum Pipe-
        lines:  A Study in Private Enterprise and Public Policy,
        1862-1906 (1956).
     Wolbert, George S.  American Pipelines (1952).

327  Chandler, Alfred D., Jr.  Henry Varnum Poor (1956).
     Fishlow, Albert.  American Railroads and the Transformation
        of the Ante-Bellum Economy.  Cambridge, MA:  Harvard U.
        Press, 1965.
     Fogel, Robert W.  Railroads and American Economic Growth
        (1964).

328  Alvarez. Eugene.  Travel on Southern Antebellum Railroads,
        1828-1860.  University, ALA:  U. of Alabama Press, 1974.
     Fish, C. R.  Restoration of the Southern Railroads (1919).
     Stover, John F.  The Railroads of the South, 1865-1900.
        A Study in Finance and Control (1955).

329  Chandler, Alfred D., Jr.  The Railroads.  The Nation's First
        Big Business (1965).
     Oberholtzer, Ellis P.  Jay Cooke, Financier of the Civil War.
        2 vols.  (1907).

330  Adler, Dorothy R.  British Investment in American Railways,
        1834-1898.  Ed. by Hidy, Muriel E.  Charlottesville, VA:
        U. of Virginia Press, 1970.

Currie, A. W. "British Attitudes Toward Investment in North American Railroads." Business History Review XXXIV.
Jenks, Leland H. "Britain and American Railway Development." Journal of Economic History XI.

331 Ambler, C. H. History of Transportation in the Ohio Valley (1932).
Filante, Ronald W. "A Note on the Economic Viability of the Erie Canal, 1825-1860." Business History Review 48 (1974): 95-102.
Gray, Ralph D. The National Waterway: A History of the Chesapeake and Delaware Canal, 1769-1965. Urbana, IL: U. of Illinois Press, 1967.
Moulton, Harold G. Waterways Versus Railways (1912).

332 Clark, Charles H. "The Development of the Semiautomatic Freight-Car Coupler, 1863-1893." Technology and Culture 13 (April 1972): 170-208.
Prout, Henry G. A Life of George Westinghouse (1922).
Westinghouse Air Brake Company, 75th Anniversary of the Westinghouse Air Brake Company...1869-1944 (1944).

333 Meyer, B. H. Railway Legislation in the United States (1903).
Nevins, Allan. Study in Power: John D. Rockefeller. 2 vols. (1953).

334 Danielian, N. R. A.T. & T. (1939).
Watson, Thomas A. Exploring Life (1926).

335 Kennedy, Charles J. "Commuter Services in the Boston Area, 1835-1860." Business History Review (Summer 1962).
Miller, John A. Fares, Please! From Horse Cars to Steam-liners (1941).

336 Gilchrist, D. T. "Albert Fink and the Pooling System." Business History Review XXXIV.
Grodinsky, Julius. The Iowa Pool: A Study in Railroad Competition, 1870-1884 (1950).
Kolko, Gabriel. Railroads and Regulation, 1877-1916. Princeton, N.J.: Princeton U. Press, 1965.

337 Benson, Lee. Merchants, Farmers, and Railroads, Railroad Regulation and New York Politics, 1850-1887 (1955).
Woodman, Harold. "Chicago Businessmen and the 'Granger' Laws." Agricultural History (January 1962).

338 Moody, John. How to Analyze Railroad Reports (1912).
Woodson, E. R. (ed.). Railway Accounting Procedure (1928).

339 Commons, John R. "Types of American Labor Unions: the Long-shoremen of the Great Lakes." Quarterly Journal of Economics XX.

Tunell, G. G.  "Transportation on the Great Lakes."  Journal
   of Political Economy IV.

340  Coon, Horace.  American Tel & Tel (1939).
     Langdale, John V.  "The Growth of Long-Distance Telephony in
        the Bell System, 1875-1907."  Journal of Historical
        Geography 4 (1978):  145-149.
     Stehman, J. Warren.  The Financial History of the American
        Telegraph Company (1925).

341  Gordon, J. H.  Illinois Railway Legislation and Commission
        Control (1904).
     James, E. J.  "Agitation for Federal Regulation."  American
        Economics Association Publications II.

342  Grodinsky, Julius.  Jay Gould:  His Business Career, 1867-1892
        (1957).
     Van Oss, S. F.  American Railroads as Investments:  A Handbook
        for Investors in American Railroad Securities (1895).

343  Glaab, Charles N.  Kansas City and the Railroads:  Community
        Policy in the Growth of a Regional Metropolis (1964).
     Riegel, Robert E.  The Story of the Western Railroads (1926).

344  Chittenden, H. M.  History of Early Steamboat Navigation on
        the Missouri.  2 vols.  (1903).
     Lass, William E.  A History of Steamboating on the Upper
        Missouri River (1962).

345  Chatburn, George R.  Highways and Highway Transportation (1923).
     Davis, Rodney O.  "Iowa Farm Opinion and the Good Roads Move-
        ment, 1903-1904."  Annals of Iowa (Summer 1964).

346  Labatut, J. and Lane, W. J. (eds.).  Highways in our National
        Life (1950).
     Winther, Oscar.  Transportation on the Trans-Mississippi West
        Frontier, 1865-1890 (1964).

347  Schmidt, Louis B.  "The Westward Movement of the Corn-Growing
        Industry in the United States."  Iowa Journal of History
        and Politics XXI.
     Throne, Mildred.  "Southern Iowa Agriculture, 1833-1890:  The
        Progress From Subsistence to Commercial Corn-Belt Farming."
        Agricultural History XXIII.

348  Wiley, B. I.  "Farming in the Lower Mississippi Valley."
        Journal of Southern History III.
     Woodson, Carter G.  Negro Migration (1918).

349  Ballagh, James C. (ed.).  Economic History [of the South],
        1865-1909 (1909).
     Bruce, Philip A.  The Rise of the New South (1905).

350   Holmes, George K.   "Peons of the South."   American Academy of
          Political and Social Science, Annals IV.
      Wiley, Bell I.   "Salient Changes in Southern Agriculture since
          the Civil War."   Agricultural History XIII.

351   Paxson, F. L.   "The Agricultural Surplus:   A Problem in
          History."   Agricultural History VI.
      Trimble, William J.   "Historical Aspects of the Surplus Food
          Production of the United States, 1862-1902."   American
          Historical Association Annual Report I (1918).

352   King, Edward.   The Great South (1875).
      Reid, Joseph D.   "Sharecropping As An Understandable Market
          Response:   The Post-Bellum South."   Journal of Economic
          History 33 (March 1973):   106-130.
      Tebeau, C. W.   "Some Aspects of Planter-Freedman Relations,
          1865-1880."   Journal of Negro History XXI.

353   Phillips, Ulrich B.   "Railway Transportation in the South."
          The South in the Building of the Nation VI (1909).
      Waller, J. L.   "Overland Movement of Cotton."   Southwestern
          Historical Quarterly XXXV.

354   Hayter, Earl W.   "Mechanical Humbuggery Among the Western
          Farmers, 1860-90."   Michigan History XXXIV.
      Hutchinson, William T.   Cyrus Hall McCormick.   2 vols.   (1930,
          1935).
      Murray, Stanley N.   The Valley Comes of Age:   A History of
          Agriculture in the Valley of the Red River of the North,
          1812-1920.   Fargo, N.D.:   North Dakota Institute for
          Regional Studies, 1968.

355   Bogue, Margaret B.   "The Swamp Land Act [of 1850] and Wet Land
          Utilization in Illinois, 1850-1890."   Agricultural History
          XXV.
      Shannon, Fred A.   The Farmer's Last Frontier...1860-1897,
          Chapter 7 (1945).

356   Arrington, Leonard J. and May, Dean.   "'A Different Mode of
          Life':   Irrigation and Society in Nineteenth Century
          Utah."   Agricultural History 49 (1975).
      Robinson, Michael C.   Water for the West:   The Bureau of
          Reclamation, 1902-1977.   Chicago, IL:   Public Works
          Historical Society, 1979.

357   Dale, E. E.   The Range Cattle Industry (1930).
      Reynolds, A. R.   "Land Frauds and Illegal Fencing in Western
          Nebraska."   Agricultural History XXIII.

358   Dalton, Anna A.   "In Praise of Oxen."   Old-Time New England
          XXIX.
      Erdman, H. E.   "The Development and Significance of California
          Cooperatives, 1900-1915."   Agricultural History XXXII.

Gates, Paul W.  The Farmer's Age:  Agriculture, 1815-1860,
     Chapter X (1960).
MacCurdy, Rahno M.  The History of the California Fruit Growers
     Exchange (1925).

359  Malin, J. C.  Dust Storms (1946).
     Webb, W. P.  The Great Plains (1931).

360  Sitterson, Joseph C.  Sugar Country:  The Cane Sugar Industry
          in the South, 1753-1950 (1953).
     Vogt, P. L.  The Sugar Refining Industry (1908).

361  Frink, Maurice, Jackson, W. T. and Wright, Agnes.  When Grass
          Was King (1957).
     Rollins, Philip A.  The Cowboy (1922).

362  Dale, Edward E.  The Range Cattle Industry (1930).
     Osgood, Ernest S.  The Day of the Cattleman (1929).

363  Hoffman, G. Wright.  Hedging by Dealing in Grain Futures (1925).
     Hubbard, Samuel T.  "The Cotton Situation."  Banker's Magazine
          L.

364  Mitchell, Broadus.  Rise of Cotton Mills in the South (1921).
     Thompson, Holland.  From Cotton Field to Cotton Mill (1906).

365  Brooks, Robert P.  The Agrarian Revolution in Georgia (1914).
     Coulter, E. Merton.  James Monroe Smith, Georgia Planter (1961).

366  Hoffman, G. W.  Future Trading upon Organized Commodity
          Markets (1932).
     Peterson, Arthur G.  "Futures Trading, with Particular
          Reference to Agricultural Commodities."  Agricultural
          History VII.

367  Closson, C. C., Jr.  "Unemployed in Cities."  Quarterly Journal
          of Economics VIII.
     Feder, L. H.  Unemployment Relief (1936).

368  Nourse, Edwin G.  American Agriculture and the European Market
          (1924).
     Rothstein, Morton.  "America in the International Rivalry for
          the British Wheat Market, 1860-1914."  Mississippi Valley
          Historical Review XLVII.

369  Hays, W. M. and Parker, E. C.  "The Cost of Producing Farm
          Products."  U.S. Department of Agriculture, Bulletin No. 48
          (G.P.O., 1906).
     Rogin, Leo.  The Introduction of Farm Machinery in Its Relation
          to the Productivity of Labor in the Agriculture of the
          United States during the Nineteenth Century (1931).

370  Ganoe, J. T.  "Beginnings of Irrigation."  Mississippi Valley
          Historical Review XIII.

Hess, R. H.  "Beginnings of Irrigation."  _Journal of Political Economy_ XX.

371  Shannon, Fred A.  _The Farmer's Last Frontier...1860-1897_, Chapter 15, (1945).
Tillson, Christiana H.  _A Woman's Story of Pioneer Illinois_ (1919).

372  Bogart, Ernest L. and Thompson, Charles M.  [Illinois] _The Industrial State, 1870-1893_ (1920).
Clark, Victor S.  _History of Manufactures in the United States_ II, Chapter 16 (1929).

373  Burns, Arthur R.  _The Decline of Competition_ (1936).
Kirkland, Edward C.  _Industry Comes of Age...1860-1897_, Chapter 10 (1961).

374  Galloway, D. F.  "Machine Tools," in Singer, Charles et al. (eds.), _A History of Technology_ V, Chapter 26 (1958).
Kingzett, Charles T.  _The History, Products, and Processes of the Alkali Trade_ (1877).

376  Edwards, James D.  _History of Public Accounting in the United States_ (1960).
Garner, Samuel P.  _Evolution of Cost Accounting to 1925_ (1954).

377  Bernal, John D.  _Science and Industry in the Nineteenth Century_ (1953).
Holley, A. L.  "The Inadequate Union of Engineering Science and Art."  American Institute of Mining Engineers, _Transactions_ IV (1876).

378  Kirkland, Edward C.  _Industry Comes of Age...1860-1897_, Chapter 8 (1961).
Wilson, G. B. L.  "Technical Gains During the Nineteenth Century (1775-1905."  _Journal of World History_ VI.

379  Hubbard, Guy.  "The Development of Machine Tools in New England."  _American Machinist_ LIX-LXI.
Strassmann, Paul W.  _Risk and Technological Innovation: American Methods during the Nineteenth Century_ (1959).

380  Bramson, Roy T.  _Highlights in the History of American Mass Production_ (1945).
Durfee, William F.  "The History and Modern Development of the Art of Interchangeable Construction in Mechanism."  American Society of Mechanical Engineers, _Transactions_ XXII.

381  Mansfield, Judson H.  "Woodworking Machinery--History of Development from 1852-1952."  _Mechanical Engineering_ LXXIV.
Rolt, L. T. C.  _A Short History of Machine Tools_ (1965).

382  Cole, Arthur H.  The American Wool Manufacture.  2 vols.
(1926).
Navin, Thomas R.  "Innovation and Management Policies--The
Textile Machinery Industry:  Influence of the Market on
Management."  Bulletin of the Business Historical Society
XXV.

383  Broehl, Wayne C., Jr.  Precision Valley:  The Machine Tool
Companies of Springfield, Vermont (1959).
Pratt & Whitney Company, Accuracy for Seventy Years, 1860-
1930 (1930).

384  Nasmyth, James.  Autobiography (1883).
Woodbury, Robert S.  History of the Milling Machine (1960).

385  Belissary, Constantine G.  "The Rise of Industry and the
Industrial Spirit in Tennessee, 1865-1885."  Journal of
Southern History XX.
Woodward, Vann C.  Origins of the New South, Chapter 5 (1951).

386  Taussig, F. W.  "The Iron Industry in the United States, 1870-
1899."  Quarterly Journal of Economics XIV.
Woodward, Vann C.  Origins of the New South, 1877-1913 (1951).

387  Chapman, H. H.  The Iron and Steel Industries of the South
(1953).
Phillips, William B.  Iron Making in Alabama.  3rd ed.  (1912).

388  Brady, R. A.  Industrial Standardization (1929).
Thompson, George V.  "Intercompany Technical Standardization
in the Early American Automobile Industry."  Journal of
History XIV.

389  Clemen, Rudolf A.  The American Livestock and Meat Industry
(1923).
Leech, Harper and Carroll, J. C.  Armour and His Times (1958).

390  Armes, Ethel.  Story of Coal and Iron in Alabama (1910).
Keith, Jean E.  "The Role of the Louisville and Nashville
Railroad in the Early Development of Alabama Coal and Iron."
Bulletin of the Business Historical Society XXVI.

391  Nevins, Allan.  Abram J. Hewitt (1935).
Temin, Peter.  Iron and Steel in Nineteenth Century America--
An Economic Inquiry (1964).

392  Beardsley, Edward H.  The Rise of the American Chemistry
Profession, 1850-1900 (1964).
Taylor, F. S.  A History of Industrial Chemistry (1957).

393  Calder, Nigel.  What They Read and Why (H.M.S.O., 1959).
Mott, Frank L.  A History of American Magazines, 1741-1905 II,
Chapter 3; III, Chapter 5; IV, Chapter.18 (1938, 1957).

394  Ubbelohde, A. R. J. P.  "The Beginnings of the Change from
         Craft Mystery to Science as a Basis for Technology," in
         Singer et al. (eds.), A History of Technology IV, Chapter
         23 (1958).
     Woodruff, William.  "Growth of the Rubber Industry of Great
         Britain and the United States."  Journal of Economic
         History XVI.

395  Letwin, William.  Law and Economic Policy in America.  The
         Evolution of the Anti-Trust Act (1965).
     Lloyd, H. D.  Wealth against Commonwealth (1894).

396  Hamilton, Walton H.  Patents and Free Enterprise (G.P.O., 1941).
     Machlup, Fritz.  An Economic Review of the Patent System
         (G.P.O., 1941).

397  Hodkin, F. W. and Cousen, A.  A Textbook of Glass Technology
         (1925).
     Scoville, Warren C.  Revolution in Glassmaking...1880-1920
         (1948).

398  Barnett, George F.  Chapters on Machinery and Labor (1926).
     Porritt, E.  "Trade Unionism and the Evolution of the Type-
         Setting Machine."  Journal of Political Economy 11.

399  Gannon, F. A.  A Short History of American Shoemaking (1912).
     Hazard, Blanche E.  The Organization of the Boot and Shoe
         Industry in Massachusetts Before 1875 (1921).

400  Kelsey, Carl.  The Negro Farmer (1903).
     Wesley, C. H.  Negro Labor (1927).

401  Bruce, P. A.  The Plantation Negro as Freeman (1889).
     Sitterson, J. Carlyle.  "The Transition from Slave to Free
         Economy on the William J. Minor Plantations."  Agricultural
         History (October 1943).

402  Rutledge, Ivan C.  "Regulation of the Movement of Workers:
         Forced Labor in the United States."  Washington University
         Law Quarterly (April-June 1953).
     Zeichner, Oscar.  "The Transition from Slave to Free Agricul-
         tural Labor in the Southern States."  Agricultural History
         XIII.

403  Du Bois, W. E. B. and Dill, A. G.  The Negro American Artisan
         (1912).
     Stavisky, Leonard.  "Negro Craftsmanship in Early America."
         American Historical Review LIV.

404  Wiley, Bell Il "Vicissitudes of Early Reconstruction Farming
         in the Lower Mississippi Valley.  Journal of Southern
         History III.

Woody, Robert H.  "The Labor and Immigration Problem of South
    Carolina during Reconstruction."  Mississippi Valley
    Historical Review XVIII.

405  Cobb, Henry E.  "The Negro as a Free Laborer in Alabama, 1865–
        1875."  Midwest Journal VI.
     Thompson, Edgar T.  "The Natural History of Agricultural Labor
        in the South," in Jackson, David K. (ed.), American Studies
        in Honor of William Kenneth Boyd (1940).

406  Hawk, Emory Q.  Economic History of the South, Chapter 15,
        (1934).
     Simkins, F. B. and Woody, R. H.  South Carolina During the
        Reconstruction (1932).

407  Foner, P. S.  History of the Labor Movement in the United
        States I, Chapters 17–18 (1947).
     Ware, N. J.  The Labor Movement in the United States, 1860–1895
        (1929).

408  Coulter, E. Merton.  The South During Reconstruction, 1865–
        1877, Chapter 5 (1947).
     Cox, La Wanda F.  "Tenancy in the United States, 1865–1900.
        A Consideration of the Validity of the Agricultural Ladder
        Hypothesis."  Agricultural History XVIII.

409  Hoxie, Robert F.  Scientific Management and Labor (1915).
     Wilkinson, Norman B.  "In Anticipation of Frederick W. Taylor.
        A Study of Work by Lammot du Pont, 1872."  Technology and
        Culture (Spring 1965).

410  Lerner, E. M.  "Southern Output and Agricultural Income,
        1860–1880."  Agricultural History XXXIII.
     Shannon, Fred A.  The Farmer's Last Frontier...1860–1897,
        Chapter 4 (1945).

411  Grob, Gerald N.  "Organized Labor and the Negro Worker, 1865–
        1900."  Labor History I.
     Matison, Sumner E.  "The Labor Movement and the Negro during
        Reconstruction."  Journal of Negro History XXXIII.

412  Jones, Eliot.  The Anthracite Coal Combination (1914).
     Yearley, Clifton K.  Enterprise and Anthracite Economics and
        Democracy in Schuylkill County, 1820–1875 (1961).

413  Cutler, J. E.  Lynch Law (1905).

414  Mulligan, William H., Jr.  "Mechanization and Work in the
        American Shoe Industry:  Lynn, Massachusetts, 1852–1883."
        Journal of Economic History 41 (March 1981):  59–64.
     Woodbury, Robert S.  Studies in the History of Machine Tools.
        Cambridge, MA:  MIT Press, 1972.

415  Clawson, Dan. <u>Bureaucracy and the Labor Process:   The Trans-</u>
<u>formation of U.S. Industry, 1860-1920</u>. New York:  Monthly
Review Press, 1980.
Edwards, Richard C. <u>Contested Terrain:   The Transformation</u>
<u>of the Workplace in America</u>. New York:  Basic Books, 1979.

Montgomery, David.  "Workers' Control of Machine Production
in the Nineteenth Century." <u>Labor History</u> 17 (1976):   485-
509.
Nelson, Daniel. <u>Managers and Workers:   Origins of the New</u>
<u>Factory System in the United States, 1880-1920</u>. Madison,
WI:   U. of Wisconsin Press, 1975.

416  Cox, La Wanda.  "The American Agricultural Wage Earner, 1865-
1900, Emergence of a Modern Labor Problem." <u>Agricultural</u>
<u>History</u> XXII.
Davis, Ronald L. F. <u>Good and Faithful Labor:   From Slavery</u>
<u>to Sharecropping in the Natchez District, 1860-1890</u>.
Westport, CT:  Greenwood, 1982.
Ransom, Roger L. and Sutch, Richard. <u>One Kind of Freedom:</u>
<u>The Economic Consequences of Emancipation</u>. New York:
Cambridge U. Press, 1977.

417  McKelvey, Blake.  "Penal Slavery and Southern Reconstruction."
<u>Journal of Negro History</u> XX.

418  Cross, Ira B. <u>A History of the Labor Movement in California</u>
(1935).
Ware, N. J. <u>The Labor Movement in the United States,   1860-</u>
<u>1895</u> (1929).

419  Ely, Richard T.  "Pullman:  A Social Study." <u>Harper's</u>
<u>Magazine</u> LXX.
Lindsey, Almont. <u>The Pullman Strike</u> (1942).

420  Commons, J. R. <u>History of Labour in the United States</u> II
(1918).
Ginger, R. <u>The Bending Cross:   Debs</u> (1949).

421  Paul, Arnold M. <u>Conservative Crisis and the Role of Law:</u>
<u>Attitudes of Bar and Bench, 1887-1895</u> (1960).
Pollack, Norman. <u>The Populist Response to Industrial America</u>
(1962).

422  Ginger, Ray.  "Company-Sponsored Welfare Plans in 1900."
<u>Bulletin of the Business Historical Society</u> XXVII.
Tolman, William H. <u>Social Engineering:   A Record of Things</u>
<u>Done by American Industrialists Employing Upwards of One</u>
<u>and One-Half Million People</u> (1909).

423  Logan, Rayford W. <u>The Negro in American Life and Thought,</u>
<u>The Nadir, 1877-1901</u> (1954).
Northrup, H. R. <u>Organized Labor and the Negro</u> (1944).

424   George, J. E.  "The Coal Miners Strike of 1897."  Quarterly
      Journal of Economics XII.
      Karsh, Bernard and London, Jack.  "The Coal Miners:  A Study
      of Mine Control."  Quarterly Journal of Economics LXVIII.

425   Branch, E. D.  Hunting of Buffalo (1929).
      Burlingame, Merrill G.  "The Buffalo in Trade and Commerce."
      North Dakota Historical Quarterly III.

426   Resseguie, Harry E.  "Alexander Turney Stewart and the
      Development of the Department Store, 1823-1876."  Business
      History Review 39 (1965):  301-322.
      Silk, Alvin J. and Stern, Louis W.  "The Changing Nature of
      Innovation in Marketing:  A Study of Selected Business
      Leaders, 1852-1958."  Business History Review (Autumn
      1963).
      Sisk, G. N.  "The Wholesale Commission Business in the Alabama
      Black Belt, 1875-1917."  Journal of Farm Economics XXXVIII.

427   Briggs, Edward P.  Fifty Years on the Road:  The Autobiography
      of a Traveling Salesman (1911).
      Marburg, Theodore F.  "Manufacturer's Drummer, 1832."  Bulletin
      of the Business Historical Society XXII.

428   Myrick, Herbert.  American Sugar Industry (1899).
      Vogt, Paul L.  Sugar Refining in the United States (1908).

429   Cowing, Cedric B.  Populists, Plungers, and Progressives:  A
      Social History of Stock and Commodity Speculation, 1890-
      1936  (1965).
      Hoffman, G. Wright.  Future Trading upon Organized Commodity
      Markets in the United States (1932).

430   McDaniel, Ruel.  "Confessions of a Free Lance Writer."  Modern
      Age VI.
      Mott, F. L.  The Golden Multitudes (1947).
      Trachtenberg, Alan.  The Incorporation of America:  Culture
      and Society, 1865-1893.  New York:  Farrar, Straus and
      Giroux, 1982.

431   Copeland, Melvin T.  "Some Present-Day Problems in Distribu-
      tion."  Harvard Business Review IX.
      Williamson, Harold F.  "Mass Production, Mass Consumption, and
      American Industrial Development."  First International
      Conference of Economic History (1960).

432   Wright, Elizur.  Politics and Mysteries of Life Insurance
      (1873).

433   Ferry, John W.  A History of the Department Store (1960).
      Pasdermadjian, H.  The Department Store, Its Origin, Evolution
      and Economics (1954).

434  Clarke, Arthur C.  Voice Across the Sea (1958).
     Smith, Willoughby.  The Rise and Extension of Submarine Tele-
       graphy (1891).

435  Huebner, G. G.  "Changes Effected by the Civil War," in
       Johnson, Emory R. et al., History of Domestic and Foreign
       Commerce of the United States II, Chapter 25 (1915).
     Unger, Irwin.  Greenback Era: A Social and Political Finance,
       1865-1879 (1964).

436  Downs, William C.  "The Commission House in Latin American
       Trade."  Quarterly Journal of Economics XXVI.
     Hillyer, William H.  James Talcott, Merchant and His Times
       (1937).

437  Sitterson, Joseph C.  "Expansion, Reversion, and Revolution in
       the Southern Sugar Industry: 1850-1910."  Bulletin of the
       Business Historical Society XXVII.
     _____.  Sugar Country...1753-1950 (1953).

438  Beale, Howard K.  "The Tariff and Reconstruction."  American
       Historical Review XXXV.
     Graham, Frank D.  "International Trade Under Depreciated Paper:
       The United States, 1862-79."  Quarterly Journal of
       Economics XXXVI.

439  Chapman, Sydney J.  The History of Trade Between the United
       Kingdom and the United States (1899).
     Clemen, Rudolf A.  The American Livestock and Meat Industry
       (1923).

440  Deerr, Noel.  The History of Sugar Growing.  2 vols.  (1949-
       1950).
     Stevens, Sylvester K.  American Expansion in Hawaii, 1842-
       1898 (1945).

441  Eustes, Frederic A.  Augustus Hemenway, 1805-1876, Builder
       of the United States Trade with the West Coast of South
       America (1955).
     Tyler, A. F.  The Foreign Policy of Blaine (1927).

442  Pletcher, David M.  The Awkward Years.  American Foreign
       Relations Under Garfield and Arthur (1963).
     Poulshock, S. Walter.  The Two Parties and the Tariff in the
       1880's (1965).

443  Feis, Herbert.  Europe, the World's Banker, 1870-1914 (1930).
     Joslin, David.  A Century of [British] Banking in Latin
       America (1964).

444  Nichols, Jeannette P.  "The United States Congress and Imper-
       ialism, 1861-1897."  Journal of Economic History XXI.
     Russ, W. A.  "The Role of Sugar in Hawaiian Annexation."
       Pacific Historical Review XII.

445   Huebner, G. G.  "The Foreign Trade from the Civil War to the
      Close of the Nineteenth Century," in Johnson, Emory R.
      et al., History of Domestic and Foreign Commerce of the
      United States II, Chapter 26 (1915).
      Saul, S. B. "Britain and World Trade, 1870-1914." Economic
      History Review VII, 2nd series.

446   Albion, Robert G.  "British Shipping and Latin America, 1806-
      1914." Journal of Economic History XI.
      Ferns, H. S.  Britain and Argentina in the Nineteenth Century
      (1960).
447   Mark, Shelley M. and Adler, J.  "Claus Spreckels in Hawaii:
      Impact of a Mainland Interloper on Development of Hawaiian
      Sugar Industry." Explorations in Entrepreneurial History,
      1st series (October 1957).
      Rowland, Donald.  "The United States and the Contract Labor
      Question in Hawaii, 1862-1900." Pacific Historical Review
      II.

448   Price-Grenfell, A.  The Western Invasions of the Pacific and
      its Continents...1513-1958 (1963).
      Russ, William A.  The Hawaiian Republic, 1894-98 (1961).

449   LaFeber, Walter.  The New Empire.  An Interpretation of Ameri-
      can Expansion, 1860-1898 (1963).
      Summers, Festus P.  William L. Wilson and Tariff Reform (1953).

450   Healy, David F.  The United States in Cuba, 1898-1902 (1963).
      Robinson, A. G.  Cuba and the Intervention (1905).

451   Adams, Brooks.  America's Economic Supremacy (1900).
      Sklar, M.  "The N.A.M. and Foreign Markets on the Eve of the
      Spanish-American War." Science and Society XXIII.

452   Clark, Victor S.  History of Manufactures in the United States,
      III, Chapter 6 (1929).
      Lewis, Kenneth B.  Steel Wire in America (1952).

453   Hepburn, A. B.  A History of Currency in the United States
      (1915).
      Mitchell, Wesley C.  History of the Greenbacks (1903).

454   Davis, A. M.  Origin of the National Banking System (1910-11).
      Larson, Henrietta.  Jay Cooke (1936).

455   Giddens, Paul H.  The Birth of the Oil Industry (1938).
      Stocking, George W.  The Oil Industry and the Competitive
      System (1925).

456   Henry, J. T.  The Early and Later History of Petroleum (1873).
      Williamson, Harold F. and Daum, Arnold R.  The American
      Petroleum Industry...1859-1899 (1959).

475  Gibbons, James S.  Banks of New York (1870).
     Sharkey, Robert P.  Money, Class and Party.  An Economic Study
         of Civil War and Reconstruction, Chapter 6 (1959).

458  Dewey, Davis R.  Financial History of the United States,
         Chapter 13 (1931, 11th ed.)
     Larson, Henrietta.  Jay Cooke (1936).

459  Patterson, Robert T.  "Government Finance on the Eve of the
         Civil War."  Journal of Economic History XII.
     Sharkey, Robert P.  Money, Class, and Party (1959).

460  Coulter, E. Merton.  The South During Reconstruction, 1865-
         1877, Chapter 9 (1947).
     Green, Fletcher M.  "Duff Green:  Industrial Promoter."
         Journal of Southern History II.

461  Clark, Victor S.  History of Manufactures in the United States
         III, Chapter 6 (1929).
     Smith, George W.  "Some Northern Wartime Attitudes Toward the
         Post Civil-War South."  Journal of Southern History X.

462  Sharkey, Robert P.  Money, Class, and Party (1959).
     Unger, Irwin.  "The Business Community and the Origins of the
         1875 Resumption Act."  Business History Review XXXV.

463  Robertson, Eugene C.  Road to Wealth Leads Through the South
         (1894).
     Woodward, C. Vann.  The Origins of the New South, 1877-1913,
         Chapter 5 (1951).

464  Cowing, Cedric B.  Populists, Plungers, and Progressives...
         1890-1936 (1965).
     Sobel, Robert.  The Big Board.  A History of the New York
         Stock Market (1965).

465  Klaw, Spencer.  "The Wall Street Lawyers."  Fortune (February
         1958).
     Smigl, Erwin O.  The Wall Street Lawyer (1964).

466  Ballagh, J. (ed.).  South in the Building of the Nation (1955).
     Davell, J. E.  History of Banking in Florida, 1828-1954 VI
         (1909).

467  Boyle, James E.  Cotton and the New Orleans Cotton Exchange
         (1934).
     Mitchell, Harry A.  "The Development of New Orleans as a
         Wholesale Trading Center."  Louisiana Historical Quarterly
         XXVII.

468  Brough, Charles H.  History of Banking in Mississippi (1900).
     Griffin, Richard W.  "Problems of Southern Cotton Planters
         After the Civil War."  Georgia Historical Quarterly (June
         1955).

469    Bagehot, Walter.  Lombard Street (1873).
       Warburton, Clark.  "Variations in Economic Growth and Banking
          Developments in the United States from 1835 to 1885."
          Journal of Economic History XVIII.

470    Boyle, J. E.  Cotton and the New Orleans Cotton Exchange (1934).
       Lehman Brothers.  A Centennial:  Lehman Brothers, 1850-1950
          (1950).

471    Adams, Charles F., Jr.  "The Currency Debate of 1873-74."
          North American Review (July 1874).
       Dorfman, Joseph.  The Economic Mind in American Civilization
          III, Chapter 1 (1949).

472    Coben, Stanley.  "Northeastern Business and Radical Reconstruc-
          tion:  A Re-examination."  Mississippi Valley Historical
          Review XLVI.
       Unger, Irwin.  "Business Men and Specie Resumption."  Political
          Science Quarterly LXXIV.

473    Paterson, Robert G.  Wage Payment Legislation in the United
          States (G.P.O., 1918).

474    Bogue, Allan G.  "The Land Mortgage Company in the Early Plains
          States."  Agricultural History XXV.
          _____.  "The Administrative and Policy Problems of the J. B.
          Watkins Land Mortgage Company, 1873-1894."  Bulletin of the
          Business Historical Society XXVII.

475    _____.  Money at Interest:  The Farm Mortgage on the Middle
          Border (1955).
       Frederickson, D. M.  "Mortgage Banking in America."  Journal
          of Political Economy II.

476    Baum, E. L. and others (eds.).  Capital and Credit Needs in a
          Changing Agriculture (1961).
       Sparks, Earl S.  History and Theory of Agricultural Credit in
          the United States (1932).

477    Barnett, George E.  State Banking in the United States Since
          the Passage of the National Bank Act (1902).
       Redlich, Fritz.  The Molding of American Banking...1840-1910 II
          (1951).

478    Anderson, George L.  "The South and Problems of Post-Civil
          War Finance."  Journal of Southern History IX.
       Malin, James C.  "The Farmers' Alliance Subtreasury Plan and
          European Precedents."  Mississippi Valley Historical Review
          XXXI.

479    Seligman, E. R. A. et al.  The Currency Problem and the
          Present Financial Situation (1908).

Sprague, O. M. W.  History of Crises under the National Banking System (G.P.O., 1910).

480  Barnes, James A.  John G. Carlisle, Financial Statesman (1931).
     Ford, W. C.  "Foreign Exchanges and the Movement of Gold, 1894-1895."  Yale Review IV.

481  Dewing, A. S.  Corporate Promotions and Reorganizations (1914).
     Nelson, Ralph.  Merger Movements in American Industry, 1895-1956 (1959).

482  Cannon, James G.  Clearing Houses:  Their History, Methods, and Administration (1900).
     Holes, Charles A.  The Baltimore Clearing House (1940).

483  Brayer, Herbert O.  "Boom-town Banker--Central City, Colorado, 1880."  Bulletin of the Business Historical Society XIX.
     Forgan, James B.  Recollections of a Busy Life (1924).

484  Crawford, J. B.  Credit Mobilier (1880).
     Steffens, Lincoln.  Aubobiography (1931).

485  Brewer, W. M.  "Poor Whites and Negroes Since the Civil War."  Journal of Negro History XV.
     Woodson, Carter G.  "Fifty Years of Negro Citizenship."  Journal of Negro History VI.

486  Schwab, John C.  History of the New York Property Tax (1890).
     Smith, Harry E.  The United States Federal Internal Tax History from 1861 to 1871 (1914).

487  Du Bois, W. E. B.  Black Reconstruction (1935).
     Wallace, John.  Carpetbag Rule in Florida (1888).

488  Kolko, Gabriel.  Railroads and Regulation, 1877-1916 (1965).
     Spearman, F. H.  Strategy of Great Railroads (1904).

489  Kirkland, Edward C.  Charles Francis Adams, Jr., 1831-1915 (1965).
     MacAvoy, Paul W.  The Economic Effects of Regulation:  The Trunk-Line Railroad Commission Before 1900 (1965).
     Miller, George H.  Railroads and the Granger Laws.  Madison, WI:  U. of Wisconsin Press, 1971.

490  Engerman, Stanley L.  "Some Economic Issues Relating to Railroad Subsidies and the Evaluation of Land Grants."  Journal of Economic History 32 (June 1972):  443-463.
     Fleisig, Heywood.  "The Union Pacific Railroad and the Railroad Land Grant Controversy."  Explorations in Economic History 11 (Winter 1973-74):  155-172.
     Goodrich, Carter.  Government Promotion of American Canals and Railroads, 1800-1890 (1960).
     Mercer, Lloyd J.  Railroads and Land Grant Policy:  A Study of Government Intervention.  New York:  Academic Press, 1982.

U.S. Federal Coordinator of Transportation, <u>Public Aids to Transportation</u>. 4 vols. (G.P.O., 1938-1940).

491    Berglund, Abraham and Wright, Philip G.  <u>The Tariff on Iron and Steel</u> (1929).
Pursell, Carroll W., Jr.  "Tariff and Technology:  The Foundation and Development of the American Tin-Plate Industry, 1872-1900."  <u>Technology and Culture</u> III.

492    Bancroft, Hubert H.  <u>History of Washington, Idaho, and Montana, 1845-1899</u> (1890):  381-390.
Himes, George H.  "Early Efforts of Road Making."  <u>Washington Historical Quarterly</u> XV.

493    Brooks, R. C.  <u>Corruption in American Politics</u> (1910).
Reinsch, P. S.  <u>American Legislatures</u> (1907).

# INDEX

**About the Author**

MEYER WEINBERG has had a distinguished career as a teacher, editor, and author. Currently he is both a Professor at the University of Massachusetts, Amherst, and Director of the Horace Mann Bond Center for Equal Education. His writings include *Race and Place: A Legal History of the Neighborhood School*, *The Search for Quality Integrated Education*, and an essay on American economic development in V. B. Singh's collective volume of comparative economic history. His award-winning two-volume work, *The Education of Poor and Minority Children: A World Bibliography*, was published by Greenwood Press in 1981. He has taught courses in American economic history and the general history of the United States.